The
National Question in
Marxist-Leninist
Theory and Strategy

The National Question in Marxist-Leninist Theory and Strategy

WALKER CONNOR

Princeton University Press
Princeton, New Jersey

Library of Congress Cataloging in Publication Data
will be found on the last printed page of this book
ISBN 0-691-07655-3 / ISBN 0-691-10163-9 (pbk)

This book has been composed in Linotron Baskerville

Clothbound editions of Princeton University Press books
are printed on acid-free paper, and binding materials
are chosen for strength and durability.
Paperbacks, although satisfactory for personal collections,
are not usually suitable for library rebinding

Printed in the United States of America
by Princeton University Press
Princeton, New Jersey

To Mary

Contents

(Notes appear at end of each chapter)

Tables, Maps, and Figure

TABLES

MAPS

FIGURE

Acknowledgments

SUSTAINED research on the present manuscript began in 1975–
1976. Many debts have been incurred in the ensuing years. I owe
a major debt to the Woodrow Wilson International Center for
Scholars for the award of a one-year fellowship. Although I had
long entertained the possibility of making a comparative study of
nationalism in Marxist-Leninist states, I became convinced that the
undertaking was feasible only after I arrived at the Center, became
aware of its special intellectual atmosphere, and was encouraged
by the aid that its library staff was prepared to offer in running
down a number of obscure works and documents. I am particularly
indebted to James Billington, Zed David, Prosser Gifford, and Mar-
cella Jones. A year at Oxford University (1977–1978) was made
possible by the award of a visiting professorship and the Rhodes
Fellowship at St. Antony's College, further supported by a grant
from the Ford Foundation. I owe special gratitude to Kenneth
Kirkwood and John Stone for making the year at St. Antony's
possible, hospitable, stimulating, and productive. A Fulbright-Hays
Senior Lecture Award to Poland during one of that country's most
momentous periods (1980–1981) provided an unusual opportunity
to observe unveiled nationalism at work throughout a Marxist-
Leninist system. I am also grateful for the invitation to visit the
Institute of Ethnography of the USSR Academy of Sciences and
for the informative discussions with its staff and director, Academician Yu. Bromley. Some sections of the book have been presented before the Slavic studies faculty of St. Antony's College, as
well as before its faculty of Far Eastern studies; before the faculty
of Slavic studies at the London School of Economics; before a
largely Soviet audience at the Eleventh World Congress of the
International Political Science Association in Moscow; before faculty seminars at Florida International University and Goldsmiths'
College (University of London); and before a graduate seminar at
Columbia University. The reactions proved most helpful. Robert
Conquest graciously commented on chapters 1 and 2, and Robert
Lewis on chapter 9. Sanford Thatcher of Princeton University Press

offered encouragement and sage advice throughout all stages of the book. I am also grateful to Alice Calaprice of Princeton University Press for the final editing of the book. Finally, my greatest debt is to Mary Connor, research associate, sounding board, typist, editor, and critic.

By Way of Introduction

WHAT follows is an attempt to trace and analyze the evolving relationship between communism and nationalism. The ultimate incompatibility between the two is constantly stressed in Marxist-Leninist pronouncements. The *Great Soviet Encyclopedia* defines nationalism as "a bourgeois and petit bourgeois ideology and policy as well as the outlook that raises the national question," and it adds that "the proletarian, communist world view is incompatible with any nationalist ideology." This incompatibility does not preclude Communists from appealing to nationalism in a prerevolutionary situation. Both Marx and Lenin condoned the manipulation of national aspirations as a means of furthering the world revolutionary movement. They felt, however, that there was no place for nationalism in a postrevolutionary society governed by the principles of scientific socialism; moreover, whether before or after the revolution, Communists must never become tainted with nationalism. The primary significance assigned to guaranteeing the immunity of Communists to the national virus is unequivocally set forth in the same *Great Soviet Encyclopedia*: "The struggle to overcome nationalism in the communist movement is *the most important task of Marxist-Leninists*" (emphasis added).

The formula for performing the task of harnessing the powerful forces of nationalism to the revolution and then vanquishing them thereafter is termed "Leninist national policy." Despite this apparently total attribution to Lenin, the policy is perceived as the product of Marx and Engels, as further refined by Lenin. To again cite the *Great Soviet Encyclopedia*: "A truly scientific theory of nations was created by Marx and Engels and developed by Lenin."

A comprehensive study of the relationship between communism and nationalism must therefore begin with the nature and role of nations and nationalism, as found in the writings of Marx and Engels and later further distilled by Lenin. An evaluation of this distillation (Leninist national policy) can then be pursued by tracing the degree to which various Marxist-Leninist parties have in fact implemented Leninist national policy and the result of such faithful implementation; and the degree to which the parties have deviated from faithful implementation, their reasons for doing so, and the results of their actions. This, in very rough outline, is the route taken in the following chapters.

IT is always wise to preface an English-language work dealing with nations and nationalism by a few warning words on terminology. The meaning of these key terms has been beclouded by their slipshod use in the English-speaking world.[1] *Nation*, as used herein, refers to a human grouping whose members share an intuitive sense of kindredness or sameness, predicated upon a myth of common descent. It therefore refers to peoples such as the Russians, Ukrainians, Armenians, Han Chinese, Tibetans, Serbs, Croats, Czechs, and Slovaks. It does not refer to any collection of people who are conscious of their multiethnic background (for example, the Czechosolvak people, the Soviet people, or the American people). Nor does it refer to a state (as used, for example, in the misnomer, the United Nations). *Nationalism* refers to identity with and loyalty to the *nation* in the same pristine sense in which the word is being employed in this work. It does not refer to loyalty to the state, which is *patriotism*. *Nationalism* and *patriotism* may often be in conflict. Thus, Soviet authorities periodically censure manifestations of Ukrainian, Lithuanian, or some other nationalism as "antistate activity."

We are not dealing just with a matter of semantics. Commonly used terminology by non-Marxist writers to describe events in the Second World has caused confusion. Thus, following Belgrade's break with Moscow, Tito was popularly described as a nationalist; he was, in fact, an avid internationalist. *Titoism* was equated with "national communism"; it was, in fact, "state-communism." Rather than advocating nationalism, Tito advocated patriotism (Yugoslavianism). The principal target of his displeasure was nationalism, whether of the Albanian, Croatian, Serbian, or Slovene stamp.

Marx was also given to slipshod terminology, often using *nation* to apply to a state or to an ethnically heterogeneous society. Not so, however, Lenin and his legatees. In Marxist-Leninist literature, one may encounter disagreement concerning the specific characteristics that are essential to a *nation* (e.g., language, territory, and the like), but the term will refer to a people with a sense of national consciousness. *Nationality*, in the Marxist-Leninist lexicon, can have one of two meanings: a people in a prenation stage of development, that is to say, a people who, for whatever reason, have not yet achieved (and may never achieve) the more august station of nationhood; or a segment of a nation living outside the state where the major body of the nation resides (for example, Albanians living within Yugoslavia). Being classified as a *nationality* rather than as a *nation* can have political implications. Thus, Albanians and Magyars (Hungarians) have been denied their own republics within Yugoslavia, republic status being reserved for *nations*. And Peking, by referring to all peoples within China, other than the Han, as nationalities, justifies its refusal to create republics on the Soviet pattern. In any case, *nationalism* in Marxist-Leninist literature is not confused with *patriotism*. It refers to placing primary loyalty in one's own nation or nationality, a priority which may be acceptable on the part of the masses in a prerevolutionary situation but which must give way to proletarian internationalism or socialist patriotism in the revolution's aftermath. And finally, Marxist-Leninists use the expression, *the national question*, to refer to the entire network of problems arising from the existence of nations and nationalities.[2] Leninist national policy is proclaimed as providing the method for solving the national question in a socialist society.

HEAVY reliance upon translations was made necessary by the diversity of peoples and states touched upon in this study. Such dependency is of course, a cost inherent in broad comparative studies. Many important comparative works, particularly in the field of nationalism, would not have been undertaken if skill in the language of each people studied were made a prerequisite. It is doubtful, for example, that there is a specialist on the Soviet Union's national question who is proficient in the language of each of the fifteen people who have union-republic status within the USSR, to say nothing of the scores of other languages spoken within that single country. Add to that the number of languages spoken throughout China, Southeast Asia, and Eastern Europe, and the need to rely upon translations, often double translations (e.g., from Tibetan to Chinese to English), becomes patent.

My inability to read a document in the original proved particularly frustrating when different translations offered conflicting renderings of key terms. However, the inability to resolve such dilemmas was not always due to lack of proficiency in the language. In many instances, the original documents have been destroyed, and in many other instances they have been doctored. Whenever ambiguity or conflict in the wording of translations was detected, the present text draws attention to the issue and cites the pertinent materials in a manner that will enable readers to judge the evidence for themselves.

As to problems of transliteration, spellings in this work generally follow those suggested by the United States Board on Geographic Names. In addition, the spelling of Chinese words follows the older Wade Giles system rather than the new romanized system recommended by Peking since 1979.

A FINAL prefatory note, this concerning the objectivity of the author, might be advisable. This work was dictated solely by my interest in the study of nationalism as a global phenomenon. It was prompted by a conviction that the experiences of sixteen states, most of them ethnonationally heterogeneous and accounting *in toto* for approximately one-third of the world's population, are simply too significant to be ignored, particularly when these states claim to have *the* formula for harnessing and dissolving nationalism. It was not knowingly prompted by any ideological motivation. Nonetheless, the fact that the book deals principally with Second World states might give rise to the opinion that the author is holding up the practices of these states against some unfairly idealistic, ultimate standard of behavior, rather than measuring them against the practices of non-Marxist-Leninist societies. There are two ways of responding:

1. The author subscribes to the notion that a defense of behavior predicated upon the fact that behavior of others is worse or no better is always an odious one. Be that as it may, the book will, I hope, make very clear that the treatment accorded to national groups within Marxist-Leninist states has varied enormously from state to state, and within individual states has also varied significantly over time. If all states of the world were listed according to the policies currently being practiced against national groups, some Marxist-Leninist states would merit placement among the very worst, while others would not fare badly.

2. Although the author disclaims any tendency to judge the policies of the Second World states by some ultimate standard, holding these states to such a standard could be justified in terms of their own claims. It is they who claim to have "solved their national question" and to have eradicated all inequality among nations and nationalities. To judge their performance against their own, oft-repeated claims is indeed, therefore, to apply an absolute standard.

Walker Connor
Belmont, Vermont
March 1983

NOTES

1. The matter is discussed more fully in Connor, "A Nation Is a Nation," 377–400.

2. The *Great Soviet Encyclopedia*'s definition is a bit confusing, because it speaks of relations among nations but not of the more significant relations between nations and the state: "NATIONAL QUESTION, the totality of political, economic, territorial, legal, ideological, and cultural relations among nations (*natsii*, nations in the historical sense), national groups, and nationalities (*narodnosti*) in various socioeconomic formations."

The
National Question in
Marxist-Leninist
Theory and Strategy

The conflict between Marxist discipline and nationalist forces, which is a fairly constant factor in contemporary communism—indeed the entire topic of Marxism, both in its theoretical aspects and in practice, deserves closer study than it has obtained.

Isaiah Berlin,
"The Bent Twig"

THE THEORY

CHAPTER 1

Three Strands of Nationalism in Marx and Engels

NATIONALISM and Marxism are philosophically incompatible. Nationalism is predicated upon the assumption that the most fundamental divisions of humankind are the many vertical cleavages that divide people into ethnonational groups. Marxism, by contrast, rests upon the conviction that the most fundamental human divisions are horizontal class distinctions that cut across national groupings. The nationalist would therefore contend that, in a test of loyalties, national consciousness would prove more powerful than all *intra*national divisions, including that of class. Marxists, on the other hand, would maintain that class consciousness would prove the more powerful. They would contend that English, or French, or German workers would necessarily come to sense that much more significant than the bonds of shared nationhood were the bonds that tied them to the proletariat of all national groups in a common struggle against the bourgeoisie of all nations, including their own. History would witness the victory of *inter*nationalism over nationalism. These two antagonistic perceptions could be contrasted diagrammatically as seen in figure 1.

FIGURE 1.   Perceptions

Marxist Perception			Nationalist Perception		
Bourgeoisie	Bourgeoisie	Bourgeoisie	(Bourgeoisie)	(Bourgeoisie)	(Bourgeoisie)
(German)	(English)	(French)	G	E	F
			e	n	r
			r	g	e
			m	l	n
			a	i	c
			n	s	h
				h	
Proletariat	Proletariat	Proletariat	(Proletariat)	(Proletariat)	(Proletariat)
(German)	(English)	(French)			

Both despite and because of the contradictory nature of the philosophical assumptions of nationalism and Marxism, the former has played a central role throughout the history of the latter. Intensive interaction between the two isms was assured by their nearly coincidental chronology. Marx was born near the beginning of the Age of Nationalism (generally considered to have been ushered in by the French Revolution and the Napoleonic Wars), and publication of his Communist Manifesto occurred quite ironically in the same year made famous by an early manifestation of nationalism's rapid spread, namely, the revolutions of 1848. From this point on, nationalism and Marxism were contemporaries.

Given their contradictory nature, it could logically have been anticipated that the role of nationalism in the history of Marxism would be that of an antagonistic force. And indeed, such was often the case. However, this is only part and perhaps the least intriguing part of the historical relationship of the two isms, for Marxists not only learned to accommodate themselves to an expediential coexistence with a world filled with nationalisms, but they also developed a strategy to manipulate nationalism into the service of Marxism. Marxists owe their major successes more to this strategy than to either the popular appeal or the predictive accuracy of Marxian ideology. Thus, paradoxical though it may be, the history of Marxism in practice indicates that nationalism has been a key force in promoting a philosophically antithetical variant of internationalism.

THE logical starting point for the study of the interaction of nationalism and Marxism is with the pertinent writings of Marx and Engels. Unfortunately, the relevant passages are irregularly strewn throughout a number of their treatises and even their personal correspondence, for neither man ever attempted a detailed exposition of the topic. The most compelling explanation for this neglect is the basic incompatibility between nationalism and a doctrine of proletarian internationalism. It bears repeating that there is an evident conflict between an ideology that maintains that the most significant cleavages are those that divide mankind horizontally into socioeconomic classes and one that maintains that the most significant cleavages are those that divide humanity vertically into national compartments.

Given, then, the commitment of Marx and Engels to a particular analysis of social history in which the role of *the* dominant element was assigned to the material productive forces rather than to abstract notions such as nationalism, and in which socioeconomic classes rather than nations were perceived as the principal vehicles of history, it is hardly surprising that nationalism would not loom large in their deliberations. In their scheme of things, both nation and nationalism were relegated to the superstructure. The nation was explained as a historically evolved phenomenon that comes into existence only with the demise of feudalism and the rise of capitalism. Prior to the capitalist stage, there were human groupings such as tribes, clans, and peoples; but it was the new economic relations, brought on by changes in the mode of production, that created nations.[1] Nationalism was mainly a device of the bourgeoisie for identifying their class interests as the interests of the entire society.[2] It constituted an attempt to dampen the class consciousness of the proletariat by obscuring the conflicting class interests within each nation, and by encouraging rivalry among the proletariat of various nations. Because of its association with a specific economic stage, nationalism could be progressive or reactionary, depending upon the level of society. At a feudal or semifeudal stage, it is progressive, but at a stage of developed capitalism it is counter-revolutionary.

To this point, the Marxist position is unambiguous and is given unequivocal support by contemporary Marxists of rather diverse stamps.[3] More obscure, however, is the question of what happens to nations in the postcapitalist period. Marx and Engels made clear in the Manifesto that the nation would survive the revolution at least for a time: "Though not in substance, yet in form, the struggle of the proletariat with the bourgeoisie is at first a national struggle. The proletariat of each country must, of course, first of all settle matters with its own bourgeoisie." And farther on in one of the Manifesto's most famous passages:

> The Communists are further reproached with desiring to abolish countries and nationality.
> The working men have no country. We cannot take from them what they have not got. Since the proletariat must first of all acquire political supremacy, must rise to the leading class of the nation, must constitute itself *the* nation, it is, so far, itself national, though not in the bourgeois sense of the word.

But since the nation is part of the superstructure and the product of specific productive forces and relations, will it not, as the state, wither away in the postcapitalist period? If so, does its termination merely mean the end of national antagonisms or does it mean the end of all national distinctions, including such cultural singularities as language? Phrased differently, does the socialist revolution presage total assimilation?

On this issue Marx proved a poor guide. His statements are obtuse, and subject to diverse interpretation. The key passage appeared in the Manifesto:

> National differences and antagonisms between peoples are daily more and more vanishing, owing to the development of the bourgeoisie, to freedom of commerce, to the world market, to uniformity in the mode of production and in condition of life corresponding thereto.
>
> The supremacy of the proletariat will cause them to vanish still faster.

The more conventional interpretation of this passage is that Marx and Engels meant that *all* national differences faced extermination. But the absence of the word *all* has also permitted another interpretation, which holds, in the words of one authority, that the authors of the Manifesto foresaw only "the abolition of sharp economic and social differences, economic isolation, invidious distinctions, political rivalries, wars and exploitation of one nation by another but . . . not the complete disappearance of all distinctions whatever."[4] Most of today's Marxist-Leninist states are multinational, so the question of whether a policy of condoning diversity rather than encouraging assimilation constitutes counterrevolutionary activity is more than a moot point.

Marx's failure to spell out the future of nations in greater detail is symptomatic of the aforementioned marginality of such entities to his major theme. His predilection for an economic interpretation of history caused him to slight the importance of psychological, cultural, and historical elements, and, therefore, to underestimate the magnetic pull exerted by the ethnic group. Since the nation was to Marx essentially an economic unit, the question of political legitimacy was reduced to economic ties. This led him to believe that ethnic minorities should and would be content to consider themselves members of the larger nation to which they were economically wedded. Marx held that workers in a modern industrialized setting were deaf to ethnonational appeals that conflicted with their economic interests.[5] Regardless, then, of dissimilarities in culture and ethnic traditions, identification with a given nation rested simply upon ties to an economic unit.

Contrary to Marx's analysis, nations and economic networks seldom coincide, and it is evident that when Marx wrote of *nations*, it was very often multinational *states* which he had in mind, as witness the following passage:

> With the advent of manufactures, the various nations entered into a competitive relationship, the struggle for trade, which was fought out in wars, protective duties and prohibitions, whereas earlier the nations, insofar as they were connected at all, had carried on an inoffensive exchange with each other.[6]

And yet, in other cases, he purposefully differentiated between state and nation.[7] Indeed, Marx's writings on nationalism are characterized by the same terminological confusion that has plagued American and British scholarship down to the present day.[8] In addition to being equated sometimes with the *state, nation* may, in Marx's usage, refer to the total population within a state regardless of ethnic composition, or it might refer to an ethnonational group, such as the Germans or Poles, which at the time bore no relation to state borders. *Nationality* is also sometimes used to refer to an ethnonational group, sometimes as a synonym for nationalism, and at still other times to connote the essentially legal notion of citizenship.[9] Such terminological imprecision both reflected and contributed to Marx's own lack of insight into the national phenomenon, and is a further reflection of his emphasis upon economic causation. Since to Marx it was the economic force-field that defined the limits of significant sociopolitical units, the state, nation, and the citizenry all became blurred.

With this essentially economic view of the nation, it is not surprising that in taking a position on the outcome of wars, annexations, secession movements, etc., Marx was often guided by what he perceived as most conducive to economic progress. Thus overseas colonialism and imperialism were justified by Marx because they offered the preindustrial peoples of Africa and Asia the most efficacious means of advancing to a higher economic stage.[10] Moreover, not a believer in the innate worth of the nation, Marx would not attempt to breathe the national idea into industrially backward people (whom he and Engels alternately referred to as "people without history," "remains of nations," "ruins of people," "ethnic trash," and worse). He preferred to see such human categories attached to more progressive nations. Still another manifestation of Marx's preoccupation with economic considerations was, other things being equal, his favoring of larger political units over smaller ones, because the former were more apt to be viable economically and more consonant with his theory of capital accumulation.[11]

Historical stage of development and the capacity for further economic development were, therefore, important considerations in determining whether a given movement was the more progressive alternative and therefore worthy of support. Support for nationalistic forces during a progressive phase in their history was quite acceptable behavior. But while condoning alliances with national movements and while acknowledging, as earlier cited, that the proletariat, in order to "first of all settle matters with its own bourgeoisie," must for a time "constitute itself the nation," thereby becoming "national, though not in the bourgeois sense of the word," Marx unequivocally insisted in the Manifesto that members of the Communist party were to be differentiated *precisely and solely* by their nonnationalistic perspective:

> The Communists are distinguished from the other working class parties by this only: (1) In the national struggles of the proletarians of the different countries, they point out and bring to the front the common interests of the entire proletariat, independently of all nationality. (2) In the various stages of development which the struggle of the working class against the bourgeoisie has to pass through, they always and everywhere represent the interests of the movement as a whole.

WHAT we have described to this point might be termed the classical position of Marx and Engels on nationalism. Its major propositions might be sketched as follows:

1. The nation and its ideology (nationalism) are part of the superstructure, byproducts of the capitalist era.

2. Nationalism (and perhaps all national distinctions) is therefore an ephemeral phenomenon which will not survive capitalism.

3. Nationalism can be a progressive or reactionary force, the watershed for any society being a point of developed capitalism.

4. Whether progressive or reactionary, nationalism is everywhere a bourgeois ideology pressed into service by that class in order to divert the proletariat from realizing its own class consciousness and interests.

5. This stratagem cannot work, for loyalties are determined by economic realities rather than by ethnonational sentiments.

6. Communists may support any movement, nationalist or otherwise, when the movement represents the most progressive alternative.

7. But Communists themselves must remain above nationalism, this immunity being their single defining characteristic.

Presuming that one accepts the soundness of the apriorisms of historical dialectical materialism, these seven precepts form a coherent, consistent stance toward nationalism. Had they been faithfully reflected throughout all of the writings of Marx and Engels, ambiguity would be limited to whether or not *all* cultural and psychological vestiges of national particularism would be eradicated in the postcapitalist era. But the unmistakable growing impact of nationalism upon world politics that took place during the lifetimes of Marx and Engels demanded a greater appreciation of the power of nationalism than had been accorded to it in their earlier tracts. After 1848 (a year of numerous ethnonational uprisings throughout Europe), issues involving nationalism came to enjoy a much more prominent place in their writings.

The new appreciation for the importance of nationalism, which was forced upon Marx and Engels by events, principally assumed the form of strategic considerations. Neither man was content to observe passively the unfolding of the inevitable processes of history that they had detected. Both were thoroughly social activists, acutely involved in advancing the proletarian movement. In the words of one authority: "Not content with theorizing about a revolution in the abstract, Marx and Engels concerned themselves deeply with the strategy and tactics of a socialist revolution, the organizing of revolutionary activity, the politics of world change."[12] With this activist bent, it is not surprising that Marx and Engels should come to realize the strategic value of ostensibly aligning their movements with the emerging aspirations of national groups. The slogan of "self-determination of nations" was to serve them well in this endeavor. It is indeed somewhat ironic that this most famous credo of nationalism should make its first appearance in a public document which was drafted by history's most famous internationalist. The expression appeared in the *Proclamation on the Polish Question*, drafted by Marx and endorsed by the London Conference of the First International in 1865. The proclamation noted the need "to annihilate the growing influence of Russia in Europe by assuring to Poland the right of self-determination which belongs to every nation and by giving to this country once more a social and democratic foundation."[13]

Marx had therefore seemingly committed the International to the principle of self-determination for all national groups. But in 1866, the year after its public endorsement in the *Proclamation on the Polish Question*, Engels, at Marx's urging, publicly disclaimed the principle's universality by restricting the status of nation to a very few, select peoples.[14] The major thrust of Engels's argument was that support for the self-determination of the Polish people did not constitute an endorsement of "the principle of nationalities," an expression then in vogue to describe the notion that any people, simply because it considered itself as constituting a separate people, had the right, should it so desire, to create its own state (i.e., what later generations would term "the right of self-determination of nations").[15] Engels's argument rested upon a sharp differentiation between *nations* and *nationalities*. Nations were described as "large," "well defined," "historical," "great," peoples of "undoubted vitality," such as the Italians, Poles, Germans, and Hungarians. Concerning such peoples, "there could, indeed, be no two opinions as to the right of everyone of the great national subdivisions of Europe to dispose of itself, . . . the right of the great European *nations* to separate and independent existence." On the other hand, "questions as to the right of independent national existence of those numerous small relics of peoples," such as Highland Gaels, the Welsh, Manxmen, Serbs, Croats, Ruthenes, Slovaks, and Czechs, constitute "an absurdity." Nowhere do the borders of nationality and state coincide; nor should they, because diversity varies "the otherwise monotonous uniformity of the national character." Even the "great" nations have politically fragmented segments (e.g., the French of Belgium and Switzerland, the Germans of Alsace and Switzerland) who do not wish to be and should not be reunited politically with "their own main stock"; such elements "form connecting links with their neighbours." Poland is also heterogeneous, with its Poles, Lithuanians, White Russians (Belorussians), and Little Russians (Ukrainians). "Therefore, if people say that to demand the restoration of Poland is to appeal to the principle of nationalities, they merely prove that they do not know what they are talking about, for the restoration of Poland means the reestablishment of a state composed of at least four different nationalities."[16] Engels's argument obscures more than it enlightens. Ethnonational sentiments are expressly repudiated by him as a justification for statehood, and the criteria that are advanced are again those that reflected his and Marx's bias in favor of large, economically viable units. But then why dress one's position in ethnonational garb by speaking of a right of self-determination on the part of *nations*? Quite evidently, the strategy of Marx and Engels called for ostensible commitment to the principle of self-determination in the abstract, while concomitantly reserving to themselves in each and every case the decision as to whether a particular movement was to be supported or opposed.[17]

At a less abstract level, Marx and Engels were in fact most niggardly in proffering support for national movements, limiting their major polemical efforts to the causes of Ireland and Poland. The two choices are significant, for they make clear that even the long-ranged, economic criteria, which according to Engels distinguished nations from nationalities, were to be ignored in the face of more pressing, realistic considerations. Thus there were too few Irish within Ireland to qualify them as a "large" nation, and even today the Irish are amongst the least industrialized peoples of Europe.[18] Indeed, in 1845 Engels, in a reference to the Irish, asserted that "such a nation is utterly unfit for manufacture as now conducted."[19] But for a number of strategic reasons involving the more important states of Britain and the United States, Engels and Marx came to believe that Irish independence was in the best interest of the international movement. It was in its relationship to the grand strategy of the movement as a whole, and not on its own merits of either an economic or national variety, that the Irish issue was to be judged.[20]

In contrast to Ireland, Poland would ostensibly meet Engels's criteria for a nation. And both Engels and Marx publicly identified the Polish as a progressive, great people and therefore deserving of independence. But in his private correspondence to Marx, Engels painted a less flattering picture of the Poles, assigning them the role of a means:

> The more I reflect about history the more convinced I become that the Poles are a doomed nation to be used as a means until Russia itself is swept by the agrarian revolution. From that moment on, Poland has no *raison d'être* any more. The Poles have never done anything in history except play heroic quarrelsome acts of stupidity. No moment could be pointed out in which Poland represented progress even vis-à-vis Russia or did anything of historical significance.[21]

Despite such reservations, Poland's cause recommended itself because of a common foe, tsarism, which to Marx and Engels loomed as the archetype of reaction. To frustrate tsarist expansionism, they consistently allied themselves with its adversaries and denied support to its accomplices. Panslavism offers a case in point. It would, in Engels's words, result in "the setting under Russian domination of a Slavic empire from the Erzgebirge and the Carpathians to the Black, Aegean and Adriatic Seas."[22] Such a leviathan should, of course, have appealed to Marx's predilection for large economic units. But since it was perceived as in the employ of tsarism, Panslavism must be mercilessly combatted for the good of the international movement in " 'a ceaseless fight to death' with Slavdom which betrays the Revolution, a battle of annihilation and ruthless terrorism . . . in the interests . . . of the Revolution!"[23]

Grand strategy was therefore to take precedence over ideological purity and consistency. Progressive national movements were to be supported only if consonant with the broader demands of the global movement. Alliances with otherwise unprogressive movements were condoned if strategically opportune. In any situation, national movements were not to be treated in isolation but viewed against this broader backdrop.

This flexibility on the national question, though certainly opportunistic by conventional standards, is, in fact, quite consistent with Marx's dialectical view of progress, within which means are always kept subservient to the end. If the interests of an unprogressive movement promote the broader interests of the international movement, support for it is, by definition, progressive. If the interests of an otherwise progressive movement conflict with those of the international movement as a whole, support for it, by definition, is counterrevolutionary. To our earlier listing of seven prescriptions of classical Marxism with regard to the national question, we can therefore add two more:

8. An ostensible alignment with national aspirations through the public endorsement of the abstract principle of self-determination is good strategy, but, at the nonabstract level, the decision whether or not to support a specific national movement must be made on an individual basis.

9. The ultimate test in determining support or nonsupport is not the relative progressiveness of the specific movement but its relationship to the broader demands of the international movement as a whole.

IF this were the extent of the impact that the spate of nationalist movements commencing with 1848 exerted upon the writings of Marx and Engels, that impact could be described as slight. Their increased awareness of the power of nationalism upon the masses would have been reflected only in a shift in strategy. While becoming manipulators of nationalism, they themselves might have remained intellectually unscathed by nationalist concepts. However, the later works of Marx and Engels are far from free of implicitly or explicitly expressed ideas which, because of their national coloration, sound strangely out of tune with classical Marxism.

Of the two men, Engels was the more immediately and markedly affected by the upsurge in national movements. Changes in his outlook are most readily discernible in those tracts in which he reviewed the abortive revolutions of 1848.[24] Socioeconomic classes were uncharacteristically slighted, their leading role as the principal vehicles of history expropriated by nations: class antagonisms were replaced by national antagonisms; warfare between nations now supplanted class warfare. Indeed, Engels's treatises on the events of 1848 read very much like a morality play, in which entire nations (more specifically, the Germans, Italians, Magyars, and Poles) had come to denote the forces of enlightenment and progress, a role previously reserved for the proletariat, while still other entire nations (particularly the non-Polish and non-Russian Slavic peoples), had now been substituted for the feudal aristocracy and the bourgeoisie in the role of darkness and reaction. The latter were described as unredeemable ethnic trash, the ruins of people, whose "chief mission . . . is to perish in the revolutionary holocaust."[25] As for "the Slavic barbarians, . . . these petty, bull-headed nations will be destroyed so that nothing is left of them but their names."[26] It is therefore explicitly asserted that it is nations—not classes—that fight the class war. "The next world war will cause not only reactionary classes and dynasties but also entire reactionary peoples to disappear from the earth. And that too would be progress."[27]

Such an indictment of entire peoples requires a stereotypical approach to nations that is hardly consonant with a class analysis. Indeed, Engels was given to the broadest assertions concerning so-called national characteristics. We have previously alluded to such generalities as "lazy Mexicans," "bull-headed" Slavs, and the like. Toward the Irish people, he was much more sympathetic, though no less sweeping, in his ascription of national traits. They were variously described in his works as *wild, headstrong, fanatical, light-hearted, corruptible, cheerful, sensuous, excitable, resilient, potato-eating children of nature* in whom *"feeling and passion predominate."*[28]

Classical Marxism, of course, would dictate against the existence of such class-transcending national traits. Even more fundamentally would it dictate against group characteristics of an immutable, transepochal type since such characteristics, as part of the superstructure, should necessarily reflect only a particular economic stage.

Yet Engels on several occasions wrote of enduring national characteristics, as witness the following passage:

> The further back we go in history, the more the characteristics distinguishing different peoples of the same race disappear. . . . Just as the Scandinavians and the Germans differed less in the seventh and eighth centuries than they do today, so also must the Irish Celts and the Gallic Celts have originally resembled each other more than present-day Irishmen and Frenchmen. Therefore we should not be surprised to find in Caesar's description of the Gauls many features which are ascribed to the Irish by Giraldus some twelve hundred years later, and which, furthermore, are discernible in the Irish national character even today, in spite of the admixture of Germanic blood.[29]

Elsewhere he noted that "the Irish are a people related *in their whole character* to the Latin nations, to the French, and especially to the Italians."[30] The genetic determinism which permeates these and many other passages by Engels would probably appear extreme within any intellectual framework, but its appearance in the works of one of the two founders of a school described as "scientific socialism" and predicated upon a theory of historical dialectical materialism borders on the bizarre.

Marx's own writings were less infiltrated by sweeping generalities concerning the characteristics and historic roles of nations, but there is no reason to believe that he did not share all of his colleague's major ideas and biases.[31] Thus, echoing Engel's denunciation of the peoples of southeastern Europe, particularly those of Slavic background, he wrote in 1853 that "this splendid territory has the misfortune to be inhabited by a conglomerate of different races and nationalities, of which it is hard to say which is the least fit for progress and civilization."[32] Though less apt than Engels to ignore in his writings the role of classes as the carriers of history, he did endorse the assignation of entire nations to either progressive or reactionary categories, and prophesied the withering away of the latter group. He concurred with Engels's prognostication that the Czechs were a "dying nationality."[33] So too the Turks, to whom he ascribed "historical guilt" and pronounced them "doomed."[34] Marx also often flirted openly with the notion of national character. He favorably reviewed a work because the author displayed "great feeling for national characteristics," such as "the straightforward Kalmuck," and "the talented Little Russian."[35] His own stereotypical imagery included portraits of the Slavs as "anti-maritime," the English as "lacking the spirit of generalization," and the Russians as devoid of "honor."[36] His description of the Irish as "being more passionate and revolutionary in character than the English" should have been particularly inconceivable to him, since the relative level of industrialization of the two peoples should, according to scientific socialism, have dictated a reverse order of things.[37]

Neither Engels nor Marx ever reconciled his many acknowledgments of the enduring vitality of national ideas and traits with his belief in classical Marxism. And perhaps neither man was aware of any need to do so.[38] But that Engels continued to be influenced heavily by national concepts is evident in a tract written in his seventieth year (1890). In it he spoke of the "natural boundaries" of states, by which he meant ethnic boundaries. He also distinguished between the forceful annexation of peoples aimed at "the uniting of scattered and related ethnic groups . . . [and] the naked conquest by force of *foreign territories*, with robbery pure and simple."[39] Elsewhere in the same article, he anticipated a period in which Russian imperialism would end and in which "Magyars, Rumanians, Serbs, Bulgars, Arnauts [Albanians], Greeks, and Turks will then finally be in a position to settle their own mutual disputes without the intervention of foreign powers, to settle among themselves the boundaries of their individual *national territories*, to manage their internal affairs according to their own judgement."[40] This late homage to the principle of the uninational state is as inconsistent with his earlier denunciations of the "principle of nationalities" and with his earlier view of Bulgars, Serbs, et al. as doomed peoples without a future, as it is with classical Marxism's emphasis upon large, transethnic unions. It therefore illustrates that national ideas persisted in their influence upon his perceptions.

Marx was not influenced to the same degree. It is difficult, however, to imagine the Marx of 1848 referring, as he did in 1869, to the Irish question as "not *merely a simple economic* question but at the same time a *national* question."[41] Moreover, in what has been described as his last great political pamphlet, he demonstrated a sense of uncertainty concerning the relative power of class consciousness relative to national consciousness. The pamphlet dealt with the Paris Commune, upon which Marx approvingly bestowed the honor of recognition as the first dictatorship of the proletariat and therefore the recommended inspirational prototype to all members of the international movement. Marx's appraisal of the motivations of the participants in this uprising is therefore of the utmost significance. On the one hand, he exaggerated, almost to the point of farce, the scanty evidence of an international orientation. With uncharacteristic solicitude for trivial detail, he stressed (1) that the Commune had appointed a person of German extraction as Minister of Labor; (2) that it numbered Poles within its ranks, and (3) that "to broadly mark the new era of history it was conscious of initiating . . . the Commune pulled down that colossal symbol of martial glory, the Vendôme column."[42] On the other hand, Marx felt compelled to take note of the manifest presence of nationalistic and xenophobic sentiments, stating that the governing apparatus "had revolted their national feelings as Frenchmen by precipitating them into a losing war which left only one equivalent for the ruins it made—the disappearance of the Empire."[43] In this tract, written nearly a quarter-century following publication of the Manifesto, it is as though his earlier convictions concerning the fundamental internationalism of the proletariat are still vying for his analytical powers with the press of contrary facts.

Though of great significance, these ambiguities surrounding the national question do not support an assertion that Marx and Engels were anything less than internationalist in their fundamental outlook. Whether or not classes had been replaced by nations as the principal instruments of Marxian history, whether or not entire peoples were perceived as exhibiting traits that transcended both economic class and economic eras, both men remained trenchantly committed to the global revolution. And nationalism, whatever its merits and shortcomings, was not to be permitted to interfere. Late in his life, Marx wrote a letter criticizing a draft of a program of the German Social Democratic Party. His displeasure was aroused, *inter alia*, by that part of the program which read:

> 5. The working class strives for its emancipation first of all *within the framework of the present-day national state*, conscious that the necessary results of its efforts, which are common to the workers of all civilized countries, will be the international brotherhood of peoples.

Behind these words, Marx detected a tendency to view "the workers movement from the narrowest national viewpoint," in opposition "to the Communist Manifesto and to all earlier socialism." While noting that it was "self-evident" that the immediate arena of an uprising by a proletariat must be its own country, he emphasized that even to that limited degree "its class struggle is national, not in substance, but as the Communist Manifesto says, 'in form.' " He ridiculed the vacuity of the phrase "the international brotherhood of peoples," which had nothing to say about how the joint struggle was to be prosecuted: "Not a word, therefore, *about the international functions* of the German working class!" He protested that the movement's enemies were correct in asserting "that the German worker's party had sworn off internationalism in the new programme."[44] Implicit is the exhortation: "Don't let it happen! It must not happen!" Similarly, we have noted that with regard to the Irish, Polish, and all other national questions, Marx and Engels regularly made clear that all such issues were to be viewed against the interests of the international movement as a whole.[45] Lenin and Stalin were quite correct when they noted with approbation that "Marx had no doubt as to the subordinate position of the national question as compared with the 'labor question.' "[46] Indeed, on balance it is for badly underestimating rather than overestimating the emotional pull and tenacity of national identity for which Marx and Engels must be faulted. This underassessment led them to exaggerate the willingness of peoples to surrender their group identity in order to assimilate into larger units of greater vitality.[47] And even in those very few situations in which nations did secede, both men believed that given time for emotions to cool, economic self-interest would soon lead the secessionists to seek some form of political reunion, probably along federal lines.[48] In summary, then, even where classes had been replaced by entire nations in the analyses of Marx and Engels, economic motivation and the world movement remained the paramount force and paramount goal, respectively.

Care should therefore be taken not to mistake the significance of the inconsistencies and ambiguities found in Marx and Engels concerning the relationships between scientific socialism and nationalism. What is significant about these inconsistencies and ambiguities is that they illustrate the basic incompatibility between classical Marxist assumptions and national realities, and also illustrate the manner in which the founders of Marxism, despite their conviction that they could manipulate national sentiments to serve their movement, came themselves to be influenced more substantively by national concepts than they were probably aware.

Concerning the national question, then, three identifiable strains were bequeathed by Marx and Engels to their ideological successors. The first strain, which we earlier termed classical Marxism, was predicated upon the primacy of class consciousness and the indispensability of class struggle, and was therefore irreconcilable with nationalism. The second strain, strategic Marxism, revolved about formal support for the right of national self-determination in the abstract, coupled with very selective support for national movements in the realm of action. Though classical and strategic Marxism were not naturally harmonious, a measure of concinnity was possible if Marxists never forgot that nationalism was a bourgeois and therefore ephemeral ideology whose progressiveness and life expectancy dwindled as society progressed from feudalism through capitalism toward socialism. The final strain, national Marxism, was reflected in references to national characteristics that transcend epochs, and to the role of nations as the principal instrumentality of historical forces. Though potentially compatible with an internationalistic, non-Marxist interpretation of history,[49] national Marxism was irreconcilable with classical Marxism's emphasis upon classes and class warfare. Indeed, the derivation of the word *classical* (from the Latin, *classicus*, meaning "of the classes of the people") causes the expression, *classical Marxism*, to be a particularly felicitous way of differentiating pristine from national Marxism.

NOTES

1. As set forth in the Manifesto: "The bourgeoisie keeps more and more doing away with the scattered state of the population, of the means of production, and of property. It has agglomerated population, centralized means of production, and has concentrated property in a few hands. The necessary consequence of this was political centralization. Independent, or but loosely connected provinces, with separate interests, laws, government, and systems of taxation, became lumped together in one nation, with one government, one code of laws, one national class interest, one frontier and one customs-tariff."

2. As explained by Marx in *The German Ideology*, which was written in 1845–1846, national consciousness was part of what he termed the "illusory communal interest," as contrasted with the true communal interest. Every state, he maintained, is based on an "illusory communal life, always based, however, on the real ties existing in every family and tribal conglomeration—such as flesh and blood, language, division of labor on a larger scale, and other interests. . . . [E]very class which is struggling for mastery . . . must first conquer for itself political power in order to represent its interest in turn as the general interest . . . (in fact the general is the illusory form of communal life)." Part 1 of *The German Ideology* is reproduced in Tucker, *Marx-Engels Reader*; the above excerpts are on pp. 123–125.

3. See, for example, the official Soviet Union opinion in Groshev, *A*

Fraternal Family of Nations, 6–7. "The nation, as a new form of community, emerged when feudalism disintegrated to be superseded by capitalism. . . . Nations appear and develop as a result of the elimination of feudalism and the rise of capitalism, which established economic links and forms a home market, thus evolving a common economic life which unites the separate parts of a nation into a single whole." For the Chinese position, see Chang Chih-i, "A Discussion of the National Question," 35: "It is recognized in Marxist Leninism that 'nations are historically determined . . . , having been formed at the time of the collapse of feudalism and the rise of capitalism.' We endorse this thesis." The article was written in 1956.

4. Bloom, *World of Nations*, 26. For a generally concurring opinion, see Rosdolsky, "Worker and Fatherland."

Earlier, in *The German Ideology*, Marx had differentiated a Communist revolution from all others by stating that a Communist revolution was carried out by the class which "is in itself the expression of the dissolution of all classes, nationalities, etc. within present society." Tucker, *Marx-Engels Reader*, 157. Elsewhere in the same treatise (p. 149), he wrote as though this dissolution was already underway within the industrialized world: "Generally speaking, big industry created everywhere the same relations between the classes of society, and thus destroyed the peculiar individuality of the various nationalities."

5. In *The German Ideology* (Tucker, *Marx-Engels Reader*, 149), Marx noted that "big industry created a class which in all nations has the same interest and with which nationality is already dead." He reaffirmed this position in the Communist Manifesto by writing, in regard to the national consciousness of the proletariat, "we cannot take from them what they have not got."

6. *The German Ideology*, in Tucker, *Marx-Engels Reader*, 145. Several other illustrations may be found on p. 147. Note also in footnote 1 the passage from the Manifesto that ascribes to a nation "one government, one code of laws, . . . one frontier, and one customs-tariff."

7. For example, in another passage from *The German Ideology* (Tucker, *Marx-Engels Reader*, 140), Marx states that "the antagonism between town and country begins with the transition from barbarism to civilization, from tribe to State, from locality to nation."

8. For further discussion, see Introduction.

9. It is left to the reader to sort out as best he can the meaning of *society*, *state*, and *nation* in the following passage from *The German Ideology* (Tucker, *Marx-Engels Reader*, 127), but *nationality* seems to be equated here with citizenship. "Civil society embraces the whole material intercourse of individuals within a definite stage of the development of productive forces. It embraces the whole commercial and industrial life of a given stage and, insofar, transcends the State and the nation, though on the other hand again, it must assert itself in its foreign relations as nationality, and inwardly must organize itself as State."

10. See the many appropriate selections from the works of Marx and Engels in Avineri, *Karl Marx*, which also contains an excellent introduction. On very similar grounds, Engels justified the American annexation of California (as well as Texas) "from the lazy Mexicans who do not know what to do with it." From "Democratic Panslavism," in Blackstock and Hoselitz, *Russian Menace*, 73.

11. Engels suggested in 1849 that 5.5 million people would be too small a population and that 12 million would be a more appropriate minimum. (Blackstock and Hoselitz, *Russian Menace*, 73.)

12. Tucker, *Marx-Engels Reader*, xxviii. One of Marx's most quoted comments, a criticism of earlier philosophers, noted that "the philosophers have only interpreted the world, in various ways; the point, however, is to *change* it." From "Theses on Fuerbach," in Tucker, *Marx-Engels Reader*, 109.

13. As cited in Carr, *The Bolshevik Revolution* 1:421.

14. The disclaimer took the form of three letters written to the editor of the British journal, *Commonwealth*, during 1866. Marx had urged Engels to write them in order to counter Proudhon's criticism of their support for Polish independence. The letters, collectively entitled "What Have the Working Classes to Do with Poland?," can be found in Blackstock and Hoselitz, *Russian Menace*, 95–104.

Criticism of the proclamation on the part of members of the International was not limited to Proudhon. For details, see Cummins, *Marx, Engels*, 94 et seq.

15. The expression had come to be associated closely with Emperor Louis Napoleon of France who was ostensibly committed to it.

16. Despite his insistence that *nations* and *nationalities* must be differentiated, Engels here confusedly interutilizes the two. Are the Poles, as he earlier stated, a *nation* who deserve their own state, or are they merely a nationality?

17. In the same year that Engels, with Marx's approval, stringently restricted the notion of a nation to a very few so-called "great" peoples, Marx drafted the program for the Geneva Conference of the First International, which referred to "the need for annulling Russian influence in Europe, through enforcing the right of self-determination and through the reconstitution of Poland upon democratic and social foundations." (As cited in Stekloff, *History of the First International*, 85.) The wording was almost identical with that of the 1865 "Proclamation on the Polish Question," except for the deletion of the phrase "which belongs to every nation." The deletion may reflect a desire not to irk further Proudhon and other critics of the proclamation on Poland, but, in any case, a "right of self-determination" would by definition apply to all nations. Although the source of his quotation is not clear, J. Braunthal (*History of the International* 1:331) notes that in the Geneva program "the right of self-determination, 'the right of every people' in Marx's words, was demanded."

18. Marx did not support Irish independence until 1867. This was well after the famine years of the 1840s, during which Ireland's population was halved to approximately four million people.

19. From "Conditions of the Working Class in England," in Marx and Engels, *Ireland*, 42.

20. Marx's writings candidly acknowledge that his support for Irish nationalism was due to its significance to the international movement as a whole. This ascribed significance was predicated essentially upon two considerations. The first was the weakest-link strategy. In Marx's words: "If England is the bulwark of landlordism and European capitalism, the only point where one can hit official England really hard is *Ireland*. . . . Ireland is the *bulwark* of English landlordism. If it fell in Ireland, it would fall in England. In Ireland this is a hundred times easier since *the economic struggle there is concentrated exclusively on landed property*, since the struggle is at the same time national, and since the people there are more revolutionary and exasperated than in England." The second reason for Marx's concern with Ireland was his conviction that the Irish question was a decisive element in the working class movement within both Britain and the United States: "[T]he English bourgeoisie has not only exploited the Irish poverty to keep down the working class in England by *forced immigration* of poor Irishmen, but it has also divided the proletariat into two hostile camps. . . . The average English worker hates the Irish worker as a competitor who lowers wages and the *standard* of life. He feels national and religious antipathies for him. . . . This antagonism among the proletarians of England is artificially nourished and supported by the bourgeoisie. It knows that this scission is the true secret of maintaining its power. This antagonism is reproduced on the other side of the Atlantic. The Irish . . . reassemble in North America where they constitute a huge, evergrowing section of the population. Their only thought, their only passion, is hatred for England. The English or American governments (or the classes they represent) play on these feelings [and] thereby prevent a sincere and lasting alliance between the workers on both sides of the Atlantic, and consequently their emancipation. . . . Thus, the attitude of the International Association to the Irish question is very clear. Its first need is to encourage the social revolution in England. To this end a great blow must be struck in Ireland." All of the foregoing is extracted from a confidential communication to the General Council of the First International and was therefore not intended for propagandistic purposes. The text can be found in Marx and Engels, *Ireland*, 160–163. For several other acknowledgments that his support for the Irish cause was dictated by its place in grand strategy, see pp. 280, 281, and 290. See also Mehring, *Karl Marx*, 390–391.

21. Letter from Engels to Marx, May 23, 1851, in Avineri, *Karl Marx*, 447. In yet a more sarcastic, historic reference, Engels wrote to Marx on April 21, 1863: "I must say that to summon up any enthusiasm for the Polacks of 1772 needs a hide like an ox." Cited in Mehring, *Karl Marx*, 340.

22. From "Hungary and Panslavism" (1849), in Blackstock and Hoselitz, *Russian Menace*, 62.

23. From "Democratic Panslavism" in ibid., 84. Marx's concurrence in this view is substantiated by the lending of his name to a piece in which Panslavism was referred to as "this ludicrous, this anti-historical movement . . . , a movement which intended nothing less than to subjugate the civilized West under the barbarian East, the town under the country, trade manufactures, intelligence, under the primitive agriculture of Slavonic serfs." The piece was probably written by Engels but appeared under Marx's name in the *New York Daily Tribune* of March 15, 1852. It is reprinted in Marx and Engels, *Selected Works* 1:341–344.

24. See, for example, his two 1849 treatises, "Hungary and Panslavism" and "Democratic Panslavism" in Blackstock and Hoselitz, *Russian Menace*, 56–84.

25. Ibid., 59.

26. Ibid., 67. Notice that Engels in 1849 was referring to these peoples as nations, though in 1866 he would insist that they were only nationalities.

Not only Slavic national groups were scheduled for destruction. "Such miserably powerless so-called nations as the Danes, the Dutch, the Belgians, Swiss, etc." faced a similar fate. See "Letter from Germany: The War in Schleswig-Holstein," in Marx and Engels, *Collected Works* 10:393.

27. Blackstock and Hoselitz, *Russian Menace*, 67. This emphasis upon nations as the carriers of history should not be confused with the Manifesto's statement that the proletariat must for a time become the nation, that is, that each working class must first settle accounts with its own bourgeoisie. In that passage the emphasis remained upon class. In the 1849 tracts of Engels, the emphasis is on entire peoples, regardless of their class structure.

28. Marx and Engels, *Ireland*, 33, 42, 211, 274.

29. From "History of Ireland" (1869-1870), in ibid., 209. Contrast the enduring nature of national characteristics as described here with the earlier-cited passage of the Manifesto concerning the vanishing of national differences.

30. "Conditions of the Working Class in Europe" (1845), in ibid., 41. Emphasis added.

31. Many of Engels's most florid passages concerning national characteristics appeared either in the *Neue Rheinische Zeitung*, which Marx served (in Engels's words) as the "dictator" of the editorial board or, years later, in the *New York Daily Tribune*, under Marx's byline. In an attack upon the Danes that was broadened to include the Swedes, Norse, and Icelanders, Engels had written in the *Neue Rheinische Zeitung*: "Scandinavianism is enthusiasm for the brutal, sordid, piratical, Old Norse national traits, for that deep-rooted inner life which is unable to express its exuberant ideas and sentiments in words, but can express them only in deeds, namely in rudeness towards women, perpetual drunkenness and wild berserk frenzy

alternating with tearful sentimentality." Marx and Engels, "The Danish-Prussian Armistice," in *Collected Works* 7:422.

32. Article in the *New York Daily Tribune*, April 7, 1853. Reprinted in Avineri, *Karl Marx*, 51–58.

33. Bloom, *World of Nations*, 41.

34. "Letter to Liebknecht," reprinted in Avineri, *Karl Marx*, 471.

35. Bloom, *World of Nations*, 13.

36. Ibid., 12, 13, 186.

37. "Letter to Sigfrid Meyer and August Vogt," April 9, 1870, in Marx and Engels, *Ireland*, 293. See also p. 162 where, in a confidential communication, Marx contrasts the "revolutionary fire of the Celtic worker" with "the nature of the Anglo Saxon worker, solid, but slow."

38. Solomon Bloom (*World of Nations*, 15) cites Marx's favorable comments to Engels concerning a book written in 1867 by Pierre Tremaux, whose thesis was that racial distinctions were related to physical environment (topography, climate, etc.), as evidence that Marx believed that this thesis supported his (Marx's) own position that national traits varied with the system of production. Marx's actual words need not support such an interpretation, however. And, in any case, there would be little chronological association between Tremaux's view of the role of the physical environment upon human traits, which operated through minute, undetectable increments over hundreds of thousands of years, and that of classical Marxism, which called for sudden radical transformations (the Law of the Transformation of Quantity into Quality).

39. "The Foreign Policy of Russian Czarism" (1890) in Blackstock and Hoselitz, *Russian Menace*, 39. Emphasis added.

40. Ibid., 53. Emphasis added. In the following sentence, he refers to "the autonomy and free groupings of the peoples and ethnic fragments between the Carpathian mountains and the Aegean sea."

41. "Letter to Ludwig Kugelmann," November 29, 1869, in Marx and Engels, *Ireland*, 281. Emphasis as in the original letter. Again, the fact that this sentiment was expressed in private correspondence is particularly noteworthy.

42. "The Civil War in France" (1871) in Tucker, *Marx-Engels Reader*, 560–561. Such tenuous linkages suggest the primacy of wishful thinking over analytical rigor. A similar note of wishful thinking is evident in Engels's 1895 introduction to *The Tactics of Social Democracy*, in ibid., 412. Though, as noted, he had by 1890 altered his stance concerning the principle of "one nation, one state," he now contrasted the situation in 1848 with that in 1895 as follows: "At that time the masses, sundered and differing according to locality and nationality, linked only by the feeling of common suffering, undeveloped, helplessly tossed to and fro from enthusiasm to despair; today the *one* great international army of Socialists, marching irresistibly on and growing daily in number, organization, discipline, insight and certainty of victory."

43. Ibid., 559. Years later, Marx acknowledged that "the Commune was in no wise Socialist, nor could it be." (Cummins, *Marx, Engels*, 167.) But that his original analysis of the Commune has been the one with enduring effect was pointed up in an interview with Regis Debray ("Marxism and the National Question," 33): "One very striking thing here is Marx's treatment of the Commune. The most elementary study of the Paris Commune's history shows its powerfully patriotic, even chauvinistic character. Yet Marx imposed his mythological interpretation of the Commune so powerfully—we still use his spectacles today—that this aspect has disappeared completely. It ceases to be a patriotic outburst against an invader. Why were Trochu and Jules Favre kicked out during the Commune? Because their breakthrough was too feeble and short-lived and they failed to lift the siege of Paris, and hence—cutting a long story short—were accused of complicity with the enemy! There is an extreme patriotic side to the Commune that Marx never discusses at all."

44. "Critique of the Gotha Program," in Tucker, *Marx-Engels Reader*, 390–391.

45. In 1849 Engels warned those Panslavists who would "join the Revolution on condition that they be allowed to form into independent Slavic states all Slavs without exception, without any consideration of material necessities, . . . [that] the Revolution does not permit the setting up of any conditions. One is either a revolutionary, and accepts the consequences of the Revolution, whatever they may be, or one is driven into the arms of the counterrevolution." "Democratic Panslavism" in Blackstock and Hoselitz, *Russian Menace*, 83. Nor was this warning restricted to those people without a history: Two years later (1851), Engels announced that "the Italians, Poles, and Hungarians must be told plainly that when modern questions are under discussion they must hold their tongues." Mehring, *Karl Marx*, 241.

46. The quote was originally Lenin's, but was cited with favor by Stalin at the Twelfth Congress of the Russian Communist Party on April 23, 1923. See Stalin, *Marxism: Selected Writings*, 158.

47. Engels had a tendency to perceive assimilation as progressing or completed nearly everywhere. See, for example, "Hungary and Panslavism" (1849), in Blackstock and Hoselitz, *Russian Menace*, 61. To both Engels and Marx, the record of a people's ability to assimilate others was a major test of that people's vitality and its fitness for a role in history. Note Engels's explanation as to why Poland had no long-run future and why Russia did: "Russian rule, with all its nastiness, with all its Slavonic filth . . . has absorbed far more civilization-building and industrial elements than Poland with its chivalrous and bearskin nature. . . . Poland could never nationalize foreign elements. The Germans in the cities are and remain German. How Russia manages to russify Germans and Jews—for this every Russian-German of the second generation serves as a glaring example. Even the Jews develop their Slavonic cheekbones." Engels to Marx, May 23, 1851, in Avineri, *Karl*

Marx, 447. The much later decision to support Irish independence was also justified in part on the successful resistance of the Irish to British assimilation and on the assimilative power of the Irish over British settlers. See, for example, Marx's speech of 1867 and Engels's "History of Ireland" (1869–1870), in *Ireland*, 140, 172.

48. In 1867 Marx wrote to Engels: "Previously I thought Ireland's separation from England impossible. Now I think it inevitable, although after separation there may come *federation*." Ibid., 143. See also his hope for "equal and free confederation" of the two countries in his confidential communication of 1870, ibid., 163. In 1882, after noting that the smaller Slavic nations of the Habsburg Empire might well someday each have their own state, Engels added: "And I am certain that six months of independence will suffice for most Austro-Hungarian Slavs to bring them to a point where they will beg to be readmitted." "Nationalism, Internationalism and the Polish Question," in Blackstock and Hoselitz, *Russian Menace*, 119.

49. Over the decades, numerous non-Marxists have maintained that a view of the nation as the primary unit of humanity is quite compatible with an international outlook. Johann Gottfried von Herder and Guiseppe Mazzini are well-known cases in point.

CHAPTER 2

The National Question
from the Second International
to the October Revolution

As a result of Marx's total failure to address himself directly to the issue of nationalism and thus resolve the many ambiguities and inconsistencies concerning its place in the Marxist scheme of things, the national question was to remain a matter of serious discord among later disciples even down to the present. Such doctrinaires on the issue as Rosa Luxembourg, Georgii Plekhanov, and Karl Radek would rally to Marx's classical strain, viewing any and all national movements as not worthy of support by true Marxists. At the other pole would be those whose ideas reflected the third or national strain in Marx. In 1898 Edward Bernstein would note "that national diversity and the historical element rooted in tradition are of far greater significance than we and our scientific teachers had originally assumed."[1] And elsewhere he apostatically averred that "the statement that the worker has no country is not part of my creed."[2] More of a threat to classical Marxism was posed, however, by the Austrian socialists, Karl Renner and Otto Bauer. In a substantive leap from Marx's seemingly unpremeditated acknowledgments that nations can on occasion substitute for classes as the principal agency of history, Renner and Bauer described nations as enduring forms of society and the essential agency of social change. Thus wrote Karl Renner in 1918:

> Social democracy proceeds not from the existing states but from live nations. It neither denies nor ignores the existence of the nation but on the contrary, *it accepts it as the carrier* of the new order. . . . Social democracy considers the nation both indestructible and undeserving of destruction. . . . Far from being unnational or anti-national, it places nations at the foundation of its world structure.[3]

And in direct contradiction of the Communist Manifesto's assertion that economic forces were causing national peculiarities to disappear, Bauer contended that nations could only come to fruition under socialism. Nations—groups based upon common descent— had been monistic units of humanity during the stage of primitive communism. But with the advent of private property, these units were decomposed. In slave, feudal, and capitalist societies alike, only the ruling class constituted the nation, and its culture the national culture:

> Just as private ownership of the means of production and in-
> dividual production develops out of the social system of primitive
> communism, and from this, again, there develops co-operative
> production on the basis of social ownership, so the unitary nation
> divides into members of the nation and those who are excluded
> and become fragmented into small local circles; but with the
> development of social production these circles are again drawn
> together and will eventually be absorbed into the unitary socialist
> nation of the future. The nation of the era of private property
> and individual production, which is divided into members and
> non-members, and into numerous circumscribed local groups, is
> the product of the disintegration of the communist nation of the
> past and the material for the socialist nation of the future.[4]

Socialism, according to Bauer, is also the prerequisite for abolishing the political domination of one nation by another:

> The construction of the great national states in the nineteenth
> century is only the precursor of an era in which the principle of
> nationality will be fully realized. . . . [S]ocialism leads necessarily
> to the realization of the principle of nationality. . . . The trans-
> formation of men by the socialist mode of production leads nec-
> essarily to the organization of humanity in national communities.
> The international division of labour leads necessarily to the uni-
> fication of the national communities in a social structure of a
> higher order. All nations will be united for the common domi-
> nation of nature, but the totality will be organized in national
> communities which will be encouraged to develop autonomously
> and to enjoy freely their national culture—that is the socialist
> principle of nationality.

In sharpest contrast, then, to the classical Marxist projection of no role for nations under socialism, this school of Marxists anticipated that the nation would be the principal organizational unit of the new order.

Rejecting both the doctrinaire/classical position and the revisionist/national one (and indeed often aiming his polemical treatises on the national question directly at some of the above-named individuals), Lenin pursued the second strain in Marx, that which we have termed strategic Marxism. Too much the devout believer to sympathize with the revisionists and too much the revolutionary to adopt the doctrinaires' "hands-off" policy with regard to national aspirations, Lenin came to appreciate, even far more than had Marx or Engels, the tactical wisdom of ostensible alliances with national forces. In pursuing this course of action, the slogan of self-determination became his principal weapon.

Following Marx's death, the formulators of the programs of scientific socialism had continued, almost as a matter of form, to insert paeans to the self-determination doctrine into their programs and declarations. Thus the program of the Second International, as endorsed by the London Conference of 1896, noted that "the Congress declares that it upholds the full right of self-determination of all nations. . . ."[5] Similarly, the 1903 program of the Russian Communist Party (then called the Russian Social Democratic Workers Party) included "the right of self-determination for all nations comprising the State."[6] Such inclusions were due more to mimicry than to commitment or even to a regard for the importance of the national question. Thus, though Lenin was closely associated with the 1903 program, he could write about the time of its drafting that "undoubtedly the class antagonism has now pushed the national question far into the background."[7] As late as 1913, he would acknowledge his previous disinterest in a letter to Gorki: "As to nationalism, I am fully in agreement with you that it is necessary to pay more serious attention to it."[8]

Lenin's growing interest in nationalism during the early years of the twentieth century's second decade was the result of several factors, including a period of domicile within multinational Austria-Hungary where he perforce became aware of the internecine national struggles within the socialist movement there; his own lengthy dispute with the Jewish Bund; and the outbreak of the Balkan Wars with their strong national overtones. By 1913 he felt the issue was sufficiently significant to direct Stalin to write a piece that would set forth the "errors" of the Austrian socialists, and he additionally had a strongly worded resolution on the national question endorsed by the Russian Marxists at their conference held in the summer of that year. But though his interest in nationalism had therefore been stimulated prior to 1914, his realization of the power that nationalism could exert on the minds of men unquestionably underwent a qualitative transformation as a result of the events of World War I.

The possibility of such a war had long been entertained by members of the International and, at the 1907 Stuttgart Congress, Lenin's faction successfully placed the congress on record as noting that such a war, by necessitating the arming of the proletariat, would hasten the downfall of capitalism.[9] The belief that the English, French, or German proletariat would turn its weapons upon its own national bourgeoisie rather than wage war upon one another was made even more explicit in the unanimously adopted manifesto of the Basel Extraordinary Congress of 1912. Yet, when war did break out, the working classes proved no less discernibly nationalistic than did the bourgeoisie. More startling to one of Lenin's convictions was the national jingoism that pervaded all socialist parties. The bitterness with which Marxist-Leninists still lace their accounts of this unforgivable apostasy is captured in the following passage written by a Soviet scholar more than a half-century after the fact: "The majority of the leaders of the second international's social democratic parties, who were joined by the Mensheviks, slid into positions of militant chauvinism. The double-dyed opportunists, petit bourgeois conciliators, and pseudorevolutionary shouters broke with socialism and met on the soil of nationalism."[10] Even Plekhanov, whom Lenin strongly admired and who, as we have noted, had hitherto been a Marxist doctrinaire on the national question, now became an arch supporter of the Russian, and thereby the tsarist, cause. The evidence was everywhere: contrary to Lenin's expectations, when juxtaposed in the clearest relief, nationalism had proved a more powerful magnetic force than had class consciousness.[11] The impact that these unanticipated developments exerted upon Lenin was a profound one, and nationalism subsequently appears seldom to have been far from his thoughts. From 1914 until his death in 1924, two recurring topics of his treatises, speeches, and private correspondence were how to combat nationalism when necessary and how to manipulate it in the interests of the international movement whenever possible.

In the course of developing an explanation for this unexpected manifestation of strident nationalism among Europe's working class, Lenin laid great stress upon the role of colonies. His thesis, which in its fully developed form would be titled *Imperialism: The Highest Stage of Capitalism*, held that the national bourgeoisies of Europe had been able to blunt the revolutionary class consciousness of their respective working classes by temporarily exporting exploitation.

Europe had been made richer by Asia and Africa, and the European proletariat had shared, if quite unequally, the benefits of this exploitation. But the division of the world into colonies was now nearly complete, and World War I was the first of a series of imperialist wars among capitalist states for one another's colonies. It followed that the contradictions among capitalist states and within capitalist states could be exacerbated by the driving of wedges between colonies and the mother countries. To offset the loss of this source of cheap labor and this monopolistic outlet for its goods, each capitalist society would necessarily pursue more intensive exploitation of its own working class, whose class consciousness would grow as a direct result. At the same time, the opportunity to gain the friendship of hundreds of millions of Asiatics and Africans appealed irresistibly to Lenin's penchant for grand strategy. The colonies appeared to Lenin as Ireland had appeared to Marx: the weakest linchpin in the capitalist machine. And the approach to this most vulnerable part of the structure was to be the same: ally yourself with the present and future national aspirations of the inhabitants by extending to them the right of national self-determination. The significance that Lenin attached to this stratagem can be gleaned from the following passage written in 1916:

> Third, the semi-colonial countries, like China, Persia, Turkey, and all the colonies which have a combined population amounting to a billion. In these countries the bourgeois-democratic movements have either hardly begun, or are far from having been completed. Socialists must not only demand the unconditional and immediate liberation of the colonies without compensation—and this demand in its political expression signifies nothing more or less than the recognition of the right to self-determination—but must render determined support to the more revolutionary elements in the bourgeois-democratic movements for national liberation in these countries and assist their rebellion—and if need be, their revolutionary war, against the imperialist powers that oppress them.[12]

And later in the same year, he added that "to suppose that a social revolution is *thinkable* without a revolt of the small nationalities in the colonies and in Europe . . . *is to abjure the social revolution*."[13]

It was therefore not without justification that Stalin, shortly after Lenin's death, defined Leninism as "Marxism of the era of imperialism," for the merging of the colonial and national questions was one of Lenin's major contributions to Marxist thought. It is worth noting, however, that in forging this link, Lenin was uncharacteristically guilty of terminological license. Despite the confusing use of key terms by Marx and Engels, their successors, including Lenin, have been unusually circumspect in their mode of expression. Indeed, as earlier noted, the precise vocabulary on nationalism, which has become *de rigeur* for Marxist-Leninists, imbues their writings with a clarity that is particularly refreshing when contrasted with the terminological confusion characterizing American and British scholarship on nationalism.[14] A major exception to this pattern of terminological precision is represented by that body of Marxist-Leninist literature that deals with the former colonial regions, or what is today termed the Third World. It is evident that the colonies and the independent states that succeeded them are, with few exceptions, comprised of several nations and/or nationalities, and the application to them of such notions as *national* self-determination or *national* wars of liberation is therefore inappropriate. Strategy here takes precedence over terminological purity, for this deviation from customary linguistic precision reflects the great strategic value Lenin and his disciples have attached to being identified as stalwart defenders of self-determination of the Afro-Asian peoples.

Whether applied to Russia, all of Europe, or to the colonies, Lenin's sense of strategy led him quite early to the conclusion that mere statements of support for the unrefined principle of self-determination did not offer a sufficient basis for differentiating Marxists from non-Marxists with regard to the national question. Self-determination had won increasing numbers of adherents from all along the political spectrum, and, in the apt choice of word by Edward Carr, Lenin realized that it was necessary not just to adopt but to "overtrump" the doctrine of self-determination as propagated by others.[15] Lenin therefore considered it necessary to state in the most unequivocal of terms that national self-determination included the right of political secession. Indeed, most of his references to self-determination appear to equate the two.[16] However, he seems to have agreed with the more comprehensive definition set forth by Stalin in 1913, which includes but is not limited to secession. "The right of self-determination means that a nation can arrange its life according to its own will. It has the right to arrange its life on the basis of autonomy. It has the right to enter into federal relations with other nations. It has the right to complete secession. Nations are sovereign and all nations are equal."[17] In any case, the 1913 pronouncement of the party (designed by Lenin) could not have been more explicit in this matter, pledging its support for "the right of the oppressed nations of the Tsarist monarchy to self-determination, i.e., to secession and the formation of an independent state."[18]

But is not the doctrine of political independence for all nations inconsonant with Marx's insistence upon the need for large states? Not to Lenin, in part because he was certain that few small nations would act against their economic self-interest. And, in the event that they did, they would soon perceive the wisdom of requesting reunion. In Lenin's words: "To defend this right [to secession] does in no way mean encouraging the formation of small states, but, to the contrary, it leads to a freer, . . . wider formation of larger states—a phenomenon more advantageous for the masses and more in accord with economic development."[19] As earlier noted, Marx and Engels also believed that economic self-interest would lead a once independent Irish or Czech nation to seek reunion with a larger multinational structure.[20] However, the reasoning which underlay Lenin's insistence that nations be promised the right to secede went beyond a faith that peoples, acting in their own economic self-interest, would either refuse secession or, having accepted it, soon suffer from second thoughts concerning its desirability. Rather, Lenin's insistence on explicitly espousing secession mirrored his interpretation of the nature of the phenomenon termed nationalism.

Lenin conceived of nationalism in purely negative terms as the response of a people to past oppression and prejudice, whether real or imagined. He was therefore convinced that the only way to combat nationalism was by the use of the carrot, not the stick. And hence the dialectic: by conceding all, or rather, by seeming to concede all to nationalism, one in fact was promoting internationalism. With specific regard to self-determination, this meant that the best way to avoid or to dissipate a grass-roots demand for independence was to proffer that independence. Phrased differently, support for the slogan of self-determination, rather than acting as a stimulant to nationalism, would prove to be an anesthetic. Thus in 1913 Lenin could write that "the right to self-determination is an *exception* from our general premise of centralism," and that "separation is by no means our plan. We do not predict separation at all."[21] While it may appear paradoxical to espouse a course of action in order to abort it, it bears reemphasizing that the basis of Lenin's conviction on this point is a key to the Marxist-Leninist image of nationalism and, by extension, to an understanding of Marxist-Leninist national policies. Lenin could readily conceive of a nationally aroused people acting in opposition to their best economic interest by fighting for independence. But with nationalistic suspicions laid to rest by the offer of independence, economic motivation would win out.

But what if Lenin proved wrong and a number of nations should elect to withdraw from Russia at the time of the revolution? Was Lenin prepared to permit secession? Lenin's position remained unclear. On the one hand, he often suggested that Finland, Poland, and/or the Ukraine might secede. As noted, however, just as Marx in the case of Ireland, Lenin thought that the proletariat of an economically unviable state would soon perceive that it was to their economic advantage to achieve reunion. Moreover, there are a few hints that Lenin would view any postrevolutionary attempt at secession as counterrevolutionary. When asked directly how he would respond to a situation in which a nonproletarian leadership was in charge of a border nation, Lenin's evasiveness hinted at something less than resignation. "What shall happen when the reactionaries are in the majority? asks Mr. Semkovskii. This is one of those questions of which it is said that seven fools ask more than ten wise men can answer."[22] On another occasion, his comments on Marx's position on the Irish question appeared to preclude any postrevolutionary nationalist movements: "If capitalism had been overthrown in England as quickly as Marx at first expected, there would *have been no room* for a bourgeois-democratic and general national movement."[23]

In any event, Lenin left his options open by making explicit that Marxists need not support each liberation movement.[24] Lenin thus made a distinction between the abstract right of self-determination, which is enjoyed by all nations, and the right to exercise that right, which evidently is not.[25] Though supporting the right of self-determination, "we are not obliged to support 'every' struggle for independence or 'every' republic or anti-clerical movement."[26] The question of support in a specific instance was left to the Communist party and, just as strongly as Marx, Lenin insisted that members of the Communist party not be tainted by nationalism.[27] As he sporadically made clear, nationalism and Marxism cannot mix: "Marxism is incompatible with nationalism, even the most 'just,' 'pure,' refined, and civilized nationalism."[28] Given his blueprint for party organization, which came to be euphemistically termed "democratic centralism," but which in Lenin's words ". . . strives to proceed from the top downward, and upholds an extension of the rights and powers of the centre in relation to the parts,"[29] Lenin had excellent reason to feel that all decisions concerning self-determination would be guided by Marxist strategy rather than by ethnicity. To keep the party centralized and free of all nationalist inclinations became a two-pronged commandment. All forms of federalism and autonomy were vehemently opposed as inappropriate to the party and were explicitly rejected in part as insurance against the formation of ethnic poles of power within the apparatus.[30] In Lenin's concise couplet: "We Social Democrats are opposed to *all* nationalism and advocate democratic centralism."[31]

But what of those nations who remained within the multinational state? The victorious Communists would introduce the policy of "national equality," guaranteeing to the members of each nation the right to use their own language and to an education in that language. These guarantees were contained in the 1903 program, and they were reasserted in 1913 by Stalin in *Marxism and the National Question*. Stalin also set forth as essential a system of regional autonomy "for such crystallized units as Poland, Lithuania, the Ukraine, the Caucasus, and so forth," while explicitly denying it to smaller nations such as the Latvians;[32] in some instances autonomous borders would reflect ethnic distribution, in others (e.g., the Caucasus and smaller or less nationally conscious groups) they would not. The following year (1914), in a private letter, Lenin made clear that he had already devised the basic content of what subsequently became official Soviet national policy, though he also demonstrated something substantially less than ardor for the policy's merit.

> In order to struggle against the stupidity of the cultural-national autonomists, the fraction must introduce into the Duma a draft law on the equality of nations and the definition of the rights of national minorities. I propose that we draw up such a project:
> The general situation of equal rights—the division of the country into autonomous and self-governing territorial units according—among other things—to nationality (the local population determines the boundaries, the general parliament confirms them)—the limits of the administration of the autonomous districts and regions, as well as the self-governing units; the illegalization of any departure from equality of nations in the decisions of autonomous districts, zemstvos, etc.; general school councils democratically elected, etc., freedom and equality of languages—the choice of languages by the municipal institutions, etc. The protection of minorities: the right to a proportional share of the expenditures for school buildings (gratis) for stu-

dents of "alien" (non-Russian) nationalities, for "alien" teachers, for "alien" departments in museums and libraries, theaters and the like; the right of each citizen to seek redress (before a court) for any departure from the corresponding equality of rights, for any "trampling upon" the rights of national minorities; a census of population every five years in the multi-national districts, a ten-year census in the country as a whole, etc.[33]

Lenin's lack of ardor for his own program of promoting national equality and cultural autonomy was a reflection of his conviction that such a policy was merely the prerequisite for a higher stage. Interspersed throughout his writings are references to "the inevitable merging of nations," their ultimate "fusion," "amalgamation," or "assimilation."[34] Consonant with Marx's position on the vanishing of national differences, Lenin viewed the movement toward assimilation as both progressive and inevitable.

But if one desires ultimate assimilation, is he not working at cross-purposes when he encourages the use of local languages and creates national schools? Does not such an approach strengthen the nationalism of the various ethnic groups? Again, as in the case of self-determination, Lenin thought not, and essentially for the same reason. Since the bitterness and mistrust which the minorities experienced toward the Russians were due to a superior-to-inferior relationship long practiced by the latter, these attitudes, which constitute the major barrier to assimilation, must be exorcised by a period of national equality, characterized by a pandering to some of the more apparent manifestations of national diversity such as language.[35] Since he considered nationalism to be the mental product of past oppression, attempts to eradicate it by force could only have the unintended effect of strenghthening it. His emphasis is ever on the voluntary nature of assimilation.[36] Although once in power he was to condone the use of force to nullify political secession, he remained convinced to the end that a frontal attack upon nationalism was improper strategy.[37]

Even if his assumptions proved incorrect, Lenin's temporary concessions to national diversity were probably not viewed by him as particularly risky because of the presence of the Communist party. To Lenin the key element was not the language but the message, a distinction later to be sloganized as "national in form, socialist in content."[38] To grant the use of local languages while maintaining control of content was to surrender little. And it would be in the higher echelons of the party that the general content of educational curricula and of the communications media would be designed. Moreover, broadcasting, writing, or lecturing in the native language would tend to assuage ethnic sensibilities and suspicions, thereby rendering the audience more susceptible to party direction, including direction toward the ultimate goal of assimilation.

Pared down, then, to its basic elements, Lenin's strategy for harnessing nationalism is reducible to three commandments:

1. Prior to the assumption of power, promise to all national groups the right of self-determination (expressly including the right of secession), while proffering national equality to those who wish to remain within the state.

2. Following the assumption of power, terminate the fact—though not necessarily the fiction—of a right to secession, and begin the lengthy process of assimilation via the dialectical route of territorial autonomy for all compact national groups.

3. Keep the party centralized and free of all nationalist proclivities.[39]

This three-pronged strategy of Lenin's is of the utmost importance, constituting the crux of his legacy on the national question. At least in their public utterances, all Marxist-Leninists (not just those within the Soviet Union) claim fidelity to that analysis of nationalism bequeathed by Marx and Engels, as further refined by Lenin. It follows that the relative adequacy of the Marxian conception of nationalism can be evaluated through an examination of the successes and failures that each of Lenin's three injunctions encountered as it was implemented in a variety of differing situations and environments. We shall begin with the Leninist precept concerning self-determination.

In reviewing the various ways in which Marxist-Leninists have actually utilized the notion of self-determination, particular attention will be paid to the experiences of the Soviet, Chinese, Vietnamese, and Yugoslavian parties. Each of these parties came to power in a state within which there were numerically significant and/or strategically located ethnic minorities. Each can lay claim to having achieved power essentially on its own initiative, without the bayonets of the armed forces of another Communist state. In their successful quest for power, each sought the support of minorities by promising them self-determination, including the right of secession. Finally, despite very important variations in timetable, each party, once in power, denied the right of secession to its minorities and ostensibly introduced a policy of regional cultural autonomy.

NOTES

1. Cited in Kernig, *Marxism* 5:41.

2. Ibid., 83.

3. From *The Right of Self-Determination of Nations (Das Selbstbestimmungs-recht der Nationen)* 1:23–24. Cited in Pipes, *Formation*, 25. Emphasis added.

4. All preceding and subsequent quotations by Bauer are from his *The National Question and Social Democracy (Die Nationalitatenfrage und die Sozialdemokratie)*, written in 1907, as translated in Bottomore and Goode, *Austro-Marxism*, 102–117.

5. Cited in Shaheen, *Communist Theory*, 26.

6. The program was approved at the Second Conference of the party in 1903. Sections pertinent to the national question can be found in Conquest, *Soviet Nationalities*, 16. The First Congress had also proclaimed its support for "the right of national self-determination." See Shaheen, *Communist Theory*, 17.

7. With characteristic flexibility, he added, "but one should not maintain categorically, lest one become a doctrinaire, that the temporary appearance of this or that national question on the stage of the political drama is impossible." Cited in Pipes, *Formation*, 35. Ten years after its endorsement, Lenin forsook all credit for the references in the 1903 program to national self-determination, ascribing these to the efforts of Martov.

8. Cited in Wolfe, *Three Who*, 591. He also began an important tract in 1913 by noting that "it is obvious that the national question has now become prominent among the problems of Russian public life [making] it incumbent on us to give more attention to the national question than we have done so far." Lenin, *Collected Works* 20:19.

9. Wolfe, *Marxism*, 279–284.

10. Moskin, "The 24th CPSU Congress."

11. These events illustrate the profundity of Rupert Emerson's remarkably succinct definition of the nation as "the largest community which, when the chips are down, effectively commands men's loyalty." *From Empire to Nation* (Boston: Beacon Press, 1960), 95.

12. From "The Socialist Revolution and the Right of Nations to Self-Determination (Theses)," in Lenin, *Right of Nations*, 81.

13. Cited in Carr, *Bolshevik Revolution* 1:434. In his last substantive words on the national question (December 31, 1922), a bed-ridden Lenin attacked the harsh treatment accorded by Stalin to the Georgians because of its potential effect upon "hundreds of millions of peoples of Asia who in the near future are to enter the stage of history in our wake. It would be unforgivable opportunism if, on the eve of this emergence of the East and at the beginning of its awakening, we should undermine our prestige there with even the slightest rudeness or injustice to our own minorities. . . . And the coming day in world history will be precisely that day, when the peoples, oppressed by imperialism, will have their final awakening, and when the

decisive, prolonged and difficult battle for their liberation will get underway." Pipes, *Formation*, 286–287.

14. See Introduction.

15. Carr, *Bolshevik Revolution*, 265. That bourgeois thinkers were coming
to accept the right of self-determination as a combination of moral imperative and truism is illustrated by its embracement about this time by
Woodrow Wilson. Within tsarist Russia, the non-Marxist Socialist Revolutionary Party had committed itself to the self-determination principle in
its 1905 program, and the Kadet platform of the following year spoke of
"cultural self-determination."

16. See, for example, Lenin, *Right of Nations*, 14, for his comment in
"The Right of Nations to Self-Determination," written in 1914: "It means
that 'self-determination of nations' in the program of Marxists cannot,
from a historical-economic point of view, have any other meaning than
political self-determination, political independence, the formation of a
national state." See also his comment in "The Socialist Revolution and the
Right of Nations to Self-Determination (Theses)," written in 1916 (ibid.,
73): "Victorious socialism must . . . give effect to the right of the oppressed
people to self-determination, i.e., the right to free political secession."

17. Stalin, *Marxism: Selected Writings*, 23. Lenin, who had urged Stalin to
write the treatise, did not subsequently take issue with it. As we shall see
below, however, Lenin was opposed to federalism at this time.

18. Carr, *Bolshevik Revolution* 1:429.

19. Cited in Low, *Lenin*, 68. He once stated his conviction that "less than
one in fifty, or even one hundred nations" would achieve independence
prior to the proletarian revolution. Ibid., 67.

20. See chapter 1, footnote 48.

21. Cited in Low, *Lenin*, 101, and Pipes, *Formation*, 45. Lenin apparently
was making the same point in 1914 when he stated that although recognizing "the right of self-determination, to secession, seems to 'concede' the
maximum to nationalism (in reality the recognition of all nations to self-
determination implies the recognition of the maximum of democracy and
the minimum of nationalism)." Lenin, *Right of Nations*, 46. See too his
comments of the following year on p. 72: "We demand the freedom of
self-determination, i.e., independence . . . not because we cherish the ideal
of small states, but on the contrary because we are for large states and for
a coming closer, even a fusion of nations," and his 1916 comment on p.
76: "The more closely the democratic system of a state approximates to
complete freedom of secession, the rarer and weaker will the striving for
secession be in practice." See also Groshev, *Fraternal Family*, 33, for Lenin's
comment: "Recognition of the right to secession *reduces* the danger of the
'disintegration of the state.' "

22. Low, *Lenin*, 99.

23. Lenin, *Right of Nations*, 51. Emphasis added.

24. See, for example, his 1916 statement: "The various demands of

democracy, including self-determination, are not absolute, but a *small* part of the general democratic (now: general Socialist) *world* movement. Possibly, in individual concrete cases, the part may contradict the whole; if so it must be rejected." Ibid., 104. On another ocassion, when referring to self-determination, he mentioned "the necessity of subordinating the struggle for this demand, as well as for all the fundamental demands of political democracy, to the immediate revolutionary mass struggle for the overthrow of the bourgeois governments and for the achievement of socialism." Ibid., 85.

25. In the words of one contemporary Soviet writer, there is "a clear distinction between two concepts: the right to self-determination, and the advisability of self-determination." See Gililov, "Worldwide Significance," 57.

26. Stated by Lenin in 1916. Lenin, *Right of Nations*, 111. See also his comments of two years earlier: "The proletariat confines itself, so to say, to the negative demand for recognition of the *right* to self-determination, without guaranteeing anything to any nation, without undertaking to *give anything at the expense of another nation.*" Ibid., 23. See also Stalin's comments in 1913: "Social Democrats, while fighting for the right of nations to self-determination, still at the same time agitate, for instance, against the secession of the Tatars, or against national cultural autonomy for the Caucasian nations; for both, while not contrary to the rights of these nations, are contrary 'to the precise meaning of the program,' to the interests of the Caucasian proletariat." Stalin, *Marxism: Selected Writings*, 50.

27. "The question of the *right* of nations to self-determination, i.e., the guarantee by the constitution of the state of an absolutely free and absolutely democratic method of deciding the question of secession, must not be confused with the question of the *expediency* of this or that nation's seceding. The Social Democratic Party must decide the latter question in *each separate case from the point of view of the interests of social development as a whole, and the interests of the proletarian class struggle for socialism.*" Cited in Wolfe, *Three Who*, 589–590.

28. Cited in Carr, *Bolshevik Revolution*, 432.

29. *From One Step Forward, Two Steps Back* (1904). Lenin, *Selected Works* 1:398.

30. See Wolfe, *Three Who*, 233–234. See also Lenin, *Right of Nations*, 65–68.

31. Cited in Groshev, *Fraternal Family*, 34.

32. Stalin, *Marxism: Selected Writings*, 64. In the same year that this famous tract by Stalin appeared (1913), Lenin produced his "Critical Ideas on the National Question," which contained all of the principal proposals advanced by Stalin, including regional autonomy. See Lenin, *Collected Works* 20:19–51. The insistence on regional autonomy was a rebuff to the position of the Jewish Bund, Bauer, and Renner, which maintained that each ethnic group should be granted autonomy without regard to geography.

33. Cited in Wolfe, *Three Who*, 585.

34. "We are for large states and for a coming closer, even a fusion of nations." Lenin, *Right of Nations*, 72. "The aim of socialism is . . . not only to bring the nations closer to each other, but also to merge them." Ibid., 76. "The proletariat supports everything which contributes to the elimination of national differences, . . . everything which makes the relations of the nationalities to each other increasingly more intimate, everything which leads to the amalgamation of nations, . . . the amalgamation of all nationalities in a higher union." Cited in Low, *Lenin*, 115–116. A Ukrainian Social Democrat was castigated for rejecting "the interests of union, of amalgamation and assimilation of the proletariat of two nations for a passing success of the Ukrainian national cause." Lenin, *Collected Works* 20:31–32. "The proletariat . . . welcomes any and every assimilation of nationalities—with the exception of those carried out by force or on the basis of privilege." Cited in Wolfe, *Three Who*, 589.

35. The dialectical nature of this approach will be examined more carefully in chapter 8.

36. See, for example, his private letter of 1913, cited in Wolfe, *Three Who*, 584, in which Lenin opined that the adoption of Russian by non-Russians "would be of still greater progressive significance if there were no *compulsion* to use it." See also Lenin, *Right of Nations*, 103, for his statement in 1916: "All this will, until the state itself withers away, be the basis for a rich cultured life, the guarantee of an acceleration of the voluntary establishment of intimacy between and amalgamation of nations."

37. One of Lenin's last acts was a critique of the oppressive policy pursued by Stalin toward Georgians, partially on the ground that the policy was counterproductive. It is reprinted in Conquest, *Soviet Nationalities*, 146–147.

38. The slogan was evidently inspired by the Communist Manifesto's passage: "Though not in substance, yet in form, the struggle of the proletariat with the bourgeoisie is at first a national struggle."

39. In 1917, two months after the February (Kerenski) Revolution, Stalin summarized the Bolsheviks' policy as follows: "Thus our views on the national question reduce themselves to the following propositions: (a) the recognition of the right of peoples to secession; (b) regional autonomy for peoples which remain within the given state; (c) specific laws for guaranteeing freedom of development for national minorities; (d) a single, indivisible proletarian collective body, a single party, for the proletarians of all the nationalities in the given state." Stalin, *Marxism: Selected Writings*, 73. However, (b) would appear to presume (c), making the latter redundant.

SELF-DETERMINATION
AS STRATAGEM

CHAPTER 3

The Soviet Prototype

HOLDING out the vision of independence for non-Russian peoples proved very instrumental in the Bolsheviks' acquisition of power. The lengthy and demoralizing war, the overthrow of tsarism, and the general air of indecision and powerlessness that hung over the provisional government had understandably led many a non-Russian to contemplate a severing of the Russian tie; and Lenin and Stalin did not pass up the opportunity to contrast, in the sharpest possible relief, their own commitment to independence movements with the vacillating and temporizing stance of the provisional government. During the hectic events of 1917, repeated statements of support emanated from the Petrograd Soviet, materially aiding the undermining of Kerensky's government. Thus at the Seventh All Russian Socialist Democratic Labor Party Conference of May 12, 1917, both Lenin and Stalin made speeches excoriating the government for not immediately extending the right of secession to the Finns and Ukrainians.[1] And in a resolution drafted by Lenin, the conference unequivocally endorsed "the right of all of the nations forming part of Russia freely to secede and form independent states."[2] Similarly, at the first All Russian Congress of Soviets in June 1917, the Bolshevik faction criticized the congress's decision to place a series of qualifications upon its demand that the provisional government issue a formal edict recognizing the right of secession.

The party's debt to this strategy was later acknowledged in a resolution which characterized it as a "decisive" factor:

> Our party took these circumstances into consideration when it made the basis of its policy in the national question the right of nations to self-determination, the right of peoples to lead an independent political existence. . . . Our Party in its work never tired of advancing this programme of national emancipation in opposition to both the frankly coercive policy of tsarism and the half-hearted, semi-imperialist policy of the Mensheviks and So-cialist-Revolutionaries. Whereas the tsarist Russification policy created an abyss between tsarism and the nationalities of old

Russia, and whereas the semi-imperialist policy of the Mensheviks and Social Revolutionaries led the best elements among these nationalities to desert Kerenskyism, the policy of emancipation pursued by our Party won for it the sympathy and support of the broad masses of these nationalities in the struggle it waged against tsarism and the imperialist Russian bourgeoisie. There can be little doubt that this sympathy and support was one of the decisive factors that determined the triumph of our Party in the October Revolution.[3]

The Bolsheviks' formal support for the right to secede did not end with their assumption of power on November 7. The following day, in its first official pronouncement, the Soviet government re-affirmed its support for self-determination:

> If any nation whatsoever is forcibly retained within the bound-aries of a given state, if, in spite of its expressed desire—no matter whether that desire is expressed in the press, at popular meetings, in party decisions, or in the protests and revolts against national oppression—it is not permitted the right to decide the forms of its state existence by a free vote . . . , [then] such incorporation, is annexation, i.e., seizure and coercion.[4]

A week later, an official document signed by the chairman of the Council of People's Commissars (Lenin) and the People's Com-missar on Nationality Affairs (Stalin) specifically committed the new Soviet state to supporting "the right of the peoples of Russia to free self-determination, even to the point of separation and the formation of an independent state."[5]

For a time it appeared that this commitment would be honored. In the interval between the Soviet takeover and the end of 1918, at least thirteen new states came into being within what was formerly the Russian Empire.[6] And the new Soviet government did in fact extend recognition to many of these new entities.

Several factors helped to account for the Soviet leadership's early willingness to preside over the dissolution of the Russian Empire. It is important to remember that the seizure of governmental power did not guarantee political control of Russia. There remained the need to consolidate power against the armed forces of the coun-terrevolutionaries and foreign states. In this situation, the Bolshe-viks' stance on self-determination had the advantage of permitting the new government to concentrate upon this more serious threat to its survival. Moreover, in that struggle with the Whites, the Soviet leaders, by identifying themselves with the national aspirations of the minorities, could expect to gain the passive support, and perhaps the positive sympathy, of the non-Russian peoples. This support was a matter of the greatest strategic import, for the White forces were almost totally located in the non-Russian regions. Aided in their courtship of the minorities by the Whites' refusal to countenance any secessionist tendencies, the Bolsheviks' continued willingness to promise self-determination unquestionably paid handsome dividends. Indeed, we have Stalin's word that it was *the* critical factor in the war's outcome:

> Do not forget that if in the rear of Kolchak, Denikin, Wrangel, and Yudenich we had not had the so-called "aliens," if we had not had the former oppressed peoples who undermined the rear of these generals by their silent sympathy with the Russian proletariat—and this comrades, is a special factor in our growth, this silent sympathy; nobody sees or hears it, but it decides everything—if it had not been for this sympathy, we should not have beaten one of these generals. While we were marching against them, the collapse began in their rear. Why? Because these generals relied on the "colonizing" element among the Cossacks, they offered to the oppressed peoples a prospect of further oppression, and the oppressed peoples were obliged to come forward and embrace us, seeing that we unfurled the banner of the liberation of these oppressed peoples.[7]

At its Twelfth Congress (April 1923), the party also went on record as recognizing the absolute essentiality of the support provided by the non-Russian peoples during the Red-White struggle. Referring to "the confidence of its brothers of other nationalities," the party resolution added that "it need hardly be shown that if it had not enjoyed this confidence the Russian proletariat could not have defeated Kolchak and Denikin, Yudenich and Wrangel."[8]

Quite aside from such strategic considerations, the Bolshevik leadership could also defend its endorsement of secession by noting that its action was, in any case, only a recognition of the existing state of things. Since most of the territories populated by the peoples who had defected were either in the hands of the Whites or of foreign occupation forces, recognition of their independence was only recognition of what could not be immediately rectified. Moreover, quite apart from these war-related considerations, there remained Lenin's thesis that Soviet support for self-determination was the best guarantee against secession and for the speedy return of those who did secede.

Despite these strategic and presumptive considerations, growing nervousness about actual developments became manifest almost immediately after the revolution, in the form of hedging on what had hitherto been the unqualified acknowledgment of the right of secession. In an article dealing with the Ukraine, which was published less than five weeks after the revolution, Stalin reaffirmed the willingness of the Soviet authorities to support secession, but he now added the proviso "if the toiling population of the region desires it."[9] The following month he made clear that this qualification was not to be construed as empty rhetoric: "All this points to the necessity of interpreting the principle of self-determination, not of the bourgeoisie, but of the toiling masses of the given nation. The principle of self-determination must be subordinated to the principles of socialism."[10]

Here indeed was an unheralded shift of major consequence in the meaning that Marxists attached to self-determination. No longer a right adhering to the nation, it had been transformed into self-determination of the proletariat. And since the Communist party was the sole group qualified to speak for the proletariat, Stalin's alteration would in practice mean that all decisions concerning self-determination would henceforth fall within the exclusive domain of the highest reaches of the party.

Marx, Engels, and Lenin, as we have documented, had often maintained that support for specific self-determination movements should be highly selective. But they had never contended that the right was concentrated in a single class of the nation, rather than in the nation as a whole.[11] Nor had Stalin. Indeed, as recently as May 1917, he had indicated that even the most reactionary of secessionist movements would not be resisted. After noting that "recognition of the right to secession must not be confused with the expediency of secession in any given circumstances," Stalin had added, by way of illustration, that he "personally would be opposed to the secession of Transcaucasia, bearing in mind the general level of development in Transcaucasia and in Russia, the conditions of the struggle of the proletariat, and so forth." His opposition, however, would not take precedence over his commitment to the right of secession: "But if, nevertheless, the peoples of Transcaucasia were to demand secession, they would, of course, secede, and would not encounter opposition on our part."[12]

The view from inside the palace was remarkedly different, however. Lenin's strategy of championing independence had always been thought suspect by a number of Bolsheviks, and the growing number of secessionist movements reinforced these reservations. Lenin was himself troubled by these developments, as indicated by the following passage which was written in January 1918:

> There is not a single Marxist who, without making a total break with the foundations of Marxism and Socialism, could deny that the interests of Socialism are above the interests of the right of nations to self-determination. Our Socialist Republic has done and is continuing to do everything possible for implementing the right of self-determination for Finland, Ukraine, etc. But if the concrete position that has arisen is such that the existence of the Socialist Republic is endangered at a given moment in respect of an infringement of the right to self-determination of a few nations (Poland, Lithuania, Courland, etc.) then it stands to reason that the interests of the preservation of the Socialist Republic must take preference.[13]

There is, to be sure, no hint in this passage of a desire to restrict self-determination to the "toiling masses." And Lenin did, in fact, resist Stalin's narrower definition as an acceptable postulation for all situations. However, a statement drafted by Lenin, which became official party policy following its adoption in March 1919, gave to the party the right to view self-determination from this narrower perspective when such a limitation appeared appropriate:

> The All-Russian Communist Party regards the question as to which class expresses the desire of a nation for separation from a historical point of view, taking into consideration the level of historical development of the nation, i.e., whether the nation is passing from medievalism toward bourgeois democracy or from bourgeois democracy toward Soviet or proletarian democracy, etc.[14]

It would be difficult to offer a better illustration of Lenin's ability to keep policy flexible so that the strategic value to the Marxist movement that could be derived from any situation could be maximized. In reserving to the party the power to determine who is entitled to speak for the nation, Lenin designed a formula that would permit the Soviet government to remain the foremost champion of independence for colonies and specified nations,[15] while concurrently denying the propriety of the self-determination doctrine to any case in which it might be detrimental to the Soviet state. In the latter situation, the party need only proclaim that separation was not in the best interest of the toiling masses, in order to brand any move in that direction as counterrevolutionary.[16] Thus, Stalin, writing in *Pravda* during 1920 in relation to the rights of the non-Russian peoples to secede, simply averred that "the interests of the masses of the people render the demand for the secession of the border regions at the present stage of the revolution a profoundly counter-revolutionary one."[17]

It is sometimes implicitly or explicitly suggested that the subsequent fortunes of the non-Russian peoples would have been qualitatively different had Lenin lived long enough to have his national policies firmly entrenched. To holders of this view, Stalin is the villain who broke faith with the non-Russians. The evidence usually advanced for this thesis revolves about the displeasure which Lenin expressed in late 1922 concerning Stalin's harsh treatment of the Georgians following their reannexation by Moscow. Lenin's displeasure was quite consistent with his conviction that minority nationalism, the product of past oppression, must be eradicated by a period of overindugent behavior on the part of the Soviet authorities. Anything which was apt to provoke the sensibilities of the minorities must be studiously avoided. It is therefore likely that the treatment accorded to non-Russian peoples, once back in the fold, would indeed have been less coercive and high-handed had Lenin lived another decade or two. But it does not follow that Lenin was any less intent than Stalin on reabsorbing, with whatever force was required, the recently seceded peoples. On this there was no disagreement. One biographer maintains that Lenin personally directed the campaigns to reacquire the various territories and their peoples.[18] Moreover, regarding the Georgians whose harsh treatment he would later protest, an earlier directive by Lenin rather cynically expressed his awareness that their militarily achieved reannexation was not justifiable in terms of the popular will. Rather than recommending a defense on the merits, he therefore instructed the propaganda apparatus to pitch its defense solely in sarcastic references to the sins of others.

> Some caustic journalists should be instructed at once to prepare the draft of a note in reply to the British Labour Party in the politest terms. In this note it should be made thoroughly clear that the proposal to evacuate Georgia and to conduct a referendum there might be a reasonable suggestion coming from sensible people who have not been bribed by the Entente, pro-

viding the same measure were applied to all nations of the globe. More particularly, in order to suggest to the leaders of the British Labour Party the great importance of modern imperialist relationships in international politics, we respectfully propose that the British Labour Party favorably consider the following measures:

First to evacuate Ireland and conduct a popular referendum there; second, to take the same steps in India; third, to apply the same measures in Korea; fourth, to take the same action in all countries where armies of any of the great imperialist powers are kept.

The note should emphasize in the politest terms possible that those willing to reflect on our proposals on the system of imperialist relations existing in international politics will also be capable of appreciating the implications of the suggestions made to us by the British Labour Party. The purpose of the note, extremely polite in form and popular style (so as to appeal to the intelligence of ten-year-old children) should be to ridicule the idiotic leaders of the British Labour Party.[19]

Sarcasm aside, Lenin's comments constituted an admission that, faced with the rash of unanticipated secessions, the Soviets had resorted to aping the imperialists.[20]

By the combined use of the Red Army and local Communist elements, the Soviet government succeeded in returning most of the minority areas to Soviet control by 1922;[21] and, with the end of World War II, it regained control over the remaining peoples of the old Russian Empire, with the exception of the Finns.[22] As described in the constitutions of 1924, 1936, and 1977 (the last is still in effect), the state is a federation of union republics. Today totaling fifteen, each of the republics bears the name of one of the country's major national groups. Of particular interest to a discussion of self-determination is that all three constitutions declare the union republics to be sovereign and possessed of the right to secede at will from the Soviet Union.[23] Moreover, one of the prerequisites for a people to gain their own union republic is that their territory touch one of the Soviet Union's external borders, in order that the right of secession be meaningful. And yet, as we have noted, the abbreviated period of meaningful self-determination had certainly ended by 1922. The emptiness of constitutional phraseology on this point is illustrated, *inter alia*, by the many political prisoners who have been found guilty over the years of separatist, "antistate" activities, despite invoking in their defense the constitutional guarantee of a union republic's right to secede.[24]

But since in fact the right to secession is not meaningful, what purpose is served by its constitutional assertion? A number of overlapping possibilities suggest themselves:

1. *For internal propaganda purposes.* Perpetuating the myth of a right of secession would be quite consonant with Lenin's view of nationalism as the product of past discrimination which is to be exorcized by a period of "national in form." One consistent element in this psychological campaign has been the attempt to convince the fourteen minorities, whose ethnic name adorns one of the union republics and who *in toto* account for approximately 75 percent of the country's non-Russian population, that they each possess their own sovereign state and that their national aspirations have therefore already been perfectly fulfilled within the union. The official claim that the republics enjoy sovereignty is supported by several attributes, theoretically enjoyed by the republics, which are customarily associated with independent states. Among them are the right to exchange diplomatic personnel with foreign states, to enter into treaty obligations, and, of course, to secede from the union. Here again, however, one encounters the Leninist distinction between the right to a right and the right to exercise that right. The attempt to sublimate the contradiction between the constitutionally guaranteed right to secession and the government's unrelenting hostility to the least hint of the exercise of that right can be seen in the following passage by a Soviet scholar:

> Experience shows that there may be different forms of statehood. Under a socialist democracy the substance of national sovereignty lies not in the mandatory state secession of one nation from another but in the freedom of choosing any desired form of state organisation. From their own experience Soviet nations know that sovereignty is best achieved and guaranteed in a fraternal multinational family and they bend every effort to develop and strengthen the Union state.[25]

2. *For general external propaganda purposes, particularly with regard to the colonial and former colonial areas.* We have noted the great emphasis that Lenin placed upon the need to convince the peoples of the Third World that the Soviets were the principal bearers of the banner of national self-determination. In order to maintain that image, it would also be necessary to maintain the illusion of full independence for the nations under Moscow's direct super-

vision. As Stalin noted in 1921: "And inasmuch as we are concerned with colonies which are in the clutches of Great Britain, France, America and Japan, inasmuch as we are concerned with such subject countries as Arabia, Mesopotamia, Turkey, Hindustan . . . the slogan of the right of peoples to secession is a revolutionary slogan, and to abandon it would be playing into the hands of the Entente."[26] Writing in *Pravda* during the same year, Stalin colorfully added:

> If Europe and America may be called the front, the scene of the main engagements between socialism and imperialism, the nonsovereign nations and the colonies, with their raw materials, fuel, food and vast store of human material, should be regarded as the rear, the reserve of imperialism. In order to win a war one must not only triumph at the front but also revolutionise the enemy's rear, his reserves. Hence the victory of the world proletarian revolution may be regarded as assured only if the proletariat is able to combine its own revolutionary struggle with the movement for emancipation of the toiling masses of the nonsovereign nations and the colonies against the power of the imperialists and for a dictatorship of the proletariat. This "trifle" was overlooked by the moving spirits of the Second and the Two-and-a-Half Internationals when they divorced the national and colonial question from the question of power in the period of growing proletarian revolution in the West.[27]

Two years later, Stalin added, "We must here, in Russia, in our federation, solve the national problem in a correct, *a model way*, in order to set an example to the East, which represents the heavy reserves of our revolution."[28] The strategic importance which the Soviet leadership ascribes to their role as the foremost champion of political independence has not perceptibly waned with the dying of colonialism. The thesis that the former colonies have acquired only the form but not the content of independence, due to the fact that the imperialists have developed more indirect techniques for perpetuating their exploitation of the Third World (that is, "neocolonialism"), has struck a broadly popular chord.[29] By thus insisting that political self-determination remains a sham in the presence of neocolonialism, the Soviets have projected the strategic advantage of being identified as the champion of independence into the postcolonial era. One manifestation of this persevering interest in their image as the sentinel of self-determination was offered by Krushchev in his famous denunciation of Stalin at the Twentieth Party Congress in 1956. Stalin's maltreatment of various national groups within the Soviet Union was attacked in part because of its negative impact upon the "justly considered" image of the socialist fatherland "as a model of a multinational state."[30] But while the image of the Soviet Union held by outsiders is therefore of keen interest to the authorities, there are two more specific situations in which that image is particularly consequential.

3. *In order to increase the appeal of a union republic to people of the same ethnic stock immediately across the Soviet Union's borders.* From the very outset, the Soviet authorities were aware that their borders would be strengthened and perhaps advanced if neighboring peoples perceived the national situation of their kin within the Soviet Union as vastly superior to their own. Thus Stalin commented in 1930:

> We must bear in mind another circumstance which affects a number of nationalities of the U.S.S.R. There is a Ukraine in the U.S.S.R. But there is another Ukraine in other states. . . . Take, further, the nationalities of the U.S.S.R. situated along the Southern frontier from Azerbaidjan to Kazakstan and Buryat-Mongolia. They are all in the same position as the Ukraine.[31]

Following World War II, the Soviets extended their territory in a manner which caused their European borders generally to coincide with ethnic distributions, thus eliminating irredentist questions in this area.[32] However, the Asiatic land borders of the Soviet Union still bisect peoples throughout their length, enabling the Soviets to make propagandistic usage of the image of an independent Armenian, Azerbaijan, Turkmen, Uzbek, Tadzhik, Kirgiz, or Kazakh state existing just across the Soviet border. In recent years, the Soviets have not pressed this advantage except with regard to the Chinese People's Republic, but the knowledge of the governments of the neighboring states that the Soviets may at any time elect to take advantage of the possibilities offered by the ethnic map in and by itself furnishes the Soviet Union with a powerful lever in any negotiations with states to the south.[33] The myth that national groups within the Soviet Union enjoy full sovereign status, including the right of secession, therefore still exerts an important influence upon neighbors.

4. *In order to aid the Communist parties of multinational states, by permitting them to point to the motherland of socialism as self-determination in practice.* If Lenin's first injunction on the national question (i.e., prior to the assumption of power, promise minorities the right of self-determination, specifically including the right of secession) was

to be applied outside of the first Marxist-Leninist state, then it was essential that the Soviet Union maintain an impeccable demeanor with regard to the honoring of that principle at home. If the non-Communist leaders of foreign states were enabled to illustrate convincingly that national groups were being forcibly retained within the Soviet Union despite earlier promises of independence, Lenin's first stratagem with regard to the national question would quite assuredly prove ineffective. But in being able to point to a constitutional guarantee of the right of secession, the Soviets could project a faithfulness to principle which would do honor to a Caesar's wife, for no non-Marxist state could boast of a similar constitutional guarantee. Maintaining such an image would be essential if the Communist parties in prerevolutionary states were to adopt successfully Lenin's stratagem of promising independence to all national groups. The fact that the Soviet authorities did in fact continue to place much store in this stratagem as a means of furthering the world revolution is heavily documented by the resolutions and directives that emanated from the Third International (the Comintern) throughout its existence from 1919 to 1943.

The Comintern was created to coordinate the activities of all Communist parties. Article 16 of the "Conditions of Admission" mandated that "all the decisions of the Congresses of the Communist International, as well as the decisions of its Executive Committee [which was located in Moscow], *are binding* on all parties belonging to the Communist International."[34] A major preoccupation of the organization was the national question, for, steeped in its own internal experience, the Soviet leadership was particularly cognizant of the power of ethnonationalism as a potential Trojan horse within the enemy camp. The opportunism that came to characterize the Comintern's approach to the national question was captured in a speech by Bukharin, made shortly after the organization's formation: "If we propound the solution of the right of self-determination for the colonies . . . we lose nothing by it. On the contrary, we gain. . . . The most outright nationalist movement is only water for our mill."[35]

Armed with this vision of nothing to lose and everything to gain, the Soviet authorities embarked on a program to convince other Communist parties of the necessity to conform to Soviet strategy on the matter. The Manifesto passed at the first conference of the Comintern (March 1919) outlined the official Communist view of the issue.

While oppressing and coercing the small and weak peoples, condemning them to hunger and degradation, the allied imperialists, like the imperialists of the Central Powers a short while ago, do not stop talking about the right of national self-determination, which is today trampled underfoot in Europe as in all other parts of the world.[36]

The Manifesto was addressed to the world's proletariat and therefore did not lay down the course of action to be followed by Communist parties with regard to the national issue. Such a blueprint for concerted action first appeared in Lenin's "Theses on the National and the Colonial Questions," which were adopted by the Comintern at its Second Party Congress in July 1920. Lenin insisted that all parties ". . . render direct aid to the revolutionary movements among the dependent and underprivileged nations (for example, Ireland, the American Negroes, etc.) and in the colonies." Otherwise, he noted, "the struggle against the oppression of dependent nations . . . as well as recognition of their right to secede, are but a false signboard."[37] Consonant with this policy, "a particularly explicit and clear attitude on the question of the colonies and the oppressed peoples" was made a prerequisite of membership.

Every party which wishes to join the Communist International is obliged to expose the tricks and dodges of its imperialists in the colonies, to support every colonial liberation movement not merely in words but in deeds, to demand the expulsion of their own imperialists from these colonies, to inculcate among the workers of their country a genuinely fraternal attitude to the working people of the colonies and the oppressed nations, and to carry on systematic agitation among the troops of their country against any oppression of the colonial peoples.[38]

Over the next few years, the Communist parties of other countries were bombarded with reminders of the need to honor this pledge. One of the more broadly aimed statements on the matter can be found in the resolutions of the Fifth Comintern Congress of 1924:

On the nationality question the Executive had ample cause to remind many sections, for which this question is of the utmost importance, of their inadequate execution of the decisions of the second congress. One of the basic principles of Leninism, *requiring the resolute and constant advocacy by communists of the right of national self-determination* (secession and the formation of an independent State), has not yet been applied by all sections of the Comintern as it should be.[39]

In a document dealing with tactics, the same congress further pressed this theme:

5. *Correct Policy on the National Question*

In a number of countries, as a result of the re-division of the world after the first imperialist war, there is greater national oppression and dismemberment. In a number of European countries, and still more in colonial and semi-colonial countries, a mass of inflammable material has been heaped up which may blow bourgeois rule sky-high. Correct communist policy on the national question, which was thoroughly analysed in the theses of the second world congress, forms one of the most important constituents in the policy of winning the masses and preparing a victorious revolution. Nihilism and opportunist deviations in the national question, which still prevail in a number of communist parties, are the weakest side of these parties, which will never be able to accomplish their historical mission if they do not overcome these weaknesses.[40]

The following year, the Comintern had occasion to berate the parties for not heeding such directives, noting that "communists have again and again made the mistake of underestimating the national question, a mistake which deprives them of the opportunity of winning over substantial, at times decisive strata of the population."[41]

In adopting this posture on the national question, the Comintern was in effect requiring that party members agitate against the territorial integrity of their respective states and/or overseas empires. This policy could remain constant only so long as it harmonized with the foreign policy objectives of the Soviet Union, for, as laid down in Lenin's "Theses on the National and the Colonial Questions," "a policy must be pursued that will achieve the closest alliance, with Soviet Russia, of all the national and colonial liberation movements."[42] In time, therefore, the directives of the Comintern concerning the national question necessarily came to mirror each major vicissitude in Soviet foreign policy.

Between the October Revolution and the end of World War II, that foreign policy underwent three major shifts, each accompanied by a corresponding change in the policies that the Communist parties were ordered to take on the national question. In the immediate aftermath of the revolution, when the authorities tended to perceive the Soviet Union as alone in a sea of equally hostile capitalist states, a policy which indiscriminately aimed at the weakening of all multinational states and empires blended well with Soviet objectives. But as the threat of fascism became increasingly ominous, the Soviets correspondingly came to appreciate that non-Fascist states might be essential allies against this more immediate danger. Strategy therefore dictated a change of course, and Communists were instructed to enter into united fronts with, and lend support to, all anti-Fascist forces. Propaganda aimed at dismemberment of non-Fascist states and their empires was shelved. This period of the united front against fascism began in 1935 and ended in August 1939 with the signing of the Nazi-Soviet Non-Aggression Pact. During the period of the pact, Moscow insisted that any course of action which might provoke Hitler was to be avoided. United fronts with anti-Fascist forces were therefore out, and mobilization efforts on the part of non-Fascist states were not to be supported. The final phase, which commenced with the Nazi attack on the Soviet Union in June 1941, was one in which no action was to be taken which would impede the prosecution of the anti-Fascist war by the Allied countries. As one means of assuring its allies that it intended no threat to their political and territorial integrity, Moscow ordered the Comintern dissolved in 1943.

These shifts in Soviet perceptions concerning the utilitarian value of one or another group of states were accompanied by intriguing alterations in Soviet propaganda concerning the proper focus for the political loyalty of the working classes. Prior to 1935, the Comintern's position was that unlike 1848, when Marx and Engels had drawn up the Communist Manifesto, the working men of the world now had a country. Loyalty of working men everywhere was owed not to their state but to "the Worker's Fatherland," that is, the Soviet Union. As ringingly proclaimed on the fourteenth anniversary of the revolution:

> Working people of the World!
> Defend with your lives the Soviet Union, the only fatherland of the workers of all countries. Use every means at your command to protect the victorious construction of socialism.[43]

However, with the need for allies who would resist Fascist expansionism, the working classes were told in 1935 that if their state's independence were threatened by Fascist invaders, resistance to such a threat would "assume the character of a war of liberation" in which the proletariat must be "in the front ranks of the fighters for [their country's] independence and fight the war of liberation to a finish, without allowing 'their' bourgeoisie to strike a bargain with the attacking powers to the prejudice of the interests of their country."[44] By 1938, with an attack upon the Soviet Union by Germany an imminent possibility, the working class, nation, and defense of state were identified as a single trinity in a rousing call to the colors.

> The nation is the many millions of workers, peasants, and working peoples generally—the people that is devoted to its country, cherishes its liberty, and defends its independence. . . . In all countries menaced by fascist invasion from without, only the working class can rally, rouse, and lead the people to a victorious struggle for national liberation. The working class is the backbone of the nation, the bulwark of its liberty, dignity, and independence.[45]

In sharpest contrast was the exhortation to the same workers, only one year later, in the period of the German-Soviet Non-Aggression Pact. In a stunning about-face, workers were now told not to rally to defense of country:

> Workers! Don't believe those who wave the flag of national unity. What can there be in common between you and those who profit by war? What unity can there be between exploited and exploiters?
>
> Don't believe those who are calling upon you to support the war under the false pretext of the defence of democracy.[46]

Yet less than two years later, in still another complete turnabout, the French Communist Party could report: "For us there is no division into communists, socialists, radicals, catholics or de Gaulle followers. For us there are only Frenchmen fighting Hitler and his agents."[47] Other parties behaved in corresponding fashion, for in the interim the Nazis had attacked the Soviet Union, and the Comintern had given instructions to give total support to the anti-Fascist effort. For most parties this meant unswerving loyalty to their own state apparatus. As set forth in the document of intention to dissolve itself, the Comintern's parting message to the workers was to continue this support. The concluding paragraph read as follows:

The Presidium of the Executive Committee of the Communist International calls on all supporters of the Communist International to concentrate their energies on whole-hearted support of and active participation in the war of liberation of the peoples *and States* of the anti-Hitlerite coalition for the speediest defeat of the deadly enemy of the working class and toilers—German fascism and its associates and vassals.[48]

Though the Soviets therefore often stressed state unity at the expense of a right of separation during the decade from 1935 to 1945, they never formally repudiated their commitment to the right of self-determination, including secession. Similarly, with regard to their domestic scene, we have noted that the myth of a right of secession, unlike its reality, was never terminated. In the postwar years, with the Fascist threat eradicated, this forbearance would permit the Soviets to regain the pose of the consistent champion of national self-determination. But as a survey of Soviet practice reveals, the ostensible commitment with regard to both the internal and external application of self-determination rested on opportunism and pretense. Candid acknowledgment was offered by the president of the Comintern, Zinoviev, while furnishing advice in 1923 to Communist parties outside of the Soviet Union: "What we ask is that those of our parties in countries where the national question is important should learn how to make use of the nationalist element against the bourgeoisie regime. Our parties must try to set in movement against the government those elements which are naturally discontented," just as the Bolsheviks exploited Ukrainian discontent against Kerensky "for the good of the proletarian revolution." He added that the Ukrainians had been told that they would be independent, not that Karl Marx had said that the proletariat had no fatherland.[49]

Soviet experience has vindicated Lenin's assessment of the serviceability of national self-determination as a key lever for gaining power in a multinational environment. But it has also exposed the fallacy of presuming that peoples, upon being offered independence, would not take it. Nations had chosen separation, and force and artifice had been necessary to bring about their return. Official Soviet history would later attempt to mask Lenin's miscalculation, maintaining that all the member peoples of the Soviet Union had acceded voluntarily.[50] Thus Article 70 of the 1977 constitution proclaims: "The Union of Soviet Socialist Republics is an integral, federal, multinational state formed on the principle of socialist federalism as a result of the free self-determination of nations and the voluntary association of equal Soviet Socialist Republics."[51] This official myth has permitted the Soviet Union to pose as the champion of self-determination abroad. But it is doubtful that it has exerted much influence upon popular perceptions within those nations who, consonant with Lenin's promises, elected to secede at the time of the revolution. Thus in 1979, more than one-half century after Lenin's death, forty-five notables living within Estonia, Latvia, and Lithuania set forth in an open letter to the United Nations their case for independence from Moscow. The letter noted that in 1920, the Soviet authorities had solemnly ceded independence to the three republics "for all time" and had relinquished "all sovereign rights" over them.[52] Lenin's stratagem for taking power thus continues to have consequences far beyond what he had anticipated.

NOTES

1. See Lenin, *Right of Nations*, particularly p. 125; and Stalin, *Marxism: Selected Writings*, 70–71. See also in Pipes, *Formation*, 68, the reference to Lenin's newspaper article which had been written to embarrass the provisional government for its failure to respond to Ukrainian aspirations.

2. Cited in Groshev, *Fraternal Family*, 36.

3. "National Factors in Party and State Development," Resolution Adopted by the Twelfth Congress of the Russian Communist Party, April 1923, in appendix to Stalin, *Marxism and National, Colonial Questions*, 279–287.

4. The entire text is reproduced in Christman, *Communism*, 2–6.

5. Entitled "Declaration of the Rights of the Peoples of Russia" (November 18, 1917), in ibid., 11–12.

6. See Farmer, "Theory," 253. For a listing of most of these states by date of secession, see Kristian, *Right to Self-Determination*, 21.

7. Cited in Carr, *Bolshevik Revolution* 1:263, who concludes (p. 264) that "the Bolshevik doctrine of nationalism proved a *vital* contribution to the Soviet victory in the civil war." For a few details on non-Russian forces who fought against the Whites, see Salov, "Soviet Nationality Policy," 89.

8. "National Factors in Party and State Development," in Stalin, *Marxism and National, Colonial Questions*, 281.

9. Clarkson, *History of Russia*, 636. The article was published on December 12, 1917.

10. Ibid.

11. As noted in chapter 2, on the occasion when Lenin was publicly

queried about the specific course of action he would recommend in the event that a nation dominated by reactionaries sought to secede, he elected to be evasive rather than to take the opportunity to restrict the right of secession to progressive movements.

12. Stalin, *Marxism: Selected Writings*, 71.

13. Cited in Conquest, *Nation Killers*, 118–119. Lenin never publicly acknowledged that his assumption that the promise of secession would in fact deter secession was erroneous. In a *Pravda* article, he placed the blame for the spate of secessions on "capitalists" who had played upon "the national distrust of the Great Russians felt by Polish, Latvian, Estonian and Finnish peasants and small owners." This development, however, would prove temporary. By recognizing the independence of the new states, "we are . . . winning the confidence of the laboring masses of the neighbouring small states. . . . It is the surest way of wresting them from the influence of 'their' national capitalists, and leading them to full confidence, to the future united international Soviet republic." See "Letter to Workers and Peasants of the Ukraine," December 28, 1919, in Lenin, *Selected Works* 3:260–261. On the other hand, some nine months earlier, Lenin had suggested his embarrassment concerning developments by playing down the significance of self-determination and its consequences: "Our criticism [of self-determination and secession] has served to exaggerate the importance of this question. The defect in our criticism was that it attached special significance to this question, which, in substance, is of less than secondary importance in the programme's general structure, in the sum total of programme demands." See "Speech Closing the Debate on the Party Programme," March 19, 1919, in Lenin, *Selected Works* 3:136.

14. "The Program of the All-Russian Communist Party" (March 1919), in Christman, *Communism*, 16–46. The cited section is on p. 27.

15. In the same 1919 party program, it was termed "necessary" that the party "recognize the rights of colonies and oppressed nations to political separation."

16. The following year (1920), Lenin restated his renunciation of the "abstract" principle of self-determination in the following terms: "The Communist Party . . . must base its policy in the national question too, not on abstract and formal principles but, first, on a precise appraisal of the specific historical situation and, primarily, of economic conditions; second, on a clear distinction between the interests of the oppressed classes, of working and exploited people, and the general concept of the national interests as a whole, *which implies the interest of the ruling class*; third, on an equally clear distinction between the oppressed, dependent and subject nations and the oppressing, exploiting and sovereign nations." "Preliminary Draft Theses on the National and the Colonial Questions (For the Second Congress of the Communist International," in Lenin, *Selected Works* 3:373. (Emphasis added.)

17. *Pravda*, October 10, 1920.

18. Shub, *Lenin*, 402.

19. Ibid., 402–403.

20. There is evidence that Lenin never accepted any of the secessions as permanent. For data indicating that Lenin tried to reverse the Finnish separation as early as January 15, 1918, see M. Fol, "L'Accession de la Finlande a l'Independance," unpublished paper (Paris: 1976), cited in Helene Carrere d'Encausse, "Determinants and Parameters," in Azrael, *Soviet Nationality Policies*, 40. Shortly after Lenin's death, party units for the western Ukraine and western Belorussia (then parts of Poland) were established within the Soviet Union. Both parties demanded reunification with the Soviet republics. Burks, *Dynamics of Communism*, 81. We will recall that the Finns and Ukrainians were the two peoples most favored for independence by Lenin in his prerevolutionary writings. For an interesting article maintaining that Lenin had never, even prior to the revolution, intended to permit any secession whatsoever, see Israel Kleiner, "On Lenin's Attitude toward the Right of Nations to Self-Determination," *Crossroads* 5 (Winter 1980):177–197. The article's conclusion is based upon Lenin's refusal to permit the Ukrainians a separate party. But Lenin had always adamantly maintained the need for a single party incorporating all national groups. For details, see chapter 12. When analyzing Lenin's position on a right of separation, one must therefore distinguish between party and nations and, with regard to the latter, between his pre- and postrevolutionary positions.

21. For detailed accounts of the various ways in which nations were reabsorbed, see Conquest, *Soviet Nationalities*, 21–35 and Farmer, "Theory," 197–281.

22. Soviet determination to reannex all the territories of the Russian Empire was indicated in 1939, when the Soviet-Nazi Non-Aggression Pact was signed. Secret protocols of the agreement gave the Soviet Union control over western Poland, Bessarabia, Estonia, Latvia, and Lithuania. Combined with the fruits of the Soviet war against Finland, these concessions would have made the western border of the Soviet Union correspond closely with that of pre-World War I tsarist Russia. Although the areas acquired under the secret protocols were lost during World War II and reacquired only with the expulsion of German forces, voices both from within and outside these regions continue to embarrass the Soviet authorities by drawing attention to the fact that it was the secret protocols with the Nazis that in effect ripped up the Soviet Union's earlier treaties that had recognized the independence of these peoples. For example, in 1920 the Soviets had entered treaties renouncing "all sovereign rights" over the Baltic republics and had recognized their independence "for all time." It is obviously embarrassing for the Soviet Union to have the Nazi-Soviet Pact re-aired and to have it pointed out that "for all time" was reduced to nineteen years. See later parts of this chapter.

23. Chapter 3, Article 4 of the 1924 constitution read "Each one of the

member Republics retains the right to freely withdraw from the Union." Article 17 of the 1936 constitution and Article 72 of the current (1977) constitution acknowledge the same right.

24. See, for example, the plea addressed to the Supreme Soviet of the Ukrainian Republic by the incarcerated V. Moroz in *Problems of Communism* 17 (July–August 1968):85–86: "My colleagues and I were convicted for 'propaganda directed at the separation of the Ukraine from the USSR.' But Article 17 of the Constitution of the USSR clearly states that each republic has the right to leave the Union."

25. Lebedinskaya, "Nationality Question," 15.

26. Stalin, *Marxism: Selected Writings*, 106.

27. *Pravda*, May 8, 1921. Reprinted in Stalin, *Marxism and National, Colonial Questions*, 115. Both the wording and the thrust of this passage anticipate Mao Tse-tung's later claim to originality in advancing a global strategy involving the city-states (the industrial states) being surrounded by and dependent upon the country-states (the Third World). Both in turn owe an intellectual debt to Lenin's *Imperialism: The Highest Stage of Capitalism*.

28. Stalin, *Marxism: Selected Writings*, 156. Emphasis added.

29. With his usual aptitude for locating the jugular, and with amazing foresight, Lenin outlined this strategy before the decolonizing period was much underway. Writing in 1920, he noted "the need constantly to explain and expose among the broadest masses of the toilers of all countries, and particularly of the backward countries, the deception systematically practiced by the imperialist powers, which, under the guise of politically independent states, set up states that are wholly dependent upon them economically, financially and militarily." "Preliminary Draft Theses on the National and the Colonial Questions (for the Second Congress of the Communist International)," in Lenin, *Selected Works* 3:377.

30. The text of Khrushchev's address is reprinted in Christman, *Communism*, 158–228. The citation is from p. 202.

31. Stalin, *Marxism: Selected Writings*, 214.

32. The major exception involved Moscow's absorption of the Bessarabian area, which left the Rumanian nation divided. However, the official Soviet position is that the people of Bessarabia are not Rumanians but Moldavians, who have their own Moldavian Soviet Socialist Republic within the Soviet Union. See chapter 7.

33. See chapter 7. The possibility that the Soviets might revert to the use of such propaganda at any time was driven home in 1981–1982, when the radio and press of the Azerbaijan Soviet Socialist Republic began publicizing the ardent aspiration for the unity of "Southern Azerbaijan" (that is, the Iranian sector) with Soviet Azerbaijan, which was allegedly broadly shared throughout Southern Azerbaijan. For several examples, see *JPRS* 80829 (May 17, 1982):2–4.

34. "Conditions of Admission to the Communist International," August 1920, in Christman, *Communism*, 62–70. Emphasis added.

35. Degras, *Documents* 1:138.

36. "Manifesto of the Communist International to the Proletariat of the Entire World," March 1919, in Christman, *Communism*, 47–61.

37. "Preliminary Draft Theses on the National and the Colonial Questions" in Lenin, *Selected Works* 3:375. Interestingly, what the Soviets translate as a "false signboard," the Chinese translate as "a deceitful pretense." See *Lenin on the National and Colonial Questions: Three Articles* (Peking: Foreign Language Press, 1967), 25.

38. "Conditions of Admission to the Communist International," August 1920, in Christman, *Communism*, 66–67.

39. "Extracts from the Resolution of the Fifth Comintern Congress on the Report of the Executive Committee of the Communist International," June 26, 1924, in Degras, *Documents* 2:106. Emphasis added.

40. "Extracts from the Theses on Tactics Adopted by the Fifth Comintern Congress," July 1924, in ibid. 2:142–156.

41. "Extracts from the Theses on the Bolshevization of Communist Parties Adopted at the Fifth Executive Plenum," April 1925, in ibid. 2:188–200.

42. "Theses on the National and Colonial Questions," in Lenin, *Selected Works* 3:374.

43. "Extracts from a Comintern Executive Committee Manifesto on the Fourteenth Anniversary of the Russian Revolution," November 1931, in Degras, *Documents* 3:179–180.

44. "Extracts from a Resolution of the Seventh Comintern Congress on the Danger of a New World War," August 1935, in ibid., 427–433.

45. "Extracts from a Comintern Executive Committee Manifesto on the Anniversary of the Russian Revolution," November 1938, in ibid., 427–433.

46. "Extracts from the Comintern Executive Committee Manifesto on the 22nd Anniversary of the Russian Revolution," November 1939, in ibid., 439–448. An article published during the same month by the secretary of the Executive Committee warned the parties against "slipping into the position of 'defending the Fatherland,' in support of the fairy-tale about the anti-fascist character of the war." Ibid., 459. This, of course, was precisely the "fairy-tale" that the Comintern had been propagating between 1935 and August 1939.

47. Ibid., 471.

48. "Resolution of the Comintern Executive Committee Presidium Recommending the Dissolution of the Communist International," May 1943, in ibid., 476-479. Emphasis added.

49. Ibid. 2:157–158.

50. See, for example, the 1982 article by the editor-in-chief of the leading party journal, *Kommunist* (Kosolapov, "Class and National Relations" in *JPRS* 82853, February 11, 1983, p. 12):

"The freer Russia is and the more resolutely our republic recognizes the freedom of secession of the non-Great Russian nations," Lenin emphasized, "the more strongly other nations *will strive* for an alliance with us, the fewer clashes there will be, the rarer the instances of actual secession will be." Splendid words! And we had the honor today to confirm for certain that history has completely justified this prediction, without making any amendment to it.

51. While the constitutions of 1924 and 1936 spoke of voluntary union, the constitution of 1977 was the first to contain a reference to "free self-determination." It is probable that Yugoslav practice was the inspiration for this inclusion. For details, see chapter 6.

52. See the article by Peter Reddaway in *The Observer* (London), January 11, 1981.

CHAPTER 4

Minorities and the Creation of the
Chinese People's Republic

SOMEWHAT ironically, in the case of China Lenin's adjuration that those who would seek political power through revolution should ostensibly identify themselves with the principle of self-determination for their country's minorities had its first disciples not among the Chinese Communist Party (CCP) but among the Nationalist Party (KMT).[1] In order to neutralize the risk of encirclement by hostile powers, the newly entrenched Soviet government in Moscow was anxious to forge friendly links with a faction that had good prospects of winning power within China. The Soviets therefore elected to place primary reliance upon the nationalist movement of Sun Yat-sen, rather than upon the embryonic CCP, although they did insist (over some resistance within both parties) that cooperation be maintained between the two groups and that Communists be permitted to join the KMT as individuals.

The KMT's new relations with the Soviet Union were soon reflected in the phrasing of its resolutions. Among the obviously Soviet expressions to enter the KMT's lexicon following the new agreement was that of self-determination, despite the fact that Sun had been an erstwhile, undisguised proponent of assimilation. As late as 1921, he had stressed that the non-Han peoples of China were destined "to be melted in the same furnace, to be assimilated within the Han nationality."[2] Yet in 1923, the same year that agreement was reached between the KMT and the Soviet Union, a KMT manifesto made mention of self-determination, and the following year the declaration of the First National Congress of the KMT furnished even more explicit recognition of the principle:

> The Kuomintang hereby formally declare: We recognize the right of all racial groups of China to self-determination; and as soon as militarism and imperialism have been expelled from the land . . . we will do our best to organize (upon the voluntary agreement of all racial groups) a free and united Republic of China.[3]

By its failure to equate self-determination with the right of secession, the 1924 declaration strongly suggests that Sun had not really undergone a fundamental change of mind with regard to the political future of China's minorities.[4] Indeed, one of the concessions that Sun had extracted for his friendship was a guarantee that it was not "the intention or the objective of the present Russian government to work for Outer Mongolia's independence from China."[5] It seems evident, therefore, that Sun was not prepared to go so far as to endorse publicly the notion of a right of secession. And Chiang Kai-shek, who succeeded to the KMT's leadership following Sun's death in 1925, found objectionable even the lip service paid to this otherwise undefined and nebulous self-determination. His position was reflected in the KMT constitution of 1931, which made no mention of self-determination and which, by asserting that "the Republic of China shall be a unified Republic forever," placed the stamp of finality upon resistance to secession.[6]

Consonant with this constitutional assertion, the KMT subsequently frowned not only upon secession but meaningful autonomy as well, and this attitude was maintained even when its control over the area and people in question was at best theoretical.[7] Under the guidance of Chiang, who, all evidence to the contrary, maintained that there simply could be no national question within China because all of its peoples were of one stock, KMT policy was in fact one of Hanification, that is to say, assimilation of all peoples into a single nation of Han.[8] Just as the White forces had done within the Soviet Union, the KMT, by its intransigence on the national question and by its general insensitivity to minority aspirations, ensured fertile soil for the introduction of the Leninist strategy of promising self-determination.

But the fledgling CCP did not immediately adopt this line of strategy. The party's earliest documents make no reference to self-determination. Indeed, a document drawn up in 1922 that itemized the nine most immediate aims of the party did not even make a passing reference to minorities.[9] Later in the same year, a party manifesto prophesied "the establishment of a Chinese Federated Republic by the unification of China proper, Mongolia, Tibet, and Sinkiang into a free federation," but again made no mention of either self-determination or secession.[10] The term "self-determination" appeared for the first time in a 1923 declaration, but it was used in reference to China's struggle against foreign imperialism rather than to a right adhering to a nation.[11] At the Sixth National Congress of the CCP (September 1928), the third of "ten great demands of the Chinese Revolution" read "Unify China and recognize [the principle] of national self-determination."[12] However, no further explanation was offered, and the coupling of unification with self-determination causes the latter to appear more in the vein of Sun Yat-sen's grudging and ambiguous concession than of Lenin's insistence upon promising independence. Indeed, the fact that this CCP congress was held in Moscow makes it likely that the passing reference to self-determination was a token concession to Soviet pressures. The total absence of any additional discussion of self-determination or of minority matters in this lengthy and otherwise detailed document would seem to be a more accurate reflection of the CCP's level of interest in the general topic. This lack of concern was further illustrated the following year when the party leadership, convening once more back in China, failed to mention either self-determination or minorities in the course of laying out its fifteen most pressing political tasks (five more than in 1928).[13]

This slighting of the minorities is partially explainable as a consequence of the party's early preoccupation with the urban proletariat of eastern China. As evidenced by the ethnic map of China (see map 1), the minorities are by and large located in China's inland frontier zones, far distant from the east-coast cities. This remoteness of the minorities, coupled with their economic backwardness,[14] prevented them from becoming a matter of vital concern to those in charge of party strategy.

But very different indeed was the view from the rural hinterland to which Mao and his colleagues repaired after the 1927 break with Chiang Kai-shek. From that vantage point, the minority areas took on a new strategic importance, for to deny them to the KMT was to lessen materially the risk of encirclement.[15] Secondly, once in the hinterland and cut off from the coast, the Communist forces could hope to receive assistance from the Soviet Union, or from any other power, only through minority territory. Finally, the military strategy and tactics that were adopted by Mao and his cohorts necessarily endowed the local populace with vital significance and, given Mao's locational situation, the local populace was very apt to be non-Han.

Although scholarship dealing with the CCP's rise to power has tended to emphasize military tactics, there is little originality either in Mao's writings on warfare or in the campaigns conducted by Chinese Communist forces.[16] Moreover, on the scene of battle, military tactics are likely to be far more impromptu than writings on the topic indicate. And even wise tactics may fail to produce

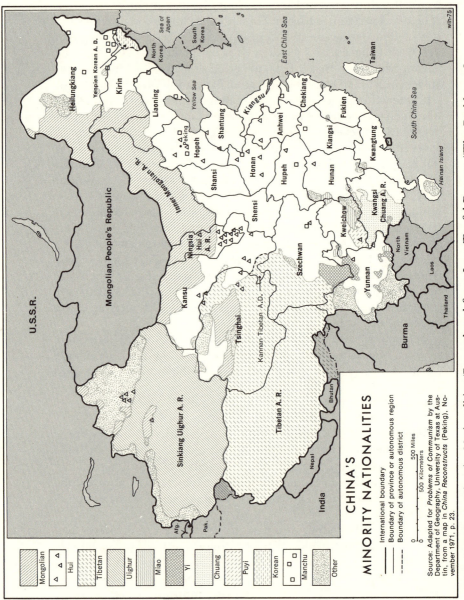

CHINA'S
MINORITY NATIONALITIES

—— International boundary
—— Boundary of province or autonomous region
- - - - Boundary of autonomous district

0   500 Miles
0   500 Kilometers

Source: Adapted for *Problems of Communism* by the
Department of Geography, University of Texas at Austin, from a map in *China Reconstructs* (Peking). November 1971, p. 23.

Legend:
- Mongolian
- Hui △
- Tibetan
- Uighur
- Miao
- Yi
- Chuang
- Puyi
- Korean
- Manchu
- Other

Map labels:

U.S.S.R.

Mongolian People's Republic

Inner Mongolian A.R.

Heilungkiang
Yenpien Korean A.D.
Kirin
Liaoning
North Korea
South Korea
Sea of Japan
East China Sea
Taiwan
South China Sea
Hainan Island

Shantung
Kiangsu
Chekiang
Anhwei
Fukien
Kiangsi
Kwangtung
Hopeh
Peking
Shansi
Honan
Hupeh
Hunan
Shensi
Kweichow
Kwangsi Chuang A.R.
Ningsia Hui A.R.
Kansu
Szechwan
Yunnan
North Vietnam
Laos
Thailand
Burma
Tsinghai
Kannan Tibetan A.D.
Tibetan A.R.
Bhutan
Nepal
India
Afg.
Pak.
Sinkiang Uighur A.R.
Yellow Sea

wlh-75

MAP 1. China's Minority Nationalities (Reproduced from June Teufel Dreyer, "The Problem of

victory in a battle, much less determine the outcome of a war. Apt to be more significant in a revolutionary war is the relationship of the revolutionary forces to the local people. We earlier noted, with regard to the postrevolutionary struggle within the Soviet Union between the Communist and White forces, that the attitude of the local people can be consequential even in an essentially conventional war. However, as boldy advertised in the rubric, "people's war," or in such metaphorical axioms as "the people are the water and our army the fish," the essentiality of the support of the local populace is many times magnified in the case of a revolutionary struggle that has assumed the guerrilla form.

The necessity of local support was articulated in 1936 by a leading figure of the CCP, P'eng Teh-huai. While in command of the First Front Red Army, then locked in combat with KMT forces, General P'eng forcefully remarked during an interview granted to Edgar Snow:

> Finally, it is absolutely necessary for the partisans to win the support and participation of the peasant masses. If there is no movement of the armed peasantry, in fact, there is no partisan base, and the army cannot exist. Only by implanting itself deeply in the hearts of the people, only by fulfilling the demands of the masses, only by consolidating a base in the peasant soviets, and only by sheltering in the shadow of the masses, can partisan warfare bring revolutionary victory.
>
> But nothing, absolutely nothing, is more important than this— that the Red Army is a people's army, and has grown because the people helped us. . . .
>
> Tactics are important, but we could not exist if the majority of the people did not support us.[17]

The "support" to which General P'eng alluded need not manifest itself in positive actions. However, whether one contemplates the creation of a base area or the actual conduct of revolutionary warfare, the passivity of the local people is the irreducible requirement. If the people do not love you more, they must at least despise you less than they do your enemy. This minimum attitude guarantees (1) that the local people will not violently resist your presence; (2) that they will not furnish information on your movements or otherwise cooperate with your enemy;[18] and (3) that food and other essential needs can be acquired locally without excessive coercion.

Apathy on the part of the indigenous people, then, is the minimal attitude compatible with successful revolutionary warfare. But between this minimum and the maximum of ideological conversion and total commitment lie great opportunities for various levels of positive cooperation with the revolutionary forces. Common manifestations of such positive cooperation are the furnishing of food and shelter, the provision of intelligence about the enemy,[19] and the offer of porters to carry ammunition and other necessary supplies (porters being almost essential for conducting successful revolutionary warfare in the relatively roadless tracts of inner Asia).

In order to achieve this progression from apathy to positive cooperation (and, perhaps, to ideological conversion), programs, such as land reform, which possessed great appeal for the mass of the local people, were inaugurated by the CCP in occupied areas; and the revolutionary forces were instructed to treat the local people with the utmost circumspection.[20] Selective terror also played a key role. This system of rewards, courtesies, coercion, and the threat of coercion were to be extended without regard to nationality. But the minorities posed a special problem. The CCP had good reason to anticipate that the minorities would not cooperate with any movement identified as Chinese, particularly with that of the Nationalists. The non-Han peoples harbored a traditional dislike of the Chinese, in large part a reflection of the latter's penchant for treating non-Han as inferiors. The KMT's program of political consolidation of all the territory and of all the peoples of imperial China was, therefore, hardly one to elicit minority cooperation. The CCP leaders could therefore expect that the minorities would remain at least coldly neutral, and they indicated their awareness of this strategic asset on a number of occasions when their forces, badly harassed by the KMT, purposefully fell back on non-Han areas.[21] But if distrust of the CCP's own image as overwhelmingly Han were to be overcome, something more was needed. And Lenin's legacy had, of course, made provision for just such an exigency in the guise of self-determination.

But before turning to the party's endorsement of self-determination during the 1930s, there remains to be considered the question of why the party failed to endorse the principle prior to this time. Even when due allowance is made for the party's early disinterest in the national question due to a combination of geographic factors and preoccupation with urban centers, there is still something enigmatic involved in the fact that the party should for ten years have slighted the long list of precedents, dating back to Marx's action of 1865, of including, almost as a matter of form, promises of self-determination in socialist programs. Their immediate concentration upon the cities of eastern China could not have blinded the CCP's leadership to the fact that the minorities' homelands accounted for more than half of China's territory, including the strategic border zones, particularly at a time when Japan, Britain, and the Soviet Union were all actively appealing to the national aspirations of one or more of China's major groups. Moreover, as earlier documented, the leaders of the Soviet Union, through the agency of the Comintern, were pressuring all other Communist parties during the 1920s to endorse publicly self-determination for their respective minorities.[22]

The otherwise unexplained slighting of self-determination by the CCP during its first ten years suggests the prevalence of grave skepticism concerning the advisability of such a step, a skepticism which could draw nourishment from the record of secessionist movements that had afflicted the Soviet Union during its revolutionary and immediate postrevolutionary periods. Moreover, the pattern of steps by which the CCP introduced the promise of self-determination into its program further indicates that there was resistance which first had to be overcome.

The opening salvo of the campaign did not occur until early 1930, a period when the leaders of the hinterland soviets were first becoming recognized as an important independent force within the party. A group of otherwise unidentified "delegates from various soviets" held a meeting in Shanghai, the principal result of which was a proposal to establish a Chinese Soviet government in the hinterland. However, the delegates also outlined Ten Great Political Programs, number five of which was the recognition of the right of minorities to secede.[23] This theme was echoed by an article that appeared in the party's journal, *Bolshevik* (Pu-erh-sai-wei-k'o), during 1931.[24] There was the clearest sense of urgency in the article's insistence that "the CCP . . . must advocate that the non-Han nationalities . . . be given the right of self-determination and even the right of secession. . . . It is in the revolutionary interest of the Chinese Soviet Government to insure actual independence and freedom of non-Han nationality states."

Consonant with this sense of urgency, a constitutional conference, meeting before the year had elapsed, adopted a constitution whose 14th article reads as follows:

The Soviet Government of China recognizes the right of self-determination of the national minorities in China, their right to complete separation from China, and to the formation of an independent state for each national minority. *All* Mongolians, Tibetans, Miao, Yao, Koreans, and others living on the territory of China shall enjoy the full right to self-determination, i.e. they may either join the Union of Chinese Soviets or secede from it and form their own state as they may prefer. The Soviet regime of China will do its utmost to assist the national minorities in liberating themselves from the yoke of imperialists, the KMT militarists, *t'u-ssu*, the princes, lamas, and others, and in achieving complete freedom and autonomy. The Soviet regime must encourage the development of the national cultures and of the respective languages of these peoples.[25]

By 1931, then, the CCP had ostensibly pledged itself to support the right of national self-determination, explicitly including the right of secession, for "all" members of every minority. But while Article 14 set forth the public stance of the CCP with regard to self-determination, a resolution passed by the constitutional conference before it adopted the constitution provides a much better insight into actual CCP intentions. Entitled "Resolution of the First All-China Congress of Soviets on the Question of National Minorities in China," it is a document that addresses itself to "the toiling masses of the national minorities," rather than to minorities as such.[26] Indeed, in the course of its relatively slender text, the phrase "the toiling masses" is repeated ten times. "The toiling masses," it will be remembered, was the precise phrase suddenly adopted by Stalin following the October Revolution as a formula for calling a halt to separatist movements and for justifying the forcible reestablishment of the state's prerevolutionary borders. There appears to be little question but that the repetitive use of the same phrase by the CCP, far from being coincidental, was intended to assure members of the party that, though promising the right of secession, the party would not permit any group to exercise that option. Apparently so that there would be no mistaking this point, the resolution contained two vitally different definitions of self-determination: the first version was that which was truly accepted by the party; the second version was the one to be publicized through the medium of the constitution. The first states:

> The Chinese workers, peasants, soldiers, and all the toiling masses shall fight determinedly against the oppression of national minorities, and strive for their complete emancipation. In view of this, the First All-China Congress of Soviets of Workers', Peasants', and Soldiers' Deputies declares that the Chinese Soviet

Republic categorically and unconditionally recognizes the right of national minorities to self-determination. This means that in districts like Mongolia, Tibet, Sinkiang, Yunnan, Kweichow, and others, where the majority of the population belongs to non-Chinese nationalities, *the toiling masses of these nationalities shall have the right to determine for themselves* whether they wish to leave the Chinese Soviet Republic and create their own independent state, or whether they wish to join the Union of Soviet Republics, or form an autonomous area inside the Chinese Soviet Republic.[27]

Then, having further stressed the party's commitment solely to the toiling masses; having urged the toiling masses of the minorities to join with those of the Han against the common exploiters; having driven wedges between the toiling masses of the minorities and their respective oppressing classes ("princes," "Living Buddhas," "lamas," "the gentry," the "t'u-ssu," and the like); having noted that the congress "openly declares before the toiling masses of all nationalities in China that it is the purpose of the Chinese Soviet Republic to create a single state for them, without national barriers"; and having noted that "the Soviet Union is the only country . . . where the national question has indeed been solved," the congress, in a seeming non sequitur, "therefore" resolved:

> In the fundamental Law (Constitution) of the Chinese Soviet Republic it shall be clearly stated that *all national minorities within the confines of China shall have the right to national self-determination, including secession* from China and the formation of independent states, and that the Chinese Soviet Republic fully and unconditionally recognizes the independence of the Outer Mongolian People's Republic.[28]

As noted, the congress did in fact carry out this directive with regard to the constitution, thereby committing the party to two distinct views as to the group in whom a so-called right of self-determination was vested: (1) that of the resolution: "This means . . . the toiling masses shall have the right . . ." and (2) that of the constitution: "All Mongolians . . . and others living on the territory of China shall enjoy the full right. . . ." The message that emanated from the conference, therefore, was that self-determination for the toiling masses presently required a purely formal commitment to national self-determination. Or, phrased differently, since, in the Marxist lexicon, self-determination for the toiling masses would be indistinguishable from the victory of communism, the resolution's message was that victory for the CCP required the public endorsement of self-determination for all minorities as a purely temporary expedient that was not to be honored. By the simultaneous endorsement of these two variant versions of the right of self-determination, the Chinese removed any question of ambiguity due to a lapse of time. Whereas, Stalin, following the revolution, had contended that the toiling masses had always been implicitly present in the Marxist view of self-determination, and whereas Lenin, following the revolution, had contended that he had truly intended to permit secession by nations without regard to class considerations but that changed circumstances had necessitated a change of position, the resolution of 1931 would seemingly deny either contention to the CCP.

The CCP's ambivalence toward supporting independence for minorities was also evident in its propaganda. Sensing at a very early date that Japanese pressure upon China might prove to be the KMT's Achilles' heel, Mao had by 1931 adopted appeals to Han nationalism, particularly the need for all Chinese to wage a war of national liberation against imperialism, as the leitmotif of party propaganda.[29] As part of that campaign, Mao harshly condemned the KMT for failing to preserve the integrity of China's imperial territory. Such a criticism was hardly consonant with the CCP's own constitutional promise to grant independence to non-Han peoples who populated huge segments of China. Yet, following the adoption of the 1931 constitution, Mao periodically pledged that the CCP "stands ready at all times to shed the last drop of blood in order to maintain the independence, unity and territorial integrity of China." He specifically charged the KMT with having conceded Inner Mongolia to Japan; Tibet, Sinkiang, and Sikang to the British; and Yunan to the French.[30] Mao's expressions of dismay are difficult to reconcile with the fact that all of these territories were populated by minorities and their separation from China had therefore already been condoned by Article 14 of the 1931 Constitution of the Chinese Soviet Republic. Mao was obviously intent upon having it both ways. So far as the Han Chinese were concerned, he was convinced that appeals to the unity and territorial integrity of "the motherland" would, in his own words, "win the sympathy and active support of the laboring masses of the whole country and all other Chinese people with even a slight amount of patriotic blood running in their veins."[31] In order to gain the support of both the Han and the minorities, the CCP therefore simultaneously projected the image of preserver of the territorial borders of imperial China when addressing the Han and of promoter of secession when addressing the minorities.[32]

Regardless of its underlying sincerity, the new minority policy, as set forth publicly in the 1931 constitution, served the CCP well through some of its most trying times. Within three years of the original pronouncement on the matter, Mao's forces began their Long March, during which they were to travel thousands of miles through southern, southwestern, and, ultimately, northwestern China. During the overwhelming portion of this two-year journey, the Communists were traversing the territory of various minorities, and they successively communicated the party's public position on self-determination to the minorities whom they encountered. A participant in the march described the impact that the doctrine had upon one people as follows:

> Near the River of Golden Sand is the mountainous country of "Independent Lololand." The Red Army sent friendly letters to treat with the Lolos and told them of our definite policy to give self-determination to the tribes of China and to preserve them. Ultimately, our negotiations were successful. In the future the Lolos will all support our party and policy, but for a while it seemed touch and go before we could establish good relations with them.[33]

The promise of national self-determination was not, of course, a magical wand which upon a single wave was capable of immediately transforming enmity into camaraderie. Given the traditional distrust that the minorities harbored toward outsiders in general and Han in particular, it would be unrealistic not to expect the CCP to have encountered resistance. And, indeed, the accounts of the participants in the Long March record a number of unpleasant experiences. On balance, however, they all make clear that the party's nationality policy was an essential factor in its survival. In view of the poorly equipped, ill-fed, tiny fraction who did complete the march, it appears reasonable to conclude that determined indigenous resistance to the CCP's passage, or limited cooperation with the KMT by local peoples, would have proven disastrous.[34] Nor did the importance of minorities terminate with the establishment of the historic base in Yenan. Continued good relations with the nearby Mongols and Hui (Moslems) were necessary in order to secure the rear and right flanks, respectively. Thus the realization of the minimum requirement with regard to the attitudes of the local populace (their passivity), obtained in large part by sporadically declared promises of ethnic self-determination, was an essential element in Mao's survival from 1927 until the evacuation of the Yenan base twenty years later.

What the CCP leaders tried to achieve from the manipulation of ethnic aspirations was not restricted to apathy, however. Having achieved, by their promise of political independence for minorities, a modicum of good will (or at least a better image than that enjoyed by the KMT), the CCP employed this entering wedge to gain further advantage. Here the leadership had a number of choices with regard to both intermediate goals and techniques. For example, the CCP could deal with a minority as a strategic unit and urge it to declare a war of national liberation against the common KMT enemy. Or it could try to entice members of the minority to join its forces, either as individuals or as tactical units. Second, the CCP could cooperate with the backward ("feudal") leadership, or work with the more progressive ("bourgeois") elite, or limit itself to operating through Communists. Third, it could defer the ideological conversion of the minorities until the revolution was successful, or it could begin indoctrination immediately. In actuality, the CCP's decisions were marked by great flexibility reflecting pragmatic opportunism, for it employed all of these approaches at one time or another. Exact numbers are unobtainable, but members of minorities did volunteer to act as porters during the Long March, and others joined the Red Army either as individuals or as units.[35] There were also numerous attempts to have entire minorities declare their independence, thereby declaring civil war with the KMT. In some cases, the attempt to create a secessionist state was taken under the leadership of members of the CCP.[36] But the CCP was not averse to working through the most conservative elements, if such an avenue promised success. In the case of the Moslem Hui, for example, the CCP took advantage of a schismatic struggle by allying itself with the most conservative relgious leaders against a modernizing movement that had the support of the KMT-allied ruling house.[37] The question of the communization of the minority masses was also approached pragmatically. As noted, the basic appeal made by the CCP to the minorities was the potential discarding of an alien political yoke. But the minorities were concurrently urged to overthrow native landlords and other national reactionaries.[38] Thus ethnic nationalism and communism were linked, but there was a clear recognition on the part of the CCP that the greater attraction—the wedge—was nationalism. Political independence was depicted as near at hand; the timetable for broad acceptance of

Marxism was left less definite. Wherever possible, the psychological groundwork for conversion was laid, but the pragmatic goal of the revolution's success was to take paramountcy over ideology. Since the Long March occurred primarily in minority territory, both the long-range necessity and inevitability of the ideological conversion of the minorities, and the lack of immediate urgency for such a conversion are clearly conveyed by Mao's statement of late 1935:

> The Long March is also an agitation corps. It declares to the approximately two hundred million people of eleven provinces that only the road of the Red Army leads to their liberation. Without the Long March, how could the broad masses have known so quickly that there are such great ideas in the world as are upheld by the Red Army?
>
> The Long March is also a seeding machine. It has sown many seeds in eleven provinces, which will sprout, grow leaves, blossom into flowers, bear fruit and yield a crop in the future.[39]

While thus engaged in parlaying its intermittent offers of national independence into necessary support for its cause, the party never fell prey to its own rhetoric but continued to differentiate between its propaganda and its more privately held commitment to maintaining the territorial integrity of the Chinese state. It is instructive, for example, to contrast Mao's public statement and the official pledge of the CCP to the people of Inner Mongolia, both of which were made in December 1935, with Mao's more private statements concerning the people of Inner and Outer Mongolia that were made just seven months later. The officially declared policy of the CCP was that "we recognize the right of the people of Inner Mongolia to decide all questions pertaining to themselves, for no one has the right to forcefully interfere with the way of life, religious observances, etc., of the Inner Mongolian people. At the same time the people of Inner Mongolia are free to build a system of their own choosing; they are at liberty to develop their own government, unite in a federation with other peoples, or to make themselves entirely separate."[40] A personal greeting by Mao at the same time noted that "we are persuaded that it is only by fighting together with us that the people of Inner Mongolia can preserve the glory of the epoch of Genghis Khan, prevent the extermination of their nation, embark on the path of national revival, and obtain the freedom and independence enjoyed by peoples such as those of Turkey, Poland, the Ukraine, and the Caucasus."[41] Yet, in a private interview during July 1936, Mao made no mention of a possible separate state for the people of Inner Mongolia, but spoke only of an "autonomous state." Later he added, "When the people's revolution has been victorious in China the Outer Mongolian Republic will automatically become a part of the Chinese federation, at their own will. The Mohammedan and Tibetan peoples likewise will form autonomous republics attached to the China federation."[42] By the expressions "autonomous states" and "autonomous republics" Mao did not mean independence. Even as then employed within the Soviet Union to describe that state's subsidiary political organs, these terms had a precise connotation—cultural autonomy but political subservience. Both Lenin and Stalin, we will recall, had, on numerous occasions, differentiated between self-determination, which to them and therefore to all true Marxist-Leninists included the right of secession, and autonomy, which did not.[43] Mao was unquestionably clearly aware of this distinction. Remember that the CCP's 1931 resolution on minorities, which was quoted earlier, made clear this same distinction between an "independent state" and "an autonomous area inside the Chinese Soviet Republic."[44] Moreover, the inclusion of Outer Mongolia among the regions to be attached to China is particularly noteworthy. As mentioned earlier, the 1931 resolution called for the constitution to stipulate "that the Chinese Soviet Republic fully and unconditionally recognizes the independence of the Outer Mongolian People's Republic." In point of fact, however, the constitution failed to make any reference whatsoever to Outer Mongolia, and Mao's 1936 comments suggest that he had had a hand in this omission. Apparently he perceived greater danger in granting formal approval to an already consummated act of secession, which the party hoped one day to reverse, than he did in holding out the phantasma of secession in an indefinite future.

A more perplexing glimpse of the two faces the CCP was presenting with regard to the national question during this phase of its history is offered by the case of Chang Kuo-t'ao. One of the nadiral points of the CCP's history coincided with the 1935 meeting in western Szechwan Province of Mao's forces coming from the south with those of Chang Kuo-t'ao, another Communist leader who had been active in central China. The forces of both men were badly depleted, and it was decided that Chang would work totally among the minorities of western China (Tibet, Sinkiang, and Szechwan), while Mao would move northeastward to Yenan and work primarily among the Han Chinese, whose support he would gain by espousing a united front of all patriotic forces to resist the

Japanese. Chang was to fail and be purged, and his entire plan would later be described as "warlordism," purportedly carried out only over Mao's strongest objections.[45] There are a number of reasons, however, to suspect that Chang's and Mao's respective courses of action constituted a two-pronged strategy, and that Mao's objections were *ex post facto* and were a result of the plan's failure rather than of its concept.[46] But, in any event, to stigmatize pejoratively an attempt to carry out the party's official program on national independence as "warlordism" is to substantiate simultaneously a lack of sincerity with regard to the many proclamations made in support of national self-determination. How else can the charge of "warlordism" be reconciled with promises of independence made to minorities by Mao even *after* the Szechwan meeting? We have noted that Mao personally promised independence to the Mongolians in December of 1935. In the same month he signed a resolution that asserted: "By its own example and sincere slogans, the Soviet People's Republic tells the oppressed Mongolians and Moslems: Organize your own state!"[47] In May of the following year, he pledged independence to the very people whom Chang was currently courting. Addressing the "Turkish Moslems" of Sinkiang (elsewhere in the address referred to as "the minorities of the Northwest"), Mao wrote:

1. According to the principle of national self-determination, we advocate that the affairs of the Moslems must be completely handled by the Moslems themselves, that, in all Moslem areas, the Moslems must establish their independent and autonomous political power and handle all the political, economic, religious, custom, ethical, educational, and other matters.[48]

In short, the party's official commitment to national self-determination, and therefore to "warlordism," survived Chang's ill-fated venture and even his expulsion from the party.

Regardless of its merits, Mao's well-known attack upon Chang for "warlordism" probably helps to account for the fact that some authorities have erroneously concluded that the party actually terminated its official support for a right of secession about this time.[49] Charges brought against Liu Shao-ch'i by the Red Guards in 1967 would, if well founded, offer retroactive substantiation for such a conclusion. The Guards urged that Liu be purged for advocating "national separatism" for minorities in 1937, the implication being that such a position could not have been compatible with official policy at that time.[50] Yet, a party document published the same year (1937) noted the need to "mobilize Mongolians, Moslems, and other minority groups for a common struggle against Japan on the basis of the principles of self-determination and self-government."[51] While the document did not explicitly mention a right of secession, it most certainly did so by inference, since the CCP remained publicly committed to its 1931 constitutional definition of self-determination which explicitly gave to minorities the right to "secede . . . and form their own state." Moreover, as we have recorded, this explicit definition of self-determination was reaffirmed in several subsequent party declarations, as well as in personal pronouncements by Mao. Indeed, in his 1937 article, Liu Shao-ch'i, who was at the time a member of the Politburo and a confidant of Mao, referred six times to "independence" as an elemental ingredient of self-determination.[52]

Comments attributed to Mao in a speech before the Central Committee of the CCP in October 1938 have also been cited as a public rejection of secession:[53]

> First, the Meng, Hui, Tsang, Miao, Yao, I, and Fan minorities must be allowed to have equal rights with the Han people. Under the principle of common struggle against Japan, they have the right to control their own affairs, and, at the same time, unite with the Han people to establish a unified country.[54]

The passage, however, is not without ambiguity. The right of national minorities "to control their own affairs" could well be interpreted, particularly by the minorities themselves, as incorporating the right of secession. Indeed, given the fact that during the preceding year (1937) the CCP had, for the second time, entered into a united front with the KMT, the wording of Mao's promise to the minorities was lavish. The party congress that Mao was addressing took place at a time when the CCP leadership was determined to avoid all potential sources of conflict between itself and the KMT, and, given the KMT's integrationist position with regard to all minorities, it is surprising that Mao was prepared to promise the latter the right "to control their own affairs."[55] In any case, by 1945, with an American victory over Japan imminent and with the CCP now in a much more powerful position relative to the KMT, Mao once more employed the specific phrase, self-determination.[56] He now demanded that the KMT grant "better treatment for the racial minorities in China, according them the right of self-determination and of forming a union with the Han people on a voluntary basis."[57] Moreover, in the course of his 1945 speech, Mao favorably cited a portion of the "Manifesto of the First National Congress of the Kuomintang" (1924) in which it was noted that "the Kuomintang solemnly declares that it recognizes the right to self-determination of all nationalities in China."[58] Whatever the meaning that Sun Yat-sen might have intended by the phrase "self-determination," the CCP, as we noted, had never repudiated its explicit 1931 constitutional assertion that self-determination for the national minorities meant "their right to complete separation from China, and to the formation of an independent state for each national minority."[59] By citing Sun's reference to self-determination and adding that the CCP "fully agrees," Mao, as late as 1945, was holding out the vision of a separate political state for any of the non-Han peoples who desired one. Furthermore, the 1945 constitution of the CCP spoke of the need "to organize and unify the . . . national minorities on its side" and pledged to struggle for the establishment of a "strong new democratic federated republic based on the alliance of all revolutionary classes *and free union of all races*. . . ."[60]

The promise of national self-determination therefore remained an integral part of the CCP's program long after 1938. As Chang Chih-i, a Chinese Communist official with special expertise on the national question, would candidly acknowledge in 1956:

> Why does the Chinese Communist Party, with respect to the tasks concerning the national question in the transition period, give prominence to safeguarding the unity of the motherland and nationalities solidarity rather than the principle constantly emphasized by Lenin—that of "national self-determination"? In the first place, as we know, the Chinese Communist Party, on the basis of the Marxist-Leninist formulation of the national question, consistently advocated self-determination and federalism from the day the Party was founded until the period of the Anti-Japanese War. It was only with the period of China's third revolutionary war [i.e., 1946–1949 (ed.)] that these slogans ceased to be emphasized.[61]

The party's ostensible commitment to self-determination therefore survived at least until 1946. And given the late 1948 statement by Liu Shao-ch'i to the effect that the CCP "advocates the complete equality of all nations (large or small, strong or weak) both at home and in the family of nations, and it also advocates the voluntary association and voluntary separation of all nations," it would seem that the party continued until the eve of total victory to hold out the grail of political separation before China's minorities.[62]

Chang Chih-i's confirmation that self-determination for minorities continued to be "emphasized" by the party until at least 1946 is intriguing, in that this emphasis is not reflected in known party declarations made after the mid-1930s. We have seen that Mao had very early exhibited an appreciation of the fact that the Han Chinese would likely regard any loss of imperial China's territory and populace as anathema, causing him to mask the party's support for separation when addressing a Han Chinese audience. And this at a time when the minorities held a very important place in party strategy. The degree of importance that the CCP assigned to the non-Han during the period is mirrored in the prophecy contained in the declaration that was issued at the culmination of the 1935 Szechwan meeting between Mao and Chang Ku-t'ao. It forecast that the bringing of the minorities under the leadership of the CCP "will be of *decisive* significance on the road ahead to the victory of the Chinese people's revolution."[63] The attitudes of the minorities might indeed prove decisive in permitting Mao's movement to survive one of its most desperate periods. But ultimately the Han, constituting more than ninety percent of the populace and inhabiting most of China's key centers, had to be won over if the CCP was to prove victorious. Developments already well underway, most particularly growing Japanese aggression against China, offered new opportunities for the CCP to win sympathizers among the Han, opportunities that would correspondingly lessen the significance of the minorities.[64]

We will recall that the plan agreed upon during the Szechwan conference called for one group to work among the minorities, while Mao proceeded to Yenan where he would initiate a proselytizing movement among the Han by stressing resistance to the Japanese invaders. Both courses of action were therefore predicated upon a profound appreciation of the political power of ethnic distinctions. In Mao's case, the Japanese were viewed as an ethnic asset, the vital "them," for Mao correctly gauged that a crusade against the alien would prove more seductive to the Han Chinese than would Chiang Kai-shek's anti-Communist campaign against fellow Chinese.[65] Moreover, he also counted upon ethnic nationalism to bring ultimate victory over the powerful Japanese. Responding to a skeptical inquiry concerning the possibility of backward China defeating highly industrialized Japan, Mao commented in 1936:

It must be remembered that the war will be fought in China. This means that the Japanese will be entirely surrounded by a hostile Chinese people. The Japanese will be forced to move in all their provisions and guard them, maintaining troops along all lines of communications, and heavily garrisoning their bases. The great reservoirs of human material in the revolutionary Chinese people will still be pouring men ready to fight for their freedom into our front lines long after the tidal flood of Japanese imperialism has wrecked itself on the hidden reefs of Chinese resistance.[66]

To Mao there was an obvious parallel between a Japanese army operating in eastern (Han) China, and a KMT army operating in a minority region of China. The intervention of the Japanese in China made it feasible to apply those concepts of successful revolutionary warfare, which were predicated upon ethnic diversity, through the medium of the majority, Han-Chinese people. As Mao succinctly phrased it: "Linking the civil war of China with the national war is a fundamental principle of the party's guidance of the revolutionary war."[67]

Mao's prospects were materially enhanced when the CCP entered, for the second time, into a united front with the KMT. Freed from the pressures of survival strategy, the CCP seized the opportunity to achieve broad-scale acceptability by wrapping itself in the attire of Han ethnonationalism. Party propaganda became unabashedly nationalistic. Thus the CCP's "Public Statement on KMT-CCP Co-Operation" (September 22,1937) read in part:

Beloved Compatriots! The Central Committee of the CCP respectfully and most sincerely issues the following manifesto to all fathers, brothers, aunts, and sisters throughout the country: [W]e know that in order to transform this glorious future into a new China, independent, free, and happy, all our fellow countrymen, every single zealous descendent of Huang-ti [the legendary first emperor of China] must determinedly and relentlessly participate in the concerted struggle. . . .
The enemy has penetrated our country! The moment is critical! Compatriots, arise and unite! Our great Chinese nation, with its long history, is unconquerable. Rise and struggle for the consolidation of national unity and the overthrow of Japanese imperialist oppression. Victory will belong to the Chinese nation.
Long live the victory of the anti-Japanese war!
Long live the independent, free, and happy new China![68]

Subsequent documents noted that "our race and nation now stand at a critical hour of survival" and spoke of the "holy national war of self-defense to drive the Japanese bandits out of China and to preserve our territorial and sovereign integrity."[69] National unity replaced the cleavage of class, and repetitive utilization of the rather clumsy and redundant phrase "the Chinese nation and the Chinese people" replaced references to "the toiling masses."[70] Indeed the party, Marx's vanguard of the working class, now explicitly became "the vanguard of the Chinese nation and the Chinese people."[71]

Han ethnonationalism was indeed "an idea whose time had come," and its timely embrace by the CCP rapidly increased support for the party among the Han people. As noted, since the Han comprised the bulk of China's population, their attitudes were necessarily of prime importance, if the CCP aspired to control of the entire country. Therefore, as the new ethnonational propaganda began to reap dividends, the significance of the minorities quite naturally sharply receded. A now realistic preoccupation with the Han people (unlike the party's earlier preoccupation predicated upon an unduly optimistic self-appraisal of its proselytical capabilities during the 1920s) could, in and by itself, account for the relative absence of references to minority matters after 1936. But it is also likely that the paucity of publicity accorded minority policies was due to a desire not to risk alienating members of the Han nation by becoming associated with policies sanctioning the severance of territory and subjects from "mother China." The fear of such a response even on the part of Han who were party members is evident in a 1937 party document authored by Liu Shao-ch'i:

> The independence and autonomy of the minority nationalities is nothing to be afraid of, for after they are given independence and autonomy, they can still join China in the common struggle against the Japanese. What is to be feared is their opposition to China and the Hans, initiated at the deception of and for utilization by the Japanese.[72]

When Liu felt compelled to write this passage, the minorities were still an important element in the party's deliberations. But with the rather radical change in the party's fortunes brought about by growing support among the Han, it is reasonable to assume that the leadership found it progressively unwise to endanger the Han's support by drawing attention to the party's promises concerning national self-determination for minorities.[73] Tempering such a risk by decreasing the number of public references to a right of secession need not have cost the CCP a corresponding loss of support among the minorities, since prior to assuming power they never repudiated their support of such a right. Given even the very sporadic references to self-determination which, as we have noted, continued almost to the eve of total victory over the KMT, it is probable that the CCP persisted in its promises of secession while engaged in less publicized dealings with the minorities and their leaders. Considering that independent states proliferated among the Hui, Mongols, Tibetans, and peoples of Sinkiang (Eastern Turkestan) during the period;[74] that their reunification by the CCP was achieved only by the use of force; and that several counter-revolutionary struggles occurred in minority areas after reunification (that is, in the early 1950s), it is evident that to the minorities the promises of independence retained their credibility into the late 1940s.[75]

In any case, immediately after assuming power in 1949, the CCP abruptly set to rest any Han or intraparty consternation concerning separatism. The document which proclaimed the establishment of the People's Republic of China (CPR) and which was to serve as a provisional constitution for the new state, was ominously silent regarding self-determination.[76] Article 2 spoke of the need "to liberate all of the territory of China, and to achieve the unification of China." Article 7 promised "to suppress all counter-revolutionary elements who . . . commit treason against the motherland." Article 10 instructed the army "to defend the . . . territorial integrity . . . of China." Those articles (50–53) dealing explicitly with minorities offered "equality" and "regional autonomy" but, unlike the Soviet constitutions of 1924 and 1936, made no mention of secession. As if to underline the change of policy, it was stipulated flatly (Article 50) that "nationalism and chauvinism shall be opposed." If further clarification of this phrase was necessary, it was furnished in unmistakable form the following year, when the People's Liberation Army was ordered into Tibet. General Lin Po explained the impending reannexation as follows: "The People's Army will soon liberate Tibet. . . . When the country has been liberated Tibetans will be given regional autonomy and religious freedom."[77] The parallel between this action and that taken by the Soviet authorities with regard to their nationalities at a corresponding point in their party's history is striking. In each instance, peoples who, during the revolution, were promised the right of political independence were subsequently reincorporated by force and offered the diminished prospect of regional autonomy.

In yet another striking similarity, Stalin's ominous statement made two years after the Soviet revolution to the effect that a demand for secession would henceforth be "a profoundly counter-revolutionary one,"[78] found a Chinese echo precisely two years following the defeat of the KMT. An editorial in *People's Daily* of October 2, 1951 stated that "any national movement which seeks separation from the Chinese People's Republic for independence will be reactionary." In a similar, if less bellicose vein, a Chinese official responsible for nationality policy within the CPR, described the first two years of the country's experience with minorities as follows: "During the past two years, the different nationalities within the big family have steadily tightened the bonds between them. They now form an *indivisible* group, a fact over which all of us must rejoice."[79] By this time, all of the minorities, including the Tibetans, had been returned to the fold, and the stress upon indivisibility, a theme subsequently to be repeated with undeviating regularity in the party's major documents, appears to have been designed to impress the minorities that the days of verbal toying with secessionism were definitely over. Thus, Article 2 of the General Program of the CPR for the Implementation of Regional Autonomy for Nationalities, which became official policy on August 9, 1952, averred that "each national autonomous area is an *inseparable* part of the territory of the PRC."[80] The same note of irreversible union was voiced in Article 3 of the 1954 constitution, which stated, *inter alia*, that "the PRC is a *single*, multinational state," that "acts which undermine the unity of the nationalities are prohibited," and that the "national autonomous areas are *inalienable* parts of the PRC."[81] More than a quarter century after the state's founding, the same theme was still echoing: Article 4 of the 1975 constitution announced that "the PRC is a *unitary* multinational state. The areas where regional autonomy is practiced are all *inalienable* parts of the PRC."[82] The same two terms (*unitary* and *inalienable*) appeared yet again in Article 4 of the 1978 constitution.[83] While faithfully repeating the phrase that "the autonomous areas are inalienable parts of the PRC," the 1982 constitution was even more explicit than its predecessors concerning any claim to a right of secession: "any acts that undermine the unity of nationalities or instigate their secession are prohibited."[84] Unlike the Soviets, then, the CCP dropped the doctrine of self-determination immediately upon assuming power, and has subsequently denied any right of secession not just in "content" (as have the Soviets), but in "form" as well.

And what of the many earlier promises of national self-determination? Chang Chih-i, the Chinese Communist official whom we earlier quoted, would, in 1956, quite correctly defend the broken promises as orthodox Marxism: "Marxists have never regarded the demand for the right to national self-determination as an invariable thing; generally it has been regarded as a factor in the struggle for democracy and socialism." After citing Lenin and Stalin to this same effect, he concluded:

> In sum, the principal aim of Marxist-Leninists in insisting on the necessity of recognizing the right of national self-determination is that of opposing imperialism by seeking to make allies of the oppressed nationalities in the socialist revolution of the international proletariat; it is clearly not their aim to advocate indiscriminately the separation of each nation nor to urge the establishment of a great number of small nation-states. On the contrary, while supporting the right to national self-determination, Marxist-Leninists have constantly stressed the question of whether or not a particular nationality, *depending on the actual circumstances of time and place and the interests of the revolution,* ought to be separate: only then can the question of its independence be decided.[85]

In an earlier passage, this same official had made clear that no right to separate could be countenanced if the time were postrevolutionary and if the place were the territory of a multinational state:

> With each nationality in the country having achieved liberation, with the system of nationalities oppression basically abolished, and with the nationalities of our country having already entered the era of nationalities equality, can "national liberation" still be regarded as the task of each national minority? Of course, it cannot. Since the system of nationalities oppression no longer exists, *the aim of national liberation has already been achieved....* This concept must be made absolutely clear, for otherwise individual reactionary elements within certain nationalities might take advantage of it.[86]

As in the case of the Soviet Union, a request that prerevolutionary promises be honored became counterrevolutionary and reactionary.

Less candid concerning the broken promises of secession was the 1957 account of Chou En-lai. In a speech of that year, he left the definite impression that the CCP had not followed Lenin's precedent in promising a right of independence to the minorities. The speech merits quotation in length, for it was released with great publicity only in 1980, and reflects the official post-Mao position of the Chinese Government with regard to nationality policy:

> With a view to integrating the struggle of the various nationalities against tsarist, imperialist oppression with the struggle of the proletariat and the peasantry against the bourgeoisie and the landlords, Lenin at that time proclaimed the slogan of national self-determination and recognized the right of the various nationalities to secede; it was all right if you wished to form an independent republic, it was also all right if you wished to join the union of socialist republics of Russia. At that time, to enable the first socialist state to take root politically, it was imperative to lay emphasis on this slogan of national self-determination and allow the various nationalities to separate. This was the only way to break free of the past imperialist political relations, and to enable the new socialist state under the dictatorship of the proletariat to establish a firm foothold. The specific conditions of the time demanded that the Russian proletariat do this.
>
> China finds itself in different historical circumstances. Although in old China, there was the reactionary rule of first the Northern Warlords and later the Kuomintang, who oppressed the working people and the fraternal nationalities, the whole country was one that suffered imperialist aggression, one that had become a semi-colony, or, in some regions, a colony. We were liberated under these circumstances. The revolutionary situation developed differently from that in the Soviet Union. We did not win political power by staging uprisings in big cities or in the industrially developed areas first; instead, we established revolutionary base areas mainly in the countryside and won liberation after 22 years of revolutionary wars. In these war years, the various nationalities in our country had come to establish close ties. For instance, there were revolutionary base areas in Inner Mongolia and anti-Koumintang revolutionary movements in Xinjiang, various nationalities had taken part in the activities led by our Party, in the guerrilla areas in southwest China, many members of fraternal nationalities in the interior had joined the Liberation Army; and the Red Army had made its revolutionary influence felt in areas in the southwest inhabited by minority peoples when it passed through these places during the Long March and had absorbed cadres from among these peoples. In short, the Chinese nation as a whole has long been a nation suffering external imperialist oppression; among our various na-

tionalities, they have shared weal and woe and cemented a militant friendship in the revolutionary wars, culminating in the liberation of this big family of nationalities. The relations among ourselves and our relations with the outside world do not require us to adopt the policy as was followed by Russia at the time of the October Revolution, which laid emphasis on national self-determination and at the same time allowed the secession of nationalities.

Historical development has provided us with conditions for national co-operation while the development of our revolutionary movement has also provided us with the basis for such co-operation. So, since liberation, we have adopted this system of national regional autonomy suitable to Chinese conditions and favourable to national co-operation. We don't lay emphasis on the secession of nationalities. If we do now, imperialism will take advantage of this.[87]

Thus, by combining ambiguity, a series of confusing chronological jumps, and the omission of key facts (most notably the CCP's many pledges to honor a right of secession), history is rewritten and the CCP's perfidy toward the minorities erased.

In retrospect, it is clear that Lenin's advice concerning the public advocacy of national self-determination prior to the taking of power served the CCP extraordinarily well. From 1927 until the evacuation of his Yenan headquarters twenty years later, Mao operated in or near minority areas, and the requirements of guerrilla warfare made the neutrality or the support of the minorities seemingly indispensable to his survival during most of the interval. The policy of appealing to ethnic aspirations for independence therefore blended well with the party's needs. (Moreover, unlike the case of the Soviet Union, which lost Finland, the manipulation of ethnic attitudes did not cost China a loss of territory.)

It is also evident that the CCP did not slavishly follow Lenin's advice or the example of the Soviet Union. The promise of secession was not carried into the postrevolutionary period, and Mao's decision to cloak his party in the ethnonational garb of the country's dominant element appears strangely out of tune with Lenin's cosmopolitan viewpoints. But it was that decision to adopt ethnonationalism not just as an ally but as a disguise which made possible the single-decade transformation of the CCP from a small and isolated faction at Yenan into the ruling group of the world's most populous state. By 1930, the Chinese Communist leaders had come to appreciate the close interrelationship between people's wars and ethnopsychology, and having once adopted the strategy of gaining power by conducting such a war, they continuously ascribed the greatest importance to the exploitation of ethnonational attitudes on the part of both the dominant and minority groups.

NOTES

1. In late 1978 China's State Council introduced a new standardized system for translating Chinese into English. Since nearly all sources used in this work antedate that change, the older Wade-Giles system has been retained throughout. For the rules of spelling and pronunciation for both the old and new conventions, see *Peking* (now *Beijing*) *Review*, January 5, 1979, 18–20.

2. Deal, "National Minority," 49–50.

3. Ibid., 56.

4. The indefinite time schedule (only after "militarism and imperialism have been expelled") for implementing even this rather tame policy is also suggestive. In "The Outline of National Reconstruction" (1924), the notion that self-determination (whatever its meaning) could only be exercised after a lengthy period of tutelage was made somewhat more explicit. See Tung, *Political Institutions*, 99.

5. "Joint Manifesto of Sun Yat-Sen and A. Joffe (January 26, 1923)" in Brandt et al., *Documentary History*, 70. The reference to Outer Mongolia is curious in that the region had comprised an independent state since 1921. Moreover, despite this agreement between Joffe and Sun, it was with Soviet guidance that Outer Mongolia was proclaimed a People's Republic the following year (1924).

6. "Article 3, Provisional Constitution of the Republic of China for the Period of Political Tutelage (June 1, 1931)." The entire text can be found in Tung, *Political Institutions*, 344–349. The actual wording was borrowed from the first article of another constitution drawn up in 1923 under the government of Ts'ao K'un. It can be found in ibid., 332–343.

7. See, for example, David Deal's account ("National Minority," 47–48) of the debate in the National Assembly of November 16, 1946. Even though the KMT was in danger of losing all minority areas, it refused to condone self-determination, but would instead grant a token measure of self-government (in the sense of home rule). See also "The Constitution of the Republic of China," December 25, 1946, in Tung, *Political Institutions*, 350–366. No reference was made to self-determination, and Article 4 stipulated that "the territory of the Republic of China according to its existing national boundaries shall not be altered except by resolution of the National As-

sembly." Article 168 promised "the various nationalities . . . special assistance . . . in their *local* self-government undertakings."

8. See Chiang Kai-shek, *China's Destiny*, 29–31, 39, 40.

9. "First Manifesto of the CCP on the Current Situation (June 10, 1922)," in Brandt et al., *Documentary History*, 54–63.

10. "Manifesto of the Second National Congress of the CCP (July 1922)," in ibid., 64.

11. "Manifesto of the Third National Congress of the CCP (June 1923)," in ibid., 71.

12. Ibid., 127–165. The cited passage is on p. 132.

13. "Resolutions and Spirit of the Second Plenum of the Central Committee (July 9, 1929)," in ibid., 166–179.

14. One might assume that the Manchus represented a major exception to this depiction of the minorities as rustics, since Manchuria, under the Japanese, had become the most industrialized region of the country. However, the process of assimilation had made such great headway among the Manchus that they had become essentially indistinguishable from the Han. As indicated in a number of documents cited below, the CCP did not therefore consider them to be a separate ethnic category.

15. The group in the hinterland began proselytical action almost immediately. Prior to 1930, two base areas were set up in the Chuang minority area near the Chinese border. Although they were destined to be destroyed soon, they subsequently became important as areas of support for the Vietnamese Communist movement.

16. See, for example, Schram, *Mao*, 156–157, in which the author notes that "virtually all of Mao's tactical principles are to be found in the classical Chinese writings on the subject, and above all in the maxims of Sun Tzu, the famous military writer who flourished about 500 B.C." Schram, in turn, cites for authority, General Samuel Griffith, who translated Sun Tzu.

17. Snow, *Red Star*, 304–305.

18. The necessity to maintain a veil of secrecy cannot be overstressed. Notice again General P'eng's colorful phrase that "only by sheltering in the shadow of the masses, can partisan warfare bring revolutionary victory."

19. As General P'eng noted in the same interview with Snow: "The partisans, being inseparable from the local mass, have the advantage of superior intelligence, and the greatest use must be made of this. Ideally, every peasant should be on the partisan's intelligence staff, so that it is impossible for the enemy to take a step without the partisans knowing it." Snow, *Red Star*, 303. For similar comments by Mao, see Schram, *Mao*, 157–159.

20. The famous eight rules to be observed by all members of the revolutionary forces in their dealings with the local populace are listed in Snow, *Red Star*, 176.

21. See, for example, Ch'en, *Mao and Chinese Revolution*, 170, 190, 195.

22. There is no reason to believe that China was ever made an exception by the Soviets. Remember that even Sun Yat-sen had made a sudden volte-face with regard to self-determination at the time of his agreement with the Soviet Union. And remember, too, the unheralded, unexplained, and unfollowed inclusion of a reference to self-determination in a CCP document drawn up in Moscow during 1928.

23. Cited in Dreyer, *China's Forty*, 63. Soviet support (and perhaps design) of these developments was made manifest in a resolution propounded by the Executive Committee of the Comintern a month after the Shanghai meeting. It called for the creation of a central Soviet government with headquarters in the hinterlands, and with its own "real Red Army." With regard to the minorities, the resolution directed that "the party should also reinforce its work among the national minorities. It should establish strong links with and take the lead in the Moslem movement in North China, in the national-revolutionary struggle in Inner Mongolia, in the struggle of the Korean workers and the Manchurian peasants, and of the tribes in South China. . . . Furthermore, given the immense importance of the growing revolutionary struggle in Indo-China, the party should extend its influence over the Annamite masses particularly in Yunnan, Hong Kong, and Canton." See "Extracts from an Executive Committee of the Comintern on the Chinese Question (June 1930)," in Degras, *Documents* 3:114–120.

24. Cited in Deal, "National Minority," 258. Some years after the CCP's assumption of power, a Chinese official by the name of Chang Chih-i would recall that "several Party representatives . . . expounded the Party's nationalities policy in public writings" following the 1927 break with the KMT. It may therefore be that the article in *Bolshevik* was merely one, and not even the first, of a number of publications signaling the need for a more forceful minorities policy. See Chang Chih-i, *The Party*, 48–49. The full title of Chang's work was *A Discussion of the National Question in the Chinese Revolution and of Actual Nationalities Policy (Draft)* (Peking: China Youth Publishing House, 1956).

25. "Constitution of the Soviet Republic," November 7, 1931, in Brandt et al., *Documentary History*, 220–221. Emphasis added.

26. For full text, see Chang Chih-i, *The Party*, appendix B.

27. Emphasis added.

28. Emphasis added.

29. See, for example, "Open Letter to the People of the Whole Country on the Betrayal of Chinese National Interests by the Kuomintang Reactionary Government," December 11, 1931, in Mao, *Collected Works*. The letter reads in part (3:38): "Brothers! Sisters! Can we allow the reactionary rule to connive freely with imperialism to carve us up like sheep? Can we watch our land being forcefully taken away by Japanese imperialism? Can we endure the cruelest kind of oppression, slaughter, and humiliation suffered by slaves in the colonies? Can we silently watch our own brothers

being whipped, killed, and slaughtered? Can we unfeelingly watch our sisters being molested, insulted, and raped? No! No! Ten thousand times no! We must rise up in unison to oppose, oppose the aggression of Japanese and international imperialism, oppose the shameless capitulation of the Kuomintang rulers, to imperialism, and its betrayal of China!"

30. Mao, *Collected Works* 3:169–171, 183–184, and 4:83–85. These three propaganda tracts were released on May 30, June 10, and November 11, 1933, respectively.

31. Ibid., 4:85.

32. Unlike the image it was projecting at the time before the Han masses, the CCP leadership at the Second All-Soviet Congress of the Chinese Soviet Republic (held in 1934) drew attention to its constitutional commitment to the right of secession. However, the leadership made clear to the party membership that its support was rooted in pragmatism rather than in principle: "The basis from which the Soviet nationalities policy proceeds is winning over all oppressed minority nationalities and rally them around the Soviet, and increasing the revolutionary forces opposing imperialism and the Kuomintang." See "Report of the Central Executive Committee and the People's Committee of the Chinese Soviet Republic to the Second All-Soviet Congress," January 25, 1934, in Mao, *Collected Works* 4:191.

33. Wales, *Red Dust*, 69–70.

34. The most significant resistance by minorities to the passage of Mao's forces was offered by the Man-tzu in northern Szechwan Province, and this was disorganized. It is also interesting that this people never afforded the CCP an opportunity to explain its policies on minorities. See Snow, *Red Star*, 213–214, and Schram, *Mao*, 186–197. K'ang K'ê-ching (wife of Chu Tê) reported "bitter fighting" between the CCP and the Hui in 1936, but credited it to the fact that "the Red Army didn't know how to approach them properly in political work." Wales, *Red Dust*, 218. This too sounds as though the problem was due to a failure to convey the party's promise of independence.

35. See Snow, *Red Star*, 282, 350, for references to various minority peoples, from both south and north China, who were serving in the Red Army in 1936.

36. Prior to the Long March, the southern element of the CCP, of which Mao was a part, created a number of soviets (base areas) within minority territory. Another leader, Chang Kuo-t'ao, later created a minority soviet in Szechwan Province, and still later (1935–1937) was to lead the attempt to create independent minority states throughout Tibet, Sinkiang, and Kansu. (See Ch'en, *Mao and Chinese Revolution*, 195–197, and Schram, *Mao*, 186–187.)

37. Snow, *Red Star*, 343–344.

38. See, for example, the 1931 resolution on minorities, cited above, which emphasized the toiling masses throughout.

39. Mao, "On the Tactics of Fighting Japanese Imperialism" in *Selected Works* 1:162–163.

40. Ibid., 50–51.

41. Quoted in Schram, *Mao*, 196. Elsewhere in his greeting, Mao added: "[T]he nation of Inner Mongolia may organize according to its own desire. It may, according to the principle of self-determination, organize its own life and form its own government. It has the right to form alliances with other nations. It also has the right to establish its separate entity. In sum, the nation is supreme, and all nations are equal." See "Declaration of the Soviet Central Government to the Inner Mongolian People," December 20, 1935, in Mao, *Collected Works* 5–6:6.

42. Snow, *Red Star*, 96.

43. Lenin had addressed himself directly to the issue in "The Socialist Revolution and the Right of Nations to Self-Determination (Theses)," written in 1916. He criticized "the reactionary nature of the ideas of Renner and O. Bauer," who contended that self-determination meant "cultural national autonomy," and he insisted that there could only be one meaning to "self-determination, i.e., the right to free political secession." See Lenin, *Right of Nations*, 73, 76.

In 1921, Stalin, in an article entitled "New Features of the National Question," sarcastically commented on the mistaken interpretation of self-determination by Kautsky, Springer, and Bauer: "When they spoke of the right of self-determination, the moving spirits of the Second International as a rule never even hinted at the right of political secession—the right of self-determination was at best interpreted to mean the right to autonomy in general." See Stalin, *Marxism: Selected Writings*, 112.

44. Considering all this, Mao's coupling of the independent states of Turkey and Poland with the pseudo-independent Ukraine and Caucasus in his 1935 address to the Mongols, would appear to be a deliberate attempt to confuse independence with autonomy, thus seemingly holding out the right of secession while simultaneously laying the groundwork for the political integration he intended.

45. Years later, CCP historians would describe Chang's crime as follows: "Most notoriously, in 1935 he opposed the Red Army's northward march, advocating a defeatist and liquidationist withdrawal by the Red Army to the minority-nationality areas on the Szechwan-Sikang border." See editors' note on p. 175 of *Selected Works of Mao Tse-tung* (Peking) 1:175. Chang's own historical account is very different. He omits any reference to the minorities and claims the dispute centered upon his criticism of Mao and others for prematurely creating the Chinese Soviet Republic. See his comments in the Introduction to the *Collected Works of Liu Shao-ch'i before 1944*, particularly p. v. Chang's expedition appears to have enjoyed some initial success. One of its members reported that in February of 1936, a "Special Independent Government of the Minorities" was established within Sinkiang Province. It claimed a population of approximately 200,000. However, the Communist forces evacuated the area in early July, so the experiment was short-lived. See Wales, *Red Dust*, 161, 231.

46. Among the reasons for such a suspicion is that Chu Teh, Mao's close associate (both before and after this adventure), accompanied Chang rather than Mao. Another reason is that, prior to the Long March, Mao's southern organization had done similar work among minorities, creating a number of soviets, at least one of which was headed by a non-Chinese. On this latter point, see Ch'en, *Mao and Chinese Revolution*, 152–154. It is assumed that if such activity constituted "warlordism" in western China, it did so also in the southern areas. Still another reason is the declaration made at the end of the Szechwan meeting, which indicated general support for Chang Kuo-t'ao's plan to work among the minorities. See discussion later in this chapter.

47. "Resolution on Current Political Situation and Party Tasks," December 25, 1935, in Mao, *Collected Works* 5–6:22. "Sincere slogans" was presumably a reference to self-determination.

48. "Declaration of the Soviet Central Government to the Moslem People," May 25, 1936, in Mao, *Collected Works* 5–6:35–36.

49. For example, George Moseley has maintained that the rights to secession and even to federal status were "gradually discarded" with Mao's rise to power in 1935. See his *Consolidation*, 4–5. See also footnote 53.

50. *Completely Purge Liu Shao-ch'i.*

51. "The Ten Great Policies of the CCP for Anti-Japanese Resistance and National Salvation," August 15, 1937, in Brandt et al., *Documentary History*, 242–245.

52. "Various Questions Concerning Fundamental Policies in Anti-Japanese Guerrilla Warfare," October 16, 1937, in Liu Shao-ch'i, *Collected Works before 1944*, 27–51.

53. See Deal, "National Minority," 122, and Dreyer, *China's Forty*, 67. This speech had not been publicly released at the time that Deal and Dreyer were doing their research. They were dependent upon an extract that appeared in the Chinese press (*People's Daily*) in 1953 and that incorrectly dated the address at November 6, 1938. It was actually delivered three weeks earlier, in October. For the entire speech, see Mao, *Collected Works* 5–6:129–158.

54. Mao, *Collected Works* 5–6:173.

55. A major segment of Mao's speech was in fact dedicated to the need to ensure long-term cooperation with the KMT. See, for example, ibid., 175 et seq.

56. Though in the context of illustrating how Lenin and Stalin had linked national self-determination to the colonial question (rather than in reference to China's minorities), Mao had in 1940 favorably quoted at length a passage from Stalin in which "the right to self-determination" was often cited. The quoted passage included a reference by Stalin to Lenin's 1916 "The Discussion on Self-Determination Summed Up," which was said to have concerned "the fundamental point of the national question, the right of self-determination." See "On New Democracy," January 1940, in Mao, *Selected Works* (New York) 3:113–114.

57. Brandt et al., *Documentary History*, 308. Once in power, the Chinese authorities attempted to expurgate this late reference by Mao to self-determination. The 1954 edition of Mao's *Selected Works* translated the passage as "give better treatment to the national minorities in the country and grant them the right of self-government." Vol. 3 (New York): 281. The 1975 version stated "give the minority nationalities in China better treatment and grant them autonomous rights." Vol. 3 (Peking): 238. Following Mao's death, the authorities acknowledged that his writings had often been purposefully altered, and this appears to be a case in point. The combination of Chinese characters which means self-determination is quite different than those combinations conveying either self-government or national autonomy. See Brandt et al., *Documentary History*, 530.

58. *Selected Works of Mao Tse-tung* (New York) 4:301.

59. See earlier discussion, this chapter, concerning the 1931 constitution.

60. Brandt et al., *Documentary History*, 422. Emphasis added.

61. Chang Chih-i, *The Party*, 67–68.

62. "Internationalism and Nationalism," November 1, 1948, in Liu Shao-ch'i, *Collected Works of Liu Shao-ch'i, 1945–1957*, 127–128.

63. The formal declaration was entitled "Decisions of the Central Committee on the Political Situation and our Tasks Following the Linking-up of the First and Fourth Armies." The section cited can be found in Chang Chih-i, *The Party*, 49. Emphasis added. The issuance of this announcement is still another reason to believe that there was general support for Chang Kuo-t'ao's plan to work among the minorities of western China.

64. Shortly after the declaration positing the "decisive significance" of the minorities, a resolution signed by Mao declared the party's commitment to preserving China's territorial integrity. See "Resolution on Current Political Situation and Party Tasks," December 25, 1935, in Mao, *Collected Works* 5–6:13. This resolution postdated by only five days Mao's promise of political independence to the Mongols and preceded by exactly five months his promise of independence to the Turkish peoples of Sinkiang.

65. The Chinese Soviet Republic at Kiangsi had declared war on Japan in February 1932, but given its isolated location and near encirclement by the KMT, this was necessarily an empty gesture. Several anti-Japanese manifestoes, calling for a united front, were issued over the following months, but the Japanese threat in the early 1930s appeared too remote to the Han of southern China to permit the manifestoes to have much significance.

66. Snow, *Red Star*, 100.

67. "Resolution on Current Political Situation and Party Tasks," December 25, 1935, in Mao, *Collected Works* 5–6:20.

68. Brandt et al., *Documentary History*, 245–247.

69. Ibid., 257, 259.

70. The phrase appeared in six of the seven paragraphs comprising a document intended as a guide for agitprop activities. See "Propaganda Outline Issued by the Central Committee on the Seventeenth Anniversary of the CCP," June 24, 1938, in ibid., 258–260.

71. Ibid.

72. Liu Shao-ch'i, "Various Questions Concerning Fundamental Policies in Anti-Japanese Guerrilla Warfare," October 16, 1937, in *Collected Works before 1944*, 45.

73. Lenin and his colleagues had never faced this dilemma, of course, because they did not elect to adopt the attire of Russian ethnonationalism as a means of gaining power.

74. The period is one of great confusion, with the Japanese (prior to their defeat in World War II) and the Soviets also appealing to separatist tendencies. The latter supported the creation of an "East Turkestan Republic" in November 1944 and a "Provisional Government of the Inner Mongolian Republic" in August 1945.

75. Beyond making promises, the CCP claims to have respected the autonomy and independence of the minorities in the liberated areas during the anti-Japanese struggle. (See Chang Chih-i, *The Party*, 53–54.) This forbearance would be consonant with the 1937 party decree to "carry out a concrete policy of assisting the minority nationalities in their endeavors to attain independence and autonomy." "Various Questions Concerning Fundamental Policies in Anti-Japanese Guerrilla Warfare," October 16, 1937, in Liu Shao-ch'i, *Collected Works before 1944*, 45. In late 1941, the CCP held an anti-Fascist Nationality Conference at which the Tibetan, Mongolian, Yi, and Miao delegates were treated precisely the same as delegates from Indochina, (Dutch) Indonesia, and Thailand—that is, as representatives of peoples over whom China had no claim. See "Comrade Mao Tse-tung Addresses Eastern Antifascist Meeting Calling on all Nationals to Strengthen Unity," October 30, 1941, in Mao, *Collected Works 7–10*:89.

76. "The Common Program of the Chinese People's Political Consultative Conference," September 29, 1949. The text can be found in Chen, *Chinese Communist Regime*, 34–45.

77. The general's statement appeared in the Chinese press on August 5, 1950 and is cited in Patterson, "Treatment of Minorities," 157.

78. See Chapter 3.

79. Li Wei-han, Chairman of the Commission of Nationalities Affairs, "Report Made at the Enlarged Meeting," 45. Emphasis added.

80. Ibid. See also Patterson, "Treatment of Minorities," 155. Emphasis added.

81. "Constitution of the PRC adopted September 20, 1954 by the First National People's Congress of the PRC." Text can be found in John Lewis, *Major Doctrines*, 197–211. Emphasis added.

82. "Constitution of the PRC adopted January 17, 1975 by the Fourth National People's Congress of the PRC." Text can be found in *Keesing's Contemporary Archives* (1975), 26966–26968. Emphasis added.

83. "Constitution of the PRC adopted March 1, 1978 by the Fifth National People's Congress of the PRC." Text can be found in *Keesing's Contemporary Archives* (1978), 29184–29188.

84. Article 4 of the "Constitution of the PRC adopted December 4, 1982 by the Fifth National People's Congress of the PRC." Text can be found in *Peking Review* 11 (December 17, 1982): 10-18.

85. Chang Chih-i, *The Party*, 69. Emphasis added.

86. Ibid., 57. Emphasis added.

87. Chou En-lai, "Some Questions," 21–22. At the time of the article's publication in 1980, the editors of the *Peking Review* maintained that it "had been suppressed for over 20 years."

CHAPTER 5

Highland Peoples in the National Liberation and Consolidation of Vietnam

In contrast with that of the CCP, the early history of the Vietnamese Communist party's position on the national question is a bit more complex because the party was operating in a colony. This made the issue at least a four-sided matter, involving the mother country, the Communist party within the mother country, the Soviet Union, and the Communist party or parties within the colony. Moreover, the doctrine of self-determination, as applied to Indochina, ran afoul of the inconsistency which had always been present in Lenin's wedding of the national and colonial questions. Promising self-determination to colonies *qua* colonies is compatible with national self-determination only if the colony contains but one self-conscious ethnic group. Otherwise, colonial self-determination could mean national self-determination *only* for the ethnic element that comes to dominate the new state. This inconsistency would pertain not just to Indochina as a whole, but to Cambodia, Laos, or Vietnam if considered alone, for each of the three states presently comprising Indochina are ethnically heterogeneous. It is necessary to consider Cambodia and Laos, as well as Vietnam, for the various organizations which Ho Chi Minh headed during his career had a kaleidoscopic dimension, sometimes claiming only to speak for the peoples of Vietnam, while at other times extending their claim to encompass Cambodia and Laos as well.

The first noteworthy Marxist-Leninist organization within Indochina was founded by Ho in 1925, and, as implied by its name, Association of Revolutionary Vietnamese Youth, was not intended to incorporate the many peoples of Indochina. A number of localized Communist movements sprang up in the ensuing years, leading Ho to call a meeting of the factions in January 1930, at which a united organization, called the Vietnamese Communist Party, was created. However, the Third International felt that an organization with a larger base would be necessary to challenge the French effectively, and Ho and his colleagues were therefore directed to incorporate Laos and Cambodia into the organization.

Ho concurred, and in October 1930 the party took the title, Indochinese Communist Party (ICP). That this decision was reached in full awareness of the importance of the fact that three different peoples were involved is evident from the party's official history: "Following the Communist International's instructions, the Session decided to change the Party's name to Indochinese Communist Party because the Vietnamese, Cambodian and Laotian proletariat have politically and economically to be closely related in spite of their difference in language, customs and race."[1] Yet another organization appeared during World War II, when Ho took advantage of the unpopularity of the Japanese and their French agents to organize the Viet Minh, a united front representing a conglomeration of nationalist and patriotic forces under the effective control of the leadership of the ICP. In order to assuage the fears of many of the Viet Minh's anti-Communist members, thereby ensuring the continued unity of the united front into the postwar period, the formal organization of the ICP was dissolved in November 1945, although it continued in fact to function through "study groups." By the time it was formally resurrected in March 1951 as the Workers Party (Lao Dong), the Communist party had *ostensibly* become once more a party geographically limited to Vietnam. It is necessary to emphasize the word, *ostensibly*, because the domination of the Communist parties of Cambodia and Laos by the leaders of the Lao Dong continued long after 1951.[2] Indeed, in its 1951 platform, the party pledged to work toward "an independent, free, strong and prosperous federation of the states of Viet-nam, Laos and Cambodia if the three people so desire."[3]

But whatever the geographic extent of their claimed jurisdiction, all of the various organizations with which Ho was associated prior to the end of World War II paid great attention to the minorities. His earliest organization, the Association of the Revolutionary Vietnamese Youth, insisted that it was the right of all people—not just Vietnamese, but "Cambodians, Man, Laos, etc."—"to govern themselves."[4] And at its founding in 1930, the ICP set itself ten "concrete tasks," number seven of which was "political independence of Indochina; the right of self-determination of peoples."[5] Moreover, in a *programme d'action*, drawn up sometime between 1930 and 1934, the ICP pledged itself to a "fraternal union of all Indochinese peoples. The right of Cambodians, Laotians and other nationalities to self-determination."[6]

None of these promises was devoid of ambiguity. A "right to govern themselves" (1929) could be taken to mean a right to total independence or merely a right to a measure of regional autonomy. In the absence of further elaboration, a "right of self-determination of peoples" (1930) might be interpreted as what we earlier termed "colonial self-determination," i.e., the right of Indochina, as a single unit, to sever the French connection. The still later enumeration of "Cambodians, Laotians, and other nationalities" as peoples to whom the right of self-determination accrued, would, had it stood alone, justify the inference that it was national and not colonial self-determination that was being promised. As noted, however, this promise of self-determination to the Cambodians et al. was prefaced with the contradictory commitment to a "fraternal union of all Indochinese peoples." Moreover, glaring in its absence from all of these documents, each of which was intended for the broadest audience possible, was any reference to a right of secession. As earlier noted, throughout this period the Comintern was consistently demanding that Communist parties outside the Soviet Union publicly proclaim the right of self-determination, making explicit that this included the right of secession. Thus in 1928, the year immediately preceding the earliest of Ho's known public stances with regard to minorities, the Comintern postulated among "the most important tasks . . . recognition of the right of all nations, regardless of race, to complete self-determination, i.e., going as far as political secession."[7] Ho was unquestionably aware of the Comintern's stand on this matter. He had been an active member of the organization for many years, attending many of the Congresses; he had been sent to China as an agent of the Comintern as early as 1925; he had, as noted, followed a Comintern directive in restructuring his party into an Indochina-wide organization; and finally, he had formally joined his party to the Comintern in the spring of 1931, thus committing it to the Leninist policy on the national question.[8]

That the ICP's ambiguity concerning its minorities policy was deliberate was acknowledged in a party article published in 1934.[9] Referring to their most recent program, the article noted that certain comrades found the slogan (*mot d'ordre*), "A fraternal union of all Indochinese peoples. The Right of Cambodians, Laotians and other nationalities to self-determination," to be incomplete, and "they would add the right of separation." Such comrades were accused of an inability to grasp the flexibility of the slogan of self-determination and of overlooking the reality of the situation which "sometimes obliges us to emphasize one part of the [national] question more than another." The article continues: "The right of peoples to self-determination is political independence, it is the right of these nations to organize themselves as will appear wise, to decide for themselves whether they unite or not with the country which had oppressed them prior to the revolution." The authors then address the question, "But why do we not emphasize here [in the program] that part [of the slogan] *including separation?*" A two-part answer is proffered.

The first explanation is associated with the charge that French imperialism was currently employing the ancient device of divide and rule by stirring up the animosity of the French proletariat toward the exploited masses in France's colonies as well as the animosities among the various peoples of Indochina. This French strategy must be countered by a transethnic united front, for "only a close union of the Anamites [Vietnamese] with the Cambodians, Laotians and other nationalities of Indochina will be able to assure the victory of the revolution over imperialism and feudalism." It is therefore necessary that "we explain to all the oppressed peoples of Indochina that we unite for the struggle until the victorious revolution throughout all of Indochina, when we shall organize ourselves after the overthrow of imperialism and feudalism."

Given the earlier acknowledgment that self-determination incorporates the right of separation, it might be assumed that this article was holding forth the option of separation following the end of French rule. However, the key sentence, although mentioning separation, is so ambiguous that it suggests a purposeful attempt to mislead: "It is natural that with the overthrow of imperialism and feudalism there arises the question of a federation of soviet republics of all the liberated nationalities on the basis of their right to self-determination and to unite or to separate." No further elucidation is offered, and it is therefore not clear whether separation refers to a right of political existence *outside* of the soviet federation, or to a purely formal right of separation *within* the soviet federation, in the fashion of the right of secession bestowed by the constitution of the Soviet Union.

The second reason that was advanced for the party's failure to spell out a right of secession in its program was that the Cambodians and Laotians (in addition to the Vietnamese) were the only peoples who qualified as nations under Stalin's 1913 definition.[10] The unstated but self-evident implication was that the other groups, not being nations, did not qualify for the right of self-determination. This dichotomizing of ethnic groups is the more interesting, since public pronouncements of the party had hitherto given no hint of such an intention. Remember that the 1929 program had referred to "Cambodians, Man, Laotians, etc."; that the 1930 program had mentioned only "the right of *peoples* to self-determination," thus implying all peoples; and that the very phrase upon which the article had focused (i.e., the excerpt from the party's most recent program) spoke of "the right of Cambodians, Laotians, *and other nationalities* to self-determination." Thus, with regard to national self-determination for the many non-Cambodian, non-Laotian minorities, a summary of the article might read "what the Party hath given (publicly), the Party hath taken away (more privately)."

Ho's party was also destined to backtrack with regard to colonial self-determination. As Moscow's fear of fascism grew in the early and mid-1930s, the Comintern instructed Communist parties to enter united fronts with all anti-Fascist forces, and to support all anti-Fascist governments. Under directions from the International to change tactics, particularly with regard to colonial self-determination, so as not to threaten the United Front within France, the ICP temporarily shelved its demand of immediate independence for all the peoples of Indochina, and now emphasized that the right to secede did not mean that it was *necessary* to secede. This new strategy of the ICP won the sobriquet "the United Front of Treason" from the Vietnamese Trotskyites.[11] This hiatus in the party's otherwise steadfast commitment to colonial self-determination proved of short duration, for from the signing of the Nazi-Soviet Non-Aggression Pact in 1939 until the French withdrawal from Indochina in 1954, anticolonial resistance was fully compatible with the Soviet Union's foreign policy, despite the remarkable vicissitudes that that country's list of enemies and allies underwent during the period. Despite its short duration, however, the hiatus is significant as an illustration that colonial and national self-determination were both held subservient to the broader interests of the global Marxist movement.

But while the ICP did demonstrate a significant level of hedging on the national question, it continued to proclaim its support for the right of self-determination. Moreover, the Viet Minh (which was under the effective domination of the party) most unequivocally pledged itself in 1943 to national self-determination for *Vietnam's* non-Vietnamese peoples. A conference held that year adopted a program, point four of which read "the right of minorities to self-determination."[12] Since the Viet Minh (whose full title, Viet Nam Doc Lap Dong Minh, translates into the Vietnam Independence League) claimed to be only a Vietnamese and not an Indochinese organization, the promise clearly pertained to those non-Vietnamese peoples who populated the highlands of Vietnam.

The Viet Minh's concern with gaining the support of the highland peoples is quite understandable. In the first of a remarkable series of parallels to the experience of the Chinese Communist Party, the early attempts of the ICP to develop a following among the numerically dominant people (who also, as in the case of the dominant element within China, were stretched along the eastern seaboard) had met with a series of failures. As in the case of the CCP, strategic necessity caused the ICP then to fall back upon regions populated by inland minorities. Indeed, the meeting that established the Viet Minh took place well within the northeastern highlands in close proximity to the Chinese border, so it was natural that gaining support of the minorities should be accorded the highest priority.[13]

Although the ICP operated almost exclusively within minority areas during the entire World War II period, its operations were not restricted to French Indochina. In Southeast Asia, as elsewhere throughout the globe, there is an almost total absence of coincidence between ethnic and political land borders. The Sino-Indochinese border segmented ethnic homelands, and the local peoples viewed the border as nonexistent.[14] Taking advantage of the border's porousness and the realities of the ethnic map, the ICP treated the region located between that populated by the Han Chinese in the north and that by the ethnically Vietnamese in the south as a single region of operations, establishing base areas on either side of the border and, when pressure demanded, retreating deeply into China's territory.[15] In ICP perceptions of the time, the minority areas of southern China would serve both as sanctuary "from the control and repression of the French and Japanese," and as "a convenient springboard from which we could easily cross back into Vietnam to operate and build up our infrastructure among the people."[16]

Although the ICP could not be aware of it at the time, the experience they gained in dealing with minorities during the World War II period would be of great value in their postwar struggles. Their World War II experience confirmed the wisdom of adopting the local dress, language, and other overt, cultural idiosyncracies;[17] of elevating ICP members belonging to the minorities to the higher echelons and utilizing them as often as possible when dealing directly with the local people;[18] and, finally, of appealing to the ethnopolitical aspirations of the minorities. A key ingredient in the ap-

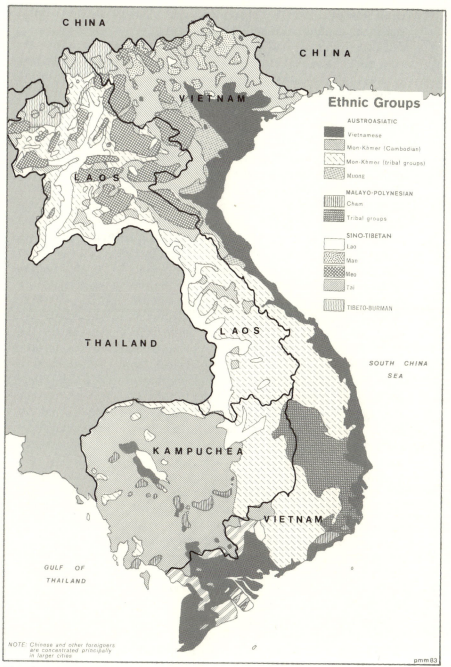

Ethnic Groups

AUSTROASIATIC
- Vietnamese
- Mon-Khmer (Cambodian)
- Mon-Khmer (tribal groups)
- Muong

MALAYO-POLYNESIAN
- Cham
- Tribal groups

SINO-TIBETAN
- Lao
- Man
- Meo
- Tai

TIBETO-BURMAN

NOTE: Chinese and other foreigners
are concentrated principally
in larger cities

pmm 83

MAP 2. Southeast Asia

peals was, of course, the aforementioned plank of the Viet Minh's platform dealing with self-determination.[19] And the promise of self-determination had paid rich dividends. The first important base area of the Viet Minh, established by Giap during World War II, was in the territory of the minorities living on either side of the Chinese-Vietnamese border. It was this haven which afforded the ICP the time and safety to create its first effective organization.

The Viet Minh's official commitment to national self-determination throughout World War II caused the abrupt about-face performed by Ho and his associates in the immediate postwar period to be all the more striking. Confident that he was on the threshold of power, Ho proclaimed the creation of the Democratic Republic of Vietnam on September 2, 1945, the same day on which Japan formally surrendered to the United States. The constitution of the new republic, adopted on November 9, 1946, made no mention of either self-determination or a right of secession, the territory of Vietnam being declared "one and indivisible."[20] Throughout the document, the term *nation* was consistently equated with the entire population. Nor did the term *nationalities* appear anywhere throughout the constitution. The only suggestion of ethnic heterogeneity found in either the preamble or in the section entitled "General Provisions" was oblique, being transmitted through the ritual phrase (which was employed twice), "without distinction of *race*, class, creed, wealth or sex" (emphasis added). Elsewhere throughout the document (Articles 4 through 70), with but one exception, the non-Vietnamese were referred to as "ethnic minorities."[21] Did this hitherto unused terminology indicate that there were no groups within Vietnam who could qualify for *national* self-determination?

Some insight into the thinking that went into this constitutional treatment of minorities can be gleaned from an important party tract written in the same year that the constitution was ratified. Entitled "The August Revolution," it was written sometime in 1946 by Truong Chinh, an important party leader who was later to become its General Secretary.[22] In consecutive paragraphs, Truong Chinh asserted that "the principle of 'the right of nations to self-determination'" gave Vietnam the right to total freedom from France, and that attempts to fractionalize Vietnam by creating a "'Nam Ky state', 'Moi state', 'Thai state', 'Nung state', etc." had to be rejected because "Viet Nam must be worthy of the name *nation*; that is to say, it is one and indivisible."[23] By thus employing the term *nation* to refer to Vietnam, national self-determination was paradoxically employed to justify the right of a multiethnic territory to secede while simultaneously denying this same right to the non-Vietnamese ethnonational groupings which inhabited that territory.

It is highly unlikely that this unusual departure from the Marxist-Leninist legacy of carefully distinguishing between *nation* and *state* was unintentional. As quite probably the party's most sophisticated theorist, Truong Chinh could be expected to be familiar with the nuances of Marxist terminology. Perhaps even more to the point was the fact that this interutilization of key terms was also at variance with all previous practices of the ICP itself. Considering, then, that several years were to elapse before the expression "self-determination" (at least to the knowledge of this writer) was to reappear in a party document, the article may well have been intended to act as a beguiling swan song, designed to paper over the discrepancy between the earlier promises of national self-determination to minorities and the reality which the party actually planned for them. As Marx or Engels might have put it, the non-Vietnamese had become a people without a history.

But this only leads to a larger question. Why did the Communists decide to drop support for the right of self-determination some nine years before the actual assumption of power in northern Vietnam and nearly two decades before victory in the south? As we have seen, the minorities were the key to the party's survival prior to 1945. But the withdrawal of the Japanese and the anticipation that the French would not attempt the reconquest of Indochina now caused the minorities to shrink in significance. The ethnic focus of the party concentrated once more upon the Vietnamese, for the only remaining obstacle to uncontested power appeared to be the leaders of the medley of Vietnamese national parties and movements. Just as had the CCP in 1937, Ho now appealed to the ethnically Vietnamese people in the most nationalistic manner, as witness the following statement made by Ho in 1946.

> Compatriots in the South and the Southern part of Central Viet-Nam! The North, Center, and South are part and parcel of Viet-Nam! . . . We have the same ancestors, we are of the same family, we are all brothers and sisters. . . . No one can divide the children of the same family. Likewise, no one can divide Viet-Nam.[24]

The passage is in curious contradiction to the 1946 constitution, the more curious because the constitution was submitted by Ho to the Vietnamese National Assembly for ratification within a week of this speech. In basing his case for a single state upon a single people with a common ancestry, Ho was clearly excluding the ethnic minorities; the constitution, we will recall, though making no mention of nations or nationalities, had at least acknowledged "distinction of race" and the presence of "ethnic minorities" within Vietnam. Yet within a week the ethnically pure state of his speech had been transformed into the "one and indivisible" multiethnic state of the constitution. A "Vietnamese people" defined in terms of common ancestry had been transformed into a "Vietnamese people" defined in terms of geographic accident. And all these metamorphoses had been facilitated by the misapplication of the concept of the *nation* to the entire population of an envisaged, ethnically heterogeneous state.[25]

Minimally, Ho's appeal to common blood was clearly one which could be expected to produce negative psychological responses among the ethnic minorities, and therefore illustrates Ho's preoccupation with the ethnically Vietnamese segment of the population. As the Chinese Communist Party had realized when launching its own successful campaign to capture the imagination of its state's dominant people, such a goal required that the Communists not be identified too closely with promises to violate the "fatherland's" territorial integrity. Indeed, the only noteworthy difference between the actions of the CCP and Ho's organization at these comparable points in their development is that while the Chinese only played down the publicity surrounding their support of self-determination, the 1946 Vietnamese Constitution, by pledging territorial indivisibility, publicly denied a right of secession. But Mao had been anticipating a protracted struggle with the Japanese, followed by a still more protracted one with the state's recognized government. Ho, by contrast, was the declared president of the Democratic Republic of Vietnam, which he expected momentarily to become the recognized state of all Vietnam.[26] Moreover, the CCP, by claiming an uninterrupted history dating from 1921, had to consider the impact that too drastic a volte-face might exert upon its reputation for sincerity among the minorities. By contrast, Ho's decision to dissolve the formal structure of the ICP, so it would not in any way impede his courtship of the ethnically Vietnamese people, had the advantage of freeing him from the onus of earlier promises made in that party's name.

Although fraught with risk, Ho's precipitate actions of 1946 were to have no discernible effect upon future relations with the minorities. Upon the outbreak of hostilities with the French, the Viet

Minh fell back once more upon its transborder base area within the territory populated by non-Vietnamese. Moreover, it was in this area and in the minority regions to the west that the major battles of the French-Indochina War (1946–1954), including the decisive battle of Dien Bien Phu, were waged. The selection of these sites by the Viet Minh for the conduct of its struggle is revealing, for the leaders were committed to a guerrilla struggle, and they were at least as aware as the leaders of the CCP that the relationship of the local inhabitants to the armed forces was of vital significance. In 1947, near the beginning of the war, Truong Chinh wrote:

> Guerrilla warfare must be the tactic of the people as a whole, not of the army alone.
>
> To achieve good results in guerrilla and mobile warfare, we must mobilize the people to support our armed forces enthusiastically and to fight the army together with them. The people are the eyes and ears of the army, they feed or keep our soldiers. It is they who help the army in sabotage and in battle. *The people are the water and our army the fish.* The people constitute an inexhaustible source of strength to the army. To increase their numbers, the troops must recruit new fighters from among the people. That is why the entire people must be armed, guerrilla movements must be initiated, the actions of the regular army and guerrilla forces must be coordinated. We must act in such a way that wherever the enemy goes, he meets the resistance forces of the entire Vietnamese people, who arms in hand, fight against him, ready to die rather than return to slavery.[27]

Here, just as in the statements of Mao and P'eng, the local people are assigned the key roles of providing food, shelter, recruits, and intelligence, while performing the equally important tasks of denying each of these to the enemy. As has been indicated, it was members of a minority who in most instances constituted "the local people" in the French-Indochina War. And, in fact, throughout the war the minorities did play all of the strategic roles assigned to them in Communist guerrilla strategy. They harbored Viet Minh forces and supplied them with food and shelter; they worked as porters (consider the importance of this contribution in massing artillery around the French position at Dien Bien Phu); they furnished information on French movements; they fought in Viet Minh ranks, both as individuals and as units.[28] The role of the minorities was unquestionably vital to the Viet Minh victory, even more important than minorities had been to the rise of the Soviet and Chinese parties.[29] Indeed, in ethnic terms it would be more accurate to describe the war as a victory of the non-Vietnamese indigenes, rather than of the Vietnamese.

Nor did the importance of non-Vietnamese peoples cease with the defeat of the French and the extension of Communist control over the northern half of Vietnam. In its subsequent campaign to bring about the dissolution of the Saigon political organization and to consolidate the country, Hanoi's representatives remained extremely active among the many minorities who populate the mountain chain that forms all of Laos except for the Mekong Valley in the west, most of South Vietnam north of Saigon except for a thin coastal strip, and the northeastern corner of Cambodia.

It would be difficult to exaggerate the strategic role performed by this area in Hanoi's victorious campaign. First, it contained the major routes by which Hanoi supplied the guerrilla forces operating within what prior to 1975 was popularly termed the state of South Vietnam.[30] Both the Ho Chi Minh and Sihanouk trails were totally within minority regions. Second, the huge highlands within South Vietnam, which comprise more than two-thirds of that former state's territory, contained or commanded most of the strategically important targets north of Saigon. Thirdly, the area contained the minority (i.e., non-Laotian, non-Khmer) regions of southeastern Laos and northeastern Cambodia which were used throughout the war as sanctuaries by anti-Saigon forces, greatly magnifying the problems associated with counterinsurgency efforts.

On balance, the Communist forces were incontestably more successful than their opponents in eliciting support from the *montagnards*, that collective term most commonly used to describe the diverse peoples who populate this highland region. In the case of Laos, the Communist movement (the Pathet Lao) was, with the exception of a handful of top leaders such as Prince Souphonophong, nearly totally composed of non-Lao. United States Special Forces made important allies among some of the hill tribes (particularly the Meo), but the vast minority areas of Laos remained definitely more available throughout the war to Hanoi than they were to the non-Communist government in Vientianne. In the case of Cambodia, prior to the overthrow of the very popular Khmer Prince, Norodom Sihanouk in 1970, broad-scale resistance to Phnom Penh was lacking in areas populated by the dominant Khmer element. However, during this period the Communist forces (Khmer

Rouge) were able to establish and maintain base areas in the minority area of the northeast, as well as in minority dominated pockets in the southwest and Thai pockets in the northwest.[31] Finally, within the hill country of what was then South Vietnam, the inability of the substantial and well-equipped forces of the United States and Saigon to stamp out the guerrilla activities of the Viet Cong and detachments of the People's Army of Vietnam (PAVN) confirms that the guerrillas enjoyed at least that minimal essential of apathy on the part of the local populace. The overall record of Viet Cong and PAVN operations in the highlands attests that the minorities were not actively impeding the Communist forces; nor were they reporting on their caches, semifixed positions, and movements to the U.S. and Saigon authorities. United States Special Forces were for a time remarkably successful in organizing significant numbers of the hill people under their personal command, but the Saigon authorities, increasingly wary of aliens (Americans) interceding between themselves and their subjects and fearing (with good cause as witness the montagnard revolts of 1965) that the program was arming potential dissidents, had completely curtailed such operations by 1970. Moreover, following U.S. withdrawal from Vietnam, montagnard hostility to the South Vietnamese forces increased. The closing months of the war witnessed several uprisings. Indeed, the last extended offensive, which drove Saigon forces out of the hill country, was ignited by local forces and appears originally to have caught the Viet Cong and PAVN units by surprise. Assessing the contribution of the montagnard efforts in bringing about the fall of the Saigon political structure, *Le Monde* commented on April 2, 1975 that "the local population played *an essential part* in expelling the government troops from the Central Highlands" (emphasis added).[32]

What were the lures selected by the Communists to elicit this support in the period from 1946 to 1975? The documents fall well short of providing a definite answer.[33] Perhaps as a consequence of the premature constitution of 1946 with its embarrassing commitment to a state that was to be "one and indivisible," the pieces of documentary evidence during the French phase of the struggle (1946–1954) are either noncommittal or suspiciously vague concerning the destiny of the montagnards. Thus, in the case of the official platform of the newly created Lao Dong Party (March 1951), one is struck by the absence of any of the words customarily used by Communist movements to convey where their current minority policy falls on the integration-secession continuum (i.e., words such as inalienable, indivisible, autonomy, self-determination, secession, and the like). The platform did note that the "Party resolutely opposes narrow-minded nationalism and is determined to smash the plots of the imperialists and traitors to sow hatred among the people and divide them."[34] But it would be difficult to read even a veiled denial of self-determination into this passage, since Lenin had prescribed the promise of independence as the necessary antidote for precisely the sort of intergroup relationship which this passage deplores. Otherwise, the platform's only reference to secession is most oblique. It could be argued that in proposing a "federation of the states of Viet-Nam, Laos and Cambodia," the party was ruling out any other states within Indochina.[35]

That a definite nationality policy was being pursued at this time is beyond dispute. In 1950 Ho credited the cooperation of the non-Vietnamese nationalities to the "cadres of the Viet Bac Interzone who have correctly implemented the policies of the Party";[36] in 1951 he condemned "erroneous tendencies . . . in the implementation of the policies on . . . national minorities";[37] and in 1952 he advised military officers that "the Government has issued policies concerning the national minorities; you and the troops must implement them correctly."[38] In none of these cases, however, did Ho give any intimation of the content of these policies with regard to the promises made to the minorities in order to gain their cooperation. Two scholarly authorities report that the Viet Minh regularly outpromised the French with regard to the degree of self-government they (the Viet Minh) would countenance.[39] If so, the Viet Minh must have been promising independence, for the French were promising what they termed "autonomous States within the French Union."[40]

The Geneva Accords of 1954, which formally signaled the end of French rule and the partition of Vietnam into two independent states, gave rise to a dilemma on the national question not faced by any other Marxist-Leninist movement. Had the Lao Dong assumed immediate control of the entire country, there is no reason to suspect that it would not have introduced the unitary structure outlined in the 1946 constitution.[41] But the Lao Dong, committed by the terms of its program to the unification of the entire country and cognizant of the continuing importance of the minorities of Laos, Cambodia, and South Vietnam to this effort, could presume that the treatment accorded to the minorities under its sway would affect the amount of influence it could exert upon these other inhabitants of Indochina's highlands. Ostensible consistency had necessarily to be maintained between what the Lao Dong was practicing at home and promising abroad, for, as we have noted in the case of the China border, North Vietnam's borders regularly bisected ethnic units and were therefore very porous from a communications viewpoint.

But what options were available to the Lao Dong? Secession of more than two-thirds of North Vietnam's territory was clearly unacceptable, but rigorous integration could imperil the support among minorities outside the state that was deemed essential if unification were to be achieved. Moreover, the strategic considerations of the Lao Dong following the withdrawal of French forces were not totally dissimilar to those faced by the Chinese Communists following the withdrawal of the Japanese troops. The main adversary was now a government dominated by members of the principal ethnic group, and undermining the power base of that government would require convincing its (ethnically) Vietnamese subjects that the revolutionary movement was the true champion of the Vietnamese nation.[42] And, as the CCP leadership had appreciated, such a task would be far more difficult to accomplish if the revolutionary movement was popularly perceived as willing to cede huge segments of territory.

It was therefore necessary to make promissory concessions to the national aspirations of the minorities, while simultaneously having due caution for the sensibilities of the dominant element. A middle course was essential, and the leadership of the Lao Dong settled on regional autonomy. Within three months of his movement's occupation of Hanoi, Ho made clear that such autonomy was to be the cornerstone of nationality policy, but he also took pains to make clear that autonomy was to be exercised "within the bloc of solidarity with Vietnam."[43] In compliance with this directive, the first "autonomous zone" was established in May 1955. Again, Ho felt constrained to use the occasion to remind the inhabitants of the region that their subordination both to the party and to the state was not to be seen as a temporary condition, but as one in perpetuity: "The Thai-Meo Autonomous Region is an integral part of the great family of Viet-Nam, making with other brother nationalities a monolithic bloc of unity. It will always enjoy the education and leadership of the Party and Government and the assistance of other brother nationalities."[44]

From a purely legalistic viewpoint, autonomous zones within North Vietnam occupied an anomalous position between 1955 and 1960, in that the 1946 constitution, which was technically still in effect, had made no allowance for the principle of autonomy.[45] Constitutional legitimacy was granted *ex post facto* by the constitution of 1960. This later constitution, unlike that of 1946, also recognized distinctions of nationality, as well as of race, class, sex, etc.[46] Indeed, the state was now defined as "a *multinational* state." And in a return to Marxist practice, the distinction between "the state" and "the nation" was now meticulously maintained throughout the constitution's body proper. On the other hand, the preamble undid much of this vocabular precision, particularly the acknowledgment of the state's multinational character, by referring to all inhabitants of Vietnam by such collective rubrics as "the Vietnamese people," "the entire Vietnamese people," and even "the entire nation." In any event, the concept of indivisibility was proclaimed in as unyielding a fashion as it had been in 1946: "The territory of Viet-nam is a single, indivisible whole from North to South" (Article 1). "The Democratic Republic of Viet-nam is a single multinational state. Autonomous zones are inalienable parts of the Democratic Republic of Viet-nam" (Article 3). Thus, unlike the Chinese and Soviets who were able to delay substituting autonomy and inalienability for promises of secession until after coming into control of the ruling apparatus for the entire state, the Vietnamese movement was forced to adopt such a stance somewhat prematurely, at a time when only half the country was under its jurisdiction.

As noted, regional autonomy was a compromise between the needs of internal and external objectives. Judging by their earlier actions, the Lao Dong would have preferred to do less with regard to minorities at home while remaining free to promise more to minorities throughout the remainder of Vietnam. But, at least at the documentary level, regional autonomy became the leitmotif of the propaganda addressed to the montagnards outside of North Vietnam. The 1961 program of the National Liberation Front (NLF), for example, promised "to set up within the great family of the Vietnamese people, autonomous regions or areas inhabited by minority peoples" and "to abolish . . . forced assimilation."[47] The 1967 program reiterated the promise of autonomy, adding the rather hazy conditions that autonomous zones would be restricted to "the areas where the minorities live concentrated and gather their required conditions."[48]

It is difficult to assess the impact such documents exerted upon the remote and largely illiterate montagnards. Much more pertinent to know would be the precise manner in which this program was translated by Communist cadre when in actual conversation with the hill people.[49] It may well be that the cadre continued to promise independence.[50] But, even if not, it is unlikely that an isolated and politically unsophisticated people would sense any meaningful distinction between a promise of autonomy and a promise of independence. Remote peoples are hardly apt to perceive independence in such imagery as sending ambassadors abroad, a seat at the United Nations, or an abstraction termed sovereignty. Rather, independence is apt to be viewed as freedom from domination by some other ethnic element, i.e., a ridding of the ethnic territory of the alien and his influences. In such a milieu, the promise to a people of freedom to use their own language, have their own schools, preserve all their own customs, etc., must to the ear of the villager be indistinguishable from the promise of political independence. Dennis Warner reports that the Viet Cong went further than this, actually promising political autonomy in "an autonomous *State* for the tribes."[51] But again, it is doubtful that it would, in any case, have been necessary to go that far in order to convey the vision of a society free of the despised Vietnamese.[52] Thus, a member of the Chru reports that during a period of more than two years in which his village was under Viet Cong control, the Communist cadre, when describing the future that awaited the Chru after the Viet Cong victory, studiously avoided references to such notions as independence, autonomy, state, political structure, and the like. Rather, the cadre promised an end to Vietnamese domination and the oppressive policies of Saigon, conjuring, by contrast, the image of a reconstituted Golden Age in which Chru could again roam unrestrictedly throughout their ancient hunting grounds (presumably without encountering a sign of Vietnamese intruders).[53] But perhaps the best evidence that remote peoples are not apt to differentiate between a promise of autonomy and one of independence is offered by an unanticipated development within the Chinese People's Republic. There, some four years after the CCP came into power and instituted a regime that consistently and publicly berated any hint of what it termed "national splittism," the authorities, in an unusually forthright assessment of the problems associated with their nationalities program, acknowledged that the right of autonomy and the right of secession were still being confused by members of ethnic minorities: "In some areas, for instance, some people among a national minority considered that the enforcement of autonomy meant a separation from the Han Chinese, and that the Han Chinese would no longer be wanted in their region."[54] Expressions such as "autonomy," "self-rule," "independence," "freedom to choose one's culture," etc., are therefore apt to trigger different images in different minds and in different milieus. This phenomenon clearly came to the aid of the Lao Dong after 1954. When its *de jure* (as well as *de facto*) control of northern Vietnam's minorities precluded it from carrying out the letter of Lenin's injunction concerning the promise of secession, the party's decision to observe the spirit of Lenin's injunction to the greatest degree possible under the circumstances, by using ambiguous terminology, proved more than adequate to the task of gaining the support from the montagnards that was essential to its victory in the south.

Soon after the victory of the "liberation forces" in South Vietnam, Hanoi began a campaign to prepare the people of the region for union with the north. As reported by Reuters, the campaign took for its motto a quotation from the recently deceased Ho Chi Minh: "Vietnam is one country, the Vietnamese are one people. Rivers can be dried up, mountains can be worn out, but this truth can never be changed."[55] This slogan is most revealing when one examines the general content of the 1947 letter from which it was, with alterations, extracted. It will be remembered that in 1946, Ho, who was at the time visualizing his immediate coming to power over the entire country, had, in one of his speeches, evoked the myth of a single ancestry common to Vietnamese and montagnard alike. The same myth formed the key element in his letter from which the motto of the 1975 reunification campaign would later be extracted:

> Compatriots of the Kinh majority [ethnically Vietnamese] people or of the Tho, Muong or Man, Djarie or Ede, Sedan or Bana, and other minorities are all of Viet-Nam's children, *all are blood brothers and sisters.* Alive or dead, in happiness or misfortune, we stand close to one another. . . . Rivers can dry up, mountains can wear away, but our solidarity will never decrease.[56]

With political actuality now having overtaken the optimistic visions of 1946, the unification campaign of 1975 clearly heralded a return to the minorities policy of the immediate post-World War II period. Under this policy, montagnards, once more a people without a history, could not aspire to ever achieving the status of a nation. They were at best a subdivision of one. The ethnic Vietnamese and the montagnards formed a single people, a single nation, and a single state, monoliths which would outlive the rivers and mountains.[57]

Consonant with this baseless myth of ethnic kinship, though not with the promises made to the minorities over a fifty-year period, Hanoi, now unchallenged ruler of all of Vietnam, quickly made manifest that even regional autonomy, much less secession, was not to be honored. Ignoring the provisions of the 1960 constitution, the government announced on December 29, 1975 its decision to dissolve the national autonomous regions, thus creating a unitary state in form as well as in content.[58] Although surprisingly close upon the heels of the Communists' assumption of total power, this action was clearly heralded by the constitution, documents, and speeches of 1946, the year in which the Vietnamese Communists first believed they were about to acquire full authority over Vietnam. Their decision to abolish the autonomous regions was therefore quite predictable.[59] But the haste with which Hanoi acted demonstrates the showcase role that the autonomous regions had been designed to play for the montagnards outside of northern Vietnam, and the absence of sincerity underlying the promises of independence and/or autonomy made to the minorities of both northern and southern Vietnam since the very beginning of the Vietnamese Marxist-Leninist movement.[60]

The history of the minorities policy of the Vietnamese Communists over the half century preceding victory was therefore one of innumerable twists and turns, pockmarked by glaring inconsistencies in the use of key terms. Were such convolutions the symptom of disinterest? The lack of guiding strategy? Unfamiliarity with or incomprehension of Lenin's writings on the national question? That all such explanations are badly wanting is evident from the following extracts of an article written by Ho, near the end of his career, to commemorate the fortieth anniversary of the Bolshevik Revolution. Both in its exposition of the manner in which nationalism must be skillfully employed to promote the cause of Marxism and in its punctilious regard for accuracy in terminology, this article has few equals outside of the collected works of Lenin himself.

> The October Revolution has brought to the people of all nations the right to decide their own fate and the practical means to implement this right. It is well known that Lenin attached particular importance to the recognition of the right of all nations to secession and to build up independent states. . . . The Soviet Union of the October Revolution recognized the independence of Mongolia and Finland, which seceded to build up independent states, Of course, for the formerly oppressed nations, the right to secession does not signify the obligation to secede from a state

where the people have overthrown the oppressors. On the contrary, it creates conditions for a voluntary alliance between free nations on the basis of complete equality of interests. . . . Therefore, the national question can no longer be viewed from an abstract and isolated point of view. Marxism-Leninism has shown that national movements effectively directed against imperialism unfailingly contribute to the general revolutionary struggle and that national claims and national movements must not be estimated according to their strictly local political and social character in a narrow-minded way, but according to the part they play against the imperialist forces in the world.[61]

Surveying their half century of stuggle, Ho and his colleagues could legitimately lay claim to having measured up fully to the cited criterion that "national movements effectively directed against imperialism unfailingly contribute to the general revolutionary struggle."

NOTES

1. Central Committee of Propaganda, *Thirty Years*, 27.
2. For substantiation on this point, see Fall, "The Pathet Lao," 178 et seq.
3. The full text of the platform can be found in Cole, *Conflict in Indo-China*, 96–106.
4. On May 9, 1929, the Association made the following fundamental and urgent demand: "Reconnaître à tous les peuples: cambodgien, man, laotien, etc. . . . le droit de se gouverner eux-mêmes." Gouvernement Générale des Affaires Politiques, *Documents* 4:56.
5. See Nguyen Kien Giang, *Les Grandes dates du parti de la classe ouvrière du Vietnam* (Hanoi, 1960), 22: "Indépendance politique du l'Indochine; reconnaissance du droit des peuples à disposer d'eux-mêmes."
6. "Vers le renforcement du parti communiste indochinois," 798. "Union fraternelle de tous les peuples indochinois. Droit pour les cambodgiens, laotiens et autres nationalités de disposer d'eux-mêmes."
7. "Programme of the Communist International, Adopted at its Sixth Congress," September 1, 1928, in Degras, *Documents* 2:471–526.
8. Ho had appreciated the concept of self-determination even prior to the creation of of the Comintern. In 1918 he wrote letters to Clemenceau, George, and Wilson, setting forth the "Annamite case" for independence under the self-determination principle which these leaders ostensibly espoused. See Ennis, *French Policy*, 201.
9. "Vers le renforcement du parti communiste indochinois," 796–800.

10. In his 1913 tract, *Marxism and the National Question*, Stalin had defined a nation as "a historically evolved, stable community of people, formed on the basis of a common language, territory, economic life, and psychological make-up manifested in a common culture."

11. See Hammer, *Struggle*, 91–92.

12. U.S. Department of State, "Political Alignments."

13. In addition to creating the Viet Minh, in itself a stratagem, the conference laid down a number of policies that the ICP was to follow. One was to "expand the organizations into the provinces where the movement is still weak and into ethnic minorities regions." Chu Van Tan, "Reminiscences," 54. The wording of the directive seems to be an acknowledgment that ICP strength at this time was greatest in the minority regions.

14. A leading member of the ICP who operated on either side of the border throughout World War II has noted that because the local peoples had "relatives, acquaintances and friends" on either side of the border, "in their souls and hearts, they did not pay any attention to the border markers or the lines that delineated the two countries on the map." Chu Van Tan "Reminiscences," 95.

15. The most important transborder element were the people variously known at the time within China as Chuang, T'ai, Nung, Sha, or Pu-yi (see Chang Chih-i, *The Party*, 38) and as Nung or Tai within Indochina. During the war, Chu Van Tan, an ICP leader who was himself a member of this ethnonational group, led a penetration deep into the Chinese segment of the group's homeland, where he visited one of the revolutionary base areas that had been set up among the Chuang by the CCP in 1929–1930. See his "Reminiscences," particularly p. 116.

16. Chu Van Tan, "Reminiscences," 95. An adequate account of the political intrigue that transpired in this remote transborder area during and immediately following World War II is yet to be written. During the war the ICP and the KMT often cooperated, and a number of ICP personnel attended KMT training schools and academies. Meanwhile, anti-KMT forces often used the Indochinese side of the border for sanctuary.

17. See, for example, Chu Van Tan, "Reminiscences," 16, where the author notes that the ICP forces operating in the Chuang area of China "had assimilated with the people and adopted their clothing, their style of speech, their pattern of work and living. They were so much like the local people that a stranger coming in from afar could not tell them apart from the villagers." Years later cadre, scheduled to be sent from Hanoi to operate among the highland peoples of South Vietnam, would first be introduced to the local customs. Consonant with the practice of some of the highlanders, certain cadre even had their teeth sharpened before arriving in the south.

18. Chu Van Tan was merely one of several non-Vietnamese to hold positions of high authority in the ICP at this time. His "Reminiscences" is studded with people in the movement who were not ethnically Vietnamese.

19. From the vantage point of 1971, Chu Van Tan was understandably hesitant to recall the precise promises made during the war to the minorities, because they had not subsequently been honored. However, he noted that the Viet Minh Program was distributed as "souvenirs" to the local people and that "we explained clearly to the people . . . the mission . . . of the ethnic minorities in this historic period." "Reminiscences," 105. With regard to the Chuang people within China, he noted that his followers purposefully "heightened the villagers' awareness of their ethnic and class backgrounds" (p. 116). The purposeful heightening of awareness of the ethnic background shared by the Chuang with their kin across the Indochinese border strongly suggests that the ICP leaders were holding out the prospect of a single, transborder Chuang state. Only a few paragraphs earlier, Chu Van Tan, with regard to the Chuang of China, had noted that "all the villagers here were ready and willing to feed, support and protect [us], because of their affection for people of their own ethnic background who spoke their dialect, were related to them."

20. English translations of the constitution, which vary only very slightly from one another, can be found in Cole, *Conflict in Indo-China*, and Fall, *Viet-Minh Regime*, 156–164.

21. The sole exception, the last reference and perhaps an unintentional slip, was *national minorities*.

22. *The August Revolution* was republished in Hanoi in 1962, and can be found in Truong Chinh, *Primer*.

23. Ibid., 62–63. The enumeration of various states (Nam Ky, Moi, etc.) was a reference to proposals by France to subdivide the territory into a complex system of federated states and autonomous regions—a system in which ethnicity would play a major role in determining political boundaries. The motives behind these French proposals would have been less suspect had they been advanced prior to France's attempt to reassert its authority over Indochina. However, the chronology of events makes it difficult to avoid the conclusion that the proposals were merely an attempt to play one ethnic group against another. Nevertheless, these French proposals should have been acceptable to Ho as fully consonant with earlier promises of his party. On France's proposals and related French activity, see Hammer, *Struggle*, particularly pp. 162, 172.

24. "Proclamation to the People upon Return from France after Negotiations," October 23, 1946, in Ho Chi Minh, *On Revolution*, 158–161.

25. By such phrases as "the nation entering upon a new stage of history," "the destiny of the nation," and "the entire nation," the constitution regularly referred to *all* people living within Vietnam regardless of ethnic background.

As a devoted student of Lenin's writings on the national question, Ho was certainly aware that the use to which the word *nation* was put in the 1946 constitution was contrary to Marxist-Leninist practice. For later proof of Ho's awareness of proper Marxist terminology on the national question, see the discussion later in this chapter concerning his article commemorating the fortieth anniversary of the Bolshevik Revolution.

26. Perhaps the best indication of Ho's reading of French intentions at this time was his trip to France to negotiate the relationship between France and the Democratic Republic of Vietnam. It would have been most unusual, had he anticipated subsequent French actions, for him to risk a visit to the "enemy's" home ground.

27. From *The Resistance Will Win*, republished in Hanoi in 1960; it can be found in Truong Chinh, *Primer*. The cited passage is from pp. 116–117.

28. For the most complete account of the essential roles played by the minorities in the French-Indochina war, see McAlister, "Mountain Minorities," 771–844. See also McAlister, "The Possibilities for Diplomacy," particularly pp. 273–280. For an interesting reference by Ho to the willingness of non-Vietnamese women to serve as porters, see "Instructions Given at the Conference Reviewing the Second Le Hong Phong Military Campaign" (1950), in Ho Chi Minh, *On Revolution*, 184–188: "Never before have such big contingents of women of the Kinh [Vietnamese], Man, Tho, Nung, and other nationalities volunteered to carry supplies to the front as in the recent campaign."

29. With regard to just the single people who played the most important role in the Viet Minh victory over the French, one authority has concluded: "In terms of the utility of their territory and the commitment of their population, the contribution of the Tho to the military success of the Viet Minh was vital, if not absolutely decisive." McAlister, "Mountain Minorities," 796.

30. Actually the Republic of Vietnam, whose capital was Saigon.

31. For an account of antigovernmental violence by minority tribesmen in the northeastern area, see the *Christian Science Monitor*, November 22, 1968.

32. One account of the March 1975 attack on Ban Me Thuot, described as "where the final drive to P.R.G. victory was set in motion," read in part: "The attacking units were led by highlands minority people who missionary sources said were members of the long-dormant FULRO (United Front for the Liberation of Oppressed Races), a group which had demanded autonomy for minority nationalities in the highlands." See *Indochina Chronicle* (July–August 1975), 5.

33. The most detailed account of the minorities during the French phase of the war tells us much about how the Viet Minh exploited rivalries between the minority groups, but it fails to tell us much concerning the political promises that were made. In some instances, the Viet Minh even proved adroit at allying itself with both minorities involved in such a local competition. See, for example, McAlister, "Mountain Minorities," 813. McAlister's account serves to remind once again of the many parallels between the experiences of the Viet Minh and the CCP. Remember the

great flexibility practiced by the CCP in forging alliances throughout its early history (e.g., the willingness to work with the conservative Moslems).

34. The platform can be found in Cole, *Conflict in Indo-China*, 96–106.

35. See earlier, this chapter.

36. Ho Chi Minh, "Instructions Given at the Conference Reviewing the Second Le Hong Phong Military Campaign" (1950), in *On Revolution*, 186.

37. "Political Report Read at the Second National Congress of the Viet-Nam Worker's Party, Held in February, 1951" in Ho Chi Minh, *On Revolution*, 188–208.

38. The passage continues: "This is a measure to win over the people, frustrating the enemy's scheme of 'using Vietnamese to harm Vietnamese.' " ("Teaching at the Meeting of Officers for the Preparation of the Military Campaign in the Northwest," September 9, 1952, in Ho Chi Minh, *On Revolution*, 226–230.)

39. Joiner, "Administration and Political Warfare," 23, and Kunstadter, *Southeast Asian Tribes*, 679.

40. In 1946, the French proposed to create a *Pays Montagnard du Sud* and later a Tai Federation for the non-Vietnamese people of northern Vietnam. See also the quotation from Truong Chinh's earlier cited 1946 article with its reference to " 'Nam Ky state', 'Moi state', 'Thai state', 'Nung state', etc." The French actually created such states in the cases of Cambodia and Laos during 1947. For their constitutions, see Cole, *Conflict in Indo-China*, 52–57.

41. About this time, an ostensibly independent organization (but actually a creature of the Lao Dong) released a program for achieving unity of the entire country. It reflected the same ambiguity that had surrounded the Lao Dong's use of key terms and concepts in 1946. In its opening sentence, the nation was equated with the entire Vietnam state: "Our Viet-Nam is an independent nation with an age-old history [but] it became a French colony." Elsewhere, *nation* was used in relation to all of the various peoples of Vietnam who as a group, but not as "nationalities," were said to have a "sacred right" to self-determination: "Viet-Nam's national sovereignty belongs to the entire Vietnamese people without distinction of nationality, class, political or religious convictions. Whether in the political, military, economic, cultural, diplomatic or any other field, the Viet-Nam nation has the sacred and inviolable right to self-determination." See "Programme of the Viet-Nam Fatherland Front," in Turner, *Vietnamese Communism*, 386–388.

42. The emphasis placed by the leadership on appealing to Vietnamese nationalism is suggested in a 1960 tract by Lao Dong First Secretary Le Duan: "The communist parties must grasp firmly and hold aloft the banner of nationalism, democracy and peace, and should not let the bourgeoisie utilize it to hoodwink the masses." That Le Duan viewed this ostensible commitment to nationalism as purely tactical was demonstrated by his further comment that the parties themselves must not be contaminated

by nationalist considerations: "The communist and workers' parties have the obligation . . . to resolutely struggle against all manifestations of nationalism and chauvinism." (Le Duan, "On Some Present International Problems," as cited in Turner, *Vietnamese Communism*, 280.)

The propaganda task of painting itself more nationalistic than the Saigon leaders was vastly eased with the arrival of large contingents of U.S. forces in the late 1960s. The American presence lent important credence to the theme that the Saigon elite were the "running dogs" and "puppets" of U.S. imperialism. Turner (*Vietnamese Communism*, 280) cites a classified party document circulated within South Vietman in 1966, which read in part: "Nationalism must be promoted, sufferings pointed out, national and class hatred provoked and aimed at the Americans and traitorous Vietnamese who sell out their country." For further details on the nationalistic propaganda of Hanoi and the Viet Cong, see Connor, "Ethnology and Peace," 51–86.

43. U.S. Department of the Army, *Minority Groups*, 5. The speech by Ho was made in January 1955.

44. "Letter to Compatriots in the Thai-Meo Autonomous Region," May 7, 1955, in Ho Chi Minh, *On Revolution*, 260–262. These twin messages of autonomy and indivisibility were also reflected in the propaganda being aimed at this time at South Vietnam. Thus the "Programme of the Viet-Nam Fatherland Front" (Turner, *Vietnamese Communism*, 388) noted: "Equality of the various nationalities in the country to be guaranteed; every attempt to divide the people to be forbidden. . . . In the reunified Viet-Nam, autonomous regions to be established wherever the minorities are in groups of sufficient density."

45. Following the creation of the first autonomous region (originally called the Thai-Meo AR but renamed the Tay Bac AR in 1962), a second such unit (the Viet Bac AR) had been created in the northeast on August 10, 1956. Still a third unit (the Lao-Ha-Yen AR) was created near the headwaters of the Red River in the spring of 1957. However, this last creation was short-lived, being allowed to lapse without publicity sometime in 1959.

46. The 1960 constitution can be found in Blaustein and Flanz, *Constitutions*.

47. The NLF, designed in the tradition of the Viet Minh, was a Communist-dominated organization designed to appeal to all "patriotic peoples." The text of the organization's 1961 program is reproduced in U.S. Senate Committee on Foreign Relations, *Background Information*, 269–274. During the 1960s and early 1970s, the degree to which Hanoi controlled the Viet Cong, the Provisional Revolutionary Government, the National Liberation Front, etc., was a controversial point in the West. However, in 1978 the former head of the Provisional Revolutionary Government acknowledged that Hanoi had directed all movements. Referring to North Vietnam and the Viet Cong, he stated: "Officially we were separate, but

in fact we were the same thing all the time; there was a single party, a single government, a single capital, a single country." *Washington Post*, November 6, 1978.

48. The entire program is reproduced in the *New York Times*, December 15, 1967. The nature of these "required conditions" and the time and manner of their "gathering" are not specified.

49. A Western clergyman, who spent many years among the montagnards and knew them well, has cryptically written: "Thus, the Montagnards not only endured the Marxist propaganda spread by persuasion or intimidation, but also received attractive promises of liberation and self-government." See Seitz, *Men of Dignity*, 100.

50. As mentioned earlier, Communist cadre were being given specific instructions for gaining the support of the minorities in the 1946–1954 period, although the party's public documents of the time gave no hint about the content of these instructions.

51. Warner, *Last Confucian*, 167. Emphasis added. Such a status would be similar to that accorded to the Cambodians and Laotians by the French in 1947. To the montagnards it would therefore probably mean the same freedom from the Vietnamese that had been accorded these other two peoples.

52. As in the case of the minorities within China, the "montagnards" have long-standing reasons to dislike all Vietnamese, whose traditional name for the mountain people ("*Moi*," translatable as "barbarian") is an accurate reflection of the attitude of the Vietnamese toward the tribesmen and their culture. However, the promises of cultural independence by Hanoi and the NLF fell on particularly fertile ground because of a policy of enforced assimilation inaugurated by South Vietnam's former President Diem. The policy, which was strongly resented and resisted by the tribesmen, was not pursued by subsequent governments, but a rather dismal record of broken promises and maltreatment continued until the downfall of the Saigon government.

53. Private conversations with Han Tho at the Woodrow Wilson International Center for Scholars, Washington, D.C., January 9 and 14, 1976. It is also worth noting that Han Tho, although an extremely well-educated individual with fluency in English, French, and Vietnamese as well as in the language of his people, and although well informed on minority matters generally (having worked for a time in this field for the Saigon government), had never seen documents putting forth the minority policy of the NLF or Hanoi. Scholarship may therefore tend to exaggerate the impact of such documents.

54. "Basic Summarization of Experiences in the Promotion of Autonomy in National Minority Areas," Report adopted at the 3rd (enlarged) Conference of the Nationalities Affairs Commission, June 15, 1953. *New China News Agency* (Peking), September 9, 1953.

55. *New York Times*, November 9, 1975.

56. "Letter Sent to the Congress of the Southern National Minorities, Held in Pleiku in April, 1946," April 19, 1946, in Ho Chi Minh, *On Revolution*, 156. Emphasis added.

57. In inaugurating the reunification campaign, Pham Van Dong, the prime minister of North Vietnam, stated that "in reality the country has already been reunified because all problems have been settled in the name of a single country, a single people and a single economy." See the *New York Times*, November 9, 1975.

58. *FBIS*, January 19, 1976.

59. Hanoi's decision to abolish the autonomous regions was made after this section on North Vietnam was written. However, except for the addition of this single paragraph dealing with the decision, no alteration in the book was made, in order to illustrate that the decision (though not its precise timetable) was a quite natural step in the evolution of Hanoi's policy.

60. While the party had denied self-determination at home, it continued to employ the term in dealings with foreign countries. For example, the 1973 "Agreement on Ending the War and Restoring Peace in Vietnam," which was signed by Hanoi, Washington, Saigon, and the Provisional Revolutionary Government, referred in both the preamble and Article 9 to "the South Vietnamese people's right to self-determination." Also, a 1975 letter from the North Vietnamese foreign minister to his Thailand counterpart stated that good relations between the two states must be based upon "respect for fundamental national rights and the right to self-determination of each people." See *Indochina Chronicle* (May–June 1975), 16.

61. "The October Revolution and the Liberation of the Peoples of the East," November 6, 1957, in Ho Chi Minh, *On Revolution*, 291–303. Ho's candor might have been fortified by the fact that the article was for publication in the USSR rather than at home.

CHAPTER 6

The Joining of the Yugoslav Nations

As applied to the area of Europe populated by the southern Slavonic peoples, the Leninist strategy concerning self-determination
of nations was soon enmeshed in the general confusion and debate
surrounding the question of which sets of people did or did not
constitute separate national entities. The end of World War I found
national consciousness among the region's masses still at a quite
inchoate stage, thus providing a forum in which contradictory assertions concerning the national identity of groups were regularly
made without risk of effective rebuttal. The group identity of the
Macedonians was perhaps the most clouded, being subjected to at
least three mutually exclusive allegations. Although an independence movement, the Internal Macedonian Revolutionary Movement (IMRO), had been active since 1896, there were (and still are)
many, particularly in Sofia, who maintained that the Macedonians
were Bulgars, while still others insisted that they were Serbians.
Controversy extended even to the identity of the Serbs and Montenegrins, though each had had its own state since at least 1878.
Thus, there were those among the literati who insisted that the
Montenegrins were merely a fragment of the Serbian nation. However, these cases notwithstanding, the most consequential assertion
concerning national identity, popular at the time of the Paris Peace
Conference, was the contention that all southern Slavs (Yugo-slavs)
comprised but a single nation. This assertion held that Croats,
Serbs, Slovenes, etc., were at best only tribes, in the sense of subdivisions or suborders of a larger ethnonational whole. This notion
had developed principally among the Slavonic peoples throughout
the southern regions of the Habsburg Empire and ultimately became the justification for creating, in the name of Wilsonian self-
determination, the state today known as Yugoslavia.[1]

Curiously, the vision of a single state for southern Slavs did not
at first appeal to the Serbian leaders who were instead intent on
erecting a Greater Serbia, a state that would incorporate Bosnia
and Hercegovina into the existing Serbian political structure but
which would nonetheless be much smaller than the state envisaged

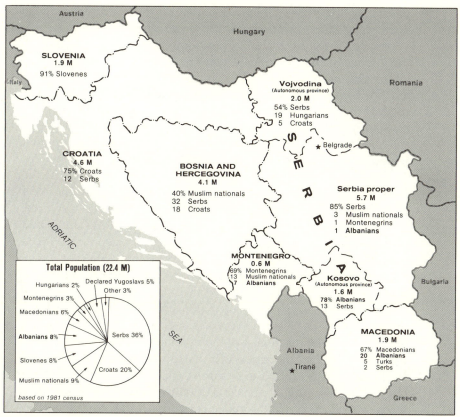

MAP 3. Yugoslavia

by the Yugo-Slav movement. However, with the overthrow of its chief ally, tsarist Russia, and under pressure from the Western powers, the Serbian monarchy finally consented to the creation of a single state called the Kingdom of the Serbs, Croats, and Slovenes.[2] The name of the proposed state would appear to be an official recognition of the country's multinational composition, as would sections of the Pact of Corfu (the agreement of July 20, 1917 which gave rise to the new state). The pact, for example, promised equal status to the individual flags and coats of arms of the Serbs, Croats, and Slovenes, and it designated the three group names of Serb, Croat, and Slovene as "equal before the law throughout the territory of the Kingdom."[3] However, by a number of references to "our nation" or "the nation," the pact made clear that the new government was committed to the notion that these three elements were only "tribal" components of a single Yugoslav nation.[4]

Despite historically different viewpoints on the national question, the two major organizations which were later to comprise the Yugoslav Communist Party (YCP) also came to embrace the position that the southern Slavs constituted a single nation. As part of the socialist movement within Austria-Hungary, a movement that was constantly embroiled in the issue of rights for national minorities, the Social Democratic Party of Croatia and Slovenia had agitated for political autonomy for the region populated by the Croatians. As contrasted with this ethnically narrow focus, the party of the Serbian Social Democrats had been traditionally among the most truly internationalist of all Marxist parties. It had, for example, been the only European socialist party which in 1914 had abided by the Leninist dictum to oppose its government's request for funds to underwrite wartime mobilization,[5] a course of action that was all the more impressive in its demonstration of the absence of national proclivities, in that it involved the survival of a state that was the product of a successful war of national liberation. Indeed, for a number of years prior to World War I, the party's leaders had openly advocated the demise of their nation's self-determined state, preferring instead the vision of a Balkan federation. The appeal of the latter was economic, a throwback to Karl Marx's bias for large units over small, regardless of ethnic distributional patterns. But despite the fact that the policies of the Serbian Social Democrats tended to transcend national consciousness, while the Croatian Social Democrats had, by contrast, long been parochially preoccupied with the Croatian cause, both groups, even prior to their union, had switched to a common perspective concerning a Yugoslav nation. Thus a declaration of the Croatian Social Democrats of May 1, 1918 asserted that "Slovenes, Croats, and Serbs are one and the same people, and that as a consequence they have all the attributes of one people, and especially in this respect . . . that they constitute an independent free state."[6] In a similar vein, the Serbian Social Democrats proclaimed in November of the same year:

> The Serbs, Croats, and Slovenes are one nation, for they have one language and identical remaining ethnic characteristics. They feel like one people and desire union. It follows that their union in one national state is a great political, economic, and cultural need which is beyond any discussion.[7]

In the light of subsequent events, these early statements that Serbs, Croats, and Slovenes constituted one nation became acute embarrassments to the YCP. Looking back from the vantage point of 1948, Tito would ridicule the early policies of the Kingdom of Serbs, Croats, and Slovenes in the following terms:

> One of the main elements in this process was the unsolved national question which the ruling clique ignored completely, persistently preaching about a tri-named people, that is, preaching that Serbs, Croats and Slovenes are one people, paying no attention whatsoever to the Montenegrins and Macedonians.[8]

No mention was made that the precursors to the YCP had shared in this "preaching." Nor did Tito note that this policy was not repudiated in the early years of the YCP itself.

The early history of the YCP's position on the national question is not easy to unravel for at least two sets of reasons. The first is that factions were operating within the party who were in sharp disagreement on the matter. As they alternated in gaining the upper hand, the party's public position developed an inconsistent pattern. The second factor impeding an unraveling is that several outside agencies also became involved in the decision-making process with regard to the YCP's national policy. The most influential of these agents was the Comintern. Though the national question was not raised at the YCP's First Congress (April 1919), the congress did take the momentous step of voting to petition for membership in the one-month-old Third International. While we have seen that the influence of this organization was certainly a significant factor in the evolution of the policies of the Chinese and Vietnamese parties, there were several reasons why the Comintern became more intimately involved in the affairs of the YCP, not the least of which was greater Soviet concern with her European borders than with her Asiatic ones. Still other agents that influenced YCP policy were the Communist parties of the other Balkan states, most notably those of Bulgaria and Greece. Interaction among the parties with regard to the national question was a result of both shared peoples (for example, the Macedonians who were divided into Bulgar, Greek, and Yugoslav components), and a continuing, though sporadic, flirtation by the parties with the idea of a Balkan federation. We have noted the Serbian Social Democratic Party's earlier interest in such a regional approach. Along with the Social Democratic parties of Bulgaria, Greece, and Rumania, they had formed a so-called Balkan Social Democratic Federation in 1910; in January

1920, at a meeting attended by delegates from the Bulgarian, Greek, and Yugoslav Communist parties, it was decided to rename the organization the Balkan Communist Federation (BCF) and to apply for membership in the Comintern. For some years thereafter, the Comintern gave the appearance of favoring the BCF over the individual parties comprising it, probably because (as we shall directly note) the Comintern leaders at this time supported the absorption of the states of southeastern Europe into a larger whole. BCF programs therefore tended to reflect Moscow's outlook, but the degree to which they reflected the dominant sentiments of the YCP is more questionable. By and large, the BCF remained more under the sway of the Bulgarian party, and often took that party's particular position on issues dividing the Bulgarian and Yugoslav parties.

The Comintern's first pronouncement affecting the YCP came in the form of a "Manifesto to the Communist Parties of Bulgaria, Rumania, Serbia, and Turkey" (April 1920).[9] The Manifesto made it abundantly evident that the Comintern planned to exploit the national divisions within the Balkans in order to weaken, and, if possible, to destroy the states that had emerged from the Treaty of Versailles.

> The new national divisions which followed the dismemberment of Austria-Hungary and the defeat of Bulgaria and Turkey have made the nationality problem in the Balkan Peninsula even more complex than it was before the war. Many more elements of foreign nationality have come under the rule of the victors. And the policy of national oppression, the policy of insatiable militarism awakens a still greater desire for emancipation, and this struggle for emancipation is taking on an ever wider scope.
>
> Against the rule of the Serbian bureaucratic and landowning oligarchy, there are rising up the Macedonian Bulgarians, the Albanians, the Montenegrins, the Croats, and the Bosnians. . . .
>
> A new period of embittered nationalist agitation, national hate, and national bourgeois wars threatens the Balkan and Danube peoples. Only the proletariat can avert a new catastrophe by its victory and free the working and peasant masses from economic and national oppression. Only the victory of the proletarian dictatorship can unite all the masses of the peoples in a Federation of Socialist Balkan (or Balkan and Danubian) Soviet Republics, and save them . . . from colonial enslavement and national disputes. The Communist Party is called by existing circumstances to play an even bigger role in the Balkan Peninsula than in

capitalist countries where there are no nationality problems. All
the efforts of the Balkan Communist parties should be directed
to fulfilling this great historical mission on communism in the
Balkans.[10]

The outlined strategy was therefore dialectical, and might be
characterized as instigating fission to create a larger fusion. The
local Communist parties were being instructed to foment dissatisfaction on the part of national groups within their respective state,
in order to promote the goal of a federation of socialist republics.
But somewhat paradoxically, the YCP elected to endorse the goal
while ignoring the prescribed means. In the program approved at
the party's Second Congress (June 1920), Yugoslavia was treated
as a given, which, as a "Soviet Republic" would join "with all neighboring peoples for the establishment of a Soviet federation of Bal-
kan-Danubian countries, which will be an integral part of the international federation of Soviet Republics."[11] In choosing to ignore
the Comintern's reference to "the Macedonian Bulgarians, the Albanians, the Montenegrins, the Croats, and the Bosnians," and by
advocating the territorial integrity of Yugoslavia, the YCP was in
effect reasserting its 1918 claim that the Serbs, Croats, and other
southern Slavs constituted a single nation. Years later, Tito would
describe this stance as the most serious error to appear in the
program.

> It can already be seen from this that the program of the CPY
> accepted at the Vukovar Congress had enormous shortcomings.
> First of all, there is no mention in the program of the national
> question. . . . In the resolution of the same congress, however,
> on the political situation and tasks of the CPY, it is maintained
> that "the CPY will continue to stand on the bulwark of national
> unity," a thought forming the basis of a complete non-compre-
> hension of the national question.[12]

The YCP's deviation from the Comintern's directive did not occasion any detectable retribution. Comintern forbearance may be
explained by the fact that the organization had not yet issued a
formal position paper on the national question, claiming universal
validity. Such a document appeared only one month after the Second Congress of the YCP, in the form of "Lenin's Theses on the
National and Colonial Question" (July 28, 1920).[13] That document,
we will remember, made explicit that "communist parties must give
direct support to the revolutionary movements among the de-

pendent nations and those without equal rights. . . . " It will also be recalled that the reason for this injunction was "to bring into being a close alliance of all national and colonial liberation movements within Soviet Russia."

When combined with the Comintern's enumeration of specific national groups within Yugoslavia made three months earlier, the "Theses on the National and Colonial Question" had the effect of declaring the YCP's national policy doctrinally unacceptable. But the issue was not immediately joined. In July 1922, the First Conference of the YCP held in Vienna produced an ambiguous resolution which, while paying lip service to the notion of "self-determination," invoked that principle "for the solution of the national and tribal differences."[14] Since tribal differences implied a single nation of southern Slavs, the resolution evidently did not contemplate a right of secession at least so far as Slavic peoples were concerned. As if to underline this point, a separate resolution warned the proletariat, particularly the Croatian proletariat, against "the dangerous infection of nationalism."[15]

Even this most recent illustration of the YCP's intention to dawdle on the national question did not trigger an overt manifestation of Comintern irritation.[16] Meeting later in 1922, the Fourth Congress of the Comintern, while noting that the national question was "the question which is quite of the most serious importance for the Yugoslav Party," refrained from direct criticism of the party's inaction on the issue.[17] But such forbearance was now quickly coming to an end. Tito reports that the first official Comintern indictment of the YCP's stand was made by its delegate at the BCF conference, held in December 1922.[18] But even this belated reprimand failed to bring about an immediate change in the YCP's position. The platform of a newly created, legal front, the Independent Workers Party of Yugoslavia (IWPY),[19] which was adopted in January 1923, included the following passage:

> It is the viewpoint of the IWPY that one of the fundamental reasons for the tribal disputes in Yugoslavia is the still unresolved economic struggle between various regional tribal centers. In the wish for national unity, [the party] will fight against each powerful and hegemonistic centralization and for the self-determination of the working people with full internal freedoms. . . . For the minorities . . . the IWPY demands full political and cultural freedoms.[20]

The reference to "tribal disputes" inferentially reasserted the proposition that the Yugoslavs constituted a single nation. And a "self-determination" linked to "national unity," with no reference to secession, could not constitute the fulfillment of self-determination in the Leninist sense for either "the tribes" or the "national minorities." It is not surprising, therefore, that in May 1923 the Comintern felt compelled to castigate the YCP for its deviation on the national question. A letter addressed to the YCP insisted that the party endorse "absolute self-determination of nationalities even to the point of actual separation from the Yugoslav state."[21]

Taken at face value, and given the fact that the dominant ethnic element accounted for less than half of the total population (in sharp contrast to the cases of Vietnam and China), the Comintern's position, in effect, was a demand that the YCP support the eradication of its state as a recognized entity. This was more than the leadership of the YCP was then willing to grant. At the Third Plenum of the Executive Committee of the Comintern held in June 1923, the Yugoslav delegate replied to criticism of the YCP's position on the national question as follows:

> The Yugoslav party is energetically fighting both against the Serbian hegemony and against the chauvinism of the Slovenian and Croatian bourgeoisie . . . [O]ur slogans in the nationality question must be against the Serbian bourgeoisie, for revision of the constitution and for the rights to self-determination of all nations and tribes. . . . [22]

There were evidently those in the YCP who still hoped that the paying of lip service to a purely abstract concept of self-determination, devoid of any hint of a right of secession, would constitute a sufficient facade of Marxist-Leninist conformity behind which the party could persevere in its policy of preserving Yugoslavia as the single unit over which it aspired ultimately to assume power. But the May directive of the Comintern, with its explicit command to endorse publicly the right of separatism, made it highly doubtful whether Soviet displeasure could henceforth be so easily sidestepped. It is therefore not surprising that many of the YCP's leaders now thought it wise to embrace the Comintern's position.

With the directive from the Comintern, the national question had become a major issue in the internal power struggles of the YCP. A leftist and a rightist faction had been maneuvering for supremacy since at least April 1921, but the national question had not been a matter of contention between them.[23] Now, however, the left faction embraced the Comintern's position, and the national question became an ideological battlefield.[24] Meanwhile, the rightists, though maintaining solid ranks against the leftist position, actually supported two somewhat different perceptions of the issue. One faction, whose chief spokesman was Zivota Milojkovic, remained loyal to the party's early stand which held that the Serbs, Croats, and Slovenes were one people. Moreover, even with regard to non-Slavic peoples, Milojkovic was an adherent of a "give-no-quarter" philosophy, holding that nationalism was to be fought wherever and whenever met. The more popular position among rightists, however, was that enunciated by Sima Markovic. Although as late as 1922 he too had accepted Milojkovic's position that Serbs, Croats, and Slovenes were merely three branches of a single people, a book, which was published by him in September 1923, now acknowledged them to constitute three different distinct nations.[25] But the matter, in any case, was not important in Markovic's view of things: "As far as our position is concerned, it is altogether the same whether the Serbs, Croats, and Slovenes are three 'tribes' of one nation or three nations."[26] There was really no mass support for the dismemberment of the state, according to Markovic.[27] Nor was federation necessary. What little ethnic discord there was, was traceable to the hegemonistic policies of the Serbian bourgeoisie and could be assuaged by provincial autonomy coupled with political and economic reform. National antagonisms could, of course, only be finally obliterated under socialism, and within a union of Balkan peoples. But autonomy and reform could at the present stage lessen national tensions and avoid separatist tendencies, thereby making it possible for the proletariat to settle their struggle with the bourgeoisie within the overriding context of a Yugoslav state. Moreover, the various "petit bourgeois" national movements would prove unreliable allies, who would impede, not aid, the proletarian revolution. In Rosa Luxembourg fashion, Markovic held that nationalism and proletarian internationalism simply could not and did not mix. In sum, flirting with nationalist movements should be viewed as unnecessary, unproductive, and dangerous.

Such a stand was hardly consonant with the Comintern's directive to exploit all national divisions by endorsing the right of secession.[28] The difference in the two positions was highlighted at the Third Conference of the YCP held in December 1923. The leftists took advantage of a temporary period of domination to push through a resolution recognizing the right of national self-determination, including the right of secession.[29] They affixed the usual addendum that recognition of the right of secession "does not assert that secession is always necessary." However, after referring to Markovic's contention that autonomy would alleviate national dissension as constituting "constitutional revision," the resolution insisted that such constitutional revision cannot be equated with self-determination, but is, in fact, "a renunciation of that right."[30] Describing this 1923 resolution, Tito would later note that "at this conference a stand of principle, basically a correct one, was taken on the national question with the point of view adopted that peoples have a right to self-determination up to the point of secession." However, he would also hasten to add that "this stand was adopted only by the 'left' and not by the 'right' in the leadership of the CPY."[31]

The debate found its way to the Fifth Congress of the Communist International which was held between June 17 and July 8, 1924. This was the congress at which parties in general were sharply criticized for failing to carry out "the resolute and constant advocacy by Communists of the right of national self-determination (secession and the formation of an independent State)."[32] The YCP was singled out for particular censure. Representatives of the party heard themselves reprimanded in a lengthy speech by D. Z. Manuilsky on June 24, 1924:

> The many mistakes made by the various sections of the Comintern in connexion [sic] with this question are due to the fact that many of our comrades are not yet rid of social democratic ideology. These mistakes can be said to be of four fundamental types, all of which are survivals of the attitude of some Yugoslav comrades, especially of Comrades Markovic and Miliokovic [sic], who are now in prison. . . . He [Comrade Milojkovic] asserts that in Yugoslavia there are no nations, but only linguistic differentiations. In his punphlet [sic], *National Question in the Light of Marxism*, and in a number of articles published in the organ of the Yugoslav Communist Party, *Radnik*, Comrade Markovic brings forward, as a practical slogan for the Communist Party, the fight for the revision of the constitution, that is to say, he placed the whole question of national self-determination on a constitutional basis. . . .
>
> At the same time there is in Macedonia a strong national movement for the re-establishment of an independent State. What is Comrade Markovic's attitude to this national movement? In his articles he expressed the opinion that the Macedonian question is not by any means a Balkan but a European problem, which cannot therefore be finally solved before a victory of the European proletariat over the bourgeoisie has been achieved. If the question is put in this way, what will be the result? Only a passive

attitude of the Communist Party to one of the most burning questions which is agitating the various Balkan nationalities at present. A careful study of the situation will show you that the origin of this kind of view is to be sought in the Second International. Markovic holds the view that the proletariat must accept the bourgeois State such as it has been created by a series of wars and violations.

In an apparent allusion to Markovic's contention that there was little support within Yugoslavia for national movements, Manuilsky went on to note that it was not enough to take national movements as one found them. The purpose of Leninist national policy was to fan national proclivities to a revolutionary heat.

I know that in the commission on the national question that will be formed at this Fifth Congress we shall be able to find those practical solutions that will stimulate the national movements in different countries and impart to them a revolutionary character. The time for declarations of a general character has passed; we now have a period for creative revolutionary work in the colonies and among national minorities. If we fulfill these tasks we will have created half the chances for the success of the international revolution to which we are devoted and which is guarded for the workers of the world by the Communist International.[33]

The Fifth Congress elected not to let the matter drop with just this oral reprimand. A formal, sharply worded resolution dealt exclusively with Yugoslavia. It noted that "the Yugoslav Communist Party must conduct a resolute and consistent struggle for the right of the oppressed nationalities to self-determination, up to political secession . . . in the form of separating Croatia, Slovenia and Macedonia from Yugoslavia and creating independent republics of them." The party "can and must" support the nationalities' demands for cultural and political autonomy, but it "must unfailingly emphasize that these are half-measures and try to extend each separate demand. The basic slogan must be the demand for the formation of a Balkan Federation of Workers' and Peasants' Republics." Milojkovic was singled out for particular censure, it being noted that "the opinion of Milojkovic, that the Communist Party must fight equally hard against any nationalism whatever, is not only opportunist, but objectively plays into the hands of Great Serb bourgeois nationalist policy."[34] As a further means of assuring compliance with the Comintern's policy on the national question, the Fifth Congress, in a separate resolution dealing with Macedonia and Thrace, downgraded the role of the individual Communist parties (most particularly those of Greece and Yugoslavia) relative to the BCF: "The Balkan Communist Federation is entrusted with the unification of leadership of the activities of the Communist Parties of the separate Balkan countries in regard to national questions, and particularly the Macedonian and Thracian questions."[35]

The attack against the positions of Milojkovic and Markovic was to be unrelenting. Hardly had the Fifth Congress dissolved, when a salvo was fired by the newly strengthened Balkan Communist Federation at a meeting apparently hurriedly convened for just this purpose. Here is an official account by a participant as reported in a Communist publication (*International Press Correspondence*) of August 7, 1924:

> The Conference declared that the position in the Balkans is not only revolutionary, but that the revolutionary crisis is reaching its acutest stage: . . . that the struggle in Croatia, Slavonia, Bosnia, and Macedonia, and especially the fight of the Croatian peasant masses against the hegemony of the Serbian bourgeoisie and against Serbian militarism is developing in the direction of an armed uprising; that the national movement of the Macedonian people is again reviving and assuming the form of an armed struggle. . . .
>
> The Communist Balkan Conference has also discussed very thoroughly the inner situation and the activity of the individual Communist Parties of the Balkan countries. It condemned in a most decided manner the right and liquidatory deviation of many leaders and groups in these parties, and especially the opportunist standpoint of Comrades Sima Markovic and J. Milanovic [Milojkovic?] in the Yugoslav Communist Party regarding the national question, which they regard merely as an ordinary constitutional question.[36]

Despite this multipronged attack, Markovic refused to submit, leading to a crisis now perceived by Stalin to be of sufficient gravity to merit his personal intervention. Stalin's speech, delivered before a commission of the Comintern which had been especially created to end the factionalism within the YCP, wasted no time with the usual preliminary courtesies.[37] It opened, "Comrades, I think Comrade Semich [Markovic] has not fully understood the essence of the Bolshevik presentation of the national question." Several specific errors were then noted: (1) the attempt to reduce the national question to a constitutional (read: nonrevolutionary) question; (2) the refusal to link the national question to the peasant question;[38] and (3) perceiving the issue in a purely Yugoslavian context and not relating it to the world revolution and the foreign policy of the Soviet Union. Stalin concluded this section of his speech by noting "that the question of the right of nations to self-determination should be regarded as an immediate and burning question."

Turning to what must be done to correct the errors, Stalin insisted that "it is imperative to include in the national [YCP] programme a special point on the right of nations to self-determination, including the right of secession." But he took particular pains to emphasize that the right of territorial autonomy should also be included for those peoples who do not secede.

> Those who think that such a contigency must be excluded are wrong. That is a mistake. Under certain circumstances, as a result of the victory of the Soviet revolution in Yugoslavia, it may well be that on the analogy of what occurred in Russia certain nationalities will not desire to secede.

Particularly when one remembers that the Soviet government had just forcibly returned to the fold most of those nations who had earlier seceded from the Russian Soviet state, it is evident that Stalin was telling the YCP that the promises that he demanded of the party need not be honored. To further ensure that this message was not overlooked, he returned to the same theme later in his speech:

> To avoid all misunderstanding, I must say that the *right* to secession must not be understood as an *obligation*, as a duty to secede. . . . Some comrades turn this right of secession into an obligation, and demand from the Croats, for instance, that they secede *at all costs*. This position is wrong, and must be rejected. We must not confuse a right with an obligation.[39]

Markovic's response to Stalin could only be construed as concessive. His demurrer to the effect that his statements had been misunderstood and taken out of context interpret better as a face-saving measure than as a counterargument. Stalin, however, appears to have been determined to undermine Markovic's credence forever, taking the trouble to again attack Markovic on the national question two months later, even though his second attack added little to the first.[40] Moreover, in the interim, the Comintern, in the most unambiguous manner, had ordered the YCP not just to condone but to generate national hostilities:

> [T]he entire Party must spread its propaganda and agitation to the utmost to convince the toiling masses of the oppressed nations of Yugoslavia that the destruction of the pan-Serb bourgeoisie is the only way towards the solution of the national question. Fear of inflaming national passions ought not to keep the Party from appealing with all its might to the masses on this most important question.[41]

In the face of this attack, Markovic and the right wing were forced to conform, joining the left wing of the party to support a resolution on the national question at the Third Congress, held in Vienna in June 1926. "Thus, the CPY as a whole finally took a correct stand of principle in connection with the national question," Tito would reminisce in 1948.[42] In 1948, however, Tito was also in favor of a federation with Bulgaria. It is therefore quite likely that his unconditional praise of the 1926 resolution was the source of some embarrassment in the post-1948 period when the federation scheme was scrapped, for in addition to declaring Yugoslavia a "multinational state" and insisting that "the Communist Party must energetically fight for the right of self-determination of all nations until [up to and including?] secession," the 1926 resolution had also declared its support for "a *Federal Workers'-Peasants' Republic in the Balkans,* since only the voluntary unity of the organized nations into workers'-peasants' states can bring about *the true solution of the national question.*"[43]

Achieving this ostensible consensus did not bring about an end to the intraparty, factional bickering. Though the national question ceased to be the battlefield, the contestants in the infighting continued to coincide with ethnic delineations, leading to a charge by the Comintern that the YCP had virtually divided into its national components.[44] In 1928, therefore, the Comintern determined that radical surgery was required. Upon its initiative, the YCP was denationalized by a purge of the leadership (both left and right) who were replaced, in the words of Paul Shoup, by "a new breed, trained from an early age in Moscow for revolutionary responsibilities, with very few ties in Yugoslavia, and little or no national perspectives to start with."[45]

Under its new leadership, the policies of the party, including its national policy, mirrored Soviet wishes of the moment. In the period from 1928 through 1934, Soviet policy toward the political regimes of the area remained ardently anti-status quo. While those regimes had long been perceived by Moscow as the artifices of the schemers of Versailles, the campaign to bring about their downfall was now made a matter of urgency. So far as the national policy of the YCP was concerned, this urgency manifested itself in support for the immediate secession of all non-Serbian peoples. At the party's Fourth Congress in November 1928, the newly entrenched leadership endorsed "the right of armed revolt against national oppression." It promised to fight "unconditionally and unreservedly for the independence of Croatia" and to "give full aid to all the mass actions leading to the creation of an independent Montenegro"; it invited "the working-class to fight with all its might for a united and independent Macedonia [and] for an independent and united Albania." It further recognized "the right of the Hungarian national minority in Vojvodina to secede."[46] Had the policy succeeded, Yugoslavia would have soon been dismembered.

It did not succeed, however. Armed revolt proved a dismal fiasco and was formally discarded in 1932. But in accordance with Comintern directions, the party continued until 1935 to call for the breakup of Yugoslavia into its numerous ethnic components. At the party's Fourth Conference, held on December 24–25, 1934, a resolution was passed which reiterated the party's dedication to "the right of self-determination up to secession for all the oppressed nationalities—the Croats, Slovenes, Macedonians, Montenegrins, etc." And in an effort to inflame opinion by raising the spectre of alien masters in the ethnic homeland, it called for the "expulsion of Serb occupiers, Serb troops, officials, and policemen, as well as Serb Cetniks, from Croatia, Slovenia, Dalmatia, Vojvodina, Bosnia, Montenegro, Macedonia, and Kosovo."[47]

A historical sketch of the YCP policy with regard to secessionism might therefore be broken down into four distinct periods: (1) from 1919 to 1923, a refusal to endorse secession; (2) from 1923 to 1926, periodic endorsement by the left wing, but continued rejection by the right wing; (3) from 1926 to 1928, endorsement by the entire party, but little or no attempt to convert it into a catalyst for action (in Soviet terminology, this might be described as propaganda without agitation);[48] and (4) from 1928 through 1935, the high-tide period, during which "Secession now!" became the party's rallying cry for all non-Serbian peoples.

The high tide of YCP support for secession was destined not to recede but to undergo instantaneous evaporation. As late as April 20, 1935, the Comintern would goad the YCP to increase its agitation for secession, complaining that the work of the party "within the national liberation movements must be far, far better."[49] But in August of the same year, and with no advance warning, the Executive Committee of the YCP would inform its membership that "the Congress of the Communist International has given a new tactical orientation," a most disarmingly innocent-sounding signal for a radical volte-face in basic strategy.[50] The Seventh Comintern Congress (July 25–August 20, 1935) had just called for a united front of all anti-Fascist forces. Recast in the new scenario as potentially useful ramparts against a Fascist *Drang nach Osten*, the states of Eastern Europe were henceforth to be nurtured rather than dismembered. Secession was to be shunned. This strategic flip-flop was accompanied by some verbal gymnastics as well:

> Remaining by its principled standpoint of self-determination of people with the right to secession, Communists take into consideration the present international situation and with the stipulation of the destruction of national inequality of rights, of the minimum guarantees of freedom of the Croatian and other peoples and of the consent of these peoples, do *not* declare for secession of that people from today's state organization—Yugoslavia.[51]

Freed of circumlocution, this resolution declared the national question solvable within the present bourgeois state, precisely the position for which Markovic had been berated by Stalin a decade earlier. A resolution of the following year (summer 1936) more openly acknowledged a turning-away from what the party itself described as "its principled standpoint of self-determination of the people with the right to secession," by noting that prior to the period of the united front, "the CPY understood and propagated the slogan of self-determination, including secession, in a completely sectarian manner. . . . Nothing was said about political territorial autonomy, for people who do not wish secession."[52] The thinly disguised suggestion was that the party had miscalculated national intentions: there was no popular desire for secession among the masses (again, a position held earlier by Markovic for which he had been heavily criticized). But if there was no prosecessionist sentiment then there was no point in stressing it in party publications and pronouncements. In short, the scene had been set for the virtual disappearance of the self-determination slogan. Its abrupt elimination from all official speeches and documents occurred in January 1937, and remained in effect until well after the Nazi-Soviet Pact of August 1939.[53] As in the cases of China and Vietnam during the same period, no formal renunciation of the principle of self-determination occurred. The phrase simply vanished. In a breathtakingly swift demonstration of substituting one diametrically opposed slogan for another, "secession" and "national liberation" were replaced by "we shall defend the [Yugoslav] fatherland."[54]

The switch in orientation from disunion to union was somewhat paradoxically accompanied by a decision to decentralize the formal structure of the YCP through the creation of Croatian and Slovenian wings. The possibility of such a development had been broached in 1934 and would seem to have been well suited to aid the YCP in accomplishing its goal at that time, namely, the fragmentation of Yugoslavia. But goals had radically altered, so that when actually initiated in 1937 the change in party structure was now expected to produce the opposite effect of promoting the state's stability. Admittedly, the new party structure had the real advantage of challenging an image of the YCP as a Serb-dominated organization. But the danger that a regional party, whose jurisdiction closely coincided with an ethnic homeland, might provide a focus for particularist, even nationalist aspirations soon manifested itself. Though the leadership of the newly created Croatian and Slovene parties obediently followed the YCP's lead in abstaining from all mention of self-determination, they manifested in other ways their displeasure with the party's unexpected metamorphosis from one demanding separation for (*inter alia*) Croats and Slovenes into one demanding loyalty to the Yugoslav state. Tension appears to have crystallized particularly about the time of Hitler's *Anschluss* with Austria (March 1938). The declaration, which was touched off by this event and which was approved by the YCP's new general secretary, Josip Tito, read in part:

> The anti-people's and hegemonistic regime of Stojadinovic is the greatest danger to the liberty of the peoples of Yugoslavia and to the independence of their country. It sows discord and prevents brotherly agreement among the peoples of Yugoslavia in these fatal hours. . . . In these difficult and fatal hours, we are addressing all democratic and patriotic citizens, irrespective of religion, nationality and party, not only the adherents of the National Agreement Block but all other patriotic forces of the Serbian, Croat, Slovene and other peoples, who . . . are willing to defend the peace and independence of the country.[55]

At this time, Croatia was the scene of substantial agitation for greater autonomy from Belgrade, and the leadership of the new Croatian Communist Party criticized the declaration of the parent organization for promoting the cause of Yugoslav unity at the expense of Croatian national aspirations. Tito replied in an open letter, charging the dissenters with "Trotskyism" and of "falling under the influence of national petty-bourgeois ideology."[56]

This period of running roughshod over national aspirations was cut short by the announcement of the Nazi-Soviet Non-Aggression Pact of August 1939. Yesterday's emotional rallying point, the Yugoslav fatherland, was no longer to be defended. Though the party was not instructed to call directly for the state's dissolution, the pacifistic, antimobilization, neutralist stance it was instructed to adopt was one designed to leave Yugoslavia defenseless.[57] Despite and in part because of the many shifts that had hitherto characterized its national policy, the YCP was unable to invent a stratagem for comfortably straddling this latest twist in Soviet policy. Vacillation and uncharacteristically guarded language prevailed. The response of the party to the so-called *Sporazum* of September 1939 is a case in point. Under the terms of the *Sporazum*, the Yugoslavian government had granted autonomy to Croatia. So as not to be perceived as opposing Croatian aspirations, the party's first response was positive, though not warm. But more indicative of the dilemma confronting a party which favors neither the strengthening nor dismembership of a regime was the proclamation of May 1, 1940, which harshly criticized the *Sporazum* while offering no hint of an alternative. To have recommended reversion to the pre-*Sporazum* status quo would have irritated Croatian sensibilities. To have refrained from criticism of the existing situation would have favored the state apparatus. So the party elected to drive wedges between Serb and Croat without offering any hint as to the course of action the party thought the Croatian masses should follow. Similarly, the party used the same proclamation to drive wedges between the Serbs and Croats on the one hand and the remaining peoples of Yugoslavia on the other: "Serbian and Croatian chauvinism is being fanned. And they are not paying any attention to the national rights of Montenegro, Macedonia, and Slovenia at all."[58] But the nature of these national rights and the methods by which they were to be secured were not suggested.

A greater insight into the strategic thinking of the leadership at this time is offered by Tito's speech before the Fifth Conference of the YCP (October 1940). Secession, the speech made clear, had no place whatsoever in Tito's future scheme of things. Indeed, the same separatist movements, which had been so ardently wooed prior to 1935, were now depicted as the catastrophic results of *rightist* errors by former YCP leaders. Holding the Soviet Union up as the model, Tito insisted that autonomy was the answer: national autonomy would permit the YCP to gain support of the people in order to carry out the social revolution; cultural autonomy would permit the ideological conversion of the masses from national particularism to, in Tito's words, "political uniformity."

> But our greatest task [over the past three years] has been to forge a solution to the chronic malady of Yugoslavia—the nationalities problem. For years the Party failed in this, as the bourgeois parliamentary parties had failed, as King Aleksander and his dictatorship had failed. The leaders of the Party in the twenties—Sima Markovic, Gorkic and their crowd—proved just as narrowly chauvinistic and pan-Serb in their outlook as the blackest reactionaries. So they failed to capture the leadership of the masses. They played into the hands of the nationalist extremes. They created Macek and Pavelic. They created I.M.R.O. and the Macedonian separatists. And all the time the answer was there, in their own hands, had they only known it; national autonomy, the condition for social revolution; diversity of national cultures—the condition for political uniformity. It needed the great teacher, Stalin himself, to point the way and vindicate the truth that the teaching of Marx and Lenin meant the liberation of the hitherto oppressed nationalities, no less than the liberation of the working classes. The Soviet Union became the model for the multinational state, the model for what Yugoslavia with its varied races must become. Never forget, comrades, that the Party which dares to bring this solution to Yugoslavia must become its master. And never forget that we, and we alone, have this solution.[59]

Had the purged Markovic been present, he would have undoubtedly found it a bit droll to hear himself criticized in a speech denigrating separatism and extolling autonomy. As mentioned earlier, he had been attacked by Stalin and the Comintern for the precise stand now defended by Tito. The critical reference to Gorkic is also perplexing, for certainly Tito and his audience were aware that Gorkic's tenure as General Secretary (1932–1937) had been almost equally divided between the period in which the party, under Moscow's direction, pressed for immediate secession by national groups and the period of the united front when, again under Moscow's directives, it pressed for unity. Objectively then, an attack on Gorkic was an attack upon both a policy of secession and one of state preservation. And it was in either case an attack upon Soviet directives. Yet, Stalin is credited with "pointing the way," and the Soviet Union is held out as "the model" for solving Yugoslavia's national question.

The contradictions in Tito's speech of 1940 were therefore numerous, and he would later conveniently forget that he had even given such an address. We have noted, for example, that in 1948 he would reflect that the YCP had come to take a correct stand on the question by 1926.[60] Elsewhere in his 1948 report, in the course of reviewing the events of 1921 through 1928, he would conclude that "after discussions and struggles against the views of Sima Markovic a correct stand was taken on the national question, with the help of the Comintern and comrade Stalin." Tito's 1948 speech implied that once the party had succeeded during the late 1920s in taking a correct position upon the national question, it never strayed from it. He thus chose to overlook both the period of the united front and his own post-united front speech of 1940 in which he criticized all hitherto national policy. At least at the time of his 1940 speech, Tito had no sympathy for the 1928–1935 policy of supporting secession. Nor had he harbored any sympathy for the notion of Yugoslavia per se. As he emphasized in his 1940 speech:

> We are not interested in the bourgeois ideal of a Fatherland to be defended, but of a world revolution to be carried through. Remember this. The greatest revolution for the Yugoslav State— a revolution which I am confident the mass of the people will accept—will be a revolution which brings national equality to Serbs, Croats, Slovenes, Macedonians, Montenegrins. And that, comrades, will in turn make possible the greater social revolution which we plan and of which the Soviet Union is our glorious model.

Secession simply would not be reintroduced into the party's platform. The promise of autonomy would suffice to gain the necessary support of the masses.

The resolution on the national question, which was shepherded through the Fifth Conference by Tito and which, unlike his speech, was designed for public consumption, was substantially less explicit with regard to repudiating secession. The general thrust of the message to the various non-Serbian peoples was an expression of sympathy for the trampling upon their national rights by the Serbs, coupled with a warning to beware of Fascists bearing gifts. But solutions were phrased in a most hazy manner. Thus it was noted that while the party supported "self-rule" for the Macedonians to protect them "against oppression by the Serbian bourgeoisie," it must at the same time accomplish the "unmasking of the Italian and Bulgarian imperialists and their agents who also want to put the Macedonian people under their yoke by means of demagogic promises." "Self-rule" (*samoodred jenje*) was also promised to the Montenegrins who, along with the Albanians, had to be protected both from the Serbian bourgeoisie and from the Italians who were trying to exploit their national discontent "by means of various promises." The German, Hungarian, and Rumanian minorities should be supported in their just struggle, but must be warned that they cannot "solve the national question in these and other regions with the help of an imperialist, conquering war." Autonomy or some analogous form of government should be introduced in Bosnia. Serbs, Croats, and Slovenes were platitudinously promised a "real solution of the national question."[61] The resolution was thus designed to hold the national groups together, temporarily alleviating any secessionist impulse by promising to each group a judicious, if purposefully nebulous, solution to their national question, a solution which could be achieved only after the current imperialist threat had receded in the face of the united resistance of all the national groups.

This temporizing stance, which had been forced upon the YCP by the embarrassing Soviet-Fascist accord, was not one that in the normal course of events would be expected to win many converts to the party. Yet in retrospect, this recourse to ambiguity was to prove an incomparable stroke of good fortune. Within six months of the resolution's passage at the Fifth Conference, Yugoslavia was to be invaded (April 1941), and from the ensuing occupation the YCP was to emerge as the ruling force of postwar Yugoslavia. A key element in bringing about this remarkable turn of fortune was the ability of the YCP to avoid identification either with the fragmentation of Yugoslavia or with the notion of the prewar Yugoslavian state. The policy of the party during 1939–1940 had been worded in a sufficiently enigmatic manner that it was able to meet these negative requirements. Had this transitional period not occurred, had the party entered upon World War II directly from either the 1928–1935 period during which it had been calling for immediate dismemberment of the state or if it had proceeded directly into the war from the 1935–1939 period during which it had been calling for the downgrading of national aspirations in the name of defense of the fatherland, the party's ability to attract converts during the occupation would have been substantially lessened.

In order to probe the manner in which its period of equivocation just prior to Axis occupation aided the YCP's march to power, it is instructive to recall that the party's earlier, less obscure positions had not resulted in any startling groundswell of popularity among the masses. The radical swings which had occurred in that policy over the years were both a partial acknowledgment of that failure and a contributing element to it.[62] Those who might sympathize with the party in one period because of its stand on the national question would perforce be repelled in another. And, at least in the case of the better informed, the party's history of extreme vacillation on the national question offered excellent cause, even for those who shared the YCP's national outlook of the moment, to suspect its sincerity on the issue. A more significant factor for the party's failure to exploit the national question, however, was that regardless of where the YCP had elected to stand, there were alternative, non-Communist organizations already there. On the one hand, the Communists had been preempted from staking out a monopolistic position with regard to the national aspirations of specific national groups, such as the Croats who could (and did) turn to their own nationalistic Peasant Party or the Macedonians who could rally around IMRO. On the other hand, there had been groups who, though in opposition to the government, had shared the government's preference for a single, integrated society. (The Socialists, for example, had continued to espouse the myth that the Yugoslavs constituted a single nation.)

Neither the notion of an integrated Yugoslavia nor that of immediate fragmentation proved equal to the demands posed by the Axis invasion. An integrated Yugoslavia had long been viewed by the more articulate members of the non-Serbian peoples as a euphemism for Serbian hegemony. In the interval since 1918, an intuitive sense of a distinctive Croatian, Macedonian, or Slovene national identity had infected a sufficient number of individuals so as to render anachronistic the idea of a single Yugoslav people. The government had acknowledged as much when it accorded autonomous status to the Croats during 1939. Any remaining claim antebellum Yugoslavia had upon the loyalties of the non-Serbian peoples suffered a further severe setback in 1941 as a result of the pathetically feeble resistance offered to the invading Germans.

But immediate fragmentation also failed to arouse mass support. Following its easy victory, the Axis powers (1) divided the territory into three "independent" states (Croatia, Montenegro, and Serbia); (2) annexed and divided Slovenia; and (3) ceded Macedonia to Bulgaria, the Albanian district to Albania, and the Hungarian district to Hungary. The division was not one designed to enchant Serbs and Slovenes, and its attractiveness to Croatians and Montenegrins would be severely compromised by the realization that the new puppet states were tainted by Fascist collaborationism.[63] Indeed, the German decision to dissect Yugoslavia proved a boon to the YCP, because only the Communists entered this period in possession of a secret, underground structure organized on a country-wide basis. It was therefore uniquely positioned to conduct effectively coordinated guerrilla resistance against the Germans throughout Yugoslavia. Their principal rivals, the Chetniks, led by Mihailovic, were essentially a Serbian group, distrusted by non-Serbs as aspiring to reintroduce Serbian hegemony, and thus restricted in their operations to areas populated by Serbs.[64]

The German invasion therefore fulfilled a precondition for the success of the YCP by giving rise to a most unhappy and unacceptable situation that the Communists were best prepared to counter.[65] Local ethnonational antagonisms would be temporarily shelved only if faced with a more ominous, more alien, common threat. And the Nazis represented ideal typecasting. They thus filled the fortuitous but indispensable role for the YCP that the Japanese had for the Chinese Communists and that the Japanese, French, and Americans had for the Vietnamese movement. Nor do the similarities between these Communist movements end there. In nurturing its image as the only force which was capable and willing to engage the alien, the YCP was aided by Mihailovic's unwillingness to commit his forces against the Germans, just as the Chinese Communists had been aided by the reluctance of Chiang to move against the Japanese forces prior to 1936. Moreover, in order to maximize their appeal to the masses, the YCP leaders, following the same pattern as their Chinese and Vietnamese counterparts, were careful to play down their relationship to the Marxist movement, stressing instead their leadership of the popular movement against the alien presence. Thus the resistance became "the Sacred National Liberation War," and a similar rubric was applied to the guerrilla forces:

> Partisan detachments are called National Liberation Partisan Detachments because they are not the fighting formations of any

political party or group—not even the Communist Party, in this concrete case, though communists are fighting in their front ranks—but they are the fighting detachments of the peoples of Yugoslavia in which all patriots capable of armed struggle against the invader should participate, regardless of their political convictions.[66]

While avoiding too close an association with international Marxism-Leninism, the YCP also took pains to avoid too close an association with the idea of Yugoslavia. Such an aloof stance was essential if the party were not to risk being labeled as Serbian chauvinists. The premeditated tendency to limit or avoid references to Yugoslavia can be seen in the two most heavily promoted slogans of the war, "Brotherhood and Unity!" and "Death to Fascism, Liberty to the People!" Abstractions, such as *brotherhood* and *the people*, are at least as apt to conjure forth images of one's own nation as to conjure forth images of the multiethnic community that shares one citizenship. This is even more true of the term *national* as it appeared in "the Sacred National War of Liberation" or in "National Liberation Partisan Detachments." Indeed, the term was quite appropriate, for national detachments were organized on ethnic, that is, national lines.[67]

It is doubtful that this stratagem caused much soul wrenching among the YCP leadership, for their actions during the first stage of the occupation illustrated a stark lack of ardor for the reestablishment of the Yugoslav state. In a memorable display of willingness to accommodate Moscow's policies, the party refrained from calling for resistance against the occupying forces of the state with whom Moscow was still joined in a non-aggression pact.[68] Such a call did not go out until after the Germans attacked the Soviet Union on June 22, 1941. Moreover, the proclamation then released was curiously devoid of conventional patriotic appeals. It was addressed to all who opposed fascism rather than to Yugoslavians. Moreover, far from being pitched to the defense of a Yugoslav fatherland, it seemed to ascribe the highest priority to the defense of the Soviet Union:

All you who are groaning under the invader's boot, you who love freedom and independence, who will not stand fascist slavery— know that the hour has come for your liberation from struggle for your liberty, under the leadership of the CPY. The struggle of the Soviet Union is your struggle as well for it is also fighting against your enemies, under whose yoke you are groaning. . . . If you love your freedom and independence, if you do not want to be foreign slaves, if you want to free yourselves from fascist slavery, help the righteous struggle of the great, peace-loving country of socialism, the Soviet Union, with all your means, unite all your forces against your oppressors, the fascist invaders, who enslaved and plundered your country. . . . Get ready quickly for the final and decisive fight, do not allow the precious blood of the heroic Soviet peoples to be shed without our participating in the struggle. . . . Mobilize all your forces against your country's being made a base for supplying the fascist rabble, which, like mad dogs, are attacking the Soviet Union, our dear socialist country, our hope and the beacon that all the toilers of the world are looking at with hope.[69]

In performing this not easy trick of eliciting common action without arousing adverse ethnic sensibilities though the triggering of prewar memories, one theme seized upon by the YCP was that of common Slavism. Though the time had long expired in which an appeal in the name of a single, South-Slav national identity could be expected to overpower the inkling of a separate Croatian, Macedonian, Serbian, or Slovene nationhood, the sense of shared Slavic roots was not totally without influence. On the one hand, the YCP could fan this sense of commonality by appealing to fear: from the beginning of the armed struggle, a recurring theme of the party's propaganda was that the Germans were embarked on a genocidal crusade against the South Slavs, and the party could buttress this accusation with references to traditional German disdain for Slavs, Hitler's personal comments on the topic, and, most poignantly, the brutal acts of the Nazi occupation forces. In a more positive vein, the theme of Slavic greatness and unity was propagated through the party-controlled press, radio, and popular song.[70]

In addition to stressing the bond linking the Slavic peoples of prewar Yugoslavia, the Slavic motif had, from the YCP's standpoint, the added advantage of reinforcing psychological ties to Mother Russia, "our dear socialist country." But in the debit column, cloaking the partisan movement with Slavic attire would decrease its attractiveness to the non-Slavic peoples. Albanians and Hungarians, already favorably predisposed toward the German and Italian forces as a result of being joined to the states of Albania and Hungary, respectively, could hardly be expected to be moved by exhortations in the name of Slavdom.[71] Indeed, as events during the war subsequently made tragically clear, appeals to a common Slavic heritage were even unable to assuage perceptibly the deep-seated hatreds among Slavic peoples.

With normal peacetime controls eradicated, the awesome depth of ethnic animosities within Yugoslavia was soon revealed. Though the World War II experience would in retrospect be officially described as an anti-Fascist struggle in which all of the national groups participated, it was, on balance, much more a civil war that pitted one national element against another. Atrocities were legion: hardly had Croatia been separated from the rest of Yugoslavia when Croatians began to practice large-scale violence against the Serbian minority within the new state. Not needing much provocation, Serbs retaliated in kind against Croats in Bosnia, Hercegovina, and elsewhere. Meanwhile, the Moslems (Slavs of the Islamic faith, who feel they constitute a separate people) were engaged in genocidal attacks against Serbs and Montenegrins, as were the Albanians.[72]

To design a united front so that it could transcend the "primal hatreds" (the phrase used by Djilas) would tax any elite's ingenuity. In fact, the YCP did not prove very successful in doing so. The number of its active sympathizers remained dangerously thin throughout the decisive period of the war. In each region of the country, Tito's united front either encountered passivity bred of fear, or found itself competing for the people's loyalty with local revolutionary forces and/or the government. For example, although Tito's movement realized greater success within Serbia than elsewhere, most of the people therein were too awed by German might to engage in physical acts of resistance. Those who were willing were divided in their loyalties to the partisans, the Chetniks, the German-installed government of Serbia, and the government-in-exile in London. As a result, both the partisans and the Chetniks found that the people "didn't flock into their embattled ranks."[73]

The principal point, however, is not the absolute number of supporters attracted by Tito's movement, but the fact that the movement was the most successful in developing a viable organization throughout diverse segments of Yugoslavia. By contrast, the government-in-exile, popularly identified with the Serb-dominated system of the prewar period, had little support outside of Serbia. So too, the Axis-approved governments of Croatia, Montenegro, and Serbia could exert no influence beyond their particular ethnic homeland. The same held true for movements, such as the Chetniks, who were popularly identified with a single ethnic group. To a significant degree, then, the role of a transregional, transethnic organization fell by default to Tito and his colleagues. Moreover, quite paradoxically, the ethnic animosities that divided the peoples of Yugoslavia aided Tito's efforts to create a country-wide movement. As atrocities mounted, beleaguered minorities became a major source of recruits who gravitated to the partisans for protection, since the YCP, at least in theory, stood above ethnic strife, preaching peace among the various national groups in order to pursue the struggle against the common enemy.[74] In the case of Croatia, for example, well over half of the movement's recruits were members of the Serbian minority.[75]

Its image and role as the coordinator of the resistance to the Fascist invaders were therefore essential to the YCP's success. And the YCP leadership did not lose sight of the fact that its maximum role could only be as the coordinator of the resistance offered by several nations rather than as the vanguard of a united people. Indeed, events throughout the war were such as to preclude any possibility of the party being lulled into neglecting the reality of the national divisions and antagonisms that underlay the fragile relationship. Although the party emphasizes in retrospect its role against the Axis occupiers, the memoirs of a member of its wartime inner circle document that the partisans were more often engaged in fighting Serbs (primarily but not always Chetniks), Albanians, Moslems, or what they termed "separatist" Croats and Montenegrins.[76] And at least one writer has reported that a larger number of lives were lost in interethnic, civil strife than were lost in struggle against the Axis forces.[77] Some measure of how deep and potentially ferocious and divisive the party viewed these antagonisms is offered by "the basic line" of the party during the liberation struggle as recorded by Tito: "The members of the Party and partisans must use propaganda and the spoken word to make the mutual slaughter of the peoples of Yugoslavia on a chauvinistic basis impossible."[78] Similarly, a wartime directive to the partisan forces within Bosnia-Hercegovina asserted that "it will continue to be the *most important task* of Communists and Partisans—to block completely the criminal plans of the invaders . . . to fan national hatred and invite mutual extermination by the Serbian, Moslem, and Croatian populations."[79]

The image of the united front as one divorced from and transcending the special interests of any particular ethnic element was essential if the partisans were to maintain an effective guerrilla capability throughout all sections of the country. And, no less than those other Marxist-Leninist movements whose histories we have sketched, the Yugoslav Communist Party appreciated the essentiality of local support in a guerrilla struggle. Thus the sea-and-fish metaphor employed by Chinese and Vietnamese leaders was also articulated by a close associate of Tito: "The people are the water. The Partisan is a fish. A fish cannot live without water. That goes for us too."[80]

Given both the indispensability of local support and the intractability of the intergroup enmity, which appeals to brotherhood and common Slavdom might reduce but certainly not obliterate, the party pitched its propaganda in terms of the identity and aspirations of the individual groups. Propaganda was quite regularly addressed to Croat, Serb, or Slovene rather than to Yugoslavians. Thus, *Borba* on November 15, 1941 heralded its editorial "Serbia [not Yugoslavia] shall be free," and it further cited a martyr just before death at the hands of the Germans: "Kill you cursed dogs, but Serbia shall nevertheless be free!" Similarly, a member of the Central Committee of the YCP was reported to have faced death in his native Slovenia on May 21, 1942 with the words: "I know that by killing me they will not kill the freedom of the Slovene people. We will win through to liberty, however fierce the enemy's rage may become."[81] Tito, too, customarily addressed his remarks to national groups rather than to Yugoslavians. Even in a speech made after the outcome of the war was no longer in doubt, Tito would repetitively address himself to "our nations" or to "the nations of Yugoslavia," rather than to Yugoslavians per se. At one point he would note: "It is the duty of every decent Serb, Croat, Slovene, Moslem, Montenegrin, Macedonian, etc. to give all he has in this hard and bloody struggle—the justest fight in the history of our nations."[82] Perhaps more surprisingly, in earlier remarks made to ostensibly Communist fighting forces, he spoke as though his audience were composed of members of national groups motivated by ethnically inspired goals, rather than Marxist-Leninists inspired by proletarian internationalism:

Here in Bosnia, you men of Serbia and Montenegro, are fighting all enemies, and will continue to do so for this is at the same time a struggle for the freedom of the Serbian and Montenegrin people. And tomorrow, when the time comes—and I assure you, comrades, that time is not far off—you will march again into Serbia, Montenegro . . . to liberate your people.[83]

A most enlightening example of the perils and difficulties associated with such tightrope walking is offered in a report of August 8, 1943 by Svetozar Vukmanovic (alias Tempo), the YCP's major representative within Macedonia. In his letter to the party's Central Committee, he recounted how the propaganda of the Communist movement there had been appealing to Macedonian sentiment for independent statehood without reference to a Yugoslavia. This was "a tremendous political mistake in that in it Macedonia was treated outside the framework of Yugoslavia."[84] Tempo felt such an orientation might prove disastrous to the long-term interests of the YCP, so he insisted upon a change. But how far could propaganda go toward promoting common Yugoslavism and still attract broad support among the Macedonians? After much wrangling, agreement was reached on the deceptively innocuous-sounding "slogan of the liberation and unification of the Macedonian people in brotherly cooperation with all the Yugoslav people."[85] Thus a phrase that at the time would ring like little more than a passing tribute to a wartime alliance could later be vested with great significance.

The wartime propaganda therefore furnishes evidence that the YCP leadership understood that only as members of distinct nations, not as fellow Yugoslavians, were non-Communists apt to join the war of liberation under the party's leadership; that the only strategically significant bond that linked members of different nationalities, other than the limited one of shared Slavism, was that of common enemies; and that mobilizing the energies of the people therefore required an appeal to national identity and national aspirations.[86] In order to ensure broad receptivity to this appeal, it is not at all surprising that the party should reintroduce the Leninist concept of self-determination into its program, from which it had been so summarily exorcized in January, 1937, during the period of the united front.[87]

As we have noted, many of the propagandistic stories that appeared in the party press throughout the war contained references to a future free Serbia, a free Slovenia, etc., so it could well be argued that (in content if not in form) the party had, upon the inception of the liberation struggle, resorted immediately to its 1926–1937 practice of promising national self-determination, including secession. Moreover, the program of the National Liberation Front of Slovena (a united front organization dominated by members of the Slovenian wing of the YCP), which was announced on June 22, 1941, declared its commitment to the "right of self-determination, including the right to secession and uniting with other people!", adding "Whosoever does not expressly recognize this right to the Slovenes and other peoples in its entirety, that [individual] is only being deceived when he claims that he fights against *imperialism* regardless of how much he preaches phrases."[88] About this same time (August 1941), the Comintern signaled the return of self-determination to official favor when, in the course of taking the Yugoslav side in a dispute between the Bulgarian and Yugoslavian Communist parties over Macedonia, it insisted that both parties must maintain a clear perspective on the self-determination of the Macedonian people.[89] Nevertheless, the central apparatus of the YCP does not appear formally to have reinstated use of the term until late 1942.

The occasion of the term's reintroduction was an article by Tito ("The National Question in the Light of the People's Liberation War") which first appeared in the December 1942 issue of the party publication, *Proleter*.[90] A eulogistic biography of Tito, published within Yugoslavia well after the war, notes that "the article was of great theoretic importance, as well as of practical and political significance in solving the national question in Yugoslavia."[91]

A scrutiny of the article hardly substantiates a claim to "theoretic importance." Indeed, in keeping with the party's precarious policy of walking the tightrope between unity and national particularism, the article is a study in ambiguities and shadowy promises. Though it refers numerous times to the coming freedom and liberation of the various national groups, it is never quite clear whether Tito is referring to postwar independence or merely to freedom and liberation from German occupation. Even while decrying deception, his words appear to have been selected carefully so that those who were so inclined would see in them the promise of independence, while the words themselves remained amenable to a quite different interpretation at some later date:

> The expression "National Liberation Struggle" would be only a phrase, even a deceit, if it would not have both general Yugoslav meaning and national meaning for each particular people, that is, if it would not mean in addition to the liberation of Yugoslavia, the simultaneous liberation of the Croats, Slovenes, Serbs, Macedonians, Albanians, Moslems, etc., if the National Liberation Struggle would not have had as its substance to really bring freedom, equality and brotherhood to all Yugoslav people. This is precisely the essence of the Liberation struggle. . . . It would not be permissible to achieve *full liberation of each people* if each of them would not have engaged in the struggle for the common victory of all Yugoslav peoples over all the enemies of the peoples. [Emphasis added.]

Despite this ambiguity and despite the many vacillations and convolutions that had hitherto characterized the party's stand on the national question, Tito now described the YCP as having been, from its very inception, the unswerving champion of self-determination. His version of the YCP's history made the party appear to be a one-issue organization; it was solely for defense of national rights that party members had been tyrannized.

> Loyal to its principle that each people has the right of self-determination, the Communist Party fought against such national policy of the Great Serbian Hegemonists during the whole period of the fight for survival of Yugoslavia. The Communist Party of Yugoslavia resisted in a most resolute way the oppression of the Croats, Slovenes, Macedonians, Montenegrins, Albanians and others. Just for that reason the Great Serbian Hegemony bourgeoisie was furious with the Communist Party, for that reason for twenty-two years Yugoslav jails were filled with our best Communist militants.

Referring later in the article to "the same spotless flag carried by the Communist Party since the beginning of Yugoslavia in the uncompromised struggle for national freedom and equality of all our people," Tito continued, "The Communist Party has never renounced nor will it ever renounce the principle laid down by our great teachers, Marx, Engels and Lenin, the principle that each nation has the right to self-determination, including separation." Here was certainly an unequivocal statement, but Tito hastened to add:

> But at the same time the Communist Party of Yugoslavia will never allow and will fight against abusing that right by the enemies of the people, who want to bring to the people medieval darkness and colonial slavery instead of freedom and independence, which is the case with Pavelich's "independent" Croatia.
>
> The Communist Party of Yugoslavia will continue to fight for a brotherly, free, equal community of all nations of Yugoslavia. It will equally fight against the Great Serbian Hegemony, which tends to continue to oppress the Yugoslav people, and against all those who try to arouse dissent and to interfere with brotherly accord in the interest of some imperialist power.

What significance can one ascribe to an unequivocal endorsement of "the principle that each nation has the right to self-determination, including separation," if the party will "never allow" this right to be exercised by the forces of "medieval darkness," the more so when the party reserves to itself the exclusive right to differentiate between the forces of darkness and those of light?

The nebulosity with which the future of the individual nations was depicted reached its zenith with the article's concluding paragraph:

> The question of Macedonia, the question of Kossovo, and Metohia, the question of Montenegro, of Croatia, of Slovenia, of Bosnia and Herzegovina, will all be easily solved to everybody's satisfaction only if it is solved by the people themselves, if the people themselves take gun in hand and join in this present National Liberation Struggle.

The ambiguity was quite purposeful. Only a few months earlier, Tito had pointed out that a program capable of appealing to all nationalists was essential at this juncture. He brushed aside talk of specific postwar developments as incompatible with that need:

> But today is not the time to talk about the postwar period. We are now in the midst of the People's Liberation Struggle. For all of us, irrespective of religion, class, or creed—that is the main and most urgent task.
>
> It is our duty to rally to our ranks *all those who love their people*. This, in turn, makes it incumbent on us to adopt a broad and flexible approach.[92]

In 1942, with the outcome of the war and the future of his movement still very much in doubt, Tito was therefore quite cautious on the national question, refusing to hint at his true postwar plans for the various national groups. But by the end of 1943, Allied troops were engaging the Germans in nearby Italy and the Nazi rollback on the Soviet front had begun. Tito's position on the national question now swiftly emerged from the shadows. As Tito described the situation:

> The allies had disembarked in Italy and Italy had capitulated. The heroic Red Army was chasing the German fascist hordes further and further over its boundaries without a stop. Hitler's defeat in the near future was inevitable. In that situation, it was necessary to see to it that the attainments of the National Liberation Struggle were made secure. It was already time to think of the creation of the first state organ as the highest authority in the country. The second meeting of the Anti-Fascist Council

of the National Liberation of Yugoslavia was convened on November 29, 1943.[93]

At this YCP-directed conference, it was declared that the peoples of Yugoslavia had unmistakably proven by their collective resistance during the war that they wished to create an "indissoluble" union. This declaration was remarkably dissimilar from the resolution that had been adopted at the first meeting of the Anti-Fascist Council of National Liberation only a year before (November–December 1942). The earlier resolution had made no reference to a united Yugoslavia but, with the customary ambiguity that had marked wartime party statements on the national question, gave the appearance of promising that each group's future would be determined in accordance with the group's own wishes: "The National Liberation Movement fully recognizes the national rights of Croatia, Slovenia, Serbia, Macedonia and all other regions. It is a movement which is as much Croatian, as it is Slovene and Serbian. It guarantees that the national rights of all the peoples of Jugoslavia will be preserved."[94] But in November 1943, with the end of the war a momentary possibility, visions of national independence no longer had any place in the party's propaganda. And yet, in an ingenious bit of sophistry, self-determination, including the right of secession, was invoked as the basis for this *fait accompli*.

On the basis of the right of all nations to self-determination, including the union with or secession from other nations, and in accordance with the true will of all the nations of Yugoslavia, tested during three years of common national struggle for liberation which has cemented the indissoluble fraternity of all the people of Yugoslavia, the Anti-Fascist Council of National Liberation of Yugoslavia passes the following decisions:

1. The peoples of Yugoslavia do not recognize and never have recognized the partition of Yugoslavia by Fascist imperialists, but have proved in the common armed struggle their firm will to remain united in Yugoslavia.[95]

A more accurate appraisal of the occupation period might well have read that "the nations of Yugoslavia have proved by their propensity to engage in interethnic, genocidal conflict with their neighbors, their firm will to achieve independent statehood." Be that as it may, here is a document, unlike Tito's article of 1942, that could lay claim to breaking new ground in the theory of national self-determination. On the one hand, it advanced the proposition that the Communist party had the power to determine when and how self-determination had been exercised. There was simply no need to hold a plebiscite or otherwise try to determine public opinion on the issue. A proper exercise of the right was whatever the party said it was. The 1943 declaration itself was to offer an illustration of the arbitrariness of such a standard. Though the declaration maintained that the right of self-determination had already been exercised, the official position later became that the people exercised that right only in the course of adopting and carrying out the declaration. Here is the official position as set forth in 1967:

> In adopting and implementing the decisions of the Second Session of A.C.P.L.Y., the peoples of Yugoslavia were actually exercising the right of self-determination, including the right of secession, in voluntarily resolving to create again a common Yugoslav State—on new, democratic and federative foundations, however.[96]

Despite the differences in these claims concerning when and how self-determination had been exercised, their important common element was the party's assertion that the exercise of the right had already taken place. Whether or not the people were aware at the time that they had been exercising that right was immaterial.[97] This *ex post facto* approach to a solution of the national question might be termed *retroactive self-determination.*

Yet another illustration of the retroactive device as applied to self-determination appeared in Tito's address to the 1943 meeting of the Anti-Fascist Council. At the very time he was prepared to inform the peoples of Yugoslavia that independent statehood was not to be, he elected also to inform them that they had already achieved political independence.

> With the setting up of the Provincial Anti-Fascist Council of People's Liberation of Croatia, and before that the Slovene Liberation Front and its executive body, the principles of equality for all the nationalities of Yugoslavia began to be put into practice, and the age-old aspirations of the individual nationalities of Yugoslavia *to govern themselves* began to be realized.[98]

Thus, whether aware of it or not, the peoples had in the past both achieved and voluntarily surrendered political independence.

A second proposition of theoretic importance was inherent in the 1943 declaration's references to an "*indissoluble* fraternity" and to a "will to *remain* united." They made clear that self-determination constituted a single, irreversible action. Once exercised, the right had run its full course. This second proposition holding that the peoples of Yugoslavia had utilized their one opportunity to exercise self-determination became a cornerstone of postwar policy,[99] as witness Article I of the Constitution of the Federal People's Republic of Yugoslavia, 1946: "The Federal Republic of Yugoslavia is a federal people's state republican in form, a community of peoples equal in rights who, on the basis of the right to self-determination, including the right of separation, *have* expressed their will to live together in a federative state." This same note of an irreversible *fait accompli* is apparent also in the opening words of the 1974 constitution: "The peoples of Yugoslavia, *proceeding* from the right of every people to self-determination, including the right to secession . . . *have united* into a federal republic . . . and *have founded* . . . the Socialist Federal Republic of Yugoslavia."

A word of clarification on the reference to separation or secession in each of these constitutions is in order. Following the example of the Soviet Union, the YCP adopted the fiction of a federation of fully sovereign republics.[100] However, unlike the Soviet case, none of the Yugoslavian constitutions have contained any acknowledgment of a right of a republic to secede. Since any right *to exercise the right* of self-determination, including secession, had already occurred, *and with that occurrence had simultaneously expired*, there was no basis for such an inclusion. Thus immutability was added to retroactivity to form the YCP's post-1943 version of self-determination.[101]

Despite its remarkable lack of consistency, the strategy of the YCP with regard to the national question thus ultimately reaped success.[102] At one time or another, the party had stood on all sides of the question: denial that any national problem existed (1919–1926); advocacy of immediate secession (1928–1935); united-front support for the state (1935–1939); indefiniteness and indecisiveness (1939–1941); balancing separatist aspirations with immediate need for cooperative action (1941–1943); and a united Yugoslavia under YCP control (1943 et seq.). But continuity of purpose existed throughout all of these vicissitudes. As we earlier noted, Tito in 1948 endorsed the position of the party that was developed between Stalin's criticism of Markovic and 1928, that is, the period culminating in advocacy of immediate secession.[103] Yet, earlier in the same speech, he acknowledged that secession was never truly countenanced by the party:

We are not speaking here of whether or not the creation of a new state, that is, unification, should have taken place. Unification of the southern Slavs ought to have taken and had to take place: that was the idea of the most progressive people in the countries which were called south Slav. The question was on what principles would that unification be effected.[104]

And in a different speech of the same year, Tito referred to the part played by the YCP during the war as follows: "The role of the Communist Party lay in the first place in the fact that it led that struggle, which was a guarantee that after the war the national question would be settled decisively in the way communists had conceived *long before the war* and during the war."[105] This continuity of purpose was what lent a measure of accuracy to Tito's assertion that "the Communist Party [after 1926] has never renounced nor will it ever renounce the principle laid down by our great teachers, Marx, Engels and Lenin, the principle that each nation has the right to self-determination, including separation."[106] The meaning of the words may have changed, but the expression, *self-determination*, lingered on.

NOTES

1. For references to the many organizations and conferences that promoted the Jugo-Slav movement, see Mittelman, "Nationality Problem," 12–15. Programs included such phrases as "The Croats and the Serbs are one nation"; "Our race, variously known as Serb, Croat and Slovene, is nevertheless, in spite of three different names, but one people—the Jugoslavs"; and "The Croats, Serbs, and Slovenes are one and the same as regards nationality and language, though they were known by different names."

2. At least one U.S. diplomat of the time (Percival Dodge) disagreed with his country's policy, stating that "all those who know well the three nations (Serbs, Croats, and Slovenes) express doubts that they could unite happily into one state." See Tudjman, *Nationalism*, 22.

3. Mittelman, "Nationality Problem," 15–16.

4. More enigmatic is why these three groups were singled out, to the exclusion of other Slavonic peoples such as the Montenegrins and Macedonians. If Croats and Slovenes, though only "tribes," merited mention in the state's official designation, then seemingly all Yugoslav "tribes" should have been extended the same courtesy. The proposed state would also include significant numbers of non-Slavic peoples, such as Albanians, Germans, and Magyars, but they could have been judiciously ignored from

such considerations on the ground that they were not part of the Yugoslav nation (as well as the fact that a state dominated by their ethnic group already existed outside of Yugoslavia).

5. Shoup, *Communism and Yugoslav National Question*, 17.

6. Ibid., 15.

7. Ibid., 19. Evidence that the Marxist party belonging to the next largest ethnic element (after the Serbs and Croats), the Slovenes, had for some time also been sympathetic to this viewpoint is indicated by the fact that their party within Austria-Hungary had been known as the Yugoslav (rather than Slovenian) Socialist Party.

8. Tito, "Political Report," 16.

9. Some scholars stress the fact that the Manifesto was incorrectly addressed to Serbia as evidence that the Comintern was poorly informed on Balkan matters at this time. While this conclusion would certainly be warranted if the name of the state at that time were Yugoslavia, the use of Serbia may well have been a quite consciously chosen abbreviation for Kingdom of the Serbs, Croats and Slovenes. Moreover, quite inexplicably, the body of the document contained a reference to Yugoslavia, which seemingly illustrates not only knowledge of the current scene but remarkable foresight as well. Elsewhere, however, the document spoke of "the triumph and consolidation of Soviet power in Rumania, Bulgaria, *Serbia*, Greece, and Turkey." (Emphasis added.) See the translation by Degras, *Documents* 1:87 for the phrase, "the white Governments of Rumania, Yugoslavia, and Czechoslovakia."

10. The cited passage is a composite extracted from Degras, *Documents* 1:85–87, and Barker, *Macedonia*, 48–49. Neither source quotes the entire document.

11. Mittelman, "Nationality Problem," 131. Opponents sardonically characterized the proposed federation as "an enlarged Austria-Hungary."

12. Tito, "Political Report," 13–14. Technically, the 1920 program did include a single rather ambiguous reference to nationalities: "The CPY also will continue forward in defense of the idea of national unity and equality of rights of all nationalities in the country." Mittelman, "Nationality Problem," 131. This was likely intended to refer to the non-Slavonic peoples. In any case, it is clear that the party was not talking about secession or even federalism, for the only mention of governmental structure (support for "the widest possible self-government of the region, district, and commune") took no heed of national distinctions or distributions. Moreover, in the debates, party spokesmen made clear that the reference to self-government was not intended to connote a federal structure, but only limited home rule. Avakumovic, *History of the Communist Party*, 47.

13. Degras, *Documents* 1:138–144. As earlier noted, the document was drafted and introduced by Lenin.

14. Avakumovic, *History of the Communist Party*, 64.

15. This warning against falling prey to nationalism, made to a group

said *not* to be a nation, is probably illustrative of the party's lack of conviction concerning its assertion that Serbs, Croats, and Slovenes comprised a single people.

16. Indeed, in an attempt to assuage both sides of a factional dispute which was troubling the YCP at this time, the Comintern approved all of the resolutions passed by the conference. However, this was part of a "package deal," and the resolutions were probably viewed as a small price that must be paid to keep the party intact. See Avakumovic, *History of the Communist Party*, 65.

17. Williams, "Communist Party in Yugoslavia," 10.

18. Tito, "Political Report," 25–26.

19. The front had been necessitated by the outlawing of the YCP in July 1921.

20. Williams, "Communist Party in Yugoslavia," 13–14.

21. Ibid., 18.

22. Ibid., 20.

23. Articles expressing somewhat dissimilar views on the topic had appeared in the party's newspaper, *Borba*; but as Tito later noted, "both the 'left' and the 'right' still had the same stand on the national question—that is, a mistaken one." Tito maintained that a serious challenge to the party's position of no secession did not occur until December 1923. See Tito, "Political Report," 26.

24. The right wing was composed primarily of Serbs, while the left was composed mainly of non-Serbs. This has led some authorities to suggest that ethnonational considerations were present in this split on the national question. See, for example, Burks, *Dynamics of Communism*, 109–110, and Tomasic, *National Communism*, 20–21.

25. Avakumovic, *History of the Communist Party*, 67–69. The book was entitled *The National Question in the Light of Marxism.*

26. Shoup, *Communism and Yugoslav National Question*, 25.

27. In a pamphlet he also published in 1923 (*The Constitutional Question and the Working Class of Yugoslavia* [Belgrade: 1923]), Markovic acknowledged that in some cases Marxists must stand "even for complete separation of certain regions." But because no strong desire for separation existed among Yugoslavia's nations, this line of action would not fit the Yugoslav case. "Since, up to now, not one political group of a nation has, *in any manner*, declared itself against the present political unity and in favor of separation, then the nationality question in Yugoslavia obviously is reduced for now . . . to a constitutional question." He further noted that although the right to separation must be recognized, it is the "idea of agreement" (of unity) that must be stressed. That is to say, the right of secession would be recognized on paper (in the constitution), but it would never be exercised. See Williams, "Communist Party in Yugoslavia," 45–49.

28. An unmistakable sign of the Comintern's determination to pursue this course of action was given just two months before the publication of

Markovic's book, when the Comintern had appealed directly to the national aspirations of the Macedonians: "Peasants of Macedonia! Revolutionaries of Macedonia! . . . Only a Workers' and Peasants' Government in Bulgaria . . . will blaze the path for the establishment of a Balkan Federation of Workers' and Peasants' Governments, which alone can bring about your deliverance. . . . For the sake of your own national freedom, you must join hands with the Bulgarian Workers and Peasants." Barker, *Macedonia*, 51. The excerpt is part of a special manifesto on Bulgaria drawn up by the Enlarged Executive of the Comintern on July 23, 1923.

29. Mittelman, "Nationality Problem," 133–134.

30. An IWPY document of this period that set forth the various positions of party members on the national question described Markovic as perceiving it as a constitutional question that "can only be resolved by an automatic revision of the constitution on the basis of full democracy." See ibid., 134–135.

31. Tito, "Political Report," 26.

32. See chapter 3.

33. Barker, *Macedonia*, 60–61.

34. Mittelman, "Nationality Problem," 135–136, and Barker, *Macedonia*, 58–59.

35. Barker, *Macedonia*, 58.

36. Ibid., 62.

37. "Speech Delivered in the Yugoslav Commission of the Executive Committee of the Comintern," March 30, 1925. This can be found in Stalin, *Marxism and National, Colonial Questions*, 200–205.

38. At the Fifth Congress of the Comintern in 1924, Czechoslovakia, Greece, Poland, and Rumania, as well as Yugoslavia, had been singled out as states within which it was necessary to link the national and peasant questions. (See Williams, "Communist Party in Yugoslavia," 31.) However, this linkage was to become de rigeur for all parties the following month (April 1925) when the "Theses on the Bolshevization of Communist Parties Adopted at the Fifth Executive Committee of the Comintern" pronounced that "the national question in colonial and semicolonial countries—and not only in these—is very largely a peasant question, since the majority of the population there are peasants." Degras, *Documents* 2:195. More explicitly, this linkage meant appealing to both the nationalistic proclivities and the land hungriness of the peasant by the joint use of the slogans, "national self-determination" and "all land to the peasants (or tillers)." In the particular case of Yugoslavia, it also meant cooperating with parties, such as the Croatian Peasant Party.

39. Interestingly, however, Georgi Dimitrov unambiguously called for the breakup of Yugoslavia at this same special meeting of the Comintern: "No serious Communist work will be possible in the Balkans until Yugoslavia disintegrates. So Yugoslavia must be made to disintegrate by our helping the Separatist movements there." Cited in Clissold, *Whirlwind*, 101–102.

40. "The National Question Once Again: Re Comrade Semich's Article," in Stalin, *Marxism and National, Colonial Questions,* 221–228. The second criticism appeared in *Bolshevik* on June 30, 1925.

41. Avakumovic, *History of the Communist Party,* 80–81.

42. Tito, "Political Report," 26.

43. Mittelman, "Nationality Problem," 139–140. Material in brackets added.

44. See Jackson, "Green International," 281–282.

45. Shoup, *Communism and Yugoslav National Question,* 38.

46. Avakumovic, *History of the Communist Party,* 108, and Mittelman, "Nationality Problem," 141.

47. Avakumovic, *History of the Communist Party,* 108.

48. Or perhaps it could be described in the terminology used by the U.S. Supreme Court in decisions involving the American Communist Party, i.e., the difference between "abstract doctrine" and "incitement to action."

49. Avakumovic, *History of the Communist Party,* 111.

50. Ibid., 116.

51. Mittelman, "Nationality Problem," 142–143. Emphasis added.

52. Ibid., 143.

53. Shoup (*Communism and Yugoslav National Question,* 40) reports that its last reference appeared in the "Declaration on the United Front," January 1937.

54. Avakumovic, *History of the Communist Party,* 172.

55. Tito, "Political Report," 40.

56. Shoup, *Communism and Yugoslav National Question,* 44.

57. Strategy included the calling of strikes in defense-related industries and the organizing of anticonscription rallies.

58. Tito, "Political Report," 42–43.

59. As reported in Clissold's (*Whirlwind,* 20) popular (nonfootnoted) political biography.

60. See discussion earlier in this chapter. Markovic had acquiesced in the new policy, and his tenure as the YCP's General Secretary (though interrupted) had survived the change of policy by two years. As in the case of Gorkic, therefore, Tito could theoretically accuse him of either stifling secession or catering to it.

61. Mittelman, "Nationality Problem," 144–145, and Shoup, *Communism and Yugoslav National Problem,* 50. One author, with predictably confused results, loosely translated self-rule as self-determination. See Vucinich, "Nationalism and Communism," 248.

62. As we documented, Soviet pressure was the immediate cause of such changes. But the inability of the party to attract mass support because of an inadequate posture on the national question was a staple of Comintern criticism from 1923 through the late 1930s.

63. In like manner, Flemings and Slovaks tended to withhold approval of the Flemish and Slovak states created during this period.

64. In his personal account of the occupation period, Milovan Djilas (*Wartime*, 23) noted that the Communists led the resistance because "no other political movement could have waged the struggle, for all were confined by regional bounds or carried away by excessive ethnic nationalism."

65. Clissold (*Whirlwind*, 10) recounts a secret directive that was supposedly drawn up by Tito just before the German attack. It called for the immediate overthrow of the monarchy and the dismemberment of the state, but it also indicated that Tito felt that this would be a good thing because of the party's far-flung organization. "Yugoslavia must first be dissolved into its several component parts, and the party will then be able to pursue its work within each of them in accordance with the directives already issued." Tito went on to note that help should therefore be accorded to all separatist movements. As contrasted with the official stand of the party at this time (see the party communiqué of January 1941, in Tito, "Political Report," 43–44, which spoke only of national equality), as well as with Tito's speech of May 1940, this sudden return to the pro-separatist stance of 1928–1935 would be inexplicable were it not for Tito's correct anticipation that the Germans were about to occupy the country: "Germany will speedily crush Yugoslav resistance and, with the help of Italy, introduce the Ustase regime in Croatia and possibly similar separatist regimes elsewhere. Steps must therefore be taken to infiltrate our own people into the new administrations for intelligence and other purposes." In short, anticipate and take maximal advantage of the inevitable! To do so, the party must presume German dismemberment of the state into ethnic components; make clear by *earlier* actions that the YCP sympathizes and supports the national aspirations of the people ("Did we not aid your recent separatist movement?"); and use the camaraderie so generated to infiltrate the new units of government and to develop revolutionary bases. That Tito did not perceive the imminent dismemberment as a desirable or acceptable development is illustrated by the directive he transmitted the month after the German invasion (i.e., May 1941). It declared the party's resolve to maintain the unity not just of the YCP but of the working classes of all of the peoples of Yugoslavia. (See Barker, *Macedonia*, 86.)

66. From the first bulletin of the Chief Headquarters of the National Liberation Partisan Detachments as cited in Tito, "Political Report," 53–54.

67. Milovan Djilas records that the forces he organized within Montenegro during the early stages of the resistance were called the Provisional Supreme Command of the National Liberation Troops of Montenegro, and he acknowledges that "the term 'supreme' was adopted to emphasize Montenegrin equality with other Yugoslav nationalities." (*Wartime*, 28.)

The name of the movement within each republic underwent numerous changes during the war, but each (with the necessary exception of that within Bosnia-Hercegovina) stressed that the movement was identified with a single people. For example, the Liberation Front of the Slovenian People, formed on April 27, 1941, became the Slovenian National Liberation Committee in September 1941, and the Slovenian National Liberation Council on February 19, 1944. (For an account of all name changes, see U.S. Senate Committee on the Judiciary, *Yugoslav Communism*, 98–100.)

A similar desire to avoid the term Yugoslavia, while appealing to each national group as such, is evident in the term used to cloak the entire united front, viz., the "*All*-national Liberation Anti-fascist Movement." Djilas (*Wartime*, 57) reports the name was the invention of Soviet officials.

See also Djilas's expression of satisfaction with the phrase "the people's revolution," which he coined to rally all Montenegrins to the cause. He notes: "That might have had a sectarian ring to comrades outside Montenegro. But Montenegrins are partial to unanimity even when they aren't Communists." (Ibid., 63.)

68. The Soviet line at this time was that nothing must be done which might provoke Hitler.

69. Tito, "Political Report," 51–52.

70. See Tomasic, *National Communism*, 72. The "Brotherhood and Union" slogan also contained pan-Slavic overtones.

71. In his dealings with the Hungarian and Albanian Communist parties throughout the war, Tito steadfastly refused to recognize the absorption of the Albanian and Hungarian minorities into their greater homelands, despite the promises to that effect made in the 1928 YCP program, a program retroactively endorsed by Tito.

72. See, for example, Djilas, *Wartime*, 11, 39–41, 48, 132, 136, 321. The number of non-Croatian compatriots killed by Croatian forces alone is estimated at 750,000. (See *Keesing's Contemporary Archives* [1971], 24733.)

73. Djilas, *Wartime*, 100.

74. Djilas offers a number of illustrations in which partisan forces appear to have engaged in ethnocidal warfare while losing sight of all other goals. Thus, in an attack upon a Moslem village, the orders issued in advance to the partisans were "to kill all adult males, drive out the population, and burn down the houses." Ibid., 158.

75. On the early importance of the Serbs who were fleeing from Ustase terrorists, see Tito, "Political Report," 56–58.

76. Djilas, *Wartime*. See, for example, pp. 11, 18, 22, 39, 48.

77. Schöpflin, "The National Question."

78. Tito, "Political Report," 63.

79. "Bulletin of the General HQ of the People's Liberation Partisan Detachments of Yugoslavia, No. 7–8," October 1, 1941. The text can be found in Tito, *Selected Works*, 57–59.

80. Tito's associate was Vladimir Dedijer. The quotation is cited in Maclean, *Disputed Barricade*, 172.

81. Stanojenic and Markovic, *Tito*, unpaged.

82. Tito, *Tito Speaks*, 22. The speech was made on March 1, 1944, well after the battle of Stalingrad and Italy's withdrawal from the war. For an

earlier speech also filled with appeals to "our nations," "the nations," etc.,
see his speech of November 29, 1943 in the same volume, pp. 5–17.

83. "Address Delivered During Banner Presentation to the First Proletarian Brigade," *Borba*, no. 26 (November 14, 1942). The English text
can be found in Tito, *Selected Works*, 99. For examples of speeches made
by Djilas that were pitched to the nationalist proclivities of the audience,
see Djilas, *Wartime*, 45, 321. Elsewhere (pp. 149, 315), Djilas complains
that too much stress in the propaganda was placed upon the notion of
"Montenegrin" and "Croatian." For an illustration of the manner in which
the traditionally impersonal category of military messages often reflected
a nationalistic orientation, see the message headed "Supreme HQ of the
People's Liberation Army and Partisan Detachments of Yugoslavia to General HQ for Serbia," in Tito, *Selected Works*, 224: "You may rest assured,
comrades, that we have forged a powerful Army which is ready to assist
you in the fight to liberate the Serbian people and frustrate the plans of
various reactionary and traitorous cliques to ride roughshod over the people of Serbia again."

84. U.S. Department of State, "Macedonian Nationalism," 57.

85. Ibid., 60.

86. An extensive survey conducted throughout Yugoslavia nearly forty
years after "the National Liberation War" documented that members of
the various national groups were very familiar with events during the war
as they occurred in their own homeland, but were nearly totally ignorant
of wartime events and leaders in other regions. (See *Joint Publications Research Service (JPRS)* 81222 [July 7, 1982]: 58–63.) It was evident that even
at this late date, people perceived the 1940–1944 period as a time of
Croatian, Serb, or Slovene struggle, rather than as a common Yugoslav
one.

87. See the earlier discussion in this chapter.

88. Shoup, *Communism and Yugoslav National Question*, 48.

89. Barker, *Macedonia*, 88.

90. The article was reprinted in Tito, *Govori I Clanci*, 113–122. I am
indebted to Mildred Pappas of the Woodrow Wilson International Center
for Scholars, Washington, D.C., for translating the article in its entirety.

91. Stanojenic and Markovic, *Tito*, n.p.

92. "Address on the Day the Fourth Montenegrin Brigade Was Founded,"
June 17, 1942, in Tito, *Selected Works*, 78.

93. Tito, "Political Report," 98.

94. Maclean, *Disputed Barricade*, 199.

95. Barker, *Macedonia*, 94.

96. Joncic, *Relations between Nationalities*," 14.

97. Even within the ranks of the YCP, powerful forces believed that the
party intended to grant independent statehood after the war. Djilas (*Wartime*, 372) reports that the Central Committee of Croatia continued to
criticize the notion of a single Yugoslav state as late as 1944, that is, after

Tito had openly proclaimed that the goal of a united Yugoslavia was beyond dispute. Earlier, the Croatian liberation front, dominated by Communists, had declared certain Italian territories to be part of Croatia, thereby, in the words of Djilas (p. 317), "assuming a sovereignty which belonged to Yugoslavia alone."

98. "Address at the Second Session, Anti-Fascist Council of People's Liberation, Jajce, Yugoslavia," November 29, 1943, in Christman, *Essential Tito*, 19. Emphasis added.

99. Concluding a major address shortly after the war, Tito listed among the major accomplishments "the creation of *indestructible* brotherhood and unity among the various nationalities of Yugoslavia . . . and the creation of a strong state community composed of the various nationalities of Yugoslavia, all of whom have equal rights." "Address at the Third Session, Anti-Fascist Council of People's Liberation, Belgrade," August 8, 1945, in Christman, *Essential Tito*, 49.

100. Article 2 of the 1943 declaration had read as follows: "2. In order to carry out the principles of sovereignty of the nations of Yugoslavia and in order that Yugoslavia may be the true home of all its peoples, and no longer an arena for the machinations of reactionary influences, Yugoslavia is being built up on a federal principle which will ensure full equality for the nations of Serbia, Croatia, Slovenia, Macedonia, Montenegro, Bosnia, and Hercegovina."

101. Although all Soviet constitutions down to the present have made allowance for secession, there was no constitutional reference to self-determination prior to 1977. However, the Yugoslavian version of self-determination as a fully consummated, irrevocable act appealed to drafters of the 1977 Soviet constitution. Article 70 reads: "The Union of Soviet Socialist Republics is a unitary, federal and multinational state formed . . . as a result of the free self-determination of nations."

102. Thirty years after World War II, a Yugoslav scholar would evaluate the significance of the party's wartime stand on the national question as follows: "During the national-liberation struggle the policy of national self-determination and of fraternity and unity were *the basic factors of the victory* over the foreign and domestic fascism and bourgeoisie. In that struggle for national liberation *national specificities were respected* and all our peoples *alone* founded their own States, while proclaiming the union into the Yugoslav federation." (Emphasis added.) See Šuvar, "Relationship between Class and National," 6.

103. Tito, "Political Report," 37.

104. Ibid., 17.

105. "Concerning the National Question and Socialist Patriotism" (speech before the Slovene Academy of Arts and Sciences, November 16, 1948), in Tito, *Selected Speeches*, 98. Emphasis added.

106. Cited above. See note 90, this chapter.

CHAPTER 7

Still Other Variations

THE INTERWAR PERIOD

THOUGH the Soviet Union, China, Vietnam, and Yugoslavia complete the list of those states in which the Leninist stratagem concerning self-determination played a key role in the rise to power of the local Communist party, the same stratagem, with varying success, was applied elsewhere. Wherever applied, the stratagem was not without great peril because of its inherent risk of alienating the dominant group within the state. Surrendering segments of the state's population and territory is seldom popular with such people. We have seen how an appreciation of this ethnopsychological factor led the Chinese and Vietnamese Communists to play down their support of the doctrine whenever they were principally interested in wooing the state's dominant ethnic element.

Such an expedient could serve in a situation where communications were poor. It is very doubtful, for example, that many Han were aware of what Mao was promising non-Han peoples during his sojourn in the hinterlands. And we have reviewed how difficult it is to ascertain with precision even today what it was that Communist cadre were actually promising the hill peoples of Vietnam between 1942 and 1975. It was this general absence of effective communications that permitted the Chinese and the Vietnamese parties to perform the chameleonic role of posing intermittently as the champion of the state's survival and of the national interests of the dominant element, and as the architect of the country's dismemberment.

While the communications network throughout Yugoslavia, even in that state's early days, was significantly superior to that of China and Vietnam, it is unlikely that many Yugoslav citizens of the interwar period were aware of the YCP's stand on the national or other questions. The outlawing of the party within two years of its inception posed a severe barrier to the YCP's desire to get its program before the masses. Yet, in retrospect, illegalization was probably a *sine qua non* of YCP success, preventing the masses from becoming cognizant of the series of zigzags and countermarches that marked prewar national policy, thus making it possible for the YCP to pose as the credible protector of the national interest of each national group during the decisive years of the occupation.

In each of these cases, then, the danger of alienating one group while appealing to the national aspirations of another was blunted by poor communications.[1] But in a series of other states, the Comintern's insistence upon support for a right of secession, though generating votes among the minorities who were promised independence, quite understandably did not enhance the local Communist party's image among the state's dominant people. Thus, during the 1920s, the Polish Communist Party, having promised, in accordance with Comintern directives, self-determination, including separation, for the state's Belorussian and Ukrainian minorities, fared much better in elections throughout areas populated by these peoples than it did in ethnically Polish regions.[2]

The same phenomenon occurred within Czechoslovakia. From its founding in 1921, the Czechoslovak Communist Party abided by the Comintern's orders to proclaim the right of secession for the Ruthenians. The 1925 elections offer one indication of the impact of this plank of their program upon the population. In each of the three provinces in which Czechs or Slovaks predominated, the percentage of the vote received by the party failed to exceed 13 percent. However, in Ruthenia, it was more than three times as great (42 percent).[3] The failure of the party to excite a larger percentage of the Slovaks is traceable to its anomalous approach to Slovak nationhood. The official governmental and generally popularly held view at the time was that the Czechoslovaks constituted a single people. But in 1924, again upon Comintern prodding, the party maintained that the Slovaks were a separate nation. Unhappiness within the party at this decision was acknowledged by the Executive Committee of the Comintern on October 15, 1924, in a document which noted that many believed it would lead to the breakup of the state.[4] This strong opposition may account for the fact that despite the party's recognition of a Slovak nation and despite its commitment to national self-determination, the party did not recommend even autonomy, much less secession, for the Slovaks. Such a step did not occur until March 1940, after the Nazis had already created a separate puppet state of Slovakia.[5] As a result of this delay, plus the fact that Slovak nationalists had a viable, non-Communist defender of the nation's interests in the Slovak People's Party, Communist self-determination, while irksome to the Czechs, exerted little magnetic pull upon the Slovak masses.

The same pattern repeated itself elsewhere. Comintern insistence that the French Communist Party stand for the independence of Alsace-Lorraine and the emancipation of French colonies did little to win converts within "la grande nation."[6] The British Communist Party was hindered by its demand for Irish liberation and the dissolution of the empire.[7] Japanese recruitment was hampered by the party's demand for the release of Korea and Formosa (Taiwan).[8] Within Greece, the Comintern's demand that the party adopt the unpopular stance of secession for the Macedonians led to a split of the party itself in 1927.[9]

The case of the United States offers some unique features. Over the objection of several of the party's leaders, the American black community was singled out quite early as one of the most promising cracks in the wall of capitalist imperialism.[10] Lenin's "Theses on the National and Colonial Question," adopted by the Comintern in 1920 as the official guide to action on the national question, had noted that it was essential "that all Communist Parties should render direct aid to the revolutionary movements among the dependent and underprivileged nations (for example, Ireland, the American Negroes, etc.)."[11] However, despite Lenin's reference to American blacks as a distinct nation, it was not until its Sixth Congress (1928) that the Comintern insisted that this Leninist viewpoint be reflected in the platform and propaganda of the American Communist Party (ACP). Prior to that time, the ACP had treated the black question as part of an overriding class question, bourgeois blacks being grouped with bourgeois whites as enemies of the working class. Moreover, when after 1928 it dropped this dichotomous view of blacks predicated upon socioeconomic class, the ACP immediately substituted an equally dichotomous view predicated upon geography. Though according the blacks the status of a nation, the party limited the right of separation to those blacks living in the "Black Belt" of the southern United States. For the blacks of this region, the ACP was instructed, "the Party must come out openly and unreservedly for the right of Negroes to national self-determination."[12] This self-determination, it was later emphasized, extended to total independence. It meant "complete and unlimited right of the Negro to exercise governmental authority in the entire territory of the Black Belt, as well as to decide upon the relations between their territory and other nations [sic], particularly the United States." It was called "incorrect and harmful to interpret the communist standpoint to mean that the communists stand for the right of self-determination of the Negroes only up to a certain point, but not beyond this, for example, to the right of separation." Some measure of the great importance that was ascribed to avoiding anything which might threaten the success of this propaganda campaign was evident in the explicit statement that Stalin's postrevolutionary proviso that self-determination applied only to the toiling masses did not apply in the case of the Black Belt. The party was informed that it "cannot make its stand for this slogan [of 'Right to self-determination'] dependent upon any conditions, even the condition that the proletariat has the hegemony in the national revolutionary Negro movement or that the majority of the Negroes in the Black Belt adopts the Soviet form."[13] Similarly, the decision to treat northern blacks in a completely separate category from southern blacks appears to have been motivated by a presumption that the northern blacks' desire for assimilation would harm the chance of igniting an effective separatist movement within the country. Therefore, rather than exploit the cleavages between whites and blacks in the north, the Comintern elected to promote optimism concerning the likelihood of racial assimilation within the northern "melting pot." As set forth by the Comintern:

> The broad masses of the Negro population in the big industrial centres of the North are, however, making no efforts whatsoever to maintain and cultivate a national aloofness, they are, on the contrary, working for assimilation. This effort of the Negro masses can do much in the future to facilitate the progressive process of amalgamating the whites and Negroes into *one* nation, and it is under no circumstances the task of the communists to give support to bourgeois nationalism in its fight with the progressive assimilation tendencies of the Negro working masses.[14]

Apparently, the northern blacks were to be encouraged to become part of an undifferentiated American nation, thus eradicating the major nonseparatistically inclined component of the black community.[15] In the case of the United States, then, Leninist national policy was so applied as to divide a nation as well as a state.[16]

The application of national policy within Germany represented yet a sharper departure from the norm. Here, rather than appealing to the discontent that is intrinsic to minorities, national policy concentrated on the discontent of a state's dominant people. World War I, the peace treaties, and their aftermath (particularly the occupation of the Ruhr by French troops) had left the German people dangerously disconsolate, and the Comintern elected to pitch its propaganda to the frustrated nationalism of this large and strategically important nation. With typical flexibility, the Comintern appreciated that the self-held view of the Germans concerning their status relative to the victorious peoples was not totally dissimilar to the self-held views of minorities relative to their state's dominant ethnic element. Speaking for the Comintern in 1923, Grigori Zinoviev criticized the German Communist Party (the KPD) for its reluctance to declare forthrightly that "we German communists (and nobody else) defend the interests of the country, the people, the nation."[17] Strange words indeed for an internationalist movement, and words not accepted without opposition. But led by Karl Radek, a majority of the KPD accepted the proposition that in its present situation, support for German nationalism was a revolutionary act. In the beginning, the principal intent behind this nationalistic approach was apparently to perpetuate and exacerbate the cleavages between Germany and the other capitalist powers. But as Hitler's star began to rise, the need to abort the Nazi movement by attracting potential support to itself became salient. Now the Comintern adopted the difficult task of appearing more nationalistic than the Nazis. Even with regard to the German irredenta, the party was to outpromise Hitler's movement.[18] An article that appeared during 1930 in the journal, *Communist International*, carried this advice:

> The German Party must concern itself more with the question of the German population in the neighboring countries . . . . We must not leave them a prey to the national socialists, but must emphasize the fact that they will not enjoy the full right of self-determination, and to join the future German Soviet State, until the chains of the Versailles system are broken asunder by the German Soviet Republic of the future.[19]

As late as 1934 with Hitler now firmly in power, from its sanctuary in Switzerland the KPD was still appealing to German nationalism, criticizing the Nazis for policies that were preventing union with the Germans of Austria, Danzig, the Saar, Silesia, etc. These irredentist and other nationalistic clamorings of the KPD could only harm the popular support of those Communist parties of Czechoslovakia, France, and Poland whose leaders often voiced dissatisfaction with the KPD's program. The primacy which the Comintern ascribed to winning over the German masses even at the expense of alienating public opinion in adjoining states is implicit in the directives to the Communist parties of those states that they support the right of secession for the German minorities of, respectively, Czechoslovakia's Sudetenland, France's Alsace-Lorraine, and Poland's Upper Silesia, Pomerania, and Danzig.[20] However, though KPD leaders had assured the Comintern as late as April 1931 that the party's appeals to the *Volk* had prevented Nazi inroads among the German masses, this wishful thinking could not long retain credibility in the face of Hitler's growing popularity. At the Comintern's Seventh Congress in August 1935, failure was attributed to past underestimation of the Fascist threat and of the strength of national sentiment. But given the thrust of the KPD's program throughout the 1920s and early 1930s, it would be more accurate to say that the Communists fully appreciated the power of national sentiment throughout *Mittel Europa*, but that, no matter how nationalistic the KPD's propaganda, the party was, as part of an international movement, unable to project an image of itself as the protector and promoter of German national interest with the same credibility as could a movement confined in reality as well as in its propaganda to the German nation. As elsewhere, Lenin's stratagem lost out to a viable, nationalist alternative.

Still another variation in the application of Leninist self-determination occurred within Rumania. There the Rumanian Communist Party (RCP) was instructed to work for the transfer from Rumania to the Soviet Union of a region populated principally by Rumanians.[21] This paradoxical use of the notion of national self-determination to bring about the division of a nation was made possible by simply asserting that the Rumanians who lived in the area of Bessarabia were in fact not Rumanians at all.

The region called Bessarabia had been annexed by tsarist Russia in 1812. Though there were sections of Bessarabia in which Rumanians were a minority, this ethnic element represented a majority overall. In 1917 local leaders took advantage of the chaotic situation to announce the region's secession in order to form what they called the Democratic Moldavian Republic. The general consensus of scholars is that Moldavia is only the name of a region devoid of ethnic overtones, and that the designation of the new state was therefore not intended to convey any ethnonational message. In any case, the state was short-lived, being absorbed by Rumania during April 1918 in what has been described as a "voluntary" action prompted in part by fear of Soviet reannexation on the part of the region's inhabitants.[22]

Consonant with their policy toward other areas and peoples that had seceded during 1917–1918, the Soviet authorities were intent on the region's reabsorption. During 1924 a multipronged campaign was launched. At its Fifth Congress held in the spring of that year, the Comintern advanced "the slogan that the communist party is fighting against the annexation of Bessarabia by Rumania and the slogan that this country [i.e., Bessarabia] has a right to self-determination."[23] The Rumanian Communist Party then took up the theme at its Third Congress held during the same year. A resolution pledged the party to support self-determination, including secession, for the workers and peasants of Bessarabia "who lived in liberty in the first period of the Russian Revolution and at present groan under the boot of the Rumanian dictatorship [and who are] striving for national revolution and union with the Union of Soviet Socialist Republics."[24] Those "who lived in liberty" during the Russian Revolution constituted an evident reference to the short-lived Democratic Moldavian Republic, but on what basis could *national* self-determination be applied to the population of Bessarabia, whose chief component was Rumanian? The answer also came in the course of 1924, when in October Moscow announced the creation of a Moldavian Autonomous Soviet Socialist Republic (MASSR) in an area immediately adjacent to Rumania. Given the Soviet practice of assigning ethnic designations to such political units, this action in effect constituted official recognition of the existence of a Moldavian nation. The Rumanian Communist Party acknowledged its recognition of such a nation at its next congress (the Fourth), in the form of a resolution that attacked the Rumanian bourgeoisie for "advancing the claim that Moldavians, who constitute a relative majority of the population of Bessarabia, are Rumanians, even when the population of Moldavia considers itself in reality an independent nationality, with a culture of its own." The party was therefore "obligated to support by all means the struggle of the masses of workers of Bessarabia for unification with the MASSR."[25] Given Stalin's perception of the strategic value of having ostensibly independent, ethnically designated political units along the Soviet Union's external borders,[26] MASSR was evidently created to act as an emotional magnet for Bessarabians, as well as a base from which to launch propaganda and other forms of activity designed to bring about Bessarabia's return.[27] If so, the ploy did not meet with much success. When the Soviets, assured of German acquiescence by the Nazi-Soviet Pact, first retook the area by ultimatum in 1940, they brushed aside the Rumanian government's plea that the political allegiance of the people be determined by plebiscite. And when Soviet forces reoccupied the area in 1944, talk of a right of self-determination was not heard. The Soviets were well aware that their attempt to employ the slogan of national self-determination to create an artificial division of the Rumanian nation had made few converts and numerous opponents, as witness the exceptional weakness of the Communist apparatus throughout Rumania, including Bessarabia, during the interwar period.[28] The Soviets had achieved their goal by military conquest rather than through a "Moldavian nationalism."

SELF-DETERMINATION IN THE POSTWAR ENVIRONMENT

Policy with Regard to Capitalist States

Soviet policy with regard to promoting self-determination underwent a significant alteration in the post-Stalin era. We have traced the Soviet prewar penchant for manipulating ethnonational sentiments within capitalist states. This same penchant was observable throughout the war and into the immediate postwar period. Soviet attempts to wrest both Sinkiang (East Turkestan) and Inner Mongolia from Nationalist China are cases in point, as are the abortive attempts to have the Azerbaijani and Kurdish peoples of Iran secede from that state. But Stalin's successors did not exhibit the same interest in exploiting the discontent of minorities within the capitalist states.

This reluctance held true not just with regard to the older states of Western Europe and North America, but with regard to the new states of Africa and Asia as well. All but a handful of these new states were ethnic mosaics and therefore rich soil in which to agitate for national self-determination. But even when national secessionist movements erupted within these regions without benefit of outside encouragement, Soviet authorities demonstrated little desire to side with them against their respective governments.

Marx, Engels, and their Leninist legatees had admittedly reserved to the party the determination of whether or not to support a particular secessionist movement. And Marx and Engels had been particularly niggardly in extending their verbal support to such movements. But given the unprecedented outbreak of ethnonational movements throughout all areas of the globe in the late 1960s and 1970s,[29] the Soviet Union's passive response, particularly when contrasted with its prewar policies, constituted a disavowal of support for self-determination, even though the government continued to pose as the foremost champion and defender of that ideal. Granted that from 1955 on, the Soviet government lent oral support to the Pushtunistan movement, which would have divided (then West) Pakistan in two, an eventuality contemplated with relish by two states the Soviet Union was courting, namely Afghanistan and India. Further, it supported the successful Bengali drive for separate statehood in the early 1970s, but appears to have done so primarily to please India and aggravate China. As against these few cases of support for secession, however, the Soviets refrained from fishing the troubled waters of those other, nearly 90 percent of all capitalist states which possessed at least one important national minority, more than 50 percent of which experienced manifestations of significant, ethnically inspired discord during the late 1960s and 1970s.[30]

Soviet reluctance to support such struggles became an issue in the polemics between the Chinese People's Republic and the Soviet Union, soon after the commencement of their rift. Though the Chinese were themselves far from consistent on the matter (e.g., denying the right of the Bengalis to secede from Pakistan while insisting on the same right for the Kashmiri of India), they took the Soviets to task for being unwilling to support progressive struggles within the Third World. In an open letter of July 1963, the Central Committee of the CCP criticized the Soviet leaders in the following terms:

> Certain persons now go so far as to deny the great international significance of the anti-imperialist revolutionary struggles of the Asian, African and Latin-American peoples and, on the pretext of breaking down the barriers of nationality, color and geographical location, are trying their best to efface the line of demarcation between oppressed and oppressor nations and between oppressed and oppressor countries and to hold down the revolutionary struggles of the peoples in these areas. In fact, they cater to the needs of imperialism and create a new "theory" to justify the rule of imperialism in these areas and the promotion of its policies of old and new colonialism. Actually, this "theory" seeks not to break down the barriers of nationality, color and geographical location but to maintain the rule of the "superior nations" over the oppressed nations. It is only natural that this fraudulent "theory" is rejected by the people in these areas.[31]

These "certain persons" were charged with taking this revisionist road because of fear that such a struggle would lead to thermonuclear war.

In recent years, certain persons have been spreading the argument that a single spark from a war of national liberation or from a revolutionary people's war will lead to a world conflagration destroying the whole of mankind. What are the facts? Contrary to what these persons say, the wars of national liberation and the revolutionary peoples' wars that have occurred since World War II have not led to world war.[32]

The reply of the Central Committee of the CPSU, also in the form of an open letter, was multifaceted and somewhat contradictory. On the one hand the Soviets cited cases to prove that they continued to support national movements: "The Soviet Union is rendering broadest support to the national liberation movement. Everybody is familiar with the practical assistance our country rendered the peoples of Vietnam, Egypt, Iraq, Algeria, Yemen, the Cubans and other peoples."[33] At best the list is not very impressive from the viewpoint of support for self-determination: only Algeria and Yemen involved an issue of political separatism; in all the other cases, Soviet assistance was channeled to the government in power.[34] But, in any event, it is difficult to reconcile this assertion of support for national liberation movements with another segment of the letter which suggested that with the end of colonialism, national liberation had moved from the stage of political emancipation into one of consolidation:

> And now that the liberated peoples have entered a new stage of their struggle, concentrating their efforts on the consolidation of their political gains and economic independence do they not see that it would be immeasurably more difficult, if not altogether impossible, to solve these tasks without the assistance of the Socialist states?
> The Marxists-Leninists always stress the epochal significance of the national liberation movement and its great future, but they regard as one of the main requisites for its further victories solid alliance and cooperation with the countries of the world system of Socialism as the main force in the struggle against imperialism, the solid alliance with the labor movement in the capitalist countries.

The general thrust of the Soviet's 1963 letter therefore suggested a policy of taking Third World states as they were, while beguiling or otherwise convincing their governments of the wisdom of close friendship with the USSR.[35] In sum, a policy with little role for Leninist national self-determination.

Certain other Marxist-Leninist governments, particularly the Chinese, proved far less hesitant to appeal in the postwar period to ethnonational discontent within non-Communist states. We have noted that the Chinese People's Republic took issue with the Soviet Union on this precise point. Peking's rationale for aiding and abetting non-Communists involved in national liberation struggles abroad was summed up in an essay by the deputy chairman of the Commission of Nationalities:

> When their class interests are encroached upon by the imperialists through national oppression, the national bourgeoisie and even certain patriotic kings, princes, and aristocrats of an oppressed nationality may sometimes fight against national oppression together with the broad masses of working people of their own nationality. In this struggle the proletariat should unite with them while at the same time they must understand that the attitude of these people towards imperialist national oppression is, in the final analysis, based on their own class interests.[36]

At about the same time of the publication of this document, Peking embarked on an ambitious program to bring about political change in a number of countries through manipulation of the ethnic media. Particular stress was placed upon the non-Communist states to the south. In addition to supporting Communist movements within Burma, India, Malaysia, and Thailand, Peking furnished assistance, including the equipping and training of guerrilla forces, to non-Communist ethnonational movements within those same states.[37]

Meanwhile, the Communist movements within Burma, Malaysia, and Thailand adopted strategies that mirrored those of the Cambodian, Chinese, Laotian, and Vietnamese movements at comparable stages of development. Each adopted the guerrilla form of struggle. Each developed its base in a minority area or areas.[38] Each promised autonomy or independence to minorities.[39]

The experience of the Communist movement within India at times converged and at other times diverged from this common pattern. In its formative years, the Communist Party of India (CPI), under Comintern direction, had been adamantly opposed to Gandhi and the Congress movement. By 1934, however, in a tactical twist reminiscent of its earlier decision to have the fledgling Chinese Communist Party ally itself with the nationalist party of Sun Yatsen, the Comintern had come to appreciate Congress as the most viable, anti-British organization, and had counseled the CPI to ally itself with the movement. Congress acquiesced, but disenchantment followed when the CPI, faithfully reflecting the foreign policy objectives of the Soviet Union, collaborated with the British authorities so as not to divert attention from the threat of fascism. Expulsion of the party from the Congress for disloyalty to the cause of Indian independence followed in 1945. During the early postindependence period (1947–1951), the party turned to guerrilla struggle, particularly of the urban variety. However, again upon the advice of Moscow, such tactics were dropped, and in 1952 the CPI became a constitutional, office-seeking political party.

To this point, the party's vacillation in policy on the national question closely paralleled that of the Vietnamese Communist Party at similar stages in its evolution. In its 1930 draft program, the CPI had guaranteed to "national minorities their right to self-determination, including that of complete separation," but it had hedged on the issue during its period of alliance with Congress and its subsequent period of cooperation with the British authorities.[40] During the period of guerrilla struggle, separatism had again been stressed. The party's 1952 return to legal status within a "bourgeois state" did not follow the Vietnamese experience, of course, and this change necessitated the redropping of support for separatism. In 1953 Moscow indicated that the party would not again revert to espousing secession by formally noting that "though for India, too, the principle of self-determination means and naturally includes the right of separation, it is inexpedient for Indian nationalities to exercise the right."[41] To paraphrase Stalin's 1920 statement, the demand for secession of India's minorities at the present stage had become a profoundly revolutionary one.[42]

The CPI realized quite substantial electoral successes in the ensuing years, but the probability of still greater successes received a severe setback following the appearance of a serious Indo-Sino rift, throughout which the Soviet Union increasingly favored the side of India. The party fractured into two wings in 1964. The one favored by Moscow now forged extremely close ties with the Congress Party of Indira Gandhi, entering into coalition governments and, in some elections, even entering into election agreements under which only one or the other party (that is, the CPI or the Congress Party) would contest certain districts, thus combining their electoral strength against opponents. In order to underline their conviction that such cooperation was beyond the boundaries of doctrinally acceptable behavior, the other, more orthodox wing of the party adopted the name, Communist Party of India/Marxist (CPI/M). Though following generally Maoist policies and though at first leaning toward China in the Sino-Soviet competition, the CPI/M announced in 1968 its autonomy from both power centers and its commitment to building a Third World Communist movement to bridge the ideological chasm separating Peking and Moscow. This action was followed by a further splintering of the Indian Communist movement, with the announcement in 1969 of a third, pro-Maoist wing, the Communist Party of India/Marxist-Leninist (CPI/M-L), which was dedicated to revolutionary action of the guerrilla variety.

The differing fundamental orientations of these three parties were reflected in their stands on the national question. The CPI was too strongly committed to the notion of an Indian Union, a bias shared with the Congress Party, to countenance the right of secession for India's numerous peoples. By contrast, the more orthodox CPI/M demonstrated the influence of Lenin's legacy on the national question. Perhaps in a purposeful leak designed to serve as a trial balloon, it was reported in the Indian press in late 1971 that the party was preparing to come out formally for the right of self-determination, including secession. Spokesmen later denied this intention, saying that the CPI/M was "opposed to a disruptive secessionist movement." However, in a remarkable analysis, the Asian News Service reported that many people were skeptical regarding this disavowal:

> Political observers believe, however, that the Marxists have yielded nothing, but have merely resorted to a clever camouflage of words. The Marxists, they point out, are opposed to secession from a *People's* democracy (a complicated way of saying a government headed by them) but have not specifically bartered their right to secede from a *bourgeois* democracy.[43]

This analysis was lent credence when campaign literature of the West Bengal branch of the CPI/M, although carefully avoiding the word *secession*, stressed that India was a multinational state and recommended that India become a "voluntary" union of the national groups which comprised it.[44] The CPI/M could not have gone much further without threatening its legal status, but this constraint did not apply to the already illegal, violence-prone CPI/M-L. Given this wing's commitment to Maoist policies, it was to be expected that it would support secessionist, national movements. However, an intraparty squabble in late 1971, which led to the purging of the general secretary, glaringly demonstrated that Maoism, in the tradition of Marx, Engels, Lenin, and Stalin, was highly selective in its support for such movements. One of the principal reasons for the general secretary's ouster had been his sympathy for Bengali secession from Pakistan, despite the fact that that movement had been stigmatized as "bourgeois" by Peking.[45] Maoism's condoning of alliances with some bourgeois nationalist movements was clearly not to be misconstrued as condoning alliances indiscriminately with all bourgeois nationalist movements.[46]

Even Peking's selective support for self-determination contrasted vividly, however, with the earlier-noted general refusal of the Soviets to take advantage of the numerous ethnonational movements occurring within non-Marxist states throughout the late 1960s and 1970s. The reasoning which underlay Moscow's decision to remain chaste despite the temptation of so many seductively bared opportunities is a matter for conjecture. Among the reinforcing factors that could help to account for it are the advent of the nuclear age and the aforementioned fear that local situations could escalate into nuclear conflagrations; a basic complacency with things as they were progressing in their natural course; the fear that identification of Moscow as an agent of instability and subversion would drive the Third World states en masse into a united anti-Soviet stance and into closer relations with Moscow's principal non-Marxist enemies; the acrid competition with Peking for influence, particularly throughout the Third World; and a policy of first-things-first coupled to the realization that the ethnonational divisions would be there to exploit at a later time should the exigencies of the moment so decree.

Despite such considerations it would have been dangerous for governments in Moscow's disfavor to assume that the Soviets were committed to refrain permanently from playing the ethnic card. Consonant with the great flexibility and opportunism that had characterized the party's attitude toward self-determination from the very beginning, the Soviet leadership abruptly reverted to a Stalinist ploy in the early 1980s. Breaking a three-decade moratorium on this type of propaganda, Moscow launched a campaign emphasizing the ostensible desire of Iran's Azerbaijani community to unite with their cousins in the Soviet Union.[47] Moreover, during the late 1970s, a number of revolutionary movements throughout Central America and the Andean states, which enjoyed at least the tacit support of Havana and Moscow, came belatedly to appreciate the strategic value of championing the ethnic aspirations of the various Indian peoples of the region.[48]

Meanwhile, Peking also did a flip-flop, but in the opposite direction. During the de-Maoization campaign of 1980–1981, the authorities indicated that they would curtail support for revolutionary movements within the non-Marxist-Leninist states of southern Asia. In addition to those reasons suggested for the Soviet tendency to accept existing state borders, the Chinese may also have been motivated by a desire to isolate Vietnam (by then a major enemy), as well as by the need to convince the United States, Japan, and other non-Marxist states that it was worthy of major military and economic assistance.

In any event, it is evident that whenever Moscow and Peking have shown a disinclination to manipulate the aspirations of ethnic minorities in non-Marxist states, their reluctance was not due to a conviction of the inefficacy of this stratagem as a means of inspiring discord. While hesitant to encourage minority unrest within non-Communist states, Moscow illustrated no such compunction in its dealings with other Marxist-Leninist governments.

Policy with Regard to Other Marxist-Leninist States

When trying to press their will upon the leaders of another Marxist-Leninist state, the Soviets have often resorted to playing upon the resentments and aspirations of minorities. This approach reminds the recalcitrant government that it is vulnerable from within as well as from without. Soviet efforts of this type were particularly extensive and long-lasting in the cause of ending the Sino-Soviet rift. Long hours of broadcasts in a number of local vernaculars were beamed from long-ranged transmitting facilities newly erected near the border for just this purpose. Newspapers and pamphlets, also in the local languages, were distributed by whatever means possible. The message was always essentially the same: The Chinese have denied your right to national self-determination. They are bent upon forcibly eradicating your culture and your identity, and assimilating you into the Han nation. Your plight contrasts badly with the situation in the Soviet Union where the various national groups have their own republics and where their unique cultures are encouraged. But the revolutionary spirit of the Mongol, Tibetan, Uighur, etc. people cannot be extinguished, and the national liberation struggle will be won. Thus a broadcast in Tibetan described in graphic terms how "the Tibetans fought for their survival and independence in 1959" and prophesied that the "struggle for their survival and independence . . . like that of other nationalities, will never be subdued."[49]

Although difficult to substantiate, Soviet activities probably went beyond mere propaganda. At least this was the charge brought on numerous occasions by the Chinese:

> In certain frontier regions of the minorities nationalities there has emerged a new special situation. There the modern revisionists are frantically fomenting disunity in the relations among our nationalities. They carry out subversive activities on a large scale, inciting and coercing huge numbers of people of the frontier minority nationalities to flee the country.[50]

For their part, the Chinese tried to minimize their vulnerability by such devices as radio jamming and forcing the Turkic peoples of western China to discard the Cyrillic alphabet (which had been adopted in place of the Arabic script only two years earlier) in order to render written materials from across the border unintelligible.[51] They were also reported to have created something of a *cordon sanitaire* by moving minorities back some miles from the border, then repopulating the zone with Han. Peking also went on the counteroffensive with charges that the Soviet Union was a prison of nations, not their nirvana as Moscow had advertised.[52] Thus, using the centennial of Lenin's birth as an opportunity to carry on their battle of invectives with Moscow, the Chinese news agency Hsinhua commented on April 21, 1970:

> Lenin pointed out: *"Nowhere in the world is there such an oppression of the majority of the country's population as there is in Russia,"* and nationalities other than Russians were regarded *"as inorodtsi (aliens)."* National oppression *"turned the nationalities without any rights into great reservoirs of fierce hatred for the monarchs."* Now the Soviet revisionist new Tsars have restored the old Tsars' policy of national oppression, adopted such cruel measures as discrimination, forced migration, splitting and imprisonment to oppress and persecute the minority nationalities and turned the Soviet Union back into the *"prison of nations."*

But despite the beaming of such messages into the Soviet Union, China was decidedly at a disadvantage in the game of ethnic diplomacy.[53]

There is little question but that the Soviets at least equally appreciated the strategic value to Moscow of the ethnically based rivalries that pockmark Eastern Europe. As contrasted with their own activities involving China's minorities, the Soviets' manipulation of ethnonational attitudes within Eastern Europe was less publicized because therein Moscow more often elected to operate through intermediaries—e.g., through Budapest when the target was Rumania and through Sofia (and sometimes Budapest) when the target was Yugoslavia. Take the case of Rumania. When in the early 1960s that country's government took advantage of the Sino-Soviet split to strike an increasingly independent stance, Hungary, certainly acting with Moscow's consent and apparently as its agent, began fomenting unrest among Rumania's Hungarian (Magyar) element. And when Rumanian authorities, undaunted by such threats, openly declared in 1964 that the principles governing the relations among socialist states should include national independence and sovereignty, equal rights, noninterference in internal affairs, and territorial integrity, organized rioting broke out among the country's Magyars. More indirect allusions to the Hungarian minority, which were made by Budapest officials during this period, further served to remind Rumania of its vulnerability and the wisdom of more closely conforming to Moscow's wishes. Still another illustration of Budapest serving as the Soviet Union's willing agent against Bucharest occurred in 1971, following a much-heralded trip to China by Rumania's President Nicolae Ceausescu, a trip that obviously displeased Moscow. But this time, in response to a Budapest official's thinly veiled threat concerning the Magyars within Rumania, a Rumanian dignitary fired back:

> Anyone who tries to pursue a policy of fostering national hatred is pursuing a policy against socialism and communism—and consequently must be treated as an enemy of our socialist nation. We must fight for national advancement. We observe the rights of the nationalities and work to ensure these rights. We wish to advance together toward communism. Therefore, we cannot permit any attempts at nationalism- or chauvinism-mongering, no matter where they come from. This should be treated as an activity inimical to the cause of socialism and communism.[54]

The manipulation of minorities to bring governments and other leaders into line was unusually visible about the time of the Soviet's 1968 military intervention in Czechoslovakia. Soviet displeasure with increasingly democratic developments within Czechoslovakia had been escalating for some months. Prior to the invasion, the Hungarian government had taken several steps to remind the

Czechoslovak authorities of the Magyars in their midst, and both before and after the invasion, Moscow preyed upon Slovak resentments toward the Czechs in order to isolate both peoples and thereby make each more manageable. The issue was not confined to Czechoslovakia, however, for the Soviet Union could anticipate that the intervention would evoke verbal and perhaps other forms of protest from the area's two most ardent proponents of state sovereignty, Rumania and Yugoslavia. As part of the broadly orchestrated use of minority issues, therefore, Hungary again raised the minorities question with Rumania, while Bulgaria intensified its propaganda campaign to wrest Macedonia from Yugoslavia to an unprecedented postwar pitch.

Ethnic diplomacy therefore became a staple in the arsenal of weapons employed by the Soviet Union with regard to Marxist-Leninist states. It bears emphasizing, however, that the purpose behind these appeals to ethnonational aspirations was quite different than the purpose which had undergirded such appeals by Marxist-Leninists before World War II and which continued to undergird such appeals by Peking and Hanoi throughout the postwar period. Whereas prewar appeals of this nature were intended to bring on revolutionary situations, postwar Soviet resort to such tactics was predicated upon a desire to maintain the status quo. This change of purpose self-evidently required a more cautious approach to utilizing ethnic sentiments; if such utilization were not to prove counterproductive, care must be taken that the antigovernmental feelings of a minority not be raised to a point that would cause the minority to later refuse to readapt to its former political status, even though the government of its state had meanwhile reentered Soviet favor. This consideration probably dictates that blatant, emotional appeals to the minority be used only in the rarest and most pressing of situations and then only as a last resort, and that the threat to make such an appeal, rather than the making of the appeal, be the standard modus operandi. Otherwise, given the unpredictable passion lurking within ethnopsychology, minorities represent a most dangerous vehicle by which to gain foreign policy objectives if one truly desires a return to the status quo ante. Moreover, as one views the response of Rumania and Yugoslavia (as well as of China) to Soviet attempts to take advantage of their multinational character, it appears that, if anything, this tampering with their subjects steeled the resolve of the targeted governments to become less, not more dependent on Moscow's will. But whatever the level of success enjoyed by the Soviet Union, in pressing the innately revolutionary force of ethnonationalism into the service of systems maintenance, the Soviets again demonstrated an unusual capacity to retain a very flexible perspective on the potentialities inherent in nationalist inclinations.

It would be misleading to leave the impression that the other Marxist-Leninist governments of Europe acted only as agents or as targets of the Soviet Union in matters involving minorities, or that they were uniformly content with the ethnic status quo. The key role that came to be played in the postwar period by the ethnographic map in the diplomatic dramas of Eastern Europe was hardly a recent development. On the contrary, one is struck by the continuity of specific national problems extending from before World War I, through the Hitlerian period, down to the present. Marxism-Leninism neither created nor succeeded in erasing these problems. Among those which persisted and which seriously ruffled the relations among Marxist-Leninist states were the conflict between Bulgaria and Yugoslavia concerning the Macedonians; between Albania and Yugoslavia regarding the latter's Albanian minority; those between Hungary on the one hand and Czechoslovakia, Rumania, and Yugoslavia on the other, all involving the Magyar minorities in the latter three states; and between Rumania and the Soviet Union over the aforementioned case of the Bessarabians.[55] These national rivalries continued to have a life of their own under Marxism-Leninism. On numerous occasions, the governments involved conducted ethnically oriented propaganda campaigns without encouragement from Moscow and sometimes despite Moscow's displeasure.

What was new in the postwar equation, however, was the absence of a threat of immediate war between neighbors as a means of settling a conflict involving national minorities. It was not the comparative strength of any one East European state that would be apt to decide such an issue. The Soviet Union remained the ultimate arbiter, and since Moscow would frown upon open hostilities between fraternal socialist states, disputes between the governments of the area over ethnic issues assumed such highly subtle forms as indirect allusions, pseudohistorical debates, and the citing of sometimes quite obscure passages from Marx, Engels, or Lenin in support of one's own position.[56] But the absence of a resort to violence by the European Marxist-Leninist states was not due to a lessening of interstate frictions involving the national question.

The most significant factor regulating the national question throughout Eastern Europe in the postwar era was, therefore, the dominating role of the Soviet Union. It was in the course of rationalizing that imbalanced relationship that the Soviets were to invent perhaps the most innovative chapter in the lengthy history of Marxism and self-determination—that dealing with the theory of "*socialist* self-determination." The theory first appeared on September 26, 1968 in a *Pravda* article written by one Sergei Kovalev, whose principal aim was to defend against critics the military invasion and occupation of Czechoslovakia by the armed forces of the Soviet Union and four lesser members of the Warsaw Pact. The article was later endorsed by Soviet Premier Leonid Brezhnev and became popularly known as "the Brezhnev Doctrine." The document set forth a notion of limited sovereignty for Marxist-Leninist states, noting that it is not merely a right but a duty for other Marxist-Leninist states to intervene in the internal affairs of a fellow Marxist-Leninist state to prevent it from backsliding into bourgeois ways.[57] Subsequent analyses of the document's case for this assertion tended to concentrate on the phrase "socialist commonwealth" as the novel and key element of the doctrine, although this expression had in fact appeared in Soviet documents and press releases with some regularity throughout the 1960s.[58] A second phrase which appeared in the article and which was much more central to the Brezhnev Doctrine was "socialist self-determination." Indeed, as the following excerpts testify, the notion of self-determination and the vital distinction between its bourgeois and socialist varieties formed the recurring theme. Referring specifically to the invasion and occupation of Czechoslovakia by the combined armed forces of the Soviet Union and its four allies, the article commented:

> We cannot ignore the assertions, held in some places, that the actions of the five socialist countries run counter to the Marxist-Leninist principle of sovereignty and the rights of nations to self-determination. The groundlessness of such reasoning consists primarily in that it is based on an abstract, non-class approach to the question of sovereignty and the rights of nations to self-determination. . . . Each Communist party is free to apply the principles of Marxism-Leninism and socialism in its own country, but it cannot deviate from these principles . . . . The antisocialist elements in Czechoslovakia actually covered up the demand for so-called neutrality and Czechoslovakia's withdrawal from the socialist community with talking about the right of nations to self-determination. However, the implementation of such "self-determination," in other words, Czechoslovakia's detachment from

the socialist community, would have come into conflict with its own vital interests and would have been detrimental to the other socialist states. Such "self-determination," as a result of which NATO troops would have been able to come up to the Soviet border, while the community of European socialist countries would have been split, in effect encroaches upon the vital interests of the peoples of these countries and conflicts, as the very root of it, with *the right of these people to socialist self-determination*. . . . As a social system, world socialism is the common gain of the working people of all lands; it is indivisible and its defense is the common cause of all Communists. . . . Naturally the Communists of the fraternal countries could not allow the socialist states to be inactive in the name of an abstractly understood sovereignty, when they saw that the country stood in peril of antisocialist degeneration. . . . Formal observance of the freedom of self-determination of a nation in the concrete situation that arose in Czechoslovakia would mean freedom of "self-determination" not of the popular masses, the working people, but of their enemies. . . . The soldiers of the allied socialist countries now in Czechoslovakia . . . do not interfere in the internal affairs of the country, are fighting for the principle of self-determination of the peoples of Czechoslovakia not in words but in deeds, are fighting for their inalienable right to think out profoundly and decide their fate themselves, without intimidation on the part of counterrevolutionaries, without revisionists and national demagogy.

One rather obvious message of the doctrine is that constraints arising from the right of socialist self-determination apply not only to nations but to Communist states. A second is that any activities viewed by Moscow as detrimental to *socialist* self-determination are by definition the handiwork of "counterrevolutionaries." And "counterrevolutionary activity" undertaken in the name of self-determination by Communist states will be no more tolerated than were similarly stigmatized activities carried out by national groups in the name of self-determination within the Soviet Union, China, Vietnam, and Yugoslavia following the consolidation of power by the Communist parties. But with the Brezhnev Doctrine, the justification advanced for denying self-determination is another form of self-determination. This development is particularly ironic in light of the manner in which Marx, Engels, Lenin, Stalin, Mao, Ho, Tito, and a host of other Marxist-Leninists had extensively manipulated the self-determination principle for more than a century.

National self-determination had been invoked to lure nations and states into the Marxist-Leninist fold. Now socialist self-determination was invoked to keep them there.

NOTES

1. So far as the case of the Soviets was concerned, their principal strategic purpose during the Kerensky period had been to cause dissension and chaos, rather than to gain popularity. The response of the ethnic Russians to their stand on secession was therefore probably not given weighty consideration. By the time the Soviets achieved power, the ethnic Russians could be consoled with the argument that recognition of secession was, at worst, only making the best of an undesirable situation which could not, in any case, be rectified until after the struggle against the Whites (a struggle in which the support of the seceded peoples was necessary). It is nevertheless of interest that Lenin never appears to have considered that his stratagem on self-determination might prove counterproductive by turning the dominant group against the Communist party.

2. See Burks, *Dynamics of Communism*, for a sophisticated analysis of the electoral fortunes of Communist parties within Eastern Europe during the interwar period. A map on page 76 illustrates election results by districts.

During the late 1920s and early 1930s, the treatment of their kin within the Soviet Union caused increasing skepticism among the Belorussian and Ukrainian communities concerning the wisdom of secession from Poland, and the party's demands switched from secession to autonomy. (See, for example, Karklins, "Interrelationship," 142.)

3. Burks, *Dynamics of Communism*, 213.

4. Degras, *Documents* 2:157. Dissension within the party over national policy did not cease as a result of the Comintern's 1924 criticism. In 1925 the party was criticized for its intraparty "national antagonisms." See "Bolshevizing the Communist International," 130, 183.

5. In that month, the head of the party, then domiciled in Moscow sent the following communiqué: "It is necessary to change our pre-war slogans. The idea of 'restoration of Czechoslovakia' today is an expression of imperialist and anti-Soviet plans. The national question today is different. It is reduced to the problem of the Czechs and the Slovaks. We emphasize explicitly that the principle of complete right of self-determination is binding for our Party. This means the right to an independent state existence." Cited in Steiner, *Slovak Dilemma*, 45.

6. For references to this aspect of French history, see Degras, *Documents* 2:220–222; and 3:218, 219, 229, 389.

7. See ibid. 1:139, 142; and 2:28, 171, 265. The call for Irish liberation

went on long after the creation of an independent Irish state. See, for example, the Comintern statement of September 1932 in ibid. 3:229.

8. See ibid. 3:97, 242.

9. See, for example, Barker, *Macedonia*, 65.

10. While strategy concerning the national question as it applied to the United States concentrated on the black issue, it did not do so exclusively. For example, it also called for the emancipation of the American "colonies" of Cuba and the Philippines. In an interesting attempt to drive wedges between Japan and the United States, it drew attention to American exclusionary policies with regard to the immigration of Orientals. For example, a Comintern manifesto of 1924 noted that "the antagonism between Japan and the United States retains its full force. . . . The prohibition on the immigration of yellow peoples gives the imperialist struggle in the Pacific the character of a racial struggle." ("Extracts from a Manifesto of the Fifth Comintern Congress on the Tenth Anniversary of the Outbreak of War," July 1924, in Degras, *Documents* 2:107–113.)

11. "Preliminary Draft Theses on the National and the Colonial Questions, in Lenin, *Selected Works* 3:373.

12. "Extracts from a Comintern Executive Committee Resolution on the Negro Question," October 1928, in Degras, *Documents* 2:552–557.

13. "Extracts from a Resolution of the Comintern Executive Committee's Political Secretariat on the Negro Question in the United States," October 1930, in Degras, *Documents* 3:124–135.

14. Ibid., 127–128. By "bourgeois nationalism" was meant "reactionary Negro separatism, for instance that represented by Garvey; his Utopia of an isolated Negro State (regardless if in Africa or America, if it is supposed to consist of Negroes only) pursues the only political aim of diverting the Negro masses from the real liberation struggle against American imperialism." (Ibid. 3:132–133.)

15. The Comintern was not so committed to the notion of black separatism that it would not drop it during the period of the united front, however. In 1936 the ACP dissolved its "League of Struggle for Negro Rights" which had been created in 1930 with a program dedicated to self-determination for the Black Belt.

16. In an interesting after-effect of the party's position on blacks, a group at the party's Nineteenth Annual Convention in 1969 tried but failed to pass a resolution calling for a "struggle for complete liberation" of American blacks. General Secretary Gus Hall was quoted as saying "Even though black people do not now constitute a nation, we do not place any limitation upon further development of the struggle . . . including their right to develop self-government and to exercise the right of self-determination." Mr. Hall was further quoted as cautioning, however, that self-determination "applied only to nations and was consequently not now applicable to the black community in the United States." See the *New York Times*, May

7, 1969. (The second quotation was not set within quotation marks in the article.)

17. Degras, *Documents* 3:29.

18. This was no easy task. As early as 1920, the party program of the National Socialists had stipulated: "We demand uniting all Germans into a great Germany by virtue of the right to self-determination."

19. Degras, *Documents* 3:122.

20. For a brief comment on the Polish case, see Fejto, *History of the People's Democracy*, 195.

21. As we earlier noted, the Comintern attempted to divide the American black community into two, but that attempt involved a minority, not the state's dominant element.

22. Fisher-Galati, "Moldavia," 235. The writer, in turn, cites for authority, Charles Clark, *Bessarabia* (New York: n.p., 1927).

23. Cited in King, *Minorities*, 235. Karklins ("Interrelationship," 140) reports that the Comintern further instructed the Rumanian Communist Party to support the national demands of the Bulgarian, German, Hungarian, and Ukrainian minorities. This represented something of a geographic overlap with the resolution on Bessarabia, since the Bulgarians and Ukrainians were located principally within the Bessarabian region.

24. King, *Minorities*, 233–234.

25. Ibid., 234. Resistance to such a resolution was apparently pronounced. Karklins ("Interrelationship," 140) cites an interwar Soviet source (I. E. Levin, *Natsional' nyi Vopros v Poslevoennoi Evrope* [*The National Question in Postwar Europe*] [Moscow: Kommunisticheskaia Akademiia, 1934], 337–338) to the effect that the Rumanian Communists proved quite unwilling to implement the Comintern's directive to support separation for the Moldavians, doing so reluctantly only at the Fourth Congress in 1928. Levin describes the policy prior to 1928 as "faulty." For additional details, see Jackson, "Green International," 310, 311, 318–321.

26. See chapter 3.

27. Fisher-Galati ("Moldavia," 417) states flatly that MASSR "was assigned by Moscow the task of working toward the reincorporation of Bessarabia through propaganda as well as through revolutionary action with Bessarabia proper." The emotional magnetism that the Soviets hoped MASSR would exert is evident in such published Soviet statements as "with the formation of the Moldavian Soviet Republic the centrifugal tendencies of the broad working masses of Bessarabia have found a concrete goal for their political, social and cultural strivings." Cited in Karklins, "Interrelationship," 137.

28. Of all East European states, only Albania had a weaker (and in that case, nonexistent) Communist apparatus. See Burks, *Dynamics of Communism*, 51.

29. For a global survey of such problems as of the mid-1960s, see Walker

Connor, "Self-Determination: The New Phase," *World Politics* 20 (October 1967):30–53.

30. For more detailed statistics and discussion concerning the ethnic composition and problems of states, see Connor, "Nation Building," 319–355, and "Politics of Ethnonationalism," 1–21.

31. Christman, *Communism*, 240.

32. Ibid., 253.

33. Ibid., 279–340.

34. The Vietnam case, as we have seen, was one led not by nationalists but by the Communist party. Moreover, Soviet aid became significant only after the party came into power in Hanoi in 1954, and all subsequent aid was channeled through that government.

35. One Soviet writer, using terms such as clans and tribes in a seeming attempt to deny the presence of nations, explained the Soviet Union's failure to support separatist movements within Africa as follows:

> In Lenin's view, self-determination, and especially separation, have no absolute significance. In solving the problem of self-determination, due consideration should be paid to the concrete historical circumstances and the special national peculiarities of the country concerned. In the actual historical situation in many African countries today, where clan separatism and tribalism play a significant part, an absolute interpretation of the principle of self-determination would lead to the review of nearly all the national frontiers and, in many cases, to the abolition of the existing political systems and the birth of hundreds of micropolitical formations.
>
> When the problem of new frontiers and the formation of new states is actually demanded by nations in their struggle for the liquidation of colonialism, then this is fully justified. But the situation is entirely different when separatist movements, paying lip-service to the slogan of self-determination, in actual fact hand over their countries to yesterday's colonialists and strengthen the position of the local reaction. This kind of separatism has nothing to do with self-determination. The majority of the African states decisively repudiate any attempts to review the frontiers on their continents. (Baratashvili, "Lenin's Doctrine," 13.)

In short, the Soviets do not find it expedient to support movements that would gain them the animosity of most or all African governments.

36. Liu Ch'un, *National Question and Class Struggle*, 5–6. Later in the same article, Liu, although referring to the national question within China, makes clear that such an alliance is temporary and that successful national revolution must be followed by the elimination of the exploiting classes.

37. For further details, see Connor, "Ethnology," particularly pp. 73–77.

38. In the case of Malaysia, this is totally true with regard to the Marxist-Leninist movement in the territories on Borneo and essentially true in the

case of peninsular Malaysia. In the latter case, the guerrillas fell back on the Thai-Malaysian border area, and for some time their principal base was on the Thai side of the border in an area populated by Malays, who were desirous of independence from Bangkok. Thus this segment of the Malaysian Communist Party operated from the minority area of another state. We earlier noted that the Vietnamese Communist Party had also created a base area in a minority area of an adjoining state (China). However, unlike that case, the Malaysian Communists established their base amongst a minority (Thailand's Malays), whose kin were the dominant ethnic element within the target state (Malaysia). For more information, see Connor, "Overview of Ethnic Composition," 11–27.

39. See, for example, the interesting article in the *Washington Post*, April 11, 1976, by a visitor to the Shan area of Burma. He notes that "the Communists offer the hill tribes and the Shan rebels promises of an independent homeland plus enough guns and ammunition to fight the government armies."

Thailand's Communist party adopted a twelve-point policy in 1961 and a ten-point policy in 1968. In each case, point five pledged autonomy to the ethnic minorities (referred to as such in 1961 and as "the various nationalities" in 1968). See Caldwell, "Revolution and Response," 146, 158.

40. Harrison, *In Afghanistan's Shadow*, 128.

41. Ibid., 129.

42. See chapter 3.

43. Printed in the *Christian Science Monitor*, November 18, 1971.

44. Ibid.

45. *Area Handbook for India*, 356.

46. Peking's highly selective approach was particularly apparent during this period because its negative view concerning Bengali self-determination contrasted so sharply with its often-articulated support for self-determination for the Kashmiri of India. Thus, in the official communiqué marking the end of a historic visit to China by a United States president (and therefore a communiqué which the Chinese realized would have a massive, worldwide audience), Peking announced that it "firmly supports . . . the people of Jammu and Kashmir in their struggle for the right of self-determination." (This was followed almost immediately by a salute to "noninterference in the internal affairs of other states.") The entire text is reprinted in the *New York Times*, February 28, 1972.

47. See, for example, the many items in *Joint Publications Research Service (JPRS)* 80867 (May 20, 1982), particularly those on p. 4. The campaign was presumably intended to exert pressure upon the Khomeini regime to be less hostile toward Moscow.

48. In a conversation held in Washington, D.C., in February 1982, a leader of Nicaragua's Miskito Indians (Steadman Fagoth Müller), told me that during their successful revolution against Somoza, the Sandinista guerrillas had gained the fighting support of himself and other Miskitos

by pledging them total autonomy following victory. Failure to abide by this pledge led to subsequent hostilities between the Indians and the Sandinistas. Propaganda materials distributed by guerrillas to Indians within Guatemala about this time also played heavily on the Indians' desire to rid their highlands of the influence of the state's Spanish-speaking elite. For information on the creation of a Tawantinsuyo Liberation Front, which would do away with Bolivia, Ecuador, and Peru in order to recreate the borders of the Inca Empire, see *Keesing's Contemporary Archives* (1982), 31308.

49. Cited in Bradsher, "Tibet Struggles to Survive," 70. For a general survey of the Soviet approach, see Osofsky, "Soviet Criticism," 907–917. For an interesting and comprehensive treatment of Soviet policies as they influenced the Uighurs, see Karklins, "Interrelationship," 161–202.

50. Liu Ch'un, *National Question*, 22.

51. In a similar move, the Tibetans were forced to adopt Chinese characters.

52. Yaroslav Bilinsky ("Assimilation and Ethnic Assertiveness," 130) reports a 1965 Peking broadcast to Ukrainian troops serving along the Chinese border. In addition to charging that Moscow intended to russify the Ukrainians, the broadcast ominously pointed out that Russian troops were stationed in the Ukraine while Ukrainians were sent far from their homeland into Asia.

53. Peking seems to have enjoyed minor success in its appeals to the ethnopolitical sentiments of minorities within Vietnam and Laos. Following the deterioration of relations with Hanoi, China appears to have supported insurrectionist movements among the minorities of both countries (including support for the movements among the montagnards of former South Vietnam). See *Keesing's Contemporary Archives* (1981), 31146, 31147, 31202, 31203.

54. Cited in King, *Minorities*, 168.

55. For details, see King, *Minorities*.

56. Even states such as Albania and Yugoslavia, which had broken formally with Moscow, had to consider that hostilities might precipitate Soviet intervention.

57. This theme was conveyed in the article's original title, "Sovereignty and International Duties of Socialist Countries." The article was reprinted in its entirety in the *New York Times*, September 27, 1968.

58. The phrase appeared several times in Kovalev's article, and was rendered more geographically specific by the expression, "the commonwealth of European socialist countries."

THE DIALECTICAL ROAD
TO FUSION

CHAPTER 8

National in Form . . .

LENIN's formula for solving the national question in a postrevolutionary environment flowed from his perception of nationalism as the outgrowth of past discrimination and oppression. The resulting milieu of national suspicion and mistrust was to be exorcised by a period of national equality.[1] This period of equality was to be one of cultural pluralism in which the more overt manifestations of each nation's uniqueness, most especially its language, were to be nurtured by the state.

In time this policy of promoting pluralism came to be known as "the flourishing of the nations." Lenin reasoned that as the policy of equality dissipated the antagonisms and mistrust that had previously estranged nations, those human units would naturally move closer together, a process that became known in the official Marxist lexicon as "the rapprochement" or "coming together" of nations. The process of coming together would continue until a complete blending was achieved, and a single identity had emerged. Leninists usually avoid terming this synthesis *assimilation*, on the twin grounds that (1) assimilation is better suited to capitalist societies, wherein the relations among national groups are characterized by inequality and oppression and where coercion is the principal means for bringing about acculturation; and (2) assimilation usually refers to absorption by the state's dominant national group and is therefore a euphemism for russification, sinification, vietification, serbification, and the like.[2] Marxist-Leninists differentiate their approach to the national question by noting (1) that national relations within a Marxist society are predicated upon absolute national equality and (2) that the process of blending together is fully voluntary, devoid of any element of coercion; and that, far from being a device for absorbing people into the state's dominant group, the blending process in a Marxist state leads to the creation of a totally new identity, a new socialist person, who, in the case of the Soviet Union, came to be called "Soviet man." The Soviet authorities therefore generally eschew the word *assimilation* when describing the final phase of the synthesizing process, preferring the Russian term *sliyaniye*, translatable as a *merging*.[3] Similarly, Peking usually avoids references to the Chinese word for assimilation, *t'ung-hua*, preferring *jung-ho*, which means a *melting together* or *amalgamation*.[4] And, in the same vein, a Yugoslav theoretician has explained that in "referring to a joint Yugoslav culture we are not alluding to assimilation of the cultures of less numerous peoples and national minorities, but to an integration of equals."[5]

In Lenin's scheme, the period of the flourishing of nations would hasten the process of *e pluribus unum*. To Lenin, language and other overt manifestations of national uniqueness were construed, on balance, as conveyors of the messages emanating from the party. In and by themselves they were merely forms. It was the party, acting through the state, which would give them content. Forms did, nevertheless, have an important role to play in enhancing the receptivity accorded to the messages. Lenin and his successors have believed that sovietization would not be resisted by minorities as an alien program identified with the state's dominant ethnic element, if it came dressed in the local tongue and other appropriate national attire. Employing the individualized national forms would convince the people that Marxism-Leninism was not just a new guise for assimilation by the dominant group.[6] In 1925 Stalin would confer upon this entire approach to the national question the official, abbreviated title of "national in form, socialist in content."[7]

Lenin's plan for achieving homogeneity by encouraging cultural distinctiveness is at least a somewhat enigmatic one. Even Stalin granted that the approach would appear "contradictory" and "paradoxical" to those uninitiated in the ways of Marxian dialectics. In 1930 he likened Lenin's national policy to the Marxist view concerning the withering away of the state and to Lenin's strategic insight concerning self-determination:

> It may seem strange that we, who are in favor of the *fusion* of national cultures in the future into one common culture (both in form and content), with a single, common language, are at the same time in favour of the *blossoming* of national cultures at the present time, in the period of the dictatorship of the proletariat. . . .
>
> It may be said that, presented in this way, the question is "self-contradictory." But is there not the same sort of "self-contradiction" in our treatment of the question of the state? We are in favour of the withering away of the state, yet we are at the same time in favour of strengthening the dictatorship of the proletar-

iat, which represents the most powerful and mighty of all forms of state power that have hitherto existed. The supreme development of the power of the state, with the object of preparing the way for the withering away of state power—such is the Marxist formula. Is that "self-contradictory"? Yes, it is "self-contradictory." But this contradiction is a living thing, and it is a complete reflection of Marxian dialectics.

Or take, for example, the way Lenin presents the question of the right of nations to self-determination, including secession. Lenin sometimes expressed the thesis of national self-determination in the form of a simple formula: "disunion for the purpose of union." Just think—disunion for the purpose of union! It even smacks of the paradoxical. And yet this "self-contradictory" formula reflects that living truth of Marxian dialectics which enables the Bolsheviks to capture the most impregnable fortresses in the sphere of the national question.

The same must be said of the formula of national culture: the blossoming of national cultures (and languages) in the period of the dictatorship of the proletariat in one country, with the object of preparing the way for their dying away and fusion into a single, common, socialist culture (and a single, common language) in the period of victory of socialism all over the world.

Whoever has failed to understand this peculiarity and this "self-contradictory" nature of our transitional times, whoever has failed to understand this dialectical character of historical processes, is lost to Marxism.[8]

It might well be argued that the actual experience of Marxists with regard to (1) the withering away of the state and (2) the response of peoples to prerevolutionary promises of self-determination should have led Stalin to a quite different assessment of the likely outcome of Lenin's prescription for solving the national question. As we are reminded by the high priority that Marxist-Leninist governments still assign to the strengthening of their respective states, and by the way in which the nations of the Soviet Union availed themselves of the right of self-determination during 1917–1918 to secede from the Russian state, paradoxes, which in the realm of theory may be readily explained away in terms of an anticipated dialectical development, may prove in the real world to be predicated upon more intractable, unilateral forces. And so, Stalin's analogies might well have led him to the conclusion that nurturing cultural pluralism would be more likely to result in a unilateral path of increasing awareness of national uniqueness than in a dialectical route toward transnational fusion.

Such a nondialectical eventuality was not considered a viable threat, because the party, through control of the state apparatus, would command the forces of political socialization. Particularly significant would be the agencies responsible for agitation and propaganda, because they would design the intellectual content of school and university curricula, of all published works (including the particularly important category of historical works), and of the telecommunications media and press, as well as of communication channels of lesser incidence, such as films, plays, operas, and graphic art. How such controls might be exercised is illustrated by a remarkably candid Chinese directive to teachers of non-Han students:

> Minority education, like other minority work, [aims at] increasing common qualities and decreasing differences. Therefore, while teaching, teachers have the possibility of strongly pushing . . . the racial viewpoint of Marxism-Leninism . . . vividly and intelligently infiltrating day by day the thoughts of each race's children, youth, and adults; seeping into the consciousness of each child, youth, and adult of each race. This will cause them to have a common language, understanding and thought; and of course will bring about common action, synthesizing them into a unified force of all the races, giving all their strength to fulfill completely the grand purpose of building the big socialist home.[9]

As to books, the same directive, in a section entitled "Give Heed to Doing Well the Translating and Supplying of Teaching Materials and Texts," pointed out that the "leading ideas in racial materials should have an eye to national unity, racial amity, and the building of socialism."

In somewhat more guarded terms, an article, which was officially approved for use in seminars addressed to the national question within the Soviet Union, assigned the same high priority to altering national psychology by controlling the message that the people receive. Though the process is referred to as "education," it is evident that all channels of communication, and not just formal education, are intended thereby:

> Educational work has tremendous significance in the struggle against the designs of class enemies and any vestiges of nationalism in *people's consciousness*. The CPSU Central Committee res-

olution in connection with the 50th anniversary of the formation of the USSR points out that internationalist education acts as one of *the central tasks of all party, soviet, economic, cultural and public organizations, and of all our cadre in the center and locally in every republic, kray, oblast, and collective.* The party draws attention to the fact that in this work . . . it must be shown more widely that the further development of international relations, the consolidation of the peoples' friendship, and the processes of the development and rapprochement of the socialist nations exert favorable influence on all spheres of Soviet society's life—economics and politics, ideology and morality, culture and everyday life. The party will continue to educate all working people in the spirit of socialist internationalism and implacability toward manifestations of nationalism and chauvinism and national narrow-mindedness and conceit in whatever form they appear and in the spirit of profound respect for all nations and nationalities.[10]

This antinationalist "education" is to be waged on the widest possible front with regard to both its socialist content and national form.[11] Implicit in the preceding quotation is the command that all sources of information (press, radio, television, school curricula, the speeches of cadre, etc.) are to be marshaled so as to promote socialist content and to ensure prior censorship of all national content. Moreover, the national form is not to be restricted to language but is to incorporate whatever aspects of traditional cultural attire are apt to prove effective at making the socialist content appear less exotic, more familiar, and therefore more compatible with a group's predispositions. The manner in which all media are to be marshaled was suggested by a Soviet official in 1982:

> Comrades! An integrated approach to the education process [of instilling (1) hostility toward "survivals of nationalism" and (2) greater friendship toward other national groups] presupposes the active employment of the entire diversity of forms and resources which the ideological front has today at its disposal. . . . I refer to the effective use of all the resources of mass information—the press, television and radio, the possibilities of the cinema, oral political and visual agitation and cultural-educational institutions.
>
> Literature and art also play an important role here. . . . And the results of these efforts are already evident. The themes of Motherland, the party, revolution, patriotism, military glory and

valor and the international solidarity of peoples have become leading topics for the creative workers of all generations.

The republic's scholars are making a significant contribution to the process of patriotic and international education and to the development of its theoretical and scientific bases. In the last ten years alone, they have prepared and defended more than 30 doctoral and candidate dissertations dealing with topical problems of national relations and education of workers in the spirit of patriotism and internationalism. . . . A number of collective and individual monographs has been published dealing with problems of establishment of internationalist maturity in the workers of the republic.[12]

Traditional religious rites, as well as forms of folk music, costumes, and dance, may also be used to cloak socialist content, as witness the manner in which the Vietnamese deputy minister of culture, shortly after the victory over South Vietnam, described the techniques for inculcating the Khmer minority of southern Vietnam with what he termed "the new culture."

"The third of five ethnic zones within southern Vietnam is inhabited by about 600,000 compatriots of Khmer descent who are mostly Buddhists. They enjoy a rather good economic life, use their own language, and have good singing and dancing skills. Their cultural activities are connected with pagodas." In this zone, nationality songs and dances must be developed and combined with religious activities at pagodas to disseminate the new culture among the working masses.[13]

The keystone of Leninist national policy has been, therefore, a plenary distinction between form and substance. While the former assumes a national coloration during the period of the flourishing of the nations, the latter must unerringly remain thoroughly socialist at all times. Here, for example, is how the First Secretary of the Soviet Communist Party described Soviet culture in 1972:

In the half century that the U.S.S.R. has been in existence, a Soviet socialist culture, uniform in spirit and in its fundamental content, has formed and flourished in our country. . . . Today we have every right to say that our culture is socialist in content and in the main tendency of its development, diverse in its national forms and internationalist in its spirit and character.[14]

All Marxist-Leninist states are ostensibly committed to the maxims laid down by Lenin for solving the national question in a postrevolutionary situation. The degree to which Lenin's legacy on the question has been canonized was reflected in the principal speech commemorating the fiftieth anniversary of the formation of the Soviet Union.[15] Part 1 was entitled "The Formation of the U.S.S.R.— A Triumph of the Leninist Nationalities Policy" and read in part:

> Thus, the fundamental interests of all the Soviet peoples and the very logic of the struggle for socialism in our country demanded the formation of a single multinational socialist state. But the creation of such a state required the Party's organizing role, its correct policy and its purposeful activity.
>
> The Communist Party did have the necessary theoretical basis for such a policy: the Marxist-Leninist teaching on the nationalities question.

As a result of the canonization of Leninist national policy, the charge that a Marxist-Leninist party is violating that policy is tantamount to a charge of apostasy. Thus a Soviet article entitled "Unmasking Mao Tse-tung's Anti-Leninist Policies" states that "as is known, the Mao Tse-tung group at the present time is resolving the nationality problem in the Chinese People's Republic from the standpoint of great power chauvinism and is abandoning the principles of proletarian internationalism and of Marxist-Leninist policies on the national question."[16] Chinese writers have responded in kind:

> Brezhnev and his ilk shamelessly try their utmost to describe what they call "national rapprochement" as "the Leninist policy on nationalities" and the continued development along the road chartered by Lenin. This is indeed the biggest insult to Lenin, the teacher of proletarian revolution, and a crude distortion of his teachings. . . . It has nothing in common with the Leninist policy on nationalities; it is an utter betrayal of Leninism.[17]

Similarly, Hungarian leaders, when pressing Prague for more autonomy for the Magyar (Hungarian) minority within Czechoslovakia, noted that better relations between the two states were "possible only on the basis of socialism and a Leninist nationality policy."[18]

With but two exceptions, Leninist national policy, sloganized in the motto that "all nations are equal," is emblazoned on the escutcheon of every Marxist state. Minimally, their constitutions reflect Lenin's insistence that all preferential treatment be avoided. The prototype was Article 123 of the Soviet Union's 1936 constitution which stipulated that "equality of rights of citizens of the U.S.S.R., irrespective of their nationality or race, in all spheres of economic, governmental, cultural, political and other social activity, is an independent law."[19] The Chinese Constitution conveys this same sentiment with admirable brevity (Article 4): "All nationalities in the PRC are equal."

The two exceptions are Cuba and North Korea. The Cuban and Korean governments do not disclaim Lenin's approach, but simply make no reference to it, since they treat their respective populations as ethnically homogeneous.[20] While this presumption is well founded in the case of North Korea, in the case of Cuba it represents a departure from earlier positions taken by the Communists with regard to the ethnic composition of the Cuban population. The most prominent division within Cuba follows racial lines, and the Cuban Communist Party, as its American counterpart, had endorsed a Comintern directive of 1928, which held that the principle of self-determination required that a separate Black republic be carved from Cuban territory.[21] Nevertheless, the Castro government's constitution treated the population as homogeneous.[22]

Elsewhere, even the absence of a statistically significant minority has not been a sufficient bar to constitutional affirmations of commitment to national equality. Thus, although the post-World War II alterations in Poland's borders transformed that country into one of the world's most ethnically homogeneous states, its constitution (Article 69) proclaims that all citizens "irrespective of nationality, race or religion, enjoy equal rights in all spheres of public, political, economic, social, and cultural life."

Although the passage from the Polish Constitution cited above lists five spheres where national equality is to be honored, those entitled "public" and "social" are superfluous. In practice, the policy of national equality, which is ostensibly supported by all Marxist-Leninist states, has three distinguishable dimensions: (1) cultural, (2) economic, and (3) political. Let us examine each in turn.

CULTURAL EQUALITY

With regard to the first dimension, the constitutions of most Marxist-Leninist states somehow suggest that the national groups have the right to preserve their particular culture, most specifically, their own language. The Albanian Constitution (Article 39), for example, states that national minorities "enjoy all the rights, the protection of their cultural development and the free use of their language"; the Bulgarian Constitution (Article 45) noted that citizens "in addition to the compulsory study of the Bulgarian language, are en-

TABLE 1. Ethnolinguistic Composition of
Marxist-Leninist States

State (Estimated 1980 population in parentheses)	Ethnolinguistic groups by Percentage of Population	
Albania	Albanian	97.0
(2,730,000)	Geg	(65.0)
	Tosk	(32.0)
	Greek	2.5
	Others	0.5
Bulgaria	Bulgar	85.8
(8,860,000)	Turk	9.1
	Gypsy	2.6
	Macedonian	2.5
Cambodia	Khmer	90.0
(8,870,000)	Vietnamese	4.0
	Chinese	4.0
	Cham	1.0
	Mon-Khmer	1.0
People's Republic	Han	93.3
of China	Chuang	1.0
(1,027,000,000)	Others	5.7
Cuba	White*	73.0
(9,980,000)	Mestizo*	15.0
	Negroid*	12.0
Czechoslovakia	Czech	65.0
(15,320,000)	Slovak	29.2
	Magyar	4.0
	German	0.5
	Pole	0.5
	Ruthenian	0.3
	Others	0.5
German Democratic	German	99.6
Republic	Sorb	0.4
(16,800,000)		
Hungary	Magyar	96.0
(10,710,000)	German	2.0
	Slovak	1.0
	Others	1.0

TABLE 1 (*cont.*)

State (Estimated 1980 population in parentheses)	Ethnolinguistic groups by Percentage of Population	
Democratic People's Republic of Korea (19,000,000)	Korean	99.0
	Others	1.0
Laos (3,720,000)	Lao	67.0
	Mon-Khmer	19.0
	Tai (other than Lao)	5.0
	Meo	4.0
	Chinese	3.0
	Others	2.0
Mongolia (1,670,000)	Khalka Mongol	76.0
	Other Mongol	13.0
	Kazakh	5.0
	Other Turkic	2.0
	Chinese	1.0
	Russian	1.0
	Others	2.0
Poland (35,580,000)	Pole	98.0
	German	1.0
	Others	1.0
Rumania (22,270,000)	Rumanian	88.0
	Magyar	9.0
	German	2.0
	Others	1.0
USSR (266,670,000)	Russian	52.4
	Ukrainian	16.2
	Uzbek	4.8
	Belorussian	3.6
	Kazakh	2.5
	Tatar	2.4
	Azerbaijan	2.1
	Armenian	1.6
	Georgian	1.4
	Moldavian	1.1
	Tadzhik	1.1
	Lithuanian	1.1
	Turkmen	.8

TABLE 1 (*cont.*)

State (Estimated 1980 population in parentheses)	Ethnolinguistic groups by Percentage of Population	
USSR (*cont.*)	German	.7
	Kirgiz	.7
	Jewish	.7
	Chuvash	.7
	Latvian	.5
	Bashkir	.5
	Mordvinian	.5
	Pole	.4
	Estonian	.4
	Others	3.8
Vietnam (52,300,000)	Vietnamese	86.0
	Chinese	2.0
	Khmer	2.0
	Mountain Cham tribes	2.0
	Tho	2.0
	Muong	1.0
	Tai	1.0
	Nung	1.0
	Meo	1.0
	Yao	1.0
	Mon-Khmer tribes	1.0
Yugoslavia (22,428,000)	Serb	36.3
	Croat	19.8
	Ethnic Moslem	8.9
	Slovene	7.8
	Albanian	7.7
	Macedonian	6.9
	Montenegrin	2.6
	Magyar	1.9
	Others	8.1

* Otherwise undifferentiated.

titled to study also their own language"; the Chinese Constitution (Article 4) states that "all the nationalities have the freedom to use and develop their own spoken and written languages, and to preserve or reform their own customs and ways"; the Mongolian Constitution (Article 83) ensures all nationalities that they have "the opportunity to develop their national culture and to receive tuition and conduct business in their own native language"; and the Vietnamese Constitution (Article 4) promises that "all nationalities have the right to preserve or reform their own customs and habits, to use their spoken and written languages, and to develop their own national culture."

The right to use or to study one's own language is not, of course, the same as the right to study *in* one's own language, the latter usually implying the privilege of having one's own schools. A number of Marxist states have constitutionally guaranteed this additional right. Again, the Soviet Union served as the prototype: Article 121 of the 1936 constitution ensured "the right to education . . . by instruction in schools in the native language." The Rumanian Constitution (Article 22) is even more explicit on this point, stating that "the co-inhabiting nationalities are ensured the free utilization of their native language as well as books, papers, magazines, theatres and education at all levels in their own language." In a similar approach, the Yugoslavian Constitution pledges (Article 171) that "members of the nations and nationalities of Yugoslavia shall, on the territory of each Republic and/or Autonomous Province, have the right to instruction in their own language in conformity with statute." The Hungarian Constitution (Article 49) hedges, by comparison, granting to all nationalities only "the possibility of education in their native tongue and the possibility of developing their native culture."

OTHER Marxist-Leninist states have committed themselves to providing education in a minority tongue, but have limited such a right to a specified national group or groups. Thus, in addition to designating Czech and Slovak as the two official languages of the state, the Czechoslovak Constitution of 1960 (Article 25) promised "citizens of Hungarian, Ukrainian (Ruthenian) and Polish nationality every opportunity and all means of education in their mother tongue and for their cultural development." Although more numerous than the Poles and Ruthenians, the German minority within Czechoslovakia was not extended this right until a constitutional amendment to this effect was passed in 1968. The Sorbs of East Germany

offer another example of a people being singled out in a constitution. Although the Sorbs account for less than one-half of one
percent of an otherwise homogeneous population, and although
there is general agreement that these people were well along the
way to complete assimilation by the 1940s, the newly formed German Democratic Republic, under direction from the Soviet Union,
purposefully set about reversing this trend.[23] Under Article 40 of
the constitution, citizens of "Sorb nationality have the right to cul-
tivate their mother tongue and culture. The experience of this right
is fostered by the state."

Lenin's prescription concerning the need for a people to enjoy
a period when the more overt characteristics of their national culture would be permitted to flourish had been formulated with an
eye to nationally conscious peoples who would resent an attempt
to foster the culture of the state's dominant people at the expense
of their own. But what of peoples totally or largely at a prenational
level of group-consciousness? Particularly in the cases of the Soviet
Union and China, newly installed Marxist-Leninist governments
were confronted with a number of remote groups, many of whom
did not even possess a written language.

Given the ultimate Marxist-Leninist goal of cultural fusion, it
might be anticipated that the authorities would elect to telescope
the process, having such peoples bypass the stage of the flourishing
of the nation. It is a testament to the influence of Lenin's thought
that authorities generally elected not to do so, preferring to provide
the group with an alphabet, to compile dictionaries and instruc-
tional materials in the local language, to conduct lessons in the
language, and the like.[24] A stage of pre- or semi-national consciousness did offer some potentiality for shaping the emerging
national identity, however, and the authorities did not hesitate to
experiment. Over the years, Marxist-Leninist theoreticians have
been prone to assign great significance to language as a controlling
factor in the formation of ethnonational consciousness, and so the
selection of one vernacular over another to serve as the officially
sanctioned language was often designed to bring about a desired
political end.[25] For example, in their early reign, the Soviet authorities, fearing the possibility of a pan-Turkic or pan-Muslim
movement that would unite the state's Asian peoples in a formi-
dable bloc, purposefully promoted several tongues, such as Ka-
ralkapak, Kirgiz, Tatar, Turkman, and Uzbek.[26] In somewhat similar fashion, the Yugoslav authorities elected to promote the concept
of a separate Macedonian language and identity, despite Sofia's

insistence that Macedonians are in fact Bulgars and that the so-called Macedonian language fostered by Yugoslavia is only a localized dialect of Bulgar.[27]

The selection of an alphabet has also often been a factor in nurturing one sense of national identity rather than another. For example, the various Turkic peoples on the Soviet side of the border traditionally employed the Arabic script. In the late 1920s, Moscow replaced Arabic with the Latin alphabet, at least in part as a means of dissuading sentiment of a transstate, pan-Turkic, or pan-Muslim nature. Still later, commencing in the late 1930s, the Cyrillic alphabet was introduced. On the other side of the Sino-Soviet border, the Turkic peoples had also traditionally employed the Arabic script. However, in 1956, at a time of good relations between the two countries, and apparently at Soviet prodding, Peking announced plans to introduce the Cyrillic alphabet. Soon thereafter relations chilled, and Peking's desire to make its population immune to the blandishments of Soviet propaganda caused it to substitute the Latin alphabet.[28] Despite the fact that the Soviets had earlier compelled their own Turkic peoples to use the Latin script, the Soviets now labeled Peking's decision to do so a manifestation of Great-Han chauvinism. The irony of Moscow's indictment was further underlined by Soviet practice with regard to the Moldavian question. Having taken the twin position that the people of Moldavia constituted a separate national group, distinct from the Rumanian people, and that the local Moldavian variant of the Rumanian tongue was in fact a separate language, the Soviets had purposefully promoted the Cyrillic alphabet rather than the Latin alphabet used in Rumania. Cultural form, as well as cultural content, has therefore been manipulated to bring about politically desirable ends.[29]

ECONOMIC EQUALITY

As noted, the policy of national equality is not restricted to its cultural dimension. Indeed, when leaders, whether inside or outside of Marxist-Leninist states, inveigh, without further specifics, against national inequality, it is presumed that they refer to economic inequality. Surprisingly, however, in their prerevolutionary writings both Stalin and Lenin had ignored economic motivation when enumerating their reasons for endorsing a policy of national equality. In his celebrated 1913 *Marxism and the National Question*,

Stalin had made no mention of economic considerations when he elaborated upon the bases for national discontent:

> What is it that particularly agitates a national minority?
>
> A minority is discontented not because there is no national union but because it does not enjoy the right to use its native language. Permit it to use its native language and the discontent will pass of itself.
>
> A minority is discontented not because there is no artificial union but because it does not possess its own schools. Give it its own schools and all grounds for discontent will disappear.
>
> A minority is discontented not because there is no national union, but because it does not enjoy liberty of conscience (religious liberty), liberty of locomotion, etc. Give it these liberties and it will cease to be discontented.
>
> Thus *national equality in all forms (language, school, etc.) is an essential element* in the solution of the national problem.[30]

Nor had Lenin made any reference to the righting of economic imbalances, when detailing in 1914 his program for "the equality of nations and the definition of the rights of national minorities."[31] Given their assumptions concerning the primacy of socioeconomic causation and the fact that they were committed to a social system that held out the promise that each individual would be rewarded "according to his work" (socialism) and, ultimately, "according to his needs" (communism), it is safe to conclude that the achievement of economic equality was simply presumed by both men. But a national sense of economic inequality is a different phenomenon than an individual one. And it is rather remarkable that men, who were so aware of the strategic potentialities inherent in the cultural and political grievances of entire nations, should so overlook the opportunity to appeal to another font of group dissatisfaction.[32]

In any case, once in power the closing of the economic gaps among groups became a highly publicized feature of national policy. The high priority which the Soviet leadership assigns to the broadest possible dissemination of this message was evident in the emphasis accorded it in the important speech of Party General Secretary Leonid Brezhnev on the occasion of the fiftieth anniversary of the formation of the Soviet Union. Several paragraphs were dedicated to drawing a sharp contrast between the situation of the non-Russian peoples in 1922 and their situation in 1972. The secretary said in part:

In summing up the heroic accomplishments of the last half century, we have every reason to say that the nationalities question, in the form in which it came down to us from the past, has been resolved completely, resolved definitively and irrevocably. . . . Now, on the 50th anniversary of our Union, the resolution of the nationalities question and the overcoming of the backwardness of the formerly oppressed nations is for Soviet people something that they take for granted, something that is second nature to them. But one must recall the scale and complexity of the work that was done in order to appreciate not only the wisdom but also the boldness and consistency of the Bolshevik Party, which set itself this goal and then achieved it. Let us for a minute imagine what the condition of the outlying national areas of our country looked like at the time of the Revolution. In terms of their economic development, Central Asia and Kazakstan were on a level that is characteristic of colonial countries. Poverty, illness and ignorance were the lot of the overwhelming majority of the population. . . . Many parts of Transcaucasia and even Belorussia, which was close to the Center, were marked by economic backwardness. All these areas, with the exception of a few large cities, were still in the dark ages, so to speak, in economic terms, in their social makeup, in cultural terms and in the living conditions of their working population. . . . It was in these conditions that the Party, at Lenin's initiative, embarked on a course aimed at the accelerated economic, cultural, social and political development of the outlying national areas. The Party saw that the practical implementation of this course was possible only on the basis of extensive and comprehensive assistance to the nations and nationalities who had been oppressed in the past from the more developed parts of the country, above all from the Russian people and its working class. . . . During the years the Union has been in existence, the volume of industrial output has increased 600 times in Kazakstan, more than 500 times in the Tadzhik Republic, more than 400 times in the Kirgiz Republic, almost 240 times in the Uzbek Republic, and more than 130 times in the Turkmenian Republic. . . . In short, on the basis of the Leninist nationalities policy and at the price of the intense labor of the entire Soviet people, we have achieved a situation in which the term "backward outlying national area," which was so common in the old Russia, has ceased to exist.[33]

Similar claims have been made by spokesmen for other Marxist-Leninist states.[34]

POLITICAL EQUALITY

The Soviet Union

As to the political dimension of the policy of national equality, all of the Marxist-Leninist states constitutionally prohibit political discrimination on the basis of nationality and/or race. Much more significant than this commonplace constitutional guarantee against discrimination is the degree to which the Marxist-Leninist states have designed their own internal political structures so as to reflect ethnonational distributions, thus catering to the ambition of national groups for their own political unit. Prior to the revolution, Lenin and Stalin had envisaged the prospect of some form of autonomy for territorially contiguous people, what Stalin termed "regional autonomy" and what Lenin had called "autonomous and self-governing territorial units." Neither man, however, had spelled out the anticipated level of home rule to be enjoyed by these subordinate entities. Indeed, at least in 1913, Stalin did not believe that the distribution of national groups would be a necessary consideration in the delimiting of the regional units. He wrote of autonomy only "for such crystallized units as Poland, Lithuania, the Ukraine, the Caucasus, and so forth."[35] As Stalin well knew, the Caucasus was not an ethnic homeland but a region of intricate ethnic diversity. Even with regard to the other likely territorial candidates for autonomous status, he correctly noted that "of course, not one of the regions constitutes a compact, homogeneous nation, for each is interspersed with national minorities."[36] By contrast, Lenin granted that "nationality" should be a consideration in the drawing of political subdivisions, but only one "among other things."[37]

In any case, the division of powers between the regional governments and the center was to be imbalanced markedly in favor of the latter. Anything smacking of the federal principle was to be avoided studiously, as Lenin had explicitly asserted in a letter of December 1913:

> We are in principle against federation. It weakens the economic connection and is inappropriate for a unified state. Do you want to separate? we say. Then go to the devil and cut yourself off altogether. . . . You don't want to separate? Then, please, don't decide *for me*, don't believe you have the "right" to federation.[38]

Despite this unambiguously negative viewpoint, opposition to the federal form dissolved almost simultaneously with the assumption of power. Lenin drafted a resolution for the Third All-Russian

Congress of Soviets, held in January 1918, which read in part that "the Soviet Russian Republic is established on the basis of a free union of free nations, as a federation of Soviet national republics."[39] Events had made the change of stance advisable; nations that had seceded now had to be assured that reunion would not result in political subservience. Federation was the best guarantee of equality.[40] But in reversing his prerevolutionary stance, Lenin made clear that federalism was to be only a temporary concession, or in his words, "a transitional form to the complete unity of the working people of different nations."[41] As such, federal relations were to be thought of not as frozen but very much in flux; the early forms would give way in the face of progress toward increasing unity. Again to quote Lenin, "In recognizing that federation is a transitional form to complete unity, it is necessary to strive for ever closer federal unity."[42]

The prolongation of the federal form within the Soviet Union down to the present would have probably proven surprising to Lenin therefore. One of the reasons for this prolongation is that, despite Lenin's early distrust of federalism, this structural system of government was subsequently perceived as blending well with the presumptions underlying his strategy of *national in form*.[43] Although the Soviet Union is one of the most centralized states in the world, the constitutions of 1924, 1936, and 1977 all referred to the constituent Soviet Socialist Republics (SSRs) as sovereign, and, as earlier noted, granted them "the right freely to secede."[44] During 1944, in an attempt to gain separate membership for each SSR in the United Nations General Assembly, this image of independent statehood on the part of the SSRs was further buttressed when they were extended the right to maintain diplomatic relations, enter into treaties, and otherwise conduct foreign policy directly with other countries.[45]

Preserving the form though not the content of a federation of sovereign republics has served a preemptive purpose. Over the years, the Soviet authorities have used this fiction to impress upon the fourteen non-Russian nations whose names adorn the Soviet Socialist Republics that the seemingly intrinsic urge of nations to possess their own state has, in their case, already been fulfilled.[46] Accordingly, Soviet writers on the national question have placed great emphasis on the "fact" of independent statehood. Thus one Soviet specialist insists that "each Soviet republic has its own statehood and broad representation in the union organs of power, which insures the equality and sovereignty of all the peoples."[47] If the nations can be convinced that their national state is already a fact, secession becomes a logical extravagance. As another Soviet writer on the national question has noted:

> Experience shows that there may be different forms of statehood. Under socialist democracy the substance of national sovereignty lies not in the mandatory state secession of one nation from another but in the freedom of choosing any desired form of state organization. From their own experience Soviet nations know that sovereignty is best achieved and guaranteed in a fraternal multinational family and they bend every effort to develop and strengthen the union state.[48]

If such a political unit were to satisfy or even blunt the desire of a nationally conscious people for its own state, it would be appropriate for each unit to be named so as to evoke a close association between itself and the national group. The history of the creation of the various SSRs is a complex one marked by periodic consolidations and fragmentations,[49] but the fact that fourteen of the present SSRs bear the name of a national group illustrates the authorities' keen appreciation that such designations can be very helpful in triggering a positive association. Moreover, the single exception is only a partial one and illustrates the Soviet leadership's awareness that ethnonational designations can exert a negative, as well as a positive psychological impact. The exception is the Russian Soviet Federated Socialist Republic (RSFSR), which is the oldest and manifestly most important of all such units.[50] As translated into English, this appellation would appear no exception at all. But, depending upon its spelling in the Russian language, the word *Russian* has two quite distinct meanings. Dating well back into the Romanov period, there had been a tradition of distinguishing between something Russian in the sense of ethnonational identity (*russkii*) and something simply pertaining to all the lands and peoples under Romanov domination (*rossiiskii*). Thus the dynasty was not the (*ethnically*) Russian Empire (*Russkaia Imperiia*) but the Empire of Russia (*Rossiiskaia Imperiia*).[51] Although consistency with the ethnonational designations of all the other republics would therefore require the ethnonational *Russkaia* form in the title of the RSFSR, the authorities quite purposefully selected and subsequently retained the *Rossiiskaia* spelling as a means of lowering the risk of having the political designation convey any hint of special privilege or status being accorded to the Great Russian people.[52]

In addition to those fourteen peoples who have an SSR named

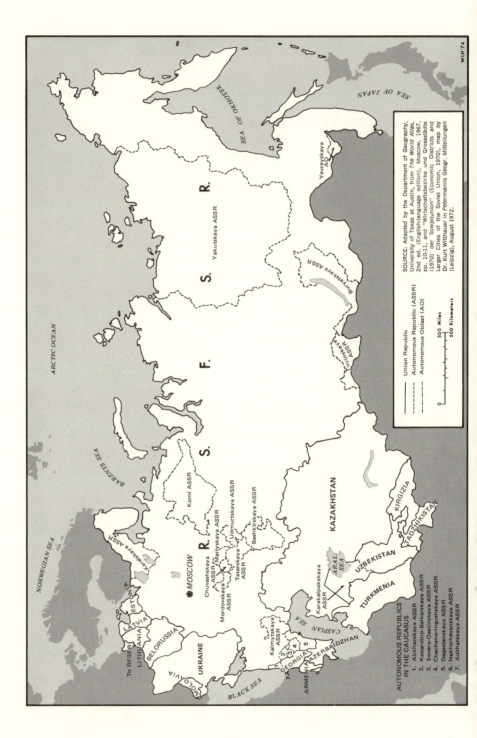

WLH '74

ARCTIC OCEAN

SEA OF OKHOTSK

SEA OF JAPAN

Yevreyskaya AO

R.

S.

Yakutskaya ASSR

F.

S.

Buryatskaya ASSR

SOURCE: Adapted by the Department of Geography, University of Texas at Austin, from *The World Atlas*, 2nd ed., English-language edition, Moscow, 1967, pp. 10–11, and "Wirtschaftsbezirke und Grossstädte (1970) der Sowjetunion" (Economic Districts and Larger Cities of the Soviet Union, 1970), map by Dr. Kurt Witthauer in *Petermanns Geogr. Mitteilungen* (Leipzig), August 1972.

Union Republic
Autonomous Republic (ASSR)
Autonomous Oblast (AO)

500 Miles
500 Kilometers
0

R.

Tuvinskaya ASSR

Komi ASSR

BARENTS SEA

NORWEGIAN SEA

Karelskaya ASSR

Chuvashskaya ASSR
Mariyskaya ASSR
Udmurtskaya ASSR
Mordovskaya ASSR
Tatarskaya ASSR
Bashkirskaya ASSR

MOSCOW

KAZAKHSTAN

ARAL SEA

KIRGIZIA

TADZHIKISTAN

Karakalpakskaya ASSR

UZBEKISTAN

TURKMENIA

To RSFSR
ESTONIA
LATVIA
LITHUANIA
BELORUSSIA
UKRAINE
MOLDAVIA

Kalmytskaya ASSR

CASPIAN SEA

BLACK SEA

GEORGIA
ARMENIA
AZERBAIDZHAN

AUTONOMOUS REPUBLICS
IN THE CAUCASUS
1. Abkhazskaya ASSR
2. Kabardino-Balkarskaya ASSR
3. Severo-Osetinskaya ASSR
4. Checheno-Ingushskaya ASSR
5. Dagestanskaya ASSR
6. Nakhichevanskaya ASSR
7. Adzharskaya ASSR

after them, nearly forty other peoples within the Soviet Union possess some form of governmental structure, whose title reflects their national identity. Stretched out below the SSR level of government in a descending order of officially ascribed importance is a series of twenty Autonomous Soviet Socialist Republics (ASSRs), eight Autonomous Regions (Oblasti), and ten Autonomous Areas (Okruga).[53]

Vital differences among these various levels of ethnically defined units are difficult to discern. At the level of pure form, the difference between SSRs and autonomous units is that only those in the first category are declared to be sovereign and to have the right to secession and to conduct foreign relations. But in a system such as that of the USSR, in which power is intensely focalized and in which the most important channels of power lie outside the governmental structure (i.e., in the party), the latitude of either regional or local governments to exercise independent policy is slight indeed, and differences between layers of government become either infinitesimal or purely theoretic.

The most tangible factor differentiating SSRs from most other units is the requirement that an SSR's territory touch upon one of the external borders of the USSR.[54] The next most definite basis for differentiation involves the numerical strength of the national group. Though subject to important exceptions, there is a definite degression in the size of the national component as one moves from the SSR through ASSR and Autonomous Region down to the level of Autonomous Area.[55] An evident though unofficial basis for refusing any form of national unit to a people, regardless of size and location, is that the group be part of a larger nation that is dominant within a state outside of the Soviet Union. For example, of the thirty largest groups within the Soviet Union, only Germans, Poles, Koreans, Bulgarians, and Greeks have been denied any governmental unit bearing their name.[56] A Jewish Oblast was created near the Chinese border in 1934, but this event took place fourteen years prior to the creation of Israel.[57]

While significant differences among the various forms of government are therefore difficult to detect, all four forms share in the political function of serving as constituencies for the election of delegates to the country's major legislature. The Supreme Soviet, described in the constitution as "the supreme body of state power," is composed of two houses, the Soviet of the Union and the Soviet of the Nationalities. The former is elected by the citizenry without regard to special categories. But by the terms of Article 110, "the

Soviet of Nationalities is elected according to the following norms: 32 Deputies form each Union republic, 11 Deputies from each autonomous republic, 5 Deputies from each autonomous region and 1 Deputy from each autonomous area."

The Supreme Soviet is generally accepted by non-Soviet scholars as another illustration of form without content. It meets periodically in very abbreviated sessions to ratify, customarily without debate, decisions made elsewhere.[58] The system of multiple constituencies for members of the Soviet of Nationalities is nevertheless quite interesting for the light it sheds on Soviet federalism. By not confining representation to the SSRs, the system is an acknowledgment that all units are essentially the same. The method of weighted voting expresses a distinction predicated upon size, but not one based on different levels of government. The Soviet system would be comparable to a United States in which towns, cities, and counties, as well as the fifty states, were to send delegates to the United States Senate. Quite aside from the merits and/or demerits of such a change, the alteration would represent a most decided step away from a federal system toward a unitary one. Nevertheless, in developing a style of government in which regional and local units are described in ethnonational terms and in which the apex of the most visible structure contains a house of "nationalities," the Soviets have clearly obeyed the dictum of *national in form*.

Yugoslavia

The Yugoslavian CP has been the only party which, immediately upon taking power, followed the Soviet precedent of adopting the federal form.[59] The plan to organize postwar Yugoslavia on the federative principle had been first announced at the second meeting of the Anti-Fascist Council of the National Liberation of Yugoslavia in November 1943.[60] Consonant with this decision, the new state was officially designated the Federal People's Republic, thereby becoming the only Marxist-Leninist state to have a reference to federalism in its title. The federal principle has subsequently been retained in form, but its content has vacillated markedly over the decades.

The new Marxist state was divided into six republics and two autonomous provinces. Five of the republics (Croatia, Macedonia, Montenegro, Serbia, and Slovenia) were ostensibly designed so as to fulfill the self-determination yearnings of the country's five principal nations to possess their own political unit. The sixth republic,

Bosnia-Hercegovina, contained a number of peoples, none of whom constituted a majority. Although there were more Albanians (variant: Shiptars) within Yugoslavia than there were Montenegrins, these people were granted only an autonomous province within the Republic of Serbia and not their own republic, apparently on the ground that a people who form part of a larger nation beyond the Yugoslavian borders could aspire only to the official status of a nationality, rather than to the higher status of a nation.[61] A second autonomous province (Vojvodina), in which there was an important Magyar (variant: Hungarian) minority but in which Serbs predominated, was also carved out of the Republic of Serbia.

Describing the changing formal structure of federalism in postwar Yugoslavia is not a simple task. The YCP experimented with an inordinate number of constitutions during its first decade in power, and each successive constitution called for substantial alterations in political form.[62] Only the first constitution (that of 1946) asserted that sovereignty was vested in the six republics.[63] All subsequent constitutions carefully stipulated that sovereignty was vested solely in the people.[64] The change in constitutional wording is noteworthy, because the notion of popular sovereignty, unlike the notion of a vesting of sovereignty in a state's constituent units, is quite compatible with the most centralized and unitary forms of government.

Why, then, was the notion of sovereignty for the constituent republics introduced in 1946? In part, the answer appears to have been to make union more attractive to the political leaders of Albania and Bulgaria, as well as to the leaders of those Macedonians living within Greece, all of whom the YCP originally hoped to entice into federation. The Yugoslav suitors thereby followed the precedent established by Lenin who, when in the course of wooing the Ukrainians, Georgians, et al. into a political union, had, we will recall, adopted the federal form on the assumption that a federal relationship would prove a less ominous prospect to the courted than would union with a unitary state.[65] A second factor was the great influence that Moscow exerted upon Yugoslavian affairs prior to 1948. Not surprisingly, therefore, the Yugoslavian Constitution of 1946 reflected the Soviet Constitution in many particulars, and those similarities extended to the conferring of sovereignty upon the constituent republics.

Great as it was, however, Moscow's influence was evidently not sufficient to placate all of the doubts that the Yugoslav leaders harbored concerning the wisdom of the Soviet prescription for handling the national question. Thus the Yugoslavian Constitution of 1946 did not follow the Soviet example of granting the right of secession to the constituent republics. As earlier noted, in 1943 the YCP had adopted the position that the national groups within Yugoslavia had already fully and irrevocably exercised their right of self-determination.[66] This remained the official stance following the assumption of power. However, the matter was resurrected during the discussions among constitutional specialists, which preceded the drafting of the constitution of 1953.[67] With unusual candor, constitutional lawyers generally conceded that the promise of sovereignty that had been guaranteed to the republics under the 1946 constitution had remained nothing but an empty phrase, while certain individual lawyers even questioned whether sovereignty could ever be meaningful in the absence of a right of secession. One extreme school of opinion would have brought form and content into greater harmony by dropping all references to the sovereignty of the republics. At the other pole were those who would have achieved this confluence by actually increasing the authority of the republics relative to the center.

In retrospect, it is clear that those wielding ultimate decision-making power sympathized more with the first group. While retaining the word *federal* in the state's official designation, all references to self-determination (with its Leninist implication of a right of secession) were avoided in the 1953 constitution, and the attribution of sovereignty to the constituent republics was replaced by its attribution to the people. Self-determination, in its fully consummated and irreversible form, was reintroduced into the constitutions of 1963 and 1974. And both of these constitutions persisted in the description of Yugoslavia as a federal state.[68] However, as earlier noted, both constitutions also followed the 1953 precedent in avoiding any reference to sovereignty being enjoyed by the constituent republics.

Some important modifications in the degree and type of decision making entered into by the republics and autonomous provinces did occur, however, in the interim between the constitutions of 1963 and 1974. The late 1960s and very early 1970s constituted a period of trial and error in which the central authorities experimented, often simultaneously, with several forms of decentralized administration. Although the republics were collectively only one competitor for the decision-making powers relinquished by the center (other competitors included economic enterprises, local governments, workers' associations, and the like), the republics were clearly the major recipients.[69] Particularly following the economic reforms of 1965 (which heralded a shift from a state-command economy to a decentralized "market socialism"), major decisions came increasingly to be debated and decided at the republic and provincial levels. Approval of this general trend by the top leadership was visible in the 1966 purge of Aleksander Rankovich, generally considered both as Tito's second-in-command and as primary advocate of preserving the highly centralized power apparatus. Tito's support was also necessary for the drafting of a new series of amendments to the constitution, adopted between 1967 and 1969, that upgraded the administrative power of the Chamber of Nationalities, the only house in the Federal Assembly whose delegates ostensibly represented the republics and provinces. Yet a stronger suggestion of Tito's approval was offered in 1969, when the Ninth Congress of the YCP adopted the principle of equal representation for each republic within the party's highest organs. But despite these portents, the amendments to the 1963 constitution that were adopted in 1971 represented a most startling departure from the customary Marxist-Leninist stress upon centralized decision making.[70] With the specified exceptions of defense, foreign affairs, foreign trade, and what was termed "the unity of economic and social affairs," primary responsibility for decision making was transferred to the republics.

Many Yugoslavs and outside observers saw in this transfer the granting of true sovereignty to the republics.[71] This might have been the case were Yugoslavia truly a constitutional system of government, within which the constitution was the supreme law of the state. But the ultimate determinant of how political authority was to be shared within Yugoslavia was not to be found in a constitution but in the momentary convictions of Tito and a few close associates. And this coterie, who had decided to stray from the Stalinist model by experimenting with economic and political decentralization, might just as readily reverse itself. If sovereignty is defined as supreme political authority, then sovereignty, as later events were to attest, remained within the same tight circle of leadership where it had been located uninterruptedly since at least 1948, the year of Yugoslavia's expulsion from the Cominform.[72] Moreover, this innermost circle of ultimate authority, through the use of very carefully selected if convoluted language, avoided conferring sovereignty upon the republics even at the level of constitutional *form*. As an authoritative, official clarification of the 1971 amendments took great pains to stress, "the republics are defined as States based on the sovereignty of the people and on the authority of, and self-management by, the working class and all working people, and as socialist, self-managing democratic communities of working people and citizens, and of equal nations and nationalities."[73] So that there might be no mistake, it was also pointed out that the autonomous provinces and the local communes were additional "socio-political communities in which the working people, nations and nationalities realize their sovereign rights."[74] These, then, were all references to a sovereign people, not a sovereign instrumentality, republic or otherwise. The sole attribution of sovereignty to a governmental unit pertained to that external form of sovereignty attributed to states in their foreign relations, and this form of sovereignty was specifically relegated exclusively to the federal level.[75]

In the months preceding ratification of the 1971 amendments, Tito gave a number of addresses in which he stressed that the forthcoming changes were not designed to abet Yugoslavia's disintegration.[76] And in an address following on the heels of ratification, he unambiguously declared that the republics did not possess sovereignty as customarily understood.

> We do not look upon the independence and statehood of the republics in the classical sense. Having decided to overcome federal statism we did not strive, nor do we now strive to create polycentric statism. . . . Any confrontation between the Federation and republics is wrong and harmful, because the two are inseparable parts of our self-managing organization. Our sovereignty is one and indivisible—be it republics or the Federation that are involved.[77]

Croats in particular failed to heed all such warnings. Significant numbers of Croatians both within and without the party apparatus misperceived the new amendments as granting sovereignty to Croatia. In support of the amendments, some 200,000 people gathered in Zagreb to chant "Long live free Croatia!" and a new local weekly demanded that Croatia be formally recognized as "the national state of the Croatian nation."[78] When convinced by such events that administrative decentralization had taken an unwanted turn, the response of the central leadership was swift and effective. Before the year in which the amendments were introduced had come to a close, the central party apparatus had reasserted its primacy and a major society-wide purge of nationalist elements had begun. Confirmation that Tito had never intended the amendments as a grant of sovereignty was embodied in the 1974 constitution. Though

Yugoslavia was by then ruled by an unquestionably recentralized power structure, the new constitution employed the precise phraseology of the 1971 amendments in describing the republics as "states based on the sovereignty of the people and the power and self-management by the working class and all working people."[79]

Aside from the question of the degree of sovereignty that should be vested in the republics, there has been the at-least-equally ticklish question of proportional versus equal representation for the republics at the federal level. From the outset, those attempting to design a federal structure, predicated upon the principle of the equality of nations, were hampered by the great variations in the numerical size of the national groups. Especially prone to criticize any suggestion of equal representation have been the spokesmen for the Serbs, who tend to distrust the entire concept of federalism, perceiving it as an attempt to deny them the prominent role which they feel should naturally befall their nation as a result of numerical superiority. The fact that Montenegro, for example, has less than one-tenth the population of Serbia, exclusive of the latter's two autonomous provinces, could, in itself, be expected to cause Serbs to discern discrimination in the principle of "one republic, one vote." In addition, the precise way in which borders of the republics were drawn might well cause Serbs to perceive thereby an attempt to lessen further the impact of their numbers through gerrymandering. Thus Serbs account for 31 percent of the population of Bosnia-Hercegovina and 12 percent of Croatia. Moreover, a further attempt to weaken the statistical advantage of the Serbs could be read into the fact that Serbia is the only republic that has been further subdivided by the creation of two autonomous provinces. In the case of Kosovo Province, a non-Slavic people, the Albanians, dominate, although Serbs account for 13 percent of the population. But in the other province of Vojvodina, Serbs account for 54 percent of the population. The Yugoslav system has regularly allocated federal representation to the provinces, as well as to the republics; so, if it be assumed that the Serbs of Vojvodina would vote as a solid block, the existence of the province would, in fact, increase the relative weight of the Serbian vote at the federal level. Nevertheless, Vojvodina only adds additional fuel to the Serbian sense of injustice, for the population of that subrepublican unit of government is in fact larger than the population of three of the five non-Serbian republics.[80] In summary, then, the Serbs have had reason to view any move toward equal representation for the republics as a ploy designed to deny them the authority befitting a people who represent more than one-third of the country's total population. At the same time, provincial and republic borders appear to them as artificial constructs that divide important segments of the Serbian nation from one another. On the other hand, non-Serbian groups have tended to perceive any move toward implementing the principle of "one man, one vote" as an attempt to return to the prewar condition of Serbian hegemony.

The early response of the YCP to these contradictory expectations concerning representation at the federal level was closely patterned after the Soviet model. A bicameral legislature was instituted, within which one house, the Federal Council, reflected the principle of "one person, one vote," while the other house, the Council of Nationalities, reflected the notion of "one republic, one vote." However, the leadership appears soon to have experienced second thoughts concerning the wisdom of bestowing such great prominence upon a political unit that emphasized national distinctions. In 1953 the Council of Nationalities was demoted to the status of a subordinate organ of one of the two houses.[81] Its constitutional standing was further reduced under the constitution of 1963, when its subordinate status was retained, despite the enlargement of the Federal Assembly from a two- to a five-chamber organization. Thus, in less than two decades, the political organ that had been designed to reflect national equality had been reduced from one of two major houses to a subordinate part of one of five.

At least at the level of pure form, however, a turning point was then reached.[82] The formal powers of the Council of Nationalities were increased by constitutional amendments in 1967, and in December of 1968 the council was elevated to become one of five houses comprising the Federal Assembly. Furthermore, when, in 1974, the decision was made to return to a bicameral assembly, the Council of Nationalities (now less ethnically termed the Chamber of Republics and Provinces) regained its original status as one of the two houses comprising the federal legislature.

This tendency, beginning in the late 1960s, to place greater stress upon the principle of "one republic, one vote" was not limited to the form assumed by the Federal Assembly. A parallel development occurred within the more important executive wing of government. In late 1970 Tito, with an evident eye to ensuring continuity in the event of his death or infirmity, proposed a collective federal presidency with equal representation for each republic. As instituted in 1972, the presidency consisted of three delegates from each republic and two from each province. As further streamlined under the terms of the 1974 constitution, this became a nine-person organ, predicated upon the absolute equality of each republic *and* province.[83] Quite expectedly, it was Serbian spokesmen who were the most critical of this trend away from one person, one vote.[84]

Even while the form of government was undergoing this swing in the direction of a federal structure predicated upon republic/province equality, still other programs carried out by the authorities demonstrated the leadership's concomitant determination to dilute the propensity of the masses to think in ethnonational terms. In this effort the regime placed great reliance upon what was termed "socialist self-management democracy." Its key element was ostensible control by the workers over their particular producing unit, or, as put forth in the 1974 constitution, "self-management by the working people in the basic organizations of associated labor." In thus stressing the producing unit as the basic sociopolitical unit of society and in then giving the workers a sense of responsibility for that unit's fortunes, the government hoped to lessen the propensity of individuals to view sociopolitical matters from the vantage point of how they affected one's own national group. The underlying presumption was that a greater degree of concern with the well-being of one's economic enterprise would necessarily deter primary preoccupation with one's nation. As Edward Kardelj, one of Tito's closest confidants, opined with regard to the concept of self-management in 1953, "This is the new factor which creates a socialist community of a new type in which language and national culture become a secondary factor."[85]

One detects here a reaffimation of faith in the classical Marxist belief that economic associations ultimately determine primary group identity. But Kardelj outlined a very different process by which ethnic fusion would take place. Whereas the more conventional Marxist-Leninist position held that a centralized supranational economy and command structure would cause people to lose their particular national identity in a larger identity that was coterminous with the politico-economic whole, Kardelj would attempt to achieve this same result by first weakening national identity through leading people to identify their interests at a subnational and subrepublican level. It was therefore a dialectic scheme in that a transnational identity was to be promoted by stimulating a subnational, functional identity. This functional approach to political representation would hopefully encourage a civic or public identity that was quite distinct from national identity. The functional approach to political representation particularly recommended itself to Kardelj over any form of territorial representation, because the fact that the major national groups tended to populate definite ethnic homelands caused national, republican, and territorial identities to reinforce each other in popular perceptions. Kardelj's shorthand for the process by which he hoped to bring about the obliteration of the individual national identities and their replacement by a new civic identity therefore appropriately became "de-territorialization." Thus, he set forth his creed in 1965:

> If what we now call the republican or command economy could be inspired only by the logic of economic laws, if it could be influenced only by stimulation based on labor productivity, then the road toward de-territorialization would be open and the real process of economic integration would be put into motion. There is no other way than to merge the national, republican, and communal interests into the interests of every individual working man and each collective. At least, I do not see any other way.[86]

The same determination to wean the citizenry from the habit of perceiving and reacting to issues in terms of ethnic competition can be detected in the authorities' decision to forestall the direct, popular election of delegates to the federal level. With regard to the election of delegates to the Federal Chamber of Republics and Provinces, for example, the 1974 constitution interposed three intermediaries between these delegates and the mass electorate.[87] Members of self-management organizations and local communities elected delegates to some five hundred communal assemblies; the assemblies, in turn, elected delegates to the assembly of their respective republic or autonomous province; in the third phase, the republic and provincial assemblies elected delegates to the Federal Chamber of Republics and Provinces. As a result of this three-tiered system, the ostensibly ethnogeographically based chamber must have been perceived by the average voter as far more remote and unrepresentative than would be the case were direct elections permitted. Made equally remote was the federal presidency, since its members were also elected by the members of the assemblies of the republics and autonomous provinces.

Even at the level of form, then, the Yugoslav authorities, during their first thirty years in power, had not strayed very far from Tito's early view of federalism. At a council of party leaders held in late 1943, just prior to the conference at which the plan for a single Yugoslav state was unveiled, Tito had played down the significance of the federal structure with the comment that "with us this will be more of an administrative division, instead of fixed borders, as with the bourgeoisie."[88] And in 1945, he had likened the borders of the constituent units to the "white lines on a marble column," adding that "the borders of the federal states in federal Yugoslavia are not borders which divide, but borders which unite."[89] His comment in 1971, the year in which the republics gained their greatest measure of autonomy at the level of form, was fully in accord with these earlier statements: "We do not look upon the independence and statehood of the republics in the classical sense . . . nor do we now strive to create polycentric statism."[90]

Czechoslovakia

The final Marxist-Leninist state to have experimented with the federal form is Czechoslovakia. There, the introduction of federalism occurred more than two decades after the Communist party first came to power. The constitutions of 1948 and 1960 had earlier made allowance for ostensible Slovak autonomy. Slovak national organs were created, including a legislature entitled the Slovak National Council.[91] However, despite the provision for such organs, both constitutions explicitly described Czechoslovakia as "a unitary state" of the two nations,[92] and the powers of the Slovak agencies were made subservient to the whims of the federal authorities. Under the 1948 constitution, for example, any act of the Slovak National Council required the prior approval of the federal prime minister and his cabinet before it could take effect.[93] So, too, members of the Slovak executive organ (the Board of Commissioners) were appointed by the federal government and subject to its recall. If anything, the constitutional standing of the Slovak agencies was further undermined by the terms of the 1960 constitution. In addition to being granted the power to delineate the authority of the Slovak National Council, the federal National Assembly was further empowered to annul any enactment of that lower body.[94]

The idea of creating a federal Czechoslovakia crystallized as part of the democratic movement that swept the state in the spring of 1968. Responding to the new milieu, the Czechoslovak Communist Party in April issued a rather lengthy document, "Czechoslovakia's Road to Socialism," which sketched the new directions in policy which the party anticipated pursuing. With regard to the governmental structure, the program called for a system that would "embody the principle of a symmetrical arrangement . . . [and thereby] on the basis of full equality, solve the status of Slovak national bodies in the nearest future."[95] The following month a special commission was established to draft a new constitution embodying a federal state.

The proposed constitution was aborted by the Soviet military incursion of August. However, somewhat enigmatically, the Soviet authorities did permit the new federal structure to come into effect in January 1969, that is to say, some five months into their occupation.

The form assumed by the new federation displayed similarities with both the Soviet and Yugoslav models. The state was divided into a Czech and a Slovak Socialist Republic, and now the Czechs, as well as the Slovaks, were endowed with a national council. The Federal Parliament became a bicameral institution, with one house (the Chamber of the People) being representative of the population at large, while the other house (the Chamber of Nations) was divided equally between representatives of the Czech and the Slovak peoples.[96]

It was perhaps not totally surprising that the Soviet authorities should acquiesce in the adoption of a federal form of government. Immediately before and after their original incursion, the Soviets had attempted to split the ranks of the Czechoslovaks by appealing to the ethnonational aspirations of the Slovaks and to Slovak disgruntlement with Czech predominance. The Soviets apparently did not want to risk the charge of perfidy by blocking those aspirations only a few months later.[97] And, in any event, the Soviets were probably predisposed by their own political structure to detect more merit than peril in the federal form. But while Soviet acquiescence in the adoption by Czechoslovakia of a federal form should, therefore, not occasion much surprise, the content of the new system made Soviet acquiescence most unusual indeed, for that system was much too decentralized to be described as "federal in form, unitary in content."[98] Only foreign and defense policy were reserved exclusively to the federal government. Authority over culture and education was reserved for the constituent republics, while both levels shared responsibilities over such sensitive areas as internal security, communications, and censorship.

The decentralizing spirit infusing this division of powers was soon rendered effete by a thoroughgoing series of purges of officeholders at both levels of government. Centrists replaced those who had been sympathetic to nationalistic proclivities. Moreover, in 1971 changes of form took place, as key powers were transferred to the central government. Most significantly, responsibility for internal security again became the exclusive prerogative of the center, which was also authorized once more to overrule any enactment of the constituent republics.[99] The Czechoslovak reformers had envisaged and had attempted to implement a federalism in content as well as in form, but more conventional Marxist-Leninists had viewed such a development as being at cross-purposes with the overriding requirement of centralized control.

China

One of the many ironies in the history of Marxism-Leninism and the national question is that the nations of the Soviet Union, who had been promised either independence or territorial autonomy, were in fact granted a federal form of government, while the nations of China, who had been consistently promised either independence or federalism, were permitted, at best, a form of territorial autonomy. As late as mid-1945, the CCP had constitutionally pledged itself to work for "the establishment of an independent, free, democratic, united, and prosperous and strong new democratic *federated* republic based on the alliance of all revolutionary classes and free union of all races."[100] However, the program announced on the eve of taking power made no mention of federalism, referring only to regional autonomy for nationalities.[101]

The inherent difficulty of explaining away this contradiction between promise and practice is manifest in the following extract from a tract written by a Chinese official in the mid-1960s:

> Although [in practice] we did not emphasize "national self-determination" but only emphasized national regional autonomy, we still endorsed and honored this principle, and in proposing "regional autonomy" we were holding to the principle of national self-determination, and we followed the spirit of this principle in resolving the question. In resolving the national question, the Soviet Union adopted "national self-determination" and in due course implemented federalism; in principle, we followed the same course as the Soviet Union, but with respect to areas in which national minorities are concentrated, we preferred not to use the federal idea but instead put into practice the method of national regional autonomy.[102]

Considering the physical remoteness of the minority areas and the previous general lack of effective Chinese control over them, Peking's policy of regional autonomy was rapidly implemented.

Eight years after taking power, the regime would boast that more than 90 percent of all minority peoples were living within some form of autonomous political unit.[103]

Three levels of autonomous government were introduced. The most prestigious, the Autonomous Region (Ch'ii) became the administrative equivalent of one of the PRC's twenty-one provinces. At the secondary level were the Autonomous Districts (Chou), and at the third level were the Autonomous Counties (Hsien).[104] Conforming to the precedent set by the Soviet Union's autonomous units, the "autonomy" is essentially formal, the units forming part of a single, highly centralized system. As Mao candidly noted in 1956: "In our fight on the question of regions, we do not take regionalism as our starting point, nor the interests of individual units, but rather the interests of the whole state. We fight this fight wherever an opportunity arises."[105]

Despite the lack of real power behind such forms, the Chinese leadership has been hesitant to confer the status of autonomous region upon its minorities. The Inner Mongolian Autonomous Region, which was created in 1947 before the CCP had come into effective control of China in general and Mongolia in particular, represents a special case. The loyalty of the inhabitants of Inner Mongolia was at that time the target of an intense competition between the KMT, the Soviets, the Mongolian People's Republic, and local Communist and non-Communist movements, and the recognition of autonomous status by the CCP was prompted by this competition. Eight years were to elapse before a second group was extended similar recognition, in the form of the Sinkiang Uighur AR. The third and fourth regions, the Kwangsi Chuang AR and the Ninghsai Hui AR, received Peking's blessing in 1958, nearly a decade after the creation of the People's Republic of China. And the Tibetan AR did not come into being until 1965.

The rationale for granting or withholding the status of an autonomous region is not obvious. It is not essential that the area touch an external border of the country, since the Ninghsai Hui AR did not do so at the time of its creation. Nor do relative numbers appear to be a determining factor. The Chuang who, as China's largest minority, are twice as numerous as the Uighurs and more than four times as numerous as the Mongols, were granted their AR long after those less populous peoples. Moreover, China's fourth largest ethnic element, the Yi (variant: Lolo) have not been accorded an autonomous region, despite the fact that they are more numerous than either the Tibetans or the Mongols. Similarly, there is no autonomous region named for the Miao or the Manchu, although both peoples are more numerous than the Mongols.[106] It would appear, therefore, that autonomous regions have been the result of ad hoc decisions predicated upon the exigencies of the moment.

In the late 1960s and early 1970s, Soviet writers unleashed a campaign of criticism against the Chinese system of autonomy, on the ground that Leninism requires federalism. A book published in Moscow during 1968 charged that by creating a unitary rather than a federal state, the CCP had violated Lenin's legacy concerning the principle of self-determination, and had also violated the party's many explicit promises, dating to 1922, that national self-determination for all non-Han peoples would be honored following victory.[107] The book was most favorably reviewed the following year in an article whose author, after noting that the nationalities of China "are deprived of their legal right to self-determination," added:

> The federal structure of the Chinese People's Republic remains a fiction. Non-Chinese peoples have been "magnanimously" allowed to build their life on the basis of the "territorial national autonomy," which in reality is merely a smokescreen to conceal the policy whereby they are forcibly assimilated.[108]

Still another article, this one appearing in 1971, charged that in being permitted only autonomy and not the right to form national states, the non-Han had been denied proper self-determination from the very beginning of the Chinese People's Republic. Particular notice was taken of the fact that ARs had no more authority than did the twenty-one regular provinces, and it was additionally noted that such large groups as the Yi, Miao, Manchus, and Koreans had not even been granted this lesser privilege of autonomy.[109] This insistence that regional autonomy falls short of Lenin's prescriptions was again repeated in a lengthy article that appeared during 1972. The article also suggested that the failure of the Chinese to follow the Soviet precedent had led them inexorably from a correct Leninist solution:

> Only the 1949 people's revolution was able to create conditions for the correct solution of the nationalities question. Victory in this revolution was achieved as the result of the common efforts and common struggle of all peoples of China.
> It seemed that it was possible then to count on special attention

to the need, to use Lenin's words, for not formal but actual equality between all nationalities and on the former oppressions and discrimination being liquidated.

This seemed all the more likely since the Soviet experience of the formation and development of the USSR was literally before China's eyes. . . . But China did not proceed along a Leninist path. . . . The idea of self-determination gave way definitively to the far more limited principle of local national autonomy. Mao Tse-tung and his supporters, following their great-Han convictions, in fact always remained loyal to petit bourgeois nationalism, imbued through and through with the spirit of the exclusiveness of the Chinese and their supremacy over all other peoples, the spirit of an attitude of arrogance bordering on racism toward the various non-Chinese nationalities living on Chinese territory.[110]

Similarly harsh criticisms of Chinese national policy continued into the post-Mao period. Thus, a 1981 Soviet work noted:

The leaders of China long ago retreated from the Marxist-Leninist solution of the nationalities question which provides, first of all, for the rights of nations to self-determination. . . . Instead of self-determination, the non-Han peoples acquired only a truncated territorial autonomy.[111]

It is difficult to accept these criticisms as little more than evidence of the extremes to which the Soviets were prepared to go in their propaganda struggle with Peking. Granted that the Soviets were correct in their charge that the autonomy permitted by Peking was decidedly more form than content. But this order of things was, as we have documented, both perfectly sound Leninist doctrine and in accord with the actual level of independence and autonomy accorded to peoples within the Soviet Union itself. Further, we have established that, prior to taking power, Lenin did not prescribe federalism and did so afterwards reluctantly as a transitional expedient. Moreover, although Moscow for a number of years was able to exert its will upon the major decisions of the Mongolian People's Republic and the states of Eastern Europe, it had not required any of these states to introduce a federal form of government.[112] Indeed, in the case of Rumania, wherein events suggest that the Soviets did insist upon a change in political structure so as to reflect ethnic distributions, the resulting structure allowed for an autonomous region, as in the case of China, and not for an experiment in federalism.

Rumania

Though Soviet influence over Rumanian affairs was assured by the presence of the Soviet armed forces as early as 1944 and though formal Communist rule was inaugurated in early 1945, it was not until 1952 that the distribution of national groups first became a consideration in the demarcating of internal borders. Under the 1948 constitution, the first to be drafted under Rumanian Communist Party leadership, the country was divided into "regions," but the regions were neither endowed with autonomy nor did they reflect ethnic distributions. The first suggestion of a new governmental policy came with the release on July 18, 1952 of the draft for a new constitution, providing for the creation of a Magyar Autonomous Region in the central sector of the country. Given the degree of Soviet influence at that time, this development certainly had the prior acquiescence of Moscow and very possibly had been initiated at the latter's prodding. From the vantage point of Moscow, the creation of an autonomous region would have the twin advantages of mollifying the leaders of Hungary, who had long been exerting pressure for the creation of Magyar autonomous zones within both Czechoslovakia and Rumania,[113] and of reinforcing a distinct identity on the part of those Magyars within the autonomous region, thereby nourishing a Trojan horse that could prove useful should it ever become necessary to remind Rumanian leaders of Moscow's capability to force compliance with its wishes.

Whatever the primary motivation to create the Magyar Autonomous Region, it certainly was not traceable to a broad-scale commitment to national autonomy on the part of the Rumanian leadership. Neither the Germans, who predominated in the area immediately to the south of the new AR, nor those Magyars who predominated in the area near the border with Hungary, were likewise rewarded with special administrative status. Moreover, the abbreviated history of an autonomous region for the Magyars illustrates a deep governmental suspicion of such administrative arrangements. The powers of the AR were sharply circumscribed from the outset; as in the case of China, there existed no discernible differences of function between the AR and other administrative units of like size. Yet, despite its weakness, there were Rumanians who resented the AR and agitated for its abrogation.[114] Their unhappiness was at least partially assuaged in 1960, when the boundaries of the AR were redrawn so as to decrease the proportion of Hungarians from 77 percent to 62 percent, and when a Rumanian geographic term was added to the title of the region, making it the Mures-Autonomous Hungarian Region. Whether these changes were originally viewed as psychological preparation for the total elimination of the AR is not known. In any case, the intent to eliminate it was announced as part of a country-wide reorganization plan in 1967 and carried out the following year.

Vietnam

The Vietnamese experience with autonomous regions parallels that of Rumania in several respects. As noted earlier the Vietnamese CP also introduced such units with reluctance.[115] With only half of the country under their sway following the French defeat in 1954, some manifestation of good faith concerning the party's earlier promises to ethnic minorities was necessary if the vital support of minorities within southern Vietnam, northeastern Cambodia, and eastern Laos was to be realized. The Thai-Meo AR (whose official name, like that of the AR within Rumania, was later to be changed to a less ethnic designation) was created in 1955; a Viet Bac AR was introduced the following year; and still a third unit, the Lao-Ha-Yen AR, came into being in early 1957.

Again paralleling the case of Rumania, the government subsequently did away with its ARs. The Lao-Ha-Yen AR survived only two years, lapsing, without formal announcement of its demise, sometime during 1959. With the surrender of the South Vietnamese forces in 1975, the propagandistic value of all autonomous zones evaporated. The two remaining ARs were now perceived as liabilities rather than assets and were summarily dissolved in the same year as Saigon's surrender.

As one surveys the forms that have been adopted in conjunction with Lenin's national policy, it is difficult to reconcile certain variations in the forms accorded groups with that ostensible cornerstone of Lenin's policy, national equality. In the sphere of cultural autonomy, for example, we noted that some state constitutions have specified those groups whose language is to be protected, thus denying by omission this right to others. The most conspicuous illustrations of differential treatment in form, however, appear in the sphere of political equality.

Applying the standard of national equality to the Leninist notion of territorial autonomy would seemingly require that all national groups be granted the same type of territorial-political unit. Yet great discrepancies exist among states. While the Soviet Union, Yugoslavia, and Czechoslovakia are, in form, ethnically delineated federations, only the first acknowledges the right of its principal constituent units to secede and to conduct foreign relations. The leaders of China, Rumania, and Vietnam were prepared to condone nothing more than autonomous regions, and even these were scrapped in the last two countries, leaving China as only the fourth state that makes any formal concession whatsoever to Lenin's principle of territorial autonomy. Minorities throughout all of the other states are denied special territorial-political status.[116]

Such discrepancies are not limited to interstate comparisons. As we have seen, even within any of the four states that formally honor the concept of territorial autonomy, there is apt to be a hierarchy of "autonomous" units bearing ethnic designations (e.g., union republics, autonomous republics, autonomous regions, autonomous provinces, autonomous districts, and the like). Some groups have been judged worthy of the highest level of autonomous unit within the state, while others have had to settle for a lower order. Still other groups, rather than having their own autonomous unit, have been forced to share a single unit with others. This is the case with the people living within the Dagestan ASSR of the Soviet Union, for example, and is true as well for most of the national groups living within China. Finally, there are those national minorities who have been denied any special political unit whatsoever. They include the Magyars of Czechoslovakia, the Manchus of China, the Turks of Yugoslavia, and the Poles of the USSR.

Consonant with their status as an aspect of form rather than of content, it is true that all such constituent units, regardless of level, are similar in their weakness vis-à-vis the overarching, highly centralized state. But this consideration renders the failure of Marxist-Leninist governments to grant all national groups an identical political unit all the more inexplicable. If the cost is insignificant, why this failure? As it is, all nations have not been treated as equals, even at the level of pure form.

NOTES

1. Technically one of inequality, since he believed that special treatment for the formerly oppressed peoples might for a time be necessary.

2. As mentioned in chapter 2, Lenin occasionally used the word *assimilation*, although he more commonly used words such as *fusion, amalgamation,* and *merger.*

3. Robert Lewis et al., *Nationality and Population,* 116. The use of the word *assimilation* may be gaining acceptance. See, for example, Bromley, *Soviet Ethnography,* 153, for a discussion of what the author calls "ethnic assimilation." See also the review of a 1981 article, translated from the Kazakh in *JPRS,* May 20, 1982, p. 22. The author writes glowingly of the assimilation process taking place throughout the Soviet Union. More recently, the editor-in-chief of *Kommunist* has noted the tendency among some Soviet researchers to use "the term 'assimilation,' although it, in my opinion, is less suitable than 'merging' for characterizing the ties of equal nations and nationalities." (Kosolapov, *Class and National Relations,"* 22.)

4. Dreyer, *China's Forty,* particularly pp. 157 and 262. For an exception, however, see Chou En-lai's 1975 comments ("Some Questions," 19): "Assimilation is a reactionary thing if it means one nation destroying another by force. It is a progressive act if it means natural merger of nations advancing towards prosperity. Assimilation as such has the significance of promoting progress."

5. Joncic, *Relations between Nationalities,* 57.

6. See chapter 2.

7. Adoption of this official nomenclature followed Stalin's remarks to the University of the Peoples of the East: "Proletarian culture, which is socialist in content, assumes different forms and methods of expression among the various peoples that have been drawn into the work of socialist construction, depending on differences of language, customs, and so forth. Proletarian in content and national in form—such is the universal human culture toward which socialism is marching. Proletarian culture does not cancel national culture, but lends it content. National culture, on the other hand, does not cancel proletarian culture, but lends it form." Stalin, *Marxism and National, Colonial Questions,* 210. Stalin's terminology was, in turn, apparently inspired by the Communist Manifesto: "Though not in substance, yet in form, the struggle . . . is at first a national struggle."

Helene Carrere d'Encausse inexplicably credits both the expression and its underlying strategic rationale to Stalin in *Decline of an Empire.* But Marx deserves credit for the first, and Lenin at least the primary credit for the second. Grey Hodnett, in comments made at the Woodrow Wilson International Center for Scholars, Washington, D.C., summer 1976, found the intellectual basis for the slogan in a statement by Lenin to the effect that there are "two cultures in each nation." Although Marxist-Leninist writers have also often found it convenient to take this passage by Lenin out of context when making a case for some aspect of national policy in a postrevolutionary environment, there is little question but that they, as well as Hodnett, read much more into it than Lenin had intended and overlook the fact that Lenin had not intended it to be applicable to a postrevolutionary situation. Lenin's precise words were: "There are two nations in every modern nation—we say to all national socialists. There are two national cultures in every national culture." "Critical Remarks on the National Question," in Lenin, *Collected Works* 20:32. The passage appeared in 1913, well before the revolution, and was never again employed in his writings. It was used to dramatically point out that aspects of the dominant culture within a capitalist society were, as had been pointed out by Marx, those of the bourgeoisie, and that the proletariat should not be fooled into accepting such standards. As Lenin made clear throughout the rest of the article, he did not mean that the culture of a nation's proletariat was national. Rather (as he went on to say immediately), the culture of any nation's proletariat must be "a common or international culture of the proletariat movement." As such, this is simply a restatement of Marx's thesis that culture is the reflection of socioeconomic class and that the workers must be encouraged to be internationalist rather than nationalist in outlook. Moreover, Lenin's reference to two national cultures in every national culture was made in the context of a 1913 appeal for unity among the leaders of the international movement (more specifically, it was an appeal for Ukrainian leaders to conform), and had nothing to do with postrevolutionary situations. Even the Soviets do not appear to ascribe true significance to Lenin's passing reference to two cultures in every nation. Although often cited in propagandistic tracts on the national question, the two-culture notion is largely ignored in more analytical works. As noted under the entry "Culture" in Kernig's encyclopedic *Marxism, etc.*, 1: 286:

> It is also worth pointing out that current reviews of ethnographic research in Soviet journals make no mention of Lenin's "two-culture" doctrine, but emphasize the persistence of distinctive ethnic features even in highly developed modern nations.

But beyond all this, it is difficult to understand why the inspiration for "national in form, socialist in content" should be sought anywhere other than in the phraseology of the 1848 Communist Manifesto to which Marx redrew attention in 1875 in his "Critique of the Gotha Program" (Tucker, *Marx-Engels Reader*, 390): "It is altogether self-evident that, to be able to fight at all, the working class must organize itself *as a class* and that its own country is the immediate arena of its struggle. In so far its class struggle is national, not in substance, but, as the *Communist Manifesto* says, 'in form'."

8. "Deviations on the National Question," June 27, 1930, in Stalin, *Marxism and National, Colonial Questions*, 261–262. Soviet scholars are even sometimes accused of not comprehending the dialectical process of blossoming and coming together. An article in *Kommunist* (*JPRS* 81900, September 30, 1982), upbraided a group of authors for "some far-fetched views" on the process: "For example, we read on p. 326 that rapprochement dominated the Soviet peoples which had reached a stage of capitalist development before the revolution, whereas in the previously backward nations

'until the final victory of socialism' (!), allegedly the leading trend was blossoming, although it is well known that these are interrelated rather than separate processes."

9. "Improve Education of Minorities." The article appeared during the Great Leap Forward, which, as will be explained later, was a period when rapid assimilation was being pressed.

10. Moskin, "24th CPSU Congress." Emphasis added. One group of Soviet scholars described the difference in ethnonational processes between a socialist and a pre-socialist society as follows:

> The subjective factor, too, plays an important part. In contrast to the spontaneous shaping and development of the pre-socialist social-economic formations, *all the elements* of life *in a socialist* society are consciously *patterned, patterned for a purpose*. The conscious activity of the people, directed by Communist parties, actuates the principles of socialist internationalism. The material results extend the objective basis for the *common socialist content* of the national element.
>
> *It is this conscious activity* that forges bonds of friendship among the peoples, giving impulse to the convergence and fusion of nations. (Zagladin, *Revolutionary Movement*, 135–136. Emphasis added.)

A leading Soviet ethnographer phrased it this way:

> The establishment of international, USSR-wide features in the minds and psychologies of Soviet nations and peoples is the principal purpose of scientific direction of the ethnic processes occurring today. The shaping of international features in the minds and psychologies of Soviet nations occurs on the basis of planned, conscious activity. The socialist multinational state and system of social and political organizations, of which the Communist Party of the Soviet Union is the core, is the moving force in scientific direction of ethnic processes presently occurring. (Kholmogorov, *International Traits*.)

The entire book was published in translated form in three issues of *Soviet Sociology*. The cited passage is from chapter 5, "The Formation of the International Traits of Soviet Nations—A Consciously Controlled Process," and can be found in vol. 12 (Fall 1973): 39. Still more concisely, the Vietnamese cadre were told at the time of the official unification of the country: "Because imperialism continues its activities against the revolution and uses its lackeys to oppose it, the lines and policies of our party and state must be intensively disseminated among the national minorities." (*Radio Hanoi*, June 30, 1976.)

11. In 1982, in an address to what was officially described as the "All Union Scientific-Practical Conference on the Development of National Relations under Conditions of Mature Socialism: The Experience and Problems of Patriotic and International Education," the First Secretary of the Latvian Communist Party noted that the propaganda effort directed at instilling greater friendship among the peoples of the USSR had greatly

intensified during the past five years: "At the present time about 62,000 lectures are held in the [Latvian] republic on these themes." The Secretary, however, called for still greater qualitative and quantitative efforts. See Voss, "Topical Questions."

12. Voss, "Topical Questions," 19–20.

13. *Ho Chi Minh City Domestic Service*, October 28, 1976. Translated and printed in *FBIS*, November 11, 1976. For a discourse by two of the Soviet Union's most influential scholars on the manner in which art can influence national attitudes, see Bromley and Kozlov, "Present-day Ethnic Processes," particularly pp. 28 et seq. See also, M. Ya. Zhornitskaya's article, "Reflections of Ethnoculture Links," 39–50.

14. The speech, delivered by First Secretary Leonid Brezhnev, can be found in *Current Digest of the Soviet Press* 24, no. 51.

15. Ibid.

16. *Aziya i Afrika segodnya*, no. 4 (1969), *JPRS* 48016, May 9, 1969.

17. "Analysis of Soviet Revisionists' Policy of 'National Rapprochement'," *Peking Review* 17 (July 19, 1974): 18–19.

18. King, *Minorities*, 129.

19. The 1936 constitution remained in effect for forty-two years and exerted a great impact upon those constitutions of other Marxist-Leninist states that were drawn up between 1936 and 1977. The 1977 Soviet Constitution purportedly marked an intermediate stage between socialism and communism called "developed" or "mature" socialism. Since no other state claims to have achieved this plateau, changes represented by the 1977 constitution should, at least theoretically, not apply to them. (The contemporary constitutions for all states can be found in Blaustein and Flanz, *Constitutions*.)

20. The Korean Constitution makes no reference to nations, nationalities, minorities, and the like. However, Article 52 does make a passing reference to "race" amidst a lengthy list of factors that should not affect the voting franchise.

21. The separatist plank was repudiated by the party in 1936, but this did not alter the question of whether or not blacks constitute a separate nation. See Booth, "Cuba, Color and the Revolution," 149–150.

22. Within the constitution, the term *nationality* is used in a most non-Leninist manner to mean citizenship. The usual antidiscrimination clauses therefore pertain only to "sex, race, color, class" or to "political opinions, or religious beliefs" (Arts. 10 and 20).

23. For a monograph dealing with this microcosmic national group, see Stone, *Smallest Slavonic Nation*, particularly pp. 161–185.

24. The many voids, typical of the limited vocabulary of primitive languages, were filled for the most part with Russian/Han words, thus causing the flourishing of the national language and the ultimate goal of cultural fusion to be on a more converging course than was true with the more developed languages such as Georgian or Armenian.

25. See, in the following chapter, the section entitled "Language Policy."

26. The breadth of Soviet activity in the language area is suggested by a leading Soviet authority: "Prior to the Revolution, about 50 peoples, among them such large ones as the Kazakhs, Turkmens and the Kirghiz, had no written literature in their own language. Dozens of peoples (the Adygheis, Karbardinians, Ingushes, Lesgins, Khants, Nenets, etc.) had no written languages at all; these were only devised in Soviet times." Bromley, *Soviet Ethnography*, 152–153. See also Salov's statement ("Soviet Nationality Policy," 92): "[I]n Soviet years more than 40 peoples, who had not had a written language in the past, today have developed a literary language."

Many of the non-Han peoples of China were also without written languages prior to the revolution. By mid-1959, the government claimed to have published 28,910,000 volumes of elementary and "anti-illiteracy" texts in non-Han tongues, including such little known languages as Hsi-po, Ha-ni, La-hu, Li-su, K'a-wa, Ching-po, I, and Pu-i. See "Correctly Translate and Publish." It may be appropriate to warn the reader, however, that 1959, a year of the Great Leap Forward, was a time of highly inflated production figures throughout all areas of Chinese society.

27. For details, see King, *Minorities*, 103–108.

28. At a conference convened some years later (1973) to urge more rapid adoption of the Latin alphabet, the Chinese acknowledged among their purposes the need for "insuring unification of the [Chinese] motherland . . . and strengthening the anti-Soviet struggle." See Karklins, "Interrelationship," 191. The change of alphabet pertained to the Kazakh, Kirgiz, Tatar, Uighur, and Uzbek peoples, all of whom had counterparts within the Soviet Union.

29. We have here been concentrating on form, but, as earlier noted, the primary reliance in Leninist national policy is placed on "education" through manipulation of content. The ability to dictate the content of a nation's written history has been particularly significant in the campaign to shape national consciousness. For example, official Moldavian history offers no evidence of Rumanian roots. And "the national histories" of the non-Russian peoples emphasize that their conquest by tsarist (Russian) forces was, on balance, a progressive act, freeing them from their own feudal, exploiting authorities.

30. Stalin, *Marxism and the National Question*, 103.

31. See chapter 2.

32. Had Lenin and Stalin been thinking in terms of economic equality for nations, their schema should have made some allowance for alterations in the previous geographical distribution of investments in order to bring about a much more egalitarian dispersal of investments throughout the country. Guaranteeing equal economic opportunities for individuals is an essentially passive or negative operation requiring assurances that discrimination will not be tolerated. By contrast, guaranteeing economic equality to national groups who tend to occupy distinct regions requires a positive

program of redistributing the investment wealth so as to equalize economic opportunities throughout the entire territory. The fact that neither Lenin nor Stalin made such proposals further suggests, therefore, that *national economic equality* was not much in their thoughts.

33. *The Current Digest of the Soviet Press* 24, no. 51:6–7. The Secretary's comments were in close harmony with the typical Soviet article on the national question, which is intended for a mass audience. See, for example, Gililov, "Worldwide Significance," which documents (on p. 61) the claim to having achieved a solution to the national question largely in terms of the strides that the Soviets had made over a half century in raising the economic situation of the poorer nations to the level of the richer ones:

> Throughout the Soviet period, the Party has ensured higher economic growth rates in the non-Russian republics than the average for the country as a whole. In 1968, growth of industrial output for the Union was 79 times the 1913 level, but in Kazakstan it was 125 times, in Kirghizie 152 times, in Armenia 146 times, and even higher in some autonomous republics (Komi Republic 223 times, Bashkira 447 times, etc.).

Gililov and authors of similar articles seem to assume that the simple recitation of such statistics constitutes prima facie proof that the national question has been solved. This may, of course, be nothing more than a propaganda ploy. However, Khrushchev's famous denunciation of Stalin at the party's Twentieth Congress (1956) suggests that the leadership has been at least somewhat conditioned to believe that advances in economic standing, as manifested in such statistics, do, in and by themselves, mute separatist tendencies. Referring to Stalin's use of ostensible Georgian separatism in order to justify a purge among these people, Khrushchev stated:

> We know that there have been at times manifestations of local bourgeois nationalism in Georgia as in several other republics. The question arises: Could it be possible that in the period during which the resolutions referred to above were made, nationalist tendencies grew so much that there was a danger of Georgia's leaving the Soviet Union and joining Turkey? (*Animation in the hall, laughter.*)
>
> This is, of course, nonsense. It is impossible to imagine how such assumptions could enter anyone's mind. Everyone knows how Georgia has developed economically and culturally under Soviet rule.
>
> Industrial production of the Georgian Republic is 27 times greater than it was before the revolution. Many new industries have arisen in Georgia which did not exist there before the revolution: iron smelting, an oil industry, a machine construction industry, etc. Illiteracy has long since been liquidated, which, in pre-revolutionary Georgia, included 78 percent of the population. (Christman, *Communism*, 205.)

34. For statements in 1966 concerning the closing of the economic gap between Han Chinese and the minorities, see the article by the deputy chairman of the Chinese Cabinet's Commission of Nationalities, Liu Ch'un,

National Question, 25–26. He noted that "it is necessary for the Party and the state to lead and help the minority nationalities," and, after commenting that "industrial, agricultural and livestock production" had already increased within the minority areas from two- to several-fold as compared to the days before liberation, he concluded that "the disparity in economic and cultural development between the minority nationality area and the Han areas has been markedly reduced." Hanoi has often expressed the need to close the economic gap between Vietnamese and non-Vietnamese as "helping the mountains to catch up with the plains," an expression attributed to Ho. For several references, see the Radio Hanoi broadcasts of the conference convened between November 17 and 24, 1969 by Hanoi to rectify problems on the part of the Dao nationality. (*Foreign Broadcast Information Service*, November 26, 1969, pp. K 11-K 62.) See also the Hanoi broadcast of January 16, 1976 for a statement by the chairman of the National Assembly Nationality Committee claiming that the country's unification and advancement to socialism are very basic conditions for helping the mountainous regions to catch up with the plains. For a detailed treatment of the Yugoslavian government's commitment to insuring economic equality for all of the state's national groups, see Joncic, *Relations between Nationalities*, 28–36.

35. See chapter 2.

36. Stalin, *Marxism and the National Question*, 101–102. Stalin went on to refer specifically to "the Jews in Poland, the Letts in Lithuania, the Russians in the Caucasus, the Poles in the Ukraine and so on."

37. See chapter 2. In his *Critical Remarks on the National Question*, written in 1913, Lenin noted that when drawing the borders of autonomous areas, "The national composition of the population, however, is *one* of the very important economic factors, *but not the sole and not* the most important factor." *Collected Works* 20:50. Lenin made clear, however, that his fears of the exclusive use of the national standard flowed from the fact that the towns and cities were often composed of nonindigenes and thus the cities might be cut off from the surrounding countryside to which they were economically wedded. He added that the boundaries of the autonomous units must be determined "by the local inhabitants themselves on the basis of their economic and social conditions, national make-up of the population, etc." The logical outcome of Lenin's prerevolutionary promises would therefore be ethnically delineated autonomous units but with minorities in the cities and larger towns.

38. Cited in Wolfe, *Three Who*, 584. About this time, he wrote: "But while, and insofar as, different nations constitute a single state, Marxists will never, under any circumstances, advocate either the federal principle or decentralization." Lenin, "Critical Remarks on the National Question," in *Collected Works* 20:45–46.

39. Pipes, *Formation*, 111. See also Carr, *Bolshevik Revolution*, 269.

40. In this regard, note the wording of Article 13 of the 1936 Soviet

Constitution which described the USSR as a "*voluntary* union of *equal* Soviet Socialist Republics." (Emphasis added.) The precise wording was carried over into Article 70 of the 1977 constitution. Lenin had stressed the expression, "a voluntary union of nations," in a 1919 *Pravda* article addressed to the workers and peasants of the then independent Ukraine. In the article, Lenin pointed out that although Marxists were in favor of the ultimate obliteration of all borders, they could wait for that to occur in the distant future. The pressing concern was that there be unity and a concerted proletarian effort. Whether this should come about "by a federal or some other tie between the states" was said to be of little concern. ("Letter to the Workers and Peasants of the Ukraine Apropos the Victories over Denikin" in *Selected Works* 3:258–263.)

41. "Preliminary Draft Theses on the National and Colonial Questions" (1920), in Lenin, Selected Works 3:374.

42. Ibid.

43. At the time of the formation of the Soviet Union (1922), Stalin had favored dropping the fiction of federation, but Lenin had insisted on its maintenance in order to attract future states that might experience a socialist revolution. (Pipes, " 'Solving' the Nationality Problem," 128.) The fact that Stalin did not subsequently abolish the federal structure during his long reign of uncontested power indicates that the federal form had indeed come to be seen as serving a worthwhile purpose.

44. Articles 3, 15, and 18, respectively, with regard to sovereignty, and 4, 17, and 72 with regard to secession. A subtle downgrading of wording with regard to sovereignty is evident in the 1977 constitution. Whereas the constitutions of 1924 and 1936 referred to "the sovereignty of the Republics," the latest constitution speaks only of "the sovereign rights of the Union republics," dropping the reference to their sovereignty per se.

45. The SSRs were also granted the right to maintain their own military formations in 1944, but this article was quietly dropped in the case of the 1977 constitution.

46. For other reasons why this fiction is maintained, particularly the reason of propagandistic value abroad, see chapter 3.

47. Ye. Modrzhinskaya, "Triumph of Proletarian Internationalism," 3.

48. Lebedinskaya, "Nationality Question," 15. For a debate between Soviet academicians on the question of whether a socialist nation requires its own national state, see the articles by P. M. Rogachev and M. A. Sverdlin; P. G. Semenov; and M. O. Mnatskanyan, all of which appeared in the Soviet journal, *Voprosy Istorii*, during 1966, and which are summarized in Howard, "Definition," 26–36.

49. For example, the Azerbaijan SSR, the Armenian SSR, and the Georgian SSR, which had been proclaimed in 1921 and early 1922, later federated and joined the USSR as the Transcaucasian Socialist Federated Soviet Republic in 1923. In 1936 this federation was dissolved, and the

three constituent republics each became an individual major political division of the USSR.

50. It accounts for more than one-half of the USSR's population and more than three-quarters of its territory.

51. For the details on the etymological history of these and related expressions, see the excellent article by Kristof, "State Idea, National Idea," particularly pp. 244–245.

52. Indeed, even the *Rossiiskaia* form has not been perceived by the leadership as thoroughly untainted by such ethnic considerations. During the drafting of the constitution for the proposed union (in 1922), it was decided to avoid any reference to *Rossiiskaia* in the title of the new state, with Lenin preferring the ethnically neutral choice of the Union of Soviet Socialist Republics. Moreover in 1925 the name of the Communist party' was changed from *Rossiiskaia Kommunisticheskaia Partiia* to the All Union Communist Party in order to increase its attractiveness to non-Russians.

53. The number of specific units has varied over time. It is also possible that the formal name of a unit may not refer to a specific group. Thus Dagestan, of the Dagestan Autonomous Soviet Socialist Republic, refers not to a people but to a region populated by several numerically small peoples. Moreover, in some cases (for example, the Chechen-Ingush ASSR), the name of the unit may be shared by two national groups.

54. This requirement, as noted in an earlier chapter, is purportedly necessary in order that the right of secession be meaningful.

55. Although some writers, citing Stalin, maintain that the minimal population required for an SSR is one million, many peoples have been so honored while their number was below that figure. Examples include the Estonians, Kirgiz, and Turkmen.

56. Prior to World War II, the Germans were an exception to this general rule, there being a Volga German ASSR. However, the distinguishing of these Germans by the addition of the word Volga in the title of the ASSR may have been an official recognition that this eighteenth-century settlement constituted a self-contained national community, distinct from the German nation of *Mittel Europa*. Stalin's subsequent suspicion concerning their loyalty to Nazi Germany might have ended this view of the Volga Germans as a separate national group.

57. As one of the largest groups in the Soviet Union (eleventh in the 1959 census, twelfth in 1970, and sixteenth in 1979), the Jews might have been expected to be assigned a higher-level unit of government. However, the Jewish people were and are widely distributed throughout the Soviet Union. The attempt to attract Jews to this new homeland met with little success, and its total population is therefore well within the range of what would be expected of an autonomous oblast.

58. See, for example, Armstrong, *Ideology*, 160–163.

59. The Yugoslavian Communist Party changed its name to the League

of Communists in 1952. However, to avoid confusion we shall herein continue to refer to it by its original name.

60. See chapter 6. The meeting occurred at a time when the defeat of the Axis powers appeared imminent.

61. In a glossary of terms appended to the 1979 constitution, *nationality* was described as "a term used for members of nations whose native countries border on Yugoslavia and for members of other nations living permanently within Yugoslavia." By the time of the 1971 census, the Albanians had also surpassed the Macedonians in numbers, thus outnumbering two groups with their own republics.

62. Constitutions were introduced in 1946, 1953, 1963, and 1974.

63. Article 9 of the 1946 constitution read: "The sovereignty of the people's republics composing the FPRY is limited only by the rights which by this Constitution are given to the FPRY."

64. Thus Article 3 of the 1974 constitution noted that "the Socialist Republics are states based on the sovereignty of the people."

65. See the discussion earlier in this chapter.

66. See chapter 6.

67. See Hoffman and Neal, *Yugoslavia*, 213ff. See also Shoup, *Communism and Yugoslav National Question*, 191–192.

68. Since 1963, the state has been officially known as the Socialist Federal Republic of Yugoslavia, an acknowledgment of its advancement from a people's republic.

69. The result of this many-sided competition for the decision-making powers that were formerly concentrated in the hands of the central party and state apparatus was a system impossible to describe in brief form. As one author described the situation, "power by the late 1960s was nowhere and everywhere, in greater and smaller accumulations, creating a quasi-anarchy of diffused decision making . . . and a free-for-all scamble to collect the pieces." Rusinow, *Yugoslav Experiment*, 253.

70. Only the 1968 springtime reforms in Czechoslovakia would represent a more radical departure, and it would be illuminating to know the impact of the short Czechoslovak experiment upon the Yugoslav leadership. The latter's sympathy with the Czechoslovak cause at that time was undisguised.

71. For several statements to this effect by one author, see Rusinow, *Yugoslav Experiment*, 279, 284, 297, and 330. In fairness, it must be said that at least one party pronouncement (cited by Rusinow on p. 281) appears to impute sovereignty to the republics. Moreover, as we shall see below, many Yugoslavs themselves mistakenly interpreted the amendments as conferring sovereignty on the republics.

72. The Yugoslav regime was not the only Marxist-Leninist hierarchy to experiment with radical decentralization of administrative power without surrendering its right to determine when and if the movement had gone too far. The simultaneously conducted Chinese Cultural Revolution, though with aims very different from those of Yugoslav decentralization,

fits this description. What most distinguished the 1968 Czechoslovak experiment is that the inner circle of power was apparently prepared to risk the loss of ultimate power in elections against non-Communist parties.

73. "The Latest Changes (1971) in the Constitution of the Socialist Republic of Yugoslavia," *Yugoslav Survey* 12 (November 1971): 5.

74. Ibid., 5–6.

75. Ibid., 5, 19.

76. *Keesing's Contemporary Archives* (1971), 24733.

77. "Speech to the Federal Assembly on the Occasion of His Election as President of the Republic, July 29, 1971," in *Yugoslav Survey* 12 (November 1971): 39–40.

78. *Keesing's Contemporary Archives* (1971), 24734, and Rusinow, *Yugoslav Experiment*, 284.

79. Article 3. Although not essential to our account, the principal reason for the center's decision to grant so many administrative powers to the republics in 1971 appears related to a need to break deadlocks at the federal level where delegates tended to vote the interests of their particular group. Thus in July 1970, the Federal Assembly failed to reach agreement on the Five Year Plans as each ethnic element zealously guarded its own cause. See *Keesing's Contemporary Archives* (1971), 24733.

80. Macedonia, Montenegro, and Slovenia.

81. It became a subsidiary organ of the Federal Council, being superseded in its role as the second house of the Federal Assembly by a newly formed Council of Producers.

82. The actual influence wielded by the Council of Nationalities, though never great, was not directly mirrored in its constitutional status. It was, for example, very weak under the 1946 constitution, despite its august standing in governmental charts, and it probably became somewhat more influential while in its subordinate status to the Federal Council. However, we are at this point dealing with form rather than content and are therefore interested principally in the organ's formal status.

83. Under the terms of Article 321, the presidency was to consist of the representative of each republic and each autonomous province, plus the president of the League of Communists.

84. See, for example, *Keesing's Contemporary Archives* (1971), 24734.

85. Shoup, *Communism and Yugoslav National Question*, 186.

86. Ibid., 258–259. For a similar statement by Kardelj made the previous year, see Rusinow, *Yugoslav Experiment*, 167.

87. The change of name from the Chamber of Nationalities to that of the Chamber of Republics and Provinces also suggests an attempt to weaken voter identification as a member of a national group.

88. Djilas, *Wartime*, 356.

89. Shoup, *Communism and Yugoslav National Question*, 116.

90. See discussion earlier in this chapter.

91. There were no corresponding organs for the Czechs. As in other

Marxist states that made allowance for autonomy but not for federalism, the state-wide governmental organs were deemed sufficient to represent the interests of the dominant Czechs.

92. Article 2 of the Fundamental Articles of the 1948 constitution and Article 1 of the 1960 constitution. The texts of both constitutions can be found in Triska, *Constitutions of Communist-Party States*.

93. Section 110. The federal authorities were specifically granted the power of "final validity" with respect to judging the wisdom of any legislative proposal of the Slovak National Council.

94. Articles 74 and 41, respectively.

95. *Keesing's Contemporary Archives* (1968), 22713.

96. An interesting innovation in voting within the Chamber of Nations called for a separate majority of each nation's delegation on certain issues.

97. The act of federation was signed with great publicity on October 30, 1968; it was implemented on January 1, 1969.

98. The new federal structure came into being under the terms of the Constitutional Act of 1968. The latter can be found in Blaustein and Flanz, *Constitutions*.

99. For an account of these developments, see *Area Handbook for Czechoslovakia*, 100 et seq.

100. Brandt et al., *Documentary History*, 422. Emphasis added.

101. "The Common Program of the Chinese People's Political Consultative Conference, Adopted September 29, 1949." The text can be found in Triska, *Constitutions of Communist-Party States*.

102. Chang Chih-i, *The Party*, 78–79.

103. Deal, *National Minority*, 156.

104. In 1970 the number of units was five, twenty-nine, and sixty-nine, respectively. See *Area Handbook for the People's Republic of China*, 247.

105. "On the Ten Great Relationships." The text can be found in Schram, *Chairman Mao Talks to the People*, 73.

106. An official population estimate, released by Peking in 1980, indicated that the Mongolians had recently grown more rapidly than the Manchu, and the two were now roughly the same size. *Peking Review* (March 30, 1980), 17.

107. Rakhimov, *Nationalizm i Shovinizm*.

108. Polyakov, "Unmasking Mao Tse-tung's Anti-Leninist Policies," 61–62; *JPRS* 48016.

109. The article is summarized in Osofsky, "Soviet Criticism." It was coauthored by V. Bogoslavskii and T. Rakhimov (the latter is also the author of the book cited in footnote 107). The charge that the Yi, Miao, and Koreans were not granted even nominal autonomy is perplexing because, although not given an AR, each had been accorded a lesser unit or units (Autonomous Chou or Autonomous Hsien). Therefore to deny that these peoples possessed any autonomy was tantamount at the time (1968) to denying any autonomy to those groups within the Soviet Union who

occupied one of the National Areas (Okruga). The change in designation of these areas under the 1977 Soviet Constitution from National Area to Autonomous Area may have reflected a desire to gain a propaganda edge over Peking. More interesting, however, is the fact that the Soviets have refused to grant any autonomous unit to the Koreans within their borders, so criticism of the Chinese for granting the Koreans only an Autonomous District is somewhat mystifying. The fourth Chinese minority mentioned in the article, the Manchu, have not been granted any form of national unit by Peking. This omission has often been attributed to the alleged fact that the Manchu have become totally assimilated. Paradoxically, however, Chinese population statistics carry the Manchu as a separate national entity, China's seventh largest minority.

110. Voropayev, "According to the Formulas," d-4.

111. Sushanlo et al., *Against Maoist Falsifications*, 136. See also the account of the Soviet propaganda campaign beamed into the minority regions of western China, reprinted in the *Los Angeles Times*, November 19, 1981.

112. As earlier noted, the CP of Yugoslavia was the only party outside of the USSR to introduce a federal form prior to 1968, and the original decision to adopt this form was made during World War II as a result of perceived necessity and before the Soviets were in a position to assert their domination.

113. The Magyars within Czechoslovakia are concentrated in Slovakia, and the Slovak leadership adamantly resisted such overtures. In its campaign for autonomous regions, Budapest had a precedent of sorts, for we will remember that Yugoslavian authorities had designated Vojvodina as an autonomous province, ostensibly because of the Magyars living there (although, in fact, the Magyars were a minority therein).

114. King, *Minorities*, 156.

115. See chapter 5.

116. There are a number of cases, of course, in which the distribution of a national minority is such as to give it preeminence within one or more of the state's regular internal administrative units (i.e., provinces, counties, districts, etc.). In such cases the group's influence within the unit may result in a situation not too different than would be the case if the unit were declared an ethnically delineated, autonomous unit. Indeed, at least in the case of Mongolia, certain provincial and district borders appear to have been drawn to preserve the cultural forms of particular minorities. Thus in the westernmost province of Bayan Ulugi, the Kazakhs are permitted to use the same language that is used in the transborder Kazakh Soviet Socialist Republic. Soviet ethnographers have expressed approval of the way in which Mongolia's internal borders have been drawn at the district (*somon*) level because "the structure of the *somon* boundaries serves to protect and preserve the separate identities of minority ethnic groups." *Area Handbook for Mongolia*, 20. A somewhat similar situation exists in the

case of the Sorbs of East Germany. Twelve administrative areas (*Kreise*) within the administrative districts (*Bezirke*) of Dresden and Cottbus are officially bilingual. In any case, we are here speaking of form, therefore limiting the discussion to ethnically identified units declared, as Lenin suggested, to be "autonomous."

CHAPTER 9

Reinforcement for the Forms

WHAT if Lenin's conviction that what was national could be confined to the sphere of form proved erroneous? As earlier noted, many of Lenin's associates had harbored grave doubts (justifiably, as it turned out) concerning his conviction that proffering the right of secession would dampen the desire of minorities for political separation. Similarly, despite periodic paeans to Leninist national policy and assertions that its application has solved their country's national question, the failure of several Marxist-Leninist governments to adopt such a key element of the Leninist schema as political autonomy and the willingness of still other governments, having once adopted the autonomous form, subsequently to jettison it, demonstrate broadly held skepticism concerning the wisdom of Lenin's formula. But even those governments that have been among the more faithful in their observance of Leninist ritual have simultaneously pursued risk-reducing policies, thereby expressing something less than certainty that the promotion of national forms would prove an effective antitoxin, rather than an intoxicant, for the poison of ethnonationalism. The major means of hedging that have been employed can be grouped under (1) language policy, (2) the recruitment and purging of elites, and (3) the redistribution and gerrymandering of national groups.

LANGUAGE POLICY

Of the three categories, the most resistant to generalities is that of language policy. The pattern is far more irregular from country to country and, within a single country, from group to group than is true in the case of either elite recruitment or population redistribution. Nevertheless, the principal theme of this section is that an evolutionary, three-stage pattern is discernible in the language policies pursued by Marxist-Leninist governments. (1) *Pluralism*: The first stage is characterized by official preoccupation with encouraging (some of) the individual languages of minorities. Official pressure to learn the state's dominant language is muted or indirect.

(2) *Bilingualism*: This stage is characterized by growing overt pressure to learn the state's dominant language, culminating in making this step mandatory. In the case of the Soviet Union, for example, study of the Russian language became compulsory in 1938. (3) *Monolingualism*: This final stage, though nowhere yet achieved, is heralded by pressures for making the dominant tongue the sole language of instruction and the sole official language.

There are a number of reasons why it is a far easier task to describe this three-step progression than it is to trace a given government's fidelity to it. First of all, the three stages overlap and reinforce one another, and are often pursued concomitantly. It is therefore often difficult to describe the current policy of a state as falling definitely within one or another stage. Secondly, although the three stages form an evolutionary or progressive whole, the policies of Marxist-Leninist governments have not evolved along the neat evolutionary route that the three-step pattern would appear to prescribe. In the realm of linguistic policy, governments have been known to leap forward or backward rather precipitously in response to favorable or countervailing forces of the moment. Thus, as we shall later see in the case of China, following both the Great Leap Forward and the Cultural Revolution, earlier demands for immediate linguistic assimilation (step 3) were replaced by a new emphasis upon the need to encourage the local languages. A final complicating factor arises from the tendency of Marxist-Leninist governments to apply language policy somewhat unevenly from group to group. Use of the local language may be tolerated or even encouraged on the part of one group, while another is concomitantly being encouraged to discard its native tongue. But despite all such irregularities, the histories of the language policies of Marxist-Leninist states demonstrate that ostensible commitment to encouraging the national languages has in practice been tempered by the encouragement of bilingualism and, further, by psychological and other inducements to adopt the state's principal language as one's own.

The prerevolutionary writings of Lenin had conceded the right of national minorities to their own language, but had said little concerning a state-wide language policy. Given his obsessive predilection for a highly centralized and efficient order, Lenin's model would seem to require a single lingua franca even during the transitional period known as "the flourishing of the nations." But beyond his privately expressed opinion that the use of the Russian language as the common medium of communication would have "progressive significance," particularly "if there were no *compulsion* to use it,"[1] Lenin offered no concrete proposals for a language policy.

The filling of this void was left to Stalin and his successors. During the first decade of party rule, the official policy was one of indigenization (*korenizatsiya*) under which the various national groups were encouraged to learn their particular language and during which overt pressure for the study of Russian was absent. Schools in which the language of instruction was not Russian flourished and were made available even for segments of a people living outside of their union republic or autonomous zone.[2] The situation began to alter in the early 1930s: schools offering instruction in a non-Russian language were increasingly restricted to a particular union republic, autonomous republic, autonomous region, or national area, while Russian language schools, by contrast, were fostered throughout the entire country.[3] Given the choice of learning in the local language or in Russian, most people living outside their ethnic homeland quite expectedly flocked to those schools offering the most universal language.[4]

Another major change took place in 1938, when Stalin made the study of Russian compulsory in all schools, thus guaranteeing that language's role as the state's lingua franca. In subsequent years, the year of study in which the pupil was introduced to the Russian language was progressively lowered. In the case of Armenia, for example, the study of Russian became a requirement in secondary schools in 1938; in 1946 it became mandatory from the second grade; and in 1957, it became mandatory from the first grade. Yet another milestone in Soviet language policy was passed in 1958–1959, when, under Khrushchev's leadership, non-Russian parents, living within their appropriate homeland, were given the option of sending their children to Russian language schools or to schools in which instruction was in the local language.[5] Taken at face value, the introduction of the "voluntary principle" would appear to be simply a governmental concession to freedom of choice, and was so depicted by the government. Viewed, however, against the broader background of the linguistic situation in the Soviet Union, there are substantial reasons why the authorities could assume that large numbers of parents would experience an urge to enroll their children in Russian language schools. Pupils attending these schools were self-evidently more apt to become more thoroughly fluent in the Russian tongue than were students attending schools in which Russian was merely a course of instruction rather than the medium of instruction. Parents desirous of eliminating any barriers to the upward mobility of their children would be apt to select the school that assured their offspring the best grounding in the country's language of success, that is to say, the language of access to the higher echelons of the party, industry, and government. (Outside of the Marxist-Leninist milieu, similar considerations were, during the same period, leading Flemish leadership within Belgium and the Quebecois leadership within Canada to oppose militantly the "voluntary principle" within Flanders and Quebec Province, respectively, despite the democratic systems within which both were operating.) The magnetism of Russian schools would, of course, be greatest for parents who anticipated a career for their offspring that might entail living outside of the homeland. But, as attested by the propensity of non-Russian, non-indigenous settlers to attend Russian rather than local language schools, Russian is the language of success within most non-Russian homelands as well.[6] Parents of indigenous stock should, therefore, be no less cognizant than settlers of the career advantages of attending the Russian language schools. Moreover, as we shall immediately note, within the Soviet Union the ostensible guarantee to an education in one's own language has not meant *all* of one's education. If parents are aware that at some point in their children's education, their offspring must transfer to a Russian language school, it is reasonable to expect parents to elect to send their children to Russian language schools from the beginning in order to mitigate a language handicap that could otherwise be expected to be encountered at a later, more significant stage in their education.

Contrary to the theory of national equality, the number of years of education available in one's own tongue varies greatly among national groups. Subject to some notable exceptions, the larger a group and the higher the level of its political unit in the "federal" hierarchy, the greater the number of years of schooling available in the local tongue. As of the late 1970s, those people living within their own union republic could conceivably complete both primary and secondary education (a total of ten years) in their national language. But such an opportunity was very rare for those living within an ASSR.[7] Most such groups had the possibility of only seven years of curriculum instruction in their own language, a few were limited to four years, and one (the Karelians) had no national language school whatsoever. Moreover, as one descended from the autonomous republics through the autonomous regions to the autonomous areas, the opportunity for the titular nationalities to attend their own language schools progressively declined. And the trend has definitely been toward even greater limitations upon such schooling. One study, limited to groups who had their own union republic, autonomous republic, or autonomous region, found that the average number of available years of instruction in the native language decreased from 6.7 to 5.0 years between 1958 and 1972.[8] If we exclude those fourteen nations with a union republic, who, as noted, all enjoy the possibility of ten years of education in their own language, the figures for the remaining thirty-one peoples covered by the study would show a drop from 5.2 to 2.74 years. That is to say, the number of years of education conducted in the language of those people having their own ASSR or autonomous region, already quite low, was nearly halved between 1958 and 1972.[9] This trend was noted and applauded in an editorial published in a Soviet journal during 1963:

> The use of the Russian language as the medium of instruction is at the present time a growing tendency in the development of the national schools in our country. In the Russian SFSR the process of the voluntary changeover of national schools to the Russian language of instruction from a certain class upwards in accordance with the desire of the parents is even now proceeding very actively in most Autonomous Republics, Autonomous Regions and National Areas. At present in the schools of thirty-six nationalities of the Russian SFSR instruction is conducted in Russian from the V, IV, III, II, or I class upwards.[10]

The guaranteed right to an education in one's own language has thus, in practice, become increasingly restricted to one of the fourteen peoples who have their own union republic. The preferential treatment accorded the languages of these fourteen peoples might be explained either as a decision by the authorities to accept these fourteen tongues as permanent features of the Soviet cultural landscape, or as a tactical decision to promote linguistic assimilation in two stages. (During the first stage, primary emphasis would be placed upon the eradication of the ninety-odd languages spoken by peoples without union republic status, while the national suspicions of that 78 percent of the non-Russian population who had such status would be tranquilized temporarily.)

The former explanation can safely be discounted since it would run counter to Marx and Lenin's insistence that assimilation is both progressive and ultimately inevitable, a dictum from which the leadership of the Soviet Union has never strayed.[11] By contrast, the hypothesis that the authorities may perceive linguistic assimilation as a two-stage process blends well with some of the more important theoretical Soviet writings on assimilation. There is, for example, a close parallel between the hypothesis and the manner in which Stalin in 1950 envisaged linguistic assimilation developing on a worldwide basis:

> After the victory of socialism on a world scale . . . we will have . . . hundreds of national [i.e., country (ed.)] languages from which at first the most enriched zonal languages will emerge as a result of lengthy economic, political, and cultural cooperation of nations, and subsequently the zonal languages will fuse into one common international language, which will of course be neither German, nor Russian, nor English, but a new language which has absorbed the best elements of the national and zonal languages.[12]

The analogical relationship of this worldwide analysis to the situation within the Soviet Union is striking. Therein (1) the lesser state languages, (2) the zonal languages, and (3) the ultimate single language find their counterparts in (1) the languages of peoples not enjoying the status of their own union republic, (2) the languages of those who do, and (3) Russian.[13]

The fact that the fourteen peoples assigned union republics (those who speak "the zonal languages") have not been subjected to the same levels of pressure for linguistic assimilation as have those who have been denied such an administrative unit should probably not be construed as more than a temporary or transitional phase. The peoples enjoying union status have not been exempted from all such pressure. Indeed, that the authorities attach no qualitative significance to union republic status per se can be seen in the fact that such pressures have been applied very unevenly from one union republic to another. The data indicate that the authorities have been applying what might be termed a "nine-to-five rule," in that five of the peoples with union republics have been less pressured with regard to language than have the other nine. The five republics in which pressure has been the least noticeable have been the three Baltic republics (Estonia, Latvia, and Lithuania) and the Transcaucasian republics of Armenia and Georgia. All five of these titular peoples have a highly developed sense of national consciousness and a proud literary tradition expressed in their own languages. The Ukrainians could also qualify on both counts, but the strong similarities between Ukrainian and Russian, reflecting their common Slavic root, have apparently led the authorities to anticipate less resistance to linguistic assimilation than would otherwise be the case. But whatever the rationale for this differential treatment, the important point is that the Ukrainians, the Belorussians (whose language is also Slavic), the Moldavians, the Azerbaijani, and the five titular peoples of the Central Asian union republics (the Kazakhs, Kirgiz, Tadzhiks, Turkmen, and Uzbeks) have not been totally exempt from the pressures to attend Russian language schools that we noted in the case of non-union republic peoples. The fact that union republics have schools offering the full ten years of primary and secondary education taught in the native language need not mean that everyone has an equal opportunity to attend such schools. The existence of schools and their availability to students are not synonymous. While the number of local language schools in the case of the Baltic republics, Armenia, and Georgia appears sufficient to accommodate all those interested in attending them, in other republics the number is inadequate. In Kazakhstan, for example, Russian is reported to be the predominant language of instruction in urban schools and in all specialized secondary schools.[14] Within Moldavia, Russian language schools accounted for 27 percent of all schools and 33 percent of all students in the mid-1950s, and the proportion of such schools jumped dramatically during the 1960s.[15] Within the Ukraine, 72 percent of all school children were taught in Ukrainian and 26 percent in Russian as of the mid-1950s, but these figures had become 60 percent and 40 percent, respectively, by the mid-1970s.[16] Such data are reflected in the comparative number of primary and secondary level school texts available in each language relative to the number of native speakers of the language. For all fourteen titular peoples, the number of texts per native speaker of the language is approximately only half (53 percent) the number available to those declaring Russian as their major language.[17] If limited to the nine least favored titular peoples, the proportion drops to approximately one-third (35 percent). The spread is quite wide, with more texts available per speaker of the Estonian and Latvian languages than for speakers of Russian, while Belorussian texts per speaker are less than one-fifth the comparable Russian figure. Again, the great disparities among groups indicate that the authorities ascribe no particular value to the languages of the titular, union republic peoples. Overall, the data suggest that in most, but not all, union republics an increasing number of titular people may not find a local language school nearby.[18]

The prevalence of Russian as the language of instruction increases as one progresses from lower to higher education. At the university level, it approaches a monopoly within some of the union republics. At this level, the number of Russian-language textbooks per speaker is more than ten times the number for all of the non-Russian titular peoples, and the disproportion would be significantly larger if the comparison were limited to the nine less-favored language groups.[19] Moreover, the competitive examinations for entrance to institutions of higher learning are customarily given in Russian, thereby providing a distinct edge to those most thoroughly trained in that language. How all this operates in a given situation is illustrated by the following petition of a Ukrainian to an official of the Ukrainian Soviet Socialist Republic:

> People of the Ukrainian nationality, whose native tongue is Ukrainian, do not enjoy the same rights in entering the *vuzy* [institutions of higher learning] as do those whose native tongue is Russian. Russian language and literature are a compulsory part of the *vuz* entrance examinations and so the graduates from Russian schools are more successful in passing this examination with higher marks than the graduates from Ukrainian schools. Furthermore, entrance examinations for special disciplines are also conducted in Russian, and this, too, makes it difficult for graduates from Ukrainian schools to pass special subjects. And so Ukrainian-speaking applicants get lower grades in the competitive examinations. Because those with higher marks in the competitive examinations are accepted by the institutions, the majority of students entering the *vuzy* in Ukraine are graduates from Russian secondary and incomplete secondary schools. . . .
>
> As a result of Lenin's instructions, higher and secondary specialized education in Ukraine was Ukrainized during the twenties and thirties. Teaching in the institutions of higher learning was conducted in Ukrainian. . . . During the period of the Stalin personality cult, this Leninist principle of higher education in Ukraine was forgotten. . . . [I]n most higher and specialized institutions of learning in Kiev, Kharkov, Odessa, Dnepropetroysk, and other cities, the instruction is still not in the Ukrainian tongue.[20]

Given this weighted balance in favor of those who are the most fluent in Russian, the option, offered to everyone by the language law of 1958–1959, to elect to send their children to a Russian language school appears admirably designed to move the population beyond bilingualism toward monolingualism. In a rather remarkable passage published in 1972, two Soviet writers acknowledged that the trend toward linguistic assimilation was readily observable, but they denied that this portended the withering away of non-Russian languages: "The observed transitions from monolingualism to bilingualism, and from there to monolingualism based on communication among nationalities, in no way imply the dying out of nationality languages."[21] How a transition from bilingualism to Russian monolingualism could be achieved except at the expense of the non-Russian languages was left unexplained.

Soviet authorities have publicly applauded the results of these language policies. The party program of 1961 approvingly noted that "the Russian language has, in effect, become the common medium of intercourse and cooperation between all the peoples of the U.S.S.R."[22] And in his speech commemorating the fiftieth anniversary of the creation of the Soviet Union, First Secretary Brezhnev complacently commented that "the rapid growth of ties and cooperation between nationalities is leading to an increase in the importance of the Russian language, which has become the language of mutual communication among all the Soviet Union's nations and nationalities."[23]

A subtle alteration in terminology between the 1936 and 1977 constitutions also signaled a move away from the flourishing of national languages toward monolingualism. The newer charter was publicized as marking the attainment of a higher, "developed" stage of socialism in the upward climb toward communism. It ostensibly reflected developments that had come about since 1936. In the area of language policy, the shift was from one based upon right to one geared to opportunity or possibility. Whereas the 1936 constitution had declared "the right [to] instruction in schools being conducted in the native language" (Article 121), the new constitution spoke rather of "the possibility to use their native language and the languages of other peoples of the USSR" (Article 36) and of "the opportunity [possibility? (ed.)] to attend a school where teaching is in the native language" (Article 45).

The reference to the possibility of using the "languages of other peoples of the USSR" portended a new emphasis upon linguistic russification. As we have seen, the actual encouragement of the non-Russian languages had not been pursued by the central authorities for some decades. But the 1977 constitution acknowledged this shift away from encouraging the local languages even at the level of form. This change was evident in officially approved articles elaborating upon the new constitution. One such article noted that "the Communist Party has consistently sought to ensure the further free development of the Soviet peoples' languages, enabling every Soviet citizen to speak any language he chooses and to bring up and educate his childern in any language, without any privileges, restrictions or compulsions to use one language or another."[24] What was meant by "without any privileges, restrictions or compulsions" was soon bared. The constitutions of Armenia, Azerbaijan, and Georgia had, since the inception of those republics, each contained a stipulation that the respective indigenous language constituted the official state language of the republic. Shortly on the heels of the new Soviet Constitution, new constitutions were drafted for each of the three republics in which the formerly assured preeminent status of the local language was replaced by a phrase holding out only "the possibility of using the native language." This change in terminology led to unanticipated protest demonstrations in the streets of the capital of Georgia, which, in turn, forced the authorities into a most unusual retreat.[25] The old phraseology was restored in all three of the republics' constitutions, but this temporary setback highlighted the intent of the authorities to perpetuate a trend toward monolingualism. Moreover, despite the failure to alter the language of the constitutions of the Caucasian republics, the new phraseology was retained in the parent Soviet Constitution. Those who had labored over the change in terminology could console themselves, therefore, with the tactical wisdom embodied in the title of Lenin's 1904 pamphlet, "One Step Forward, Two Steps Back."

DESPITE the much shorter incumbencies of other Marxist-Leninist governments, a survey of their activities in the area of language policy uncovers these same crosscurrents: an early public preoccupation with the development of the individual languages, with no overt pressure to learn the state's predominant tongue; subsequent encouragement of bilingualism; and periodic manifestations of a desire to bring about monolingualism.

Consider China: In its early years in power, the CCP publicly placed great stress upon the flourishing of the non-Han languages. Its first iterim constitution, for example, asserted that "all national minorities shall have freedom to develop their spoken and written languages."[26] Consonant with this pledge, the government encouraged the use of several local languages, in some instances giving to what were formerly purely oral languages their first written formulation.[27] But despite the Common Program's reference to "*all* national minorities," the effort to encourage local languages was in fact a highly selective one. As late as 1965, only twenty-two of the fifty-four officially recognized minorities had their own written language.[28] Many of those groups who were slighted were numerically quite small. However, numerically important groups such as the Hani, Pai, Tuchia, and T'ung were also excluded from the list of peoples with their own language. The most important illustration of an unwillingness on the part of the CCP to encourage the revitalization of a national language involved the important Manchu people. As earlier noted, the Manchus, who were already highly sinified, were also denied an autonomous political unit. Nevertheless, they are regularly listed as a minority in official publications and should therefore have fallen under the injunction that "all national minorities have the freedom to develop their spoken and written languages."[29]

In addition to its selective approach to encouraging languages, the CCP has ardently championed bilingualism. A high-level official review of the results of the first three years of minority policy made clear that bilingualism was a progressive and desirable development that was not to be impeded, and it hinted ominously that compulsion to achieve bilingualism was a likely future possibility: "Active assistance should be given to those who voluntarily desire to study the Han language or another language of a more advanced minority, but there must be no compulsion to do so at the present time."[30] Bilingualism was therefore the next step, and compulsion would be applied only to the degree that persuasion failed. Consonant with the goal of bilingualism, Chinese was made part of the curriculum within the autonomous areas, and students were led to realize that knowledge of Chinese was an essential element in upward mobility.[31]

Pressures for monolingualism have also been evident. As in the case of the Soviet Union, special and higher education have been made available principally in the state's dominant language.[32] Although a number of so-called "Institutes for Nationalities" were created to offer special and higher education to minorities, the multinational composition of their student bodies justified the use of Chinese as a lingua franca. In 1961 the number of national groups represented at a single such institute ranged from seven to forty-six. (Both the mean and median number of groups represented per campus was twenty.)[33] Moreover, we have noted that several important groups were not permitted instruction in their native language. This selectivity was given a further boost in 1968, when it was announced that there would be no further effort to develop a national language for people who already spoke Chinese.[34]

While ostensibly encouraging the flourishing of national languages, the CCP was, then, concomitantly encouraging bilingualism and monolingualism. But even this quite telescoped schedule appeared needlessly time consuming to some members of the hierarchy, and demands for immediate linguistic assimilation surfaced during the Great Leap Forward (1958–1959), and again in the late 1960s as part of the Cultural Revolution.[35] Following each of these periods of orchestrated revolutionary fervor, there was a retreat in favor of the policy of national flourishing. However, none of these subsequent periods of support for the right of nations to their own language were characterized by the same level of commitment as was the immediate postrevolutionary period (1949–1952), and the long-ranged policy trend has been in the direction of linguistic assimilation.[36] Tributes to the concept of national flourishing were very much a part of the de-Maoification campaign of 1981–1982, but the minorities could recall similar promises that were followed by efforts at linguistic assimilation.[37]

The Vietnamese experience demonstrates the same trend but on a much more telescoped timetable. Although Article 4 of the 1960 constitution had guaranteed that "all nationalities have the right . . . to use their own spoken and written languages," this right was not extended to schooling. Even during the period when the VCP controlled only northern Vietnam and badly needed the support of non-Vietnamese peoples in the south, in eastern Laos, and in northeastern Cambodia (1954–1975), only four of the thirty-seven officially recognized national minorities under its control were given any schooling in their own language. And for these four exceptions, all education beyond the fourth grade was in the Vietnamese language.[38] Despite constitutional assertions to the contrary, then, the VCP embarked immediately upon a program aimed at monolingualism. Moreover, as evident in the following excerpt from a 1968 article by the minister of education, there was pressure to achieve the desired goal of linguistic assimilation as rapidly as possible:

In reforming our educational system, we are now putting forward many positive guide-lines and measures in order to enable the younger generation to speak and write Vietnamese better with each passing day. Besides, *with the same aim in view*, we have together with our fraternal minority nationalities completed the creation of the Thai, Meo, Tay, Nung scripts and urged them to use their own languages in daily life and at school in the highlands simultaneously with the Vietnamese language.[39]

Considering that linguistic assimilation was so assiduously promoted while the outcome of the struggle in the south was so very much in doubt, it is not at all surprising that with total victory, allusions to non-Vietnamese languages would disappear from major documents. Thus, in his address to the first party congress to be held after victory over the south, VCP First Secretary Le Duan spoke of the need to "rapidly eradicate illiteracy in newly liberated regions and mountain and ethnic minority areas," but made no mention of the language in which the minorities were to become literate.[40] The Vietnamese language was simply assumed.[41]

A somewhat similar pattern can be discerned in Yugoslavia, although an important complicating factor is present. That factor involves the relationship of the Serbian and Croatian languages and the question of whether the two are separate and distinct or one and the same. As spoken, the two are quite similar. The principal difference is found in their written style, Serbian being expressed through the Cyrillic alphabet, Croatian through the Latin. It will be recalled that in its early years, the YCP had embraced the position that "the Serbs, Croats, and Slovenes are one nation, for they have one language and identical remaining ethnic characteristics," but that with evidence of growing Croatian consciousness and with prodding from the Comintern, this position was discarded well before World War II.[42] In the early postwar years, with the accent on the flourishing of nations, the issue of whether Serbian and Croatian were one or two languages did not arise. However, in 1954, a meeting of notables at Novi Sad, evidently acting with prior governmental sanction, issued a declaration insisting that Serbian, Croatian, and Montenegrin formed a single language, and further called for a single Serbo-Croatian dictionary. This return to the party's position of 1918–1926 did not go unchallenged. In 1967 all nineteen major cultural organizations within Croatia jointly issued a counterdeclaration, arguing that Croatian constituted a separate language and charging that the attempt to impose a single state language was a move toward "etatism, unitarianism, and hegemonism."[43] A group of Serbian intellectuals responded in kind, maintaining, at least as fervidly as their Croatian counterparts, the individuality of their own tongue. Party and governmental authorities, although reacting acrimoniously at the time to both of these declarations, subsequently retreated by allowing the entire issue to pass quietly into history.[44]

The attempt to declare Serbian-Croatian a single language had apparently been but one aspect of a larger program to make the language the lingua franca for the entire state. During the late 1950s, a new stress was placed upon its study as either a first or second language. Such an emphasis would run somewhat contrary to the equal status constitutionally granted to Slovenian and Macedonian. As the principal language within one of the six constituent republics, both languages were recognized as official tongues, technically on a par with Serbian-Croatian. However, the primacy in reality enjoyed by Serbian-Croatian is shown by the fact that while only an estimated 10 to 15 percent of those who speak Serbian-Croatian are bilingual, a majority of both Slovenes and Macedonians are fluent in the state's principal language.[45]

The Serbian-Croatian language was also pushed very strongly in the minority schools during the 1950s, and by mid-1960 minority students were introduced to it by their third year of primary education.[46] Moreover, whenever the population mix permitted it, minority language schools were combined with schools in which Serbian-Croatian was spoken. In such cases, there were only sections or individual classes within which instruction in the minority language took place, an environment very conducive to the furtherance of monolingualistic education.[47] Moreover, the better minority students had additional reason to opt for education in the dominant tongue, for, with the exception of those preparing to teach in the minority language schools, there were no facilities for higher level education in the minority languages.[48]

Rumania, too, followed the established pattern in setting language policy. Prior to 1956 schools for the Magyar minority proliferated. But following that date, such schools were consolidated with Rumanian-language schools wherever feasible.[49] As in the case of Yugoslavian consolidated schools, training in the minority language was limited to special classes conducted within an overarching institutional milieu favoring the majority language. And in 1959, the one university in which Magyar had been the language of instruction was merged with a nearby Rumanian university. Nearly a decade later, a formerly high-level member of the Communist party who was of Magyar descent complained in an open letter to the authorities that, despite contrary promises, the number of schools in which Magyar was the language of instruction was steadily decreasing, as part of an officially but not publicly espoused policy of discouraging the use of non-Rumanian languages.[50]

In these and other cases,[51] then, the flourishing of national languages has come to be tempered in practice by the encouragement of bilingualism and, further, by psychological and/or institutional inducements to adopt the state's principal language as one's own. Those desirous of an education in their own language often find this realizable, if at all, at only the lower levels of education. Higher education is customarily restricted to the dominant language.

Although we have emphasized the state's control over the schools as the principal lever for promoting linguistic assimilation, it is not the sole means at the government's disposal.[52] Control over post-educational opportunities, the state's monopoly over the publishing industry, and the ability to infuse the vocabulary of minority languages with words and phrases drawn from the dominant tongue are all involved.

Whether by purposeful design or not, posteducational career opportunities encourage linguistic assimilation. Given the centralized nature of decision making in Marxist-Leninist states, it could not be otherwise. While whatever measure of linguistic autonomy that is present operates within a geographically circumscribed area, the decisions that most influence upward mobility are made at the central level and reflect the authorities' predilection for state-wide linguistic uniformity. Ambitious members of smaller groups or those members of larger groups who plan to leave their homeland in pursuit of success are, of course, as we noted at the outset, aware of the need for fluency in the state's dominant language. But this same imperative operates even in the case of those members of large groups who elect to remain in their own ethnic region. The examinations or other avenues to a profession are apt to be conducted in the state's principal language, while subsequent performance in the profession is also apt to require exclusive use of the lingua franca.[53] For example, within the Ukraine (the homeland of a Soviet people second in number only to the Russians), a critical tabulation of spheres of activity in which Russian had become the customary means of communication included (1) "official life and official relations"; (2) "Party, Communist Youth League, [and] Trade Union" activities; (3) "economic life and economic relations"; and (4) business administration.[54] Admittedly, in part because their Slavic language is very similar to Russian, Ukrainians have been under more pressure to adopt Russian than have the indigenous peoples of Armenia, Georgia, and the Baltic republics. But even in those less pressured societies, the spurs to adopt Russian can be quite compelling, as witness the following description of how affairs are conducted within Latvia: "In the republic's city, regional, and most of the local municipal organizations, as well as in all enterprises, all business is conducted in Russian. . . . There are many collectives where the absolute majority is Latvian; however, if there is only one Russian in the collective, his demand that meetings be conducted in Russian is met."[55] But perhaps the firmest evidence of the lowly status of the indigenous languages is the fact that Russians living within non-Russian union republics experience little need to learn the local language. Thus in 1979 only 3.5 percent of the Russian population was able to speak a non-Russian language, although 17.4 percent of all Russians lived outside of their own union republic.[56] Contrary, then, to the Leninist postulate of the equality of national languages, each Marxist-Leninist state has in practice what might be termed "the language of success," and has promoted conformity in its use even while formally committed to the flourishing of many tongues.

The state's monopolistic power over all publications is still another major tool in forging language policy. That power is both quantitative and qualitative in its impact. In addition to determining the number of titles and the number of copies of each title to be issued in a given language, the government also determines what classifications of subject matter are or are not to be published in one of the state's minority tongues.

Data available on the Soviet Union attest to great discrepancies among national languages in all three categories. The favored position of Russian is particularly stark. In 1970, for example, 60,000 titles were published in Russian as compared to only 3,000 titles in the runner-up Ukrainian language.[57] Even within the Ukraine, the number of titles published in Russian exceeded those in Ukrainian by 51 percent.[58] Similarly, the total number of copies of books issued in the two languages country-wide favored the Russian language by 1.03 billion to 93 million, a ratio of eleven to one as contrasted with a four to one ratio of those who claimed Russian rather than Ukrainian as their first language.[59] Broadening our investigation to include all peoples with union republic status, we encounter the usual great discrepancies. Consonant with their favored status that we found when examining language schools, the two least populous titular peoples, the Estonians and Latvians (who together account for only one percent of the country's population), each had more books per capita published in their language than was true even for those claiming Russian as their principal tongue. The number of per capita copies published in the Lithuanian language was 77 percent of the Russian figure, and the corresponding figure for the Georgian language was 66 percent. Otherwise, the per capita figure for books published in any non-Russian language was less than half that of the Russian figure, ranging from 43 percent in the case of Turkmen to less than 20 percent in the case of Belorussian.

Numbers alone do not convey the relative advantage enjoyed by the Russian language. Also important is the range of subject matter available in one language relative to another. If, for example, books in advanced anatomy are published only in Russian, the aspiring doctor has little choice but to master that language. An analysis of subject matter presented in the various Soviet languages has documented a hierarchy similar to that related to the number of years of education in the national language available to the different national groups. A full spectrum of topics was published only in the Russian language. But there were great variations in the position of the other languages. With but very few exceptions, the number of subjects covered in a particular group's language correlated with the group's status in the federal structure: the groups with union republic status had several subjects available in their languages, those with autonomous republics had somewhat fewer, and so forth down to those groups at the lowest rungs of the administrative ladder.[60] The need for the intellectually curious to learn, if not to adopt, Russian was therefore inversely related to the federal status of their ethnic group. Overall then, published materials within the Soviet Union demonstrate marked inequalities of both a quantitative and qualitative nature with regard to the language of publication.

State monopoly over published materials, when combined with state monopoly over the oral communications media, has also offered Marxist-Leninist governments an unusual opportunity for impregnating minority languages with words and grammatical forms borrowed from the dominant language. To a government intent on promoting bilingualism and linguistic assimilation, the advantages of such a development are obvious. A large number of shared words makes the mastering of an adequate vocabulary in the dominant language less onerous and the study of that language a correspondingly more simple task. Moreover, by making the dominant language appear less exotic to eye and ear and more closely related to one's customary speech, common syntax and vocabulary weaken or avoid potential psychological barriers to learning the other tongue. Finally, the influx of words and grammatical principles from the dominant language can be viewed in and of itself as a step toward linguistic assimilation, by contributing (in Leninist terms) to the *coming together, fusion,* or *merger* of the state's languages. This is how a prominent Soviet scholar has described the process:

> In the process of bilingualization there occurs a direct interaction and mutual influencing of national languages and the lingua franca, a reinforcement and further development of their social functions. In cases of bilingualism, the linguistic systems of nationalities influence and mutually enrich one another. Word borrowings in bilingualism leads to enrichment *of the vocabulary of the language of the local nationality.* Bilingualism has a direct as well as a mediated influence upon the shaping of the stylistic systems of languages, and promotes mass-scale or individual deliberate selection of loan words and phrases.
>
> Bilingualism accelerates the gradual process whereby bilingual socialist nationality communities become monolingual.[61]

Word borrowing is, to be sure, not something peculiar to Marxist-Leninist societies, but a phenomenon that affects all but the most isolated language groups. It is clear, however, that the author does not perceive the process of linguistic interaction as one to be left to develop in response to its own imperatives. While he speaks of mutual enrichment, his reference to monolingualism confirms that he perceives the coming together of the languages as a unidirectional flow in which "the language of the local nationality" absorbs the vocabulary and characteristics of the dominant language.[62] This view of language development is the same as that advanced by Stalin in 1950:

> Further, it would be absolutely wrong to think that the result of the mixture of, say, two languages is a new, third language, which does not resemble either of the mixed languages and differs qualitatively from both of them. As a matter of fact one of the languages usually emerges victorious from the mixture, retains its grammatical system, its basic word stock, and continues to advance in accordance with its inherent laws of development, while the other language loses its quality and gradually dies out.
> . . .
> True, the vocabulary of the victorious language is somewhat

enriched at the expense of the vanquished language, but this strengthens, rather than weakens, it.

Such was the case, for instance, with the Russian language with which the languages of a number of other peoples mixed in the course of historical development, and which always emerged the victor.[63]

These same sentiments were expressed with much greater brevity by a Soviet scholar more than a decade after Stalin's death: "The road to language unity leads through the widespread acquisition of one of the most prevalent national languages, which under Soviet conditions is the Russian language."[64] Stalin's ideas on linguistics thus survive Stalinism.

Soviet attempts to make the various minority languages more closely resemble Russian apparently began in the late 1930s and were escalated in the postwar period. One element in the campaign was the requirement that the various Moslem peoples, who had earlier been forced to replace their Arabic script with the Latin alphabet, now adopt the Cyrillic form.[65] This requirement concerning the Cyrillic alphabet was also extended to the Moldavians, who had previously used the same Latin alphabet as did their kin across the border in Rumania. Thus, only the Armenians, Estonians, Georgians, Latvians, and Lithuanians—the five peoples consistently least pressured to assimilate linguistically—were exempted from adopting the Cyrillic alphabet. Still another aspect of this campaign to russify the non-Russian languages was the ordering of linguistic institutes in the various union republics to alter the grammar and orthography of the local language in order to increase conformity with Russian.[66] Meanwhile, gaps in the vocabularies of minority languages were filled, wherever possible, with words borrowed from the Russian.[67]

Primitive languages, being the most in need of additional vocabulary, offer the government the greatest opportunity for injecting words of the dominant language. While most of the languages of the western Soviet Union and Eastern Europe are quite sophisticated, with a well-developed lexicon, this is not true of the minority languages of Asia. As a result, the efforts of the Chinese government in this area are more wide-ranging and evident. Yet, considering its own policies, the Soviet government has quite inconsistently chastised the Chinese for engaging in similar activities:

Chinese words are forcibly incorporated into the languages of non-Chinese peoples and international terminology which has long been a part of their language is forbidden. The goal of the

Maoists is to isolate the languages of the people of China from world civilization, to confine their development to the Chinese language and to convert these languages into a dialect of Chinese.[68]

For their part, the Chinese, perhaps because their widespread activities are difficult to disguise, have been much more open than has the Soviet Union concerning such activities.[69] At least on occasion they have also been more prone to acknowledge that word borrowing is expected to lead to monolingualism. Thus a governmental directive issued in the late 1950s notified the non-Han peoples that they must "grasp the tendency for spoken and written languages to draw closer to the Chinese languages. Any plea for the preservation or purity of the existing minority languages must be resolutely attacked."[70] But despite significant variations in the degrees to which Peking and Moscow cloak their goals, the principal point is that both governments have pursued the policy of infusing minority languages with words drawn from the dominant language and that they have been aided in this venture by their monopoly over published works, including the particularly important category of dictionaries.[71]

In summary, Marxist-Leninist governments have been actively advancing a policy of bilingualism and linguistic assimilation while maintaining the official position of encouraging the flourishing of all of the national languages.[72] Would Lenin have branded such language policies "revisionist"? Given both his goal of ultimate assimilation and his flair for strategic flexibility, it is very conceivable that, had he lived another fifty years, Lenin might have condoned such activities *if he had become convinced that he had been in error concerning his belief that the period of flourishing would lead dialectically to voluntary amalgamation.* Recall his condonation of force and other devices in order to reclaim peoples who had, contrary to his earlier expectations, availed themselves of the right of secession. But having acknowledged that Lenin might have subsequently altered his position, it cannot be gainsaid that the state activities under review certainly represent a violation of Leninist national policy as set forth during his lifetime. We have noted his endorsement of a single lingua franca as "progressive," subject to the further condition that its adoption should be truly voluntary. No impediment was to be placed in the way of a people's use of its own language. Here, for example, is what he wrote concerning the Ukrainians in late 1919:

In view of the fact that Ukrainian culture (language, school, etc.) has been suppressed for centuries by tsarism and the exploiting classes of Russia, the Central Committee of the Russian Communist Party enjoins all members of the Party by all means to remove all hindrances to a free development of the Ukrainian language and culture. In view of the centuries long oppression, one can observe nationalist tendencies within the backward parts of the Ukrainian masses; in treating these tendencies members of the Russian Communist Party must show greatest patience and caution and counter them by explaining in a friendly way that the interests of the toiling masses of Ukraine and Russia are identical. The members of the Russian Communist Party on the territory of the Ukraine must implement the right of the toiling masses to learn and to use their native tongue in all Soviet institutions, and always counteract attempts to relegate the Ukrainian language to an inferior position. On the contrary, they should aspire to transform the Ukrainian language into an instrument of communist education of the toiling masses. Measures should be taken at once so that all Ukrainian institutions will have a sufficient number of employees with a command of the Ukrainian language and that in future all the employees will be able to speak the Ukrainian language.[73]

A more unambiguous statement of the nature of the local language as pure form and, as such, a thing to be conscientiously nurtured in order to increase its capacity for conveying the socialist message would be difficult to construct.[74] The discrepancies between this position of Lenin and those policies of Marxist-Leninist states are flagrant. Both the Chinese and Soviet authorities are therefore quite justified in their accusations that the other government is guilty of distorting Leninist national policy, and the accusation could be validly aimed at several additional Marxist-Leninist governments.

Have these distortions been simply the byproducts of pragmatically inspired policies aimed at eliminating impediments to economic efficiency and state integration, or do they represent a conscious departure from Leninist principles? If given its preference, any government—Marxist and non-Marxist alike—could be expected to opt for a single lingua franca (bilingualism) in preference to babelization, and monolingualism in preference to either. To governmental planners, translations of countless documents, ranging from literary masterpieces to directions for the use of machinery, represent a time-consuming and expensive extravagance. Moreover, language frontiers represent serious hindrances to the mobility of labor. Efficiency and industrialization thus exert pressure for linguistic assimilation within any modernizing state.[75] But to Lenin's successors, a trend toward linguistic assimilation signifies much more than just greater efficiency and convenience. In 1950, for example, Stalin insisted that an ecopolitical society could not endure in the absence of a common tongue: "[W]ithout a language understood by a society and common to all its members, that society must cease to produce, must disintegrate and cease to exist as a society."[76] Departing from Lenin's notion of language as belonging to the realm of pure form, his successors have perceived it as vested with real content. They contend that it is a major controlling factor in the determination of primary group identity. Thus a move toward linguistic assimilation is a move toward ethnic assimilation.

Although unrealized at the time, the ascription of a special importance to language was present in Stalin's famous 1913 definition of a nation: "A nation is a historically evolved, stable community of language, territory, economic life, and pyschological makeup manifested in a community of culture."[77] If language is an essential element of the nation, then it follows that when a language disappears, the nation disappears with it.

Stalin's definition has been the starting point for all subsequent Marxist-Leninist analyses of the nation. Though not often attributed to him following his posthumous purge in 1956, it has never been officially repudiated and continues to be cited by authorities both within the Soviet Union[78] and other Marxist-Leninist states as well.[79] Its impact is very apparent in treatises dealing with the relationship of linguistic to psychological assimilation. Thus a study undertaken in the Ukraine detected a higher incidence of narrow, nationalistic sentiments among those who read only Ukrainian-language publications, despite the similarity of content in the Ukrainian and Russian press.[80] And in the course of accusing the Soviet authorities of actively pursuing a policy of russification, a Chinese editorial quoted a Soviet publication, *The Handbook of World Population*, to the effect that "groups of people who have changed their language in the course of time usually also change their ethnic (national) identity."[81] In the same vein, a leading Soviet scholar has written:

> Linguistic assimilation leads not only to change of native language but to important changes in national self-identification. The national language and national self-identification are closely related ethnic determinants. While changing one's native language does not in itself signify a reorientation of ethnic self-awareness, it

does already testify to profound ethnic changes and the development of assimilative processes. If linguistic and ethnic affiliation do not coincide, the result is inevitably a change in one's national self-awareness.[82]

Elsewhere the author makes clear that bilingualism, though itself not constituting linguistic assimilation, is a lower transitional phase in this same sequential process that culminates ultimately in psychological assimilation. After noting how bilingualism leads to "deliberate selection of loan words and phrases," the author concludes:

> Bilingualism accelerates the gradual process whereby bilingual nationality communities become monolingual.[83]
>
> However, the strengthening of bilingualism and the rise in the social functions of the lingua franca do not justify the *premature* conclusion that the Russian language is serving a "new linguistic community," the Soviet people, as the universal Soviet language.
>
> The bilingualism that has come into being in our country does *not yet* signify that the Soviet people have become a single linguistic community. It only testifies that even in so distinctive a sphere of national culture as language, a harmonious relation between the national and the new historical community of people has been established.[84]

More concisely, a member of the Soviet Academy of Sciences has written: "Groups of people who change their language also change their ethnic affiliation in the course of time, usually in the second or third generation."[85] And a leading Soviet demographer, while making this same linkage between ethnic and linguistic assimilation, perceives no time lag between the two. The two are treated as synonymous: "The process of ethnic assimilation occurring among all the peoples of the USSR is indisputable. Specifically, the fact that the 1959 census showed more than 10 million persons—i.e., every eighth non-Russian—listing as his native tongue a language other than that of his nationality is an indicator of how far this assimilation has proceeded."[86] Still more recently, a study by two of the Soviet Union's most influential empirical investigators of that country's linguistic trends and processes also underlined this conviction of a direct link between language and ethnonational identity. It concluded as follows:

> The spread of bilingualism "in breadth" and "in depth" has [an] essential effect in transforming nations' national identity. Bilingualism is a factor which, helping to eradicate ethnic prejudices,

furthers the strengthening friendship and co-operation among the Soviet nations and the building of a single international community, namely the Soviet people.

The development and functioning of bilingualism in any one ethnic milieu is an objective process but one closely linked both with language policy and with the Soviet Union's general national policy, which is a most important factor affecting the peoples' historical development. The control over language processes (the development of bilingualism included) exercised by both the Communist Party and the Soviet state offers broad possibilities for affecting the social and ethnic development and convergence of the nations and nationalities of the USSR in a purposeful way.[87]

Official avowals of their Leninist orthodoxy to the contrary, then, the actions of Marxist-Leninist governments and the writings of their theorists betray a conviction that language is much more than just form.

THE RECRUITING AND PURGING OF ELITES

Though significant, language is not the sole, nor even the most important form involved in the transmission of socialist content. More important is the human conduit between the upper reaches of the party and the masses. If Lenin's strategy concerning the nationalization of forms were to be honored, ethnonational ancestry would necessarily be a major consideration in the recruitment of the visible elite (those whom the masses perceive as being in authority). Otherwise, as Lenin noted, the party ran the very real risk that Marxism would be popularly perceived as a new guise for alien domination.

There are evident parallels between Lenin's plan to rule through a visible elite recruited from the local ethnic group and the quite common practice of colonial powers of ruling their overseas possessions through indigenous chieftains. The differences, however, are more fundamental than the parallels. For example, the colonial powers were interested in the colonial peoples only to the degree that the latter participated in or did not thwart the economic and strategic aim of empire. There was certainly little interest in the peoples themselves or in their social and political integration. By contrast, Leninist national policy aims at converting the populace to Marxist ideology and to full integration into the socialist society.

Second, beyond insuring that the local leader was not apt to act in any way detrimental to the mother country's interests, colonial authorities were little concerned with his social and political inclinations. By contrast, the ideologically and politically integrationist purpose behind Leninist policy causes the inclinations of all members of the visible elite (the Marxist-Leninist term is *cadre*)[88] to be a major concern. Third, since the colonies were not considered integral parts of the parent state and their inhabitants were not considered citizens, colonial authorities felt no need to design a political structure that mirrored the empire's ethnic mix. By contrast, Leninist national policy, being a blueprint for nurturing Marxism within a single, integrated, multinational structure, would seemingly mandate that the visible central organs of authority reflect the ethnonational complexity of the entire population, while the more localized, visible power structure reflects the unique national coloration of the immediately surrounding populace. In particular, one would expect that the visible power structure within an ethnically delineated constituent unit (a union republic, autonomous republic, autonomous region, autonomous area, and the like) would be manned by members of the titular group. Thus Ukrainians would tend to monopolize leadership in the Ukraine SSR, Croats in the Croatian Republic, Yakuts in the Yakut ASSR, Mongols in the Inner Mongolian Autonomous Region, and so forth down to the lowest level of ethnically delineated political district. To do otherwise would risk undermining the very raison d'être of such administrative units, namely, to convince each national group that it has its own, autonomous political organization.

One of the earliest dilemmas facing a small revolutionary movement that takes power in a populous state is the choice between temporary utilization of the ruling apparatus of the previous regime on the one hand or a large measure of chaos on the other. The Bolsheviks opted for the former, employing the traditionally Russian-dominated apparatus of the tsars as a stop-gap measure, while concomitantly training their own cadre. The replacement of old by new cadre did not proceed very rapidly, however, and, five years after the revolution, Lenin fervently denounced this slow rate of personnel changeover in terms of its injurious consequences for national policy.[89] After noting that the present bureaucracy was in fact "the same Russian apparatus [that] was borrowed from Tsarism and only barely anointed with the Soviet chrism," Lenin predicted that unless changes were made, the minorities could not be defended against "the incursions of that hundred percent Russian, the Great-Russian, the chauvinist, in reality, the scoundrel and despoiler, which the typical Russian bureaucrat is." As to the new cadre, many of whom were not ethnically Russian, Lenin immediately added that "there can be no doubt that the insignificant percent of workers who are Soviet or Sovietized will drown in this Great Russian sea of chauvinist riffraff like a fly in milk." As against those who dismissed the reality of this danger on the ground that "the People's Commissariats which deal with matters of national feeling and national education are autonomous," Lenin questioned whether it was possible in fact to keep the operations of these commissariats immune from Great Russian domination and "whether we have shown enough concern in adopting measures really to defend the people of other nationalities from the truly [ethnically] Russian *Derzhimorda*."[90]

In a follow-up memorandum, Lenin warned that the need for unity would be used by the Russian-dominated apparatus as a pretext for perpetuating its domination (and, therefore, Great Russian domination) over the various non-Russian peoples. To combat this threat, decentralization of the apparatus would be essential, and Lenin was prepared, if necessary, to go so far as "to retain the Union of Socialist Soviet Republics only in the military and diplomatic spheres." The dangers of such decentralization, he maintained, could be neutralized by the authority of the nation-transcending, ethnically neutral party. In any case, those dangers were not as dire as those that a continuation of present trends held both for the Soviet Union and for the entire world movement:

> The harm which can befall our government from the absence of unification between the national apparatus and the Russian apparatus will be incomparably smaller, infinitely smaller, than that which can befall not only us but also the whole International, the hundreds of millions of the peoples of Asia who in the near future are to enter the stage of history in our wake. It would be unforgivable opportunism if, on the eve of this emergence of the East, and at the beginning of its awakening, we should undermine our prestige there with even the slightest rudeness or injustice to our own minorities.

Here is vintage Lenin. The nationalization of cadre was to be defended not as a good in itself, but because a strategic appreciation of nationalistic proclivities throughout the globe demanded it.

Lenin was not alone in perceiving Great Russian discrimination being practiced against the non-Russian peoples within the new

Soviet state.[91] Yet, as we know, Lenin's call for confederalizing the nonparty apparatus was not heeded. Indeed, Stalin used the issue to undermine some of his opponents. By exaggerating the reforms desired by the advocates for the non-Russian nations, Stalin equated their stand with Marxian heresy, in that it subordinated the proletarian question to the national question, and the industrial regions to the agricultural borderlands, instead of vice versa. Moreover, it risked the possibility that "a crack may develop in the system of proletarian dictatorship."[92]

Despite Stalin's unwillingness to countenance decentralization of the apparatus, the 1920s and early 1930s (the period of "indigenization") did witness a great growth in the recruitment of local nationals into the local apparatus. Lenin's plan for a series of cadre, each one national in its language and ethnicity, appeared well on its way to realization. But though this growth in national cadre took place with Stalin's blessing, he apparently remained distrustfully alert, less "a crack . . . develop in the system of proletarian dictatorship." And when, having concluded that the conditions were appropriate for the final consolidation of power in his person, he unleashed the massive purges of the 1930s against all detectable challenges to that focalized authority, he made the national cadre a major target.[93] Charges of "nationalist deviation," "bourgeois nationalism", "separatism", "anti-state activity," and the like were leveled against members of the cadre from the Ukrainian SSR in the west to the Buryat ASSR in the east. The purge extended throughout the entire apparatus from the highest to the lowest level, both within and without the party. It extended as well to those outside the apparatus (particularly members of the intelligentsia) who might serve as alternate sources of leadership. The scope of the purge is still staggering to contemplate; it is generally estimated that approximately one million nonparty members were arrested.[94] The number of additional cadre who were dismissed from their positions without incarceration was still higher.

No region was immune from the purge, but the Ukrainian Republic, perhaps because of its size and its buffer location relative to Nazi Germany, was treated more severely than most.[95] In 1938 Nikita Khrushchev, though ethnically Russian, was appointed by Stalin to head the Ukrainian Communist Party.[96] Under him, the Ukrainian apparatus was to undergo further purging, but this is how he described the situation in the party at the time of his appointment:

The Party had been purged spotless. It seemed as though not one regional or executive committee secretary, not one secretary of the Council of People's Commissars, not even a single deputy was left. The Party leadership was almost totally demolished. We had to start rebuilding from scratch.[97]

Though Khrushchev speaks here only of the party, the purge was equally severe upon the scientific, industrial, cultural, and academic cadre.[98]

While Lenin's plan for a cadre, national in form, had not been realized in the era between the revolution and the great purge, it was never again to come so close to realization. With local leadership decimated, Russians and lesser numbers of other non-local peoples were placed in positions of responsibility. This practice of so-called "borrowing" from other national groups, combined with sporadic purges (which, though of a much less drastic scale than those of the 1930s, nevertheless served as a significant reminder of the dangers of "nationalist deviation") characterized official personnel policy during the remainder of Stalin's rule. In the struggle for power following his death, Lavrenti Beria openly appealed to the resentment that Russian domination of the apparatus had incited among the non-Russian peoples. Under his prodding, the Presidium on June 22, 1953 resolved "to put an end to the mutilation of Soviet nationality policy" and specifically:[99]

> To organize the preparation, education, and wide selection for leadership positions of the members of local nationalities, to abandon the present practice of selecting leaders who are not of the local nationality, and to relieve individuals who do not have the command of the native language, and have them recalled by the CPSUCC.[100]

Although hidden from our understanding by the veil of secrecy that masks all Politburo infighting, this policy that enjoyed the momentary endorsement of the uppermost party organization and that, if implemented, would have led to a realization of the Leninist model led instead to the formation of a successful coalition against Beria by the other members of the Presidium. This is how Khrushchev described the matter:

> Beria stressed the principle of drawing the Republic leadership from the local population. . . . It so happened that Beria's position on this question was correct and that it coincided with the position of the All-Union Central Committee, but he was taking this po-

sition in order to further his own anti-Party goals. He was preaching that the predominance of Russians in the leadership of the
non-Russian Republics had to be reversed. Everyone knew that
this was right and that it was consistent with the Party Line, but
at first people didn't realize that Beria was pushing this idea in
order to aggravate nationalist tensions between Russians and
non-Russians, as well as between the central leadership in Moscow
and the local leadership in the Republics.[101]

Although Khrushchev here carefully avoids criticizing the policy
of renationalizing the cadre, it is evident that he and his colleagues
did in fact find such a policy odious. If such a policy would, as
Khrushchev maintained, lead to increased tensions between Russians and non-Russians and between the central and local leadership, it would do so whatever the motivation behind its implementation. Moreover, despite his claim of feeling that "Beria's position
on this question was quite correct," Khrushchev immediately con-
troverted this assertion by recording his comments on the matter
to Georgi Malenkov: "Surely you must see that Beria's position has
an anti-Party character. We must not accept what he is doing. We
must reject it."[102]

Although Beria's stand on the national cadre proved to be the
immediate cause of his undoing within the privacy of Kremlin
politics, the fact that the highest central authorities had acknowledged the injustice inherent in Russian domination of the nominally
national apparati and had in fact taken some steps to rectify the
situation made an immediate return to the Stalinist status quo a
most unlikely eventuality, particularly so because of the highly competitive struggle for power that marked the post-Stalin interreg-
num.[103] Added to these considerations was the decision to de-
nounce publicly the atrocities attributed to Stalin, for, in any such
denunciation, the injustices that had been perpetrated against the
national groups would necessarily loom large.[104] Denunciation implies a desire for rectification. All in all, then, it is not surprising
that the period following Beria's downfall was one of general amel-
ioration of the worst excesses of the Stalinist era. So far as personnel
policy was concerned, the major developments were a gradual increase in the number of local cadre within the non-Russian areas
and the making of membership in the local national group a criterion for certain high positions (most notably the first secretaryship
of the local Communist party).[105]

An alteration in this post-Stalinist trend was heralded in 1959 by the purging of a number of local cadre for "nationalistic tendencies." Two years later definite limitations were placed upon the degree to which nationalization of the cadre would be permitted. The 1961 Party Program announced that "the growing scale of Communist construction calls for the continuous exchange of trained personnel among nations." Heretofore, the Soviet authorities had in fact never tried to make their cadre fully national in form, and, during the 1930s appeared more intent upon russifying them. But the 1961 program was nevertheless the first official repudiation of the national-in-form formula with regard to cadre policy. Moreover, tied as it was to a higher stage in the evolution of communism (that is, "the growing scale of communist construction"), a subsequent return to a policy of nationalized cadre would appear by definition to be ruled out as "unprogressive" or "reactionary."

"Exchange of trained personnel" implies a *quid pro quo* process, with an equal number of indigenous cadre being transferred to positions of equal status within such traditionally Russian strongholds as Moscow or Leningrad. However, "exchange" in practice has proven to be a euphemism for what on balance is a unidirectional movement of personnel. It has not so much meant the trading of personnel as it has the need to make room for Russians and lesser numbers of other nonindigenous cadre.[106] As such it has remained a key to official policy since 1961. Thus a *Pravda* editorial of September 5, 1965 warned: "Any display of national separateness in the training and use of workers of various nationalities in the Soviet Republics is inadmissable." Four years later, on January 24, 1968, a *Pravda* article complained:

> One still encounters people who underestimate the great strength of the fraternal assistance and mutual aid among the peoples of our country and the significance of the exchange of cadres among the peoples of the USSR, people who sometimes express distrust for cadres of other nationalities and take a non-objective attitude toward other nationalities.

Again, two years later, in still another *Pravda* article, readers were reminded that the "interrepublic exchange of cadres" remained a key element in the "coming together" of the Soviet nations.[107]

These recurring references to the importance of cadre exchange serve to remind one and all that the nationalization of cadre cannot go too far. So, too, do the periodic purges of leaders on charges of local nationalism. However, even in tandem, the need-to-exchange-cadre slogan and the purges do not constitute firm guidelines, thus leaving the central authorities with great latitude in determining when and where nationalization has gone too far.[108] And, in fact, the degree of nationalization permitted by the authorities has varied substantially both with regard to place and time. The percentage of nonindigenous cadre within Armenia, for example, has been steadfastly less significant than the number within the Ukraine.[109] In the case of any national group, cadre policy is apt to be somewhat cyclical: a purge of local leaders on a charge of nationalist proclivities is usually followed by a drive to increase the "exchange" of cadre, followed in turn by a quiet redress in favor of local cadre which progresses until a new charge of nationalist proclivities heralds the beginning of yet another cycle.[110]

Assessing the ethnic composition of cadre is not an easy task. Even if the ethnic composition of the cadre operating within a single union republic were static, it would likely prove impossible to express that composition in precise numerical terms. The concept of cadre is so amorphously generic with regard to both sphere and level of authority as to resist quantification. However, though it too suffers from several inadequacies, the ethnic breakdown of membership in the Communist party is probably the best single index to the ethnic composition of the cadre that is available.[111] While many cadre are not members of the party, it is the case that most party members are cadre.[112] Joining the party is broadly viewed by pragmatists as an avenue for getting ahead, that is to say, for being appointed to cadre status.[113] Moreover, given the stake of the hierarchy in the existing distribution of power, those in authority can be expected to reward conformity and acceptance of the present power structure; and membership in the party is viewed by authorities as a positive endorsement of the status quo (commonly expressed as loyalty to the state).[114] From this perspective, membership in the all-union CP reflects great discrepancies in the ethnonational composition of the country's cadre.[115] Russians, who account for 52.4 percent of the total population, account for 60.6 percent of party membership. Otherwise, only the Georgians are significantly overrepresented (1.4 percent of the population, 1.7 percent of the party). Armenians and the two non-Russian Slavic peoples (the Ukrainians and Belorussians) are represented fairly, but the other ten nations with union republic status are all badly underrepresented. Moldavians are the most seriously underrepresented (1.1 percent of the population, 0.4 percent of party membership), followed by Tadzhiks, Turkmen, and Uzbeks.[116]

Somewhat older data available on the ethnic composition of the parties of the individual republics indicate that malrepresentation has been the rule in the local parties also.[117] In ten of the fourteen union republic parties for which data were uncovered, the percentage of the titular people who were party members ranged from a low of 37.7 percent (Kirgizistan) to a high of 76.1 percent (Georgia).[118] In all but two of the ten cases (Georgia and Kazakhstan),[119] the titular nationality was underrepresented relative to its percentage of the entire population of the republic; the percentage of malrepresentation ranged from 6.1 percentage points (Kirgizistan) to 17 points (Lithuania). Unlike the case of the all-union party, the two non-Russian Slavic peoples (Ukrainians and Belorussians) were badly underrepresented. In six of the seven cases for which data were available, the Russians were overrepresented in the party; as contrasted with their number living within the particular republic,[120] the overrepresentation ranged from 2.4 percentage points (Azerbaijan) to 12 points (Tadzhikistan).[121] In only three cases (Azerbaijan, Georgia, and Uzbekistan) are longitudinal data available for determining trends, but all three cases suggest a gradual improvement in the representation of indigenes since 1960. Fragmentary information from other sources lend credence to the existence of such a trend.[122] However, the principal point, manifest in the preceding data, is that with the exceptions of the Armenians and Georgians, those nations who have ostensibly been granted their own independent state (union republic) remain at a marked disadvantage in terms of representation among that state's cadre.[123]

While cadre policy has been a matter of great concern to the highest authorities of the Soviet Union, it is dangerous to ascribe any and all modulations in that policy to the decisions of those authorities. As we shall later have occasion to note in our discussion of internal migration policy, the image of an all powerful, highly efficacious political system with a nerve center whose will is tantamount to actual state practice and vice versa can be detrimental to analysis. Though the opinion of those in the uppermost echelons of the party who are responsible for cadre policy is the major force in determining the criteria actually employed in the appointment of cadre, it is not the sole one. Operating at any one time within a bureaucracy will be a host of individuals and commissions interpreting and applying personnel directives in accordance with their innermost predispositions and biases. As cited above, we have Lenin's word for it that governmental officials of Marxist-Leninist states have not been free of the ethnocentric impulse to "take care of one's own." This impulse was sufficiently prevalent in 1971 to cause the party through *Pravda*, to warn officials against hiring and promoting personnel on the basis of national origin.[124] The manner in which official cadre policy and what we might term "bureaucratic ethnocentrism" can complement one another is apparent in the following account of events within Latvia. After noting that the Orgbureau, the second secretary of the Latvian CPCC, and the first secretary of the Latvian CPCC are regularly staffed by Russians appointed by Moscow, the account continues:

> The Orgbureau and these "high commissars" from Moscow have continually directed the republic's cadre politics so that all leading positions—and primarily all party, state, and economic department head positions—are given to Russian newcomers. These people in turn grant other newcomers preference for registration in cities, provide apartments, and appoint them to better jobs.[125]

The Great Russian bureaucrat, against whom Lenin railed, has not been the sole practitioner of bureaucratic ethnocentrism. Thus a letter sent by twenty-six Jewish residents of Vilna to the leadership of the Lithuanian Communist Party in February 1968 complained bitterly of the tendency to employ Lithuanians in preference to others. Here are two excerpts:

> When the Deputy Minister of Trade, Kazbaras, was reproached for not observing the Leninist principle of selecting cadres on the basis of their political and technical qualifications, he replied publicly: "To be a Lithuanian in Soviet Lithuania is a political qualification."

> The President of the Pedogogical Institute, Uogintas, bluntly told one of his instructors: "It matters little that today you excel others in the German or English languages, in physics or mathematics, chemistry or music. We will develop our own cadres so that tomorrow Lithuanians will be more qualified than you." All Uogintas did was to give public expression to a principle that had been in force for a long time in cadre policy.[126]

Five years later, a group of members of the Communist party of Georgia complained that "[i]n Abkhazia [an ASSR within Georgia] a half-baked 'theory' according to which responsible posts should be filled only by representatives of the indigenous nationality has gained a certain currency."[127]

This phenomenon that we have termed *bureaucratic ethnocentrism* has been more prominently in evidence in the case of Yugoslavia.

One of the major causes of discontent within pre-World War II Yugoslavia had been Serbian domination of the power structure. As in the case of the Russians, it was therefore to be expected that the need for immediate expertise in matters of government should favor the Serbs. Moreover, it will be recalled that Serbs and the Montenegrins (many of whom insist that the Serbs and Montenegrins are one people) had formed the backbone of the partisan movement even within Croatia. As a consequence, the spoils of victory, in the form of governmental and party office, quite naturally fell disproportionately to Serbs and Montenegrins.[128]

The YCP did try to redress the balance through the training and assignment of non-Serbian cadre. However, the party never went through a period similar to that of the early "indigenization" phase in the Soviet Union, when the authorities there had attempted to nationalize the cadre of the individual republics and autonomous provinces. From the beginning, the emphasis in Yugoslavia was on multiethnic cadre.[129] As noted, the end result of this policy was that Serbs and Montenegrins tended to be overrepresented within party and state organizations.[130]

There was an offsetting factor so far as Croats and Slovenes were concerned, in that their regions were far more industrialized and modernized than Serbia. Here expertise favored the indigenous people, and the decision of Tito's government to promote what it termed "self-management" immunized somewhat the individual industrial enterprises from the control of the Serb-dominated state and party apparati.[131] But although Serbs did not come to be overrepresented in the industrial cadre of Slovenia and Croatia, their prominence within the political power structure has rankled, and periodically they have been the target of bitter criticism. Tito was apparently never in sympathy with this imbalance for it ran counter to his strategy of lessening the sense of ethnonational competition through the dual tactics of socialist self-management and evenhandedness. However, it became known in the mid-1960s that bureaucratic ethnocentrism had its champions at the highest levels of officialdom, when Aleksander Rankovich, considered at the time to be the second most powerful person within Yugoslavia and the likeliest successor to Tito, was purged. Rankovich was accused *inter alia* of conspiring to undermine economic decentralization because of a conviction that decentralization would favor Slovenia and Croatia over Serbia, and of conspiring to place Serbs in as many influential positions as possible. A committee established to investigate the charges found that there was "a network of collaborators who

very often interfered in the whole work of . . . cadre policy."[132]
Despite the great publicity given Rankovich's sin, the Hydra-like
phenomenon of bureaucratic ethnocentrism did not disappear following his purge. Serbian overrepresentation within the state and
party apparati continued, as did Slovene and Croatian resentment.[133] The magnitude of this imbalance in the case of Croatia is
illustrated by the ethnic composition of that republic's party. In
1972, the Croats, who represented 80 percent of the republic's
population, accounted for only 65 percent of the party's membership, while the percentage of Serbs within the party was more than
double that people's percentage within the population as a whole.[134]
And a decade after the Rankovich affair, Yugoslavia was again
reminded that bureaucratic ethnocentrism can reach the highest
levels of power, when charges circulated that Tito's wife had been
in collusion with high officials to ensure that certain positions should
be filled by Serbs.[135]

But more important than a few high officials are the core of mid-
to high-level bureaucrats who are responsible for carrying out the
day-to-day directives of higher authorities. The difficulty of dis-
lodging an entrenched ethnic element from these ranks is illustrated by the failure of the rather extensive, post-Rankovich, official
efforts to bring about a radical redressing of ethnic imbalances
throughout the ruling structure. More than a decade later, Croats
were still chafing under what they broadly considered to be disproportionate Serbian influence even within Croatia.[136]

The personnel problems faced by the Chinese Communists at
the time of taking power were very different than those faced by
either the Soviet or Yugoslav parties at the comparable point in
their histories. In some ways, the situation within most of the minority regions of China was more reminiscent of that of an overseas
colony than that of a section of the contiguous territory of a state.[137]
Throughout history, Peking's (and Nanking's) authority had rested
lightly and had been exerted through traditional, local leaders. For
their part, the local people tended to be illiterate and premodern.
As a result of their physical remoteness, their daily lives had remained largely unaffected by forces emanating from outside of
their region. There was, therefore, no experienced, ready-made
bureaucracy, either Chinese or local, that the Communists might
utilize to make their rule immediately effective over the non-Han
peoples.

Sending large numbers of Chinese cadre into an area whose
populace was unaccustomed to such an alien presence ran the risk

of causing the people to perceive the CCP as the vanguard of Great Han imperialism. The CCP leadership, being ardent students of Lenin's policy concerning the national question, was fully attuned to this danger and to Lenin's prescription for its avoidance through the use of national forms. Thus an official governmental report issued in 1953 noted: "The problem of national forms is an important one which affects the rights of the nationalities and their development. Many of our tasks can only be carried penetratingly among the masses of the national minorities through the use of appropriate national forms."[138] And Mao had personally made clear in a statement during 1949 that cadre constituted a key form in this strategy: "Thoroughly solve the race question, fully isolate racial reactionaries; this is impossible without a large number of Communist cadres who were born in the minority areas."[139]

Impelled by this view of things, the authorities launched a massive campaign to recruit and train cadre in the shortest possible time.[140] The high priority ascribed to this program is reflected in the pronouncement of the Minister of Education that "the training of national minorities cadres should be taken as the foremost task in our national minority educational policy."[141] But as a stop-gap measure until the program would bear sufficient fruit, it was decided to utilize those traditional leaders who were prepared to cooperate, backed up by Han Chinese cadre.[142] National cadre were therefore to be introduced as rapidly as possible. But although the authorities spoke of the "nationalization" of all organs within the national areas and specifically defined this goal as meaning "that the people of all nationalities practicing autonomy should principally use their own cadre, their own language and speech, and their own appropriate national forms in the management of the internal affairs of the nationality," the authorities explicitly indicated that they had no intention of pursuing this policy to the degree that the Soviets had during their immediate postrevolutionary period of "indigenization," much less to the degree that Lenin had advocated in his last comments on the matter.[143] While stating that "nationalization" would make each national group "the master of his home,"[144] government spokesmen concomitantly insisted on the seeming negation of that slogan, namely, that Han cadre were to be viewed as permanent members of that household:

If it is considered that by assuming control of one's own homeland and by nationalization, there is no further need for leadership of the Chinese Communist Party . . . and there is no need

TABLE 2. Minority Cadre, 1949–1963

Year	Number of Available Cadre[a]	Annual Increment[b]
1949	10,000	
1951	50,000	20,000 (1950–51)
1952	100,000	50,000
1956	215,000	28,750 (1953–56)
1957	370,000	155,000
1959	480,000	55,000 (1958–59)
1963	500,000	5,000 (1960–63)

[a] As cited in Deal, "National Minority," 191.
[b] Averaged where appropriate. Inclusive years in parentheses.

for the support of the Han people and cadres—then it will be an obvious mistake which must be prevented and rectified.[145]

Despite the high priority given to the recruitment and training of minority cadre, accomplishments proved disappointing. Official reviews of minority policy in 1953, 1956, 1962, and 1971 commented on the inadequacy in numbers of cadre from the non-Han populace and the pressing need to rectify the situation. The rather fragmentary figures on available minority cadre that were released prior to the Cultural Revolution point to radical annual fluctuations in recruitment. For example, while some 155,000 minority cadre reportedly were trained during 1957 alone, only 20,000 cadre were added over the four-year period from 1960 to 1963.

Whatever the causes of these great variations, the cumulative impact of the low-output years had been devastating. As indicated in table 2 the total number of minority cadre available in 1963 (500,000) represented approximately one percent of the total non-Han population, only a fraction of the number that would be necessary to man all of the cadre positions within the minority regions. Moreover, this total pool of cadre remained relatively constant well into the 1970s, in large part because the special institutes for the training of national minorities became casualties of the Cultural Revolution and were closed between 1966 and 1971.[146]

The schools were reopened as part of a much broader campaign to expand markedly the pool of indigenous cadre. By late 1982 the Chinese press was boasting of the great strides that had been made. In the case of Tibet, for example, indigenous cadre were said to have grown from 200 in 1951, to 7,508 in 1965, to 20,023 in 1978, to 29,046 in 1981.[147] The use of quotas was encouraged in some areas in order to insure proper representation for indigenous cadre.[148] Authorities acknowledged, however, that indigenous cadre remained in short supply. The First Secretary of the Sinkiang regional party, for example, noted in late 1982: "We must persistently implement the policy of vigorously training and promoting minority-nationality cadres. This is not only the requirement of instituting autonomy in nationality regions; it is also the key to solving China's nationality issue."[149]

The shortage of minority cadre has been reflected in Chinese cadre policy in three ways: (1) *An absence of major purges*. The minority cadre have not been totally free of purges. In 1957 and 1958, and again during the Cultural Revolution of the late 1960s, purges did in fact occur.[150] But not on a scale remotely approaching those in the Soviet Union. In China the number of minorities purged has been small and the percentage subsequently reinstated has been large.[151] Considering the willingness of the authorities to assent to the denunciation of other individuals (including such luminaries as Liu Shao-chi and Lin Piao), and groups (including, during the Cultural Revolution, the Communist party membership), it is evident that the relative immunity of non-Han cadre was not due to a lack of appreciation for the periodic purge as an implement of policy. (2) *The continued utilization of traditional leaders*. Although the use of traditional leaders was intended to be only an interim measure and was periodically attacked by the more radical wing of the party, the services of such people continued to be utilized into the post-Cultural Revolution period. This tenure was the more remarkable because it straddled numerous years during which massive numbers of Han cadre, with very badly needed expertise, were being purged throughout the Han area of China under such slogans as "better red than expert." The ideological gymnastics necessary to maintain these "class relics" in office during periods when ideological purity, regardless of cost, was elsewhere Peking's order of the day attest to the inordinate need felt by the authorities for the services of these local leaders. (3) *The imbalanced assignment of native cadre*. Apparently as a means of maximizing the impact of the relatively small numbers of available national cadre, the authorities have assigned them disproportionately to highly visible offices at the grass-roots level where contacts with the masses are most numerous.[152] The indigenous cadre are heavily concentrated at the village level, where they tend to occupy such highly visible positions as school teachers and members of the health service, as well as more showcase slots in state and party administration.[153] The severe shortage of national cadre is suggested by the disproportionately fewer number (only 20 percent of the total native cadre as of 1963) who have been trained and assigned to the important but less visible industrial and agricultural sectors.[154]

As in our previous cases, the cadre policy of the Czechoslovakian Communist Party has also been strongly influenced by the fact that the regions of the country historically varied substantially with regard to the level of urbanization, industrialization, literacy, and the like. Being more advantaged than the Slovaks in terms of formal education and technological tradition, as well as in numbers, the Czechs have tended to dominate all aspects of the apparatus (political, economic, and educational) from the state's origin in 1918. The short-lived, World War II, independent Slovak state represented only a temporary reprieve from this Czech dominance so far as the Slovak people were concerned. Czech preeminence quickly reestablished itself in the postwar period and continued into the era of Communist party control. Many Slovak Communists had hoped for a truly federal structure in which Slovaks would have greater freedom from Czech domination, but this element was effectively silenced through a number of purges, ostensibly for "bourgeois nationalism," during the early 1950s. The Communist leadership did embark on an investment program that favored the less developed Slovakia, and a significant closing of the economic gap between Czechs and Slovaks was accomplished. However, since economic decisions continued to be made at Prague, and since Czechs had more experience in the management of industrial enterprises, top managerial posts tended to be filled by Czechs.[155]

In purely quantitative terms, however, the Slovaks appear to be better off than other minorities we have studied.[156] The number of Czechs living within Slovakia has never been large. Slovaks account for approximately 85 percent of the population of Slovakia, and Magyars, Poles, and Ruthenians account for most of the remainder. Moreover, Slovak representation in the local wing of the Communist party (the Slovak CP) quite accurately reflects Slovak strength within the region.[157] If the state and party apparati were truly decentralized, then, the Slovak situation would be quantifiably quite reasonable. But we have earlier seen that the plans for a truly decentralized system that crystallized during 1968 were subsequently thwarted by Moscow's opposition.[158]

Figures that surfaced during 1968 offer an unusual glimpse of the degree to which Czechs had come to monopolize the state-wide apparatus. Although the Slovaks then accounted for 29.6 percent of the state's total population, their percentage of personnel in the country's foreign service was only 14 percent; in the Ministry of Agriculture, 9.8 percent; Ministry of Construction, 6 percent; Ministry of Transport, 5.1 percent; Ministry of Foreign Trade, 5 percent of the posts abroad and 2 to 3 percent of those at home; Ministry of Heavy Industry, 4.5 percent; Ministry of Health, 4.3 percent; Ministry of Finance, 3.4 percent; State Planning Commission, 1.5 percent; Ministry of Fuel, 1.3 percent; Ministry of Education, 1.2 percent; and the Ministry of Justice, zero percent.[159] During 1968 the state-wide CP did declare itself in favor of reforming cadre policy, and it is reasonable to assume that some improvements in the ethnically badly distorted situation have occurred.[160] However, given the magnitude of Czech entrenchment reflected in the above figures, it is likely that what we have termed bureaucratic ethnocentrism has continued to insure a highly disproportionate allocation of cadre positions to the Czechs.[161]

It is perhaps worth emphasizing at this juncture that in the matter of cadre policy, just as in other aspects of national policy, Marxist-Leninist governments have displayed great variety in the vigor with which they have applied policy to one group or another. In the case of the Soviet Union, for example, a study has documented great divergencies among the union republics in the relative number of top-echelon, nonindigenous cadre found in both the state and party apparati and in both showcase positions and real seats of authority.[162] At one end of the spectrum, the representation of Armenians in the higher offices of the Armenian SSR hovered about the 90 percent mark, while the corresponding offices within Kazakhstan are nearly divided equally between the titular national group and nonindigenous peoples. Similarly, although the Chinese have placed very few non-Han in positions of authority, Mongols and Hui have done much better in this regard than have the peoples of Tibet and Sinkiang.[163]

Some of the factors that help to explain these variations in the prosecuting of cadre policy are quite tangible. One factor is the percentage of nonindigenes living within the region: appointing a markedly disproportionate number of nonindigenes to office risks drawing the attention of the masses to their unfavorable situation. Yet another consideration is whether a people is located safely in the interior or on the border, and, if the latter, the status of relations between the two bordering states. A less tangible but probably more influential factor is the relative trust (or distrust) that the authorities place in a given minority's loyalty. Thus the tendency of Armenians to perceive Turks as *the* arch enemy of their nation has dovetailed with the general, anti-Ankara stance of Moscow to make Soviet rule rest lightly on Armenian shoulders.[164] In turn, the absence of antistate turmoil within Armenia has given Moscow less cause for concern and commensurately less perceived need for hedging devices.[165] On the other hand, a history of incidents of an antistate coloration (e.g., those among the Tibetans) will, from the viewpoint of the central authorities, quite naturally add to the wisdom of having larger numbers of nonindigenous cadre spread throughout the structure as a precaution against the future outbreak of such incidents.[166]

Despite the apparent tendency of the authorities to correlate larger numbers of nonindigenous cadre with greater security, the actual number of such outsiders in the apparatus is not necessarily of key importance, since even one strategically placed individual could conceivably apprise the center of fissiparous forces at work. Moreover, a final aspect of cadre policy, one that comprises *the authorities' ultimate hedge against nationalistic, antistate activities* remains to be discussed. Not every agency and office is of equal significance. If, as we have maintained, the regimes, by employing a series of hedging devices, have demonstrated serious doubt that Lenin's formula could indeed neutralize nationalism and solve the national question, then the functions of certain agencies and offices could be expected to make their staffing a matter of special concern. In particular, the authorities would want to be certain of the loyalty of the military and other security forces.

The issue of the ethnic composition of security forces within a multinational setting is an old one. More than a century ago, for example, John Stuart Mill voiced his concern that a despotic government of a multinational state might employ troops of one ethnic strain against fellow citizens of another. According to Mill, in such event the soldiers "will have no more desire to ask the reason why, than they would have in doing the same thing against declared enemies."[167] Mill's statement was part of a biting criticism of the multinational state per se. But those in authority within multinational states and empires have drawn quite different conclusions from the sort of scenario described by Mill. Rather than viewing it as a reason for dismantling their polyethnic unit, they have perceived in it the key to maintaining the integrity of the unit against ethnically inspired dissonance. The twin first principles of how to maintain control over a multinational polity have come to be (1) deploy all troops outside their ethnic homeland, and (2) restrict the higher levels of the military command structure and the more sensitive positions responsible for internal security (particularly the secret police) to members of the most loyal ethnic group.[168] "The most loyal ethnic group" can be assumed to be that group with the largest vested interest in perpetuating the status quo, that is, the politically dominant group. In most instances, this means the numerically dominant ethnic element.

Marxist-Leninist states have also lived by these principles. Lenin had established the precedent of deploying the troops of one ethnic group in the homeland of another at a very early point. In January 1918, at a critical point in Bolshevik history, Lenin had ordered a detachment of Latvian troops to Petrograd (Leningrad). In the words of one biographer, "Lenin knew that the Lettish troops had no particular sentimental ties with the Russian people and would carry out their orders with the loyalty of a pretorian guard."[169] Consonant with this precedent and its underlying rationale, minority members of the military forces of Marxist-Leninist states are, as a matter of policy, regularly assigned to posts outside their ethnic homeland.[170] The practice has given rise to complaints, as witness the following message from Latvia:

> During World War II, two Latvian divisions and a special aviation battalion heroically fought as part of the Red Army. Today, however, there are no separate Latvian military units; Latvian youths in the military are purposely not assigned to the Russian units stationed in Latvia, but are scattered throughout the Soviet Union as far from Latvia as possible.[171]

There may be an ethnic pattern involved in the deployment of troops that goes beyond simply assigning minorities outside of their homelands. The Soviet forces that quelled national unrest within Georgia in 1956 and within Lithuania in 1977 were composed principally of Asians.[172] Since such personnel are readily distinguishable from Russians, their use as antinational forces safeguards against popular resentment being aimed at Russians.[173] There would be less chance of unfurling the banner, "Russians, get out of [the specific homeland]!" as happened, for example, within Uzbekistan in 1969.[174]

The policy of deploying troops outside of the homeland has also been a major source of irritation within Yugoslavia. When Rankovich's behind-the-scenes efforts in support of cementing Serbian-Montenegrin control of the apparatus became public knowledge in the mid-1960s, the military authorities reluctantly consented to permit 25 percent of all recruits to be assigned to units within their own republic.[175] In the early 1970s, angry Croatian spokesmen made known that this agreement was not being honored, and that only 15 percent of new recruits were being assigned locally.[176] However, at this juncture (a short-lived period of overt, militant Croatian nationalism), many Croatians demanded far more than that a certain minority of recruits be permitted to serve their military service within the ethnic homeland. Some voices urged that the army be federalized, while extremists demanded no less than a separate Croatian army. The head of the student organization in the capital of Croatia is said to have publicly insisted that "a state without its own army is not a state."[177]

Proponents of this position might have found a precedent in the experience of the Soviet Union. In 1944, as part of a campaign to gain separate membership status in the United Nations for each of its union republics, the Soviet government had been very intent on painting its union republics as independent states. It therefore amended the constitution of 1936 (Article 18b), so that "each Union Republic has its own military formations."[178]

In the Soviet case, the amendment proved all form and no content, and was not carried over into the constitution of 1977.[179] But in the Soviet case, there were no pressing reasons for the government to contemplate actual decentralization of the armed forces. In contrast, a Soviet attack aimed at resubordinating Belgrade to Soviet influence had been the specter haunting Yugoslav authorities since the split in 1948, and the threat seemed much more imminent following the Soviet intervention in Czechoslovakia in 1968. With an insufficient army to constitute a credible deterrent against such an eventuality, the Yugoslav authorities stressed that the country's forces would in such case revert to guerrilla warfare. As exemplified by the rise to power of the Chinese and Vietnamese parties, guerrillas operate most effectively in their own ethnic environment, wherein they can anticipate receiving the sympathetic protection of the local people. Such a consideration would be particularly meaningful within Yugoslavia, where the deep-seated animosities between Serbs and Croats could be expected to prove, at least for some, more intense than their dislike of a Soviet intrusion. Finally, it could be assumed that Croats, Slovenes, etc., would fight most determinedly in defense of their own ethnic homelands. Yet despite such important considerations, the entreaties of the Croatians to decentralize the army along ethnic lines failed to elicit support among the highest authorities. The regime feared that locally recruited armies might provide the muscle for separatist movements.

The Minister of Defense warned that "we must be alert in the full sense of the word when it comes to people who are working on splitting the Yugoslavs' People's Army because they also want to split the country."[180] And this warning was echoed by Tito in a speech of July 1971, in which he coupled a need for a decentralized, regional command structure to combat a potential invasion by superior forces with the caveat that "if there is no unity, the nationwide defense may become an instrument of civil war."[181] The leadership's response to this self-perceived dilemma was to create a territorial defense force, separate from the army, under the rubric of the "General People's Defense." Self-defense units were created in every community, so an invading force would presumably be met by a guerrilla struggle conducted throughout the country by the citizens-in-arms. However, the citizens are in arms only while training. With the partial exception of border areas, the arms are kept under lock. One observer has found this manner of maintaining the "territorial forces' arms a crucial weakness in the system," and he has added, "Obviously, the government is nervous about the substantial number of unregistered weapons for reasons that are not hard to guess. At the same time, it wants to have an armed citizenry."[182] Judging by their unwillingness to arm the people's militia, as well as by their refusal to permit a majority of those in the regular forces to serve in their home republic, it would appear that the authorities have perceived the internal threat of nationalism as of more immediate concern than the external threat of Soviet intervention.[183]

In addition to deploying troops outside of their ethnic homelands, Marxist-Leninist governments have also tended to staff the higher military offices and the secret police with members of the most loyal ethnic group.[184] Not surprisingly, given the uneasiness with which governments greet disclosures concerning their security organizations, such data are extremely fragmentary. In the cases of China and Vietnam, detailed information is almost totally lacking. It can quite safely be assumed, however, that Han Chinese and ethnic Vietnamese (the Kinh) each enjoy an effective monopoly within the security apparatus of their respective states. In either country, the government has relied virtually exclusively upon members of the dominant ethnic group to fill positions of real (in contradistinction to ostensible) responsibility throughout the society, and the sensitive area of security probably constitutes the single most unlikely exception to this policy.[185] Recalling the essential role played by minorities in the coming to power of the CCP and the

VCP, the subsequent lack of faith shown in these peoples by the Communist leadership might appear unjustified. However, since the appeals made to the minorities during the revolution had been aimed at their nationalistic inclinations, the very history of success enjoyed by those appeals became with victory a vivid reminder that the minorities harbor antistate, counterrevolutionary proclivities.

These same policies emerge from the data available on other Marxist-Leninist states.[186] In each country, members of the most loyal ethnic group enjoy a disproportionate preeminence among the officer corps and the high command of the army, an agency which, as noted, is assigned a key role in matters of internal security.[187] Thus one study established that as of 1972 all of the commanders-in-chief of the Soviet Union's military districts were Russian.[188] Slavs, principally Russians, dominate the officers' corps and elite organizations such as the strategic rocket forces. Central Asians are most apt to be assigned to construction or transportation units.[189] Yugoslavia shows a similar pattern. Data released in Yugoslavia in the early 1970s indicated that Serbs and Montenegrins (43 percent of the total population) accounted for 85 percent of all army officers, a percentage said to have been increasing steadily since the creation of the state.[190] A similar though less drastic situation prevailed within Czechoslovakia, wherein the Slovaks (30 percent of the population) accounted for only 20 percent of all military officers and for an even smaller precentage of people at the higher levels of the Ministry of Defense.[191]

Information concerning the ethnic composition of the secret police is inherently difficult to uncover. However, it is known that within the Soviet Union, the head of the KGB for each of the union republics is customarily a Russian.[192] In the capital of Latvia, where the Letts accounted for 56.8 percent of the population, they reportedly accounted for only some 300 of the 1,500 personnel in the Ministry of Interior, the agency responsible for internal security.[193] A most unusual glimpse of the ethnic composition of what was described as "the leading personnel" of the Ministry for Internal Affairs of Yugoslavia was offered in 1971. It revealed that Serbs and Montenegrins (43 percent of the total population) accounted for 70 percent (61 and 9 percent, respectively) of all such high officials within the ministry responsible for internal security.[194] Moreover, although 73 percent of all Serbs live within the Republic of Serbia, only some 36 percent of the ethnically Serbian officials came from Serbia. The largest Serbian component (43 percent) consisted of members of the Serbian minority within Croatia, and the remaining 20 percent came from Bosnia.[195] Thus the higher echelons responsible for internal security were not only disproportionately staffed with Serbs, but with Serbs who could be expected to harbor the most unrelenting fear and resentment toward Croats, and therefore the greatest determination to keep the Croats a submissive part of the Yugoslav state.

Rumania's design for keeping the Ministry of the Interior in the hands of a specific ethnic group has been more undisguised and more thorough. In the mid-1950s, during the period when Leninist national policy was being paid ostensible homage in the form of a Magyar autonomous region, Interior was one of the few ministries to be designated "national." This designation meant that employment was restricted to those of ethnically Rumanian heritage.[196]

The domination of the secret police by the state's preeminent national group has also been a factor within Czechoslovakia and was one of the many irritants that helped to trigger Slovak discontent during the 1960s. In response to Slovak pressures, Article 8 of the Constitutional Law of 1968 anticipated that under the new federal system "internal order and state security" would no longer be the exclusive prerogative of the central government. Rather, authority over it would be shared by the center and the two constituent republics. If implemented, this measure would truly have vested the Slovaks with a substantial measure of autonomy with regard to security within Slovakia. However, the high priority assigned by the Soviet leadership to an uncontestably centralized system for internal security was soon demonstrated, when, in 1970 under Soviet prodding, the entire authority for security was reinvested in the federal Ministry of the Interior.

When analyzing the degree to which the Marxist-Leninist states have employed cadre policy as a hedge against nationalist proclivities, there is one office whose function renders it more critical than that of the security apparatus: the person or persons with responsibility for implementing and monitoring cadre policy. Within Yugoslavia, for example, the great impact that Aleksander Rankovich was able to exert upon cadre policy flowed not so much from his influence over the secret police (whose role with regard to the national question is the essentially negative one of deterring national dissonance), as upon his position as party secretary in charge of cadre. Had Rankovich been Croatian or a member of some other non-Serbian nationality, it is likely that Serbian domination of the state apparatus (including the security apparatus) would have been far less pronounced.

Within the Soviet Union, the responsibility for cadre policy within each of the major non-Russian national areas usually rests with the second secretary of the local Communist party. The ethnicity of the second secretary is therefore a matter of great import. The policy of the authorities in this matter must be seen in conjunction with their policy toward the ethnicity of the local first secretary. In the months following Stalin's death—that period during which Beria, as part of his strategy for gaining power, was openly appealing to the sense of resentment of Russian domination on the part of the non-Russian peoples—the Presidium of the state-wide party had resolved to make membership in the local national group a criterion for eligibility to the first secretaryship. In Khrushchev's words, this was a "decision that the post of First Secretary in every Republic had to be held by a local person and not by a Russian sent from Moscow."[197] What Khrushchev did not acknowledge, however, was the decision, either made concomitantly or shortly thereafter, to neutralize any peril in such a practice by making the second secretaryship responsible for cadre policy and then making certain that a Russian was appointed to the position. A detailed study of the backgrounds of the individuals who have served as second secretaries since the mid-1950s uncovered a steady increase in the number of cases of an in-tandem relationship of a first secretary drawn from the local group and a second secretary of Russian background.[198] Moreover, the second secretaryship was never filled by someone from the local Russian "settler" community but by a Russian sent from Moscow. Further, the tour of duty of the outsider was for a relatively short period. All of these precautions are admirably designed to insure that the second secretary would not form close personal ties or regional sympathies. Thus immunized, his control of cadre policy assured him the wherewithal to preclude any local leader, such as the first secretary, from developing an effective personal or national following.

THE REDISTRIBUTION AND GERRYMANDERING OF NATIONAL GROUPS

The division of a state's territory into a number of distinct ethnic homelands poses serious problems to state integration. National groups tend to view their respective ethnic homeland as much more than territory. It is perceived by the group as its cultural hearth and, very often, as its geographic cradle. The result is an emotional, almost reverential attribution, evident in such familial metaphors as the fatherland, the motherland, the sacred soil of our ancestors, the native land, the homeland, land where my fathers died, and the like. In Bismarckian terminology, blood and soil become mixed. The national group is convinced that it has a unique and exclusive title to this piece of territory believed to be its cultural preserve, and an intrusion by aliens, even though those aliens be compatriots, is apt to meet with deep resentment. This exclusionary attitude, combined with the numerous reinforcing reminders of a distinctive national identity with which the homeland is laden, has caused the distribution of people into distinct ethnic territories to be a major barrier to acculturation and assimilation. And homelands have also provided fertile soil for the germination and maturation of the idea of national self-determination.

Governments of multinational states have therefore traditionally attempted to blur their ethnic delineations. In contrast, Lenin's policy of regional autonomy required that the ethnic homelands be given greater prominence. As a dialectical step toward the eradication of national particularism, the various ethnic homelands were to be granted political status and territorial precision during the period of the flourishing of the nations. As in the cases of linguistic and cadre policy, however, Marxist governments in practice have demonstrated, by introducing hedging devices, a lack of faith in the wisdom of Lenin's program. In particular, they have manifested a desire to dilute the ethnic purity of the homelands.

Dilution holds both short-term and long-term attractions to governments. In the short-run, it lessens the risk of an ethnic homeland developing into an effective base for antistate activities. (For example, the fact that the Mongols today account for less than ten percent of the population of the Inner Mongolian Autonomous Region makes it far less likely that an effective, indigenous movement to separate Inner Mongolia from China will develop than would be the case if the Mongols were a majority.) Over the longer run, dilution should, at least theoretically, increase the likelihood of acculturation and assimilation by offsetting any tendency of the autonomous borders to encourage physical and cultural isolation.

There are two fundamental strategies available to a government that is intent upon effecting the ethnic dilution of an administrative unit. The first of these—population redistribution—can be subdivided into three alternatives. The government can weaken the ethnic concentrate through policies aimed at bringing about (1) an in-migration of nonindigenes; (2) an out-migration of indigenes (thereby increasing the proportion of the population represented by minorities already present); or (3) some combination of (1) and (2).

The other fundamental strategy for effecting ethnic dilution involves gerrymandering, that is, the drawing of borders so as to circumvent their ostensible raison d'être. In the case of borders purportedly drawn to conform with ethnic distributions, gerrymandering consists of purposefully deviating from the geographic contours of the territory within which an ethnonational group predominates. The deviation might involve an expansion beyond the ethnic contours so as to incorporate alien persons, or it might involve purposefully falling short of those contours so as to leave a segment of the titular group outside. (The consequences of the latter technique are magnified in the case of Marxist-Leninist states, because of the practice of tying national privileges, including the use of the national language, to residence within one's own titular unit.) To achieve maximal impact, both types of gerrymandering can be used in concert, one part of the border excluding a segment of the national group and another part incorporating alien persons.

Gerrymandering and redistribution can be viewed as alternatives. (If people cannot be induced to move across a border, the same effect can be realized by moving the border. Conversely, if borders are resistant to change, the same ethnic effect can be realized by relocating populations.) There is, however, no reason why gerrymandering and redistribution cannot be used to supplement one another. And, in fact, Marxist-Leninist governments have made intensive use of both strategies. Resort to these strategies is self-evidently anti-Leninist, since the guiding principle for granting regional autonomy to compact national groups should be "one people, one autonomous unit."[199] Yet, as a result of gerrymandering and population redistribution, the ethnic homogeneity of the ostensibly ethnically delineated constituent units within Marxist-Leninist states has been severely compromised.

The Soviet Union

The Soviets demonstrated a flair for gerrymandering from the outset. In the Central Asia area, for example, the authorities feared that excessively large and unmanageable, self-aware groups might evolve through the growth of a Bukharan, Turkic, and/or Muslim national identity. Therefore, after a short interlude during which the Soviets consolidated their power, the region's political borders were drawn so as to divide the inhabitants into a number of units and thus encourage a sense of separate national identity on the part of the Kazakhs, Kirgiz, Tadzhiks, Turkmen, and Uzbeks, all peoples whose sense of national consciousness at that time was in a very inchoate state. By contrast, in the Caucasus the authorities were confronted with the Armenians and the Georgians, each of whom had a developed sense of national consciousness that had already manifested itself in separatist movements. This situation was therefore met with the opposite stratagem of grouping these two peoples, along with the Azerbaijani, into a single Transcaucasian Federated Republic, a solution that prevailed until 1936. Moreover, when this unit was dissolved into three union republics, the prevailing distribution of ethnic groups was quite evidently not a burning consideration.[200]

Some appreciation of the general lack of interest in creating ethnically homogeneous units that has characterized Soviet planning from the very beginning can be gleaned from the following data: in not a single union republic, as originally created, did the titular group account for 90 percent of the population. Within the fourteen non-Russian union republics, the proportion of the total population represented by the titular group ranged from 49.4 percent to 88.7 percent, with a mean representation of 69.6 percent and a median of 69.3 percent.[201]

Concentrating exclusively on the union republics would obscure the magnitude of initial gerrymandering. The RSFSR contains more than three-quarters of the country's territory and more than one-half of the country's population. It also contains sixteen of the country's twenty ASSRs, whose combined population in 1970 accounted for 7.7 percent of the USSR's total population. At the time of the creation of these republics, Russians represented a majority of the population in at least three of them.[202] In at least an additional seven cases, there was no single ethnic group that accounted for a majority. The official titles of three of these republics contained the names of two distinct ethnic groups, thereby acknowledging a degree of ethnic heterogeneity.[203] The title of another contained no ethnonational reference whatsoever, its highly heterogeneous population being grouped under the name of the region, Dagestan. But in six of the twelve republics bearing a single ethnic designation and therefore ostensibly designed to conform with that group's distribution, the group after whom the republic was named did not even represent a majority.[204]

Almost equally injurious to the principle of "one nation, one autonomous unit" was the large number of people left outside of the republic bearing their designation. In the case of one of the fourteen peoples given their own union republic (the Armenians), a majority of the nation remained outside. On the average, the excluded segment of all groups approximated fifteen percent of the total. (The mean was 14.5 percent; the median, 16.7 percent.)[205]

For those people ostensibly assigned their own republic within the RSFSR, the statistics were even more unfavorable. In the typical situation, approximately one-third of the group was left outside of the republic's borders (a mean of 33.2 percent, a median of 31.2 percent). In only two of the twelve autonomous republics were the borders so drawn as to incorporate more than 90 percent of the titular group's membership, and in two others they excluded a substantial majority of the titular group (62.7 percent and 73.2 percent). Recalling that residence within one's own autonomous unit became a prerequisite for schooling conducted in one's native language, the impact of this initial gerrymandering upon the rate of acculturation must have been considerable.

Subsequent redistribution of populations within the Soviet Union has further vitiated the image of the Soviet Union as a country whose internal borders reflect ethnic distributions. Particularly pronounced has been the impact of migrations by the state's dominant group. During the period between the creation of the union republics and 1959, the proportion of the population represented by Russians increased in thirteen of the non-Russian union republics. In the fourteenth union republic (the Moldavian SSR), it remained stable. On the average for all fourteen union republics, the percentage of the population accounted for by Russians rose 9.2 percent, from 7.5 percent at the time of creation to 16.7 percent in 1959.[206]

During the same period, the Russian portion of the population also rose in fourteen of the fifteen autonomous republics within the RSFSR for which there are data. On the average for all fifteen republics, the Russian portion of the total population rose a precipitous 15.1 percent, a jump from approximately one-third of the population (32.1 percent) at the time of creation to approximately one-half (47.2 percent) by 1959.[207]

As indicated by table 3, column 5, the dispersal of Russians continued in the intercensal period, 1959–1970. In twelve of the fourteen SSRs, the percentage growth in the absolute number of Russians substantially exceeded the growth of Russians within their own republic. The percentage point increase of Russians within the twelve republics that can be assumed to be attributable to mi-

Table 3. National Composition of Union Republics, 1959–1970

	2	3	4	5	6	7	8
1 Union Republic	% of republic's population represented by titular nation*	% change in absolute number of titular nation within republic, 1959–70	% of republic's population represented by Russians*	% change in absolute number of Russians within republic, 1959–70	% of titular nation living outside republic*	% of USSR population represented by titular nation	% change in absolute number of titular nation within USSR, 1959–70
Armenian SSR	88.6 (+0.6)	+42.3	2.7 (−0.5)	+17.9	38.0 (−6.3)	1.5	27.7
Azerbaijan SSR	73.8 (+6.3)	+51.4	10.0 (−3.6)	+1.8	13.8 (−1.4)	1.8	49.0
Belorussian SSR	81.1 (−0.1)	+11.6	10.4 (+2.2)	+42.1	19.5 (+2.0)	3.7	14.4
Estonian SSR	68.2 (−6.4)	+3.6	24.7 (+4.6)	+39.6	8.1 (−1.6)	0.4	1.8
Georgian SSR	66.8 (+2.5)	+20.4	8.5 (−1.6)	−2.7	3.5 (+0.1)	1.3	20.5
Kazakh SSR	32.4 (+2.6)	+52.8	42.8 (−0.4)	+39.2	21.5 (−3.3)	2.2	46.3
Kirgiz SSR	43.8 (+3.3)	+53.5	29.2 (−1.0)	+37.2	11.5 (−2.1)	0.6	49.8
Latvian SSR	56.8 (−5.2)	+3.4	29.8 (+3.2)	+26.8	6.1 (−1.2)	0.6	2.1
Lithuanian SSR	80.1 (+0.8)	+16.6	8.6 (+0.1)	+16.0	5.9 (−1.6)	1.1	14.6
Moldavian SSR	64.6 (−0.8)	+22.1	11.6 (+1.4)	+41.3	14.6 (−0.2)	1.1	21.9
Russian SFSR	82.8 (−0.5)	+10.1		——	16.5 (+2.3)	53.4	13.1
Tadzhik SSR	56.2 (+3.1)	+55.1	11.9 (−1.4)	+30.8	23.7 (−1.1)	0.9	52.9
Turkmenian SSR	65.6 (+4.7)	+53.4	14.5 (−2.8)	+19.0	7.1 (−0.7)	0.6	52.2
Ukraine SSR	74.9 (−1.9)	+9.7	19.4 (+2.5)	+28.7	13.4 (−0.3)	16.9	9.4
Uzbek SSR	64.7 (+3.6)	+53.3	12.5 (−1.0)	+34.3	15.9 (−0.2)	3.8	52.9

* Change from 1959 to 1970 in parentheses.

gration ranged from 2.9 percent in the case of Lithuania to 29 percent in the case of Belorussia.[208]

Yet despite this very substantial emigration by Russians, column 4 records that their proportion of the population decreased in eight of the fourteen republics and virtually stagnated in still another. Only within the six westernmost republics did the Russian component increase its share of the total population. The principal explanation lies with the striking variations in the natural increase of peoples during the period (column 8). The Russians and the titular peoples of the republics located within the western sector of the USSR increased at a much slower rate than did the titular peoples of Asia and Transcaucasia.[209] Elsewhere the gap in the rate of natural increase between the Russians and the indigenous peoples proved insurmountable. Even when the figure for Russian inmigration was added to the natural increase in the Russian community already present in a republic, the total was not sufficient to offset the natural increase of peoples such as the Azerbaijani (49 percent), the Kazakhs (46.3 percent), the Kirgiz (49.8 percent), the Tadzhiks (52.9 percent), the Turkmen (52.2 percent), and the Uzbeks (52.9 percent).[210] The gap between such figures and the 13.1 percent all-union growth rate of the Russians was simply too wide to be bridged by an otherwise quite impressive level of Russian inmigration. Had it not been for the very substantial in-migration of Russians during the period, the trend in the ratio of titular people to Russians would have been abruptly reversed. As it was, the 1960s proved a stand-off, the Russian portion of the population of the average republic remaining remarkably constant. (The mean percentage change was +0.2 points; the median, −0.5.)

The trends evident during the 1960s continued throughout the 1970s (table 4). The net out-migration of Russians from the RSFSR continued, albeit at a reduced rate. The percentage of the entire Russian nation living outside of that republic increased by nearly one percentage point, from 16.5 to 17.4. As in the 1960s, the dispersion was quite broad. With the exception of the Kirgiz SSR and the three Transcaucasian republics, all republics appear to have experienced in-migration of Russians.[211] For the ten republics experiencing in-migration, the percentage point increase in the absolute number of Russian inhabitants that can be attributed to migration during the 1970s ranged from 2.4 percent in the case of Kazakhstan to 15.7 percent in the case of Moldavia. (For the ten republics, the mean was 9.1 percent and the median was 8.3 percent.)

TABLE 4. National Composition of Union Republics, 1970–1979

	2	3	4	5	6	7	8
		% change in absolute number of titular nation within republic, 1970–79		*% change in absolute number of Russians within republic, 1970–79*			*% change in absolute number of titular nation within USSR, 1970–79*
Union Republic	*% of republic's population represented by titular nation**		*% of republic's population represented by Russians**		*% of titular nation living outside republic**	*% of USSR population represented by titular nation*	
Armenian SSR	89.7 (+1.1)	+23.4	2.3 (−0.4)	+6.1	34.4 (−3.6)	1.6	16.6
Azerbaijan SSR	78.1 (+4.3)	+24.7	7.9 (−2.1)	−6.9	14.0 (+0.2)	2.1	25.0
Belorussian SSR	79.4 (−1.7)	+3.8	11.9 (+1.5)	+20.9	20.0 (+0.5)	3.6	4.5
Estonian SSR	64.7 (−3.5)	+2.5	27.9 (+3.2)	+22.1	7.1 (−1.0)	0.4	1.3
Georgian SSR	68.8 (+2.0)	+9.6	7.4 (−1.1)	−6.3	3.9 (+0.4)	1.4	10.0
Kazakh SSR	36.0 (+3.6)	+27.1	40.8 (−2.0)	+8.9	19.3 (−2.2)	2.5	23.7
Kirgiz SSR	47.9 (+4.1)	+31.3	25.9 (−3.3)	+6.5	11.5 (0.0)	0.7	31.3
Latvian SSR	53.7 (−3.1)	+0.1	32.8 (+3.0)	+16.5	6.6 (+0.5)	0.5	0.6
Lithuanian SSR	80.0 (−0.1)	+8.2	8.9 (+0.3)	+13.1	4.9 (−1.0)	1.1	7.0
Moldavian SSR	63.9 (−0.7)	+9.6	12.8 (+1.2)	+22.2	14.9 (+0.3)	1.1	10.0
Russian SFSR	82.6 (−0.2)	+5.4	10.4 (−1.5)	—	17.4 (+0.9)	52.4	6.5
Tadzhik SSR	58.8 (+2.6)	+37.2	10.4 (−1.5)	+14.8	22.8 (−0.9)	1.1	35.7
Turkmenian SSR	68.4 (+2.8)	+33.5	12.6 (−1.9)	+11.5	6.7 (−0.4)	0.8	33.0
Ukraine SSR	73.6 (−1.3)	+3.4	21.1 (+1.7)	+14.7	13.8 (+0.4)	16.2	3.9
Uzbek SSR	68.7 (+4.0)	+36.7	10.8 (−1.7)	+11.4	15.1 (−0.8)	4.8	35.5

* Change from 1970 to 1979 in parentheses.

Once more, however, as in the 1960s, the Russian portion of the population decreased within a majority of the republics. Again, only in the six westernmost republics did it increase. Elsewhere, in-migration was unable to offset the discrepancy between the natural increase of the Russians and the larger natural increase of the titular peoples. For all fourteen republics, the percentage of the population represented by Russians underwent a mean decline of 0.2 points and a median decline of 0.8 points.

The overall scene in 1979 with regard to Russians living within territories nominally assigned to non-Russians was as follows: Russians accounted for a substantial percentage (more than 7 percent) of the population of each of the union republics other than Armenia. (See table 4, column 4.) The range was from 2.3 percent in the case of Armenia to 40.8 percent in the case of Kazakhstan. Even including Armenia (and excluding the Russian Republic), Russians accounted for a mean percentage of 16.7 of the population of the union republics and a median percentage of 12.3. As to the autonomous republics within the RSFSR, the percentage represented by Russians ranged from 14.7 to 73.5, with a mean of 45 and a median of 44.1. In five of the sixteen ASSRs, the Russians constituted an absolute majority, and in four others they were the largest single ethnonational group.

Not all of this dispersion occurred after 1917. Russians had dispersed over large areas of the country under the Romanovs. However, there has been a dramatic increase in the dispersal of Russians since 1917. As we have seen, the percentage of Russians has grown in all fourteen non-Russian union republics since the revolution. Meanwhile, the Russian share of the population of traditionally Russian territory has decreased from an initial 86.2 percent to a 1970 figure of 77.3 percent.[212]

The magnitude of this redistribution is all the more striking because the migration has taken place within a society ostensibly committed to regional equalization. As noted earlier, the economic equalization of ethnic homelands was a fundamental aspect of Leninist national policy, and over the years Soviet leaders and writers have regularly cited figures purportedly demonstrating a closing of the gap between richer and poorer republics.[213] The economic equalization of homelands would, of course, tend to freeze the existing ethnic distribution, rather than to encourage the greater mixing of peoples. If economic opportunities were in fact approximately the same throughout the Soviet Union, there would be no economic motivation to migrate from one's ethnic hearth.

Numerous claims to the contrary, the Soviets have not stressed regional economic equalization as a primary goal. In the most intensive and sophisticated study of Soviet demographic patterns yet conducted, Lewis, Rowland, and Clem establish that other considerations have weighed more heavily. Specifically, they note that the highest priority in allocating investments and in locating industries has been assigned to strategic considerations. And the second most important standard has been economic rationalization, in terms of the presence of raw materials, support industries, markets, infrastructure, and the like.[214] These yardsticks, while perfectly understandable and rational, have nothing to do with promoting the economic equalization of ethnic homelands. Moreover, even at the level of form rather than of substance, the goal of regional equality was discarded by early 1978. With the reaching of the stage of "developed socialism" that had been heralded by the 1977 constitution, regional gaps were alleged to have been eliminated and the "utmost efficiency of the whole economy" made the single criterion for investment.

> One basic feature of economic development under developed socialism is that the policy of distributing the productive forces and investments no longer hinges on the need to eliminate the backwardness of the country's outlying regions, as in the early period of socialist construction, but on the need to ensure the utmost efficiency of the whole economy.
>
> Productive forces and investments are now being distributed taking account of the fact that the gaps between the development levels of the central areas and the outlying regions have been eliminated. It is only natural that, in the future, special attention will be focused on areas that are particularly important for boosting the economy of the whole country.[215]

While there is no universally accepted standard for measuring regional economic discrepancies, the claim that interregional gaps had been eliminated within the Soviet Union would not survive even the most unsophisticated analysis. In 1970, for example, the per capita product of the wealthiest republic was more than two and one-third times that of the poorest.[216] But allowing that regional equalization had been achieved, the necessary consequences of the newly announced policy would be to recreate gaps. In effect, then, the dropping of a policy of regional equalization constituted a public admission that a key aspect of Leninist national policy would no longer be pursued even at the level of form.

The fact that the Soviet authorities have not in practice encouraged regional equalization does not in itself establish that they have actively promoted ethnic diffusion. However, it is inconceivable that such a massive and consequential redistribution of population as we have described could have occurred in the absence of official approval. The infusion of large numbers of Russians into non-Russian homelands has clearly been viewed as desirable by the authorities, as indicated by the 1961 party program:

> The appearance of new industrial centers, the prospecting and development of mineral deposits, virgin land development, and the growth of all modes of transport increase the mobility of the population and promote greater intercourse between the peoples of the Soviet Union. People of many nationalities live together and work in harmony in the Soviet republics. The boundaries between the Union republics of the U.S.S.R. are increasingly losing their former significance.

Consonant with this plank in their program, the authorities have done discernibly little to combat the continuing influx of Russians into non-Russian areas. There has been no visible attempt made by the authorities to persuade Russians living outside of the RSFSR to relocate in labor-shortage areas within that republic. On the contrary, recruitment policies have continued to favor the out-migration of Russians from the RSFSR, thus contributing further to the regional imbalances between labor supply and demand that they insist they are anxious to correct. Even in cases where a sufficient pool of skilled labor has been available within non-Russian republics, the authorities are known to have recruited Russians from outside.[217] The government has also demonstrated little interest in redrawing the borders of autonomous units so as to offset the erosive, invalidating effects that gerrymandering and migration have exerted upon ostensibly ethnopolitical borders. For example, northern Kazakhstan has been a favored target of Russian migration, and rather minor adjustments in the Kazakhstan-RSFSR border in favor of the latter would transfer a large percentage of the Russian community presently within Kazakhstan to its ethnically appropriate republic. In this and numerous other analogous cases, the authorities have not chosen to undertake such adjustments.[218] In the rare instances when alterations in the borders of the union republics have taken place, ethnic homogeneity has not necessarily been advanced thereby.[219] Finally, although the official position of the government is that those nations possessing union republics have been thereby enabled to "quickly achieve national statehood and promote their own economy, culture, and language,"[220] and although the authorities, as a means of lending credence to this claim, have constitutionally granted to the union republics the three most significant attributes of sovereignty (namely, the right to conduct foreign relations, to maintain their own armed forces,[221] and even that ultimate right to withdraw from the union), it is instructive that the republics have never been granted, even at the level of pure form, the lesser right, claimed by all truly sovereign states, to control immigration policy. Official acts of both omission and commission have thus condoned, intensified, and perpetuated ethnic heterogeneity in the non-Russian units.

This is not to say that migratory patterns have always faithfully reflected the wishes of the central authorities. Increasingly during the late 1970s, Soviet scholars and members of the government bureaucracy bemoaned the absence of a single, integrated, "rational" migration policy.[222] Economic progress was being impeded by severe labor shortages in the eastern and northern sectors of the RSFSR, while Russians continued to migrate to other republics with labor surpluses. The bright lights of the more cosmopolitan cities of the westernmost republics had continued to exert a magnetic pull upon Russian migrants, but a region of greater concern to the Soviet planners was Central Asia. Although the republics there contained the country's greatest pool of underutilized manpower, they had, as we have seen, continued to attract Russian migrants. Concern at the highest echelon of authority became clear at the Twenty-sixth Party Congress in February 1981. In his report to the congress, General Secretary Brezhnev noted that "to this very day, people often prefer to go from the north to the south, or from the east to the west, although a rational deployment of production forces demands movements in the opposite directions."[223] Rather than emphasizing the need to curtail migration to Central Asia, however, Brezhnev emphasized the need for this region's indigenes to migrate to the regions of labor shortage: "In Central Asia and a number of areas of the Caucasus there is, on the contrary, a surplus of manpower, especially in the countryside. That means that the population of these parts must be more actively involved in the development of the country's new territories."[224] While here speaking of the need for migration to parts of the RSFSR, in another part of his speech Brezhnev indicated that he did not intend that migration to the other republics should cease. He did so by stressing the need for all republics to make life more attractive for nonindigenes.[225] The general secretary's prescription for Central Asia therefore appeared to be one of "Indigenes out, nonindigenes in!"

Further confirmation that the authorities did not desire to impede immigration into the Central Asian Republics nor to induce non-indigenes to emigrate from them was made explicit in an article written later in the same year by the leading demographer of the Soviet Academy of Sciences:

> Let us note that the influx of migrants from different regions of the country to the republics of Central Asia is not adverse in itself. *Such a process is necessary.* The fact that the counterflow in its size was appreciably less and *inadequately involved in the migratory turnover the indigenous inhabitants of the Central Asian republics,* is adverse.[226]

In short, the answer to the pressing demand for labor within sectors of the RSFSR was not to be sought through creating impediments to Russian migration into other republics but through fostering migration to the RSFSR by other titular peoples.

Russians, of course, are not the sole agents of ethnic dilution. The presence of non-Russian, nonindigenes is also an important element helping to account for the ethnically heterogeneous character of the union republics. Depending upon the union republic, their share of the population in 1979 could account for from 5.3 percent to 30.8 percent.[227] In four of the fourteen republics (Armenia, Georgia, Moldavia, and Tadzhikistan), the Russians were not the largest nontitular people (they were the Azerbaijani, Armenians, Ukrainians, and Uzbeks, respectively).[228] Such settlers have in effect done double duty as agents of ethnic dilution, having simultaneously contributed to the dilution of their own titular republics and the republics in which they have settled. As to their own titular republic, any portion of a national group, simply by living anywhere outside of its union republic, thereby increases the proportion of Russians and other national groups within that republic. That is to say, any out-migration of the indigenous ethnic element automatically increases the proportion of nonindigenes, even if the latters' actual number remains constant. At the same time, the émigrés will obviously contribute to the heterogeneity of the republic in which they settle.

As table 4, column 6 attests, in 1979 the percentage of four of the fourteen peoples with union republics living outside of their republic exceeded the comparable figure for the Russians.[229] And, for all fourteen peoples, the median and mean percentage of those living outside of their republic (13.9 in each case) compare not too unfavorably with the Russian figure of 17.4. We should not credit all of these settlers with having a double impact upon the ethnic dilution of the non-Russian republics, however, for a substantial percentage of them were living within the RSFSR. Thus, easily the largest group of non-Russians living outside of their appropriate republic were Ukrainian, but 62 percent of all such Ukrainians lived within the RSFSR. Similarly, 25.6 percent of all emigrant Armenians, 19.8 percent of all emigrant Azerbaijani, 55.5 percent of all emigrant Belorussians, 40.9 percent of all emigrant Kazakhs, and 23.1 percent of all emigrant Moldavians lived within the RSFSR. While each of these emigrant communities materially helped to account for the ethnic heterogeneity of their native homeland, they did not contribute to the further ethnic dilution of the other non-Russian republics.

There is, moreover, a major difference in the settlement pattern of Russians and of those non-Russians who have a union republic. While the Russians are broadly dispersed throughout the Soviet Union as a whole, non-Russians living outside of their union republic tend to be located nearby.[230] As the dominant ethnic element throughout the state's history, who gave their name to the official title of the state under the tsars and to its popular appellation even today, the Russians have tended to view the entire state as their homeland.[231] By contrast, the other nations have tended to remain close to that particular segment of the country that they consider their ethnic hearth.[232] Indeed, as noted, many of these non-Russians, although living outside of their union republic, are living within the ethnic hearth. They are the product of gerrymandering rather than migration.

In any case, however, the fact that those members of titular nations who live outside their republic tend to be concentrated in adjacent republics does not negate their significance as a hedge against Lenin's policy of territorial autonomy. As noted, any portion of a national group, simply by living anywhere outside of its union republic, contributes to that republic's ethnic heterogeneity. As to the republic of settlement, a minority drawn from the region is more apt to harbor deep suspicions and historic grievances against the titular nation than would Russian immigrants from outside the region. As a result, the former can be relied upon to keep an alert eye open to any symptom of ethnic autarky on the part of the titular group. And if, as a result of the division of a people into two republics, an irredentist note should be introduced into the relations of the two titular groups, so much the better.[233] Therefore, the intraregional, interrepublic distribution of non-Russians lends itself readily to the ancient principle of *divide et impera*.[234] And thus, the proportionately large number of Azerbaijani in Armenia, Armenians in Azerbaijan, and Armenians and Azerbaijani in Georgia unquestionably helps to account for the past equanimity with which the central authorities have tolerated the fact of the relatively few Russians in the Caucasus.[235] Moreover, as we have repeatedly noted, national privileges, including access to some education in one's native language, have, as a matter of right, been confined to those living within the union republic bearing their ethnonym.[236] Therefore, the forces of acculturation and (if Soviet theorists who link national change to language change are correct) assimilation operate even with regard to peoples living immediately outside of their home republic.[237]

The acculturation consequences of living outside of one's republic were rather graphically described in early 1972 in a letter addressed to the Communist parties of several states outside the Soviet Union by a group living within the Latvian SSR who described themselves as "seventeen Latvian communists." Although their letter was primarily a protest against what was perceived as the russification of the titular group, the writers quite candidly acknowledged that non-Latvian, non-Russian peoples suffered from a still more unfavorable status:

> Those Lithuanians, Estonians, Jews, Germans, Poles, and other minorities (except Russians) residing in Latvian territory do not have their ethnic heritages at all respected. Until 1940 (until the establishment of Soviet rule) in Latvia these minorities had their own elementary and secondary schools where they studied in their own language. They issued their own language newspapers, magazines, books; they had their own clubs, theaters, and other cultural and educational institutions. Now, in disregard of pertinent Marxist-Leninist principles dealing with ethnic questions, and contrary to the statements of USSR leaders that ethnic problems in the Soviet Union have been solved and that each nationality has been guaranteed complete freedom and equality, nothing of that kind is evident. In every republic the Russians have everything, people native to their republics have something, but others nothing at all.[238]

Soviet specialists have neither been blind to the acculturational impact of dwelling outside of one's homeland nor hesitant to describe the impact as "assimilation." In the words of the director of the Institute of Ethnography of the Soviet Academy of Sciences:

> *[E]thnic assimilation* evolved naturally during the Soviet period owing to the territorial mixing of the various national groups and the increase in economic, cultural and other links. Assimilation processes, however, mainly involve territorially dispersed groups (Jews, Mordovians, Karels, etc.) and groups of individuals settled in territories occupied by a different nationality. . . . On the whole, peoples living within their own Union or Autonomous Republics as a rule steadfastly preserve their mother tongue and their sense of national identity.[239]

Non-Russians living outside of their own republics thus tend to become russified and, in turn, to act in a sense as surrogate Russians for the further russification of the republic in which they are domiciled.[240]

Recently, another important difference emerged between Russians and non-Russians living outside of their appropriate union republic. Whereas a net influx of Russians into other republics continued during the two decades from 1959–1979, this did not hold true for twelve of the other fourteen titular peoples. The percentage of the nation living outside of its particular union republic actually declined for ten of the titular groups and remained essentially static for two others.[241] While in some cases the decline was quite small (and may be either statistically insignificant or attributable to assimilation rather than migration), the overall picture, with the two exceptions of the Belorussians and Georgians, is for non-Russian peoples either to remain stationary or to migrate to their titular republic.[242]

As was noted earlier, in recent years the diluting effect of Russian in-migration upon the ethnic composition of the eight union republics within Asia and Transcaucasia has been neutralized by the much greater natural increase on the part of several titular groups. In and by itself, the decrease in the proportion of Russians within these union republics should perhaps not be a matter of pressing concern to the authorities. They might find consolation in the expectation that the high birth rates among the non-European peoples will decrease over the long term as the people become more subjected to urbanization and the other processes collectively known as modernization.[243] And even though the percentage of the population represented by the titular nation has increased in all eight of these union republics since 1959 (column 2, tables 3 and 4), in no case does a republic merit being called ethnically homogeneous.

On the average, the titular group accounts for approximately two-thirds of the republic's population.[244] In no case does it account for over 90 percent of the total population, and in two cases it fails to account for a majority.[245] On the other hand, the gap in the natural increase of Russians compared with the titular peoples of Transcaucasia and Asia is impressive (6.5 percent versus an average of 26.4 percent during the 1970–1979 period) and is unlikely to narrow appreciably in the near future. When coupled with a decline in the relative number of non-Russian peoples living outside of their respective republics, the resulting overall demographic trend should be a matter of concern to those desirous of maintaining ethnic heterogeneity within the union republics. Given the unlikelihood of a radical decrease in the growth rate of the Transcaucasian and Asian titular peoples in the near future, the trend toward ethnic homogeneity that characterized every Transcaucasian and Central Asian union republic in the 1959–1979 period appears destined to continue.

There are three means by which the authorities could slow the move toward ethnic homogenizing of the union republics: (1) increased gerrymandering; (2) inducing a still greater proportion of Russians to live outside of the RSFSR; and/or (3) reversing the trend among the titular nations by inducing or directing large numbers to migrate from their respective republic. Several considerations should cause the authorities to place primary reliance upon the third course of action. As noted, each person who emigrates from his ethnic homeland does double duty by decreasing the proportion of the titular group in his home republic, and by increasing the proportion of minorities in the republic to which he migrates. Moreover, emigration avoids *a*, if not *the*, major barrier to acculturation and assimilation, namely, the psychological milieu that encapsulates the ethnic homeland.

A series of Soviet studies unanimously concur on the significance of residence relative to one's homeland.[246] For example, the incidence of interethnic marriages is much greater among parties who meet on ethnically neutral territory. In other words, members of the indigenous element customarily demonstrate greater unwillingness to enter interethnic marriages than do immigrants.[247] Moreover, when the child of an ethnically mixed family chooses his/her national identity (which a person must do at the age of sixteen as part of the application for an internal passport), the most influential factor, when present, is the ethnic homeland. The relative strength of the principal variables can be sketched as follows:

(1) A child will normally select the national identity of the father rather than of the mother. (2) However, if either parent is Russian, the child will tend to adopt the Russian identity. (3) But even though the father is Russian (that is, even though situations (1) and (2) reinforce one another), if the family lives in the homeland of the mother, then the child will tend to select the nationhood of the mother.[248] In short, severing non-Russians from their homeland substantially increases the likelihood of their assimilation. Therefore, encouraging out-migration of non-Russians recommends itself for both short-range (the double impact effect) and long-range (assimilation) reasons.

To foster this out-migration, the Soviet authorities have a broad arsenal of potential weapons. *In extremis*, the government could conceivably resort to naked coercion. If convinced that the advantages were sufficient to risk tarnishing the carefully nurtured public image of "a fraternal family of nations voluntarily united on the principle of national self-determination," the government might elect to affect rapid, radical alterations on the ethnic map through simple edict backed up by force. Thus, in retaliation for real or exaggerated antistate activities during World War II, the Balkar, Chechen, Crimean, Tatar, Ingush, Kalmyk, Karachai, and Volga Germans were all forcibly ejected from their homelands and deported well to the east under orders from Stalin.[249] However, actions of this type are undisguisably at odds with Leninist national policy, and resort to such extreme methods as a rule has been eschewed.[250]

Aside from naked coercion, there are several devices that the authorities can press into service as means of influencing population distribution. One potentially very powerful lever stems from the obligation of all students at institutes of higher learning and at technical and vocational schools to spend three years following graduation in a governmentally assigned position anywhere within the Soviet Union.[251] In practice, enforcement of this obligation has been extremely lax. Students have demonstrated an ingenious talent for finagling assignment in a desirable area (usually one's ethnic homeland) or for otherwise circumventing the requirement. But, with tighter controls, this program could become a major agent of ethnic diffusion. In 1974, 2.8 million new graduates came under this requirement.[252] Presuming that these figures were apportioned equitably among national groups, the government had the legal right to order more than 400,000 Ukrainians out of their republic for a period of three years.[253] If we treat the annual number of graduates as a constant (actually the number is growing), 1.2 million Ukrainians could be on outside assignment at any one time. Moreover, given the dual impact of the migrants upon their old and new republic of residence, it would require a movement of 2.4 million Russians (or other, non-titular peoples) to exert a similar impact upon the ethnic mix of the non-Russian republics. If we apply this reasoning to all non-Russians living within their respective titular union republic, it becomes evident that more than 2.5 million non-Russians could legally be assigned outside of their republic at any one time, thus having an impact comparable to a migration of over 5 million Russians.[254] And all this still ignores the qualitative factor, for the young and well educated would be the most likely source of national leaders. The absence from the homeland of the young national elite would materially decrease the likelihood of a nationalist movement arising.

In addition to the postgraduation requirement, two other noteworthy means remain for bringing about ethnic redistribution. Indeed, the actual degree of ethnic redistribution that has been realized within the Soviet Union is greater than the census data indicate, in that the census reports prisoners and those on military duty at their last civilian address rather than at the site of their assignment. The distortion caused by this practice is particularly pronounced in the case of members of the state's large military establishment. We will recall that minority personnel on military duty are posted outside their homeland as a matter of established policy. The number of persons on active military duty in 1975 has been estimated at over 3.5 million.[255] Again assuming an equitable apportionment among nations, 1.1 million non-Russian service people were posted outside of their republic. Not all of the service people would exert what we have called a double impact, because thirty-one divisions were stationed outside of the USSR in Eastern Europe and a disproportionate number of the remaining divisions were in the RSFSR, particularly along the Chinese border. Nevertheless, hundreds of thousands presumably did have such a doubling effect. Moreover, military posting leads to some permanent resettlement outside of one's republic, and this development is clearly endorsed by the authorities who offer encouragements to take one's discharge at the site of one's final post.[256]

It is apparently also general policy to incarcerate persons alleged to have committed serious crimes against the state within prisons that are located outside of the prisoners' republics. This practice evoked the following satirical comment from a Ukrainian dissident:

Ukraine, according to its constitution, is also a sovereign state which even has representatives in the United Nations. Her courts sentence thousands of Ukrainian citizens and send them to be detained beyond her borders—a policy unparalleled in history. Perhaps Ukraine, like the principality of Monaco, has no room for camps? Room was found for seven million Russians, but for Ukrainian political prisoners there is no room in their native land.[257]

The number of contemporary detainees is not known. At one time, the total ran to several millions, but it is unquestionably lower today.[258] In any case, in this category numbers are of secondary importance to some of the individuals grouped thereunder. Among the prisoners are the social activists who have overtly denied the state in the name of their nation. The authorities evidently feel that the symbolic influence of such national martyrs is less when they are incarcerated some distance from the ethnic homeland.

We have thus far discussed means by which the authorities can bring about migrations that they desire. In addition, they have tools for dissuading migration that is deemed undesirable. Most noteworthy is the requirement that settlement in a locale requires prior permission from the authorities, registration with the police, and the entering of proof that one has abided by this procedure in the internal passport which is carried by all Soviet citizens and which must be presented upon demand.[259] Although at first glance all such devices might appear purely negative in their impact upon migration, they may in fact be means for redirecting the migrational urge into governmentally approved channels. Thus, if rural youth, desirous of moving to a city, are denied access to cities within their homeland, they are, as a consequence, apt to migrate to a city outside of their homeland, rather than to smother the urge to live in an urban environment.

Although the Soviet government has had the weapons to control internal migrations, it has not been prepared to utilize them effectively.[260] We have noted that the requirement that college graduates accept a three-year assignment of the government's choosing has been very laxly enforced. Similarly, the fact that a number of urban areas, specifically designated by the government as "no-further-growth-zones," have continued to attract large numbers of new settlers casts serious doubt upon the level of enforcement of the requirement that migration requires both prior official approval and registration with the local authorities upon arrival.[261] But these are shortcomings of will rather than of weapons. If the authorities place a sufficiently high premium on attaining an objective that required strict controls over the quantity and quality of migration, then greater and more efficient use of the weapons would follow. Snuffing in advance any ethnonationally inspired dangers inherent in Lenin's policy of autonomy for compact ethnic groups by diluting the ethnic composition of the republics has been such a primary objective from the beginning. And thus far the means employed have been sufficient to the task. Extant policies have sufficed to induce impressive numbers of Russians to migrate into non-Russian areas. This continuing migration, combined with the aftereffects of earlier gerrymandering, imbues the republics with a high degree of ethnic heterogeneity even today. However, there is no evidence that the authorities have become any less enamored of the ideal (set forth in the 1961 Party Program) of having "people of many nationalities live together"; and should they conclude that the large natural increases in the number of Transcaucasian and Asian peoples must be locally offset or that the possibility of a future manifestation of ethnonationalism should be countered by greater mixing of the peoples, then more effective utilization of the powers already at their disposal can be anticipated.

As noted, Brezhnev's speech at the Twenty-sixth Party Congress in 1981 appeared to herald just such a development. In addition to noting that Central Asians *must* partake in the development of the eastern and northern RSFSR, the General Secretary had stipulated that nonindigenes located anywhere in the Soviet Union must be accorded more privileges:

> The composition of the population of the Soviet republic is multinational, and it is natural that all nationalities have the right to due representation in their party and state bodies. . . . In recent years the number of citizens of nonindigenous ethnic groups have considerably increased in a number of republics. They have their specific requirements in the spheres of language, culture and everyday life.[262]

Given the fact that Russians were certainly not unduly underprivileged with regard to representation, status, and language, the General Secretary's comment presumably referred to non-Russian émigrés and was prompted by a desire to counter the recent tendency for them to return to their homeland.[263]

The spate of follow-up conferences and publications designed to clarify the points on migration that had been made at the Twenty-sixth Congress made evident that the ruling apparatus had indeed signaled its intention to make migratory processes more responsive to its will.[264] An article by the editor of *Kommunist*, for example, suggested that the government enforce its right to direct graduates of institutes of higher learning to serve for a period in any sector of the country:

> The acute need for personnel of a number of sectors of the national economy and of some regions of the country, especially those being newly developed, was noted at the 26th CPSU Congress. . . . It is no secret to anyone that a portion of the student youth, including those of higher education institutions, are disposed to work only in the customary national environment. . . . [N]othing bad would happen if the graduates of teknikums and higher educational institutions, no matter what nationality they are, after their studies would go wherever they are actually needed and where they would acquire not only practical experience in the received specialty, but also an additional supply of proletarian internationalism.[265]

Perhaps the most comprehensive outline of the emerging policy appeared in a book appropriately entitled *Law and Demographic Processes in the USSR*.[266] The author, after depicting migratory activity over the previous two decades as haphazard and nonrational, insisted that Soviet law must be utilized to insure that demographic patterns serve the needs of Soviet society. He repeated Brezhnev's edict that large numbers of people from Central Asia must be shifted to the labor-short eastern and northern sectors of the RSFSR.[267] Among the administrative tools that he felt should prove particularly helpful in bringing about this and other desirable migration patterns were the aforementioned internal passports and resident permits required of all citizens. He further noted the recent tendency for Armenian and other non-Russian émigrés to return to their titular republics, and, in conformity with the directives of the Twenty-sixth Congress, maintained that this trend must be countered. Also in conformity with the directives of the congress, the author asserted that the law must encourage family size to remain within a range of four-to-five in number, a formula that would have the effect of encouraging larger families among Russians and other European peoples, while encouraging smaller families among Asians.[268] The author also maintained that any attempt to increase investment within a region in order to employ a local labor surplus, at a time when there were labor shortages in other regions, constituted a violation of Article 16 of the constitution which stipulated, in the author's words, "that the USSR economy constitutes a single national economic complex, which encompasses all the sectors of production, including labor resources within the country." From this perspective, any attempt to circumvent or resist interregional migration could be branded as antistate activity.

China

The practice of circumventing the possible perils inherent in a system of autonomous units through gerrymandering and the redistribution of population has been more conspicuously demonstrated in the case of China. The CPR's less camouflaged approach reflects a much more favorable statistical situation and a greater willingness to take radical action to achieve a desired end. The ethnic demography of China is quantitatively so different from that of the Soviet Union as perhaps to bring into play the Marxist "Law of the Transformation of Quantity into Quality," a paraphrase of which might read that at some point a sufficient quantitative difference transforms itself into qualitative difference. With the most loyal nation (the Han) accounting for 94 percent of the total population (as contrasted with the 52 percent figure for the Russians in the Soviet Union) and with an absolute excess of Han available in overpopulated China (the Han number some seven to eight times the number of Russians and more than the total population of any state, excluding the PRC itself), the Chinese authorities have had at their disposal the means for thoroughly diluting the non-Han homelands. And with their proven penchant for essaying radical surgery (as witness the Great Leap Forward in the late 1950s and the Cultural Revolution of the late 1960s), it would be surprising if the CCP shied away from taking advantage of the Han's numerical superiority.

The less concealed character of Chinese practices is due to the scope and character of their activities rather than to candor. As earlier noted, the Chinese insist that they are undeviating practitioners of Leninist national policy, and a major dimension of the polemics between Peking and Moscow has involved charges, countercharges, and denials concerning apostasy on the national question. Indeed, though Chinese actions have been less concealed, Peking has provided far less satisfactory statistical data on population distribution than has Moscow. At best the data tend to be very old and are usually of dubious validity. For example, a 1965 Chinese publication indicated that Uighurs accounted for 78.8 percent of the population of the Sinkiang Uighur AR and that Tibetans accounted for 94.5 percent of the population of the Tibetan AR, although in each case the titular group was by this time rapidly moving toward minority status.[269]

Gerrymandering has been consistently practiced by the CCP from the outset. As mentioned, the first autonomous region was that of Inner Mongolia, created in 1947 while the struggle for supremacy over China was still in progress. As originally delineated, the AR housed two to four times as many Han as it did Mongols.[270] In 1955 the authorities added the predominantly Han provinces of Suiyan and Chahar (Huhehot) and part of a third, Ningsia, thereby increasing the ratio of Han over Mongols to eight to one. In 1969 the AR's territory was just as abruptly decreased by approximately one-third, as huge segments of territory were severed from both its eastern and western flanks.[271] Erstwhile Mongolian inhabitants of their own AR found themselves part of either Heilungkiang, Kirin, Liaoning, or Kansu Province, or, more paradoxically, part of the Ningsia Hui AR. (See map 1.) The partition not only further numerically disadvantaged those Mongols within the truncated AR, but left a majority living outside its borders.[272] The impermanence of such borders was again underlined in 1979, when as part of the post-Cultural Revolution rewooing of the minorities, the region was returned to its 1955–1969 size. While this alteration at least had the effect of placing a majority (about 70 percent) of all of China's Mongols within their own autonomous region, it left the Mongols but a small fraction (estimates range from 10 to 20 percent) of the region's total population.[273]

By contrast with Inner Mongolia, the Tibetan AR, at the time of its creation in 1956, did contain a population composed principally of the titular national group. In this instance, gerrymandering took the form of excluding a majority of the titular national group, even though all Tibetans tend to populate a contiguous territory.[274] Large segments of Tsinghai and Szechwan provinces, as well as smaller sectors of southern Kansu and western Yunan provinces, should seemingly have been included in the Tibetan AR. The concentration of Tibetans in these regions is suggested by the fact that in 1965 there were five Tibetan Autonomous Districts (ADs) and a sixth "Mongol-Tibetan-Kazakh" AD within Tsinghai, two Tibetan ADs within Szechwan, one within Kansu, and one within Yunan.[275]

Here clearly the system of autonomous unit was used to fractionalize a people rather than to consolidate it.

A Chinese explanation for refusing to consolidate the Tibetan homeland was offered in 1982:

> The three-member delegation sent to Beijing by Dalai Lama this year requested that the central authorities accord Tibet the same treatment as is provided for Taiwan in the Chinese Government's nine-point principle, and that all the areas inhabited by Tibetans in Sichuan, Qinghai, Gansu and Yunan be incorporated with Tibet to establish a unified big Tibetan autonomous region. The central authorities' response to these questions is very clear: both Tibet and Taiwan are integral parts of China, but there are big differences between the two. Tibet has been liberated for more than three decades. . . . The nine-point principle, therefore, is not applicable to Tibet.
>
> Neither is the request for merging all the areas inhabited by Tibetans realistic. For centuries, the Tibetan people have lived in separate communities within four other provinces in addition to Tibet itself. Just like other minority nationalities in China, they exercise national regional autonomy and are organized into an autonomous region, several autonomous prefectures and autonomous counties. It is not reasonable to change the historically determined administrative divisions simply according to the distribution of nationalities.[276]

This stance, of course, was wholly inconsonant both with the prerevolutionary promises of the Chinese party and with Leninist national policy.

Unlike the Tibetans, more than 90 percent of China's largest minority, the Chuang, were consolidated within a single AR bearing their name. However, this action was carried out in a manner that relegated them to the status of a minority. In 1958 the name of Kwangsi Province was changed to Kwangsi Chuang AR, despite the fact that the Chuang constituted only one-third of the province's population.[277] It is difficult to discern any basis for choosing this particular geographic configuration for the AR, other than the desire to dissipate the strength of the Chuang. Numbering some 8 million, twice that of the next largest minority, the Chuang were certainly sufficiently numerous to merit an essentially homogeneous AR. Moreover, the group's distribution posed no problem to designing such a homogeneous unit. With the exception of some 100,000 of their members located in Kwantung Province, the Chuang had settled in a single contiguous area covering the western two-thirds of Kwangsi Province and a small salient in eastern Yunan. Prior to 1958, more than 70 percent of the Chuang living in Kwangsi were in their own autonomous district, wherein they accounted for two-thirds (67 percent) of the population.[278] Had the authorities in fact desired to make the proposed AR's borders coincide with the Chuang ethnic homeland, a slight adjustment outward in the borders of the AD was, therefore, all that was required. But the authorities elected to incorporate the heavily Han-populated eastern third of Kwangsi, thus assuring the Chuang a minority status. Moreover, the authorities elected not to incorporate the half million Chuang of adjacent Yunan. Rather, in the same year in which the Kwangsi Chuang AR was created, the Chuang of Yunan were incorporated into a newly established Wen-shan Chuang and Miao AC, wherein Chuang represented only 32 percent of the population, while Han accounted for nearly one-half.[279] Thus, by keeping the borders of (former) Kansu and Yunan provinces intact, the authorities managed to dissect a half million Chuang from those in Kwangsi and to make each of the two resulting segments a minority within its respective autonomous unit. We have just reviewed how a similar decision to respect established provincial borders resulted in the fractionalization of the Tibetans. By contrast, no such respect for provinces was evident in the northern area surrounding Inner Mongolia, where, as we have seen, borders were altered with abandon and even entire provinces were liquidated. Indeed, curiously enough, Chou En-lai answered early criticism of the decision to incorporate eastern (Han) Kwangsi into the Kwangsi Chuang AR by citing the precedent of the incorporation of the entire province of Suiyuan into the Inner Mongolian AR in 1955.[280] The premier did not attempt to answer the paradox highlighted by his faulty analogy, namely, why should the preservation of provincial borders be more esteemed than the principle of ethnic autonomy in the one case (Kwangsi) and sacrificed in the (ostensible) name of ethnic autonomy in the other? The yardstick for measuring the relative sanctity to be accorded provincial borders had evidently been the contribution they made to effective gerrymandering. Given this opportunistic approach to provincial borders, Chou's defense for the incorporation of the Han of eastern Kwangsi into the new AR amounted to little more than a statement that earlier gerrymandering in one section of the country justified subsequent gerrymandering elsewhere.[281] Overall, the decision to replace the Chuang Autonomous Division within Kwangsi with the Kwangsi-

Chuang Autonomous Region points both to the importance of gerrymandering in CCP thinking and the rather narrow line between an autonomous district and a region. The authorities preferred to give the Chuang an AR in which they were a minority rather than have them in an AD in which they were a majority.

In the case of the creation of an AR for the Hui, one must acknowledge that their broad dispersal throughout China made their concentration within a single unit quite impossible.[282] One should therefore not be too perplexed by the fact that the Ninghsia Hui AR, as created in 1958, contained only 10 to 15 percent of the total Hui population. However, one might be inclined to ponder why this relatively small group of some half million Hui should be honored with an autonomous region rather than an autonomous district.[283] But whatever the reason, the new AR was so gerrymandered that Hui accounted for only one-third of the total population.[284] An additional act of gerrymandering was executed in 1969, when the AR was extended to the Mongolian border through the appropriation of a rather substantial section of former Inner Mongolian territory. This territorial transfer was a double-edged weapon, simultaneously severing a number of Mongols from their parent AR, while also further undercutting the already weak ratio of Hui within the Ninghsia Hui AR. As noted, the territory was returned to the Mongolian AR in 1979. But this return to the pre-1969 status quo still left the Hui a definite minority within the autonomous region bearing their name. Preliminary data derived from the 1982 census indicated that the Hui accounted for 31.7 percent of the AR's total population, while Han Chinese accounted for 68 percent.[285]

Gerrymandering has therefore been a major factor by which the Chinese authorities have diluted the strength of the titular national groups in four of the five autonomous regions. It has also been practiced widely at the next level of autonomy, the district. In 1965, the official designation of seven of the twenty-nine ADs contained the names of two ethnic groups and one bore the names of three. Moreover, all ADs contained at least two significant ethnic groups (what the Chinese source called "constituent nationalities") and one contained seventeen. The median number of "constituent nationalities" per autonomous district was seven and the mean was eight.[286]

Nor did gerrymandering end with the district. Even at the smallest level of autonomous unit, the county, there were eight that bore the name of two ethnic groups. Three others were apparently still more ethnically complex; they bore no ethnic designation, each being officially referred to simply as a "Multinationality Autonomous County."

GERRYMANDERING has thus been widely practiced. But in diluting the ethnic composition of autonomous units, the authorities have not relied soley upon this tactic. Migration policy has also been a major factor. Most noteworthy in this regard has been the resettlement of millions of Han in minority regions.

Official encouragement of Han migration into traditionally non-Han areas began shortly after the CCP's victory. In 1951 the director of the Nationalities Affairs Commission described such movements as "beneficial both to nationalities solidarity and to the construction of the autonomous regions."[287] Prior to the Great Leap Forward, however, the number of migrants was not too substantial.[288] But so far as that program's impact upon ethnic redistribution was concerned, it might well have been termed the Great Leap Westward. In October 1958 the authorities initiated a policy of massive resettlement of young Han in the steppe area. Particular stress was to be placed on Inner Mongolia, Kansu, Ninghsia (which ironically would be renamed Ninghsia Hui AR less than two weeks after this policy was announced), Sinkiang Uighur AR, and Tsinghai.[289] With the partial exception of Kansu, these were the homeland regions of the non-Han peoples. Though Tibet was absent from this list, Chinese press reports at this time heralded an expansion of that region's population from the current one million to ten million by 1965, thereby confirming that massive in-migration by Han was planned.[290] The only important non-Han homelands into which a large-scale influx of Han was not contemplated were in the southern provinces of Kwangsi, Kweichow, and Yunan. These exclusions were apparently attributable to the authorities' conviction that those regions already contained a satisfactory number of Han for implementing national policy.[291]

This campaign to resettle Han in western areas was officially called *hsia fang* (literally, send down), a rubric that suggests its mandatory character.[292] The program survived both the Great Leap and the Cultural Revolution, undergoing a particular surge during the latter when universities were closed and students were transported by the trainload to rural areas where, according to Mao, they were to be reeducated by the peasants. Peking radio reported the number of those resettled in the seven years between 1968 and 1975 at 10 million and anticipated that another 2 million would be added each year.[293] The portion that settled in the non-Han areas was not given, but it can safely be assumed that it was substantial. Indeed, during this period, the majority status of the only two peoples who had ever enjoyed that role in their own AR (the Tibetans and the Uighurs) was threatened if not eclipsed.

As early as 1969, the CPSU's theoretical journal, *Kommunist*, had maintained that Tibetans now accounted for but one-third of the population of Tibet.[294] This figure may badly underestimate the percentage of Tibetans, just as Peking's 1972 figure of 90 percent probably grossly exaggerated it.[295] One less partial demographer, after noting that the percentage of Chinese had been persistently increasing, remained undecided whether the break-even point had been reached by the late 1960s.[296] In any case, given the rather small Tibetan population of 1.2 million, the large numbers of Han resettled in the interior, the special importance ascribed by Peking to settling their border areas with the most loyal nation, and repeated reports of Han migration to Tibet, it would appear likely that if the break-even point had been approached in the late 1960s, then it must surely have been crossed by the mid-1970s.[297]

There is somewhat more agreement on the ethnic changes that have occurred within Sinkiang. Beginning with a percentage of only 3 to 5 percent of the province's population in 1949, migration of Han raised their percentage to 40 percent around 1980. As a result, the Uighurs had lost their majority status. By making the Uighur AR coextensive with Sinkiang Province, the authorities had incorporated significant numbers of other non-Han peoples within the AR. In 1953 these peoples were *in toto* about one-fifth as numerous as the Uighurs, and the percentage appears to have increased.[298] According to preliminary data derived from the 1982 census, the Uighurs accounted for 45.5 percent of the AR's population, the Chinese for 40.4 percent, and the other national groups for 19.1 percent.[299] If the large military forces were included, the Chinese might well be the largest element.[300]

Moving non-Han out of their homeland does not appear to have played an important role in Peking's population policies. Non-Han have been removed from the immediate area of a frontier shared with another country, and some very remote peoples have been resettled in regions where centralized control could be more easily effected.[301] But in such cases, resettlement appears to have occurred within the same general region of the country, that is to say, within the same ethnic homeland. It is quite possible that the planners have perceived no need to redistribute large numbers of minority peoples throughout the country, because they have more than the necessary number of excess Han to accomplish a safe dilution of non-Han through unidirectional migration. Moreover, the center's sense of security in this matter should certainly be strengthened by the realization that the world's largest army operates principally in the frontier regions. Thus, in addition to our earlier calculations concerning the number of Han in traditionally non-Han areas, we must add potentially as many as 3.6 million uniformed individuals who were further diluting the non-Han population.[302]

In summary, then, a policy of extensive gerrymandering and migration has made the titular national group a certain minority in four of the five autonomous regions and a most probable minority in the other. Furthermore, these same techniques have been carried over to the next lower level of administrative unit, the autonomous district. According to Chinese data, in only eight of the twenty-nine autonomous districts existing in 1965 did the titular group represent a majority of the population. In two others, the titular group reportedly accounted for precisely 50 percent. This left nineteen of twenty-nine districts in which the titular element was a minority.[303] Moreover, five of eight exceptions were districts principally populated by Tibetans. All five were part of the contiguous Tibetan homeland and should logically have been made part of an enlarged Tibetan AR. They, too, are therefore the result of hedging against the principle of autonomy rather than of honoring it. And in one of the remaining three possible exceptions, the dominant Li (56.3 percent of the district's population) had to share the ethnic designation of the district with the Miao, even though the Miao accounted for only 2 percent of the population.[304] Thus, out of thirty-four autonomous regions and districts within China, we are reduced to two that could possibly be said to reflect Lenin's plan to grant territorial autonomy to concentrated peoples. In one of these, the titular group represented a bare majority (56.4 percent), and in the other 81.4 percent. Neither would therefore qualify as ethnically homogeneous.[305] Autonomous and minority status bear a close relationship within China.

Yugoslavia

In contrast with both the Soviet Union and China, the internal borders of Yugoslavia have remained quite stable under Communist rule.[306] Any evidence of significant gerrymandering by Belgrade must therefore be sought in the actions of the YCP at the time of the federation's formation. We will recall that five of the six newly created republics were each ostensibly designed to satisfy the desire of one of the major Slavic peoples for its own state. In all five of these new republics, the titular group accounted for a majority, although the degree of ethnic homogeneity varied considerably. (See table 5, column 2.) Only in Slovenia and Montenegro did the titular group exceed 90 percent of the population. Elsewhere the most significant minorities were the Albanians and Hungarians within Serbia (where they respectively accounted for 8.1 and 6.6 percent of the population), the Albanians within Macedonia (17 percent), and the Serbs within Croatia (14.5 percent).

The last of these regional minorities indisputably held the most significance for any scheme of a united Yugoslavia. Serb-Croat rivalry had been the cancer of the prewar state. Even the monarchy's late-hour grant of autonomy in 1939 had not been enough to immunize the Croats against Hitler's subsequent bribe of a Croatian state unencumbered by any ties to the Serbs. Within this new state of Croatia, Serbs found themselves the target of officially condoned, if not sponsored, pogroms, a heinous testament to the Croats' desire to rid the homeland of an alien presence.

Given this very recent series of events, there arises the question of why the YCP leadership did not show more interest in reducing or eliminating the Serbian minority within the area designated by them to become a Croatian Republic. Certainly the preservation of the status quo ante bellum was not the result of oversight or an act of omission, for the status of the minority within Croatia was one of several pressing matters involving ethnic distributions in the new state that demanded decisive action on the part of the leaders. Many of these issues arose from the large number of Serbian refugees who had fled war zones, occupation forces, and/or genocide by compatriots (the last largely, but far from entirely, at the hands of the Croats). In addition to the question of permitting the return of Serbs to Croatia, the authorities were also faced with the issue of Serbs desiring to return to Vojvodina and Macedonia. With regard to the latter, the authorities were still vacillating well into the spring of 1945, first prohibiting a return and later reversing themselves.[307] Their final decision to allow Serbs to return to Macedonia was likely influenced by the need to bring their position on Macedonia into line with that on Croatia, for there is no evidence that the possibility of prohibiting Serbs from returning to Croatia was ever entertained. And again, this was not simply a case of

TABLE 5. National Composition of Republics and Provinces

1	2	3	4	5	6	7
Republic	% of Republic's population represented by titular nation, 1948[a]	% of titular nation living outside Republic/Autonomous Province, 1948[a]	% of Republic's population represented by titular nation, 1981[a]	% of titular nation living outside Republic/Autonomous Province, 1981[a]	% of population born outside Republic/Autonomous Province, 1971[b]	% of Yugoslavia's population represented by titular nation, 1948[c]
Bosnia-Hercegovina	—	—	—	—	1.0	—
Serbs	44.3	—	32.0	—		—
Moslems	30.7	2.5	39.5	18.5		5.1 (8.9)
Croats	23.9	—	18.4	—		—
Croatia	79.2	21.4	75.1	22.0	3.5	24.0 (19.8)
Macedonia	68.5	2.5	67.0	4.5	1.8	5.1 (6.0)
Montenegro	90.7	19.7	68.5	30.6	2.4	2.7 (2.6)
Serbia	73.9	26.3	66.4	24.0	3.4	41.5 (36.3)
Serbia Proper	92.1	—	85.4	—	4.0	—
Vojvodina (Magyars)	25.8	13.6	18.9	9.7	—	3.2 (1.9)
Kosovo (Albanians)	68.5	33.6	77.4	29.1	—	4.8 (7.7)
Slovenia	97.0	4.6	90.5	2.3	2.5	9.0 (7.8)

[a] Derived from data in the 1981 census (Socijalisticka Federativna Republika Jugoslavija, Savezni Zavod Za Statistiku, *Nacionalni Sastav Stanovnistva Po Opstinama* [Statisticki Bilten Broj 1295], Belgrade, May 1982).

[b] Data derived from Table II, "International Migration," *Yugoslav Survey* 18 (February 1976): 5.

[c] 1981 in parentheses.

oversight, for those Serbs desirous of returning to Croatia were carefully processed through the Ministry of Transportation in Belgrade.[308]

The authorities therefore chose not to avail themselves of an excellent opportunity to diminish substantially if not eradicate the Serbian minority within Croatia through resettlement. Resettlement could have been justified as a desire to avoid any possibility of a recurrence of the interethnic bloodletting of the wartime period, as well as a desire to make the proposed republics true nation-states. It also could have been justified in terms of the party's 1934 commitment to the "expulsion of Serb occupiers, Serb troops, officials, and policemen, as well as Serb Chetniks, from Croatia, Slovenia, Dalmatia, Vojvodina, Bosnia, Montenegro, Macedonia, and Kosovo."[309] At a more politically pragmatic level, it could have been justified as necessary on other grounds, for this opportunity to make Croatia more ethnically homogeneous presented itself precisely at a time when the authorities were searching for hundreds of thousands of people to quickly resettle lands formerly in the hands of Germans and Hungarians within Vojvodina.[310] Had the more than three thousand people who were transplanted into Vojvodina been drawn from Serbs within Croatia, the Serbian community in that republic could have been depleted by more than half. Population transfers between Croatia and Bosnia-Hercegovina offered additional possibilities for substantially reducing the Serbian community within Croatia. That the authorities elected to return Serbian families to Croatia, rather than to resettle them, along with other members of the Serbian community who had remained within Croatia, in other regions of the country, strongly suggests an official decision to perpetuate a Serbian minority within Croatia as a hedging device against any recrudescence of Croatian secessionist sentiment.[311]

The anomaly of the Republic of Bosnia-Hercegovina within an otherwise ethnically defined system of republics is also related to the Serbo-Croatian rivalry. Although the territory of Bosnia-Hercegovina had not been part of the autonomous province of Croatia created under the monarchy in 1939, it had formed part of the state of Croatia as deeded by the Axis powers.[312] The prospect of being deprived of this large territory is not one that Croatians would contemplate with favor, but the prospect of the territory's independence would at least be seen as eminently preferable to its transfer to the despised Serbs. On the other hand, the Serbs could hardly be expected to endorse Croatian control of an area in which

Serbs accounted for 44.3 percent of the population; Moslems, another 30.7 percent; and Croats, only 23.9 percent.[313] Partition or independent republic status were therefore the two possible compromises.

There is, however, no evidence that partition between Serbia and Croatia was ever seriously contemplated. On the contrary, the party had indicated as early as 1940 that some form of separate, autonomous status was in store for the region.[314] The Serbian community within Bosnia-Hercegovina was easily the largest Serbian element left outside of the Serbian Republic in the postwar period, accounting in 1948 for 17.4 percent of all Serbs within Yugoslavia.[315] Had the YCP leaders truly been bent on satisfying Serbian aspirations for their own republic, they could have raised the percentage of all Yugoslav Serbs living within the Serbian Republic from 73.7 percent to 91 percent, either by partitioning Bosnia-Hercegovina or by grafting it outright to Serbia.[316] The decision instead to create this sole nonnationally defined republic was part of a much larger plan to weaken the relative numerical advantage of the Serbs by gerrymandering.

Yugoslavia is unique among Marxist-Leninist states in offering an illustration of gerrymandering as a means of weakening the state's largest ethnic element. Elsewhere, as we have seen, gerrymandering has been employed to weaken minorities and thus to enhance the power of the largest group. But unlike those other Marxist-Leninist states, Yugoslavia does not possess what the Germans call a *Staatsvolk*, that is to say, a national group which, because of history and/or numerical superiority, occupies an uncontested cultural and political primacy within the state, therefore giving to the state its peculiar national cast.[317] As the most numerous people and with the site of the state's capital located within their ethnic homeland, the Serbs had indeed managed to exert the most power under the prewar monarchy. But far from being uncritically accepted, this preeminence had been a constant source of friction and a major catalyst in the growth of Croatian separatism. The YCP therefore decided to reduce the probability of a postwar reassertion of Serbian hegemony by diffusing the Serbian numerical advantage throughout a number of different administrative units.[318]

The largest Serbian communities to be severed from the Serbian Republic were the two already discussed, those in Bosnia-Hercegovina and Croatia. The total number of Serbs recorded in the other three republics in 1948 accounted for less than one percent of all Serbs within the country. However, although not recorded as such, Montenegrins were thought by some authorities, including certain members of the Communist leadership, to consider themselves Serbs. Here, for example, is how Milovan Djilas, himself a Montenegrin and then a member of the YCP's innermost circle, assessed the party's wartime appeals to Montenegrin nationalism:

> I sensed that the Chetniks also profited from the Communists' excessive stress on Montenegrin, as distinct from Serbian nationality. . . . Serbianism was the most vociferous and emphatic sentiment of the Montenegrin Chetniks—all the more so in that the Montenegrins are, despite provincial and historical differences, quintessential Serbs, and Montenegro the cradle of Serbian myths and of aspirations for the unification of Serbs.[319]

In a similar vein, a non-Marxist academician wrote of the Montenegrins in 1969 that "the majority of them reject the concept of a separate Montenegrin nation and culture. . . . [A]ttempts to foster the idea that the Montenegrins are not Serbs but a distinct nation have thus far not been successful."[320] Whatever the validity of this claim that Montenegrins consider themselves to be Serbs (and there are data to support either side of the issue),[321] in separating the Montenegrins from Serbia and in giving them their own republic, the authorities decreased the likelihood of Montenegrin numbers contributing further to that traditional Serbian conviction of being the state's most important people.

The YCP's plan to gerrymander the Serbian community operated within the new Serbian Republic as well. Only Serbia was to have autonomous provinces carved from its territory. Kosovo Province in the south and Vojvodina Province in the north, together representing more than one-third of both the land area and population of the Republic, were granted autonomous status.[322] It is difficult to disagree with one author's conclusion that "all this was meant to keep Serbia from being disproportionately larger than Croatia and to bring about a balance between Serbs and Croats."[323] This conclusion concerning the purpose behind the creation of the provinces is particularly convincing in the case of Vojvodina, for Serbs accounted for more than half of the population therein.

Vojvodina, formerly part of Austria-Hungary, had been claimed by the Serbs in 1918 on the basis of ethnic demands.[324] The precise validity of this claim is uncertain, because the region contained large numbers of Magyars and Germans as well. During World War II, the region had been made part of Hungary. Despite the party's prewar support of the right of the Magyars to secede from Yugoslavia, upon assuming power the YCP moved quickly to reassert Yugoslav sovereignty over the entire area.[325] The German community was summarily expelled, and plans were made to expel the Magyars also. But although many Magyars fled the region and many others are reported to have been slaughtered by the partisans, over 400,000 remained.[326] However, the proportion that this element represented within the region was rapidly decreased to about one-fourth of the total, as more than 300,000 Serbs (principally from central Serbia, Bosnia-Hercegovina, and, as earlier mentioned, from Croatia) were hastily resettled in Vojvodina.[327]

A province ostensibly created to give autonomy to the Magyars thus became dominated by Serbs. Moreover, even following this huge influx of Serbian settlers, the authorities could have created an autonomous unit in which Magyars predominated. The Magyars are concentrated in the north near the Hungarian border.[328] Nowhere in the southern sector do they constitute more than 25 percent of the population and generally they constitute less than 10 percent. In contrast, the Magyars are a majority in ten of the northern provinces and a near majority in others.[329] Since in 1948 there were many more Magyars within northern Vojvodina than there were Montenegrins within the Republic of Montenegro, an autonomous province limited to northern Vojvodina could not be discounted on the basis of insufficient population. But the new borders simultaneously recommended themselves to the authorities on two grounds: (1) they made the Magyars a very manageable minority and squelched in advance any Hungarian irredentist claim to Vojvodina; and (2) they reduced the Serbian community within Serbia proper by nearly one-fifth (1.1 million in 1981).[330]

There was a stronger *prima facie* case for granting autonomy to Kosovo Province, in that Albanians had comprised two-thirds of the region's population at the end of the war.[331] Although part of prewar Yugoslavia, Kosovo had been ceded to Albania by the Axis powers. The YCP had called for an "independent and *united* Albania" in 1928, and had further called for the expulsion of Serbs from Kosovo in 1934, but neither of these promises was honored after World War II.[332] The grant of autonomy to Kosovo following its reannexation was probably motivated in part by a desire to placate the Albanian inhabitants who had resisted reincorporation into Yugoslavia with arms, and also in part to make union with the Yugoslavian federation a more attractive eventuality for Albanians still outside Yugoslavia.[333] But it also served the authorities' aim of decreasing the number of Serbs within Serbia proper. Nearly 200,000 Serbs lived within the borders of the new autonomous unit. Significantly, most of them could have been quite easily excluded from it, for, as in the case of Vojvodina, Kosovo's frontiers were so drawn as to incorporate districts, abutting Serbia proper, in which Serbs overwhelmingly predominated.[334] Moreover, a rather large area immediately across the Kosovo-Macedonian border was excluded from the autonomous region, despite the clear predominance of Albanians therein.[335] It appears, then, that in drawing the borders of the autonomous provinces, the authorities were guided more by the desire to create minorities and politically dilute the Serbs than they were by the desire to give political expression to ethnic homelands.

This structuring of republics and provinces so as to undermine the foundation of Serbian chauvinism and, what is the other side of the same coin, to reassure the non-Serbian communities that domination by any ethnic group was a thing of the past sheds important light on the trend toward equal representation for each republic and province that occurred within the executive branches of both the party and state apparati during the early 1970s.[336] This trend was broadly seen as bolstering the autonomy of the national groups. But, as we have seen, this equating of republic/province with the nation is much too simple. It presumes (1) that the republics/provinces are essentially ethnically homogeneous nation-states; (2) that a given national group is concentrated nearly exclusively within a given republic; and (3) that the titular national group within a republic/province dominates the power structure and exerts exclusive authority over delegates to federal and party posts. Gerrymandering has largely invalidated (1) and (2), and cadre policy and party discipline has been designed to thwart (3). Again, a more evident reason for granting equal status to each republic was to weaken Serbian influence and thus allay non-Serbian anxieties.[337] Equal status in effect gave each republic/province 12.5 percent representation, resulting in a gross underrepresentation for a people (the Serbs) accounting at the time for 40 percent of the population. Moreover, a representative from Serbia proper could not speak for the 42 percent of all Serbs living in Kosovo, Vojvodina, or one of the other republics. Serbs themselves quickly perceived the trend as inimical to Serbian interests and voiced strong dissent.[338]

With the single exception of the large postwar resettlement in Vojvodina, programmed migrations do not appear to have played an important role in governmental policies. During its first two decades in power, the YCP was intent upon achieving the economic equalization of all regions through intensive investment in the more backward republics. As earlier noted, such a policy, if successful, tends to freeze existing ethnic patterns rather than to encourage interregional migrations. However, the policy did not succeed in narrowing the gaps among regions and was dropped in favor of gearing investment to maximal likely return.[339] Although this latter type of policy does induce migration from the poorer to the richer regions, its impact upon ethnic redistribution is that of a side-effect rather than a primary aim.

The actual number of people who have been involved in an interrepublic/interprovincial migration in postwar Yugoslavia is quite impressive. In 1961, 1,358,000 individuals (7.3 percent of Yugoslavia's total population) were living in a republic or autonomous province other than the one in which they were born. The rate of such migration continued to increase over the next decade, although at a dwindling tempo. In 1971 there were 1,685,000 individuals (8.2 percent of the population) who had changed their republic/province.[340]

The impact that these migrations, combined with differential natural growth rates, exerted upon the ethnic heterogeneity of the republics over the first third of a century of the YCP's rule can be seen by contrasting columns 2 and 4 in table 5.[341] The biggest loss in numerical superiority was suffered by the Montenegrins, who dropped from 90.7 percent to 68.5 percent of Montenegro's total population. This drastic alteration was brought about by extensive Montenegrin out-migration to Serbia. (The absolute number of Montenegrins within Montenegro actually decreased between 1953 and 1971.)[342] This left only Slovenia with an incontestable claim to being a national area. However, the percentage of Slovenes had undergone a noteworthy decrease from 97 to 90.5 percent, and, as the most economically advanced republic, it was drawing increasing numbers of immigrants during the early 1980s. Should this trend continue, Yugoslavia would soon be devoid of *any* ethnically homogeneous units. It is doubtful that such a development would prove to be of much concern to the authorities, for diffusion of groups across administrative borders (table 5, columns 3 and 5) and suffusion of groups within any single unit (columns 2 and 4) had been employed as a hedging device by the YCP since the inception of the federation.[343]

Czechoslovakia

The Czechoslovak approach to national autonomy is unique in that neither gerrymandering nor migration has been a major stratagem in regulating relations between its *major* national groups. With

the expulsion of most Germans following World War II, the relations between Czechs and Slovaks became the state's major ethnonational issue. Though relations were far from amicable and, as
we have seen, were marked by Slovak demands for a true federation,
they were not exacerbated by the existence of large settler communities within one another's homelands. The two peoples remain
surprisingly geographically distinct: Slovaks account for approximately three percent of the entire population of the traditionally
Czech regions of Bohemia and Moravia; Czechs account for only
one percent of the population of Slovakia.[344] Moreover, since 1948
the government has attempted, with very real success, to close the
economic gap between the more industrialized Czech area and the
more rural Slovakia, and, as a result, there has been little economic
incentive for interregional migration.[345]

There is, however, a major difference concerning the ethnic
homogeneity of the two homelands. The Czechs make up nearly
94 percent of the population of their region, and, with the possible
exception of the aforementioned Slovaks, there are no significant
minorities present.[346] By contrast, Magyars account for more than
12 percent of the population of Slovakia. They are located in an
elongated stretch along the southern border that Slovakia shares
with Hungary, and a single, contiguous, autonomous unit could
have been created to incorporate most of them.[347]

At the end of World War II, both Communist and non-Communist members of the Czechoslovak government were in favor of
expelling the 300,000 Magyars, as they had done to some 2.5 million
Germans.[348] The Hungarian government, however, refused to cooperate unless the territory inhabited by their kin in Czechoslovakia
was also to come under Hungarian sovereignty.[349] Barring this
territorial grant, the Hungarian authorities insisted that the Magyars of Slovakia be granted an autonomous region, a proposal in
turn rejected by Czechoslovakia both before and after the effective
monopolization of power by the Communists in 1948.

Shortly after taking control, the Communists redistricted the
country. Slovakia was divided into six provinces, so drawn that the
Magyar community fell within five of the six and did not constitute
a majority in any. Nor was there any special allowance made for
the Magyars at the next lower level of administration, the district.
Nevertheless, Magyars were a majority within six districts. In 1960
a second redistricting occurred, which reduced the number of provinces from six to three. Parceled out among all three, the Magyars

found themselves further weakened at this provincial level.[350] More injurious to Magyar representation, however, was the redrawing of district borders. Districts were so joined that the number in which Magyars predominated fell from six to two.[351]

There is little question but that the Magyar community popularly perceived all of this as an exercise in gerrymandering. In the freer atmosphere of 1968, the semiofficial Magyar organization, the Cultural Association of Hungarian Workers in Czechoslovakia, publicly complained about what it termed the "mixed-nationality districts":

> The new districts established in the 1960 territorial reorganization are hindering rapprochement and fraternal coexistence between nations and nationalities. Rather than strengthening the unity between nations and nationalities, they are a cause of friction. They slow down the practical enforcement of nationality policy and implementation of the resolutions of party and state organs. Experience has shown that districts inhabited predominantly by one nationality are more prosperous and successful in the political and economic fields.
>
> The further inprovement of political and economic life, and the settlement of the nationalities question and the guaranteeing of their equality, make necessary the establishment of compact units—*homogeneous from the point of view of nationality*—in areas inhabited by the nationalities, through reorganization of districts along appropriate geographic lines.[352]

This demand for a territorial reorganization received support from Budapest. In a speech signaling a treaty of friendship between Czechoslovakia and Hungary, the first secretary of the Hungarian CP remarked that "some remnants of this past have survived to this day, and their elimination is possible only on the basis of socialism and a Leninist nationality policy."[353] To those familiar with Lenin's national policy, this invocation was an unmistakable call for some form of territorial autonomy for the Magyars.

Although all of this pressure for Magyar autonomy was exerted at a time when Slovaks were themselves intensely involved in a campaign to win greater freedom from Prague and the Czech populace, their response to Magyar aspirations was totally unsympathetic.[354] Magyar loyalty was brought into question, and the request for redistricting was branded as "nationalistic" and "irredentist."[355] Following the Soviet intervention and the dismissal of Dubcek, there was talk for a time of altering administrative borders in a manner more agreeable to the Magyar minority, but nothing further came of it.

CZECHOSLOVAKIA completes our list of states that ostensibly conform to the Leninist precept of territorial autonomy for compact national groups. We will recall that the only other two states to experiment with such a system—Rumania and Vietnam—subsequently jettisoned it. But even during their brief experimentation, the authorities in each of these two states introduced hedging devices similar to those encountered in the cases of the USSR, China, Yugoslavia, and Czechoslovakia.

Rumania

Rumania was the more hesitant of the two states to experiment with territorial autonomy. Despite being under Communist control since 1944 and despite the enactment of a Marxist-Leninist constitution in 1948, the state had no autonomous unit prior to 1952. The system of regions into which the country was divided before 1952 had purportedly been drawn without regard to ethnic distributions.[356] Whether or not this was the case, the end result was such as to rather effectively gerrymander the more than 1.5 million Magyars. Moreover, when what was to prove the rather abbreviated grant of territorial autonomy was made in 1952, it applied only to a small part of the total area populated by Magyars.

There are basically two sectors of the country in which Magyars predominate: one is centered in the middle of the state and is surrounded by Rumanian-dominated territory; the other stretches along the Hungarian-Rumanian border and is therefore the most susceptible to irredentism. Magyars in the latter area have consistently been denied autonomous status and, in addition, have consistently been denied majority status in any adminstrative unit. The borders of such units were altered (in some cases quite radically) in 1950, 1952, 1960, and 1968. But following all of these reorganizations, the Magyars living near Hungary saw their strength dissipated throughout anywhere from three to seven administrative units.[357]

Rumania's sole concession to the concept of territorial autonomy was therefore limited to an area far removed from the state's frontiers. The Magyar Autonomous Region was established by the 1952 constitution. As originally delineated, Magyars accounted for 77 percent of its population, but nearly two-thirds (64.4 percent) of the country's Magyars remained outside.[358] Pro-Budapest activities on the part of the Magyars at the time of the Hungarian uprising in 1956 focused attention on this minority's primary loyalty and ignited further doubt on the part of the Rumanian authorities concerning the wisdom of permitting even this safely contained autonomous region. Dismantling, however, took place in stages over the next decade. In 1960 the unit's name was changed to Mures-Autonomous Magyar Region, and the addition of the Rumanian word (Mures) heralded the addition of more Rumanians. In a flagrant case of gerrymandering, two districts in which Magyars were strong majorities (85.3 percent and 90.2 percent) were detached from the region, while three other districts, in which they were definite minorities (25.6 percent, 22.1 percent, and 13.7 percent), were added. The overall result of this gerrymandering was to increase the proportion of Rumanians within the autonomous region by 15 percent (from 20 percent to 35 percent) and to decrease the proportion of Magyars by precisely the same amount (77 percent to 62 percent). As an augury of further things to come, a reference to the autonomous region as "the territory occupied by the compact Magyar Szekler population" was deleted from the Rumanian Constitution.

The region was entirely eliminated under the territorial reorganization act of 1968. Somewhat ironically, its demise was an outgrowth of a redistricting plan that President Ceausescu had pledged would recognize "the national composition of the population." We have already learned that this criterion was not applied to the Magyars along the borders with Hungary. As to those living in or near the former autonomous region, the new redistricting plan itself underwent a substantive change. At first, a single county incorporating all of the area's principal concentrations of Magyars had been promised. Later it was decided to divide this interior community between two counties. Although Magyars were a decisive majority in each of the two resulting counties (79 and 88 percent), it appears that the decision to create two rather than one administrative unit was predicated upon a desire to fragment the Magyar community, thereby denying it a single focus or rallying point for concerted activity. The decision is certainly not traceable to a concern that the originally proposed, single county would be disproportionately large. Its population would, in fact, have approximated the country-wide average and would have been substantially less than that of several other counties. As it was, the two counties actually created ranked thirty-fifth and thirty-ninth in size out of a total of thirty-nine such units.

Even though Magyars were thus gerrymandered into two small counties in which they were a majority, into seven others in which they were an important minority, and into still another seven in which they were present in noteworthy numbers, their territorial concentration continued to worry the authorities. Over the next decade there were increasing complaints from leaders of the Magyar minority concerning governmentally sponsored efforts to resettle Rumanians in traditionally Magyar regions and to entice Magyars to move to Rumanian and German districts.[359]

Vietnam

Our remaining case of a Marxist-Leninist party that experimented with territorial autonomy is the Vietnamese Communist Party. It did so at a time when its sovereignty covered only the northern half of Vietnam and at a time when it was necessary to convince the highland people of South Vietnam (as well as those of eastern Laos and northeastern Cambodia) that total victory by the Communists would bring independence or at least autonomy in its wake.[360] Consonant with this propagandist requirement, the VCP created it first autonomous region within a year of the withdrawal of French forces. And in announcing its creation, Ho Chi Minh stressed that the Thai-Meo Autonomous Region was a prototype to which all peoples could aspire: "The compatriots in the Northwest have the particular honor of having their autonomous region established first. Hence, they have the particular task of striving to set an example to other autonomous regions which will be formed one after the other."[361] The party's subsequent actions appeared to bear out Ho's words, for a second and a third region were created in each of the two following years.

Given the biethnic title of the first autonomous region, there was reason for immediate skepticism concerning its purpose as set forth by Ho: "The aim of the founding of the Thai-Meo Autonomous Region is to enable the brother nationalities gradually to run all their own activities so as rapidly to develop their economy and culture and realize equality among nationalities in all respects."[362] It was not at all made clear why members of a national group would be any more enabled "to run all their own activities" in a multiethnic autonomous region than they would in an otherwise unitary multiethnic state. In point of fact, the Thai-Meo AR was far more ethnically complex than even its biethnic title suggested. Twenty-five officially recognized national groups were included within its frontiers.[363] The second autonomous region to be created (the Viet Bac [North] AR) was also ethnically omnifarious, containing fourteen different ethnic groups.[364] No figures on the ethnonational composition of the third autonomous region (the Lao-Ha-Yen AR) were located, but the area that it occupied was one of intense ethnic diversity, and it can safely be assumed that it too was ethnically very heterogeneous.[365]

The pockmarked ethnic map of non-Vietnamese North Vietnam would tax the most well-intentioned cartographer assigned the task of drawing ethnically homogeneous regions, but the autonomous regions sanctioned by the VCP bore scant resemblance to the type of unit Lenin had envisaged when he referred to territorial autonomy for compact national groups. The scale on which the autonomous regions were constructed (the first two to be created alone accounted for 40 percent of North Vietnam's total territory) dictated in advance that they would not reflect ethnic distributions. Given the patchwork quilt nature of the area's ethnic map, a government intent on honoring the spirit of Leninist national policy during the phase of the flourishing of nations would necessarily have worked with smaller, more numerous, and multilayered administrative units.[366] A government that recognized thirty-seven distinct ethnic minorities could hardly hope to satisfy Lenin's requirement by creating three autonomous regions.

Subsequent events were to demonstrate that the VCP had little respect for Lenin's view of territorial autonomy as an important ingredient for resolving the national question. That the VCP leadership perceived autonomy solely in terms of its propaganda impact upon minorities beyond its immediate control became evident in 1975. Hardly had the VCP's victory over the entire territory of Vietnam taken place, when the autonomous regions within North Vietnam were declared extinct.[367] The first official announcement of their abolition asserted that the decision had been made "with the approval of the highland people" who considered it a "reasonable measure."[368] While it is very questionable whether the highland peoples were in fact consulted in advance, it is probably true that the minorities had not developed a sense of intimate identification with and loyalty to these multiethnic autonomous regions and, as a result, did not grievously mourn their passing. Nevertheless, Hanoi felt compelled to rewrite history, deleting all references to autonomy from the *Selected Works of Ho Chi Minh*. In the words of a former member of the VCP inner circle:

> In order to cover up their crime of abolishing the autonomous regions and oppressing the minority nationalities, they have deleted President Ho's articles on the northwest autonomous region and the northern Vietnam autonomous region and his speeches to the people of various nationalities.[369]

The VCP has also engaged in population redistribution on a gigantic scale. As in the case of the Chinese and Rumanian parties, VCP leaders have displayed anxiety over the fact that the state's borderlands were populated by minorities.[370] "Indigenes out" and "most-loyal-nation in" became a two-pronged means of rectifying the situation even prior to victory over the south. By 1972, more than 70 percent of all the mountain peoples who formerly engaged in what was officially called "nomadic agriculture" had been resettled in lowland communities.[371] Meanwhile, more than one million Vietnamese had been moved into the North and Northwest Autonomous Regions, where they constituted more than one-third of the population.[372]

Large as these migrations were, they proved rather meager relative to the population redistribution in store once the consolidation of power over the entire country was completed. In 1976 alone, more than a million Vietnamese were moved to what were termed "new populous areas" or "new economic zones," expressions which, with few exceptions, referred to the traditional homelands of non-Vietnamese. Both northern and southern areas were affected. Recapping the successes of 1976, the chairman of the State Planning Commission recounted that "hundreds of thousands of people from the Red River Delta had gone to new economic zones in mountain provinces in the north or in the southern provinces."[373] From the former southern capital alone, more than 700,000 Vietnamese were resettled in rural areas during the year, most of them in the highland province of Song Be.[374]

Still greater reshuffling of peoples was called for by the 1976–1980 Five Year Plan. As one leading figure, long associated with minority policy, exclaimed: "New populous areas must be set up in the mountainous region."[375] This project would be aided by the erection of a road network throughout the "remote border areas."[376] Specifically, the plan called for the movement of 4 million people out of the crowded plains between 1977 and 1980.[377] Meanwhile, 700,000 montagnards engaged in swidden agriculture in the south (that is, about one-third of the total non-Vietnamese population within former South Vietnam) were scheduled for resettlement in lowland communities.[378]

Looking beyond the Five Year Plan to the last two decades of the twentieth century, the state planners anticipated that it would be "necessary to send ten million people" from the Red River Delta and the central lowlands into the northern mountain regions, the highlands, and the Mekong region. It would also be "necessary to resettle 1,500,000 nomads."[379] As in China, the minorities were destined to become minorities within their traditional home-lands.[380]

To recapitulate our findings thus far: (1) the Communist parties of all Marxist-Leninist states are committed in principle to Leninist national policy; (2) but in practice only a very few have introduced that policy's *sine qua non* of a system of territorial autonomy; and (3) those few have manifested a fundamental skepticism concerning the sagacity underlying Lenin's policy by encumbering it with a series of hedging devices. Thus hedged, the practices of the states with regard to their national question differ dramatically from the practices prescribed by Lenin.

Not surprisingly, such marked discrepancies have not gone un-noticed. Thus, in the early 1960s, intraparty dissatisfaction with Soviet national policy became sufficiently audible as to require con-demnation by the center. In a warning to the dissenters, "an au-thoritative statement" noted that the dissension had taken three principal forms, with objections to (1) the expansion of the non-indigenous population—that is, Russian immigration; (2) Russians in key positions; and (3) the "voluntary principle" in the study of national languages.[381] In reverse order, these categories conform with the present chapter's subdivision into (1) language policy, (2) the recruitment and purging of elites, and (3) the redistribution and gerrymandering of national groups.

NOTES

1. Wolfe, *Three Who*, 584. Emphasis in original. For a similar position expressed by Lenin on the issue of language preference, see "Critical Remarks on the National Question" (1913), in Lenin, *Collected Works* 20:20–21.

2. For example, Ukrainian students within the RSFSR were provided with their own schools.

3. Exceptions were made to the general rule of eliminating special schools for pockets of non-Russian people living outside of an autonomous unit bearing their ethnic designation. In late 1970, there were Rumanian, Hungarian, and Polish schools within the Ukraine; Polish schools within Lithuania; Armenian and Azerbaijani schools within Georgia; Uzbek and Kirgiz schools within Tadzhikistan; and Ukrainian schools within Moldavia.

In some cases (particularly those of Armenian and Azerbaijani schools within Georgia), such exceptions to general policy appear to have been a means of compensating for an absence of Russians. Given their own schools, Armenians and Azerbaijani would be less likely to leave Georgia for their own nearby republics. (For further discussion, see the section entitled "The Redistribution and Gerrymandering of National Groups.") In any case, the trend has been toward the eradication of such exceptions. Between 1958 and 1965, for example, the number of Ukrainian language schools within Moldavia declined from thirty-eight schools with an enrollment of 5,300 students to seven with an enrollment of 1,900. See Bilinsky, "Mykola Skrypnyk," 138. However, as will be noted below, officials may have signaled a reversal of this trend in the early 1980s.

4. The resulting impact of residence outside an ethnic homeland upon linguistic assimilation has been great. In 1970, 94.6 percent of all people living within their own union republic declared the language of their nation to be their "mother tongue," as contrasted with only 65.7 percent of members of the same nations living outside of their union republics. For people living inside/outside an autonomous republic or region, the corresponding figures were 92.3 percent and 68.1 percent. The Belorussians represented an extreme case: while 90.1 percent of those living within the Belorussian SSR declared Belorussian to be their "mother tongue," only 40.8 percent of those outside did so. See Bruk and Guboglo, "Converging Nations," 62–63.

For a knowledgeable and balanced account of linguistic policy within the USSR, see Bilinsky, "Education of Non-Russian Peoples," 411–437.

5. Although Russian was made a required subject in all non-Russian language schools, the local language was not made a requirement in Russian language schools. Thus in the case of the Russian language schools within the Ukraine, Ukrainian was the optional course, which might not even be offered in the absence of a sufficient demand. Some parents had three options, since their neighborhood might also have contained a school in which Russian was the predominant medium of instruction but in which some courses were taught in the local vernacular. However, such mixed-language schools were apparently designed to serve as a transitional step to fully russianized schools.

6. See the further discussion of the favored status of the Russian language within non-Russian homelands later in this chapter.

7. Despite the existence of twenty ASSRs, in 1980 the only corresponding titular groups having the possibility of ten years of education in their own languages were the Tatars and Bashkirs.

8. Silver, "Language Policy," 11.

9. While the years 1958 and 1972 were selected because of the availability of corresponding data and not because the former year corresponded with the introduction of the voluntary principle, it is nevertheless interesting that this decrease occurred immediately upon the heels of the introduction of the new program.

The fact that people with a union republic retained the opportunity for ten years of schooling in their own language was reflected in 1970 data, showing that while only 35.4 percent of those living within their own union republic were bilingual, 58.2 percent of those within their own autonomous republic or region were in this category. See Bruk and Guboglo, "Converging Nations," 69.

10. *The Russian Language in the National School* (Moscow), 6 (1963): 4–5. Cited in Dzyuba, *Internationalism?*, 178.

11. As shall be made clear throughout the remainder of this chapter and even more explicitly in the next, open debate concerning national policy within the Soviet Union has never contained challenges to the desirability of assimilation but has been concerned only with the degree to which attainment of that goal should be artificially accelerated.

12. Stalin, *Marxism and Linguistics*, 46.

13. For further discussion, see chapter 10.

14. Katz, *Handbook*, 230.

15. Ibid., 426.

16. Bilinsky, "Mykola Skrypnyk," 124.

17. From data in Pool, "Soviet Language," 228–229, originally compiled by Rosemarie Rogers of M.I.T. Pool's article includes a table (pp. 230–231) indicating that the number of titular peoples who do not attend their own language schools is actually quite meager. Much of the table's key data appear to be derived from a Soviet writer and are quite at odds with the data on schooling offered for each union republic in Katz, *Handbook*. The reliability of this Soviet source is further called into question by his statement that the local language is already the "main" medium of higher education in Uzbekistan, Georgia, Azerbaijan, Lithuania, and Armenia (as cited in Pool's article, p. 223). Estonia definitely and Latvia probably should be added to this list, but Uzbekistan and Azerbaijan should be removed.

18. See Bruk and Guboglo, "Converging Nations," 85, for a statement by two of the Soviet Union's leading linguistic theorists to the effect that "the consistent converging of the nations and nationalities of the Soviet Union is an objective process, and the Communist Party pays constant attention to the development of the school, in which the firmest foundations for mastery of a second language are laid."

19. Pool, "Soviet Language," 228.

20. Cited in Nogee, *Man, State, and Society*, 517–519.

21. Cited in Pool, "Soviet Language," 243.

22. The text of the program is reproduced in its entirety in Schapiro, *U.S.S.R. and the Future*.

23. *The Current Digest of the Soviet Press* 24, no. 51 (1972):8.

24. Khalmukhamedov, "Soviet Society," 30.

25. For references to the demonstrations and their cause, see the *International Herald Tribune*, April 18, 1978, and May 5, 1978, and the *New York Times*, April 25, 1978.

26. Article 53 of the Common Program of the Chinese People's Political Consultative Conference, which was adopted on September 29, 1949.

27. See chapter 8, footnote 26. According to the *Peking Review*, March 10, 1980, p. 22, since 1949 "ten minority nationalities [had] created their own written scripts and five [had] renovated their written language."

28. From data in *People's Handbook*, as it appears in translated form in appendix A in Hu, *Education of National Minorities*, 24–28.

29. For a listing of China's minorities, including the Manchus, see *People's Handbook*, 115–116.

30. "Basic Summarization of Experiences," 19.

31. *JPRS* 576-D. CGO :2597-D, 9. This is a translation of an interesting, untitled article on Chinese national policy that appeared originally in *Aussenpolitik (Zeitschrift fuer internationale Fragen)* (Stuttgart), no. 11 (November 1958).

32. The Yen-pien University may be an exception. Korean was reportedly the language of instruction there in 1954. (Hu, *Education of National Minorities* 20.) Given its location near the border with North Korea and the Soviet Union, and the competition between the latter and China for influence in North Korea, this exception may have endured.

33. From data in appendix B in Hu, *Education of National Minorities*, 29–30. The total number of minority people attending any type of institute of higher learning in 1958 was only 22,400, that is to say, less than one-tenth of one percent of all such people. (From table in Hu, *Education of National Minorities*, 8.) In 1978 the number had grown to only 36,000. (*Peking Review*, March 10, 1980, p. 22.)

In an article on China that appeared in the leading Soviet journal, *Kommunist*, T. Rakhimov stated: "In the national regions the bulk of the children are without school education. Teaching in technical and higher educational establishments is carried on in Chinese and most of the students are Chinese." Cited in "The National Minorities of Western China," *Central Asian Review* 15, no. 3 (1967): 256. China's own figures for 1978 showed 2.5 million minority youths in secondary schools and 7.5 million in primary schools, out of a total minority population of some 45 million people.

34. Deal, "National Minority," 200.

35. For comments on language policy during the Great Leap Forward,

see Schwartz, "Communist Language Policies," particularly p. 182; Deal, "National Minority," 19–204; Patterson, "Treatment of Minorities," particularly p. 157; and Dreyer, *China's Forty*, 160–161. On language policy during the Cultural Revolution, see Dreyer, *China's Forty*, particularly p. 233. See also, by the same author, "China's Minority Nationalities in the Cultural Revolution," *China Quarterly* 8 (July–September 1968): 96–109.

36. A post-Cultural Revolution editorial in *People's Daily* of May 22, 1971 stressed the necessity to "quickly overcome all the obstacles which prevent the national minorities from reading the works of Chairman Mao in Chinese." Cited in Dreyer, *China's Forty*, 233.

37. For details, see chapter 10.

38. See, for example, Kahin, "Minorities in Vietnam," 584.

39. Nguyen Van Huyen, "Vietnamese Language," 56. The Thai, Meo, Tay, and Nung are the four peoples who were granted four years of education in their own languages.

40. *Summary of World Broadcasts* (British Broadcasting Corporation), Far East/5394/C/3, December 20, 1976.

41. The Laotian leadership, which was heavily influenced by Hanoi, also moved quickly toward linguistic assimilation after taking power. "The Program for Building a Peaceful, Independent, Neutral, Democratic, United and Prosperous Kingdom of Laos," which was ratified on December 24, 1974, while referring (Article 2) to the need "to achieve equality in all fields—political, economic, cultural and social—among the ethnic groups," also (Article 8) set forth the need "to use Lao spoken and written language in all schools."

42. See chapter 6.

43. Vucinich, "Nationalism and Communism," 271. George and Patricia Klein ("Nationalism vs. Ideology," 270) draw attention to the fact that while the 1974 constitution gave nations and nationalities the right to use their languages and alphabets (Article 170) and the right to instruction in the language within their own region (Article 171), it did not contain a reference to the equality of languages, as had the previous constitution.

44. The constitution of 1974, for example, skirted the issue by avoiding any reference to specific languages. In establishing the official languages of the state, Article 246 merely notes that "the languages of the nations shall be used officially, while the languages of the nationalities shall be used in conformity with the present Constitution and federal statute." However, evidence that the issue remains very much alive is offered by George Schöpflin's 1978 report that the Serbs are irritated by the decreasing use of the Cyrillic alphabet and the increasing use of the Latin alphabet for public signs throughout the country. (See Schöpflin, "National Question.")

45. *Area Handbook for Yugoslavia*, 89–91. During the late 1960s and early 1970s, numerous complaints were voiced by Slovenes, Macedonians, and other non-Serbo-Croatian speakers concerning discrimination practiced

against their languages. See, for example, Rusinow, *Yugoslav Experiment*, 245 and 252.

46. Shoup, *Communism and Yugoslav National Question*, 194.

47. In the decade from 1956–57 to 1966–67, the number of Albanian elementary schools increased from 856 to 959. However, all other minority language elementary schools dropped from 607 to 474. Hungarian schools (from 263 to 221) and Turkish schools (from 181 to 58) suffered the largest losses. See "Schools for National Minorities," *Yugoslav Survey* 9 (May 1968), table 2: 107.

48. *Area Handbook for Yugoslavia*, 168. The University of Pristina, which became a center for Albanian nationalism in the early 1980s, may represent an exception.

49. See King, *Minorities*, 153, for some pertinent statistics. Rumanian sources claim that of "29,422 kindergartens, general education schools, lyceums and vocational schools" operating in 1980–1981, 3,276 (11 percent) used minority languages as follows: 2,502 used Hungarian, 679 used German, and 97 used some other language. Unfortunately, the article did not break these institutions down by grade level, nor did it differentiate between mixed and unilanguage schools. See the article by Corneliu Tudor in *Saptamina* (Bucharest), July 23, 1982, *JPRS* 81624 (August 25, 1982): 63. For an account of the manner in which Hungarians were increasingly deprived of education in their own language, see Schöpflin, *Hungarians*, 10–11.

50. *International Herald Tribune*, February 1, 1978. Actually, there have been some public statements in which officials suggest that the government is pursuing a policy of discouraging minority languages. President Nicolae Ceausescu has justified such a policy as ensuring truly equal opportunity to the minorities. See the excerpts from several of his speeches, dating from 1968 to 1973, in Schöpflin, *Hungarians*, 19.

51. The question of schooling for ethnic minorities within both Czechoslovakia and Hungary was aired during 1968. In response to a demand by the Magyar minority within Czechoslovakia that Magyar schools be administered by Magyars, the press countered with a series of complaints about education of Slovaks within Hungary. Particularly emphasized were the declining number of Slovak language schools and the poor quality of Slovak language instruction. (King, *Minorities*, 117 et seq.) For some statistics on Magyar schools within Czechoslovakia, see Milan Reban, "Czechoslovakia: The New Federation," in Klein and Reban, *Politics of Ethnicity*, 239. Although the Germans are now a recognized minority within Czechoslovakia, there are no German-language schools.

Bulgaria has aped the Soviet model, allowing school instruction in minority languages but requiring everyone to study Bulgarian. Higher education is conducted in Bulgarian.

Albania has been the most cavalier toward Leninist precepts. Most of the Communist party's leaders hail from the southern part of the country populated by the Tosks, and the party made Tosk dialect the official language and the only language used in publications, although the Geg dialect was the language of approximately two-thirds of the population.

For an account of how German is replacing Sorbian in Sorbian schools, see the review article by Oschlies, "Bleak Prospects for the Sorbs," 17–19.

52. Surveys taken within the Soviet Union indicate that schools clearly constitute the principle avenue for acquiring proficiency in a second language. See the data reproduced in Lubrano et al., "The Soviet Union," 57.

53. A major force working for linguistic assimilation is compulsory military training. Conscription laws are in effect in all Marxist-Leninist states, and the need for a single language of command, plus the practice of ethnically integrating units, cause the armed forces to serve as a principal mechanism for increasing knowledge of the dominant language. Soviet data indicate that 14.4 percent of bilingual Moldavians acquired their second language while in military service. (Lubrano et al., "The Soviet Union," 57.) However, the figure would be much higher if restricted to *males* over twenty years of age.

54. Dzyuba, *Internationalism?*, 156–157.

55. Saunders, "Against Russification," 434. The excerpt is from a letter addressed to Communist parties outside of the Soviet Union by a group describing themselves as "seventeen Latvian Communists." All statements and statistics in the letter appear quite accurate when checked against other sources.

56. Data derived from the 1979 census. Many of the 3.5 percent who could speak a foreign language lived within the RSFSR. See the discussion later in this chapter of the large number of Russians living within autonomous republics, regions, and areas located, in turn, within the RSFSR.

57. Table A.22 in Katz, *Handbook*, 459.

58. Derived from table 2.2 in Katz, *Handbook*, 36.

59. What such figures mean in practice was expressed in a study addressed to the First Secretary of the Ukrainian Council of Ministers by the Ukrainian scholar Ivan Dzyuba, *Internationalism?*, 163.

We have already said enough about the fact that Ukrainian publishing lags catastrophically behind Russian publishing, that its Ukrainian-language production is unfairly small in relation to the percentage of the Ukrainian population, and that Russian-language production is overwhelmingly predominant on the readers' market in the Ukraine. At the same time, Ukrainian-language production not only fails to be properly publicized, but even the basic spontaneous demand for it frequently remains unsatisfied. Everywhere you hear complaints about the shortage of some Ukrainian book or other.

60. Hall, "Language Contact in the USSR."

61. Kholmogorov, *International Traits*, 16–17. Emphasis added. As the

last sentence in the citation appeared in translation, the words *bilingual* and *monolingual* were in reverse order. I took the liberty of correcting this assumed error because the sentence is otherwise a nonsensical redundancy and would not harmonize with the rest of the treatise. For what follows the sentence, see the discussion later in this chapter.

62. Elsewhere Kholmogorov notes that bilingualism "does *not yet* signify that the Soviet people have become a single linguistic community." See *International Traits*, 17.

63. Stalin, *Marxism and Linguistics*, 28.

64. N. V. Mansvetov in *Voprosy istorii* 34, no. 5 (1964): 51, as cited in Dzyuba, *Internationalism?*, 189–190.

65. The switch from the Arabic to the Latin is explainable as a means of limiting the influence of external ideas, such as pan-Turanism and pan-Islamism. But the subsequent switch to Cyrillic cannot be so explained.

66. See, for example, Lubachko, *Belorussia*, 175. Also, in a private communication, Alice Calaprice, a granddaughter of the late distinguished Armenian scholar Manoug Abeghian, related that her grandfather had been assigned to supervise the altering of the orthography of the Armenian language, in order to "modernize" it. She noted that her grandfather, after whom the Institute of Literature in Erevan is named, performed the task with great reluctance.

67. The entire effort to restructure languages received a great impetus with the publication of Stalin's *Marxism and the Question of Linguistics* in 1950. Publication was followed by a neo-Pavlovian movement in which language was seen as the key trigger in conditioned response. It was presumed, therefore, that through the control of language, the state could regulate the behavior of its citizens. (For an interesting summary of this school, see Tucker, *Soviet Political Mind*, 159–166.) Though the thoroughgoing environmental determinism on which this official school rested was somewhat hedged following Stalin's death, the continuing impact of the school's high regard for language as a key conditioner of behavior is evident both in the works of Soviet scholars such as Kholmogorov and Bruk and in the actual linguistic policies pursued by the government, which we have outlined.

68. Polyakov, "Unmasking Mao," 45.

69. See, for example, Chang Chih-i, *The Party*, 92–93, where a Chinese official directs his subordinates to develop written languages for the minorities and advises them to use Han (Mandarin) words wherever appropriate. See also the June 1959 issue of *Nationalities Research* (Peking), 5, where an official complains of resistance to the use of Han words in minority language textbooks.

70. Deal, "National Minority," 202.

71. We will recall that the Yugoslav government, in its efforts to convince its population that Serbian and Croatian were a single language, placed great stress upon the publication of a Serbo-Croatian dictionary. Croatian

scholars subsequently protested vehemently, insisting that sufficient words were unique to Croatian to confirm that it formed a distinct language.

72. We are here interested in the policies of governments, most specifically the degree to which they reflect Leninist concepts, and not the degree to which these policies have been successfully implemented. However, in order to avoid creating an improper impression, it should be noted that the authorities have regularly expressed great frustration concerning the slow inroads made by the Russian language. Census data, dealing with choice of mother tongue and with proficiency in the Russian language, support this pessimistic assessment. In 1970 a majority of non-Russians (60 percent) denied any fluency in Russian. (From data in Bruk and Guboglo, "Converging Nations," 66.)

73. Cited in Nogee, *Man, State, Society*, 518, in turn a citation from *The Chornovil Papers*.

74. There are some remarkable parallels between Lenin's linguistic policy and that applied by Spain to the Philippines nearly four centuries earlier. Pursuing a policy of "national in form, Catholic in content" between 1550 and 1688, the Spanish administrators employed the local tongue in their proselytizing and in religious services, on the assumption that the new religion would appear less exotic and more acceptable if it were expressed in the local tongue. (See Ascuncion-Lande, "Multilingualism," 677–692.

75. Not all governments have succumbed to this pressure, of course. Switzerland is the best-known case in point.

76. Stalin, *Marxism and Linguistics*, 23.

77. Stalin, *Marxism and the National Question*, 10.

78. In a public discussion following my lecture at the University of Moscow in 1977, a Soviet professor noted that Stalinism was dead but that Stalin's definition of the nation was still valid.

In 1966, the Soviet journal, *Voprosy istorii* (*Problems of History*) carried a series of articles addressing the question, "What is a nation?" While some authorities disagreed with one or another aspect of Stalin's definition, all used it as their point of departure, and all agreed that language was a necessary element of a nation. See Howard, "Definition," 26–36.

79. See, for example, the statement by the Vietnamese Minister of Education, Nguyen Van Huyen, "Vietnamese Language," 42: "Every people have their own economic, political and cultural life, their own psychology and language."

80. L. M. Drobizheva in *Istoriia SSSR*, no. 3 (1969):61–79, as cited by Szporluk, "Ukraine and Ukrainians," 43.

81. *Peking Review* 17 (July 19, 1974):19. The same quotation appeared in a later publication within the Soviet Union. (B. Ts. Urlanis, ed., *Naseleniye mira; spravochnik* [Moscow, 1965], 213, as cited by Dzyuba, *Internationalism?*, 189.)

82. Kholmogorov, *International Traits*, 5. See Robert Lewis et al., *Nationality and Population*, 115, for additional, Russian-language source material

expressing this same relationship between language and identity. In a similar statement of direct causality, a leading Vietnamese scholar has succinctly noted: "The fate of a language of a people is always linked to the destiny of that people." (Dang Thai Mai, "Vietnamese Language," 64.)

83. See footnote 61.

84. Kholmogorov, *International Traits*, 17. Emphasis added.

85. Kozlov, "Concept of Ethnic Community," 79. A few Soviet writers have denied this causal linkage between language and identity. See, for example, Dzhafarov, "The Transformation," 7.

86. V. I. Perevedentsev, "History and Demography," 19. Some American scholars have agreed with their Soviet counterparts on this matter. See, for example, Lubrano et al., "Soviet Union," 59. After reviewing some Soviet survey data, the authors conclude: "The observance of ethnic rituals and issues of ethnic identity are related directly to bilingualism and suggest that in some ways ethnic differences may be breaking down."

87. Bruk and Guboglo, "Converging Nations," 88–89. For similar statements, see pp. 52, 54, 57, 73, and 74. In the same volume (Grigulevic and Kozlov, *Ethnocultural Processes*), another well-known Soviet specialist, L. N. Terentieva ("Ethnocultural Changes among the Peoples of the Volga, Urals, and Far North of Europe"), referring to "the processes of assimilation," wrote (p. 117): "An important stage in this process is linguistic assimilation. . . ." And elsewhere (p. 125), the author added: "An important index of the convergence of peoples (and at the same time a basic condition of it) is the spread of a single lingua franca."

88. The use of the word *cadre* to refer to the visible elite was popularized by Stalin. As such, it is a generic term, incorporating all those in overt, officially sanctioned positions of leadership throughout every social sphere from public office, to industry, education, arts, and the party. Moreover, within any of these spheres, it extends from the highest visible level of power to the lowest. For further discussion of the meaning of *cadre* within the Soviet context, see Kernig, *Marxism, Communism* 1:370. For a discussion of its essentially identical meaning within Chinese society, see John Lewis, *Leadership in Communist China*, 187.

89. All of the following citations are from one or another of three memoranda dictated by Lenin on December 30 and 31, 1922. They contain a sharp criticism of Stalin and were not widely published until after the latter's death. Together they constitute Lenin's final legacy on the national question. They can be found in full in Wolfe, *Khrushchev*, 271–276 and, with some variations in translation, in Pipes, *Formation*, 282–287. The memoranda are particularly significant, because, in the words of Lenin's personal secretary, he considered them collectively "as a document of guidance and attached great importance to it." See the letter of L. Fotieva, dated April 16, 1923, in Wolfe, *Khrushchev*, 277.

90. Derzhimorda was a reference to a character in Gogol's *Inspector General*, essentially a brutal martinet.

91. Interestingly, charges of discrimination extended even to the presumably sovietized Red Army. See Pipes, *Formation*, 291.

92. "For us, as Communists, it is clear that the basis of all our work is the work for strengthening the rule of the workers, and only after this comes the second question—an important question, but subordinated to the first—the national question. We are told that one should not offend the nationalities. This is entirely correct, I agree with this—they should not be offended. But to create from this a new theory, that it is necessary to place the Great Russian proletariat in a position of inferiority in regard to the once oppressed nations, is an absurdity. . . . It is clear, however, that the political basis of the proletarian dictatorship is in the first place and above all in the central, industrial regions, and not in the borderlands, which represent peasant countries. If we should lean too far in the direction of the peasant borderlands at the expense of the proletarian region, then a crack may develop in the system of proletarian dictatorship." Speech at the Twelfth Party Congress, April 1923, cited in Pipes, *Formation*, 290–291.

93. The wide-ranging purges were certainly not restricted to non-Russian leaders. The "enemy" forces were both personal and impersonal, individual and collective, old (the settling of grudges) and new. The single most authoritative study of the purges is that of Conquest, *Great Terror*. See also Brzezinski, *Permanent Purge*, particularly the section entitled "The Nationalities," 77–82, and appendix 2, 180–189.

94. These are the figures used by Edward Crankshaw, for example. See his note in Khrushchev, *Khrushchev Remembers*, 75. Robert Conquest (*Great Terror*, 17) concludes that approximately a million people were executed between 1936 and 1938, and that "over the whole Stalin period not less than 12 million people must have died in the camps."

95. Interestingly, Roy Medvedev (*Let History Judge*, 344) is of the opinion that Azerbaijan and Georgia were the two hardest-hit areas, despite the *relatively* small number of Russians within those republics from which the authorities could draw to replace the purged cadre. See table 4 for the percentage of the population represented by Russians in each republic.

96. Khrushchev's comments concerning Stalin are always suspect, but he maintains that he argued with Stalin that he should not be given the appointment because he was not a Ukrainian. Stalin is reported to have brushed aside this protest as unimportant. See Khrushchev, *Khrushchev Remembers*, 106.

97. Ibid., 108.

98. See Szporluk, "Nationalities and Russian Problem," particularly p. 31.

99. The Presidium was the name given for a time to the Politburo.

100. Saunders, *Samizdat*, 430.

101. Khrushchev, *Khrushchev Remembers*, 330.

102. Ibid. In addition to his general lack of zeal for such a policy, as

exemplified throughout his career, Khrushchev must have also been aware of the danger that such a policy held for his personal future. A resuscitated Ukrainian elite could be expected to despise Khrushchev as the Russian chauvinist who had presided over the executions and imprisonment of so many of their conationals during the Stalinist era.

103. As noted, at the June 1953 plenum of the party's Central Committee, Beria had pushed through a resolution "to end the mutilation of Soviet national policy." The difficulty in subsequently closing this pandora's box is shown by the fact that nineteen years later a complaint concerning Great Russian domination of the Latvian apparatus made much of the fact that the same 1953 plenum had acknowledged that Russian domination of the Latvian apparatus was a distortion of Leninist national policy. The obvious though unstated conclusion was that if it constituted a distortion in 1953, it did so also in 1972. See the *New York Times*, February 27, 1972.

104. The unwillingness of the party's uppermost echelon to make real concessions concerning the national cadre is reflected in Khrushchev's famous attack on Stalin and Stalinism at the Twentieth Party Congress in February 1956. Although placing great stress upon what he termed the "monstrous . . . acts whose initiator was Stalin and which are rude violations of the basic Leninist principles of the nationality policy of the Soviet state," Khrushchev limited his particulars to the enforced dispersion of certain national groups during World War II. No reference was made to the decimation of the ranks of national cadre during the 1930s, nor to the subsequent replacement of those who were purged by Russians. Indeed, earlier in the speech (probably as a defense for his own role in the purges), Khrushchev had insisted: "We must affirm that the Party had fought a serious fight against the Trotskyites, rightists and bourgeois nationalists." For the entire text of the speech, see Christman, *Communism*, 158–228.

105. The decision to restrict the first secretaryship to a Communist of the local national group was made by the Presidium in 1953, while Beria was an active competitor in the power struggle, but it continued to be honored following his death. See discussion later in this chapter.

106. In some situations, the major nonindigenous ethnic element within the cadre may not be Russian. Thus in the case of the Abkhazkaya ASSR, which is located within Georgia, the exchange of cadre is largely synonymous with the need to accept Georgians. See, for example, Kipnis, "Georgian National Movement," 199.

107. July 16, 1971.

108. One specialist on Soviet minorities has described how the policy of cadre "exchange" reinforces Soviet linguistic policy: "In practice, it [cadre exchange] means that the Russians and the non-Russians, *provided that they have become fully proficient in Russian*, should be employed anywhere in the USSR without the necessity of learning the local language." See Szporluk, "Nations of the USSR," 91.

109. One influential factor is the size of the nonindigenous element

within the area. Thus it would be more difficult to rationalize the appointment of large numbers of Russians to highly visible positions within Armenia, where Russians account for only 2.7 percent of the population, than it would in the case of Kazakhstan, where Russians account for 42 percent of all the inhabitants.

110. While within the Asian republics members of the local national group have been appointed to an increasingly diversified array of positions, any suggestion of sympathy for local nationalism has been followed by a reversal of this tendency. A seemingly minor illustration occurred in 1982, when the board of editors of the leading Uzbek-language literacy journal elected to serialize a novel with anti-Russian overtones. Although the board had been staffed entirely by Uzbeks for many years, a direct result of the board's indiscretion was the appointment of a Slav. For an account of the incident, see Sheehy, "Uzbek Novel."

111. Though the need to use the ethnic composition of the local party as index to the composition of all cadre is unfortunate, this choice was influenced by the availability of data and a still greater dissatisfaction with other possible selections. Concerning the latter point, we were not particularly interested in highly visible legislative bodies or offices, since they are the most apt to serve as showcases for the authorities and are thus unlikely to constitute a reliable guide to the ethnic mix of the cadre as a whole.

112. A 1957 Chinese article, though using extremely rounded-off figures, suggested that cadre and party membership figures were identical. It noted that there were 40,000 minority peoples who were members of the Communist party and an equal number of cadre operating at the village level or above. (Cited in Dreyer, *China's Forty*, 159.) Although it is unlikely that such a perfect one-for-one relationship exists, the fact that it was reported in this way illustrates that an extremely close relationship between party membership and cadre status did in fact exist.

113. For the intimate interrelationship of membership and "careerism," see Rigby, *Communist Party Membership*, 8, 11, 45, 46, 47, 517.

114. Perhaps the best evidence of the prevalence of such a perception among the authorities is the frequency with which those who challenge the distribution of positions of influence among the national groups are charged with antistate activities and stripped of cadre and party status.

115. See the table, "National Composition of the CPSU," in *The Communist Party of the Soviet Union* (Moscow: Novosti Press Agency Publishing House, 1977), 101.

116. Russian domination of the party apparatus is particularly evident at the highest level of power, namely, the Politburo and the Secretariat of the Central Committee. See, for example, Rockett, *Ethnic Nationalities*, 134, and d'Encausse, *Decline of an Empire*, 140–141.

117. The data were extrapolated from information found in Katz, *Handbook*. Where available, the pertinent information on a given republic's party

can be found in that work, within the chapter dedicated to the particular union republic, under the subheading of *Demography*.

118. It is very likely that the percentage in the case of Armenia (for which data were not available) would be the highest.

119. Kazakhstan may not be seen as a potentially dangerous situation by authorities, since, even with overrepresentation, the Kazakhs accounted for a minority (40 percent) of total party membership.

120. Again, Georgia is the exception.

121. It is likely that the Russians are more heavily represented in Estonia and Lithuania, and, very conceivably, in Latvia.

122. This long-range trend need not contradict our earlier description of the process as cyclical. An analogy might be the classical view of the manner in which capitalist economies proceed. Moreover, the trend has not always been evident. For example, in 1980 Latvian demonstrations protested the appointment of the first Minister of Education of the Latvian SSR to be of Russian background. See *L'Alternative* (Paris), January–February 1981, 45.

123. D'Encausse (*Decline of an Empire*, 127, 132) contends that there are no more "reserved" positions for Russians at the union republic level and that even the key security posts at that level are now manned by indigenes. Control, she contends, is today maintained by control of the center rather than immediate control of the republics. However, while it is possible that certain important security positions may be held by indigenes within certain republics, such as Georgia or Armenia, this is not the general pattern. Nancy Lubin, who spent a year in Uzbekistan, uncovered fascinating personnel data showing exclusive Russian control of a series of sensitive and semisensitive functions, security being one. See Lubin, "Ethnic/Political Implications," 125–128. Moreover, despite d'Encausse's contention that there are no reserved positions, later (*Decline of an Empire*, 142 et seq.) she acknowledges that the second secretary of each republic's party is such a post.

124. *New York Times*, July 19, 1971.

125. Saunders, *Samizdat*, 432.

126. Significantly, the letter made clear that the tendency of Lithuanians to exclude non-Lithuanians did *not* apply to Great Russians: "We are not speaking to you about the noble Communist ideals, *about the equality of men and nations*, about proletarian internationalism. All these slogans have been thrown into the dustheap of demagogy long ago. They have been replaced now by one slogan: 'Love for the Great Russian people, and what is left from that "love" let us divide up among ourselves.' " (Emphasis added.) The letter is cited in full in Decter, "Jewish National Consciousness," 32–36. However, for an interesting account of how Uzbeks, when given the opportunity, practice bureaucratic ethnocentrism against the Russians, see Lubin, "Ethnic/Political," 246–247.

127. Cited in Rakowska-Harmstone, "Dialectics of Nationalism," 12.

128. As of 1969, the federal bureaucracy was heavily weighted in favor of the Serbs and their closest ethnic ally, the Montenegrins. Thus Serbs

	% of Total Population	% of Federal Bureaucracy*
Serbs	40.5	77.5
Montenegrins	2.9	7.6
Croats	23.1	9.0
Slovenes	8.3	3.0
Macedonians	5.8	3.0

* From data in Dyker, "Yugoslavia: Unity out of Diversity," 88.

and Montenegrins, with 43.4 percent of the population, accounted for 85.1 percent of federal workers. When all allowances are made for the location of the federal capital in Serbia and for the primary role played by the Serbs and Montenegrins in the World War II partisan movement, this lopsided representation, a quarter of a century after the war, offers an excellent illustration of the power of bureaucratic ethnocentrism within Yugoslavia.

129. A 1946 law gave the federal government the right to transfer industrial personnel from one republic to another. Under this authority, thousands of cadre were redistributed over the next twelve years. Later, as the state moved toward decentralizing economic decision-making, this authority lapsed.

130. The exception appears to be Macedonia, wherein the principal indigenous people were overrepresented, possibly because of the absence of significant numbers of other Slavic peoples. The principal minorities were Turks and Albanians, both of whom were badly underrepresented among cadre.

131. The immunization was far from total, and in 1970–1971 Croats complained loudly about the disproportionate number of Serbs in Croatian enterprises and factories; Tito himself complained about those Croatians who appeared to be preoccupied with "ethnic head-counting" in factories. (See Rusinow, *Yugoslav Experiment*, 291, 292, 298, 299.) Moreover, the country's banking interests remained disproportionately in Belgrade and therefore in Serbian hands.

132. *Keesing's Contemporary Archives* (1966), 21567. Describing the controls exercised by Rankovich and his network, the head of the Croatian party noted that they extended to "every aspect of social life, from the appointment of company directors to the very composition of the government." Cited in Fejto, *People's Democracy*, 236.

Describing how bureaucratic ethnocentrism operated in the case of Rankovich, Rusinow (*Yugoslav Experiment*, 157) commented: "In addition, his wartime experiences in building OZNa seemed to confirm the prejudice that comes easily to any Serbian, the conviction that his fellow Serbs were the most reliable instruments for the building of a strong, independent Yugoslav State and for the protection of socialism as he understood it." Even when due allowance is made for the dangers of mind reading and ethnic generalizing, the statement does present Rankovich's motives in a fair light.

133. See, for example, Schöpflin, "Ideology of Croatian Nationalism," 123–146. The author notes (pp. 140-141) that in 1971 the Croats remained convinced that "Croatia is being run by Serbs." Tudjman (*Nationalism*, 147) indicates that Croat representation in the Federal Administration was even lower in 1978 (6 percent) than it had been in 1968.

134. Lendvai, "National Tensions in Yugoslavia," 5. These figures in fact represent a slight worsening of the situation following Rankovich's purge. In 1958 the Croats, with 79.6 percent of the population, represented 68.6 percent of party membership, while Serbs, with 15 percent of the population, represented 27.7 percent of party membership. For 1958 data, showing serious overrepresentation of Serbs in the provincial parties of Vojvodina and Kosovo, see the tables in Shoup, *Communism and Yugoslav National Question*, 270-272. Tudjman (*Nationalism*, 145) offers figures showing that malrepresentation did not substantially change between 1972 and 1978.

In the afterglow of Rankovich's dismissal, the power to appoint and dismiss party functionaries had been granted to the republics, but this power was soon relocated in the party's central apparatus as part of the general recentralization movement of the early 1970s.

135. See, for example, *The Guardian Weekly* (Manchester, England) 117, no. 18 (October 30, 1977):6. A year earlier, a group of hijackers living outside of Yugoslavia but self-identified as belonging to the "Headquarters of the Croatian National Liberation Forces" issued a declaration which noted in part: "The total command staff of the Yugoslav military forces, serving inside Croatian national territory, is composed of members of the Serbian nation. Serbians constitute the wide majority of the police force in Croatia. Key positions in judicial bodies, administration, law, the Party, and the economy are likewise occupied by Serbs." For the entire declaration, see the *New York Times*, September 11, 1976.

136. See Schöpflin, "National Question." Rusinow (*Yugoslav Experiment*, 180) described the importance of these midrank individuals as follows: "Those in leading or middle-rank positions in the Party, State and economic apparatuses ... were a doubly powerful group because they occupied the best institutional positions from which decision-making at all levels could be informally and surreptitiously influenced in one direction while dutiful public statements gave lip-service to its opposite." Elsewhere (p. 185) he relates how a Croatian, though holding the highest position in a ministry, was regularly bypassed by his Serbian staff.

137. The model that follows excludes the Manchus and Koreans. Other-

wise, it fits the Chinese non-Han peoples of 1949 to varying degrees (for example, it fits the Tibetans better than the Chuangs, the Miao better than the Mongols). Moreover, the model is not totally inappropriate to many of the peoples of Central Asia living within Russia at the time of the October Revolution.

138. *Basic Summarization of Experiences in Promotion of Autonomy*, 20.

139. Cited in "Yunan Racial Cadres Give Up," 23.

140. For details of the campaign, see Dreyer, *China's Forty*, 108–114.

141. Deal, "National Minority," 192.

142. The most famous local leader to be thus co-opted was the Dalai Lama of Tibet prior to his flight in 1959.

143. "Implement Further the Policy of Autonomy."

144. *Basic Summarization of Experiences in Promotion of Autonomy*, 20.

145. *People's Daily*, September 9, 1953. Again in 1957, however, the party was forced to remind the minorities that it had never promised to remove Han cadre from minority areas. See Dreyer, *China's Forty*, 156.

146. The Vietnamese authorities have also acknowledged a persistent shortage of cadre. For example, on December 29, 1975, an announcement of the decision to dissolve the autonomous regions within the country was combined with a statement of need for many more local teachers and cadre. See *FBIS*, January 19, 1976.

147. Jing Wei, "Tibet," 14. See also *JPRS* 83059, March 11, 1983, which speaks of the increase in Tibetan cadre even within the local armed forces.

148. See, for example, Chen Ren, "Respect Minority Nationality Customs," 114.

149. "Sinkiang Nationality Unity," 64.

150. Dreyer, *China's Forty*, 152, 226, 228. Deal, "National Minority," 109.

151. Prior to the Cultural Revolution, there had been a remarkable continuity among the better-known leaders of the non-Han peoples. Although a number of these leaders became targets of heavy criticism during the many-sided Cultural Revolution, the purge appears to have been aimed at specific entrenched individuals rather than at national policy as such. In any case, a far smaller proportion of minority cadre was purged in the minority areas than was true of the Han cadre in those areas. See Hirata, "Leadership in China's Minority."

152. This policy of disproportionately assigning local cadre to the highest showcase level and "in those departments which are closely associated with the production and life of minority nationalities" continued into the 1980s. See "Strengthen National Unity, Create a New Situation in National Work," *JPRS* 83059, March 11, 1983, p. 176. Although the Chinese have tended to employ indigenes in the more visible positions, Robert Scalapino ("The CCP's Provincial Secretaries," 28–29) points out that with the exception of the Tibetans, all of the minorities in the mid-1970s were underrepresented even in the very visible office of party secretary at the provincial/autonomous level.

153. Deal ("National Minority," 157), for example, reports that in one region, 97 percent of the minority cadre were operating below the county level. See also Dreyer (*China's Forty*, 246) for evidence of this same concentration at lower levels in the post-Cultural Revolution period. See too, Nichols, "Minority Nationality Cadres," 233 et seq. The 1982 constitution institutionalized the assignment of indigenes to high-level, showcase slots. Article 113 stated that either the chairman or vice chairman of the standing committee of the people's congress of each autonomous unit (region, county, or district) must be an indigene, and Article 114 extended the same requirement to the administrative head of the unit. (For text, see *Peking Review*, December 27, 1982.)

154. Deal, "National Minority," 158, 191, 192. One of Deal's more extreme examples (p. 177) involves the ethnic profile of those involved in trade. In 1963, there were reportedly 600,000 cadre involved in trade within minority areas. But only 12,000 of them (2 percent) were non-Han.

155. The desire to increase Slovak control over enterprises within Slovakia led the Slovak CP increasingly to demand economic decentralization. As one article has noted: "The probable effects of a decentralization of economic decision making upon the nationality question were apparent. They meant, first and foremost, that rather than tolerating professionally competent managers of Czech nationality from Prague, Slovaks would come increasingly to occupy such positions of authority. The overall effect would be to create a unified Slovak ethos among workers as well as managers in the enterprises of Slovakia, with understandable antipathy towards Czechs who since the founding of the Republic, had insisted upon asserting their presence." (Zaninovich and Brown, "Political Integration," 70.)

156. The Slovaks have certainly fared better than the Magyars of Rumania. We are not interested here in a detailed examination of Rumanian cadre policy, because, as earlier noted, none of that country's minorities has enjoyed ostensible political autonomy since the abolition of the Mures Autonomous Magyar Region in 1968. However, prior to the Hungarian Revolution of 1956, and apparently as the result of Soviet prodding, the Magyar minority did comprise a large percentage of the local cadre. In that year, Rumanians accounted for 20 percent of the population of the AR and for 22 percent of the region's political cadre. Magyars accounted for 77 percent of the population and approximately the same percentage of the cadre. (From data in King, *Minorities*, 150, 152, 156.) The situation has subsequently been radically altered in favor of Rumanians. See the complaint of a former member of the party's Central Committee that nearly all important posts in predominantly Magyar regions go to Rumanians who cannot even speak Hungarian. (*International Herald Tribune*, February 1, 1978.) See also Schöpflin, *Hungarians*, for a general discussion of the Magyars' plight.

157. In 1969 they represented 86.9 percent of the total. The percentage of Slovaks in the party state-wide was, nevertheless, disproportionately

low: they represented 29.6 percent of the state's total population, but only 16 percent of the party's enrollment state-wide.

158. See chapter 8.

159. Skilling, *Czechoslovakia's Interrupted Revolution*, 482–483.

160. Particularly so, since Husak, who became first secretary of the Communist party following the 1968 purge, was a Slovak.

161. Attitudes toward bureaucratic ethnocentrism were reflected in a poll conducted among delegates to a party congress in 1968, prior to the Soviet intervention. Proposed reforms in cadre policy were thought unsatisfactory by 38.1 percent of the Czech delegates (presumably because the reforms were too extensive) and by 23.3 percent of the Slovaks (presumably because they were too tepid). (Skilling, *Czechoslovakia's Interrupted Revolution*, 511–512.) During the same period, however, requests from the Magyar minority within Slovakia for better representation in the power structure evoked bitter reactions from the Slovak populace. (Ibid., 608.)

162. Teresa Rakowska-Harmstone, "Study of Ethnic Politics," 31.

163. Dreyer, *China's Forty*, 160, 270.

164. During the periods when Soviet policy has been one of wooing rather than threatening Turkey, Armenian unhappiness has been evident.

165. There may also be good reason for the authorities to trust cadre of the local nationality, while having no reason to trust their national group as such. In the case of Estonia, for example, the Soviets after World War II superimposed an elite structure largely drawn from Estonians who had been raised and trained within the Soviet Union. Their faithfulness to Moscow led to their being called "Yestonians."

166. A response that in fact can be seen in the case of Tibet following the Khamba rebellions in 1958–1959.

167. *Considerations on Representative Government.* Cited in Connor, "Self-Determination," 32.

168. These were well-followed rules in the case of the overseas empires of the nineteenth and early twentieth centuries. Enlisted men were rarely assigned to their home region, and officers were drawn almost exclusively from the mother country.

169. Shub, *Lenin*, 320.

170. For references to this practice in the Soviet Union, see Barghoorn, *Politics in the USSR*, 270; in China, Deal, "National Minority," 162–163. Dreyer (*China's Forty*, 271) reports a minor exception in the case of China, noting that Tibetan members of the army who are cited for bravery "have invariably performed their meritorious deeds in Tibet." However, such assignments are not typical, and the publicity given to the local site of the heroics is unquestionably designed to encourage Tibetan allegiance to the regime. The few Tibetans who are assigned to Tibet are rendered harmless by their integration into essentially Chinese units. In one presumably typical unit, there were reportedly seven hundred Chinese and twenty Tibetans. (Dreyer, *China's Forty*, 314.)

171. Saunders, *Samizdat*, 436.

172. Kipnis, "Georgian National Movement," 203, 214. Reflecting perhaps the favored status of the Georgians that we noted with regard to language policy, a nearby military unit in Georgia at the time of the national unrest in 1956 was staffed with Georgians. The outfit was reportedly alerted in response to the trouble, but Khrushchev countermanded the order and the other non-Georgian troops were rushed from a lengthier distance. The situation appears to have convinced the authorities of the dangers of having troops stationed on home territory, for the Georgian unit was soon disbanded. (See Kipnis, "Georgian National Movement," 203, and Azrael, *Emergent Nationality Problems*, 22.) Leonid Plynshch (*History's Carnival*, 60) refers to a strike at Novocherkassk at which Central Asians were ordered to fire upon workers after Russian and Ukrainian forces refused to do so. This may be the same incident referred to in the *Peking Review* (July 4, 1969), 26, where it is noted that following a Ukrainian demonstration in the summer of 1963 "Soldiers of the Ukrainian millitary district refused to carry out the Soviet revisionist authorities' orders to slaughter their class brothers. These authorities then brought in troops from two other military districts to carry out a ruthless suppression." A Rand study (Wimbush and Alexiev, *Ethnic Factor*, 21–22) maintains that military units trained for guarding penal institutions and for suppressing riots, civil disturbances, etc. are disproportionately manned with Asians.

173. At the time of the Soviet military intrusion into Afghanistan in late 1979 and early 1980, several commentators noted that a high percentage of the Soviet forces were Asian. In this case, such troops would have the advantage of mitigating the perception of the intrusion as an invasion by Europeans. Most Soviet Asians (for example, Turkmen, Uzbeks, Tadzhiks) have ethnic counterparts within Afghanistan. Not surprisingly, however, there were numerous reports that the Soviet Asian forces proved unwilling to fight fellow Asians and Moslems, so the number deployed dropped rapidly. See, for example, the *New York Times*, August 7, 1981.

174. See Katz, *Handbook*, 310, for a reference to the Uzbekistan case. Central Asians tend to perceive all Europeans in their homeland as "Russians."

175. Lendvai, "National Tensions," 12. Vucinich ("Nationalism and Communism," 270) gives the agreed-upon figure as 20 percent.

176. Lendvai, "National Tensions," 12.

177. *New York Times*, February 7, 1972.

178. There had been "national military formations" prior to Soviet involvement in World War II, but such formations were eliminated by 1939. See Barghoorn, *Soviet Russian Nationalism*, 20–21. However, see the reference to a Georgian unit in note 172.

179. The Soviet leadership probably was reinforced in its conviction that soldiers should not be permitted to serve among their own people by the activities of the Hungarian forces in 1956, and by the often-stated as-

sumption of Poles during 1981–1982 that, in the event of Soviet military intervention, the Polish army would heroically resist.

180. Lendvai, "National Tensions," 13.

181. Ibid., 12.

182. Doder, *The Yugoslavs*, 146. Quite inappropriately, therefore, the *New York Times'* eulogistic obituary for Tito noted that "the trust embodied in the arming of every able-bodied man in a country with a terrible history of ethnic rivalries was his prescription for continued independence." *New York Times*, May 5, 1980.

183. A majority of the senior officers in the military are reported to have such a perception. A poll conducted by the Defense Ministry in 1971 reportedly uncovered that 54 percent of all high-ranking officers, 40 percent of low-ranking officers, and 47 percent of all non-commissioned officers believed that nationalism was the greatest threat to Yugoslavia, greater than an invasion by the Soviet Union. (Cited in Enloe, *Ethnic Soldiers*, 173.)

184. We have noted that the official Cuban position is that it is a homogeneous society without a national question. However, as the following citation suggests, there are parallels between the cadre policy of Cuba and that followed by the multinational Marxist-Leninist states:

> Complaints about racial "tokenism" in revolutionary leadership and policies are illegal though legitimate. Only 9 percent of the 100 members of the Central Committee of the Communist Party of Cuba, appointed in 1965, were black and mulatto, the same proportion as in the Cuban Senate and the House of Representatives in 1945, with little change since then. Then, as now, this is about one-third of what would be expected from their share of the population, and suggests little impact by revolutionary rule in increasing the representation of blacks among the political elite. Within the Cuban Armed Forces in the 1970s, there were disproportionately many blacks serving as troops and disproportionately few officers—the result of both historical conditions and selective military service legislation. (Dominguez et al., *Enhancing Global Human Rights*, 54.)

185. For references to the policy of the Chinese government to fill nearly all responsible positions with Han, and purposely to exclude non-Han, see Diao, "Minorities and the Chinese," 174, 184; Hung-mao Tien, "Sinicization," 8; Deal, "National Minority," 155–156; Moseley, *Consolidation*, 47, 76, 117; and Dreyer, *China's Forty*, 155. The Soviets have often charged that the Chinese relegate the non-Han to nonresponsible positions. See, for example, Karklins, "The Uighurs," 349. In both China and Vietnam, there have, of course, been isolated or token exceptions, such as the Mongol, Ulanfu, and the Nung, Chu Van Tan, who proved their faithfulness to the movement and have been figures of great prominence. In 1979, a Tibetan became head of the Tibetan Autonomous Region, replacing a Chinese who had held that post since 1971 (*New York Times*, September 2,

1979), and this appears to have heralded a new policy. A draft for a revised Chinese Constitution, released in 1982, made it mandatory that the heads of all autonomous units "shall be persons of the nationality or nationalities exercising regional autonomy in those areas" (*FBIS*, April 28, 1982), and this was upheld by Article 114 of the constitution adopted in late 1982. However, the leadership had earlier confirmed in an article their conviction that Han cadre should continue to hold positions of responsibility in all regions. (See the *Peking Review*, March 10, 1980, pp. 22–23.) The article is a posthumously released speech by Chou En-lai, delivered in 1957, but the editors make clear that the speech contains the guidelines for future minority policy. See also the *International Herald Tribune*, October 31, 1981, for the report of a visit by Fox Butterfield to the Sinkiang-Uighur AR. The report deals largely with improvements in the situation of the minorities as contrasted with the period of the Cultural Revolution. Despite these improvements, however, Butterfield noted that all real power of decision-making remained in Han hands. The first secretary, six of eight deputy secretaries, and all military leaders were Han. By contrast with the Chinese decision to place more local nationals in showcase positions, in 1979 the Vietnamese authorities purged the leading minority figures from the movement. See *Keesing's Contemporary Archives* (1979), 29876.

186. Schöpflin (*Hungarians*, 14), reports that the Magyar minority within Rumania appears to be excluded from employment in the Ministries of Foreign Affairs, Defense, and Interior.

187. The importance ascribed to the armed forces as an agent of internal security varies from state to state and from one period to another. During the Cultural Revolution in China, for example, the People's Liberation Army was the chosen agency for keeping within prescribed levels the orchestrated chaos that was permitted to paralyze the party and much of the state apparatus. Whenever the PLA itself became infected, authorities moved rapidly to correct the situation.

The significance ascribed to the army as an arm of internal security within the USSR is suggested by the fact that the responsibility for it, the secret police, the procury, and the judiciary are all concentrated in a single agency (the Administrative Organs Department) of the Communist Party's Central Committee Secretariat. (See Schapiro, "Keynote Compromise," in Nogee, *Man, State, Society*, 171.)

188. Rakowska-Harmstone, "Study of Ethnic Politics," 31. The analysis is based on the surnames of the commanders, and the fact that one or more of these generals may have been of Ukrainian or Belorussian background cannot be discounted; the patronyms of these three Slavic peoples are similar. However, Ukrainians and Belorusians are often used as surrogate members of the "most loyal" national group outside of the Slavic regions. There they tend to be viewed as Russians by the indigenous population and can also be so viewed for our purposes. In another study (cited in d'Encausse, *Decline of an Empire* 162), Rakowska-Harmstone concluded

that of the Soviet generals appointed between 1940 and 1970, 91 percent were Slavs, and perhaps as many as 65 percent were Russians. Ellen Jones ("Minorities in Soviet Armed Forces," 306–307) reports that an "analysis of the military members of the Supreme Soviet reveals overwhelming Slavic dominance—98 percent of this group listed a Slavic nationality. A similar pattern emerges from a name analysis of 73 key MOD [Ministry of Defense] officials."

189. See Wimbush and Alexiev, *Ethnic Factor*, 23–28. The authors note that Russians dominate the officer corps and the Ukrainians are heavily overrepresented among noncommissioned officers. See also the *New York Times*, sec. 4, October 7, 1979, and Azrael, *Emergent Nationality*, vi.

190. Lendvai, "National Tensions," 9, 12. A. Ross Johnson (*Role of the Military*, 19) offers estimates showing that Serbs and Montenegrins accounted in 1970 for 66 percent of all general officers and 67.4 percent of all officers. The trend was reportedly sharply reversed following a public outcry of Croat spokesmen. (See Dyker, "Yugoslovia: Unity out of Diversity?", 88.) This alteration was seemingly called for by Article 242 of the 1974 constitution which stipulated that "as regards the composition of the officer corps and promotion to senior commanding and directing posts in the Yugoslav People's Army, the principles of proportional representation of the Republics and Autonomous Provinces shall be applied." However, by tying proportional representation to the republics and provinces rather than to national groups, the constitution did not rule out the possibility that the Serbian majority within Vojvodina, the same group's plurality within Bosnia, and its minority within Croatia and Kosovo might prove to be the major source of recruits from those republics and provinces. As noted later, something similar to this pattern had in fact been followed in the staffing of the Ministry of the Interior. Doder (*Yugoslavs*, 148) reports that the ethnic composition of the officer corps did not change radically following the adoption of the 1974 constitution because of the lack of attractiveness that a military career has traditionally held for Croats and Slovenes. However, he contends that the uppermost echelons were rapidly altered in favor of the Croats. For a round-table discussion by Yugoslav military officers concerning the problems of recruiting a better ethnic mix, see *JPRS* 81121 (June 4, 1982): 105–112.

191. Skilling, *Czechoslovakia's Interrupted Revolution*, 482–483. Reform during 1968 did not proceed fast enough to silence Slovak critics. General Martin Dzur (a Slovak who was elevated to Minister of Defense as part of the reform movement) was criticized in a Slovak newspaper on August 8, 1968 for failing to treat national identity as the "decisive" and "primary" criterion in setting cadre policy for the defense establishment.

192. Spechler, "Russia and the Russians," p. 11.

193. Saunders, *Samizdat*, 433–434.

194. Dyker, "Yugoslavia: Unity out of Diversity?", 88. These data are particularly interesting because they reflect the situation some five years

after Rankovich had been purged, *inter alia*, for staffing the secret police with Serbs. Following Rankovich's purge, the authorities granted the republics "co-responsibility" for public order, including the appointment of public prosecutors. But this power was rescinded, along with other powers over cadre policy, in the early 1970s. In any case, the ethnic composition of the security forces indicates that "co-responsibility" had not led to significant changes of personnel.

195. We will remember that during World War II, the Serbs of Croatia and Bosnia were often involved in internecine struggles with the Croats and Moslems of Croatia and Bosnia.

196. *Soviet Analyst* 6, 13 (June 30, 1977): 7.

197. Khrushchev, *Khrushchev Remembers*, 330.

198. By 1977, this was the situation in twenty-five of the thirty-four union and autonomous republics for which data were available. (See Miller, "Cadre Policy in Nationality Areas," 3–36.) As noted, the Chinese have followed a similar practice. In those cases in which the most prominent position is filled by a member of the local ethnic group, the vice chairman, vice governor, vice county magistrate, etc. is regularly a Han.

199. As noted, Lenin had written that drawing borders to reflect ethnonational distribution could not be carried so far as to defy economic logic. For example, cities in which nonindigenes predominated would not be granted separate status but would remain part of the region of which they were an essential part. But even by drawing attention to such necessary exceptions, he drove home the fact that ethnonational distribution was to be the overriding standard, and that borders and homelands would closely coincide.

200. Particularly flagrant violations of the "one nation, one republic" rule involved territories in which Armenians predominated but which were nonetheless made part of the Azerbaijani and Georgian Republics. The Nagorno-Karabak Autonomous Region, for example, was made part of Azerbaijan, although Armenians accounted for more than 80 percent of the population. Subsequent demands for its union with Armenia have been met with purges. See Sheehy, "Recent Events in Abkhazia."

Data on the ethnic composition of the Asian republics at the time of their creation also suggest something less than total commitment to establishing ethnonational units. In each case, significant portions of the titular group were left outside of the unit and large numbers of other peoples were included. As a result, Uzbeks constituted only 76.1 percent of their SSR's population; 17.4 percent of all Uzbeks lived outside. For the Turkmen, the corresponding figures were 71.9 and 5.8; for Tadzhiks, 71.2 and 24.8; for the Kirgiz (then an ASSR), 66.2 and 13.3; for the Kazakhs (an ASSR), 57.4 and 6.6; for the Karakalpaks (an AR), 38.1 and 21.7 percent. (See Zhdanko, "National State Demarcation," 152.) Thus in one case the titular group was not even a majority within its newly granted unit, and in no case did the titular group account for 80 percent of the unit's population.

201. Derived from data principally found in table 9 of Clem, "Population Change," 160. A modest allowance should be made for error. Individual union republics were created sporadically between 1922 and 1940, and census data were not always available for the specific year of creation.

202. Derived from data in ibid. Statistics on one of the republics (the Tuva ASSR) at the time of its creation are not available.

203. The name of one of the three (the Karelo-Finnish ASSR) was subsequently changed to the Karelian ASSR. However, the lack of reality that may exist behind the ethnonational designations of administrative units was here presented in the sharpest relief, for at the time of the unit's creation less than one percent of the population was Finnish. Moreover, the Karelians were themselves but a fraction (less than one-fourth) of the total population.

204. As noted in the case of Central Asia (note 200), the gerrymandering extended as well to the autonomous republics outside of the RSFSR. In the case of the Transcaucasian Abkhaz ASSR, the titular group accounted for only 27.8 percent. In still another Transcaucasian case, the Adzar ASSR was declared an autonomous unit within the Georgian union republic, although the Adzars are Georgians whose ancestors converted to Islam during the long period of Ottoman domination. It is not at all clear whether these people consider themselves a separate national group or merely a religious minority within the Georgian nation.

205. From data in table 5 in Clem, *Population Change*, 144. Needless to say, not all of the excluded people lived in immediately adjacent territory, and there are many, therefore, who could not have been included in the appropriate ethnic unit. But as noted above in the case of the Armenians, large numbers who were in contiguous territory were excluded.

206. Derived from data in table 8 in Clem, *Population Change*, 159. The median accretion in percentage was 6.9 percent, a change from 6.7 percent to 13.6 percent.

207. The median increment was 20.7 percent, representing an increase in the proportion of Russians from 25.3 percent to 46 percent.

208. Column 5 minus the 13.1 percent growth of the Russian community within the USSR (column 8). The mean figure for the twelve republics was 18 percent and the median was 19.5 percent.

We are here using the rough formula: gross increase minus natural increase equals immigration. This formula presumes that the natural increase of Russians was approximately the same in all republics, and such was indeed the case. The average Russian family size in each republic fell within the narrow range of 3.2 to 3.6 persons, with a USSR-wide average of 3.4. (Data on family size from table 4.3 in Newth, "Demographic Developments," 87.)

Though significantly smaller, a net immigration of Russians into the

ASSRs of the RSFSR also occurred during the 1958-1970 period. The percentage gain of Russians in absolute numbers within the ASSRs was 11.6, as compared with a growth of 9.98 percent in the number of Russians within the traditionally Russian areas of the RFSFR. The pattern is more skewed than in the case of the union republics, however. There appears to have been a net out-migration of Russians from seven of the sixteen, a small in-migration into two others, and a substantial in-migration into the remaining seven.

209. The only partial exception would be the Moldavians, whose growth rate very slightly exceeded that of the Georgians.

210. Similarly, the percentage of Russians went down in six of the ASSRs within the RSFSR, despite a net Russian in-migration.

211. Kirgizia experienced no net in- or out-migration; Armenia experienced a very small net outflow; and Azerbaijan and Georgia underwent a significant out-migration. See footnote 208 for details concerning the assumptions underlying the determination of the rates of in- and out-migration of Russians.

212. Table 5 in Clem, *Population Change*, 144. Here, traditional Russian territory refers to all of the RSFSR minus those areas designated as ASSRs.

213. See chapter 8.

214. Lewis et al., *Nationality and Population*, 116 et seq.

215. Khalmukhamedov, "Soviet Society," 29. For some data on planned investment under the tenth Five Year Plan, broken down by republic, see p. 30 of the same article.

216. See table A.15 in Katz, *Handbook*, 452. For a review of several studies, all pointing to significant regional disparities, see Clem, "Ethnic Dimension of the Soviet Union." Authors of the studies include Leslie Dienes (1972), Iwan Koropeckyj (1965), Allan Rodgers (1974), Gertrude Schroder (1973), and Peter Zwick (1976).

217. For the example of Estonia, see Parming, "Roots of Nationality Differences," 36. This is how the process was described in a book written within the Ukraine in 1965:

> As we all know, the most important branches of industry and construction in the USSR are centralized. The Union and Union-Republican Ministries completely neglect such an important matter, which Lenin had stressed, as the training of permanent cadres of specialists in the territories of the various Republics. (This, after all, would also be economically more profitable.) This is why specialists (not only engineers and technicians but also skilled workers) are being sent *en masse* from Russia to the Ukraine, while Ukrainians are sent to other Republics. The constant inflow of this Russian element in the present conditions in the Ukraine is a powerful encouragement to growing Russification. (Dzubya, *Internationalism?*, 110.)

218. The constitution (articles 78 and 84) asserts that the territory of a

union or autonomous republic cannot be altered without its consent; but this is an empty phrase that has not stopped the central authorities from making changes whenever they have desired.

219. Thus a transfer of territory from Kazakhstan to Uzbekistan during the 1960s involved an area in which there dwelled more Kazakhs than Uzbeks. (See Newth, "1970 Soviet Census," 219.)

220. Bagramov, "Soviet Nationalities Policy," 76.

221. This right was ostensibly in effect for thirty-eight years prior to its omission from the constitution of 1977.

222. See, "Soviets Debate Manpower and Demographic Policies," U.S. State Department Bureau of Intelligence and Research Report No. 1117 (January 24, 1979): 6. See also the article by David Shipler in the *New York Times*, January 9, 1979 which is dedicated to official concern with the labor imbalance between Central Asia and the European sector of the USSR.

223. *FBIS*, February 24, 1981, p. 36.

224. Ibid. The "new territories" were all located within the RSFSR.

225. See discussion later in this chapter.

226. Rybakovskiy, "On the Migration." Emphasis added. A slight net out-migration had come to characterize the Central Asian republics in the late 1970s, but apparently Russians and other Europeans were heavily represented in this turnabout, and the authorities were not content with an out-migration that would increase the homogeneity of the republics.

227. One hundred minus the sum of columns 2 and 4 in table 4. The mean was 16.9 percent and the median, 16.5 percent.

228. In addition, Armenians and Russians each accounted for precisely the same percentage of the population within Azerbaijan.

229. However, if to the Russian out-of-republic figure was added the approximately six percent of the Russian population living within the ASSRs of the RSFSR, then only the Armenians would surpass the Russians in terms of the proportion of the nation living outside of its republic.

230. See Robert Lewis's statement that "over 90 percent of the nationalities associated with union republics are found in, or immediately adjacent to, their republics." "The Mixing of Russians," 150.

231. The two other groups who are widely dispersed throughout the Soviet Union are the Jews and the Tatars.

232. For nine of the fourteen titular peoples, the proportion of the entire nation living within its union republic in 1970 was greater than at the time of the republic's creation, and, in the case of a tenth people, the population had remained nearly constant.

233. For a manifestation of Armenian interest in a sector of Azerbaijan populated by Armenians, see Matossian, "Armenia," 158.

234. Stalin was very attuned to this principle. For example, in a report delivered before the Twelfth Congress of the CP on April 23, 1923, he noted that the Armenians and other minority peoples within Georgia were in a situation where "the Georgians dominate" and "feel there is no par-

ticular need to reckon with these small nationalities," whom they consider "less cultured, less developed." In Azerbaijan "there is also a tendency, sometimes quite unconcealed, to think that the Azerbaijanians are the native population of the country and the Armenians are the intruders." "From very early times Transcaucasia has been the scene of massacre and strife and, under the Mensheviks and nationalists, the scene of warfare. You know of the Georgia-Armenian War. You also know of the massacres which took place at the beginning of 1904 and the end of 1905." Similar reminders of past maltreatment were further noted by Stalin between Turkmen and Kirgiz, Turkmen and Uzbek, and Armenians and Tatars. (See "Report on National Factors in Party and State," in Stalin, *Marxism: Selected Readings*, 146–147.)

235. We earlier noted that the Armenians have proven a relatively untroublesome group to Soviet authorities because of their preoccupation with the despised Turks and their tendency to view Moscow as something of an ally in this competition. Somewhat similarly, the Georgians have traditionally perceived themselves as surrounded by hostile, Muslim peoples, and have therefore also looked for support from outside of the region. At the same time, the Armenians and Georgians (though neither group is Muslim) have tended to view one another suspiciously as a competitor for dominance in the Transcaucasus. However, charges of bourgeois nationalism aimed at a number of Armenians and Georgians in the 1970s may have heralded a less complacent attitude toward these peoples by Moscow. See Matossian, "Armenia," 159, and Dobson, "Georgia," 184. At the Twenty-fifth Congress of the CPSU (1976), Armenia, Georgia, and Azerbaijan were singled out as areas for stepped-up industrial development. This might well signal an influx of Russians into the area. See Berner et al., *Soviet Union 1975–76*, 43.

236. But see later in this chapter the discussion of the possible impact of the Twenty-sixth Congress upon this restriction.

237. For example, even though there were some Armenian-language schools operating within the adjoining Georgian Republic, only 84.8 percent of the Armenian community within that republic claimed Armenian as their principle or native language in 1970, as compared to 99.8 percent of those Armenians residing within their own republic. Similarly, only 62.3 percent of Georgians outside of the Georgian Republic claimed Georgian as their native language, as contrasted with 99.4 percent of those living within Georgia. (From data in Katz, *Handbook*, 151, 172, 174.)

238. For the complete text of the letter, see Saunders, *Samizdat*, 427–440. The citation is from p. 438.

239. Bromley, *Soviet Ethnography*, 153. See also, Terentieva, "Ethnocultural Changes," 119.

240. See, for example, Kipnis, "Georgian National Movement," 200: "Today, part of the Armenian intelligentsia, chiefly in Tbilisi, is Russian-speaking and acts in Georgia as the carrier of Russian culture and Russian

influence. This is an additional cause of Georgian-Armenian conflict which anyway has a long historic tradition." As an acculturated, highly dispersed group, the Jews are particularly vulnerable to being perceived as agents of russification.

241. Based on data in column 1 of tables 3 and 4. For all fourteen non-Russian titular peoples, the percentage living outside their republic underwent a mean percentage point decrease of 1.8 and a median decrease of 1.1. The largest decrease was experienced by the Armenians (9.9 percent), and the largest increase was that of the Belorussians (2.5 percent).

242. Stationary here means relative to one's union republic and does not preclude intrarepublic migration.

243. Actually, as can be seen by contrasting the data in column 8 of tables 3 and 4, the rate of natural increase did drop for all titular peoples during the 1970s, as contrasted with the 1960s. However, with the single exception of the Georgians, the rate of increase for each of the titular people whose republic is in the Caucasus or Asia grew relative to the growth rate of the Russians. That is to say, the Russian rate of increase fell proportionately faster than did the rate among Asians and Caucasians.

244. In 1979, the mean percentage was 64.6 and the median was 68.6.

245. Still greater grounds for complacency are offered by the ASSRs within the Russian republic. In only two of the sixteen cases does a single non-Russian people account for a majority of the population.

246. For a convenient reference to several of these studies, see Silver, "Inventory of Propositions."

247. See, for example, Kholmogorov, *International Traits* 11:283 for intermarriage data on Latvia; and Evstigneev, "Ethnically Mixed Marriages," 41, 43, for data on marriages in the capitals of Estonia, Latvia, and Lithuania.

248. See Evstigneev, "Ethnically Mixed Marriages," 376 and N. Terentieva, "Ethnic Self-Identification," 45, 47.

249. These cases were all mentioned by Khrushchev in his famous denunciation of Stalin at the Twentieth Party Congress in 1956. He added: "The Ukrainians avoided meeting this fate only because there were too many of them and there was no place to which to deport them. Otherwise, he would have deported them all." Christman, *Communism*, 202. While the released account of this speech indicates that this comment on the Ukrainians was greeted with some laughter and, therefore, may not have been intended to be taken seriously, there is no gainsaying that widespread Ukrainian cooperation with the German forces, particularly during the early stages of the Nazi invasion, was a matter of great concern to the authorities. Khrushchev himself was said to have threatened the expulsion of all Georgians from Georgia in response to nationally inspired unrest in Georgia during 1956. See Kipnis, "Georgian National Movement," 203.

250. There are, of course, degrees of coercion, and a measure of coercion

has entered into other migrations as well. This is how Khrushchev described his Virgin Lands project of the 1950s:

> You can imagine the difficulties that the Virgin Lands campaign posed for a family which had to be picked up and moved from the home where it had lived for generations. It was a great hardship for them, but we had to resettle many such families—Ukrainians, Belorussians, and Russians—thousands of kilometers from the graves of their ancestors. Enormous material expenditures went into the resettlement campaign. Among other things, we had to build settlements in the Virgin Lands. (*Khrushchev Remembers*, 387.)

In a footnoted commentary on this passage, Edward Crankshaw notes that under the program, "half a million 'volunteers' were moved from European Russia."

251. The obligation does not extend to evening students.

252. Robert Lewis, "Population Redistribution," 45–46.

253. The assumption of an equitable apportionment of graduates is made in order to simplify the analysis. There are, of course, significant differences in levels of education among republics and among national groups. (See tables A.18 and A.19 in Katz, *Handbook*, 455–456.)

254. The number of Russians living outside of the RSFSR in 1979 totaled 23.9 million.

255. Other estimates run as high as five million. (See Azrael, *Emergent Nationality*, 16.)

256. Personal conversation with Vladimir Brovkin, a former officer in the Soviet army, at the Woodrow Wilson International Center for Scholars, Washington, D.C., 1976. This is how a Ukrainian described the situation:

> Millions of young Ukrainian men come home after several years' service nationally disoriented and linguistically demoralized and become in their turn a force exerting an influence for Russification on other young people and on the population at large. Not to mention that a considerable number of them do not come home at all. It is not hard to imagine how tremendously damaging all this is for national development." (Dzyuba, *Internationalism?*, 137.)

See also the comment of Plynshch (*History's Carnival*, 179) that the Ukrainians "do not understand why retired army officers from Russia settle in Ukrainian cities and are given privileges when Ukrainian boys who have finished their army service are sent to Siberia and Kazakhstan."

257. Moroz, *Report from the Beria Reserve*, 3. The "seven million Russians" alludes to the number of Russians in the Ukraine at the time of the 1959 census.

258. An estimate by an incarcerated dissident, smuggled out of the USSR in 1979, placed the current number of people in forced labor camps as "at least five million." (*New York Times*, September 15, 1979.)

259. The system of registration is known as the *propiski* system.

260. As noted, the most serious example of government inability to entice people to an area and then to keep them there has been the failure to populate Siberia with sufficiently large numbers to support the region's rapid development.

261. These migrations, for the most part, involve Europeans moving to European cities. The regulations could be more easily (and, one suspects, are) enforced in situations involving Europeans and non-Europeans.

262. *FBIS*, February 24, 1981, p. 38.

263. A number of the sources cited in footnote 264 subsequently confirmed that this had indeed been the secretary's intention. Brezhnev's reference to the language needs of non-Russian émigrés might suggest a return to the policy of the 1920s which permitted non-Russians, living outside of their republics, to have their own schools. (See discussion earlier in this chapter.) However, the emphasis upon the adoption of the Russian language at the time of the Twenty-sixth Congress made such an extreme reversion unlikely.

264. See, for example, Deshdamirov, "The 26th CPSU Congress," 43–58; Rybakovskiy, "On the Migration," 2–10; Kenigshteyn, "Regulation of the Processes," 96–97; Suskolov, "The 26th CPSU Congress," 111–115; and "The International and the National in the Soviet People's Way of Life," *JPRS* 81223 (July 7, 1982):38–54. The last article is an account of a conference in response to the Twenty-sixth Congress. Brezhnev personally demonstrated the importance he ascribed to his comments on migration by restating and expanding upon them at a conference in Uzbekistan in the spring of 1982. (See *FBIS*, March 25, 1982, pp. R2–R4.)

265. Kosolapov, "Class and National Relations," 20.

266. Galina Il'inichna Litvinova (Moscow, 1981). The following summary is based on chapter 4, "Migration and Labor Resources." Litvinova, a prestigious member of the Soviet Academy of Sciences, died shortly after the publication of this book, but an article which she coauthored and which restated all the major points of her book was published posthumously the following year. (See Litvinova and Urlanis, "Soviet Union's Demographic Policy," 38–46.)

267. The new determination to control migratory processes had already been reflected in the eleventh five-year plan, which noted that "along with the priority development of a network of professional technical institutes in the republics of Central Asia and the Transcaucasus, it is also necessary to send the youth of these republics for training in other regions of the country with the agreement of the interested departments." Cited in Shister, "Sources for the Replenishment," 26–40. The author added immediately: "One must send a larger number of youth (especially rural) to the country's all-union leading construction projects" which were located within the RSFSR. Still another author, in a follow-up article to the Twenty-sixth Congress, noted that the period of mature socialism "inevitably entails the increase of the mobility of the population, the creation of multinational

labor collectives and the extensive exchange of personnel among republics." (Nagornaya, "National Relations," 2–3.)

268. Brezhnev had spoken of financial supports for the second and third child. Such an optimally sized family was larger than the typical Russian family and smaller than the typical Asian family. Nancy Lubin, who spent 1978–1979 in Uzbekistan, has reported that the literature disseminated there suggested a desire to increase the number of children born of non-indigenous parents relative to the number of Uzbek children. (See Lubin, "Ethnic/Political," 59–60.)

269. Percentages derived from the data in table 5 in Deal, "National Minority," 143. Soviet writers have often accused the Chinese of falsifying their data on national groups. T. Rakhimov, for example, noted that an earlier Chinese figure that placed the number of Mongols at 5 or 6 million later became 1.5 million. (Cited in Osofsky, "Soviet Criticism," 912.) Data released by the Chinese in 1980 (*Peking Review* [March 3, 1980]) constituted very rough estimates. Data from the 1982 census were still fragmentary as of this writing (March 1983).

270. Hung-mao Tien, in "Sinicization," offers the 2:1 estimate, while Hyer and Heaton, in "Cultural Revolution," 117, report a 4:1 ratio.

271. The AR was simultaneously reduced from a military region to a military district directly subordinate to Peking.

272. In 1973, C. L. Sulzberger (*New York Times*, October 28, 1973) stated that there were 1.6 million Mongols outside of the AR and 420,000 within it. The imbalance may not have been this great. Chinese statistics gave the number of Mongols within the AR in 1965 as 1.2 million (Deal, "National Minority," 143), this out of an approximate total figure of 2 million. Following the 1969 partition, there were probably still more Mongols within rather than without the AR. Preliminary statistics from the 1982 census indicated 2,489,780 Mongols within the reenlarged AR and 921,877 outside. (Figures extrapolated from "Nationalities with Over One Million Population," and "Nei Monggol Issues Census Figures" in *JPRS* 82402, December 7, 1982, pp. 104 and 107, respectively.)

273. For the 10 percent figure, see Theodore Shabad's article in the *New York Times*, September 17, 1979. For the 20 percent figure, see the *Korean Herald*, July 22, 1979. Given Han migration into the area during the Cultural Revolution, 10 percent seems the more likely figure. A Soviet source gave an 8.4 percent figure as of 1981. (Suchanlo et al., *Against Maoist Falsifications*, 137.) Initial results of the 1982 census suggest that Mongols accounted for 12.9 percent of the AR's total population. (Extrapolated from "Nei Monggol Issues Census Figures," *JPRS* 82402, December 7, 1982, p. 107.)

274. Chinese sources give the total number of Tibetans in 1957 as 2.77 million and the number within the Tibetan AR in 1965 as 1.2 million. (Moseley, *Consolidation*, 3, and Deal, "National Minority," 143, respectively.) Even disallowing any natural growth of the overall Tibetan community

between 1957 and 1965, this indicates that only 43.3 percent of all Tibetans were living in their AR as of 1965.

275. Districts (*chou*) are the secondary level of autonomous unit, intermediate between the region (*ch'ü*), and the county (*hsien*). See chapter 8.

276. An Zhiguo, "Policy toward Dalai Lama," 53–54.

277. Chinese 1965 figures credit the Chuang with 7.3 million of the AR's 19.5 million people, or 37.3 percent.

278. Moseley, *Consolidation*, 53.

279. Ibid., 94.

280. Dreyer, *China's Forty*, 154. The criticism came principally from the Han who were to be incorporated.

281. In a speech in 1957, Chou stated:

> In the case of founding a Zhuang [Chuang] autonomous region, we tried to bring the Han people to see the point in the same light. A single compact Zhuang autonomous region was out of the question. This is because even if we combined the places inhabited by the Zhuang nationality in Guangxi, Yunnan, and Guizhou to form a Zhuang autonomous region, the newly formed region would still include more than one million Han inhabitants, and the two Yao autonomous counties in it would have over 400,000 people of their own, the Hans and Yaos together numbering about 2 million. Therefore you still wouldn't have had a pure, unitary national autonomous region.

You may not "have had a pure unitary national autonomous region," but you would have had an autonomous region in which the titular people represented a clear majority.

The speech was released in 1980. (*Peking Review* [March 3, 1980].) Curiously, Chou referred to the Kwangsi Chuang Autonomous Region in this speech purportedly made in 1957, although that AR was not formally created until 1958.

282. There is a significant settlement of Hui in at least fifteen provinces, as well as in the Ninghsia Hui AR.

283. Chinese data give the number of Hui living within the Ninghsia Hui AR in 1965 as 600,000. The same source listed four autonomous districts in which the titular group exceeded this figure. (Furthermore, in one of the four cases the group had to share the official name of the district with a second national group.) See table 5 in Deal, "National Minority," 143–145.

284. Six hundred thousand of a reported 1.8 million in 1965.

285. " 'Ningxia Ribao' Reports Regional Census Figures," *JPRS* 82440, December 10, 1982, p. 72.

286. Table 5, Deal, "National Minority," 143–145.

287. Diao, "Minorities and Chinese," 172.

288. The case of Sinkiang illustrates the rather low level of Han migration prior to 1958. The Chinese had substantial historical reasons to fear

both truly indigenous separatist movements and Soviet machinations in this westernmost province. Moreover, in 1949 the Han accounted for only 3 to 5 percent of the province's population. (Osofsky, "Soviet Criticism," 913, and Hung-mao Tien, "Sinicization," 10.) Yet according to one source, only a quarter of a million Han were resettled in this strategic region between 1953 and 1957. (Drew, "Sinkiang," 209.)

289. Dreyer, *China's Forty*, 164.

290 Deal, "National Minority," 178.

291. Ibid., 179.

292. Unhappiness on the part of urban youth forced to live in remote, backward, rural regions was rife, and an unknown but substantial number managed to return illegally to their home areas, particularly during both the Great Leap Forward and the Cultural Revolution. The situation inspired an anonymous wag to describe Peking's problem in new words to the old song, "How're You Going to Keep Them Down on the Farm?" Two lines read:

Can they who in a Great Leap Forward leapt,
Now settle for a single backward steppe?

293. January 18, 1975. Reported in Dreyer, *China's Forty*, 252. The projection of 2 million per year appears to be borne out by an estimate in the *New York Times*, December 5, 1978, stating that 16 million had been sent down since 1968, although only 10 million remained there.

294. Cited in Bradsher, "Tibet Struggles," 750–762.

295. *Peking Review*, December 1, 1972, p. 21. The total population figure of 1.25 million cited in this article was lower than the figure given in 1965.

296. Shabad, *China's Changing Map*, 323.

In an otherwise quite broad survey of Chinese migrations, Leo Orleans (*Every Fifth Child*, 79–92) curiously omits migration to Tibet. He does indicate by map (p. 80) that Tibet has been a major target area of Han resettlement, but his estimates of migrants into border areas (pp. 89–91) do not refer to Tibet. On the other hand, he includes Tsinghai, a region of important Tibetan settlement but one that is not on the border. This oversight may account for a later map (pp. 110–111), that shows Tibet to be over 90 percent Tibetan. However, he does estimate that an influx of Han into Tsinghai had increased the percentage of Han in that province from 56.7 to 66.5 percent between 1953 and 1970.

297. There is general agreement that the Han purposefully increased their majority over the Tibetans and other minorities within neighboring Tsinghai between 1953 and 1970. (See, for example, Shabad, *China's Changing Map*, 323; Orleans, *Every Fifth Child*, 90; and Hung-mao Tien, "Sinicization," 10.) It would be curious if the authorities were not at least as interested in diluting the Tibetans along the Indian, Nepalese, and Bhutan borders.

As a final consideration, it should be noted that if the large Han-dominated contingents of the People's Liberation Army serving in Tibet were added to our calculation, then the relative strength of the Tibetans would be significantly lowered.

298. For the 1953 census figures, see Orleans, *Every Fifth Child*, 90, or Drew, "Sinkiang," 208. In 1965, there were five autonomous districts within the Sinkiang-Uighur AR (two Mongol, one Hui, one Kirgiz, and one Kazakh). The total number of titular peoples in these ADs alone accounted for 13.6 percent of the reported AR's total population, and they were 17 percent as numerous as the Uighurs within the AR. (Derived from data in table 5 in Deal, "National Minority," 143–147.) This substantial non-Uighur population highlights the distortion in official Chinese figures. If, as claimed, the Uighurs accounted in 1965 for 78.8 percent of the AR's population and proper allowance is made for other non-Han peoples, the percentage represented by Han would have been less than 5.5 percent. Even the most conservative estimates (those of Drew and Orleans) place the Chinese percentage several times higher.

299. "Xinjiang Releases Population Census Results," *JPRS* 82402, December 7, 1982, p. 111.

300. This may well be the case even without considering the military. Several analysts believe that the Han were an absolute majority as early as 1965. (See Shabad, *China's Changing Map*, 315; Hung-mao Tien, "Sinicization," 10; Lal, "Sinification," 15–16; and Polyakov, "Unmasking Mao," 45. The last, a Soviet citizen writing in 1969, noted: "The result of the intensive Sinification of Sinkiang has meant that the share of Chinese in its population has grown from 3 to 45 percent during 1959–1966. Prior to 1949, there were virtually no Chinese in Tibet while today the Chinese constitute almost one-half of all its inhabitants." The fact that the estimates on Sinkiang agree with the analysis of numerous "third party" scholars suggests that the statement with regard to Tibet may also be a fair approximation of the situation in the late 1960s. For much more conservative estimates of the Chinese influx, see Orleans, *Every Fifth Child*, 89, and Drew, "Sinkiang," 208.

301. See, for example, Moseley, *Consolidation*, 117, and Deal, "National Minority," 180. Soviet writers have also contended that Peking has resettled the borders. The following extract is from an article that appeared in the CPSU theoretical journal *Kommunist* during 1967: "[T]he settlement of Chinese is being carried out in such a way as to isolate the non-Chinese nationalities from the outside world, even to the extent of re-settling them in the interior of China. In some sectors the local population has been completely replaced by military units and military colonies." Cited in "National Minorities of Western China," 255.

302. In September 1977, the Institute for Strategic Studies estimated the total number serving in the Chinese armed forces as just under 4 million, 300,000 of whom were in the navy. See *Keesing's Contemporary Archives* (1977), 28725–28726. In 1981 a member of the Chinese Politburo

visited Sinkiang-Uighur AR, where he is reported to have "repeatedly stressed" that army personnel stationed there "must love the frontiers and settle contentedly in the frontier lands." *International Herald Tribune*, May 29, 1981.

303. Extracted from table 5, Deal, "National Minority," 142–147. A thirteenth autonomous district was added prior to 1982, but no data concerning its composition were located.

304. The Han-nan Li and Miao Autonomous District.

305. The two are the Yen-pien Korean AC and the Liang-shan Yi AC.

306. There have been a few very slight alterations involving the exchange of a few villages between Montenegro and Bosnia-Hercegovina (1949), the latter and Croatia (1953, 1956), and Croatia and Slovenia (1956).

307. Shoup, *Communism and Yugoslav National Question*, 111.

308. Ibid., 113.

309. See chapter 6.

310. For details, see below. As it turned out, perhaps a fourth of the new settlers within Vojvodina had been born in Croatia, but larger numbers had been born in Bosnia-Hercegovina and in Serbia (proper). This breakdown is deduced from data in table 6 in "Internal Migration," *Yugoslav Survey*, 17 (February 1976): 8.

311. Recall that the Serbs from Croatia had proven the most loyal component of Tito's partisan movement.

312. For a series of maps showing the internal borders of Yugoslavia between 1918 and 1946, see Hoffman and Neal, *Yugoslavia and New Communism*, 56–57.

313. See table 5, column 2.

314. See chapter 6. Milovan Djilas offers a later date. He reports that as late as 1943 the leaders had plans to make Bosnia-Hercegovina an autonomous province within the Republic of Serbia. However, they became afraid that "autonomy under either Serbia or Croatia would have encouraged further strife." (Djilas, *Wartime*, 356.) According to his account, the final approval for separate republican status was routinely agreed upon in January 1944.

315. In 1948, the number was 1,136,000. See Shoup, *Communism and the Yugoslav National Question*, 266.

316. The commingling of Serbs and Croats in some areas of Bosnia-Hercegovina would have made the drawing of ethnic borders a most difficult task. However, there were large areas, such as that south and southwest of Sarajevo, in which Croatians predominated and which could easily have been affixed to Croatia. See the ethnic map in Hoffman and Neal, *Yugoslavia and New Communism*, 30. And, of course, intraregional population transfers could also have been undertaken.

317. Usually, but not always, the existence of a *Staatsvolk* is reflected in the name of the state. Marxist-Leninist examples include Albania, Bulgaria, Cambodia, China, the German Democratic Republic, Hungary, the Dem-

ocratic People's Republic of Korea, Laos, Mongolia, Poland, Rumania, and Vietnam. In a number of cases, the popular name of a state reflects the presence of a *Staatsvolk* even though the official name does not (for example, the use of England as a synonym for the United Kingdom). Russia is the sole Marxist-Leninist example of this tendency. The only Marxist-Leninist states whose official or popular name does not suggest a *Staatsvolk* are Cuba, Czechoslovakia, and Yugoslavia.

318. Rusinow (*Yugoslav Experiment*) reports that some party leaders favored Sarajevo (the capital of Bosnia-Hercegovina) as an ethnically more neutral capital than Belgrade for the new federation.

319. Djilas, *Wartime*, 149.

320. Vucinich, "Nationalism and Communism," 268.

321. Vucinich (ibid.) rests his case principally upon the statement that "after World War I, those [Montenegrins] who favored complete integration with the Serbs under the Karadjordjevic dynasty (fusionists or *bjelasi*) prevailed against those who favored a separate Montenegro within the Yugoslav federation (federalists or *zelenasi*)." By contrast, Phyllis Autry (*Yugoslavia*, 56) maintains that there were many Montenegrins who were adamantly opposed to either of these solutions: "Many Montenegrins were opposed to the incorporation of their country in a Yugoslav state in 1918, and the new government had to be enforced on the people." As its name implied (Kingdom of the Serbs, Croats, and Slovenes), Montenegrins were treated as Serbs in the new state. During World War II, the independent Kingdom of Montenegro was established as part of the Italian Empire of Benito Mussolini. Djilas himself acknowledges that there were what he terms Montenegrin "separatists" of both right and left leanings during the war, as well as those in favor of unification with Serbia. (Djilas, *Wartime*, 18, 19, 22, 66, 76.) Moreover, Djilas recounts how he made a stirring wartime speech before a politically broad spectrum of Montenegrins, in which he stressed "the traditional Montenegrin defiance, and a self-sacrificing devotion to homeland." (Ibid., 44.) Shortly thereafter he wrote a letter to the party's Central Committee, emphasizing the need for "a platform for the struggle of the Montenegro people." (Ibid., 63–64.) In sum, Djilas here is acknowledging that a separate Montenegrin identity does exist, despite his above-cited assertion that it does not. (On page 27, he also acknowledges that at least some of the partisan forces of Montenegro literally fought under a Montenegrin flag.) The confusion surrounding this issue is indicated by Hoffman and Neal (*Yugoslavia and New Communism*), who on page 31 treat the Montenegrins as a distinct national group despite an ethnic map on the facing page that treats Montenegrins and Serbs as identical. The Montenegrin masses have done little to dispel this confusion. When given the opportunity to identify themselves as Montenegrin in the postwar censuses, nearly all Montenegrins did so. On the other hand, the drop in absolute numbers of Montenegrins between 1961 and 1971 censuses (from 513,833 to 508,843) undoubtedly indicates that

a substantial percentage of those who formerly declared themselves Montenegrins subsequently changed to Serbian. (Montenegrins should have shown a growth of approximating the 10.6 percent increase for the entire country during the decade, so some 12 percent of all Montenegrins presumably changed their identity.) Such a change would suggest that, to many, the concept of being a Montenegrin has had more of a geographical significance than it has had as a fundamental ethnic identity. On the other hand, those identifying themselves as Montenegrin grew by a healthy 13 percent between 1971 and 1981, well ahead of the country's overall growth of 9 percent. Overall, then, the data suggest that Montenegrin opinion on whether they are or are not a separate people is both mixed and fluctuating, and that generalized statements must necessarily be erroneous.

322. Kosovo was originally classified as an autonomous region, being elevated to autonomous province in 1963.

323. Pavlowich, *Yugoslavia*, 186. If actually stripped of these two provinces, Serbia would be slightly smaller in area than Croatia (21,582 square miles versus 21,723) and somewhat more populous (5.25 million versus 4.43 million).

324. King, *Minorities*, 133.

325. See chapter 6.

326. The possibility of a population transfer was raised with Hungarian authorities at the Paris Peace Conference, but nothing came of it. (See Shoup, *Communism and Yugoslav National Question*, 103.) Milovan Djilas reports that the plan to expel the Magyars was dropped at Soviet insistence. Stalin vetoed the expulsion because he knew Hungary was about to come under a Marxist-Leninist government. (See Djilas, *Wartime*, 424.)

327. Table 4 in "Internal Migration," 8. By 1981, the Magyars accounted for only 18.9 percent of Vojvodina's population. See figure 6, column 4.

328. See map in King, *Minorities*, 133.

329. Ibid., 128, 136. There are fifty-seven districts within all of Vojvodina. Rusinow (*Yugoslav Experiment*, 17) writes that the creation of autonomous Vojvodina within Serbia was "a compromise between Serbian claims to all those territories in which the populations are partly to largely Serbs, and Croatian historic and ethnic claims to Syrmia." (The latter is a section of Vojvodina.) A Serbian claim to the entire area appears difficult to substantiate, however. For one thing, the province included some districts in which Serbs were practically nonexistent (in one, Magyars account for more than 90 percent of the population). Although Croats have been undergoing a net out-migration from the province since 1961, claims that they were deprived of a section of their homeland continue. (See Tudjman, *Nationalism*, 116.)

330. See Shoup, *Communism and Yugoslav National Question*, 15, where the author notes that "the autonomous regions were not considered areas where minorities could enjoy a homeland analogous to that available to the Slav nationalities, but were thought of rather as regions of mixed

nationality, which required special status in the light of the difficult problem of adjusting relations among groups with different national origins." In the case of Vojvodina, this "difficult problem" of adjustment could have been largely avoided, however, simply by joining southern Vojvodina to Serbia proper. This official raison d'être simply does not ring true, therefore.

331. 68.5 percent in the 1948 census. See table 5, column 2.

332. See chapter 6.

333. These were the years when Belgrade envisaged a larger federation including Albania and Bulgaria.

334. In two such districts, Albanians accounted for approximately 5 percent of the population. (See map in King, *Minorities*, 131.)

335. Ibid., 132.

336. When the state's Federal Executive Council was created in 1953, the law required that all republics should be represented, but did not specify either proportional or equal representation. By 1971 the law was changed to give each province two representatives. Finally, in 1974, each republic and province was allowed one representative. Similarly, when the party created a new Executive Bureau in 1969, it consisted of two delegates from each republic and one from each province; but, as altered in January 1972, each republic and province was accorded a single delegate.

337. Those who perceived the trend as a design for strengthening the republics should have been troubled by its continuance after 1971, that is to say, after the authority of the center had been successfully reasserted and the decision-making powers of the republics had been curtailed. It was in 1972 and 1974 that the provinces were elevated to coequal representation with the republics and the standard of one vote for each of the eight constituent units was introduced within the executive branch of the party and state, respectively. The standard has subsequently been maintained.

338. See, for example, *Keesing's Contemporary Archives* (1971), 24734.

339. Although regional equalization had been dropped some years earlier, Tito did assert at the Eleventh Congress of the YCP, held in June 1978, that greater emphasis must be placed upon developing insufficiently developed areas, particularly Kosovo. (See *Keesing's Contemporary Archives* [1978], 29237.)

340. From data in "Internal Migration," 6. The percentage would be somewhat higher if the total Yugoslav population was limited to those living within the country. By 1969 the number of Yugoslav *Gastarbeiter* working within Western Europe had reached 800,000 and soon thereafter surpassed the one million mark.

341. The relative strength of Serbs and Croats within their republics had remained essentially the same from 1948 to 1971, but underwent a sharp drop (4.1 and 4.3 percent, respectively) during the 1970s. However, the principal cause for these statistical changes appears to be due to a large

number of people declaring themselves as Yugoslav, rather than to a migration of peoples.

342. This willingness to leave "the homeland" for Serbia may be the strongest indication that many Montenegrins consider themselves ethnically to be Serb. However, the trend reversed itself during the 1970s, and the Montenegrin proportion of the population increased by 1.3 percent.

343. During the early 1980s, the authorities were extremely troubled by the exodus of Serbs from Kosovo Province, allegedly under great, coercive pressure to do so from the Albanian people located there. (The proportion of Serbs in the province had dropped from 18.4 to 13.2 percent during the decade.) At the party's Twelfth Congress, held in 1982, the current presiding executive officer of the party charged those responsible for the problem with desiring "the implementation of ethnically, nationally pure territories." See, for example, *Keesing's Contemporary Archives* (1982), 31672–31673, and *FBIS*, August 13, 1982, p. 15.

344. For official population data, see table I in Toma, "Czechoslovak Question," 17.

345. For official data on interregional migration between 1950 and 1965, consult table 3, in Toma, "Czechoslovak Question," 19. For data on the closing of the economic gap between the regions, see Ulc, *Politics in Czechoslovakia*, 17–18.

346. Next in order after the Slovaks are the Germans, who account for only one percent of the Czech region.

347. See map in King, *Minorities*, 113. Only one important pocket, located in easternmost Slovakia, is not contiguous.

348. The new party platform of the Slovak Communist Party explicitly contained such a plank. (See King, *Minorities*, 55.) Seemingly inconsistently, Stalin supported the Slovak CP's position on expulsion. (We have earlier noted Milovan Djilas's statement that Stalin refused to permit the expulsion of Magyars from Yugoslavia.) The explanation apparently lies in the fact that the Communists were not yet in power in Czechoslovakia; that they aspired, therefore, to increase their base of support; and that they could expect to do so by becoming identified with the popular goal of ridding the Slovak homeland of Magyars. Stalin's seeming inconsistency therefore actually harmonizes quite well with Lenin's strategy for manipulating national sentiments prior to the assumption of power.

349. The area in question had been annexed by Hungary during 1938 and 1939.

350. The provincial borders of 1948 and 1960 are shown on the map in King, *Minorities*, 113.

351. Apparently gerrymandering under the 1960 redistricting plan was not limited to Slovakia. Ulc (*Politics in Czechoslovakia*, 154) notes that a "remarkable case of socialist gerrymandering took place in 1960 when the predominantly Polish speaking district of Cesky Tesin was abolished and divided into two districts, each with comfortable Czech majorities."

352. Cited in King, *Minorities*, 116. Emphasis added.

353. Ibid., 120.

354. Perhaps worse off than the Magyars are the more than 300,000 gypsies who are largely concentrated in the easternmost province of Slovakia. These people are not even recognized in the census, much less extended recognition as a nationality. (See Ulc, *Politics in Czechoslovakia*, 14.)

355. Similar charges had been brought in 1956, when many of Czechoslovakia's Magyars had attempted to cross the border to aid their kin against Soviet troops. Indeed, it must be noted that the charge of irredentism had some basis in fact. We have noted that Budapest desired the area in 1945–1946. Visions of a greater Hungary were also raised in 1956, and in 1968 some among the Magyars called for reunification with the motherland. (See, for example, King, *Minorities*, 79, 81, 118.)

356. Unless otherwise indicated, the following data on the Magyars within Rumania are extracted from King, *Minorities*, 146–169. There are maps on pp. 151, 155, and 160 that depict the state's internal administrative borders as reorganized in 1950, 1952, 1960, and 1968.

357. In general, those administrative units that touched the border were more perpendicular than parallel to it. King (*Minorities*, 149–150) notes that the resulting east-west configuration of the borders conformed with the prevailing direction of valleys and transportation routes. However, the world offers several illustrations of internal borders (for example, West Virginia) and external borders (the case of the Hungarian-Rumanian border being most in point) running counter to such considerations. A government wanting to grant territorial autonomy to the Magyars of this region would therefore not be apt to be dissuaded by the local topography.

358. Most of the Magyars remaining outside were part of the earlier-discussed community along the Hungarian border.

359. See, for example, Gabriel Ronay, "The Growing Plight of Hungarians in Transylvania," *The Times* (London), November 16, 1977, and Kövari, "Accident and Necessity," 232. The latter reports that this dual movement gave rise to the cynical joke among Magyars that the second largest Hungarian city was Bucharest.

For a commentary on the enactment of laws that permit Bucharest to order Magyars to take employment outside their traditional regions, see Schöpflin, *Hungarians*, 19.

360. See chapter 5.

361. "Letter to the Compatriots in the Thai-Meo Autonomous Region," May 7, 1955, in Ho Chi Minh, *On Revolution*, 261.

362. Ibid.

363. Moseley, *Consolidation*, 157–158, and Kahin, "Minorities in Democratic Republic," 582. The ethnic complexity of the region may help to account for its change of name in 1962 to the ethnically neutral Tay Bac (Northwest AR).

364. According to the 1960 census, the largest group was the Tho (variant: Tay), followed by the Nung, Yao, and Meo. (See the introduction by Mai Elliott in Chu Van Tan, "Reminiscences," 4.)

365. It was located in the upper reaches of the Red River, between the two earlier-created autonomous regions.

366. Despite the great expanse of territory covered by the autonomous regions, some important national groups (most notably the Muongs, who were the second largest minority within North Vietnam) were not included in them.

367. Actually, only two such regions still existed at the time of the declaration. The Lao-Ha-Yen AR had been quietly dissolved sometime in 1959, only two years after its creation.

368. Radio Hanoi, December 29, 1975, as reported in *FBIS*, January 19, 1976.

369. Hoang Van Hoan, "Selected Works," 49.

370. One manifestation of this fear was that "land reform" and other policies that were apt to prove unpopular were delayed or never introduced in the border areas while the country remained divided. (See, for example, Hoang Van Chi, *From Colonialism to Communism*, 167.) See also the party's newspaper, *Nhan Dan*, June 21, 1957 (*JPRS*, DC-198), in which it is noted that the people in the border area where China, Vietnam, and Laos intersect "do not yet really believe in our regime." Finally, in the speech announcing the termination of the autonomous regions, the central and local authorities were instructed to "pay greater attention to the mountainous regions by practically helping the highlands and remote areas along the border where the compatriots live far away from the central-level economic, political, and cultural centers and where the influence of the old economy and culture is still great." (Radio Hanoi, December 29, 1975, as reported in *FBIS*, January 19, 1976.)

371. Kahin, "Minorities in Democratic Republic," 583. This type of slash and burn (swidden) agriculture is common among the mountain peoples of the region, so the number resettled must have been quite large. Kahin reports it included a majority of the Meos.

372. The one-million figure was reported in a 1968 Vietnamese publication. (Viet Chung, "National Minorities and Nationality Policy in the DRV," in Nguyen Khak Vien, ed., *Mountain Regions and National Minorities in the Democratic Republic of Vietnam*, Vietnamese Studies No. 15 [Hanoi: Foreign Languages Publishing House, 1968]. It is cited in Moseley, *Consolidation*, 158.) According to the 1960 census, the population of the Northwest AR was approximately one-half million and that of the North AR was 1.5 million. Thus, the new Vietnamese settlers equaled one-third of the total population of the two ARs. The relative impact of this influx of one million upon ostensible autonomy is suggested by the fact that the 1960 census listed the largest minority (the Tho) as only 503,998.

373. *Keesing's Contemporary Archives* (1977), 28278.

374. Ibid. and *FBIS*, November 2, 1976.

375. *FBIS*, July 2, 1976.

376. Turley, "Vietnam Since Reunification," 51.

377. *Keesing's Contemporary Archives* (1977), 28278.

378. See *FBIS*, January 18, 1977. See also the October 22, 1976 issue for an announcement by Hanoi concerning resettlement of nomadic members of minorities in the province of Dak Lac.

379. *Nhan Dan*, December 7, 1976, as reported in *Summary of World Broadcasts* (British Broadcasting Corporation), December 22, 1976, p. A30. The seriousness with which the authorities contemplated the plan to resettle 10 million people is shown by the fact that it was reiterated by the deputy chairman of the State Planning Committee in January 1978. (See *Keesing's Contemporary Archives* [1978], 28910.)

380. Meanwhile, the government was employing yet another type of enforced migration to bring about a more ethnically homogeneous state by pressuring the large Han Chinese community to flee the country. The so-called "boat people," whose pathetic plight following their departure from Vietnam was given world coverage in the late 1970s, were principally Chinese from the southern part of Vietnam. Still other Chinese, living in the north, were pressured into fleeing to China, and tales of their maltreatment at the hands of the Vietnamese became a factor in the deteriorating relations between the two countries. (See *Keesing's Contemporary Archives* [1980], 30075–30084.) In all, more than one-quarter million people fled from Vietnam to China. (*Keesing's Contemporary Archives* [1981], 31149.)

Soviet sources meanwhile contended that evidence had surfaced indicating that, during its period in power (1975–1979) the Pol Pot government had increased the ethnic homogeneity of Cambodia through genocide. For a Tass-originated account of the systematic eradication of the Cham minority, see the *Rutland (Vermont) Daily Herald*, August 29, 1980.

381. Cited in Conquest, *Nation Killers*, 137.

CHAPTER 10

A Question of Tempo

THOSE claiming faithfulness to Lenin's national policy concur concerning the ultimate outcome of the national question: merger into a single, nationless whole. However, the faithful have been riven concerning (1) the timetable according to which merging is to occur and (2) a proper role for the vanguard in that historical process. On the first point, Lenin had been very indefinite, and on the second, almost uncommunicative.

Although Lenin's prerevolutionary writings had been peppered with allusions to the inevitability of merging, fusion, amalgamation, assimilation, and the like, the time element had been ignored. Consonant with the Manifesto's dictum that "national differences and antagonisms are daily more and more vanishing" and that the victory of the proletariat "will cause them to vanish still faster," Lenin perceived the movement toward homogenization as progressing incrementally. The exact moment at which the process culminated was therefore apparently not of any greater concern to Lenin prior to the October Revolution than it had been to Marx and Engels before him. From the changed, postrevolutionary position of the decision-maker, Lenin had made a passing reference to the probability that "national and state differences . . . will continue to exist for a very, very long time even after the dictatorship of the proletariat had been established on a world scale."[1] But this statement was made in the euphoric days when worldwide revolution was believed imminent. Beyond advising that the process of homogenization would be a drawn-out one, it offered scant hint as to the timetable of that process's likely evolution within a Marxist society that was in turn within a world in which capitalism proved unexpectedly tenacious.[2]

This unanswered question of tempo is inseparable from the issue of a role for the vanguard. Lenin had envisaged a natural coming together of the nations as memories of national oppression faded. Beyond insuring the equality and flourishing of nations, this process would seem to prohibit any tinkering by the state. And indeed, periodic speeches by Marxist-Leninist leaders describe the manner in which the dialectically antithetical vectors of flourishing and merging interact as "an objective process" toward which the party's basic line is one of laissez faire. In the words of Soviet First Secretary Brezhnev:

> The further drawing together of the nations and nationalities of our country is an objective process. The Party is against the forcing of this process—there is no need for this, since the progress is dictated by the course of our Soviet life. At the same time, the Party regards as impermissible any attempt whatsoever to hold back the process of the drawing together of nations, to obstruct it on any pretext or artificiality to reinforce national isolation, because this would be at variance with the general direction of the development of our society, the Communists' international ideals and ideology and the ideas of communist construction.[3]

The line between not "forcing" the "objective process" of drawing together on the one hand, and insuring that "any attempt whatsoever to hold back the process" will be dealt with as "impermissible" on the other hand, represents a flimsy line indeed. An attempt to defend any aspect of the flourishing of nations (for example, the retention of the national language in schools or the retention of a particular autonomous unit) could be, and on numerous occasions has been, perceived as obstructing the merging process. The artificiality of this division had earlier formed the nub of a harsh criticism of a speech that had been delivered in 1961 by Brezhnev's predecessor, Nikita Khrushchev. The critic (a Ukrainian, whose criticism was later distributed among members of the highest echelon of the Ukrainian party) took particular aim at Khrushchev's statements to the effect that "Communists will not conserve and perpetuate national distinctions. We will support the objective process of the increasingly closer rapprochement of nations and nationalities proceeding under the conditions of communist construction on a voluntary and democratic basis." The criticism noted:

> First of all, an objective process is a process that takes place by itself, independently of human intentions. But a process directed by the Party and the State (and this is said by Khrushchev and in countless official publications on the subject . . .) is no longer an objectively proceeding but an intentionally induced and "predetermined" one. Secondly, what sort of "voluntariness" and democracy is it when the choice has been made beforehand by the

leadership; voluntariness indeed if it follows a plan—a "directed" voluntariness! If the leadership supports (and directs) the "process," just try to come out against what the leadership supports (and directs)! And if you cannot come out against it (as indeed you cannot) where is "voluntariness" and "democracy"?![4]

It was perhaps to be expected that political elites, whose ideology and founding fathers had assigned a positive role to human endeavor in aiding the otherwise "objective processes" of history, would find irresistible the temptation to speed up the process of merging. The situation would be quite different had Lenin ascribed some positive value to national pluralism. But Lenin had made clear that the pluralism, which for a time was to be encouraged, had no intrinsic value beyond serving as a necessary transitional phase leading to a higher stage at which national identities had withered away. To many Marxists, therefore, attempts to telescope this process would be as logical as telescoping the revolutionary process itself.

The situation also would have been quite different had Lenin specifically prohibited any tampering with the process. But Lenin had never stated that merging should not be actively promoted. Quite the contrary, those who were inclined to promote the fusion of nations could find support in several citations from Lenin, whose only restriction was that coercion not be employed because it would prove counterproductive. Thus, said Lenin, "the proletariat supports everything which contributes to the elimination of national differences." Elsewhere he would add that the proletariat "welcomes any and every assimilation of nationalities—with the exception of those carried out by force or on the basis of privilege."[5]

Given then (1) their proclivity for influencing historical developments, (2) the absence in Marxist-Leninist ideology of any ascribed intrinsic value to pluralism, (3) that ideology's designation of the elimination of national differences as belonging to a higher order of things, and (4) Lenin's blessing upon efforts to accelerate the otherwise objective process of homogenization, it is not surprising that the Communist parties of multinational states have in fact become involved in efforts to compress the merging process.

This tampering with the homogenizing process has not gone unopposed. Beyond his single proscription concerning the use of coercion, Lenin offered no firm guidelines as to what constituted proper versus improper efforts to hasten the demise of nations. As a result of his lack of specificity, those who at any one time have been in favor of taking a step toward assimilation, those who have opposed such a step, and even those who have favored a step in the direction of reencouraging national flourishing have all been able to find support for their cause in Leninist scripture. Programs, varying greatly in the degree to which they fall between the two poles of assimilation and pluralism, have been cloaked under the single rubric of Leninist national policy. Indeed, rather than exemplifying a steadfastness of purpose, the national policies of Marxist-Leninist states, despite their unswerving ostensible loyalty to Leninist national policy, exemplify a near constant state of flux on the continuum between emerging assimilation and emerging pluralism. Sometimes the vacillations in one or the other direction are quite radical and readily apparent; at other times, they are quite subtle and almost imperceptible.

When trying to trace the vacillations in the national policy of a given government, a number of signposts aid the investigator. Three areas that obviously deserve particularly close scrutiny are those in which the govenments have concentrated their hedging efforts, namely the areas of language policy, cadre policy, and population distribution. Is the government at the moment promoting the increased usage of the dominant language or the flourishing of the national languages? Greater or lesser exchange of national cadre? Greater or lesser geographic diffusion of national groups? Officially expressed attitudes toward the ethnically delineated administrative units are also very significant litmus tests of current thinking on the national question. Talk of downgrading the units or public questioning of their continuing value are often heralds of a desire to speed up the assimilation process. Equally revealing can be the current official view of a pre-Communist national hero such as the Kazakh, Kenesary Kasymov, or the Mongol, Genghis Khan.[6] The launching of a denigration campaign against such figures customarily heralds pressure for more rapid progress toward assimilation.

Constitutions can also provide important insight into the current thinking of the hierarchy with regard to policy on the national question. Granted, the constitutions of Marxist-Leninist states are not usually considered by scholars to be a reliable reflection of reality. Although a panoply of individual and collective rights are usually guaranteed therein, those same rights are difficult to discern in the society. Moreover, in the area of national policy we have noted that flux rules, while constitutions, by contrast, may remain unchanged for decades. Nevertheless, scrutinizing constitutions about the status of minorities can provide important clues to the prevalent thinking at the moment of drafting, concerning the amount of pressure that should be exerted to bring about homogenization. The same is true of party programs, the statements of leaders, and officially sanctioned publications, all of which can serve as evidence regarding the authorities' current position on the application of more or less assimilationist pressure.

The earliest clue to an impending shift in national policy is usually found in the use of the codified phrases, *great nation chauvinism* and *local nationalism*. Great nation chauvinism ostensibly refers to the penchant of a state's dominant ethnic element to act arrogantly toward minorities. Depending upon the state, it is therefore apt to be more specifically called Great Russian chauvinism, Great Han chauvinism, Great Serb chauvinism, etc. Local nationalism ostensibly refers to nationalism among a minority. Although these meanings are never totally absent, great nation chauvinism is more accurately understood in the Marxist lexicon as a shorthand for those who are pressing the merger of nations too rapidly, while local nationalism is a surrogate for a charge of too strongly defending the right of nations to continue flourishing. Therefore, if great nation chauvinism is described as the enemy of the moment, officialdom favors a slackening of the pressure for assimilation. If local nationalism is the principal enemy, more pressure for assimilation is in the offing.

The Soviet Union

Under the sway of Stalin (who, following the revolution, had become the party's recognized authority and leading spokesman on the national question), the early resolutions of the Soviet Communist Party made passing references to both types of what they called "harmful deviations," but indicated that great nation chauvinism was more harmful than local nationalism. Thus a resolution adopted at the party's Tenth Congress in 1921 noted in part:

> On the one hand, the Great Russian Communists working in these [non-Russian] regions . . . not infrequently minimize the importance of national peculiarities in Party and Soviet work, or else ignore them altogether . . . [which] leads to a deviation from communism towards the dominant-power spirit, the colonizing spirit, the spirit of Great-Russian chauvinism. On the other hand, the native Communists . . . not infrequently exaggerate the importance of national peculiarities in Party and Soviet work . . .

[which] leads to a deviation from communism towards bourgeois-democratic nationalism. . . . The congress emphatically condemning both these deviations as harmful and dangerous to the cause of communism, deems it necessary to point out the particular danger and the particular harm of the first deviation, the deviation towards Great-Power spirit, the colonizing spirit. . . . The congress therefore considers that one of the main tasks of the Party in the border regions is to eliminate the nationalist, and particularly the colonizer, vacillations among the Communists.[7]

Again in 1923, the party adopted a resolution drafted by Stalin which referred to the need to combat both chauvinism and local nationalism but made it "the first immediate task of our Party to wage determined warfare on the survivals of Great-Russian chauvinism."[8] Lest someone should miss the point or question the seriousness of the party's intention in this matter, the resolution elsewhere again reminded everyone that the leadership was "condemning both these deviations as harmful and dangerous to the cause of communism, and drawing the attention of the members of the Party to the particular danger of the deviation towards Great-Russian chauvinism."[9] Moreover, in his accompanying address to the Congress, Stalin denounced Great Russian chauvinism in terms usually reserved for such enemies as imperialism or revisionism.

Great Power chauvinism is growing in our coutry daily and hourly—Great Power chauvinism, the rankest kind of nationalism, which strives to obliterate all that is not Russian, to gather all the threads of administration into the hands of Russians and to crush everything that is not Russian. . . . Great-Russian chauvinism, which creeps along without face or form, insinuating itself drop by drop changing the mind and soul of our political workers, so that one can hardly recognize them. It is this danger, comrades, that we must lay at rest at all costs. . . . That is the first, and the most dangerous, factor hindering the amalgamation of the peoples and republics into a single union. It must be understood that if a force like Great-Russian chauvinism begins to flourish and gets its way, farewell to the confidence of the formerly oppressed peoples; we shall never secure collaboration within a single union, and we shall never have a Union of Republics.[10]

The general thrust of Stalin's speeches during this early period of Soviet rule found expression also in actual Soviet policies. This, it will be recalled, was the period of indigenization, during which the flourishing of the nations was actively prosecuted by the government. However, even during the indigenization period, Stalin made clear that the stress upon Great Russian chauvinism should not lead to complacency concerning the threat of local nationalism. In his famous 1925 speech in which he introduced the notion of national in form but socialist ("proletarian") in content, he inveighed against the danger of "an exaggeration of local peculiarities," while making no reference to chauvinism.[11] The oversight was apparently significant. Stalin subsequently exemplified a growing distrust of non-Russians, and a number of people were executed or imprisoned during the late 1920s for complaining about Russian political and/or cultural hegemony.[12]

Despite this backsliding, Stalin did not immediately cease his support for the flourishing of nations. Indeed, his most extreme statement concerning the long-ranged character of assimilation was made in 1929. Differentiating between bourgeois and socialist nations, Stalin noted that it was only the former that disappears under socialism. Then, after citing Lenin's 1920 statement to the effect that national and state differences "will continue to exist for a very, very long time even after the dictatorship of the proletariat has been established on a world scale," Stalin added:

> From these passages it is evident that Lenin does not assign the process of the dying away of national differences and the merging of nations to the period of the victory of socialism in one country, but exclusively to the period *after* the establishment of the dictatorship of the proletariat on a world scale, that is, to the period of the victory of socialism in all countries, when the foundations of a world socialist economy have already been laid.[13]

The passage of Lenin, to which Stalin here alludes, was a passing comment extracted from a lengthy pamphlet that otherwise had nothing to say concerning the national question. Standing alone as it does, it is susceptible to diverse interpretations, and forms a rather slender reed to support conclusions concerning Lenin's anticipated schedule for the merging of nations. As earlier noted, the statement was made in 1920 when a successful world revolution was believed to be near at hand. The theme of the pamphlet from which it was extracted (*Left-Wing Communism—An Infantile Disorder*) was that doctrinaire Marxists must adopt flexible tactics, so as not to abort the impending victory. Given this optimism, Lenin's passing statement that national peculiarities would survive the worldwide victory of socialism was little more than a restatement of his conviction that assimilation could not be accomplished overnight. Had Lenin lived to see his faith in the immediacy of revolutions proven badly misplaced, there is no reason to assume that he would have expected the process of the rapprochement of nations to adopt a static state of "hold" until such time as world revolution should in fact occur. Moreover, contrary to Stalin's rather remarkable contention, Lenin nowhere had assigned the merging of nations "exclusively" to the period following the victory of socialism in all countries. As we know, his dialectical scheme called for flourishing and rapprochement to occur simultaneously and to begin in any socialist country upon the introduction of a policy of national equality. Indeed, in harmony with the Communist Manifesto, he held that assimilation occured (albeit at a slower rate) under capitalism.[14]

But Stalin went even further, seemingly denying that merging would begin even with the victory of world socialism.

> It would be a mistake to think that the first stage of the period of the world dictatorship of the proletariat will mark the beginning of the formation of one common language. On the contrary, the first stage, during which national oppression will be completely abolished, will be a stage marked by the growth and flourishing of the formerly oppressed nations and national languages, the consolidation of equality among nations, the elimination of mutual distrust, and the establishment and strengthening of international ties among nations.
>
> Only in the second stage of the period of the world dictatorship of the proletariat, to the extent that a single world socialist economy is built up in place of the world capitalist economy—only in that stage will something in the nature of a common language begin to take shape. . . . It is possible that, at first, not one world economic centre will be formed, common to all nations and with one common language, but several zonal economic centres for separate groups of nations, with a separate common language for each group of nations, and that only later will these centres combine into one common world socialist economic centre, with one language common to all the nations.[15]

Despite what superficially appears to be a relegating of the entire merging process well into the period of world socialism, Stalin's analysis contained all of the necessary ingredients for the immediate commencement of the merging process within the Soviet Union. His principal theme is that assimilation will occur in a series of stages, with smaller groups being absorbed into a number of larger groups, which, in turn, will be incorporated into still larger nations, until a total fusion of humankind occurs. Consonant with classical Marxism, the crucible or unit within which assimilation is at any one time and place occurring is the economic nexus. Thus, what he terms zonal economic centers will each develop its own, single zonal language. As the principal language of a major economic zone, Stalin would presumably hold that Russian would become such a zonal language, a presumption that he would in fact make explicit in 1950.[16] But if economic forces determine the extent of the force field of assimilation, would not the multistage process of smaller into larger logically be proceeding within the Soviet Union during the stage of socialism in one country? Indeed, as Stalin would also make explicit in his 1950 piece, the Russian language had been absorbing lesser languages of the Russian Empire for centuries.[17]

Stalin's seemingly straightforward 1929 assertion that "the beginning of the dying away of nations and national languages" will occur only after the world victory of socialism was therefore not without ambiguity. Its release on the eve of the decade that would see the mass purging of party members for nationalist deviations, as well as a general trend away from the flourishing of nations toward russification, is susceptible to at least two explanations. Either he was about to undergo a rapid and radical transformation of viewpoint, or else his comments were intended to serve as a smoke-screen to hide the looming pogroms from their victims until the last possible moment.[18] Considering that he was about to embark on a program of downgrading the national language schools and of decimating the national cadre, the following comments of Stalin have a particularly hollow ring:

> What is needed is to cover the country with an extensive network of schools functioning in the native languages, and to supply them with staffs of teachers who know the native languages.
>
> What is needed is to nationalize—that is, to staff with members of the given nation—all the administrative apparatus, from Party and trade-union to state and economic.
>
> What is needed is widely to develop the press, the theatre, the cinema and other cultural institutions functioning in the native languages.[19]

Despite the rapidly approaching period of the purges, the party, under Stalin's direction, would once again endorse dutifully the view that the principal enemy was Great Russian chauvinism. A resolution of the Sixteenth Congress, held in 1930, reasserted anew that "in the present stage, the greatest danger is the Great-Power deviation."[20] However, a hint that a change was pending could be detected in the statement that "at the same time, the deviation towards local nationalism, which undermines the unity of the peoples of the USSR and plays into the hands of the interventionists, is becoming more active."

The hint indeed proved portentous. At the next party congress, held in 1934, the relative danger of the two deviations was described by Stalin as follows:

> There is a controversy as to which deviation represents the major danger, the deviation toward Great-Russian nationalism, or the deviation toward local nationalism. Under present conditions this is a formal and therefore a purposeless controversy. It would be absurd to attempt to give ready-made receipts for the major and minor danger suitable for all times and for all conditions. Such receipts do not exist. The major danger is the deviation against which one has ceased to fight and has thus enabled to grow into a danger to the state.[21]

Although these words indicate that local nationalism had overtaken great nation chauvinism as a threat to the state, the rest of the report, most particularly the attack on Ukrainian nationalism that followed immediately, left no doubt that local nationalism had not merely overtaken but had surpassed chauvinism as the principal enemy.

Great nation chauvinism did not regain its former eminence as enemy number one during the remaining Stalinist years.[22] Cadre were "denationalized," histories were rewritten to extol the virtues of the Great Russians and the debt owed to them by the non-Russian peoples; the use of the Russian language was promoted in all social endeavors; attempts were made to bring scripts, grammars, and vocabularies of non-Russian languages into the greatest possible harmony with Russian; the citizenry was regularly warned against nationalist deviations; and officials spoke increasingly of the new, supranationalist Soviet man who had evolved. In short, the trend became lopsidedly in favor of assimilation.[23]

We have previously reviewed how, following Stalin's death, first Beria and then Khrushchev set out to reverse this trend.[24] Under Beria's influence, the party's Central Committee resolved in 1953 "to end the mutilation of Soviet nationality policy"; criticism of past

hegemonistic practices (that is, Great Russian chauvinism) took place
within the upper reaches of republican parties; and leading party
officials were removed from at least two republican parties for
"abuses of Leninist nationality policy."[25] Khrushchev's commitment
to this same redressing of the balance seems little more than opportunism, for it barely survived his famous denunciatory speech
against Stalinism, made at the Twentieth Congress in 1956. A major
portion of that speech dealt with Stalin's perversion of Leninist
national policy, and the congress itself went on record as unambiguously committed to national flourishing.[26] Economic reforms
carried out in 1957, however, downgraded the republics in the area
of economic planning and management. During 1958, expressions
such as the "coming together" and "merging" of nations were increasingly heard.[27] In the same year, the government inaugurated
the "voluntary" principle with regard to attending either national
or Russian language schools.[28] During 1959, a number of non-
Russian leaders were purged for "nationalist deviations."[29] If additional evidence that a reverse swing of the pendulum was now
in progress was required, it was provided by the 1961 Party Program.

The program was a masterpiece in doublespeak, bowing in the
direction of national flourishing while laying out a blueprint for
accelerated assimilation. Thus the section dealing with the national
question, after opening with the uncompromising sentence, "Under socialism the nations flourish and their sovereignty grows
stronger," immediately promised the loss of both national identity
and sovereignty:

> The boundaries between the Union republics of the U.S.S.R. are
> increasingly losing their former significance. . . . Spiritual fea-
> tures deriving from the new type of social relations and em-
> bodying the finest traditions of the peoples of the U.S.S.R. have
> taken shape and are common to Soviet men and women of dif-
> ferent nationalities. Full scale communist construction constitutes
> a new stage in the development of national relations in the U.S.S.R.
> in which the nations will draw closer together until complete unity
> is achieved.[30]

Elsewhere, after noting that "the obliteration of national distinctions and especially of language distinctions, is a considerably longer
process than the obliteration of class distinctions" (which had, of
course, already disappeared), the program made clear that the
party planned to speed up the process of obliterating national dis-

tinctions as much as practical. In the realm of economics, for example, the program noted that "inter-republic economic organs may be set up." In the realm of culture, the program noted that "attaching [as it does] decisive importance to the development of the socialist content of the cultures of the peoples of the U.S.S.R., the Party will promote their further mutual enrichment and rapprochement, the consolidation of their international basis, and thereby the formation of the future single world-wide culture of communist society." With regard to education in any particular language, the party pledged itself to "ruling out all privileges, restrictions or compulsion in the use of this or that language," an approach which we have seen was tantamount to education in Russian for those who aspired to upward mobility. Finally, although mentioning "chauvinism of all types," the program made no specific mention of great nation chauvinism, while directing its sharpest barbs and most dire warnings against "national narrow-mindedness" and "national aloofness."

> [The Party pledges] to conduct a relentless struggle against manifestations and survivals of nationalism and chauvinism of all types, against trends of national narrow-mindedness and exclusiveness, idealization of the past and the veiling of social contradictions in the history of peoples, and against customs and habits hampering communist construction . . . . Manifestations of national aloofness in the education and employment of workers of different nationalities in the Soviet republics are impermissible. The elimination of manifestations of nationalism is in the interests of all nations and nationalities of the U.S.S.R.

In his speech of support for the program, Khrushchev reasserted that the "complete unity of nations will be achieved as the full-scale building of communism proceeds." His seemingly contradictory comment to the effect that "even after communism has in the main been built, it will be premature to declare a fusion of nations" was probably not viewed by the leadership as a prophesy of a long, drawn-out process, for the early 1960s were halcyon days when the economic gap between the Soviet and United States economies was believed to be closing rapidly and the formal advent of communism within the Soviet Union was believed to be only two decades away. As one American scholar summed up official Soviet thinking on the national question at this time, "there seemed to be an implicit intention of pressing for as rapid and complete Russification of the non-Russian peoples of the Soviet Union as possible."[31]

Khrushchev's ouster was followed by a retreat from the rapid assimilation model. The republics were reinvested with the economic powers that they had enjoyed prior to Khrushchev's rule, and some officials of the republic were given ex officio status on decision-making bodies at the federal level.[32] More significantly, talk of the merging or the "complete unity" of nations was shelved, and a more equitable balance between drawing together and flourishing came once more to characterize the speeches of party and state leaders.[33] The change was one of degree rather than one of direction. For example, no attempt was made to drop the "voluntary" principle in education that had been inaugurated under Khrushchev, and a number of trends outlined in the previous chapter (for example, the assignment of Russians to the second secretaryships of the republics) continued unabated. The shift was nonetheless quite substantial, as can be gleaned from a comparison of Khrushchev's speech to the Twenty-second Congress of the party in 1961 with Brezhnev's speech to the Twenty-third Congress in 1966. Khrushchev noted, "We come across people, of course, who deplore the gradual obliteration of national distinctions. We reply to them: Communists will not conserve and perpetuate national distinctions." By contrast, five years later Brezhnev would promise that "in solving any problem, whether it be of the political, economic, or cultural development of our country, the Party will continue to show solicitude for the interests and national differences of each people."

There are indications that the authorities were truly searching for some sort of new balance between flourishing and assimilation in this immediate post-Khrushchev period. In 1966–1967, a leading Soviet journal, in a most unusual simultaneous airing of differing opinions, published a series of articles reflecting a quite broad spectrum of opinion concerning the immediate direction that Soviet national policy should take. Both those in favor of much more rapid assimilation and those in favor of extreme foot dragging were represented.[34] More suggestive of uncertainty on the part of the authorities as to the most efficacious approach to take to the national question was the decision of the late 1960s to permit and *to publish the findings of* a series of sociological studies concerned with the relations of nations within the Soviet Union. Opinion surveys, modeled after what American social scientists call "the social distance scale," asked non-Russians their opinions concerning such matters as working or marrying with Russians. Using "harder" data, other studies examined the actual incidence of ethnic intermarriage in terms of numerous variables, as well as investigated the variables accounting for the choice of national identity selected by the off-spring of mixed marriages. Even when due allowance is made for the shortcomings of such studies (particularly the questionable va-lidity of responses to sensitive questions within a highly regimented society), the fact remains that these studies contained a great deal of data that contradicted the official myth of "the fraternal friend-ship of the peoples of the USSR."[35] Under the principle of "dem-ocratic centralism," such free debate and objective inquiry is per-mitted only until higher echelons have reached a decision on the issue. It would appear then that Khrushchev's ouster was followed by a serious reexamination of national policy to determine the ideal mixture of permitted flourishing and programmed assimilation.

Having probably been made increasingly sensitive to the perils of relinquishing an uncompromising pose toward nationalism by numerous manifestations of nationalism within the Soviet Union as well as within the states of Eastern Europe,[36] the Soviet leadership soon swung toward the pole of assimilation. Although Brezhnev's report to the party's Twenty-fourth Congress in 1971 spoke of the further drawing together of the nations as "gradual" and "in con-ditions of careful consideration for national special features and for the development of socialist national cultures," a lengthy section of the address entitled "The Molding of the New Man Is One of the Party's Main Tasks in Communist Construction" heralded a reemphasis upon assimilation. Moreover, not only was the speech free of any charge of great nation chauvinism, but it contained a paean to the Great Russians.

> All the nations and nationalities of our country, above all the Great Russian people, played a role in the formation, strength-ening and development of this mighty union of equal peoples that have taken the path of socialism. (*Applause.*) The revolu-tionary energy, selflessness, diligence and profound internation-alism of the Great Russian people have rightfully won them the sincere respect of all the peoples of our socialist homeland. (*Pro-longed applause.*)[37]

Once in motion, the swing toward the pole of assimilation main-tained its momentum. Brezhnev's speech on the fiftieth anniversary of the founding of the Soviet Union called for a new commitment to homogenization. After quoting an appropriate passage from Lenin, the General Secretary called for a marshaling of forces to promote actively the obligation of national distinctions and the removal of national barriers.

> Lenin spoke out very clearly on this score: "The proletariat cannot support any reinforcement of nationalism—on the contrary, it supports everything that helps to obliterate national distinctions and to remove national barriers, everything that makes the ties between nationalities closer and closer" (*Complete Collected Works*, Vol. XXIV, p. 133).
>
> In resolving questions of the country's further development along the path outlined by Lenin, the Party attaches great importance to the continuous systematic and thorough cultivation of a spirit of internationalism and Soviet patriotism in all citizens of the Soviet Union. For us, these two concepts constitute an inseparable whole. Needless to say, they are being cultivated in the working people by Soviet life itself, by all our reality. But conscious efforts by the Party and all workers on the political and ideological front are also necessary here. Our work in this area is a highly important part of the general cause of the construction of communism.[38]

Consonant with this injunction, a recharged militancy against national deviations became apparent. The number of trials for nationalist proclivities rose, and several non-Russians were removed from high-level posts in their home republics.[39] Editorials, articles, and a new law on industrial associations made evident that the powers of the republics were once more to be curtailed.[40]

All of these activities in the early 1970s were played out against preparations being made for the new Soviet Constitution. When finally unveiled, that instrument proved very much in harmony with the spirit of the party program that had been designed by Khrushchev sixteen years earlier. Whereas the earlier document had committed the party to the active pursuit of national homogenization, this role was now formally assigned to the state apparatus as well: "The state helps enhance the social homogeneity of society, namely . . . the all-round development and drawing together of all the nations and nationalities of the USSR."[41]

As we have noted, the new constitution elsewhere eliminated the technical right of the union republics to maintain their own militia and reduced the use of one's native language from a right to a possibility. In his report on the constitution to the Supreme Soviet, Brezhnev acknowledged that there were those who would prefer more radical surgery to bring about the merging of nations. Brezhnev did not dispute the desirability of the actions advocated by this assimilationist school, restricting his criticism to the observation that the implementation of such policies at the present stage of Communist construction was premature. His comments therefore offered an illuminating glimpse of the future.

Allow me to talk also about those *proposals that the Constitutional Commission found incorrect in substance.*

Some proposals clearly put the cart before the horse, failing to reckon with the fact that the new Constitution is the Basic Law of a state of socialism—albeit developed socialism—and not of communism. . . . As is known, a new historical community of people—has come about in the USSR. Some comrades—just a few, it is true—have drawn incorrect conclusions from this. They propose the insertion in the Constitution of the concept of an integral Soviet *nation* and the elimination of the Union and autonomous republics or sharp restrictions on the Union republics' sovereignty, depriving them of the right to secede from the USSR and of the right to conduct foreign relations. The proposals to abolish the Council of Nationalities and to create a unicameral Supreme Soviet follow the same lines. I think that the erroneousness of such proposals is clear. The social and political unity of the Soviet people does not at all imply that national distinctions have disappeared. Thanks to the consistent implementation of the Leninist nationalities policy, we have, in building socialism, at the same time—for the first time in history—successfully resolved the nationalities question. The friendship of the Soviet peoples is indestructible, and in the process of communist construction they are steadily drawing closer together, mutually enriching their spiritual life. But we would be embarking on a dangerous path if we were to begin artificially to force this objective process of the drawing together of nations. V. I. Lenin persistently warned against this, and we shall not depart from his behests. (*Applause.*)[42]

Despite the usual disclaimer of any intent to force artificially the merging process, this was a period when Brezhnev was unquestionably planning to promote assimilation more actively. As noted, the constitution authorized a positive role for the state in promoting the drawing together of nations. Moreover, although in his speech Brezhnev had explicitly denied that a Soviet nation was yet a reality, in an article published the following month he suggested that the homogenizing trend among Soviet peoples was reaching that quantity-into-quality point at which those traits held in common would become of "decisive importance."

> The formation of a historically new social and international community—the Soviet people—has become an important characteristic of developed socialism in our country, an indicator of the growing homogeneity of Soviet society and the triumph of the nationalities policy of the CPSU. This means that the common features of Soviet people's behavior, character and world-view which do not depend on social and national distinctions are gradually assuming decisive importance in our country.[43]

Still another straw in the wind appeared the following month in an officially endorsed article explaining what the new stage of developed socialism signified for the national question. The author equated the "homeland" with the entire Soviet Union and posited a love for it that transcends love of one's own national area.[44] More pointedly, he suggested that a further downgrading of the republics in economic matters was in store and that this step was discerned as hastening the process of drawing together:

> The country's integral economic complex serves the interest of the whole Soviet people as well as every individual socialist nation. Its development is essential for the all-round progress of the economy of every Union Republic, the objective material basis for the drawing together and stronger friendship of the socialist nations and nationalities.[45]

That the 1977 constitution should signal an acceleration of the merging process was certainly ideologically sound. If the process began under capitalism, quickened (as predicted by the Communist Manifesto) under socialism, and culminated under communism, then a period of mature socialism (the highest/last stage of socialism) should be characterized by a higher stage in the process of fusing or merging of nations than was true during a period of immature socialism. Indeed, it is likely that the expression "mature socialism" was inspired by Lenin's 1913 discourse on "mature capitalism," a discourse differentiating less developed capitalism from mature capitalism precisely on the basis of their varied impact upon the assimilation process.[46] During the former occurs "the awakening of national life and national movements, the struggle against all national oppression, and the creation of national states." Mature capitalism, by contrast, is characterized by "the development and growing frequency of international intercourse in every form," which underpins developed "capitalism's world-historical tendency to break down national barriers, obliterate national distinctions, and to *assimilate* nations—a tendency which manifests itself more and more powerfully with every passing decade, and is one of the greatest driving forces transforming capitalism into socialism."

Consonant with this historical perspective, Soviet literature, in the years following the adoption of the 1977 constitution, began to emphasize that the period of mature socialism was to be one characterized by more rapid strides toward fusion. As stated in *Pravda*, "The processes of the consistent rapprochement and all-around cooperation among all Soviet peoples and the strengthening of their fraternal friendship are intensified in the mature socialist society."[47] Nor was this objective process to be permitted to develop according to its own imperatives.[48] We have already noted the new stress Moscow placed upon managing migratory patterns at this time. We have also noted the rash attempt, following the ratification of the 1977 constitution, to deprive the languages of the Armenians, Azerbaijani, and Georgians of their official status. This attempt was part of a broader program reflecting the authorities' determination that the adoption of Russian would accelerate during the period of mature socialism. At an all-union meeting in Tashkent in May 1979, delegates from all of the republics dutifully endorsed a series of proposals aimed at intensifying and improving instruction in the Russian language at all levels of education, beginning with nurseries. In his opening address, Uzbekistan's First Secretary noted: "Under mature socialism a qualitatively new stage in the increase in the role of the Russian language is beginning."[49] And later in his speech, the Secretary referred to the Russian language as "an extremely important factor in the communication of all peoples and nationalities and in the acceleration of the process by which they are moving closer to each other."[50] Still greater efforts at spreading the Russian language were called for at the Twenty-sixth Party Congress (March 1981), and this led to the subsequent convening of a series of so-called "scientific-practical" conferences that were held throughout the various republics in order to discuss the means for implementing the party's injunctions. Among the practical steps called for was a substantial increase in the number of mixed language schools wherein (in the words of the Latvian First Secretary) "problems of ideopolitical, international education of children are successfully solved."[51] Apparently as a means of making this accelerated program more palatable, the Russian language now became cloaked in such euphemisms as "the language of Lenin" and "the language of the October Revolution."[52] And an Uzbek secondary school teacher of Russian, in an article provocatively entitled "Fusing Heart to Heart," termed Russian "the language of unification."[53] Yet another portent that the fusing process under mature socialism was to be implemented more rapidly than had been the case during the previous stage of socialism was a slight change of wording in the "national in form, socialist in content" formula, as presented in guidelines for the training of agitprop cadre responsible for lecturing on the national question. The guidelines called for the "creation and development of new, socialist customs and traditions—national in form, deeply international in their character and content."[54] The following month, a lengthy unsigned piece in *Kommunist* referred to the writer's conviction that "new prospects are opening up for the Soviet peoples *in the immediate future*, particularly in the question—a natural question of the Soviet people—of the future merging [*sliyaniye*] of nations."[55]

One of the more unvarnished articles concerning the national question to appear at this time was written by the editor-in-chief of *Kommunist* for another journal.[56] He attacked those who shied away from the concept of fusion, citing Lenin's dictum that "the goal of socialism is not only . . . the convergence of nations, but also their merging." He immediately added: "Such a clear statement does not permit any misinterpretations." Despite this unambiguous mandate, the author noted that there were those social scientists who had tended "to ignore Lenin's idea of the merging of nations or, worse than that, . . . to depict it as an echo of great power chauvinism." The author then suggested that this apostasy had deeply penetrated influential scholarly and scientific circles: "If we speak frankly, just a few years ago the comrades, who had insisted on the development of this idea [of merger] in an unabridged form and its comparison with practice, got into a difficult situation in some scientific collectives and editorial boards and were forced to overcome a certain psychological resistance." He acknowledged that defenders of merger had not been helped by those who had prophesied that merger would mean the eradication of all racial distinctions. Nations would disappear but physical differences, while undergoing "substantial changes," would never be totally eradicated. With regard to the tempo of the merging process, the author cited Brezhnev's comments concerning the party's opposition to both the artificial obliterating and exaggerating of national peculiarities, and he also cited the party's assertion that "the obliteration of national differences, especially linguistic differences, is a considerably longer process than the obliteration of class boundaries." On the other hand, he urged social scientists to analyze "constantly" the factors touching on the national question and to offer "timely practical conclusions." He added: "The problems, *which are growing ripe in this sphere*, should not take us by surprise or be shelved." (Emphasis added.) Overall then, the article was a clear call to social scientists to aid the process of fusion.[57]

Brezhnev's death on November 10, 1982, does not appear to have occasioned a turning away from the emphasis upon fusion in the period of mature socialism. Less than three weeks after the Secretary's demise, Konstantin Chernenko, a member of the Politburo, reasserted in an article the party's commitment not just to the rapprochement of nations but to their merger, and he hinted at the future eradication of the administrative organs of the national groups: "At the present historical stage and in the future the USSR represents the optimum state form for the cohesion of Soviet nations and ethnic groups in order to attain our program goals. At the same time, we do not regard the established national state structures as something fixed and immutable."[58] The opening segment of the first speech made by the party's new General Secretary after taking office was dedicated to the national question.[59] In it, Yuri Andropov spoke of the need to follow "a steadfast course towards the drawing together of all nations and nationalities inhabiting the country." In his most explicit comments concerning the route ahead, the General Secretary stated:

> Comrades, in summing up what has been accomplished, we, naturally, give most of our attention to what still remains to be done. Our end goal is clear. It, to quote Lenin, "is not only to bring the nations closer together but to fuse them." The party is well aware that the road to this goal is a long one. On no account must there be either any forestalling of events or any holding back of processes that have already matured.

Whereas his predecessor had warned against artificially accelerating or impeding the process leading to fusion, the new General Secretary warned only against impeding it.

CHINA

Because the Soviet authorities face few if any domestic problems as risk-laden as those arising from the states's multinational composition, significant alterations in that country's national policy are explicable almost exclusively in terms of the authorities' momentary assessment of the national question and how best to confront it. That is to say, the national question in and by itself is of such pressing concern to the authorities that discernible policy changes in this area are not apt to be the subordinate byproduct of decisions in other policy-making areas. Not so in the case of China. There the problem of national minorities is of lesser moment due to relative numbers (minorities accounting for 7 percent of the population of China, and nearly 50 percent of that of the Soviet Union), and the fact that the minority regions (particularly the border areas) have been ethnically diluted through the resettlement of Han. The national question has therefore not loomed as large in the deliberations of the Chinese authorities, and many of the government's most consequential actions toward the non-Han can only be understood as subordinate aspects of a larger domestic or foreign policy decision. Thus the two most radical shifts in Chinese national policy are better understood as the application of the country-wide Great Leap Forward (1958–1959) and the Cultural Revolution (ca. 1966–1971) to the national minorities than they are as responses to developments in the national problem itself. But despite the fact that national policy within China is more apt to be treated as a subsidiary or subordinate issue, the history of Chinese national policy, because of its indisguisable, extremely eccentric fluctuations, is particularly revealing of the scale of opinion that can coexist within a leadership that unreservedly and undeviatingly proclaims its fidelity to Leninist national policy.

The early approach of the CCP to the country's national question showed great respect for national peculiarities. Although the 1949 constitution noted that both "[n]ationalism and chauvinism shall be opposed," its Article 53 made clear that the emphasis was to be upon the flourishing of the nations:

> All national minorities shall have freedom to develop their spoken and written languages, to preserve or reform their traditions, customs, and religious beliefs. The people's government shall assist the masses of all national minorities in their political, economic, cultural, and educational development.[60]

This was the period of the Chinese version of "indigenization," when the strategic thinking of the leadership on the national question was colorfully captured in the official description of its national policy as "No Struggle."[61] Not only were local languages and other aspects of culture promoted, but differential time schedules for achieving socialism on the part of Han and non-Han peoples were officially approved. In practice the latter meant that minorities could be at least temporarily excused from unpopular "reforms," such as land collectivization.

The mood of this early period is perhaps best captured by the honors lavished upon the Mongol's greatest national figure, Genghis Khan. While the Khan's momentary standing with the Peking authorities might seem a somewhat frivolous, minor issue, that standing has in fact been one of the most reliable and easily read barometers of official policy on the national question. During the period, much publicity was given to the return of his bones to the mausoleum from which they had been removed years earlier to protect them from the Japanese invaders. Their return was heralded as illustrating "the profound concern of the Chinese Communist Party and of Chairman Mao for the minority nationalities."[62]

This period of courtship would survive from 1949 to 1957, but subtle shifts within the period are detectable. Thus, although an official summary of the experience of the first four years of national policy at first glance appears to swing further in the direction of the flourishing of nations than had the 1949 constitution, in that it proclaimed that Great Hanism "at the moment constitutes the major danger for the proper relationships among various nationalities," the overall thrust of the document was in fact in the other direction.[63] It prescribed "active assistance" for those who desired to learn Han rather than their own language, and cautioned those who believed that autonomy would lead to the elimination of Han cadre and settlers from minority regions.[64] While noting the tactical advantage of carrying out the party's tasks through "the use of *appropriate* national forms," it unambiguously warned that "respect for national forms is not to be carried to the stage of the preservation of even such forms which obstruct the progress and development of the nationality."[65]

The 1953 report can therefore be viewed as a decision to move slightly away from the erstwhile emphasis upon national flourishing. Flourishing would be continued but in a more carefully circumscribed manner; assimilation was to be encouraged but not pushed.

This slight leaning in favor of assimilation continued over the next two years. The preamble of the 1954 state constitution promised that the government would "pay full attention to the special characteristics in the development of each nationality." On the other hand, it did not single out Han chauvinism as the principal threat to an effective national policy as had the report issued the previous year. The 1954 constitution pledged instead "opposition to both big-nation chauvinism and local nationalism."[66]

An abrupt shift back toward the proflourishing stance of the 1949–1953 period was signaled by Mao himself in April 1956. In an address to the Politburo, Mao listed ten major problem areas (that he identified as "the ten great relationships"), among which was numbered "the relationship between the Han nationality and the national minorities." Though Mao maintained that on this issue "our policy is stable," it is evident that he intended a relaxation of controls over the minorities. Unlike the constitution, which was itself less than two years old, Mao's speech singled out Great Han chauvinism as the principal adversary: "Our emphasis lies on opposing Han chauvinism. Local nationalism exists, but this is not the crucial problem. The crucial problem is opposition to Han chauvinism."[67]

Mao's willingness to adopt a softer line toward the minorities at this particular juncture was, at least in part, but one aspect of his short-lived willingness to go along with Khrushchev's attacks on Stalin and Stalinism. Mao's speech on the "Ten Great Relationships" took place only two months after Khrushchev's famous denunciation of Stalin. In his speech, Mao noted:

> In the Soviet Union certain defects and errors that occurred in the course of their building socialism have lately come to light. Do you want to follow the detours that have been made? It was by drawing lessons from their experience that we were able to avoid certain detours in the past, and there is all the more reason for us to do so now.[68]

In particular, Mao singled out past Soviet errors about the treatment of the peasants and national minorities. And it was in regard to the latter that he made his case for emphasizing the cultural flowering of China's national groups. "We must sincerely and actively help the minority nationalities to develop their economy and culture. In the Soviet Union the relationship between the Russian nationality and the minority nationalities is very abnormal; we should draw a lesson from this."[69] Still another section of Mao's speech to the Politburo presaged a more favorable climate for national flourishing. In discussing the relationship between "the Center and the Regions" Mao, although explicitly warning that decentralization must not be permitted to encourage "separatism" or "striving for an independent kingdom," called for increased decision-making at the local level.[70]

The leadership's support for national flourishing carried over into the party's general program, which was issued in September of the same year. The program directed that special effort be made "to train cadres from among the national minorities" and asserted that "social reforms among the nationalities must be carried out by the respective nationalities themselves in accordance with their own wishes, and by taking steps in conformity with their special characteristics." While declaring its opposition to both "great-nation chauvinism and local nationalism," the program added that "special attention must be paid to the prevention and correction of tendencies of great-Hanism on the part of Party members and government workers of Han nationality."[71]

Consonant with the mood of both Mao's speech to the Politburo and the party program was a new slogan, "Let a hundred flowers blossom and a hundred schools of thought contend," which also made its appearance during 1956. It represented an invitation to the masses to engage in criticism, an invitation that the leadership presumed would act as a pressure valve to prevent minor grievances from developing into full-blown, antiparty attitudes as had occurred in Hungary. This departure from the usual stress upon ideological conformity was met with general skepticism and restraint until Mao lent it his personal public endorsement in a speech before the Supreme State Conference in February of 1957. Mao began his speech by noting that there were "two types of social contradictions—contradictions between ourselves and the enemy and contradictions among the people."[72] Unlike the former, the latter represented nonantagonistic contradictions, and giving voice to them could therefore be beneficially accommodated within the new China.

Mao then invited popular criticism on a broad range of issues, and one of the twelve sections into which his speech was divided was entitled "VI. The Question of the Minority Nationalities."[73] Given his 1956 speech to the Politburo, the section was unexceptional. Mao noted that "in certain places, both great-Han chauvinism and local nationalism still existed in a serious degree," but echoing his words of 1956, he emphasized that "the key to the solution of this question lies in overcoming great-Han chauvinism." He also reaffirmed the party's policy of permitting minorities to pursue a slower tempo on the path to socialism and he cautioned that "we should not be impatient." Breaking new ground, however,

Mao described both great-Han chauvinism and local nationalism as "contradictions among the people," thereby explicitly including them in the category of issues open to public criticism.

The Hundred Flowers campaign had an unintended effect. The hoped-for trickle of criticism appeared but soon became torrential. Scorching attacks were made on the most sacrosanct of objects, even extending to Mao and to the vanguard role of the party. Now aware that the Hundred Flowers campaign was a Pandora's box, the authorities moved swiftly to replace the lid. When Mao's speech of February 1957 was formally published in June of the same year, six criteria by which to measure whether criticism was legitimate or treasonable had been added to the original text:

1. Help to unite the people of our various nationalities, and not divide them;
2. Are beneficial, not harmful, to Socialist transformation and Socialist construction;
3. Help to consolidate, not to undermine or weaken, the people's democratic dictatorship;
4. Help to consolidate, not to undermine or weaken, democratic centralism;
5. Tend to strengthen, not to cast off or weaken, the leadership of the Communist Party;
6. Are beneficial, not harmful, to international Socialist solidarity and the solidarity of the peace-loving peoples of the world.[74]

Given (1) the key roles in Marxist-Leninist theory and practice of (a) socialist/communist construction, (b) the dictatorship of the working class, (c) democratic centralism, (d) the vanguard role of the Party, and (e) proletarian internationalism; and (2) the relative numerical inferiority of the minorities, it is astounding that the national question should appear on such a list at all. But it is incredible that it should head it.[75]

At least part of the explanation must lie with the unanticipated level of discontent that had been voiced by the minorities. As reported in the Chinese press, the minorities responded to the call of the Hundred Flowers by giving vent to broad and deep-seated dissatisfaction with the Chinese version of autonomy. The following are typical of the statements that appeared in the press at this time: "The Chinese Communist Party's policy of regional autonomy for the nationalities is that of 'divide and rule.'"[76] The present system of regional autonomy is "as useful as a deaf ear."[77] "All the principal responsible persons of Party committees at various levels are Han nationals [which is] contradictory to having the autonomous nationalities run their own affairs."[78] Cadre of the local ethnic groups are "traitors to their nationality" and "jackals serving the Han."[79] "The minority nationalities run the house but the Han people give the orders."[80] "Many rights in theory, few in practice."[81]

The publication of such complaints heralded a radical swing in Chinese national policy. Along with other "poisonous weeds" that had been discovered growing among the hundred flowers, elements harboring such counterrevolutionary sentiments were to be torn up by their roots. Not bothering to pause near that midpoint at which great and local nationalisms are described as equally pernicious, the authorities now abruptly replaced Great Han chauvinism with local nationalism as the arch foe. At a meeting of the Nationalities Affairs Commission held in November 1957, the principal speaker dwelled exclusively on the threat of local nationalism.[82] This brand of nationalism was said to have permeated the highest ranks of the party apparatus in the various minority regions, and it was further declared that "in certain areas there even exists to a grave extent the separatist tendency, the tendency toward secession from the big family of the motherland."[83] Moreover, whereas Mao had described the contradictions between the minorities and the center as nonantagonistic, the speaker now noted that contradictions between "local nationalists . . . and ourselves are contradictions between the enemy and ourselves." Further, while denying that assimilation was part of the party's policy, the speaker made clear that fusion was now to be given increased encouragement:

> The gradual fusion of the various nationalities on the basis of equality is the natural law governing social development. . . . Certain signs of fusion have appeared among the nationalities. . . . This fusion is desirable . . . and we shall never oppose the natural fusion among the nationalities, because such is the progressive trend of historical development.[84]

Following this conference, a full-scale attack was launched against local nationalism. Allegations that widespread separatist and anti-Han attitudes had been uncovered among the nationalities were highly publicized to justify the radical switch in emphasis.[85] In January 1958, an article ordering drastic revisions in the education of minorities in order to obliterate local nationalism described the manifestations of local nationalism as follows:

1. Hatred for and opposition to the Party as the instrument of Han Chinese chauvinism.
2. Opposition to the Government's relocation of Han Chinese.
3. Rejection of Government, Party, and Han Chinese activist leadership.
4. Demand by separatists for independence "even at the expense of Socialism."[86]

If any doubts remained that the authorities had become committed to a new direction with regard to the national question, they were surely laid to rest by the National People's Congress in February 1958. There, a joint statement signed by nineteen delegates representing minority national groups was read, whose motif was accurately reflected in its title, "The Building of Socialism Is Impossible without Opposition to Local Nationalism."[87]

The attack on local nationalism had not long been underway when the authorities launched the Great Leap Forward. As noted, the Great Leap was an all-embracing, country-wide program, and it can certainly not be attributed to official preoccupation with the national question. However, the post-Hundred Flowers assault upon the dangers of local nationalism did offer something of a bridge between the permissive attitude toward national flourishing that had characterized the 1949–1957 period and the effort to achieve nearly instantaneous assimilation that was to characterize the period of the Great Leap. As applied to the national question, the Great Leap can be thought of as an attempt to complete in one all-out, intensive effort the process described in the Communist Manifesto as "national differences and antagonisms between peoples are daily more and more vanishing." In the words of one Chinese authority, "the less differences among peoples, the faster development can be."[88] Struggle was to be waged against all symptoms of non-Han, national individuality. Different tempos on the road to socialist construction were no longer to be tolerated.[89] National dress, dance, and the like were discouraged. The Chinese language was introduced as the language of instruction for all grades. Intermarriage with Han was encouraged and, in some areas, reportedly forced. Huge numbers of Han were ordered into minority areas. Multinational communes were created that ensured that the minorities could not remain aloof from acculturating and assimilating influences. The study of national culture and national histories was ordered curtailed. (One historic casualty was Genghis Khan who was now reviled as a brutal despot.) Regional autonomy was attacked as "outmoded" and "unnecessary."

Quite expectedly, the authorities maintained that this seeming repudiation of Lenin's thesis that assimilation was to be reached via the route of national flourishing was no repudiation at all. Although somewhat gossamer, the underlying argument was not totally devoid of reason. Through the Great Leap Forward, the authorities hoped to short-circuit the historical process, thereby propelling China well along the road to communism while permitting it to hurdle stages that had been more sluggishly traversed by the Soviet Union. Since Lenin (as Marx before him) had presumed that progress toward communism would be accompanied by progress toward national fusion, a great leap toward the former demanded a corresponding jump toward the latter. For example, intermarriage was at this time encouraged on the ground that since Lenin had described the merging of all nationalities as progressive, intermarriage was necessarily a sign of "a heightened socialist consciousness."[90]

This bit of sophistry, of course, overlooked Lenin's oft-stated conviction that heavy-handed attempts to bring about assimilation directly, rather than dialectically, would prove counterproductive by arousing the suspicions and enmities of the minorities. And, indeed, this was the result of the Great Leap. Even before the end of 1958, while the country-wide Great Leap Forward remained in full swing, there were public acknowledgments of minority dissatisfaction and indications that the short-lived experiment in "assimilation now" had been discarded.

The realization that the goal of immediate fusion and its attendant radical prescriptions were proving counterproductive and had best be scrapped did not trigger an unambiguous, major shift in policy toward support for national flourishing. The promotion of immediate assimilation was replaced by its promotion at a more leisurely pace. No paeans were paid to national peculiarities. Rather, it was simply acknowledged that the onslaught upon them had been precipitate. The attacks upon traditional, minority leaders that had been made during the Great Leap Forward offers a case in point. The mounting post-Hundred Flowers attack on national distinctions had been accompanied by increasing references to the national question as a class question whose solution was therefore tied to class struggle. The real conflict was not between Han and non-Han but between classes. Eradicate the oppressing class within each national group and the national question was solved. Among other things, this approach would require that Peking discontinue using traditional local leaders, as it had hitherto been doing in the case of the more remote peoples. Attacks upon these leaders had backfired, however, as the local people tended to rally to their traditional symbols of authority, who thereby became an effective focus of resistance.[91] The first inklings of a retreat from this confrontation were not predicated upon a denial of the validity of the thesis that the national issue was a class issue, but rather that there were other dimensions of the national question that could not be ignored. Thus an article in December 1958 noted that "exclusive emphasis on the class question, mechanical application of the methods used in other parts of China, neglect of nationality characteristics and neglect of historical nationality barriers will all lead to disputes among the nationalities themselves."[92] In the months that immediately followed, a series of articles blamed the excessive attacks made on minority leaders and institutions on overzealous Han cadre, who allegedly had not really understood the party's policy on the national question and who, in some cases, had been guilty of Great Han chauvinism. The words of one article, "go slowly and relax a bit," best captured the predominant guiding standard of this period of retreat.[93]

The word *predominant* rather than *exclusive* must be used to describe policy at this juncture, because from the inception of the Great Leap Forward to well after Mao's death in 1976, it is evident that at least two factions—one pressing for a total scrapping of Lenin's dialectical formula for achieving national fusion and the other urging a slower approach, more in keeping with Lenin's precepts—were vying for predominance. While the former clearly had the upper hand during the early stages of the Great Leap, even this period of preeminence was not devoid of ambiguity. Consider, for example, the matter of regional autonomy. Consonant with the goal of rapid assimilation, voices had been raised demanding an end to the autonomous status of minorities. Yet contrary to this demand, grants of ostensible autonomy to peoples actually increased during the period. Indeed, the number of autonomous regions within the country was doubled during 1958 with the creation of the Kwangsi Chuang AR in March and the Ningsai Hui AR in October. Since the well-publicized preparations for the creation of these units preceded the inauguration of the Great Leap, it may well be that the authorities were influenced by the image of perfidy that would result from too abrupt an abandonment of a pledge. But these two important, highly trumpeted manifestations of a continuing commitment to implementing at least the form of Lenin's gradual, indirect approach to the national question, at a time when the extremists clamored for an end to autonomy, are evidence that the gradualists were not without influence.

The competition between gradualists and ultraists that surfaced at the time of the Great Leap was, of course, not restricted to the national question. It was part of the larger dispute over the form, direction, and tempo that Chinese policies should take with regard to all aspects and regions of the society. The decision as to whether the prevailing modus operandi was to be one of Great Leaps and Cultural Revolutions or one predicated upon more evolutionary progress and pragmatic considerations would pervasively affect the life style of Han and non-Han alike. But the fact that it was policy concerning the national question that became the first public battlefield of the two contending factions is not without significance. The adverse results of the Great Leap in minority areas had become unmistakably evident more quickly than had the social and economic dislocations occurring elsewhere throughout the country, thus supplying the gradualists with the wedge for their attack upon the radicalism inherent in the Great Leap. Unquestionably their hand was strengthened in this matter by the rapidly deteriorating relations with the Soviet Union and India, which lent the need to mollify the peoples near the borders an additional sense of urgency.

The early victory of the gradualists did not prove conclusive. What followed was more of a muting of Great Leap rhetoric than a call for the status quo ante. The multinational communes were decentralized; the unique traditions of national groups were reextended recognition in matters of eating habits and the like; the drive to have Chinese introduced everywhere as the language of instruction was quietly dropped; traditional leaders who had been scheduled to be purged under the party line that "the national question is a class question" were now promised "a bright future" by the country's leading newspaper; and cadre, as noted, were instructed to curb their zeal. But there was no overt attack on the recent experiment in rapid assimilation, per se, which, as part of the Great Leap Forward, was associated with Mao's prestige. Moreover, in the latter half of 1959, the ultraists mounted a counteroffensive. Following the purge of Defense Minister P'eng Teh-huai, who had criticized Mao personally for the excessiveness of the Great Leap, there were indications of a move back toward the policy of rapid assimilation.[94] For example, the study of Chinese, rather than the local languages, was again pressed.

This revival also proved inconclusive, and a lengthy period followed during which public statements on the national question reflected a guarded stance because their authors were not certain which faction would prove victorious. A *Red Flag* article in May 1960 noted that real advances on the national question had been achieved under the Leap's system of communes, but it coupled this with quotations of a 1949 speech on the advantages of a policy of regional autonomy made by Liu Shao-chi (in 1960 the leading gradualist and expected successor to Mao), thereby indicating that the party's original postrevolutionary, gradual approach to the national question had been the correct one.

A year of near silence of published expression on the national question occurred. When this silence was broken in April 1961, there was a suggestion that the ultraists had the edge. Appropriate policy was now described as follows:

[P]romote Marxism-Leninism and the thought of Mao Tse-tung on the theory of the nationalities question and the Party's nationalities policies, promulgate the proletarian view on nationalities, criticize revisionism, bourgeois nationalism and bourgeois nationalist studies, promulgate our Party's solution to the nationalities question and the accomplishment of its nationalities work, reflecting the three great red banners of the general line, the Great Leap Forward, and the people's communes.[95]

The criticism of (1) revisionism, (2) bourgeois nationalism, and (3) bourgeois nationalist studies might well be viewed as attacks upon (1) those contending that the Soviet model should be followed with regard to the national question, (2) those defending continuing regional autonomy, and (3) those defending continuation of the encouragement of national flourishing. However, the obliquity of the criticism and the absence of the customary, less ambiguous word indicators, such as class struggle and local nationalism, suggest a persisting uncertainty over the outcome of the struggle.[96] And indeed, late in 1961, only a few months after the publication of this article, another piece, appearing in the same journal, made clear that the gradualists had once more won the day. The article, written by a vice chairman of the Nationalities Affairs Commission, stated forthrightly that the notion that regional autonomy was no longer appropriate for China since the country had entered the stage of socialist construction was not only "incorrect" but "against Party policy." National flourishing was declared to be back in vogue: administrative organs of the autonomous units were instructed to use the local language in all documents except those intended for country-wide use, and Han cadre were told to improve their facility in the local language through intensive study. The traditional elites were not to undergo a purge and, in a picturesque command, cadre were told that in dealing with the ruling elites of the minorities they were to use the technique of "gentle winds and light rains," presumably in preference to the cyclonic winds and torrential downpour that had characterized the treatment of the elites during the Great Leap.[97]

The new emphasis upon gradualism was propagated through numerous articles and speeches and was given visible support by the party's highest luminaries, short of Mao himself, when Liu Shao-chi, Chou En-lai, Chu Teh, and Teng Hsaio-p'ing attended a conference on the national question held in Peking in the spring of 1962. Their attendance demonstrated the importance they ascribed to publicizing and implementing the new go-slow policy. A major reason for their concern was that the party's inconclusive backing-down from the excessively pro-assimilationist stance of the Great Leap had failed to quell turmoil in the minority regions. Unrest had continued among the Tibetans, and Kazakhs had engaged in a major revolt.[98] Mongols, among whom dissatisfaction had also surfaced, were given a special assurance that national flourishing was back in style when Genghis Khan was removed from the list of villains in time for an official commemoration of his eight-hundredth birthday.

The gradualists maintained their predominance throughout 1962 and 1963, but a statement attributed to Mao on August 8, 1963, heralded yet another twist in policy on the national question. "In the final analysis," stated Mao, "a national struggle is a question of class struggle."[99] The description of national struggle as a form of class struggle, a canon of the Great Leap period, had fallen into disuse in the post-Leap period. But now references to the linkage began to appear with increasing frequency. And the June 1964 issue of the party's principal theoretic journal, *Red Flag*, carried an article by the vice chairman of the Nationalities Affairs Commission entitled "The Present Day Nationalities Question in Our Country and the Class Struggle."[100]

Yet, while the title reflected a revitalization in the fortunes of the ultraists, its contents indicated that they had not achieved preeminence. The article was marred by serious inconsistencies, the result of trying to straddle the two opposing viewpoints. But on balance, it reflected a bias in favor of the gradualist position. Extensive lip service was paid to the proposition that the national question is a class question and can only be solved by the defeat of the feudal and bourgeois classes of each nation who "always put their own class interests above those of the people of the whole nationality."[101] But somewhat ingeniously, the linking of national and class struggle was now used to defend regional autonomy and the survival of national peculiarities, on the ground that class and not cultural differences were the wellspring of antagonism among nations. More difficult to understand is how the perception of the national question as an aspect of class struggle could be made compatible with the author's insistence that "our Party's work among the upper strata of the minority nationalities is to win them over to the anti-imperialist, patriotic united front. . . ."[102] The class struggle approach should logically have demanded the upper strata's elimination, rather than the position "that the establishment by the Party of a united front with the upper strata of the minority nationalities serves the revolutionary cause of the workers, peasants and other labouring people as well as the socialist revolution and socialist construction."[103] The only matter on which the article appeared to side with the ultraists was the question of whether Han chauvinism or local nationalism represented the principal threat. We will recall that the post-Leap gradualists placed primary blame for minority discontent upon the overzealousness of Han cadre, thus nominating Han chauvinism as the greater evil. By contrast, the 1964 article, while noting that both phenomena are "class contradictions" and therefore "fundamentally irreconcilable with socialism and the proletarian view of nationality," reserved all further criticism for local chauvinism.

> In recent years, in many minority nationality areas, local nationalists have become very active. Working hand in glove with the imperialists, foreign reactionaries, modern revisionists, and the counter-revolutionaries within the country, they have used all means to stir up antagonism between the nationalities and vainly attempted to break the unity of the motherland and restore the system of oppression and exploitation. Their main attack has been directed against the unity of the motherland, solidarity among the nationalities, Party leadership, and the socialist cause, their slogan being "Against the Han, for independence, and no reform!" Thus the contradiction between the local nationalists

and the people of the various nationalities has become a contradiction between ourselves and the enemy.[104]

The heavier criticism thus heaped upon local nationalists could be viewed as a harmless sop to the ultraists and one that would be acceptable to the gradualists since it was aimed at those particular leaders of the Kazakhs, Tibetans, Hui, and other groups who had actually staged revolts against Peking, rather than being aimed at the upper strata in general.[105] In any case, this vacillating document ultimately makes clear its author's overall predilection by concluding with a timetable for assimilation that the gradualists would surely applaud:

> As the common cause of socialism of all the nationalities of the motherland develops, agreement between them will become greater and greater while differences between them will become less and less. This is an immutable law of social development and an indication of progress. However, during the entire long period of socialist society, national characteristics and differences will continue to exist. It is only after the realization of communism and elimination of classes, with the gradual fading away and merging together of nationalities, that these characteristics and differences will fade away.[106]

Subsequent events were to establish that the strategy of the gradualists—paying formal homage to Mao's statement that "in the final analysis, a national question is a question of class struggle," while concomitantly pursuing a gradualist policy—was fated to fail. Indeed, the author of the article, Liu Ch'un, was destined for later purging because of his failure to follow a correct Maoist policy on the national question. However, the strength of the gradualists within the highest reaches of the party at this time is demonstrated by their ability to resist, for more than two years after its utterance, the radicalism inherent in Mao's 1963 statement linking national and class questions. Throughout 1964 and 1965, formal deference to the statement remained an empty gesture, exerting virtually no impact upon actual policy.[107] But all this changed abruptly with the inception of the Great Proletarian Cultural Revolution in 1966.[108]

A key theme of the Cultural Revolution was the attack upon "the Four Olds," identified as customs, ideas, culture, and habits. While the campaign was waged country-wide, an assault upon traditional customs, culture, and habits portended greater consequences for minorities than it did for Han, in that it would necessarily herald the end of national flourishing. Regional autonomy, toleration of national differences, different tempos for achieving socialism, and cooperation with traditional local leaders were all now violently attacked, and demands for proceeding with immediate assimilation were again raised. As during the Great Leap Forward, the most far-reaching measures demanded by the radicals were not carried out, and extremists operating in minority areas were often ordered by the central authorities to curtail their activities.[109] The chaos orchestrated through the medium of the Red Guards was not without restrictions, particularly where national security was involved.[110] It is therefore probable that the periodic orders to Red Guards to refrain from zealotry in the minority areas was due to a concern to maintain security in the border regions. On the other hand, unlike the period of the Great Leap, those favoring rapid assimilation could now savor the humiliation and purging of the most renowned figures who had publicly defended a gradualist approach to the national question. The list included no less a personage than the chief-of-state, Liu Shao-ch'i.[111] The most prominent gradualists were not, of course, purged solely or even principally because of their attitude toward the national question. It was their reluctance to prescribe radical therapy for all aspects of Chinese society that enraged their opponents. However, given the relative numerical insignificance of the non-Han peoples, it is remarkable how much emphasis was placed upon the alleged deviations of the gradualists with regard to the national question. Thus, the General Secretary of the party (Teng Hsiao-p'ing) was accused of abetting the 1959 Tibetan revolution. And a pamphlet aimed at bringing down the chief-of-state was entitled *Completely Purge Liu Shao-ch'i for His Counter-Revolutionary Revisionist Crimes in United Front, Nationalities, and Religious Work.*[112] After citing from Liu's writings of 1937, 1948, and 1954—all of which had reflected what at the time was the current position of the party and Mao—the authors charged him with being a proponent of "national separatism."

Those who were purged for favoring a more gradual approach to the national question included a number of non-Han, some of whom had long been among the most honored and trusted members of the CCP's elite. Typical of the allegations were charges that they had promoted "national splittism" and had been "trying to establish an independent kingdom."[113] However, beyond such extreme accusations, the principal allegation made against both Han and non-Han gradualists was that they had undermined the thought of Mao Tse-tung on the national question. The absence of references to Leninist national policy in the allegations is both revealing and appropriate, since the national policy of the gradualists, while falling well short of Lenin's prescriptions, was manifestly more in accord with those prescriptions than was the policy advocated by the ultraists. As the allegations of the ultraists made clear, the dictum of Mao that had been purportedly trampled upon by the gradualists was his 1963 pronouncement that the national question was a class question, and not his more Leninist-sounding statements from the pre-Hundred Flowers period.

Having achieved the upper hand, the ultraists agitated for having this non-Leninist approach sanctified by inclusion in the party and state constitutions. The party constitution of 1956 was attacked for stressing "only the special characteristics of the nationalities and the conducting of social reforms according to their own wishes, but not the party's leadership and the socialist revolution." It was further charged that this approach had fostered bourgeois nationalism rather than internationalism.

> By emphasizing nationalism to the exclusion of patriotism and internationalism, it in reality creates national schism. The broad revolutionary masses maintain that the following directive from Chairman Mao should be stressed in the new party constitution of the Ninth Congress. "National Struggle is in the final analysis a question of class struggle." The unity of all nationalities on the basis of the thought of Chairman Mao Tse-tung and on the socialist road should be stressed.[114]

The ultraists had their way through omission rather than commission, for the constitution that was unanimously adopted the following year (1969) by the Ninth Congress made no reference whatsoever to the non-Han peoples.[115] When contrasted with the previous party constitution's pledge to "make special efforts to raise the status of the national minorities, help them to attain self-government, endeavor to train cadres from among the national minorities," etc., this silence clearly betokened assimilation.

A draft state constitution, circulated during 1970, reflected the worsening plight of the minorities, although it did not go as far in this direction as the more extreme radicals would have liked. It did, for example, recognize the existence of autonomous regions, even though it did so only in a passage emphasizing that the regions were inalienable parts of a "unified, multinational state."[116] Similarly, the minorities were extended "freedom to use their spoken and written languages," but this was far more preferable to the extreme ultraists than had been the wording of the 1954 constitution that had granted, in addition to "the freedom to use," the freedom to "foster the growth of their spoken and written languages." However, most satisfying to the ultraists must have been the elimination of any reference to the 1954-recognized right of the minorities "to preserve or reform their own customs or ways." This omission left little doubt that national flourishing was considered a thing of the past.

The ultraists remained preeminent from 1966 until 1971. As the latter year wound down, a number of public disclosures and announcements suggested that yet another shift in the power struggle had occurred. Clues included a series of personnel changes in the leadership of the autonomous regions, a *People's Daily* article calling for more minority cadre, and numerous uncritical references to the cultural differences among national groups. During 1972 indications of a changing national policy multiplied. The Central Nationalities Institutes, closed down during the Cultural Revolution, were reopened; national forms were once more described in favorable terms; and selective quotations by Mao from the pre-Hundred Flowers period began to slip into print. Even more symptomatic of a shift was the reelevation to good standing of Teng Hsaio-p'ing, along with a number of non-Han leaders such as Ulanfu who had been purged during the Cultural Revolution. The reinstatement of these gradualists was made official by their presence at the Tenth Party Congress, held in the summer of 1973. And yet, a party constitution passed at this congress ignored the minorities almost as much as had the party's 1969 constitution. They were only mentioned in a statement requiring the party to "lead the people of all nationalities of our country in carrying out the three great revolutionary movements of class struggle, the struggle for production, and scientific experiment."[117]

This rather cavalier treatment of the national question, combined with the reference to class struggle, would appear a throwback to the period of the Cultural Revolution. And it may be an indication that the gradualists had not yet consolidated power. On the other hand, it may indicate a desire to placate Mao, or at least not to draw attention to the fact that a number of his ideas were now officially discredited. Quite aside from the potential impact upon the outcome of the power struggle, denigrating Mao could have dangerous repercussions for any ruling clique, gradualist or ultraist. During the Cultural Revolution, Mao's words, as revealed through the famous "little red book" of *Quotations from Chairman Mao*, had been elevated to immutable truths that the populace was expected to memorize as sources of inspiration for overcoming all problems. A sudden discrediting of what had hitherto been treated as divinely inspired, holy writ could exert an inestimable impact upon the populace at large. Not surprisingly, then, references to Mao's statement linking class and national struggle, so ubiquitous from 1965 through 1971, had quietly merely sunk from public view during 1972. And when, following the Tenth Party Congress, the gradualists stepped up their attack upon the national policy that had been pursued during the Cultural Revolution, Mao was spared. For example, the post-mortem attack upon Lin Piao, who, during the Cultural Revolution, had been the principal wielder of day-to-day power and, at the time, Mao's designated successor, criticized Lin for undermining the party's position on the national question, while making no reference to Mao's intellectual contribution to this aberration.

Consonant with this desire to avoid direct criticism of Mao, when the authorities decided to publicly repudiate his "national struggle equals class struggle" thesis, they employed the Soviet Union as a surrogate culprit. In an article entitled "Analysis of Soviet Revisionist's Policy of 'National Rapprochement,' " it was asserted that national distinctions would long survive the eradication of classes:

> Viewed from the long-term historical development the integration of nations and the extinction of nation conform to the law of historical development. But Marxist-Leninists maintain that the elimination of classes will come first, followed by the elimination of the state and finally that of nations. Lenin pointed out that mankind "can arrive at the inevitable integration of nations only through a transition period of the complete emancipation of all oppressed nations." Referring to Lenin's attitude towards the problem of nationalities, the great Marxist-Leninist Stalin pointed out that "Lenin never said that national differences must disappear and that national language must merge into one common language within the borders *of a single* state *before the victory* of socialism *on a world scale*. On the contrary, Lenin said something that was the very opposite of this, namely, that 'national and state *differences* among peoples and countries . . . will continue to exist *for a very, very long time* even *after* the dictatorship of the proletariat has been established on a *world* scale.' "[118]

Despite this commitment to a lengthy period of national flourishing, official documents continued to reflect an unwillingness to return to the phraseology of the pre-Hundred Flowers period. For example, the long-awaited state constitution, finally unveiled in 1975, did not vary substantially from the 1970 draft. It did reassert the Leninist dictum that "all nationalities are equal," but it aped the 1970 draft in granting only the right to use one's own language but not the right to foster it. In specific guarantees to the minorities, it fell short of the 1954 constitution.

This wariness on the part of the gradualists seemed to evaporate with the death of Mao in 1976. Even before the year of his death ended, the publication of his 1956 speech to the Politburo (in which he had pledged to "sincerely and actively help the minority nationalities to develop their economy and culture" and in which he had identified Great Han chauvinism as the principal evil) signaled a return to the minority policies of the early postrevolutionary period. Paeans to national flourishing now became common, and when plans were announced for yet another state constitution, this one designed to mark the complete victory of the gradualists over the ultraists, the minorities could sanguinely anticipate that the new constitution would be a marked improvement over that of 1975.

At the opening session of the Fifth National Congress, convened in early 1978 to approve the new constitution, Premier Hua Kuo-feng reestablished "great nationality chauvinism" as the principal enemy; affirmed that "regional national autonomy must be conscientiously implemented"; pledged to "try very hard to train cadres from minority nationalities"; to guarantee "without fail" the rights of minority peoples to equality and autonomy; and "to stress the use and development of the spoken and written languages of the minority nationalities."[119]

The new constitution underlined the renewed significance ascribed to the minorities. The preamble alone contained two references to "all our nationalities" and another to "all the nationalities." Article 4 confirmed the equality of all nations and the right of regional autonomy for compact communities. In addition, unlike the 1975 constitution, the new document conferred upon the minorities not just the freedom to use their own languages but the freedom "to use and develop their own spoken and written languages." It further signaled an official return to the flourishing of nations by granting to minorities the freedom "to preserve or reform their own customs and ways." In addition, Article 40 pledged "the higher organs of the state [to] take into full consideration the characteristics and needs of the various minority nationalities, [and to] make a major effort to train cadres of the minority nationalities."

Over the months and years that followed, the gradualist approach appeared secure.[120] On September 29, 1979, in the course of delivering the official speech in celebration of the thirtieth anniversary of the formation of the People's Republic, the speaker, after criticizing the excessiveness of the Great Leap and the Cultural Revolution, stated that Mao's 1956 speech "On the Ten Major Relationships," the major documents of the 1956 Party Congress, and Mao's 1957 speech "On the Correct Handling of Contradictions among the People" together offered "the guiding principles for socialist revolution and socialist construction in our country."[121] Recall that Mao in his 1956 speech had identified "opposition to Han chauvinism" as the cornerstone of national policy; that the 1956 party program had declared that "special attention must be paid to the prevention . . . of great-Hanism"; and that Mao's 1957 speech had also stressed the need for "overcoming great-Han chauvinism."[122] Other auguries of a return to pre-Great Leap policies followed. In October 1979 the Nationalities Committee of the National People's Congress, which had been abolished during the Cultural Revolution, reconvened. In an address to the committee, the rehabilitated Mongolian leader, Ulanfu, pointed out that "the socialist stage is a time in which all nationalities develop and flourish." He also made a strong case for meaningful autonomy, noting that "autonomous organs should not exist in name only."[123] At a more practical level, mosques were reopened, university examinations were offered for the first time in the local languages (although the first year for any accepted minority candidates would be one of intensive Chinese study), and a number of non-Han were appointed to high, if largely showcase, positions.[124]

In early 1980, *Red Flag* and all major newspapers carried a speech by the deceased Chou En-lai, a legacy that was now characterized as an "article, which expounds the national policy of the Chinese Communist Party, [and] is a Marxist work of immediate significance."[125] The speech, reportedly delivered on August 4, 1957, was said to have been refused publication in 1958 (the period of the Great Leap Forward) and had been subsequently "suppressed for over 20 years."[126] In general, the content of the speech was in tune with the 1978 constitution: Han chauvinism was depicted as a more pressing danger than local nationalism, and both were described as "contradictions among the people" rather than between the people and enemies of the people; differential tempos to achieving socialism were upheld; some nationalities were to be spared birth control requirements applied to the Han; individual languages were to be encouraged, and peoples without a written language were to be assisted in developing one; the language of the dominant group in an autonomous area was to become "the area's first language"; indigenous cadre should represent "a proper ratio of the cadres" in autonomous areas; and "the customs and habits of all nationalities must be respected." In sum, national flourishing was reaffirmed. Interestingly, however, the speech also emphasized the progressive nature of assimilation in the absence of coercion.

> The Hans are so numerous simply because they have assimilated other nationalities. . . . Assimilation is a reactionary thing if it means one nation destroying another by force. It is a progressive act if it means natural merger of nations advancing toward prosperity. Assimilation as such has the significance of promoting progress. . . . The Huis are so huge in number just because they have succeeded in absorbing people from other nationalities. To absorb and expand—what's wrong with that?

The posthumous publication of Chou En-lai's speech was therefore a reminder that, while the CCP had returned to a policy of national flourishing, assimilation remained the ultimate goal of the party. Moreover, the new constitution's several references to a unitary state and to the unity of all nationalities represented a further reminder that autonomy had strict limitations and that the authorities would remain vigilant for signs of "splittism."[127] Finally, given the history of the party's vacillations on the national question, the minorities could not be certain that the constitutional guarantees of 1978 would prove any more durable than had those of 1954. Indeed, the ephemeral nature of the 1978 guarantees was highlighted the following year, when articles and big character posters written by the editor of an unofficial journal were declared to constitute "counterrevolutionary crimes," despite the defendant's invocation of Article 45 of the new constitution, which stipulated that "citizens enjoy freedom of speech, correspondence, the press, assembly, association and the freedom to strike, and have the right to 'speak out freely, air their views freely, hold great debates and write big-character posters.' "[128] Although minorities were in no way involved in the trial, the case's pertinence to the national question was underlined by the fact that the defendant was specifically charged with violating Article 56 of the constitution: "Citizens must support the leadership of the communist party of China, support the socialist system, safeguard the unification of the motherland and the unity of all nationalities in our country and abide by the constitution and the Law." The case in effect made Article 56 paramount to all other articles, with the result that a claim to freedom of speech, assembly, association, and the like could not prevail against a charge of undermining "the unification of the motherland and the unity of all nationalities."

Since the policy of the gradualists concerning the national question had enjoyed official sanction since 1976, the further solidification of power by this element, signified by the 1981 ouster of Hua Kuo-feng from the party's leading office, was not immediately followed by any marked shift in national policy. At the same Central Committee session at which Hua's resignation was announced, a lengthy resolution on Mao's achievements and errors was adopted, in which past mistakes on the national question were acknowledged. The resolution read in part:

> In the past, particularly during the 'Cultural Revolution', we committed, on the question of nationalities, the grave mistake of widening the scope of class struggle, and wronged a large number of cadres and masses of the minority nationalities. In our work among them we did not show due respect for their right to autonomy. . . . It is necessary to persist in their regional autonomy and enact laws and regulations to ensure this autonomy.[129]

A draft for a revised constitution, circulated the following year, was in accord with this desire to enact laws to ensure autonomy. It appeared to support the augmentation of powers of all autonomous units and, following current Soviet practice, required that the head of each autonomous unit henceforth be a member of the indigenous people.[130] And a new party constitution, also released during 1982, proclaimed that the party "persists in the policy of regional autonomy." Perhaps more important than this formal recommitment to autonomy was the general importance ascribed to the minorities in the party constitution, a vivid contrast with the constitution of 1973. In the preamble, "the people of all nationalities" was now repeatedly used in lieu of the more conventional "the Chinese people" or "the Chinese workers and peasants."[131]

The post-Mao period was therefore marked by a return to the flourishing of nations. But this recommitment to national flourishing, as well as the constitutional concessions to autonomy, while certainly indicative of a major shift away from the extreme "assimilation now" policies of the Cultural Revolution, must be viewed against the broader framework of post-Mao national policy. The article authored by Chou En-lai, which had been released in 1980 and described as embodying the national policy of the current party leadership, had indeed approved regional autonomy and an expanded use of indigenous cadre. But it had also defended the past gerrymandering and resettlement policies that had left all autonomous units severely diluted from an ethnonational aspect. Moreover, the article had emphasized that Han cadre were to be important fixtures in all autonomous units, particularly in positions calling for what he termed "leading cadres."[132] And finally, as we have noted, the article had quite candidly championed the desirability of assimilation.

Confirmation that the newly ensconced leadership indeed favored those aspects of Chou's policies that fostered control over the minorities could be detected in the unraveling of events during late 1982 and early 1983. As the new elite consolidated its power, a somewhat subtle shift away from its previous pro-minority stance occurred. Whereas in 1979, publicity had focused on those 1956–1957 speeches of Mao in which Great Han chauvinism had been singled out for censure, the preamble of the new state constitution, adopted in December 1982, noted that "it is necessary to combat big-nation chauvinism, mainly Han chauvinism, and also necessary to combat local-national chauvinism." Moreover, while the new constitution did reserve to the indigenous peoples a number of showcase positions in the government of the autonomous units, it also introduced for the first time in a constitution a harsh warning against any separatist activities; Article 4 read in part that "any acts that undermine the unity of the nationalities or instigate their secession are prohibited." Furthermore, restrictions on family size, formerly restricted to the Han, were extended to the minorities.[133] And although the campaign to increase the number of non-Han cadre continued, a number of articles and speeches emphasized that Han cadre were to remain indefinitely as part of the power structure in minority areas.[134] Finally, references to all the nationalities as members of a single Chinese nation reflected Chou En-lai's view of assimilation as a progressive development.[135]

YUGOSLAVIA

The early, postrevolutionary national policy of the YCP was a reflection of the still fresh memories of the World War II period. Intense national passions, manifesting themselves in outbreaks of genocide, had surfaced during the Axis occupation. The YCP was therefore fully sensitized to the danger of encouraging awareness of national distinctions. In this charged atmosphere, a policy of indigenization, such as that introduced by the Soviets and, to a lesser degree, the Chinese during their early years in power, could be particularly counterproductive to the creation of a viable state. On the other hand, the party had pledged respect for a right of secession at least as recently as December 1942 and had been promising the lesser right of regional autonomy since November 1943. Too rapid a repudiation of respect for national aspirations could be perceived as duplicity and therefore also prove counterproductive. Moreover, a policy that did not appear to pander to national peculiarities could hardly be expected to attract the inhabitants of Albania, Bulgaria, and northern Greece to join with Yugoslavia in forming a single political entity, a goal that the YCP endorsed at the time.

The strategy selected by the party in order to straddle these two contradictory needs (that is, the need to carefully contain nationalistic proclivities while not seeming to depart from earlier promises) was to bypass the stage of indigenization and to embark directly upon the policy that was currently in effect in the Soviet Union. As would later be acknowledged by Stalin's successors, that policy was one under which form and substance were virtually at total variance. The Yugoslav Constitution of 1946 resembled the Soviet Constitution of 1936 (the so-called "Stalin's Constitution") in the many privileges and rights it bestowed upon the national groups and republics. Aping the Soviet myth-model, it defined the republics as sovereign and made a chamber of nationalities one of two coequal houses at the apex of the formal governmental structure.[136] It guaranteed "the sovereignty, equality, and national freedom of the peoples of the FPRY and their people's republics" and acknowledged "the special characteristics" of each "people's republic."[137] But, as in the case of "Stalin's Constitution," these constitutional tributes to the concept of national flourishing amounted to little more than a mask for a highly centralized system. A more accurate indicator of the intentions of the authorities at this time was the adoption of a coat of arms in the center of which "five torches are laid obliquely, their several flames merging into one single flame."[138] The discrepancy between forms and reality during this early period was so blatant that when the authorities called for a revision of the first constitution, some members of the redrafting commission did not fear to describe the federal structure as being merely a façade, constitutional guarantees to the contrary, with the republics having few if any powers.[139]

Unlike the cases of the Soviet and Chinese parties, then, the YCP embarked immediately upon a policy weighted heavily in favor of integration rather than national flourishing. Moreover, it is evident that the decision to favor integration was not due simply to Soviet insistence, for, following Yugoslavia's expulsion from the Cominform and the corresponding loss in popularity enjoyed by Soviet models, the goal of assimilation became less camouflaged. A new constitution (the Constitutional Law of 1953) eliminated all references to the sovereignty of the republics. Moving farther from the Soviet model, it also demoted the Council of Nationalities to a subordinate part of the house that had hitherto been its coequal. The name of its replacement, the Council of Producers, was also not without significance, for the new emphasis upon the production unit as a focus for identity was designed, in its architect's words, as a "new factor which creates a socialist community of a new type in which language and national culture become a secondary factor."[140] Consciousness of membership in the enterprise was seen as a method of diminishing national consciousness, thereby promoting a natural merger of peoples.

There were nonconstitutional straws in the wind at this time also. Going beyond the Soviet notion of the exchange of cadre between republics, a Yugoslav campaign was launched in the early 1950s to have artists, performers, writers, and the like partake in interrepublic exchange programs. Presumably the authorities hoped that breaking down cultural isolation would hasten the development of a single culture. Another indication that assimilation was being encouraged became evident with the 1953 census. Unlike that of 1948, the new census offered the option of listing one's national identity as "Yugoslav." (By contrast, censuses in the Soviet Union had never offered the option of a nation-transcending identity [such as "Soviet" or the nonethnic spelling of "Russian"].) Still another portent was the increasing frequency with which nationalist proclivities were attacked beginning in 1953; party membership, the creative arts, and education (including textbooks) were particularly criticized.[141] A still more ominous omen of looming assimilation, at least so far as the Croats were concerned, was the 1954 declaration that Serbian, Montenegrin, and Croatian constituted a single language, accompanied by the announcement of the formation of a committee to prepare a single dictionary reflecting this unity.

The impact of this assimilationist pressure was most visible in the case of nationalities (that is, those without republic status). The consolidation of their schools with those in which Serbian/Croatian was the language of instruction underwent a rapid growth during the 1950s. In other schools, the number of years of instruction in Serbian/Croatian underwent a progressive increase. And the provincial culture committees for minorities, after a steady deterioration in their influence, were formally abolished in 1957.

The decision to pursue assimilation more openly and more vigorously following the rupture with Moscow had unquestionably been related to that development. The rupture provided both the opportunity and the need for a more undisguised approach to merging. On the one hand, Moscow was now cast in the same unifying role of the outside threat that the Axis powers had so ably performed during the recent wartime period; anyone who resisted integrationist pressures could henceforth be branded as "cominformist," a new synonym for "traitor." At the same time, the new adversary role played by the Soviet Union highlighted the danger of national divisions within Yugoslavia. Given the history of Moscow's directives to the YCP concerning the manner in which the national question was to be exploited, particularly those during the 1920s and '30s, Belgrade could well expect Moscow to renew its interest in the Trojan horses represented by the various national groups within Yugoslavia. Rapid strides toward assimilation could thwart such a Soviet tactic. Moreover, in evaluating the likelihood of achieving such rapid strides, the YCP could find grounds for optimism in the fact that the concept of a single people was not totally alien to the Yugoslav tradition. There were numerous precedents for maintaining that the major ethnic elements within the country (the Slavs) comprised a single nation. Recall (1) that this was the presumption underlying the creation of Yugoslavia in 1919; (2) that the adoption of the country's new name (Yugoslavia) in 1929 was intended as a testament to this single national identity;[142] (3) that several factions, including the Socialist Party, persevered in this position; and (4) that the YCP had itself supported the one-nation concept until forced to recant in 1925 under great pressure from Stalin and the Comintern.

Many factors therefore accounted for the YCP's decision to promote assimilation more openly. Yet, even while doing so, the leadership's cautious language manifested a continuing fear of triggering national reactions on the part of the individual nations. With each step taken toward assimilation, reassurances were given that no attempt was being made to obliterate the nations and their cultures. References to assimilation were eschewed, as were references to less offensive Leninist terms, such as rapprochement, fusion, merger, and the like. The practices of using innocuous-sounding substitutes and that of coupling references to concrescence with reassurances concerning the continuing viability of national cultures were apparent in a speech delivered in early 1958 by the president of the Cultural Exchange Assembly (itself an organ specifically designed to foster a merging of the cultures). The president stated in part: "Although in the process which is developing in Yugoslavia the structure of the nations is changed in the direction of *ever-greater inter-relatedness*, the independent cultural development of each nation was, and remains, the condition for cooperation and the further drawing together of our peoples."[143]

The party program of 1958 was only slightly more forthright. It noted with evident satisfaction the growth of a "socialist Yugoslav consciousness" and elsewhere averred support "for the steady consolidation of the brotherhood and unity of the peoples of Yugoslavia."[144] Still elsewhere, however, it advanced the customary assurances that there was no intention to obliterate the nations and their republics.

Despite the program's verbal equivocation, in invoking a "socialist Yugoslav consciousness" the YCP leadership displayed a growing willingness to acknowledge publicly the course of action that it had been actively pursuing for some years. It was hardly a coincidence that a Yugoslav consciousness, elevated to the level of an established *ism* by the coining of the term Yugoslavianism (*Jugoslovenstvo*), was also a key element in a work written by the YCP's leading theoretician, Edvard Kardelj, and published in the same year as the party program.[145] Although defenders of the prerogatives of the individual national groups would later find statements in the work that they would find compatible with their own cause, the overall thrust of the document was definitely intended as a justification for, and a prophecy of, assimilation. Kardelj avoided laying out a precise timetable for the disappearance of national groups, but he definitely predicted their demise: "Just as the nation appeared on the basis of the specific division of labor in the epoch of capitalism, so will it disappear gradually from the historical stage as a definite social historical category with the appearance of new forms and dimensions of the social division of labor which the socialist, that is, communist social order will bring."[146] Kardelj then referred to the disappearance of nations as an "objective," but one that cannot be "attained by an imposed or artificial merger of language and culture, as Stalin thought, but by the further development of productive forces and a higher level of human civilization, adapted to these new productive forces of humanity."[147] Kardelj's objection to Stalinist tactics was not due to any fondness for national distinctions.[148] Following Lenin's lead, he opposed blatant attempts at assimilation because of a belief that they would prove counter-productive. People would not become "denationalized" through being denied their language, he asserted, but through a perceived need, nurtured by changes in socioeconomic relations, for membership in a larger community, one transcending their national group.[149] In short, national distinctions were to be tolerated for a time, but since, under socialism, nations no longer had a progressive socioeconomic role to perform, they were destined to disappear.

The foregoing, of course, is all good Leninism, and Leninist terminology, such as "rapprochement" and "merger," is liberally interspersed throughout Kardelj's work. In futher harmony with Lenin (and Stalin), Kardelj also indicated that while the process of merging is a worldwide one, it will proceed by stages through ever larger regional groups. One of these way-units would be "Yugoslavian." If this were all he had to say, Kardelj's scenario would be compatible with a very slow rate of assimilation leading to the obliteration of local nations within a regional group identity only at some very remote future date. However, by employing the view that the South Slavs are intimately related, Kardelj was able to project a telescoped schedule for amalgamation:

> There is no doubt that the ethnic and cultural kinship of the Yugoslav peoples is a very important factor in their rapprochement. This very factor, even in the past, was one of the driving forces in the struggle for their unification. ... Ethnic kinship and cultural affinity of the peoples of Yugoslavia, it is understood, give to this organism a characteristically appearing form and strength, facilitating the process of its internal cohesion.[150]

Kardelj acknowledged that this ethnic and cultural kinship was only "one of the driving forces" leading to a single "organism." Otherwise, he noted, the rapprochement would have already occurred. Consonant with Marxist theory, socioeconomic forces were pinpointed as the principal factor. But, because of the particularly tight "ethnic and cultural kinship" of the South Slavs, the new socioeconomic forces would be able to bring about the merger of the nations of Yugoslavia much more quickly than would otherwise be the case. By thus returning to a position quite close to that held by the YCP prior to 1925 (that is, that the Croats, Macedonians,

Montenegrins, Serbs, and Slovenes were offshoots of a single stem), Kardelj was able to predict/justify an accelerated merging.

The official position of the authorities was therefore (1) that a Yugoslavian consciousness was developing and this was a progressive and desirable development, and (2) that this new sense of group consciousness did not represent a threat to the survival of the individual cultures. At a more realistic level, the launching of *Jugoslovenstvo* was both a signal that increased pro-assimilationist activity was in prospect, and a trial balloon to test reaction to such integration. With regard to the former, an early intimation of an impending stress upon integration was offered at the Seventh Party Congress in 1958. There, a rather innocuous phrase that could be interpreted to permit the individual republic wings of the party some very limited discretion in decision-making was rescinded in the name of keeping the party a "united organization."[151] Moreover, following the publication of the party's 1958 program, with its official blessing upon an emerging Yugoslav consciousness, a series of articles advocating a single Yugoslav culture began to appear. Yet another development was the 1960 appearance of the dictionary predicated upon the oneness of the Croatian, Montenegrin, and Serbian languages. The 1961 census also reflected a benign official view toward a Yugoslavian identity. We have noted that the 1953 census permitted people to describe their national identity as Yugoslavian and that the overwhelming number of people assigned this designation were the Moslems. But even though "Moslem" had subsequently been designated a national category for the purposes of the census, the 1961 census still retained the category of Yugoslav. Tito lent his own weighty prestige to *Jugoslovenstvo* in early 1962, when in a speech he spoke of the need for "a uniform socialist culture."[152]

On the other hand, the launching of the *Jugoslovenstvo* campaign provoked a serious backlash. Official complaints of foot dragging concerning the authorities' call for cultural cooperation were numerous, and charges of parochial nationalism became common.[153] Although the authorities continued to support *Jugoslovenstvo*, an early concession to the growing reaction could be seen in a draft constitution, circulated in 1961, that would no longer permit a person to use the category of *Yugoslav* to describe his/her national identity.[154] Still another measure of the seriousness with which the authorities perceived the growing national reaction was offered in late 1961 when opposition to *Jugoslovenstvo* was somewhat legitimized by the airing of an open exchange of views between a proponent and an opponent of Yugoslavism in the party's official news-paper, *Borba*. The opponent was quite outspoken, accusing certain "centralists who do not know what republics and what people are" of attempting to eliminate the republics. He also made a ringing defense of nations as something far more than "only capitalist or bourgeois phenomena" and "more than a number of particular, economic, geographical, and cultural characteristics."[155]

Not surprisingly, the issue of Serbian hegemony was also raised in the course of the debate that appeared in *Borba*. Nor was it surprising that the proponent of *Jugoslovenstvo* was Serbian, while the opponent (a Slovene) was not. Serbs were disproportionately found among the advocates of a Yugoslav consciousness, and op-ponents tended to perceive in it a resurrection of prewar Great Serbian chauvinism. The old animosities that had been the bane of prewar Yugoslavia and the motive power behind the genocidal horrors of the wartime period were resurfacing, giving the au-thorities cause for grave concern. In May 1962 Tito remarked that "it is simply revolting when one sees how chauvinism is beginning to spread among our youths."[156] In September of the same year, Tito felt compelled to reassure the non-Serbs that assimilation was not in prospect. Speaking before the Federal Assembly, he noted: "When we speak about integration, we do not think of the inte-gration of nationalities, of their assimilation or negation."[157] Before the same body, Kardelj made a specific reference to the party's vigilance against hegemonism: "Our federation is not a frame for making some new Yugoslav nation, or a frame for the kind of national integration which various advocates of hegemonism or denationalizing terror have been dreaming of."[158] About this same time, regional leaders of the YCP were giving assurances to their particular groups that merging was not an immediate prospect and that nations would continue to exist during the stage of socialism.[159]

Resistance to integration and the national passions that showed signs of revitalization in its wake were causing the leadership to have second thoughts. In early 1963 Tito still voiced support for *Jugoslovenstvo*, but with a decidedly defensive tone. To reporters he cited letters from children indicating their wish to be identified as Yugoslavs and he added that "our cultural life should develop within a Yugoslav framework." However, the implication was that few adults shared this vision, and he lamented that "there are even individuals who simply don't dare to call themselves Yugoslavs."[160] Moreover, less than two weeks later, Tito publicly complained that "there are not a small number of people in particular republics, and among them some Communists, who find it difficult to speak the word 'Yugoslav'."[161]

Tito's reference to the children who desired to be called Yugoslavs proved to presage the resuscitation of a right to have one's national identity listed under that rubric. Unlike the draft constitution of 1961, the constitution of 1963 did not rule out adopting "Yugoslav" as a national designation. Indeed, despite the increasing indicators that Tito and Kardelj were having second thoughts about the wisdom of stressing *Jugoslovenstvo*, the 1963 constitution was, if anything, more heavily weighted in favor of integration than had been the Constitutional Law of 1953. The weak status of the republics was maintained, and the principal governmental symbol of nationhood, the Council of Nationalities, already demoted to serving as a subordinate part of one of the two houses comprising the federal legislature, found its prestige further sapped when no change was made in its subordinate status despite the transformation of the legislature from a two-house into a five-house organization.

But then the pendulum reversed direction. Sometime between final approval of the 1963 constitution and the Eighth Party Congress that convened in December 1964, the growing doubts of Tito and Kardelj persuaded them to throw their weight behind those who opposed the integration drive. Absent from the Eighth Congress were all references to *Jugoslovenstvo*. Indeed, if one were to judge solely by the speeches of Tito and Kardelj, they had never entertained such a notion. Tito, for example, took to task "certain people, including even some communists" who suffered from "the confused idea that the unity of our peoples means the elimination of nationalities and the creation of something new and artificial, that is a single Yugoslav nation, rather on the lines of assimilation and bureaucratic centralization, unitarianism and hegemony."[162] Proof that these words were not just another verbal smokescreen designed to pacify the non-Serb national groups, but were in fact intended to signify official renunciation of the policy attacked at the congress as "integral Yugoslavism" could be found in the new powers assigned to the republican branches of the YCP. As noted earlier, in the name of absolute party unity the previous congress, held in 1958, had stripped these branches of even the most nominal powers of decision-making. But now each of the branches was empowered to convene its own congress prior to any congress of the entire YCP, a procedure that would seemingly ensure that each republic's delegation would arrive at the country-wide congress with a national stance on all important issues staked out in advance.

Moreover, each republican branch of the party was now empowered to "determine the policies, positions, and tasks of the League of Communists of the socialist republic in harmony with the policy of the League of Communists of Yugoslavia."[163] A speech at the congress, elaborating upon these new powers, explained that the purpose was "to express more precisely the independence of the League of Communists in the socialist republics on the basis of the national character of the economic development of the republics."[164]

Developments in the wake of the Eighth Congress further underlined the commitment of Tito and Kardelj to a new direction in policy. The shift in 1965 from a command to a market economy was acknowledged by Kardelj to be linked to the national question.[165] Centralized planning had nurtured local nationalism, as growing complaints concerning the distribution of scarce resources among republics and autonomous provinces were readily translatable into an escalating sense of ethnic high dudgeon. The answer was believed to lie in decentralization, or what Kardelj had termed at the Eighth Congress the "de-territorialization" of economic decision-making.

Still another indication of Tito's commitment to the new policy occurred in 1966, when the purge of his erstwhile heir apparent, Aleksander Rankovich, was made the occasion to brand him and, by implication, all who resisted the new decentralization program, as Great Serbian chauvinists. This specific charge against Rankovich might have been unfair. (Little evidence for this charge was publicized, and Rankovich had, in fact, made a speech earlier in the year that was critical of Serbian nationalism.) However, he was certainly a centrist who had resisted decentralization, and it is a measure of the priority that Tito and Kardelj ascribed to the new policy that they were prepared to fan distrust of Serbian chauvinism in order to ensure compliance with the program. "Centrists", "hegemonists", and "unitarians" now became synonymous with Great Serbian chauvinists, and it was evident at this juncture that great nation chauvinism had replaced local nationalism as the arch foe.

Throughout the remainder of the 1960s and the 1970s, institutional changes appear to have increasingly strengthened the autonomy of the nations.[166] Constitutional amendments between 1967 and 1971 upgraded materially the powers of the Council of Nationalities, and the constitution of 1974 reestablished that council as one of the two houses of the federal legislature. The concept of one republic (or province), one vote was introduced as the principle of representation in the executive branch of the federal govenment and in the Presidium of the party. At the time of Tito's death in 1980, national autonomy had certainly become far more realized than it had at any point during the 1945–1964 period.

The national policy first articulated at the Eighth Party Congress held in 1964 therefore certainly represented a radical change in design. But did it represent a change of purpose or simply a change in the choice of means? In a speech delivered at the time of Rankovich's purging, Tito was quoted as saying: "It is impossible to create a single nation here." Some scholars have found in this and similar utterances a full renunciation of the ultimate goal of assimilation,[167] but such a conclusion appears unwarranted. In the Marxist-Leninist lexicon, it would indeed be impossible to create a new nation within the Yugoslavian socialist society, since nations arise only under capitalism. A new Yugoslav people (just as "the new Soviet man") would necessarily be a higher order of things than a nation. Denials of attempts to create a new nation in a postcapitalist society are therefore not meaningful. Moreover, the authorities took pains to dramatize that decentralization should not be construed to indicate any slackening of the unrelenting war against national propensities. Thus, during early 1966 great publicity was given to the trial and conviction of a group charged with organizing a Croatian Liberation Movement. And only two weeks before Tito's statement concerning the impossibility of creating a single Yugoslav nation, he had, in the course of otherwise acclaiming the inherently liberal character of the decentralization movement, pointedly warned that "we will not be liberal towards various separatist and nationalist trends."[168]

The open break with the policy of *Jugoslovenstvo*, which the YCP had pursued with varying degress of candidness between 1945 and 1964, was therefore not, at least in the eyes of Tito and Kardelj, an admission that the forces of local nationalism had emerged victorious. On the contrary, dropping the campaign for Yugoslavianism had come to be viewed as a necessary first step to dampen nationalism. Kardelj's speech at the Eighth Congress had depicted local nationalism as having fed on the specter of Great Serbian chauvinism, dressed up (in the eyes of local nationalists) in the garb of *Jugoslovenstvo*. As noted, Kardelj had also perceived centralized planning as having fostered nationalism. Centralization, whether of the economic or psychological (*Jugoslovenstvo*) variety was therefore scrapped. Atomization would bring about the "deterritorialization" of the wellsprings of national rivalry and thereby wean the population away from perceiving issues in ethnonational terms.[169] The anticipated result would be a weakening of national consciousness.[170]

More indicative of the leadership's long-range perspective than occasional statements concerning the impossibility of creating a single nation was their unwillingness (some hedging terminology to the contrary) to forswear either the inevitability or the desirability of ultimate assimilation. Thus in late 1966, only a few months after Rankovich's purge, at a time when the anti-*Jugoslovenstvo* campaign was at its height, Tito spoke approvingly of the founders of the Yugoslav Academy of Sciences and Art for their commitment to "rapprochement among South Slav peoples."[171] The general tendency at this time, however, was to hedge on the issue. For example, a 1967 pamphlet by a person vested with important responsibilities for national policy aped Tito in remarking that "it would be impossible to seek to create a uniform Yugoslav nation." He added:

> Any attempt of this sort would amount to forcible assimilation in defiance of individual historical traditions and heritages and the existence and functioning of a whole series of national institutions. . . . Any attempt to create a uniform Yugoslav nation would rouse the problem of a uniform Yugoslav language and of the creation of unified cultural and other institutions. Consequently, such a possibility belongs to an already completely superceded past. It might have been possible only in the 19th century, at the time of the emergence of the great European nations, of a still underdeveloped state of enlightenment and cultural, educational and other national institutions.[172]

If one glosses over the Marxist view of nations as products of the capitalist era, and the fact that the nineteenth century was everywhere part of that era, the passage certainly appears to be an unambiguous renunciation of Lenin's predictions concerning the coming together and fusion of nations. However, in the conclusion of the pamphlet, significantly entitled "The Prospects," a quite different scenario is sketched:

> The development of the material base of socialism should contribute to the universal enrichment of all working people and all national collectivities, reducing the disparities existing in the economic development of individual national and other areas and mitigating the contradictions that stem therefrom. This will make for an increasingly dynamic and comprehensive development of

the social superstructure in education, culture, artistic creation, social services and in all other sectors of life for each people and national minority. The general improvement of the material base of society should also make for a quicker emancipation of social relations from all statist, bureaucratic and administrative vestiges, leading to the strengthening of social self-government by way of an increasing participation of the direct producers and wide circles of citizens in decision-making on all social questions. This at the same time will make possible an increasing rapprochement between the peoples of Yugoslavia on voluntary bases, through integration and other forms of association; not however, in terms of the assimilation of the few and undeveloped by the better developed, but in terms of a growing need of the richer and more comprehensively active social and national environments for expanding cooperation and mutual exchange as equal and equivalent partners.[173]

This is a view of the future that Lenin could surely have endorsed.

Another Yugoslav specialist on the national question peppered a 1975 article on the question with references to Lenin, but limited his comments concerning ultimate assimilation to very guarded references such as "just as it [the working class] could not automatically abolish itself as a class . . . it cannot 'abolish' overnight the nation as well."[174] By contrast, much more frank references to the coming obliteration of nations appeared in a party-endorsed series of articles published in 1976. Written by the Secretary of the Executive Committee of the YCP Central Committee Presidium, unambiguously entitled "The National Question and the Communist and Workers Movement," and given prominence in the party organ *Borba*, there appears little question but that the series was ascribed utmost significance by the leadership.[175] Supporting his points with numerous invocations of the name of Lenin, the author suggested that the process of obliteration is already underway, because "socialism in its social and political-economic sense and content is developing during the process when the classes, the nations, the state and commodity production are being rendered obsolete." Lest the message be overlooked, the concluding paragraph to the series again hits at the ephemerality of nations:

Proceeding from the Marxist view, according to which the national question is essentially a class question, or rather the nation is a form of the society's class structure and that the nation will disappear along with the disappearance of the class, one comes to the acceptable conclusion that the contradictions of the class and national interest will be accompanied by socialism until its disappearance as a categorical structure of society."

This new candidness on the part of the party suggests a shift of official opinion in favor of playing down national flourishing and offering more encouragement to assimilation.[176] However, the articles's several references to the total obliteration of national peculiarities only with the achievement of communism ruled out a shift sufficiently radical to reembrace the program of *Jugoslovenstvo*.

In addition, then, to establishing that the change in policy initiated in 1964 was one of strategy but not of goal, the newly found willingness of the party to publicize its faith in the inevitability of the merging of nations reminds us that policy on the national question was in flux throughout. Although, in contrast with the many severe vacillations in policy experienced by the Soviet Union and China, Yugoslavia had undergone only one overall tipping of the balance between the two approaches of encouraging either national flourishing or more direct assimilation, forces in favor of each approach were continually active.[177] Sometimes the resulting changes in emphasis were visible, as when Tito, stung into action by the national agitation within Croatia in the early 1970s, purged the party of nationalists and recentralized control even while retaining the form of republican (and therefore national) representation within the Presidium. At other times, shifts have been camouflaged.[178] But the most overt evidence that *Jugoslovenstvo* had not fallen completely out of grace with the leadership even after that concept had been officially discarded is that as late as 1969, polls were being conducted to test attitudes concerning the desirability of renewed efforts to overcome national differences and "to create a unitary Yugoslav nation." The suspiciously highly favorable attitudes reported toward such efforts suggest that the polls were designed more to prepare the public to accept a return to *Jugoslovenstvo* than to record actual opinions.[179]

Those favoring *Jugoslovenstvo* may have been heartened by an unexpected jump in the number of people who declared their identity as Yugoslavian in the 1981 election. However, although the increase led to broad speculation and incrimination (including charges that the figures had been falsified by "centrists"), the total number of declared Yugoslavians represented only 5 percent of the population. Meanwhile, members of the Serbian community continued to bemoan the trend toward disintegration following

Tito's death and, in so doing, made clear their preference for a reintegrating movement.[180]

CZECHOSLOVAKIA

There are a number of parallels between the histories of the Slovaks and the Croats. At the time of the concurrent creation of their states (Czechoslovakia and Yugoslavia, respectively), each was considered to share a single nationhood with the state's predominant people. In each case, a sense of separate nationhood ripened during the interwar period. In each case, the country's Communist party, pursuant to orders from the Comintern, came, during the 1920s, to recognize and support this separate nationhood.[181] But also in each case, this strategic appeal to nationalism was largely aborted by the presence of an alternative, non-Communist party.[182] In each case, the state's bourgeois government had tried in the late 1930s to quell the growing national aspirations of the group by conferring a large measure of autonomy. And in a final parallel, this palliative had failed in both instances, as each people, under Nazi aegis, formed an independent state during World War II.

From the viewpoint of designing a national policy that struck the most effective balance between encouraging assimilation and national flourishing, the Czechoslovak party, at the time of assuming power (1948), therefore faced the same paradox as had the Yugoslav party (in 1945). On the one hand, there was the close cultural affinity and a myth of shared ancestry between the Czechs and Slovaks. As we have seen in the case of the Yugoslav authorities, such a relationship could be reasonably perceived as making assimilation a relatively modest undertaking that should be pressed. On the other hand, recent decades had seen the growth of an undisguised sense of unique nationhood on the part of the Slovaks, as well as manifestations of strong separatist sentiments. Lenin's prescription for this syndrome was, of course, a lengthy period of national flourishing. As in our other country studies, actual policy was to undergo fluctuations between these two paths.

During the 1945–1948 period (before the party had achieved domination), the leadership of the Slavic wing of the Communist party had advocated a substantial measure of autonomy for Slovakia in nearly all spheres, including the military. This stance was to cost them dearly, for following the consolidation of Communist power, the leadership of the more powerful and centrist-minded Czech wing of the party used this indiscretion to subject the Slovak wing to a thorough-going purge on the charge of harboring bourgeois national sentiments. The Stalin-like purge blended well with the overall national policy of the party. Not surprisingly, the party had immediately adopted the then current model of the Soviet Union, namely, one of promoting assimilation while paying lip service to national autonomy. The purge, which had probably run its full course, ameliorated soon after the denunciation of Stalin in 1956. But the policy of encouraging assimilation survived Stalinism. The 1958 Party Congress called for "the completion of the cultural revolution and the strengthening of the unity of the peoples."[183] Close on the heels of this intimation that even nominal national flourishing was coming to an end came the 1960 constitution, which gerrymandered Slovakia into three territorial components (each made responsible to Prague) and which nearly stripped Slovak institutions of what little autonomy they had enjoyed. The accelerated timetable for achieving assimilation was also reflected in the publications of party theorists. In the words of one scholar, these works quite incautiously predicted "the development of a homogeneous, cohesive, and assimilated national community within one generation."[184] This projection was based on the classical Marxist assumption that an integrated economic society leads to an integrated people. But the party was assigned a most active role: on the negative side, First Secretary Novotny called for the waging of "intolerant struggle against demonstrations of any nationalism" and, on the side of positive action, he called for the obliterating of all national distinctions through the mass intermarriage of Slovaks with Czechs.[185] Gustav Husak (a Slovak leader who had been purged for bourgeois nationalism in the 1950s but who was to become the CzCP's First Secretary following the Soviet intervention in 1968) was seemingly not far from the mark when he described the intentions of the party's leadership at this time as the "degradation of a [Slovak] nation."[186]

We have perceived the dangers in such a blatant espousal of rapid assimilation elsewhere. In China the authorities had been forced to retreat hastily from the rapid assimilation posture of the Great Leap Forward and the Cultural Revolution in the face of resistance on the part of minorities. And we have just recorded that the reaction to the *Jugoslovenstvo* campaign had caused Tito and his colleagues to order an about-face. The experience of the Czechoslovak party proved to be similar. Slovak writers, supported by the leadership of the Slovak wing of the party, staged a counteroffensive. Much of their campaign centered upon absolving targets of the antinationalist purge of the early 1950s and upon ridding the Slovak nation of the taint of massive collusion with the Nazis. Novotny resisted for a time, but by December 1963 the party's Central Committee was prepared to acknowledge that the attacks upon Slovak Communists had been "unsubstantiated in toto."[187] The Slovak leadership continued to press its anti-assimilationist drive, allying itself during the late 1960s with the anticentralist, liberal movement within the country's Czech population. The difference in views between these allies was shown in a poll conducted just prior to the Soviet intervention. While 91 percent of all Slovak respondents believed that the most important intrastate issue was the equality of the two nations, only 5 percent of Czech respondents agreed.[188] Slovak leadership had come to the conclusion that only a true federalism could insure the Slovak nation's best interests, and on March 5, 1968 the Slovak National Council voted *unanimously* to support federalism as the only acceptable system. Despite a decidedly less favorable view of federalism on the part of the Czechs, we have reviewed how a true federalism was in fact approved by the Czechoslovak authorities and allowed to come into being by the Soviets.[189]

If the Soviets had in fact permitted the spirit of the new federal system to operate, 1968 would have inaugurated a period of true national flourishing.[190] However, we know that through party purges and changes in the constitution, the Soviets brought about the reestablishment of a centralized system. The CzCP's new First Secretary, Husak, who, with an eye to his reputation as a proponent of Slovak rights, had unquestionably been selected by the Soviets as a means of insuring Slovak cooperation, was soon under pressure to swing policy back toward the assimilationist goal.[191] In 1971 he told the Fourteenth Party Congress that "we must consolidate a common consciousness among the nationalities of Czechoslovakia, a single Czechoslovak consciousness founded on our socialist order."[192] The congress obliged:

> The Party will increasingly promote socialist relations between our peoples and the national minorities, as well as the universal Czechoslovakian consciousness in the spirit of both proletarian internationalism and socialist patriotism, mutual respect, co-operation, equality and fraternity. It will fight determinedly to extinguish all expressions of nationalism and socialism.[193]

This official endorsement of "Czechoslovakism" was not followed by a radical raising of the level of assimilationist pressure, and it may well be that Husak was merely mechanically complying with Soviet directives. However, references to a single Czechoslovak identity continued to appear, and, in 1976, a Yugoslav reporter commented that "the 'theory' on the existence of 'objective conditions for creating a single socialist nation' [not just in Czechoslovakia, but] in the 'countries of the socialist community' is being increasingly more present in the Czechoslovak publications and press, and these 'possibilities' are directly or indirectly being increasingly written about and publicly discussed."[194] The article continued:

> "The Soviet Union's experience," it is further said, points to a path of "bringing closer together, of overcoming differences, of merging, of removing the specific traits of nations" and, finally, of creating a "socialist nation." If in a multinational state, such as the USSR, "a single-Soviet Nation had been formed," why should not a "single nation" be created in the countries of the "socialist community?"

The article then went on to cite Soviet authors (who, in turn, had been cited in the Czechoslovak press) to the effect that as a consequence of economic and military integration of the eastern European states under CEMA and the Warsaw Pact, the "objective conditions are being created in the countries of the socialist community for a merging of nations and states." The reader was left to draw the obvious inference: if the growing economic and cultural ties between the states of Eastern Europe were transforming the diverse amalgam of Magyars, Rumanians, Germans, Poles, et al. into one national group, then the much more intensive intra-Czechoslovakian economic and cultural ties must have achieved much greater strides in transforming the culturally more akin Czechs and Slovaks into a single nation.

The party's commitment to a merging of the nations was also apparent in an article, written by a deputy premier, that appeared in the party's journal, *Tvorba*, in late 1977.[195] After citing that portion of Brezhnev's speech on the 1977 Soviet Constitution in which the General Secretary had said that the constitution did not signify "the disappearance of national differences *yet*," the article added: "The new USSR Constitution, which reflects the highest stage of socialism's development—is a constitution 'of a society of mature socialist relations'—expresses also the long-range tendencies of our constitutional development. We are going in a good, correct direction."

Developments Elsewhere

Czechoslovakia was evidently not the sole country to be urged by Moscow during the 1970s to adopt a policy of rapid assimilation under the rubric of "a single socialist nation." The expression also became quite common at this time within two other states that were particularly susceptible to Soviet pressure—Bulgaria and East Germany. In the former the rapid integration of all minorities into "a single socialist nation" was alternately described as "a basic task" or "a foremost task" of the party.[196] Under this program, language instruction in non-Bulgarian languages was effectively curtailed and all Moslems—Turks and Bulgars alike—were pressured into adopting conventional Bulgar names.[197] As the country's largest minority, the Turks came in for particular attention.[198] Adherence to Turkish customs and the Moslem faith were attacked as manifestations of "Turkish bourgeois nationalism" that must be eradicated in order to "make the Turkish population part of the Bulgarian nation."[199]

Whereas in Bulgaria, the concept of a single socialist nation was used to justify the rapid assimilation of minorities, in East Germany the same concept was used during the 1970s to rationalize the disintegration of an existent nation. Prior to 1970, the Communist party of East Germany (the SED) had depicted itself as the vanguard of the entire German nation, and a steadfast goal of the SED had been a reunited Germany in a "socialist state of the German nation."[200] However, at the Eighth Party Congress in 1971, SED General Secretary Honecker denounced as "mere rhetoric" the "so-called 'unity of the German nation',", maintaining that "a new type of nation, the socialist nation" had come into being in East Germany.[201]

While the renunciation of reunification represented a clear departure from previous East German policy, the reference to a socialist nation, in and of itself, was quite consonant with Marxist–Leninist terminology and need not have heralded a significant change of attitude with regard to national identity. However, an article that appeared during early 1974 in *Einheit* (the publication of the SED's Central Committee) demonstrated that the concept of a socialist nation could have the most profound consequences for national identity in a situation in which a nation became politically divided between a Marxist-Leninist and a bourgeois state.[202] After setting forth the classical Marxist proposition that the forces of production (most particularly the economic nexus and the relationship of the socioeconomic classes operating within that nexus) are more important in determining the geographic contours of a nation than are "ethnic" factors such as language, cultural history, and ethnopsychology, the author of the article concluded that if the primary factors are altered for part of a nation, the national consciousness of that part will also alter. No longer will the two share a common sense of nationhood. And since the economic nexus and the sociopolitical unit coincide most nearly with the state, it follows that when a nation is divided into socialist and bourgeois states, two separate sets of national identity will develop.

The line of argument was not entirely new. As early as 1929, Stalin had noted that the bourgeois nation disappears with the coming of the socialist revolution and is replaced by the socialist nation.[203] But beyond a few comments to the effect that attitudes among socialist nations are fraternal and beatific, as contrasted with the competitive and oppressive relations that characterize the relations among bourgeois nations, little clarification concerning the magnitude or specifics of the difference between the two classifications of nations had been advanced.

The lack of specificity concerning vital distinctions between socialist and bourgeois nations suggests that the concept of the socialist nation had been introduced by Stalin as a pragmatic response to developments rather than to a deep conviction that vital distinctions in fact existed. Introduction of the term had been a necessary consequence of the admission that nations were to continue into the socialist era. That is to say, just as it had been deemed expedient to differentiate other factors (such as the state, economics, ethics, etc.) within a Marxist-Leninist society from counterparts in a capitalist society by affixing the adjective "socialist" to them, so too were nations in a Marxist-Leninist society to be distinguished. Socialist nationhood was merely a phase through which the nation must pass on its way to eradication. It was at best the nation at a higher stage of history. It could not be an entirely new nation, since nations, according to Marx, were created only during the capitalist stage.

The best evidence that Marxist-Leninist leaders had heretofore not ascribed any vital peculiarities to socialist nations is that in those many cases in which a political border divided a nation between a bourgeois and a socialist state, the latter's government had not maintained that the two segments had thereby been transformed into two totally different phenomena. Rather, the common nationhood of the two segments was stressed as a means of influencing the transborder element and of convincing it that it should join the socialist state. Thus, under Stalin, the bourgeois Azerbaijani, Finns, Uighurs, Ukrainians, etc. were appealed to in terms of their kinship with the segment of their nation residing within the USSR. We have reviewed how Ho Chi Minh and his successors appealed between 1954 and 1975 to the common nationhood existing between the Vietnamese of bourgeois South Vietnam and socialist North Vietnam. The Communist party of China remains committed to reabsorbing the bourgeois people of Taiwan into the Great Han family. And thirty years after the division of Korea, General Secretary Kim Il Sung would proclaim:

> Reunifying our divided country is the greatest national duty and the most important revolutionary task for our Party and people. ... The country's reunification is a unanimous ardent desire of all our nation. ... Our people have lived as a homogeneous nation in the same land for thousands of years. They have one spoken and written language, and their history and cultural traditions are the same. Our country has no national minority. That any people who have lived as a homogeneous nation in a unified state for ages should be divided into two in our times, is impermissible *either from the viewpoint of the communist ideas or from the standpoint of the nationalist ideas.* ... Reunifying the country is an undertaking for the good of the whole nation, and a national task feasible only when the whole nation unites efforts and struggles for it in firm unity. ... Although we, the communists, and the nationalists in south Korea live under different social systems and differ in ideologies and political views, there can be no contradiction between them as long [far?] as the reunification question is concerned. Now when even countries and peoples with differing social systems are fighting in concert for a common goal, why cannot we communists and the south Korean nationalists of one and the same descent and nation join hands in the bid for reunification?[204]

In all of the preceding cases, the involved Communist party perceived support for the unification of a nation or nations as furthering its own power, and it was therefore in the party's interest to stress that the bonds of nationhood bridged the bourgeois-socialist divide. But when the East German authorities became persuaded that the theme of reunification was more of a liability than an asset, in that a vastly greater percentage of East Germans were casting covetous looks at the life style of Germans to the west rather than the other way around, an attack upon the validity of the common national bond followed.[205]

The assertion that an entirely new nation had come into being in socialist East Germany was, as noted, at odds with classical Marxism. Yet, this major deviation had been indubitably approved in advance by, and may well have been hatched within, the Soviet Union, for its premise that the political division of a nation subsequently gives rise to separate nations was rapidly accepted as dogma by at least one other state heavily influenced by Moscow. Witness the following statement excerpted from an official Bulgarian publication:

> It is a generally known truth that the nation is a product of the bourgeois epoch, of the transition from the feudal to the capitalist social system. It is usually formed as a development already existing for centuries or, as it more seldom happens, as the result of a division of a nationality, or as a result of the unification of several nationalities. *The formation of a new nation is, of course, possible also later, as a result of the division of a nation already created by that time, of the formation of two states, etc.*[206]

The purpose behind the first two sentences was to repudiate a Yugoslav claim that there were living within Bulgaria large numbers of people who were allegedly part of a Macedonian nation, on the ground that presocialist, Bulgarian history disclosed that the people in question were part of the Bulgar nation. The purpose behind the last sentence was to deny any claim over those people living within Yugoslavia, whom the Yugoslav authorities called Macedonians, on the ground that "what nations and what nationalities exist in the territory of Yugoslavia is a purely internal question, a question of the peoples of that country."[207] The important point, however, is that the incompatibility between the first and last sentences was not addressed. As had been true at the time of the original surfacing of the doctrine within East Germany in 1974, the incompatibility between alleging that a socialist state gives rise to a new nation and Marx's restricting of nation formation to the capitalist era was sidestepped in silence.

The nature of the change in the national consciousness of the East Germans that the formulators of the doctrine of a new socialist nation hoped to achieve soon manifested itself. Alterations in the 1968 constitution, as approved on September 27, 1974, demonstrated an attempt to de-Germanize the population by eradicating all references to a German nation. Gone were the opening words of the preamble "Impelled by the responsibility of showing the entire German nation the path into a future of peace and socialism. . . ." In Article 1, the German Democratic Republic, formerly described as "a socialist state of German nationhood," had become "a socialist state of workers and farmers." In Article 6, the word *German* (before people) and the ending phrase *of all Germans* had been deleted from the opening sentence: "The German Democratic Republic has eradicated German militarism and Naziism from its territory in keeping with the interests of the *German* people and the international obligations *of all Germans*." Totally omitted was paragraph 2 of Article 8, which had read:

> The establishment and cultivation of normal relations and cooperation between the two German States on the basis of equality are the *national concern* of the German Democratic Republic. The German Democratic Republic and its citizens strive to overcome the partition of Germany imposed upon *the German nation* by imperialism, and support the step-by-step rapprochement of the two German States until the time of their reunification on the basis of democracy and socialism.[208]

The West German interpretation of what the SED hoped to achieve by all of this was summed up in the critical comment of the Federal Minister for Inner-German Relations: "In the opinion of the Federal Government a nation, and therefore the German nation, cannot be created or abolished by mere act of law."[209]

The response of the East German people to this attempt to de-Germanize them was overwhelmingly negative.[210] In 1975 more than two-thirds of the East German population refused to identify the people of West Germany as a "foreign nation."[211] Socialist organizations within East Germany expressed their unhappiness with this attempt to sever them from their German roots, and voices of protest were heard even within the SED.[212]

In less than four months, the attempt to purge *German* from the vocabulary was abandoned. During February 1975 the party newspaper, *Neues Deutschland*, carried a lengthy treatise whose main burden was to distinguish between the concepts of nationality and nation.[213] Consonant with Soviet usage, a nationality was described as a group at a prenation stage, characterized by an amalgam of "ethnic peculiarities," such as common language, culture, and traditions. According to the authors, "the birth of German nationality coincided essentially with the evolution and full development of feudal society." By contrast, the German nation began to form only "in the fifteenth and sixteenth centuries on the basis of the capitalistic mode of production." This bourgeois German nation continued to evolve and indeed has continued to do so even down to the present day in West Germany. However, the introduction of a Marxist-Leninist political and social system within East Germany following World War II had given rise to a new socialist nation of a different order than the bourgeois nation from which it had sprung. Thus, by reverting to the two-nation thesis that they had advanced in early 1974, the authors maintained that all Germans shared a common nationality but not a common nationhood.[214]

In a book published the following year, one of the authors of the *Neues Deutschland* article more expansively described the tempo of growth of a new nation within East Germany:

> To the extent that the foundations of socialist society in the GDR were established, national relations and national processes also changed. In this process of revolutionary transformation the presuppositions and elements of a socialist nation were created. Already in the mid-1950s, a socialist nation began slowly to develop in the GDR. At the beginning of the 1960s, when the foundations of socialism had been laid and the establishment of the developed socialist society had begun, this process reached a certain level of maturity. At present, when socialist relations of production prevail and the politico-moral unity of the people is assured under the leadership of the working class, we can speak of a highly developed stage of the socialist nation.[215]

Thus adorned with historical vindication, the concept of a new socialist nation became a cornerstone of East German policy. At the same time, the distinction made between nationality and nation permitted the authorities to quit the dangerous course of denying German roots to the party and the socialist state. Thus, the Party Program of 1976 proclaimed that the party was not the representative merely of a socialist nation but of an "independent socialist *German* nation."[216] The return to official grace of the German heritage permitted the authorities to seek increased legitimacy for their socialist order by portraying it as the progressive extension of the German past. During the late 1970s, the authorities played the German card with great frequency. Prussian history, shown in a favorable light, became a subject of a lengthy television documentary and of academic treatises. When the Soviets took an East German on a space mission, it was gleefully reported that "the first German in space is a citizen of the German Democratic Republic," and the cosmonaut was publicly linked with some of the greatest luminaries of German history.[217]

The concept of one socialist German nation had the attractive possibility of permitting the SED to have it both ways: (1) an opportunity to deny a German nationalism shared with West Germans that had led East Germans to view the East German state as artificial, imposed, and ephemeral; (2) an opportunity nevertheless to appeal to the German nationalism of its populace as a means of shoring up the party's popularity. By wedding Marxism-Leninism to German nationalism in this manner, the SED hoped to achieve a legitimacy in the eyes of their subjects that had hitherto largely escaped them.[218]

Along with Bulgaria, Czechoslovakia, and East Germany, Vietnam was one of the states most sensitized to Moscow's influence during the late 1970s. Here too the notion of a single socialist nation became the slogan of the day. Hardly had the struggle ceased in the south when Premier Pham Van Dong announced that reunification was necessary "in the name of a single country, a single people, and a single economy."[219] We have earlier reviewed how the slogan selected for a reunified Vietnam was "Vietnam is one country, the Vietnamese are one people," a phrase extracted from a speech by Ho Chi Minh in which he had evoked the baseless myth of a single ancestry common to all of the peoples of Vietnam.[220]

Consonant with this myth, although not with reality, *nation* now came to be equated with the entire people. And yet, the term *nationality* continued to be applied to the Cham, Chinese, Khmer, montagnard and other non-Kinh (ethnically Vietnamese) peoples. For example, in a 1976 speech specifically addressed to the problem of minorities, the Vice Minister of Culture described the state's population in the following terms: "Dear Comrades, the unified Vietnamese nation is a great family of both ethnic majority and minority nationalities."[221] in short, at one and the same time, a differentiation between the concepts of nation and nationality that was being advanced in East Germany to support a case for *one nationality but two nations* was being employed in Vietnam to support a case for *several nationalities but one nation.*[222]

Armed with the myth of a single Vietnamese nation, Hanoi proclaimed a policy of assimilation. During October 1976, at what was termed a "southern cultural conference on the development of the cultural movement in the mountain areas," the Vice Minister of Culture announced plans for the assimilation of what he described as the "approximately 30 nationalities with different languages, customs, and habits and with a population of 2.5 million living in the mountain areas, deltas, coastal areas and border zones."[223] He noted in part:

> It is necessary to eradicate all the outmoded customs and superstitions which the Americans and puppets sought to develop and spread among the ethnic minority nationalities, while gradually bringing the new culture to each area inhabited by the people of each ethnic minority nationality in accordance with their ability to assimilate this new culture. . . . The state has the duty to bring new, progressive culture to these people, guide them in engaging in new cultural activities, eliminate the vestiges of the former regime's enslaving culture, increase cultural exchanges among various nationalities throughout the country, assimilate what is good and beautiful in the cultures of these nationalities in order to build a new culture with socialist objectives and *Vietnamese national characteristics*.[224]

In a similar vein, VCP First Secretary Le Duan informed the party's Fourth Congress that "the Party's policy on nationalities consists . . . in creating conditions for the complete eradication of all differences in economic and cultural knowledge between the ethnic minority and majority people."[225]

Later in his address, Le Duan suggested that the assimilation drive should be gradual:

> Of course, backward, unscientific, superstitions, customs and habits must be changed, but the change must be gradual and in keeping with the mass line; we must use explanation and persuasion and wait with perseverance for the masses to understand, and absolutely refrain from using arbitrary or rude measures.

But despite these Leninist-sounding words, the party had already embarked upon a program of extremely rapid assimilation for all minorities in both the north and the south. We have earlier reviewed how the party, immediately following its victory over the entire country, disbanded the autonomous regions in the north.[226] Earlier promises to the contrary, it had refused to introduce such administrative units in the south. Again contrary to earlier promises, the VCP had by 1976 embarked on a massive resettlement program that would move millions of Vietnamese into minority homelands, thereby causing the non-Vietnamese to become overnight minorities within their own locales.[227] In 1976 also, the VCP conducted a purge of those members of the highest echelon who had been most closely associated with the gradual, Leninist approach to the national question, most of whom were members of one or another minority.[228]

The treatment of the Chinese community during this period is particularly revealing of Hanoi's desire to create an ethnically homogeneous state. As an ethnically self-aware people, conscious that members of their nation predominated in the Chinese People's Republic immediately across the border, the Chinese could be expected to resist loss of identity through assimilation into a single Vietnamese nation. At the time of the country's reunification in 1975, close to 1.5 million Chinese (popularly called Hoa by the Vietnamese) lived throughout the northern and southern sectors. During the period when South Vietnam was a separate state (1954–1975), a decree had been in effect that forced the Hoa to adopt Vietnamese citizenship. However, in several pronouncements made during the 1960s, the Hanoi-dominated National Liberation Movement had promised that this law would be abolished and that all Chinese could freely determine their own citizenship. In the re-registration drive of January 1976, however, those Hoa who did record their citizenship as Chinese were subjected to loss of jobs, reduced food rations, and the like. Judging from refugee reports, the Chinese in the north were also subjected to discriminatory treatment beginning at about this time, and the general distrust with which the VCP viewed their Hoa minority was signaled in early 1977 when people of Chinese descent were forcibly removed from the area of the border shared with China.[229] As relations between the two countries deteriorated and Peking took up the cause of the Hoa, the treatment of the Chinese within Vietnam appeared to become even more severe. By 1978 hundreds of thousands of Hoa were fleeing the country by boat or by crossing the Chinese border.[230] Refugee reports establish that they did so with Hanoi's encouragement. Moreover, when the VCP claimed that the refugees were all unrepentant capitalists who were fleeing socialist reforms, and the party newspaper, *Nhan Dan*, pointedly asked on May 29, 1978 why Peking was so interested in "a handful of Vietnamese bourgeoisie of Chinese descent," Peking cogently retorted that Vietnam's description of the Hoa refugees as capitalists hardly jibed with the fact that 95 percent of the refugees had fled from northern Vietnam, where socialist reforms had taken place during the 1950s.[231] Particularly unusual for a Communist publication was an article that appeared in the August 1978 issue of the party journal, *Tap Chi Cong San (Journal of Communism)*. In words well chosen to foster ethnic animosity, the article identified the Chinese community of South Vietnam prior to 1975 as the principal exploiter of the Vietnamese people.

> The bourgeoisie of Chinese descent [had] controlled nearly all important economic positions [including] more than 80 percent . . . of the food, textile, chemical, metallurgy, engineering and electrical industries and nearly achieved a trading monopoly— wholesale trade 100 percent, retail trade more than 50 percent and export-import trade 90 percent. They completely controlled the purchase of rice and paddy. . . . They could manipulate prices. . . . They built a closed world based on blood relations. . . . This was truly a state within a state.

One would have to return to Marx and Engels's peoples without a history to find in Marxist literature so close an association of a specific people with the forces of reaction. The Hoa community evidently had no more role to play in the future of the single socialist Vietnamese nation than the southern Slavs had had in Marx's scheme of things.

WE began this chapter by noting that debates among Marxist-Leninist elites concerning the relative stress to be placed at any one moment upon national flourishing rather than upon more direct assimilationist techniques were merely debates over means and not over ends. They involved a tactical question of tempo but not disagreement concerning the ultimate merging of nations. But it is, of course, only superficially true to say that disagreement is only over tempo; it is more likely that the debate disguises a difference of opinion concerning ends. In a Marxist-Leninist state it would be deemed apostasy to deny the progressive nature and therefore the desirability of the merging of nations that both Marx and Lenin had described as inevitable. Consequently, debates over the ultimate destiny of nations customarily masquerade as debates over tempo. Those who caution a slow pace, who defend national flourishing, who cull Lenin for any citable hint of a prophecy of the long-term survival of nations may well be in favor of the indefinite perpetuation of a nation. This is most likely to be the case when the defender of national flourishing is a member of a minority. The point, however, is that Lenin's peculiar formula for achieving the desired goal of assimilation by promoting national flourishing has permitted both (1) those who would violate his strategy by promoting immediate assimilation, and (2) those who would violate his intended objectives by perpetuating nations for all time to cloak themselves in Leninist garb. The former could cite Lenin's many statements to the effect that Communists support everything that advances assimilation. The latter could cite his many references to the necessity of encouraging national flourishing. Thus Lenin's dialectical formula provided the camouflage for those who would ignore its strategy and for those who would defeat its ultimate purpose. But this is only one of the inherent shortcomings of Lenin's national policy.

NOTES

1. " 'Left-Wing' Communism, an Infantile Disorder" (1920), in Lenin, *Selected Works* 3:349.

2. Equally indefinite with regard to timetable was Lenin's 1919 statement: "To be international it is not enough for it to proclaim a world Soviet republic, or the abolition of nations, as Comrade Pyatakov did when he said: 'We don't want any nations. What we want is the union of all proletarians.' This is splendid, of course, and eventually it will come about, but at an entirely different stage of communist development." "Speech Closing the Debate on the Party Programme," March 19, 1919, in Lenin, *Selected Works* 3:136.

3. Speech commemorating the semicentennial of the formation of the Soviet Union. *Current Digest of the Soviet Press* 24, no. 51 (1972): 9.

4. Dzyuba, *Internationalism?*, 182–183. Dzyuba wrote his critical work in 1965, the year after Khrushchev's ouster.

5. See chapter 2, note 34. As mentioned previously, in a private letter in 1913 Lenin had noted that "the Russian tongue would be for a number of unfortunate and backward peoples of progressive significance—no doubt of it. But do you see that it would be of still greater progessive significance if there were no compulsion to use it." Cited in Wolfe, *Three Who*, 584.

6. For a fascinating account of Kasymov's irregular image in Soviet history, see Tillett, "Nationalism and History," 36–45. Genghis Khan's place in Chinese Communist history will be treated later in the chapter.

7. "The Immediate Tasks of the Party in Connection with the National Problem," Resolution Adopted by the Tenth Congress of the Russian Communist Party, March 1921. The resolution, which was drawn up by Stalin, is reprinted in Stalin, *Marxism and National, Colonial Questions*, 270–279. The citation appears on p. 278. Although in the formal resolution Stalin referred to local nationalism as "bourgeois-democratic nationalism," in his oral comment to the Congress he spoke of "the deviation towards local, native nationalism." See ibid., 104.

The ascription of particular opprobrium to Great Russian chauvinism in the 1921 resolution had been heralded two years earlier in the 1919 Party Program: "The proletariat of the nations which have been oppressing nations must exercise special caution and pay special attention to the survivals of national sentiment among the toiling masses of oppressed or non-sovereign nations."

8. "National Factors in Party and State Development," Resolution Adopted by the Twelfth Congress of the Russian Communist Party, April 1923, reprinted in Stalin, *Marxism and National, Colonial Questions*, 279–287. Citation from page 283.

9. Ibid., 286.

10. "Report on National Factors in Party and State Development," April 23, 1923, in ibid., 154–155. However, in response to criticism from the floor, Stalin rejected the notion that equality demanded for a time special treatment for the non-Russians vis-à-vis the Russians (a position that could find support in the writings of Lenin). He also defended retention of criticism of local chauvinism, that is, arrogance displayed by Georgians and others toward non-Russian peoples. (Ibid., 168–169.)

11. "The Political Tasks of the University of the Peoples of the East," May 18, 1925, in Stalin, *Works* 7:145.

12. Barghoorn, *Soviet Russian*, 37, and Szporluk, "Nationalities and Russian Problem," 29. Szporluk cites Robert Sullivant (*Soviet Politics and the Ukraine*, 132) as noting that by 1926 Stalin "was beginning to identify Russia and Russian institutions with Marxism and Bolshevik rule."

13. "The National Question and Leninism," March 18, 1929, in Stalin, *Works* 11:361.

14. See discussion later this chapter.

15. Stalin, *Works* 11:363–364.

16. "After the victory of socialism on a world scale . . . we will have . . . hundreds of national languages from which at first the most enriched single zonal languages will emerge as a result of lengthy economic, political, and cultural co-operation of nations, and subsequently the zonal languages will fuse into one common international language, which will of course be neither German, nor Russian, nor English, but a new language which has absorbed the best elements of the national and zonal languages." Stalin, *Marxism and Linguistics*, 46.

17. See chapter 9.

18. The fact that Stalin's essay was ostensibly a reply to several pieces of correspondence and was not made public until 1949 does not materially detract from the likelihood of the latter explanation. It is customary for such open letters by the leaders to be circulated broadly within the apparatus. Moreover, Stalin reiterated most of the same basic points publicly the following year before the Sixteenth Party Congress. See his report in Stalin, *Marxism and National, Colonial Questions*, 256–266.

19. Stalin, *Works* 11:370.

20. The resolution is reproduced in Stalin, *Marxism and National, Colonial Questions*, 287.

21. "Extract from the Report on the Work of the Central Committee of the CPSU Delivered at the Seventeenth Party Congress," January 26, 1934, in ibid., 267–268.

22. The overall trend under Stalin is visible in the reports of the party congresses. Whereas, as we have noted, the Sixteenth Congress declared "Great-Russian chauvinism" as the principal enemy and the Seventeenth Congress formally declared both deviations equally pernicious, the Eighteenth Congress (1939) declared "nationalist deviations" the most invidious.

23. For details on this trend during the Stalinist years, see Barghoorn, *Soviet Russian*.

24. See chapter 9.

25. Rakowska-Harmstone, "Dialectics of Nationalism," 17, and Harned, "Latvia," 115.

26. Hodnett, "What's in a Nation?" 2. For Khrushchev's speech see Christman, *Communism*, 158–228.

27. Hodnett, "What's in a Nation?" 2.

28. See chapter 9.

29. Strangely out of tune with Khrushchev's programs at home was his speech in Leipzig, East Germany on March 7, 1959. In it, Khrushchev opined that national distinctions would survive even the worldwide victory of communism and the withering away of the state:

> With the victory of communism on a world-wide scale, state boundaries will become extinct, Marxist-Leninism teaches us. In all probability only ethnographical boundaries will remain for the time being, and even they will no doubt only be conventional. On these boundaries, if they can be called such at all, there will be no frontier guards, no customs officials, no incidents. They will simply record the historically evolved fact that this or that nationality inhabits a given territory.

Adding to the remarkableness of the speech was its publication in *Pravda* on March 27, 1959.

30. The program is reprinted in its entirety in Schapiro, *USSR and Future*. Part 4, "The Tasks of the Party in the Field of National Relations," is on pp. 301–303.

31. Barghoorn, *Politics in USSR*, 77.

32. Rakowska-Harmstone, "Dialectics of Nationalism," 18.

33. Two years after Khrushchev's ouster, a number of speakers at a meeting of the Ukrainian Writers Congress complained of the pressures exerted on them during the early 1960s to publish in the Russian language, as part of a program to hasten assimilation. In a most unusual apology, a secretary of the Russian Federation Writers Union who was present stated: "I as a Russian could not understand the haste with which we suddenly began to talk about the merging of cultures." He acknowledged that there

had been "those among us who proceeded with undue haste and have been responsible for some not very pleasant feelings and moods around the issue." See the *New York Times*, January 29, 1967.

34. Among the participating authors was one who had previously recommended the immediate abolition of the republics, another who had not only defended the republics but had called for an extension of their powers to be guaranteed by the anticipated, new constitution, and still another who had daringly written that "only stupid people can suppose that the time has already come to curtail the development of the national statehood, culture, and language of the people of the USSR." See Hodnett, "What's in a Nation?" particularly pp. 7, 8, and 11. See also Howard, "Definition."

35. For a listing of twenty-three such studies, see the bibliography appended to Silver, "Inventory of Propositions."

36. Events in Czechoslovakia and Yugoslavia during the late 1960s unquestionably exerted great impact.

37. *Current Digest of the Soviet Press* 23, no. 14 (1971): 3.

38. Ibid. 24, no. 51, (1972): 10.

39. See the subsection entitled "Recent Manifestations of Nationalism" under each of the chapters in Katz, *Handbook*. The most highly publicized demotion for nationalist deviations involved the Ukrainian party's First Secretary, Shelest.

40. Rakowska-Harmstone, "Dialectics of Nationalism," 20. See also Shyrock, "Indigenous Economic Managers," 101. See also Berner et al., *Soviet Union 1975–76*, 55, whose authors detect less publicity accorded the flowering of nations and more on their "approximation" during 1975–1976.

41. Article 19. "All-round" was substituted for "continued" in the interim between the appearances of the original draft of the constitution and the final product. The substitution may be quite significant to the issue of tempo, since the use of "continued" might have been construed as projecting an indefinite prolongation of national "development."

42. Emphasis in original. The speech, delivered on October 4, 1977, appeared in *Pravda* and *Izvestia* the following day. The new constitution had been in preparation for many years, and it reflected a search of the constitutions of other states for appropriate ideas and phrases. Thus the use of the word *possibility* in relation to use of language was foreshadowed by the Hungarian Constitution (see chapter 8), and the notion of self-determination as a fully exercised, irreversible act (Article 70) was borrowed from Yugoslavia.

43. The article appeared in *World Marxist Review*, no. 12 (1977); *Pravda*, November 23,1977; and *International Affairs* (Moscow), no. 1 (1978). The citation is from the last, p. 5.

44. "Soviet men and women, whatever their nationality, have an all embracing, international awareness of their homeland, which is not and cannot be confined solely to their own Republic, but applies to the whole socialist country." Khalmukhamedov, "Soviet Society," 27.

45. Ibid., 29.

46. "Critical Remarks on the National Question" (1913), in Lenin, *Collected Works* 20:27–28.

47. Fedoseyev, "60 Years of the USSR."

48. In harmony with many other articles of the period, Fedoseyev's piece in *Pravda* (ibid.) stressed the need for social engineering ("scientific management of social development") with regard to "the internationalization process in all spheres of our life." As a member of the CPSU Central Committee and vice president of the Academy of Sciences, Fedoseyev's words carried the stamp of official sanction. In a later piece ("The USSR," 26–30), he suggested that the need for state control over the objective process of rapprochement be stressed in all lectures on the national question that were then being prepared to commemorate the forthcoming sixtieth anniversary of the formation of the Soviet Union:

> However, the effect of this [process], which is contributing to the rapprochement of the nations under the conditions of developed socialism, is realized far from automatically. Like any other complex and multi-aspectual process of socialist building, it requires a constant improvement in the scientific control of social development, primarily centralized planning in combination with the broad initiative of the union and autonomous republics, an increase in the creative assertiveness of the masses and a rise in their consciousness and cultural level and an emphatic struggle against all manifestations of localism and departmental preference (it is recommended that this point of the lecture also be illustrated as far as possible with figures, facts and concrete examples on the basis of local material).

49. *FBIS*, May 25, 1979, p. 109.

50. Ibid., 110.

51. Voss, "Development of National Relations."

52. One "scientific-practical" conference, held in the capital of Tadzhikistan in February 1982, was even entitled "Let Us Study the Language of Lenin, the Language of October."

53. See *JPRS* 81266 (July 13, 1982). An article appearing in a Kazakh journal about this same time notes (in the words of a reviewer) "the importance of the Russian language in the process of mutual assimilation and underscores bilateral borrowing of words and concepts between Russian and nationalities languages as an affirmation of the process of assimilation itself." See *JPRS* 80867 (May 20, 1982): 22.

54. Voss, "Development of National Relations," 17.

A sophisticated account of a conference on the national question under mature socialism suggested that forms were scheduled to lose some of their national coloration (Baranva, "International and National," 54–60, emphasis added):

The dialectics of the international and the national were traced in the spiritual sphere, and the qualitative differences in the internationalization of the spiritual sphere under socialism and capitalism were shown. Internationalization in a socialist society occurs within a process of a reciprocally conditioned flourishing and rapprochement of nations *within a predominant trend of their growing closer*. Under these conditions the proportion of the international increases, moreover, not only in the economic and socio-political fields, but also in the cultural sphere (although, of course, the ways and rates of internationalization of the economy and culture are different). For a socialist culture, national in form and socialist in content, the determining factor is the content. *But the form does not remain unchanged either.* It becomes more international within a situation of reciprocal influences of socialist cultures. Consequently, with regard to culture this same principle is operative. Lack of recognition of this position leads to a denial of the validity of the law of internationalization, which is unsound theoretically and unsupported by the overall practical experience in the development of Soviet culture.

55. "We Are the Soviet People," *JPRS* 82130, November 1, 1982, p. 10.

56. Kosolapov, "Class and National Relations." The excerpts are from pp. 12, 18, 21, and 22.

57. Another article in the same issue of the journal outlined an extremely broad and ambitious agenda for the social sciences in solving the national question. See the unsigned "The Strengthening of the Social and International Unity of Soviet Society: Urgent Questions of Scientific Research Developments," *JPRS* 82853, February 11, 1983, pp. 4–9.

58. Chernenko, "60 Years," 13, 14.

59. Andropov, "Sixty Years of the USSR." The excerpts are from pp. 2, 4.

60. "The Common Program of the Chinese People's Consultative Conference," September 29, 1949, can be found in Chen, *Chinese Communist*, 34 et seq.

61. Hyer and Heaton, "Cultural Revolution in Inner Mongolia," 116.

62. Cited in Dreyer, "Chinese Communist Policy," 178.

63. "Basic Summarization of Experiences," 16.

64. Ibid., 16, 17, 19.

65. Ibid., 20. Emphasis added.

66. The 1954 constitution is reproduced in Christman, *Communism*, 133–157.

67. *On the Ten Great Relationships*, April 25, 1956. This translation is from that in Schram, *Chairman Mao Talks*, 74. A similar translation can be found in Ch'en, *Mao*.

68. *Keesing's Contemporary Archives* (1977), 28212. The speech, as cited by *Keesing's*, had been printed in *People's Daily* on December 26, 1976, well after Mao's death, and was described by the world press (including *Keesing's*) as never before published. Yet the translation of the speech which

was published by Stuart Schram in 1974 was just cited. The matter is made more intriguing by the fact that the version published by Schram (as well as that published by Jerome Ch'en in 1969) did *not* contain these adverse references to prior Soviet practice. The version released in 1976 can be found in full in the *Peking Review* 20, no. 1 (January 1, 1977), and in Mao, *Selected Works* (Peking) 5:281–307.

69. Mao, *Selected Works* (Peking) 5:296. Again, this passage did not appear in the earlier versions and may well have been added ex post facto. For an official acknowledgment that Mao's official works were often altered, see *The Times* (London), January 6, 1981.

70. Schram, *Chairman Mao Talks*, 73. The references to separatism were deleted from the translation released in 1976. In Mao's *Selected Works* (Peking) 5:292, this section of his address had become "The Relationship between the Central and Local Authorities."

71. John Lewis, *Major Doctrines*, 117.

72. As published, the speech became known as "On the Correct Handling of Contradictions among the People." It can be found in Mao, *Selected Works* (Peking) 5:384–421.

73. Ibid., 406–407.

74. An early translation of the speech appeared in the Chinese (English-language) magazine, *China Reconstructs*. (This translation can be found in Freemantle, *Mao Tse-tung*, 264–297.) It was prefaced in *China Reconstructs* by an acknowledgement that "[t]he author has gone over the text based on the verbatim record and made certain additions." Moreover, the speech is dated July 1, 1957, thereby further acknowledging that it had been altered since its original delivery in February. By contrast, as the speech was later published in Mao's *Selected Works* (Peking) in 1977, no such acknowledgment was appended, and the February date was employed, even though the post-February revisions had been incorporated.

75. Mao did go on to say that "of these six criteria, the most important are the socialist path and the leadership of the Party." However, all the other criteria (numbers 1, 3, 4, and 6) could have been subsumed under these two, so we are still left to puzzle the perplexing question of why such prominent public stress was placed on the national question.

76. *Yunan Daily*, August 25, 1957.

77. Cited in Dreyer, *Chinese Communist Policy*, 224.

78. *People's Daily*, December 26, 1957.

79. Cited in Dreyer, *Chinese Communist Policy*, 224. This response might be termed "the Uncle Han" syndrome.

80. *Kuang Ming Daily*, January 17, 1958.

81. Cited in Dreyer, *Chinese Communist Policy*, 224.

82. The speed with which policy changed direction is illustrated by the fact that less than three months earlier (August 4, 1957), Chou En-lai had delivered a speech on the national question noting: "We oppose two types of chauvinism, namely, big-nationality chauvinism (in China, chiefly Han

chauvinism) and local-nationality chauvinism, with our attention to combatting Han chauvinism in particular." (For additional details on the speech, which was not published until 1980, see later this chapter.)

83. Deal, "National Minority," 137.

84. Ibid., 138.

85. Typical was the statement attributed to a Hui spokesman that "the mother country of the Huis is not China." (*Kuang Ming Daily*, January 17, 1958.)

86. Cited in Hu, *Education of National Minorities*, 18.

87. *People's Daily*, February 13, 1958. The statement had been read at the fifth session, held on February 10.

88. Dreyer, *Chinese Communist Policy*, 241. The following account of the minorities during the Great Leap Forward draws heavily from documents cited in Dreyer's well-documented narrative, pp. 240–247.

89. A partial, intended exception to this policy may have been the Tibetans, who were only recently promised by the authorities that they could continue their traditional structure under the Dalai Lama. However, Han cadre on the scene, reacting to Peking's general line, acted much as cadre in other minority areas, frightening supporters of the Lama and resulting in his flight to India in March 1959.

90. Dreyer, *Chinese Communist Policy*, 242–243.

91. During this period, rebellions erupted among the Hui, Yi, and Tibetans. But unrest was reported among nearly all of the remote peoples.

92. *Yunan Daily*, December 24, 1958. Emphasis added.

93. Dreyer, *China's Forty*, 178.

94. P'eng, we will recall, had been a major figure in the pre-1949 struggle of the CCP. See chapter 4.

95. Cited in Dreyer, *China's Forty*, 181.

96. Not much importance should be attributed to the article's reference to the Great Leap and the communes for, in deference to Mao, both continued to be paid lip service long after they had been discarded or altered beyond recognition in all but name.

97. The article is cited in Dreyer, *China's Forty*, 185.

98. More than 70,000 Kazakhs fled to the USSR during 1962–1963.

99. Mao Tse-tung, *Statement Calling on the People*, 5. Mao's reintroduction of this theme in a statement referring to another country rather than to the domestic scene may itself be a hint that the outcome of the competition between the two factions was currently very much in doubt. In any case, subsequent articles applied Mao's words to the Chinese scene.

100. The article was given broad circulation and was published by the Foreign Languages Press in 1966 as simply "The Nationalities Question and Class Struggle." All subsequent pagination refers to this 1966 version.

101. Liu Ch'un, *National Question*, 11.

102. Ibid., 17.

103. Ibid., 18.

104. Ibid., 20.

105. However, the gradualists had, of course, maintained that these leaders had been provoked into rebellion by the ill-conceived policies of the ultraists.

106. Liu Ch'un, *National Question*, 27.

107. Major pieces of evidence of the continuing gradualist policy on the national question included a very moderate speech on the subject by Chou En-lai in 1964 and the establishment of the Tibetan Autonomous Republic in September 1965.

108. Although the Cultural Revolution was officially launched at the Eleventh Plenum of the Central Committee in August 1966, it had been apparent for some months prior to that meeting that the ultraists were in the ascendancy.

109. In addition to further deterioration in relations with the Soviet Union and India, stepped-up U.S. involvement in Vietnam was another matter for concern with the border regions. The major supply lines between industrial China and Vietnam passed through the homelands of the Chuang and less numerous minority peoples.

110. Witness the center's immediate and effective reactions whenever clashes between factions endangered the unity of the People's Liberation Army or threatened disruption of research and development on modern weapons.

111. The major gradualist to avoid the purge was Chou En-lai, who, as Chinese specialists of the time regularly pointed out, was Mao-like in his ability to survive changes in the fortunes of the two major factions striving for control of the state apparatus.

112. The pamphlet, dated April 1967, was attributed to the "Red Army" Corps of the K'angta Commune of the Central Institute for Nationalities.

113. In addition, the Mongol, Ulanfu, was charged with having eulogized the once-more-discredited Genghis Khan. See, for example, Hyer and Heaton, "Cultural Revolution," 124.

114. *Survey of China Mainland Press*, no. 4151:3.

115. See the interesting article on the draft constitution by Stephan Pan in the *Christian Science Monitor*, May 13, 1969.

116. See *Area Handbook for the People's Republic of China*, 237. The 1954 constitution had also identified China as a "unitary multinational state" and described the autonomous regions as "inseparable." However, in 1954 the concept of autonomy had been viewed in a favorable light and a full section of the constitution (Section 5) had been dedicated to it.

117. Cited in Dreyer, *China's Forty*, 148.

118. *Peking Review* 17 (July 19, 1974): 18.

119. *Hsinhua News Agency*, March 6, 1978. Reprinted in the *Peking Review* 21 (March 10, 1978): 8–40.

120. If further proof of the reversion to national flourishing was needed, it was proffered on May 12, 1980, when Genghis Khan was once again

rehabilitated. On that date, *People's Daily* praised him as a "leader of Chinese and foreign peoples, an outstanding military strategist and statesman."

121. *Keesing's Contemporary Archives* (1980), 30495.

122. See discussion earlier this chapter. It is, of course, also significant that Mao's 1957 speech, as finally published, contained the warning that any action that could be interpreted as divisive would be strenuously dealt with.

123. *Hsinhua*, October 17, 1979. Reprinted in *FBIS*, October 19, 1979.

124. For an account of the effect of some of these changes upon the Sinkiang-Uighur AR, see the *International Herald Tribune*, October 31, 1980.

125. The speech was reprinted in two segments in the *Peking Review* 23 (March 3 and March 10, 1980) under the title "Some Questions on Policy Toward Nationalities."

126. Ibid. (March 3, 1980), 14. The reported date of the speech is interesting in that it postdated the publication of the altered version of Mao's Hundred Flowers speech by two months (see earlier discussion). Since Chou's speech was an affirmation of the policy supported by Mao in 1956 and early 1957 but seemingly repudiated by him in June 1957, the date of Chou's speech suggests that Mao's determination, as a result of the criticism unleashed by the Hundred Flowers campaign, to set a totally new course for China in all matters, including the national question, was not yet fully realized by some of his closest associates. As to the 1980 charge that Chou's speech had been suppressed for twenty years, this was in keeping with the current tendency to blame past errors on the national question on those responsible for the Great Leap and Cultural Revolution. Thus an editorial in the *Peking Review* of January 21, 1980 (p. 4), noted:

> The Party and government have always attached great importance to work among the national minorities. Effective measures have been taken to protect their rights, develop their economies and cultures and raise their living standards by taking into consideration their special needs.
>
> However, the government's correct policies were sabotaged during the Cultural Revolution and an abnormal situation emerged. For instance, the equal rights enjoyed by these minority nationalities were infringed upon.

127. Commenting on the meaning of "autonomy" in the new constitution, John Gittings remarked: "Autonomy certainly does not mean self-determination—something Chinese Communists used to promise rather vaguely before 1949. It means following the same path as the rest of China but more slowly and making allowances for 'local conditions'." (*Manchester Guardian*, September 24, 1979.) The new constitution had also pledged to "accomplish the great cause of *unifying* our motherland" through the acquisition of Taiwan, which was described as "China's sacred territory." To accomplish this, the leadership subsequently promised that Taiwan could

enjoy "autonomy" in a reunited China. (*New York Times*, January 10, 1979.) This projected autonomy would seem to validate Gitting's definition.

128. As the prosecutor noted: "Freedom of speech of the individual citizen must be based on the four basic principles of insisting on the socialist road, the dictatorship of the proletariat, the leadership of the Party and Marxist-Leninism Mao Tse-tung thought. The citizen has only the freedom to support these principles and not the freedom to oppose them." (*New York Times*, November 5, 1979.)

The ephemeral nature of the constitutional guarantees was further highlighted when the right to write big-character posters was withdrawn. However, this ephemerality should not be taken to mean that the constitution has no significance. One non-Chinese writer, after noting that the 1978 constitution superseded one that had been in effect for only three years, has stated: "What functions does a constitution serve in the Chinese political system? It is a sham not worth the paper on which it is printed. It is an artifice of propaganda designed to impress and mislead foreigners. Does it have legal as well as political significance? The 1954 Constitution was not revised for two decades, why then was its 1975 successor so quickly overtaken by events?" (Cohen, "China's Changing Constitution," 796.) This analysis appears too harsh. The constitution of a Marxist-Leninist state is, of course, partly designed for propaganda purposes both within and without the country. But, as noted, a constitution can afford valuable clues to the prevalent thinking of the moment. Moreover, all Chinese constitutions prior to 1978 were, in effect, Maoist documents, and a fundamental reason for the new constitution was to declare a changing of the guard, that is, a clear declaration of a commitment to gradualism and pragmatism following the death of Mao.

129. *Keesing's Contemporary Archives* (1982), 31319.

130. *FBIS*, April 28, 1982, p. K4.

131. *FBIS*, September 9, 1982, pp. K1 et seq.

132. Chou En-lai, "Some Questions," 22.

133. See, for example, the *New York Times*, February 10, 1983.

134. See, for example, Jing Wei, "Tibet," 47; "Yunnan's Sun Yuting Talks about Nationality Work," *JPRS* 82615, January 11, 1983, p. 60; and Xinjiang Nationality Unity Gathering Reported," *JPRS* 82440, December 10, 1982, p. 67.

135. See, for example, "Xinjiang Nationality," 60: "The people of all nationalities in Xinjiang are fine sons and daughters of the Chinese nation." See also Li Hongran, "Lu Xun," 75 et seq., where the various national groups are subsumed under "the Chinese race" throughout the article. Finally, see "Stress the Key," 111, where the First Secretary of the CPC Committee of the Uighur AR asserts: "It must be recognized that China is a multi-national country and that the Chinese nation is a whole—the Han nationality can't do without the national minorities and the national minorities can't do without the Han nationality."

136. The principal difference between Yugoslav and Soviet constitutions was that the former did not grant the theoretic right of secession to the republics.

137. Articles 10 and 11.

138. Article 3. A sixth torch was added to the coat of arms after the Moslems of Bosnia-Hercegovina were elevated to the status of a nation.

139. Shoup, *Communism and Yugoslav National Question*, 192.

140. See chapter 8.

141. Shoup, *Communism and Yugoslav National Question*, 189.

142. Rusinow (*Yugoslav Experiment*, xvii) notes that the first act of the government under the new name was "to redefine Serbs, Croats, and Slovenes (the first already subsuming Montenegrins, Macedonians and Bosnian Moslems) as 'tribes' of one Yugoslav nation." There was, of course, nothing new in this definition, since it was the official state position from the beginning.

143. Cited in Shoup, *Communism and Yugoslav National Question*, 198.

144. *Programme of the League of Yugoslav Communists*.

145. Kardelj, *Development of Slovenian National Question*. Although published simply as a revised edition of a work originally published in 1938, the book contained a lengthy introduction that represented the first important postrevolutionary theoretical work on nationalism by a leading member of the YCP. The use of this device to publish such a significant tract may itself have been a manifestation of a desire to avoid riling national groups by making it appear that the party planned no radical innovations but was merely pursuing a decades-old policy on the national question.

146. Ibid., 61. Translation as it appears in Frey, "Yugoslav Nationalisms," 27.

147. Elsewhere (p. 398), Kardelj, in reference to nations, spoke of the necessary process of their "dying out as a special force in general."

148. Kardelj's intense dislike of nationalism is well conveyed in the following passage:

Nationalism in our conditions is one of those reactionary ideological factors which draws peoples backwards, shuts out socialist perspectives, hinders the formation of socialist consciousness, and cripples that practical socialist creative activity. . . . As such, nationalism is a reactionary force which undermines many of the results of the National Liberation War and revolution, deforms equal relations among the peoples of Yugoslavia, and would significantly cripple the socialist enthusiasm which initiated the revolution if socialist forces did not actively fight against its manifestations and sources. (Kardelj, *Development of Slovenia*, 39. Cited in Shoup, *Communism and Yugoslav National Question*, 205–206.)

149. Ibid., 398–399.

150. Ibid., 53–54.

151. Shoup, *Communism and Yugoslav National Question*, 213.

152. Rusinow, *Yugoslav Experiment*, 135.

153. See, for example, Shoup, *Communism and Yugoslav National Question*, 195.

154. Officially sanctioned discussions of the draft treaty confirmed that this was not an oversight, but was specifically intended as a prohibition. A contributing factor to the decision may have been the embarrassingly small percentage (1.7 percent) of the populace who were currently demonstrating a willingness to take advantage of the "Yugoslav" category under the 1961 census.

155. Shoup, *Communism and Yugoslav National Question*, 197, and King, *Minorities*, 250.

156. Shoup, *Communism and Yugoslav National Question*, 190.

157. Rusinow, *Yugoslav Experiment*, 135.

158. Ibid.

159. See, for example, the excerpt from a 1962 speech by a leading Macedonian Communist in King, *Minorities*, 250–251.

160. *Kommunist*, January 14, 1963.

161. Shoup, *Communism and Yugoslav National Question*, 224.

162. Cited in Rusinow, *Yugoslav Experiment*, 167, and King, *Minorities*, 250.

163. Article 28 of the statute adopted at the Eighth Congress.

164. Shoup, *Communism and Yugoslav National Question*, 213.

165. See chapter 8.

166. For details, see chapter 8.

167. See, for example, King, *Minorities*, 250–251.

168. Speech of July 5, 1966 to foreign correspondents, as cited in *Keesing's Contemporary Archives* (1966), 21568.

169. For a fuller analysis of Kardelj's strategy, see chapter 8.

170. The assumption of a direct relationship between national consciousness and a perception of being discriminated against is certainly compatible with Leninist thought. See chapters 2 and 8.

171. *New York Times*, November 13, 1966.

172. Joncic, *Relations between Nationalities*, 54–55. Dr. Joncic was Federal Deputy of the Chamber of Nationalities and Director of the Research Program on the Relations between Nationalities in Yugoslavia.

173. Ibid., 75.

174. Šuvar, *Relationship between the Class and the National*, 4.

175. The series, written by Dr. Aleksander Grlickov, appeared in *Borba* in four installments during July 1976. The following citations are from the issue of July 22.

176. Tito's own speeches offer hints that he had never strayed from the goal of assimilation. In a speech of May 8, 1971, he stated: "There is only one Yugoslav League of Communists and only one Yugoslav working class." In an interview in Croatia during October 1972, he stated: "We must strive toward unification at a cultural level, that is towards a close

mutual co-operation and assistance, and must strive not to divide our people." And on October 30, 1975, in a most uncharacteristic misuse of terms, Tito spoke of "the whole nation" as being "determined to defend its achievements and its freedom if they are threatened." *Keesing's Contemporary Archives*, 24735, 25795, 27635.

177. For example, acknowledgment of the existence of those in favor of a return to *Jugoslovenstvo*, a year after the purge of Rankovich for this sin, was made in 1967 by Joncic (*Relations between Nationalities*, 54) who offered a remarkably mild rebuke: "According to some, the increasingly dynamic economic development and the creation of large industrial centres with mixed populations is leading towards the creation of a uniform Yugoslav nation. However well-meaning, or superficial and one sided this view may be, essentially it is a negative one." And Rusinow (*Yugoslav Experiment*, 246) reports that at a May 1968 meeting of the Serbian party's Central Committee, two speakers openly criticized the fact that a supranational notion of Yugoslavianism was no longer being promoted.

178. One of the standard gauges that we have employed in other Marxist-Leninist states, the relative criticism of local nationalism or chauvinism, is not as accurate in the case of Yugoslavianism. Because of the relative numerical equivalency of the nations (that is, the absence of a clearly predominant nation) plus the undisguised national animosities, the authorities are more hesitant to make a target of one people. Thus, even at the time of the purge of Croatians in the early 1970s for blatant, nationalist, antistate activities, a series of trials of Serbs for chauvinism was also conducted. Throughout 1974, 1975, and 1976, charges brought against Croats and Albanians for nationalist and separatist activities were regularly balanced by trials of Serbs for "Chetnik" activities (the latter had become a synonym for Great Serbian chauvinism). See, for example, *Keesing's Contemporary Archives*, 27021, 27635, 27636, 17754, 17940, 281977, 29098, 29236.

179. Croatians were reported to favor such efforts over either codevelopment of a "feeling of belonging to a specific nation" plus belonging to the "Yugoslav socialist community," or development of "the feeling of belonging to a specific nation as the most relevant expression of historical tradition, culture, and political freedom." (For the specific results, see table 49 in Denitch, *Legitimation of a Revolution*, 204.) That such a favorable view of *Jugoslovenstvo* represented a valid survey of attitudes within Croatia only months before the surfacing of militant Croatian nationalism resists credibility. Moreover, the percentage of all Yugoslavians who identified themselves as Yugoslav in the 1971 census was only 1.3 percent. Polling on national attitudes appears to have fallen into disfavor in the 1970s, probably due to the national animosities that surfaced during the Croatian events of the early 1970s. Similar passions surfaced between Serbs and Albanians during the early 1980s.

180. See, for example, the account of a round table on "federalism,

autonomy, and self-management," sponsored by the Marxist Center of the Central Committee of the Serbian CP in Momcilo Djorgovic, "Those Who Are Bothered by Federalism," *JPRS* 81669, August 31, 1982, pp. 55–58. Complaints were voiced about the way in which the autonomy of the republics and provinces had been permitted to lead to "etatism, nationalism, autarchy, and the stagnation of self-management." One panelist noted how far removed Yugoslav federalism had become from that of Lenin: "The Leninist concept of a federation is a way to bring nations closer together and unite them, not a way to separate them." The difference in perceptions between the panelists and the leadership of the country-wide party was underlined by the fact that at the Twelfth Congress of the Yugoslavian League of Communists, which convened only a few days after this round table, the President of the Presidium sharply and repeatedly stressed the need to combat "centralist tendencies." (See *Keesing's Contemporary Archives* [1982], 31672.) The convening of the round table immediately before the Twelfth Congress suggests an attempt by the Serbian party to influence decisions at the congress.

181. For a somewhat sketchy account of the national policy of the Czechoslovak Communist Party during the interwar period, see Steiner, *Slovak Dilemma*, 41–47.

182. In the case of the Slovaks, the national party was the Hlinka People's Party.

183. Toma, "Czechoslovak Question," 18.

184. Ibid., 18–19.

185. Ulc, *Politics in Czechoslovakia*, 16.

186. See the review by Yeshayahu Jelinek of a number of monographs published within Czechoslovakia, "Between Nationalism and Communism," 334–341. The citation is from p. 341.

187. Toma, "Czechoslovak Question," 21.

188. Ulc, *Politics in Czechoslovakia*, 16.

189. See chapter 6. One poll indicated that federalism was supported by 73 percent of the Slovaks but only by a bare majority of Czechs. See Ulc, *Politics in Czechoslovakia*, 16.

190. The very liberal Constitutional Law of October 27, 1968 had unambiguously stated (Article 4, paragraph 3): "All forms of pressure toward de-nationalization [of all peoples and nationalities] are prohibited."

191. The selection of a Slovak as First Secretary was particularly essential because the deposed Secretary, Alexander Dubcek, had been the country's first Slovak to hold that position.

192. Ulc, *Politics in Czechoslovakia*, 17.

193. Renner, "National Minorities in Czechoslovakia," 36.

194. This review of assimilationist articles from the Czechoslovak press was reported by the Yugoslav *Tanjug* reporter in Prague. The great significance attributed to the report by Yugoslav authorities was shown by its

publication in both *Borba* and *Politika* on June 8, 1976. Yet, quite enigmatically, the report refrained from any suggestion of criticism or acclaim.

195. Laco, "The Czechoslovak Federation," 3, 16, 17.

196. See, for example, the *Bulgarian Situation Report* (Radio Free Europe) of April 28, 1976; May 14, 1976; and December 8, 1977.

197. Although Albania was certainly not susceptible to Soviet influence at this time, it is interesting that Tirana in 1976 also decreed that all persons whose names did not conform to the party's "political, ideological and moral standards" must change them or have them changed by the authorities. (See the *Washington Post* of February 26, 1976, and the *New York Times* of February 27, 1976.) The timing of the decree suggests that the Bulgarian example must have played a role in the decree's formulation.

198. Two other significant elements had been assimilated at the statistical level prior to 1970. Before World War II, Moslems of Bulgarian stock (who describe themselves as "Pomaks") had been listed in the census as a separate group. Although identifying Moslems as a separate national group has (with the single exception of the 1953 census) also been the practice within Yugoslavia, the Bulgarian CP has steadfastly treated Moslems of Bulgarian stock in all censuses as Bulgars. A second important group, the Macedonians, were treated as a separate national group in the 1956 census but were thereafter declared to be Bulgars. However, real, in contradistinction to statistical, assimilation of these two groups was also a goal of the "single socialist nation" program.

199. *Bulgarian Situation Report* (Radio Free Europe), December 8, 1977, p. 5.

200. The 1963 Party Program, for example, had specifically called upon its members to "unify Germany," and the 1955 and 1964 treaties of friendship between East Germany and the USSR had each mentioned German reunification as a goal.

201. Ludz, "SED's Concept of Nation," 207.

202. Kosing and Schmidt, "Concerning the Development," 179–188. The article is treated at some length in Possony, "Communism and the National Question," 51–68. Kosing, a member of the Institute of Sociology, became East Germany's principal theoretician on the national question during this period.

203. See discussion earlier this chapter. The expression, *socialist nation*, had been used by the Austrian socialist, Otto Bauer, as early as 1907 in *The National Question and Social Democracy*. To Bauer, nations came to true fruition only under socialism, and a socialist nation was therefore a higher and more enduring form of nationhood. For an English translation of Bauer's passages on socialist nations, see Bottomore and Goode, *Austro-Marxism*, 107–109.

204. Emphasis added. The speech was given on October 9, 1975 on the occasion of the thirtieth anniversary of the founding of the Workers' Party

of Korea. Excerpts of the speech appeared in a full page advertisement in the *New York Times*, October 24, 1975.

205. There are numerous reasons why the East German leaders turned their backs upon reunification, but, in toto, they amounted to the fact that the magnetism exerted by West Germany upon East Germany was far more powerful than any countervailing influence. From an East German perspective, the following were some of the more compelling reasons for denying any bonds between the two populations: persistent defections; large numbers of requests for emigration permits; the perceived need for the Berlin Wall and the heavily guarded, fenced zone along the entire common border with West Germany; the popularity of West German over East German television, radio, and published materials; a serious public morale problem; and the continuously widening gap in living standards in favor of West Germany (despite the fact that the East German economy was outperforming the economies of other Marxist-Leninist states). In light of all this, West German Chancellor Willy Brandt's newly introduced policy of *Ostpolitik*, which anticipated an increase in the quantity and quality of contacts between the peoples of West and East Germany, represented a pressing threat to East German authority, and can therefore be viewed as an immediate cause of the decision to repudiate the link of common Germanness.

206. "For All-Round Development of Bulgaro-Yugoslav Relations." Emphasis added.

207. Ibid., 8.

208. Emphasis added.

209. *Keesing's Contemporary Archives* (1974), 26836.

210. A scholar in an Eastern European country and in a position to learn of such things informed this writer that the pressure for the de-Germanization campaign originated in the USSR. SED leaders for a time resisted, stating that the people would object. They reportedly relented only under severe pressure from Moscow.

211. Ludz, "SED's Concept of Nation," 208.

212. *Süddeutsche Zeitung*, February 19, 1975.

213. Kosing and Schmidt, "Nation and Nationality in the DDR." Notice that these were the same two authors who had produced the 1974 piece introducing the two-nation doctrine. For press reaction to this latest piece within West Germany, see *German Press Review*, February 26, 1975.

214. No attempt was made to explain the SED's pre-1974 acceptance of membership in the German nation. As late as 1969, for example, the General Secretary, in reference to relations between East and West Germany, had stated: "History teaches that it is possible to have international relations between sovereign states of one nation." (Ludz, "SED's Concept of Nation," 215.) And we have seen that the constitution in effect until the fall of 1974 had made several references to a common German nation.

215. Kosing, *Nation in History*. The citation is reproduced in Ludz, "SED's

Concept of Nation," 219–220. A Russian translation of Kosing's book was published in Moscow in 1978. A. Ye. Zharnikov ("National and International," 11–17) cites it favorably as helping "to scientifically explain the fact of existence of two German nations which preserve one nationality."

The Soviet commitment to the concept of two German nations can surface in odd ways. Thus a Soviet listing of the world's population by ethnonational category gives a consolidated figure for all Germans. But of the sixty-one peoples listed, only the German category is accompanied by an explanatory footnote. In this case, it read: "*Since the founding of the German Democratic Republic a socialist nation of that country has begun to take shape." See Bruk, "Post-War Dynamics," 230.

216. *New York Times*, May 23, 1976.

217. *New York Times*, December 18, 1978.

218. Whether they could succeed in this quest is another matter. On January 12, 1977, the *Stuttgarter Zeitung* reported that more than one hundred thousand applications for emigration to West Germany had been made to the East German authorities, despite the risk of penalties such as loss of job.

219. *New York Times*, November 9, 1975.

220. See chapter 5.

221. The speech was delivered during October 1976, and this section was carried by the *Ho Chi Minh Domestic Service*, November 2, 1976. Translated in *FBIS*, November 12, 1976.

222. The flexibility with which the Vietnamese authorities employed key terms at this time is illustrated by a June 1976 statement of the VCP's First Secretary Le Duan: "Nation and socialism are one. For us Vietnamese, love of country now means love of socialism." (Cited in Turley, "Vietnam Since Reunification," 36.) This terminological legerdemain, if successful, would transfuse the more bloodless concept of socialism with the emotion inherent in nationalism (identity with one's people) and patriotism (love of country).

223. *FBIS*, November 2, 1976.

224. Ibid., November 2 and 11, 1976. Emphasis added.

225. *Summary of World Broadcasts, Far East*, December 31, 1976. As in the previously cited speech, this address contained several symptoms of ethnic arrogance, such as two references to the need to give the minorities a "civilized" way of life.

226. See chapters 8 and 9.

227. See chapter 9.

228. The list of those purged included General Le Quang Ba (former Chairman of the Commission for Nationalities), General Chu Van Tan (a member of the Muong people who was very instrumental in creating the base areas for the Viet Minh in China during World War II), and Tran Dinh Tui (long-term specialist in "nationalities affairs"). They were dropped

from the CP's Central Committee in 1976 and were reportedly arrested in 1979. (See *Keesing's Contemporary Archives* [1979], 29876.)

229. For a general outline of the treatment accorded the Chinese community during this period, see *Keesing's Contemporary Archives* (1979), 29468–29473.

230. It is estimated that 250,000 crossed the Chinese border between April 1978 and summer 1979. Meanwhile, the largest share of so-called boat people fleeing from the southern sector were also Chinese. (See *Keesing's Contemporary Archives* [1980], 30075.)

231. *Keesing's Contemporary Archives* (1979), 29470 and 29472.

CHAPTER 11

. . . And National in Content

LENINISM VERSUS PRACTICE

The Leninist claim to have discovered the formula for expunging
nationalism can be evaluated from several perspectives. If evaluated
from the perspective of the results of the policies actually followed
by one or another Marxist-Leninist state, then Leninist national
policy has failed as a strategy for the quelling of nationalism. Numerous incidents, periodic trials of people accused of nationalist
deviations, and what few opinion surveys are available attest to the
presence of vigorous nationalism.[1] Indeed, even while maintaining
that they have solved their national question by the application of
Leninist national policy, party leaders have often acknowledged
that nationalism remains *a*, and often *the* principal obstruction to
the building of communism. Thus the Party Program of the Communist party of the Soviet Union proclaims:

> Nationalism is the chief political and ideological weapon used
> by international reaction and the remnants of the domestic re-
> actionary forces against the unity of the socialist countries. Na-
> tionalist sentiments and national narrow-mindedness do not dis-
> appear automatically with the establishment of the social system.
> Nationalist prejudice and survivals of former national strife are
> a province in which resistance to social progress may be most
> protracted and stubborn, bitter and insidious.
>
> The Communists consider it their prime duty to educate the
> working people in a spirit of internationalism, socialist patriotism,
> and intolerance of all possible manifestations of nationalism and
> chauvinism.[2]

The paradox inherent in calling for vigilance against nationalism
well after the national question ostensibly has been solved was apparent at the celebration of the fiftieth anniversary of the Soviet
Union. In listing the principal accomplishments of the Soviet experience, General Secretary Brezhnev emphasized the total solving
of the national question as a major attainment:

In summing up the heroic accomplishments of the last half century, we have every reason to say that the nationalities question, in the form in which it came down to us from the past, has been resolved completely, resolved definitively and irrevocably. (*Stormy applause.*) This achievement can rightfully be ranked among such victories in the construction of a new society in the U.S.S.R. as industrialization, collectivization and the cultural revolution.

A great brotherhood of people of labor, people who are united, regardless of national origin, by a community of class interests and goals, has come into being and has gained strength in our country; it has developed relations unprecedented in history, relations that we can rightfully call the Leninist friendship of peoples. (*Applause.*) This friendship, comrades, is our priceless property and one of the most significant gains of socialism, a gain that is most dear to the heart of every Soviet person. We Soviet people will always cherish this friendship as the apple of our eye! (*Prolonged applause.*)[3]

Much later in the same speech, however, the General Secretary suggested that the question was far from being resolved "completely," "definitively," or "irrevocably":

As I have already said, we have completely resolved the nationalities question in those aspects that we inherited from the prerevolutionary past. But nationality relations even in a society of mature socialism are a reality that is constantly developing and putting forth new problems and tasks. The Party constantly keeps these questions in its field of vision and resolves them in good time in the interests of the whole country and of each individual republic, in the interests of communist construction.

It should not be forgotten that nationalistic prejudices and exaggerated or distorted manifestations of national feelings are extremely tenacious phenomena that are deeply embedded in the psychology of people with insufficient political maturity. These prejudices continue to exist even in conditions in which objective preconditions for any antagonism in relations between nations have long since ceased to exist.[4]

This willingness to etch into the sharpest relief the fundamental discrepancy between the official posture and reality—a discrepancy hardly disguised by an allusion to an otherwise undifferentiated distinction between pre- and postrevolutionary nationalism—indicates that the vitality and perniciousness of nationalism within the Soviet Union were perceived by the General Secretary as having reached a point at which pretending that nationalism was not present constituted a greater risk than did the damage that might flow from puncturing the official myth of having solved the national question.[5]

Multinational Marxist-Leninist states have certainly not been unique in experiencing national unrest. Multinational states throughout the globe, regardless of official ideology, have recently been swept with nationally inspired ferment.[6] No state can convincingly lay claim to be a model for combatting nationalism. But the fact that other states have fared no better (and in many instances have fared worse) in managing problems associated with ethnonational heterogeneity in no way strengthens the claim that Leninist national policy has proven an effective answer to the national question.

Defenders of the Leninist formula would be on firmer ground if they contended that Leninist national policy has nowhere been given a fair test. As we have seen, only a handful of Marxist-Leninist states have made institutional concessions to carrying out Leninist policy. And these few states have then rendered their version of Leninist national policy soulless by their machinations in the areas of language policy, cadre policy, and population redistribution and gerrymandering. We have further reviewed how these governments have periodically fluctuated radically in the direction of immediate assimilation. A return to a tempo that is more in keeping with the spirit of Lenin's formula does not undo the damage done to the basic strategy. Lenin, we will recall, had insisted that nationalism was a byproduct of past "great nation" chauvinism and oppression and that the task of Communists was to convince minorities that communism was not the continuation of assimilation by nonbourgeois means. But an undisguised step toward assimilation (whether Stalin's antinationalist purges, Mao's Great Leap Forward and Cultural Revolution, or Tito's program of *Jugoslovenstvo*) has the effect of placing minorities on their guard long after a retreat in policy has been effected. Lenin's worst fears come to be realized: whatever party credence on the national question has been cultivated during a period of national flourishing is destroyed. In effect, the ability of the party to implement a Leninist policy is poorer than it was at the time of taking power, for subsequent avowals of respect for national peculiarities are apt to be greeted with skepticism by minorities who recall that past avowals of a similar nature were followed by determined attempts at rapid assimilation.

COERCION VERSUS PERSUASION

We must therefore conclude that Lenin's formula for solving the national question in a postrevolutionary situation has nowhere been accorded a fair testing. But it does not follow that this failure to carry out Lenin's prescriptions can be ascribed solely to faithlessness on the part of his nominal followers. At the outset of the previous chapter we noted that Lenin (1) viewed assimilation as an inevitable, historical process; (2) at least inferentially condoned actions that would speed up the process; and (3) specifically prohibited only those actions that were "coercive." Since nationalism to Lenin was a psychological response to oppression and inequality, he concluded that coercion would counterproductively nurture it.

The authorities of even those few states that have continued to pay institutional lip service to Leninist national policy have not refrained from employing physical coercion to dispel nationalism, so the protestations of any government that it has never knowingly violated Lenin's policy must be viewed as cynical.[7] But would nationalism be an insignificant force today within Marxist-Leninist states if authorities had refrained from the methods of physical coercion? The prevalence of national unrest within a host of democratic, open societies strongly supports a negative answer.[8] Lenin's program fallaciously presumed a discontinuity between persuasion and coercion, when what is really involved is a continuum. The one blends imperceptibly into the other, particularly in the perceptions of the minorities. For example, where is the line to be drawn between persuasion and coercion in the choice of language within the Ukraine? If Russian language schools, because of state favoritism, become the best schools; if Russian becomes the language of career-determining examinations; if Russian, because of the presence of large numbers of immigrants, becomes the everyday language within Ukrainian cities; if Russian becomes the local language of business and success; if the best (newswise) newspapers are in Russian; if many books and journals are made available only in Russian; if all this—is one being persuaded or coerced into adopting Russian as his/her principal language? "Either you adopt Russian or forget about becoming an engineer" is more in the nature of an ultimatum than a free choice, or, in any case, has tended to be so viewed by members of national minorities. And given Lenin's view of nationalism as a response to perceived oppression, the perceptions of the minorities, and not the motivation of the authorities, logically should have been made the criterion for adopting a specific course of action.

It is indeed difficult to imagine what type of governmental action, whose purpose is to speed the coming of assimilation, would not be viewed as coercive by minorities. It is therefore probable that the actualization of Lenin's vision of overcoming national suspicions would require that the central government refrain from all such initiatives. Lenin appears to have come to this realization at a very late hour. Shortly before his death, he warned that a solution to the national question might require decentralization of decision-making to a point at which all matters other than military and foreign policy would become the prerogative of the individual republics.[9]

Lenin's willingness to contemplate with equanimity such a decentralized structure is totally out of harmony with opinions expressed throughout all earlier periods of his life and is at sharp odds both with the fundamental tenet of Marxism concerning the progressiveness and inevitability of ever-larger, integrated, ecopolitical units, and with Lenin's personal disdain for federalism.[10] This sole and very late departure from his otherwise steadfast advocacy of a highly centralized system should therefore not be assigned too much weight when assessing Lenin's convictions.[11] Given Lenin's pragmatic leanings, it is safe to conclude that, had he lived, the need for a strong economy (required both to establish a military-industrial complex that was able to withstand capitalist encirclement and to prove the rectitude of scientific Marxism by outperforming capitalist economies) would have reinforced his Marxist predilection for a large, highly centralized system. Strategic priorities, the freedom to allocate scarce investment capital in the geographically most rational manner, the free movement of labor and other factors of production, and the need for a lingua franca would all exert pressure for focalized planning and controls.

What Lenin's aberration does accomplish is to draw attention to one of the dilemmas of Leninist national policy. If nationalism must be exorcised by convincing minorities that a new period of national equality has dawned, a period in which there is no place for coercive pressure to assimilate, and if nearly any decision involving langauge, education, the movement of peoples, and the geographic distribution of investments is apt to be viewed as violating the principle of national equality and/or the principle of noncoercive assimilation, how can Lenin's formula be compatible with the needs of an industrialized state, most particularly a Marxist-Leninist state, that for ideological, structural (governmental ownership of the means of production), and competitive reasons places an inordinate emphasis upon centralized planning and control? Lenin's convictions concerning the proper way to quell nationalism appear to dictate a confederal system more decentralized than even the famed Swiss model rather than the system of focalized government that has been the rule in Marxist-Leninist states.[12]

Lenin's implicit condonation of all noncoercive efforts to bring about assimilation directly (nondialectically) was logically at odds with his view of nationalism as a psychological phenomenon. The latter had accounted for his dialectical scheme for achieving assimilation via a period of the flourishing of nations. This scheme was based on a recognition that assimilation would require a lengthy period of constraint rather than of activism on the part of the authorities. The incompatibility between this dialectical strategy and support for "noncoercive," direct assimilation would seem to be irreconcilable.

It is conceivable that Lenin's general predilection for urging Communists to take action to accelerate the development of progressive historical forces caused him to overlook this inconsistency. The success of the October Revolution confirmed Lenin's belief that revolutionary stages could be telescoped by proper action. But revolutions and assimilation differ drastically in this regard. As noted, activity perceived by a minority as an attempt to induce assimilation will retard rather than compress the process. Lenin's failure to prohibit noncoercive activity aimed at achieving assimilation directly was therefore tantamount to counteracting all of the effort so laboriously expended on promoting the dialectical approach termed "national flourishing."

This most atypical lapse of strategic coherence on the part of Lenin is not easily explained away. If, for the sake of debate, one were to accept the validity of a firm distinction between coercive and noncoercive actions and, further, were to allow that there may be some actions that a government might take to advance assimilation directly (nondialectically), there remains Lenin's puzzling failure to offer guidance for differentiating between permissible and impermissible actions. As reviewed in the previous chapter, the absence of guidelines has permitted those who desire the indefinite survival of nations, those who desire their rapid obliteration, and all those holding any of the myriad possible positions intermediate between these two extremes, to all disguise themselves behind the single mask of Leninist national policy. From the viewpoint of the implementer of actual policy, Lenin's formula proved to be no formula at all. Those who wished to tinker were free to do so.[13] It is difficult to comprehend why Lenin did not foresee the result, for perhaps the only truly inevitable feature of Leninist national policy was that there would be those in authority who would find the absence of restrictive guidelines an irresistible invitation to meddle with the assimilation process. Since such unrestricted tampering would undermine the rationale behind national flourishing, Leninist national policy (as Marx said of capitalism) contained the seeds of its own destruction.

EQUALITY VERSUS REALITY AND PERCEPTIONS OF REALITY

But what if Lenin had prohibited all effort to bring about assimilation directly? Would his dialectical approach then have brought about the desired end? Indeed, far from being certain that in such case the ultimate goal of assimilation would be realized, we are left with strong doubts concerning the attainability of even the intermediate goal of national equality. We will recall that Lenin's plan for achieving assimilation was dependent upon first achieving equality. Only by convincing nations that all inequality had been eradicated could the groundwork for psychological assimilation be laid.

Lenin does not appear to have considered national equality a difficult accomplishment. Beyond his deathbed warning involving the chauvinistic tendency of Russian bureaucrats to preserve their dominant status over other peoples, he had little to say concerning the obstacles to achieving national egalitarianism. His silence suggests too sanguine or naive a view of this task for, a great deal of propaganda to the contrary, national equality remains beyond the accomplishments of Marxist-Leninist states.

Consider economic equality. In all states, discrepancies—sometimes very sharp discrepancies—persist. In the case of the Soviet Union, the persistence is in part attributable to the fact that in matters of investment the authorities have been guided more by the concept of most efficient utilization of scarce investment capital than by national equality.[14] But had they emphasized for a time the standard of national equality, it is likely that results would soon have dictated a reversion to the standard of maximal return. Yugoslavia did follow just such a pattern.[15] After having pumped large sums into the poorer south without satisfactory results, the authorities came to the conclusion that the living conditions of all citizens could best be elevated by investing scarce investment funds in a manner most apt to promote the economic growth of the country as a whole.[16]

Were minorities dispersed evenly throughout a country, the goal of national equality could be achieved (at least theoretically) through antidiscrimination policies, without causing economic dislocation. But the fact that national groups populate distinct regions of a country introduces a complicating element. Large states, whether ethnically heterogeneous or homogeneous, exemplify marked regional distinctions in economic level. Sharp differences in income between Italy's poor south and wealthy north, between Canada's poor Maritime Provinces and Ontario, or between Castile and the wealthier Spanish Basqueland have little to do with ethnic discrimination. There is, in effect, something of a rule of uneven regional economic development. Among the overlapping explanations for such variations can be climatic factors; soils; topographic barriers to transportation; relative proximity to power resources, raw materials, and markets; the availability of support industries; the presence of a sufficiently large work force possessed of the necessary technological tradition; and the age and condition of the present industrial plant, as well as the type of industry for which the plant was designed.

The aggregate impact of such factors often militates against any attempt to overcome regional imbalances. It would be unrealistic to expect those responsible for planning within the Soviet Union, China, Vietnam, or Yugoslavia to approve the expenditure of untold amounts of scarce investment capital in an attempt to develop a modern industrial infrastructure in Tadzhikistan, Tibet, the Vietnamese highlands, or Kosovo. Limited investment funds, plus the security interests and economic well-being of the state as a whole, have dictated that planners adopt the more reasonable standard of comparative return. Firm evidence that we are not dealing here with something explicable simply in terms of favoritism for the state's dominant group is offered in the case of the Soviet Union by the fact that the inhabitants of Estonia, Latvia, and Lithuania, and probably those of Armenia and Georgia as well, enjoy a higher per capita income than do those living in the RSFSR.[17] Within Yugoslavia, Croats and Slovenes enjoy a higher living standard than do the politically dominant Serbs. The quest to achieve maximal economic growth for the state as a whole has exerted its own imperative upon the planners, and, as Lenin should have anticipated, economic equality of national groups has been correspondingly slighted.

There is yet another congenital problem in the pursuit of national equality: the difficulty, if not the impossibility, of discovering a universally acceptable formula to achieve equality between unequals. The question of whether seemingly fair equality of access to opportunity on the basis of individual merit does not perpetuate inequality among groups has become endemic to multiethnic states. Group quotas have been introduced into Marxist and non-Marxist states alike as a means of decreasing the proportion of a group or groups within the more desirable professions. Thus the percentage of Jewish students within Soviet institutes of higher learning has been cut as a matter of policy, ostensibly as a means of insuring increased social mobility for other groups. Similarly, following the Cultural Revolution, the Chinese CP reverted to its practice of establishing quotas at universities for non-Han who would otherwise not qualify.[18] As anyone familiar with the debates concerning recent affirmative action programs in the United States, Malaysia, and elsewhere can attest, quotas are certain to be seen as unfair by those groups adversely affected by them.

It can further be expected that any group that enjoys an advantage in income and living standards over another will insist that any formula that merely aims at closing the gap is simplistic and deficient. To them, the higher income is the result of greater effort and acumen, and a formula that does not recognize and reward such factors is inherently unequal. Thus the Slovenes of Yugoslavia, though enjoying the highest standard of living of any of the state's national groups, tend to be unhappy because they feel they would have an even higher income were it not for the fact that moneys they have generated through their industriousness are quite unfairly used to raise living standards outside of Slovenia.[19]

The obstacles to achieving national equality are therefore seemingly insurmountable. But had Lenin nevertheless conjured and bequeathed some ingenious strategy for surmounting all of the preceding obstacles, he would still have encountered the gulf between reality and its perception. It is the latter, not the former, that has social consequences, and reality and perceptions are often at serious variance. For example, Russians often complain that their living standard is below that of many other Soviet peoples, while statistics indicate a reverse order of things.[20] Thus even if national economic equality were achieved, it is doubtful that national groups, perceiving the world through the distorting lens of an ethnic prism, would so view it.

We conclude, therefore, that due to a number of complexities which Lenin failed to anticipate, national economic equality has not been achieved and is not apt to be achieved. Even if it were, there would remain the problem of perceptions. Turning now to cultural and political equality, we find that they have been equally elusive.

The gaps between the ideals of cultural and political equality on the one hand and reality on the other are particularly conspicuous in cases such as the Soviet Union, China, Rumania, and Vietnam, in which a single national group enjoyed a clear numerical and cultural preeminence long before the coming of communism. Should not Lenin have anticipated such a development? In planning the revolutionary takeover of tsarist Russia, he was envisioning Communist control over a sprawling empire (1) that had resulted from the expansion of the Great Russians from their original hearth in Muscovy; (2) whose history was therefore principally the history of the Russian people; (3) whose capital (whether Moscow or Saint Petersburg) had remained within the Great Russians' hearth; (4) in which Russians were the largest ethnic element; (5) in which Russian was the language of most of the population, the official language, and the only approximation of a country-wide lingua franca; (6) within which Russians had disproportionately manned the ruling apparatus and the elite structure generally; and (7) whose name (Empire of Russia) conferred official recognition of the cultural and political preeminence of the Russian people.[21] In such an environment, was it not to be expected that as the bloodless abstraction termed the "new Soviet man" took flesh, he (she) should come increasingly to resemble a Russian? And that a socialist society that arose within Russia would be quite different from one arising within China, in that each society would exemplify a number of either Russian or Chinese characteristics?

Lenin did anticipate that the new Soviet man would be Russian in speech.[22] Presumably, he felt that since the Russian language had become the established language throughout most of the empire, the linguistic mold had already been cast. The forces of history were well on their way to bringing about the progressive stage of full linguistic assimilation, and it would be counterhistorical to undo this progress by requiring all Russian speakers now to switch to Esperanto or some other ethnically neutral language.[23] Still another pragmatic consideration that may have influenced Lenin was the realization that downgrading the language of the dominant group would run the very real risk of alienating the most important national group in the state, a group whose support would be crucial to the success of the Communist experiment.[24]

The adoption of the historically dominant language as today's lingua franca and tomorrow's single language was therefore to be expected. But where does this leave the principle of cultural equality? If the lingua franca (the language of success) is the traditional language of another group, that group and its culture are automatically endowed with favored status. The problem is hardly unique to Marxist-Leninist states. In multilinguistic states as diverse as Canada and India, questions concerning the official language, the language of business, the language of entrance examinations, and the language of government have been volatile issues. And charges of ethnonational discrimination have been everyday occurrences.

The need to invoke the past in order to motivate the masses has also conspired to cause the new Soviet man to resemble the state's dominant group in ways other than language. Lenin had not anticipated such a development. For a time following the October Revolution, the tendency was to brand all that had preceded the revolution as reactionary. Little that was worthy of admiration or emulation was discovered in the political and cultural history of the Russian Empire. Traditions held no value in the Brave New World. The new Soviet man was to be totally new. This clean-slate approach admittedly constituted a form of cultural equality, but in a most perverse form, predicated as it was upon equal disparagement of cultural traditions rather than on their equal esteem. The approach was also at odds with Marx's low estimation of people without a history. To Marx, people without a history were people without a future.[25] While such a prognosis proved to be an exaggeration, it is certainly true that throughout history the evocation of a people's glorified past has been the most commonly utilized goad for spurring the masses on to greater sacrifice and dedication. Stalin soon recognized the implausibility of mobilizing a country without resort to a cultural tradition, and during the 1930s the great political, military, and artistic figures from prerevolutionary times came again to be venerated.

But what figures? Quite expectedly, those whose actions and views were compatible with the existing boundaries of the new Soviet state, therefore those who had been associated with the expansion and consolidation of the Russian Empire, and, consequently, people who were almost exclusively Great Russian. As the most important political figures in the history of the empire, the tsars (including Ivan the Terrible) were now discovered to have possessed progressive qualities.[26] The military figures of history who were now reelevated to the status of heroes were necessarily those who had contributed to the expansion of the empire, not those non-Russian leaders who had led their people in resisting its encroachment.[27] Nationalist authors, poets, and artists of the past who were to be honored were necessarily Great Russian nationalists, since the nationalism of any other group questioned the historic legitimacy of the new Soviet state. The audacity with which the authorities claimed Russian writers for Marxism-Leninism and then made them the heritage of all Soviet peoples is suggested (and applauded) by a Soviet author with regard to the Korean community in the eastern RSFSR: "The Korean readers received in their native language the works of the classicists of Marxism-Leninism, political and popular literature, the works of A. S. Pushkin, L. N. Tolstoi, I. C. Turgenev, N. V. Gogol, A. P. Chekhov, M. Gor'kog, V. Maiakovski, and others."[28]

Sculpting the new Soviet man in the image of the dominant national group has been carried farther than exigencies would seem to dictate or than Lenin would probably approve. Excessiveness has been particularly apparent in the praise heaped upon the state's dominant ethnic element, in attributing god-like national characteristics to it, and in elevating it to a model to be emulated by other national groups.[29] In the case of the Soviet Union, the growing role of the Great Russians as the vanguard of the nations was apparent before World War II, and it was made explicit in a famous toast by Stalin shortly after the Nazi surrender:

> I would like to propose a toast to our Soviet people, and in particular to the health of the Russian people.
>
> I drink first of all to the health of the Russian people because it is the leading nation of all the nations belonging to the Soviet Union.
>
> I propose a toast to the health of the Russian people because it earned in this war general recognition as the guiding force of the Soviet Union among all the peoples of our country.
>
> I propose a toast to the health of the Russian people not only because it is the leading people, but also because it has a clear mind, a firm character and patience.[30]

Following Beria's ouster in 1953, an article in the July 12, 1953 issue of *Izvestia* affirmed that the vanguard role of the Russian nation had survived Stalin. After proclaiming that "a decisive role belongs to the great Russian people," the article continued: "The Russian people rightfully merited recognition as the most outstanding, the directing nation of the U.S.S.R." And by his comments before the Twenty-fourth Party Congress in 1971, General Secretary Brezhnev testified that this vanguard role had survived not only Stalin but Stalinism as well:

> Recently many fraternal republics celebrated their half-century jubilees. This was an impressive demonstration of the flourishing of socialist nations, of the monolithic unity of all the peoples of our homeland. Next year we shall celebrate the 50th anniversary of the Union of Soviet Socialist Republics. In terms of its political significance and its social and economic consequences, the formation of the U.S.S.R. holds an outstanding place in the history of our state. (*Applause.*)
>
> All the nations and nationalities of our country, above all the Great Russian people, played a role in the formation, strengthening and development of this mighty union of equal peoples that have taken the path of socialism. (*Applause.*) The revolutionary energy, selflessness, diligence and profound internationalism of the Great Russian people have rightfully won them the sincere respect of all the peoples of our socialist homeland. (*Prolonged applause.*)[31]

If anything, official extolling of the virtues of the Great Russian nation became more commonplace after the Twenty-sixth Congress, held in 1981. Andropov, in his first major speech as General Secretary of the CPSU, expressed "special words of gratitude to the Russian people [without whom] in none of the republics would the present achievements have been conceivable."[32] The gushiness that characterized this latest outpouring of admiration for the Russians, even in the more sophisticated Soviet publications, is illustrated by an anonymous article in the party's leading theoretic journal, *Kommunist*:

> It is impossible not to single out the special role of the Russian people in the establishment and development of the Soviet people. The name of the first among equals of the fraternal peoples has been firmly and justly attributed to them. Not, of course, because the Russian people are numerically the strongest or possess some qualities which are unaccessible to others. They have won respect and authority for their revolutionary services, self-

lessness and spiritual generosity. It is no exaggeration to say that the Russian people have become the backbone of our new internationalist community of people. The rulers of czarist Russia made great endeavors to install in Russians a sense of "superiority" over a contemptuously hostile attitude toward "outsiders." But nothing could eliminate sensitivity to other people's troubles from the soul of the Russian people, who became a good friend to all the country's peoples, large and small. The misanthropic ideas of chauvinism and racism never took root in practice on Russian soil, and superpatriotic intoxication never turned the heads of indigenous Russians. . . . The Russian people were undoubtedly the decisive force in the victory of the Great October Socialist Revolution, on the battlefields of the civil war and in the restoration of the national economy, the industrialization of the country and the collectivization of the countryside—that is, in the building of socialism as a whole—and subsequently in the victory over fascist Germany. They also made and are continuing to make an invaluable contribution to our society's postwar development.[33]

It is not difficult to imagine the response of an Armenian, Georgian, Lett, or Ukrainian to such statements. As one Soviet citizen wrote with regard to expressions of this type:

Like all manifestations of great-power chauvinism, it provokes reaction, aggravating the nationalist sentiments of smaller nations. Naturally they can only be suspicious and distrustful of the nation held up by Semanov and his friends (with no authority whatsoever) as a dominant superior race whose whole history is sacred. This kind of approach hardly promotes the ideas of internationalism nor does it strengthen the state.[34]

A similar vanguard role has been claimed for the Han, Rumanians, and Vietnamese within the states in which they predominate. Considering the materially more one-sided numerical advantage enjoyed by these peoples within their respective states, the prospect that the emerging Soviet man within each of these societies would take on the characteristics of the state's dominant people was even greater than in the case of the Soviet Union. A Chinese magazine is reported to have described such an outcome in a most candid manner:

The Chinese make up 94 percent of the whole population of China, and from the point of view of the political, economic and cultural development they are the most advanced. Consequently, the merging of the nationalities should be realized on the basis of one nationality. It is China we are speaking of, so the basis should be the Chinese. . . . The characteristics of the Chinese nation are being transformed [*sic*] into the general national characteristics of the national minorities.[35]

In a similar vein, Vietnamese Communist Party First Secretary Le Duan addressed the party's Fourth Congress in December 1976:

The new socialist man is the new Vietnamese whose most outstanding features are his collective mastership, labour, love for socialism and his spirit of proletarian internationalism. This man is the embodiment and development of what is best and noblest in the Vietnamese mind and character forged through 4,000 years of history.[36]

Although one could well argue that the potential damage of flaunting officially endorsed favoritism of a single nation is much less in such cases where the minorities represent a much smaller percentage of the entire population, one wonders why any party has felt compelled to adopt a line that must necessarily rankle the sensibilities of the country's minorities. One possible explanation is that the theme of national superiority actually reflects the innermost convictions of the power elite, most of whom have been members of the most favored nation.[37] Another explanation involves the need to ensure the fidelity of the dominant group. Unlike minorities, whose loyalty to a state they perceive as dominated by another people is always suspect, manifestly dominant people within a state (whether Russian or Frenchman, Han Chinese or [Israeli] Jew, Vietnamese or Englishman, Rumanian or [Castilian] Spaniard) perceive the state as essentially the political expression of their particular nation and therefore worthy of their unconditional loyalty. The destiny of the dominant nation, as well as its history, is perceived as indissolubly linked to the state. Such considerations cause Communist parties to staff their state's security forces disproportionately with members of the dominant group. They also underlie our depiction of the dominant group as the most loyal nation.[38]

Loyalty to a state and loyalty to a regime are not synonymous, however. And to the degree that the policies of a regime run counter to the dominant group's perception of the state as "our state," the regime risks alienating itself from the largest and most powerful part of its population. National equality is precisely such a policy. Having been the beneficiary of the former inequality and being convinced that that particular allocation of prestige and power was both deserved and just, the dominant group perceives the introduction of a policy of equality as innately unfair.[39] Indeed, despite the fact that the dominant groups have each enjoyed a special status under Marxism-Leninism, their perception of their status is quite different. For example, one collectively authored document (*A Nation Speaks*) that surfaced in *samizdat* (underground) in the early 1970s described the Great Russian people as the most "underprivileged nation in the USSR."[40] The voices of Great Russian discontent have grown more strident over the years and have involved a broad range of often waspish complaints such as the "disorderly hybridization" of nations; the diverting of capital investment funds away from the RSFSR to other republics; the destruction of Russian village life and the denigration of the Orthodox religion, said to constitute the twin pillars of the Russian soul; the "yellowing" (*ozheltenie*) of the armed forces (that is, the increase in the proportion of Asians); the fact that the Great Russians are the only major people without their own party; and the fact that they are also the only major people without their own republic.[41] Han people, living within autonomous regions of China, have also complained of the preferential treatment accorded to the minorities.[42] Similarly, the Serbs perceive themselves as discriminated against and, therefore, are definitely not one of the more contented peoples within Yugoslavia.[43] Indeed, among both Russians and Serbs there has been a small but growing number who speak of breaking off from the other nations and going it alone.[44]

In assessing the potential consequences of alienating the dominant group by fostering a policy of national equality, a regime would have to consider the pervasive presence of members of the group throughout all echelons of the power structure. As we have seen, cadre policy, buttressed by (1) inherited prerevolutionary personnel patterns, (2) imbalanced national demographic statistics, (3) bureaucratic ethnocentrism, and (4) a conviction that the dominant nation was the most loyal nation, has resulted in the preeminence of the state's major national group throughout the bureaucracy. The preeminence has extended to the most sensitive arms of government, including the secret police. To risk offending the national sensibilities of such strategically placed people would be perilous indeed. Thus when Aleksandr Solzhenitsyn, following his expatriation from the Soviet Union, was asked what force represented the greatest threat to the survival of the Soviet regime, he pointed to the sense of national consciousness shared by Russians in positions of power:

> In our country, I count on that degree of enlightenment which has already developed in our [Russian] people and must inevitably extend also to the spheres of the military and the administration. A people, after all, is not just a throng of millions down below, but also its individual representatives occupying key posts. There are sons of Russia up there too, and Russia expects that they will fulfill their filial duty.[45]

It is, of course, during periods of severe crises that the loyalty of the major group is most essential. It was therefore not a coincidence that the paeans to Russian superiority became particularly pronounced during World War II; nor was it a coincidence that Stalin's famous toast of gratitude to the Russians occurred in the immediate afterglow of that struggle, for the Russians had necessarily borne the major responsibility for victory. Although one may well disagree with Solzhenitsyn's prediction of a coming war between the Soviet Union and China, his warning to the Soviet leadership that the survival of their regime has and does hinge upon the support of the Russian nation does not appear far from the mark:

> To someone brought up on Marxism it seems a terrifying step—suddenly to start living without the familiar Ideology [of Marxism-Leninism]. But in fact you have no choice, circumstances themselves will force you to do it, and it may already be too late. In anticipation of an impending war with China, Russia's national leaders will in any case have to rely on patriotism, and on patriotism alone. When Stalin initiated such a shift during the war—remember!—nobody was in the least surprised and nobody shed a tear for Marxism; everyone took it as the most natural thing in the world, something they recognized as Russian. . . . [T]he hour of peril will come, and you will appeal to your people once more, not to world communism. And even your own fate—yes, even *yours!*—will depend on us.[46]

Advantageous numbers and positions of power enjoyed by the major group therefore encourage the regime to accord it the status of *primus inter pares*.[47] But the Leninist legacy also contributes to this tendency. Lenin realized that the loyalty of the minorities was inherently suspect, and this realization led him to dangle the carrot of independence before minorities everywhere as a means of furthering the revolution. There was indeed always something of an inconsistency in the logic underlying this piece of Leninist strategy and that which underlay the postrevolutionary introduction of national equality. The proven efficacy of the lure of independence in a prerevolutionary situation confirms the disloyalty of minorities to the state. People whose temporary coooperation was purchased by the promise of separation from the state cannot, following a reneging on that promise, be expected magically to have developed a fondness for that same state.[48] Moreover, the party's memory of the disloyalty displayed by the minorities does not necessarily dim with time. Self-determination for peoples everywhere remains a basic foreign policy theme of long established Marxist-Leninist regimes, and is therefore a continuous reminder of the disloyalty of minorities. Moreover, the fact that Marxist-Leninist regimes regularly appeal to the unhappiness of minorities within rival Marxist-Leninist states confirms their keen awareness that minority disloyalty does not subside with the revolution.[49] In short, Marxist-Leninist ideology and practice cause the regimes to be unusually sensitized to the endemic disloyalty of national minorities. Dominant nations are the only ones who can benefit from such a fixation.

It is therefore understandable how one group tends to reassert its dominance following a Marxist-Leninist takeover of power. Lenin's optimism concerning the attainability of cultural and political equality might have been more justified if nations more closely approximated one another in size, education, cultural traditions, and the like. But nations are most unequal with regard to such considerations. And even had Lenin, Mao, Tito, et al. been able to convince a traditionally dominant group that it should be prepared to surrender its vanguard status in the name of true equality, they would still have encountered a dilemma discussed earlier in connection with economic equality, namely, the difficulty of developing formulae designed to insure equality among unequals. For example, the issue, raised earlier, of whether the principle of national equality is honored or violated by the introduction of quotas (as contrasted with a system based upon individual merit) is not confined to national economic equality. The ethnic composition of the political and cultural elites will also be heavily influenced if quotas are applied to university admissions, government service, and the like.

Still another question involving an appropriate formula arises from the disparities in size among nations, this one involving political representation. We have seen in the case of Yugoslavia how the formula "one people (or republic), one vote" was viewed as unfair by the numerically superior Serbs, while "one person, one vote" proved unacceptable to Croats, Slovenes, etc. Late in his life, Tito opted for the standard of one republic, one vote, but the growing disenchantment of the Serbs, to which we earlier alluded, indicates that the turmoil surrounding the two conflicting formulae is far from spent.[50]

Finally, as in the case of economic equality, the overcoming of all of the previously mentioned obstacles to real equality in the political and cultural spheres would still leave Lenin confronting the problem of perceptions. Even if the principle of proportionality were strictly observed, the numerical superiority of the dominant group would make it the most heavily represented in positions of power and thus make it appear to minorities to be in control of the state and party apparatus. Moreover, the location of the capital within the homeland of the dominant group (which is true in all Marxist-Leninist states) adds to this perception. We have seen, however, that the dominant nation that does in fact enjoy advantageous status may nevertheless feel it suffers discrimination. That is to say, contrary to facts, the vanguard nation may perceive itself as the pariah nation. This being the case, it should not be surprising that less-favored nations perceive the situation in Orwellian terms: "all nations may be equal, but. . . ."

We conclude, therefore, that even the intermediate Leninist goals of economic, political, and cultural equality of nations defy realization. But for the purpose of more fully examining Lenin's legacy on the national question, let us presume that equality can be achieved and stabilized.[51] This would bring us to Lenin's differentiation between form and content.[52]

FORM VERSUS CONTENT

As we have seen, Lenin's solution to the national question was predicated upon a plenary distinction between form and content.[53] Only the form was to be national; the content must be exclusively socialist. But can such a plenary distinction between the two be upheld? Do not national forms, in and by themselves, help to reinforce and perpetuate that sense of group uniqueness which, according to the Communist Manifesto, should be "daily more and more vanishing?" Did Lenin err in not appreciating that forms have a content of their own?

Lenin was convinced that the content of scientific socialism would be more readily acceptable to the masses if presented in national garb. However, even if Lenin were correct and the socialist messages, transmitted through national forms, were absorbed by the masses of the various nations, it would not follow that these same people would necessarily acquiesce in the loss of their national identity as required by the merging and fusing of nations. If the masses, encouraged by the government's support for national forms, continued to think of themselves as Russians, Ukrainians, Georgians, Hans, Tibetans, Serbs, Croats, Vietnamese, Czechs, Slovaks, Rumanians, Magyars, Poles, etc., then, depending upon which conviction was felt as primary, there would emerge either national socialists or socialist nationalists. But not nationless socialists.

Lenin's ostensible disciples have shown far less assurance concerning the ideological passivity of national forms. As we have seen, most Marxist-Leninist states have shied away from Lenin's policy with regard to forms. The four states that do honor national forms have demonstrated their distrust of those forms by saddling them with a series of hedging devices.

The difference between Lenin's perception of forms and the perceptions of his successors is particularly glaring in the case of language. Indeed, if Lenin is to be faulted for ascribing too little "content" to the matter of language, his successors are to be faulted for ascribing too much power to this "form." Far from perceiving language as simply a medium for communicating the tenets of Marxism-Leninism, his successors have tended to perceive language as the key to national identity.[54] The notion that "a person is what he speaks" is obviously exaggerated, since peoples have been known to lose their language without a corresponding loss of national identity.[55] On the other hand, a national language is much more than the passive form that emerges from Lenin's writings on the national question. It is, first of all, a constant reminder of group uniqueness. Moreover, in their desire to resist acculturation and assimilation, national groups often make rallying points of their more tangible manifestations of uniqueness, particularly language. In such cases, the national language is elevated to the symbol of the nation and becomes the principal battleground against the forces of assimilation. Flemings, Quebecois, and Tamils—as well as Ukrainians and Letts—have phrased their urge for group self-preservation largely in terms of preserving the language. In such cases, language becomes infused with emotion. Recall, for example, the seemingly irrational response of the Croats to the proposal for a single Serbo-Croat dictionary and the equally peevish response of Serbs to the increasing use of the Latin alphabet on signs throughout the country.[56] Anything viewed as a threat to the language can become equated with a threat to the survival of the nation. Language, in addition to being an enduring reminder of national uniqueness, can therefore also become a sensitized outer defense perimeter that the forces of assimilation must not be permitted to penetrate. Form has become saturated with national content.

Similar considerations surround Lenin's plan for regional autonomy. The rationale for creating administrative units along ethnonational lines was intended to blunt the urge of nations to possess their own state. But was it reasonable to presume that the impulse toward national self-determination could be satisfied by mere form? Further, was it not to be expected that the very existence of political units bearing ethnic designations would whet the collective appetite of individual ethnic groups for a true realization of an independent nation-state? Demarcating the borders of the administrative unit gives geographic precision to the more shadowy notion of the ethnic motherland. Constitutionally declaring the unit to be "sovereign" or "autonomous" legitimizes the idea of self-rule. Giving the unit an ethnic designation conveys the idea that the unit's proper raison d'être is the safeguarding and promotion of the national interests of the people so designated. Adorning the unit with its own government as well as other appurtenances of political individuality (seals, flags, and the like) conditions the people to think in terms of their particular unit rather than in terms of the entire state. The recording and publicizing of census and other data broken down by administrative units furthers this tendency, as do repetitious references to "our sovereign/autonomous (Ukrainian, Tibetan, Croatian, Slovak, etc.) republic/region/province/area/district." Dialectical reasoning to the contrary notwithstanding, was it not likely that the national, geopolitical form would produce a nationalist rather than an internationalist orientation?

Surely Lenin's successors feared that the consequences would be far different than what Lenin had anticipated. Most Marxist-Leninist parties simply refused to initiate regional autonomy. The Slovak leadership, for example, has adamantly rebuffed all entreaties from Budapest and the concerned minority to grant any form of autonomous status to the Magyar community within Slovakia, while concomitantly demanding a true federal status vis-à-vis the dominant Czechs.[57] Rumania, which under Soviet and Budapest pressures granted autonomous status to a segment of its Magyar minority (meanwhile refusing such status to the remaining Magyar community and the entire German minority), dropped even this limited application of Leninist national policy as soon as it was propitious to do so.[58] Vietnam abrogated its autonomous regions almost simultaneously with victory over the southern part of the country, strongly suggesting that the authorities had long planned to take such a step the moment the external propaganda value of the autonomous regions ended. Those states that have maintained a system of regional autonomy have shown their fear that the forms might encourage nationalism by employing such risk-reducing measures as nonindigenous cadre, nonindigenous security forces, population transfers, and gerrymandering.

Beyond all this, the reservations of the Chinese, Rumanian, and Vietnamese parties toward autonomous units extended even to the labeling of such units. From the outset, the Chinese leadership purposefully chose names that would play down the connection between the unit and a single ethnic group, either by including two or more ethnonyms in the unit's official title or by combining an ethnonym with an ethnically neutral geographic term. The authorities took for granted that naming a unit after a particular group would lead that group to conclude that it had an exclusive or primary interest in the unit. In turn, such sentiment would be more conducive to separatism than to recognizing the hegemony of the state and party apparatus. This is how Chou En-lai phrased it in 1957:

> We don't lay emphasis on the secession of nationalities. If we do now, imperialism will take advantage of this. Even though it will not succeed, it can add troubles to the co-operation among our nationalities. In Sinkiang, for instance, before liberation, when some reactionaries engaged in separatist activities to set up a so-called eastern Turkestan, imperialism took advantage of it. In view of this, at the time of founding the Sinkiang Uighur Autonomous Region, we did not approve of the name "Uighuristan." Sinkiang embraces not just the Uighurs but 12 other nationalities as well. It is impossible to form a "-stan" for each of the 13 nationalities. So the Party and government, with the consent of our Sinkiang comrades, decided on the founding of the Sinkiang Uighur Autonomous Region. ... As to the two characters Sin Kiang, they just mean the new land, *and do not connote aggression.* The names Tibet and Inner Mongolia are names of

both places and nationalities. These names [i.e., the matter of names] may sound a thing of minor importance but they are very important in connection with the national regional autonomy in China for they have the connotation of national co-operation.[59]

Chou did not explain why a smaller Uighuristan AR that more closely reflected the ethnic distribution of the Uighur people could not have been created instead of one that coincided with the borders of Sinkiang Province. Or alternatively, why the large unit that was decided upon could not have been called Turkestan (or Eastern Turkestan) AR, a historical term that would have had special meaning to most of the non-Han peoples of the area, who like the Uighurs, were of Turkic background. As in the case of the Ningsia Hui AR and the Kwangsi Chuang AR, the CCP preferred to include an ethnically neutral geographic word in the unit's title.[60] Chinese determination to avoid popular equating of a unit with one's own ethnic group carried over to the titling of the lesser levels of autonomous districts and counties as well. All were prefaced by a geographic term. Moreover, in the case of the autonomous districts, seven designations contained two ethnonyms and one contained three. Even at the still smaller, county level, six of the official designations contained two ethnonyms, two contained three, and three of the districts were simply called "multinationality" units (for example, the Lung-sheng Multinationality A.H.).[61]

Similar concern for nomenclature was shown by the Rumanian CP during the abbreviated period when it tolerated an autonomous region within its jurisdiction. As first established, the unit was known as the Magyar Autonomous Region. However, concomitant with its ethnic dilution through the redrawing of its borders in 1960, the unit was renamed the Mures-Autonomous Hungarian Region. Mures, a Rumanian word referring to a geographic region, held no emotional significance for Magyars. The Vietnamese CP acted in an analogous manner. At the time of its creation in 1955, the first autonomous unit, the Thai-Meo AR, bore the name of two ethnic groups. A second unit, created in 1956, bore no ethnic designation, simply being referred to as the North (Viet Bac) AR. A title so totally devoid of ethnic symbolism recommended itself to the leadership even over a multiethnic one, for in 1961 the Thai-Meo AR was renamed the Northwest (Tay Bac) AR. Even these alterations did not totally reassure the Rumanian and Vietnamese leaders, who, as we know, later did away completely with all autonomous units.

Soviet and Yugoslav authorities have not shown a similar level of concern for the issue of "What's in a name?"[62] However, they certainly offer other confirmation of their belief that regional autonomy inspires national particularism rather than a merging of nations, for in both states certain administrative units were created for the specific purpose of encouraging a separate nationalism by the people encased therein. For example, the Soviet authorities furnished the Kazakhs, Kirgiz, Tadzhiks, Turkmen, and Uzbeks with their own administrative units as a means of discouraging a larger movement of a Bukharan, pan-Turkic, or pan-Muslim complexion.[63] Similarly, in creating a Macedonian Republic, the Yugoslav authorities intended to strengthen a Macedonian identity at the expense of a possible Bulgar one. More recently, they have encouraged the growth of a Bosnian national consciousness, although Bosnia-Hercegovina was originally perceived as the only nonethnically inspired republic in the federation. But the most significant illustration of the importance that both the authorities and the people ascribe to a republic surfaced during 1981-1982, when Albanians agitated to have Kosovo Province elevated to republic status. The demand was vehemently criticized by the central authorities, who perceived such status as part of a planned sequence terminating with secession and union with Albania. The official reaction was given by a member of the party Presidium:

> A republic of Kosovo is not possible within the framework of Yugoslavia—neither in terms of our Constitution, nor in terms of Yugoslavia's national composition, nor in terms of what was achieved by the national liberation war, especially in view of the fact that the establishment of a republic of Kosovo in Yugoslavia would in essence mean the downfall of Yugoslavia.[64]

The qualms of those in power concerning the peril of regional autonomy were, of course, quite realistic. Rather than being beguiled by the forms, spokesmen for minorities quite predictably have emphasized discrepancies between form and content and have campaigned to bring the two into conformity. Thus, concluding what is probably the most comprehensive criticism of national policy to emerge from within the Soviet Union, a Ukrainian wrote of "this desire to see the socialist Ukraine as truly existing and genuinely equal among the socialist family of nations, this feeling of a socialist

Ukraine as a national reality and not simply as an administrative-geographic term and a bureaucratic stumbling-block."[65]

Given this quite natural tendency of people to believe that they have a claim to all that is constitutionally guaranteed to them, it is not at all surprising to find dissident members of those peoples assigned a union republic within the Soviet Union often invoking the right of secession.[66] More surprising is that they should feel that they have the right, nowhere granted, to control immigration policy. As noted, Soviet authorities have acknowledged widespread objections to nonindigenous immigrants, particularly Russians.[67] Rallies with the basic theme of "Russian, Go Home!" (read: "Leave our Republic") have occurred.[68] In a number of instances, forces within the SSRs have been known to inveigh against increased investment for their republic because increased industrialization would lead to increased immigration.[69] Nor has this conviction of a right to control immigration been limited to the constitutionally "sovereign" SSRs. Thus "executives" within the Adzhar ASSR (located within Georgian SSR) were accused of urging the Adzhar party to reject plans "to build new factories and plants and to develop resorts and tourism, basing their advice on the premise that this would lead to immigration of people from other republics."[70] Moreover, in the case of China's autonomous units, which, even at the level of form, had been extended precious little power, people came to perceive the mere establishing of such units as an acknowledgment of the indigenous people's right to exclude Chinese. In 1953 the Nationalities Affairs Commission complained that in a number of areas there were those who "considered that the enforcement of autonomy meant a separation from the Han Chinese, and that the Han Chinese would no longer be wanted in their region.[71] The Chinese authorities were to find this linkage between autonomy and an implied right to ethnic isolation a difficult one to eradicate, for similar attitudes were expressed following the Great Leap and Cultural Revolution.[72]

We are here dealing not just with the natural tendency to demand that content come to reflect form, that is, to demand that that which has been promised be delivered. When the form is an autonomous, ethnically defined unit, expectations do not remain confined to specifically enumerated powers. Simply dwelling within one's autonomous ethnic unit—no matter how circumscribed the authorities declare the unit's powers to be—instills a sense of possession of fundamental proprietary rights. Form becomes the father of content.

The tendency to wish to rid the homeland of an alien presence is admittedly a near universal that has also surfaced in multinational states that have not introduced ethnically based administrative units. So too, secessionist movements have afflicted numerous unitary political systems. It might therefore be contended that Lenin's scheme of territorial autonomy cannot be faulted for having nurtured nationalism, since the result would have been the same in any event.

The answer to such a contention is threefold. First, Lenin did not view nationalism as inevitable. His view of the autonomous form was not that of an essentially passive or harmless device, which he indifferently approved with the attitude that "Since it can do no (additional) harm, why not grant it as a sop to the minorities?" He was ideologically opposed to any type of federalism or pluralism, but came to believe that the granting of territorial autonomy was a necessary device to blunt the nationalist urge. This it failed to do. Second, had Lenin not committed his more faithful legatees to the policy of territorial autonomy, it is quite likely that they would have broken the link between peoples and homeland (that psychological intermingling of blood and soil that nineteenth-century German nationalists abbreviatedly sloganized into *"Blut und Boden!"*). We have noted that Marxists are well aware that people outside of their homeland are most apt to assimilate.[73] Given this awareness plus the uncompromisingly hostile view of nationalism held by true Marxist-Leninists, it is reasonable to presume that, if unfettered by Lenin's proautonomy scheme, leaders who ordered the elimination of the kulaks or who ordered the Cultural Revolution would not have blanched at ordering the mass relocation of peoples in order to maximize intermingling and minimize the notion of homelands. Indeed, Stalin did not hesitate to move entire peoples out of their homelands during World War II. Tito summarily expelled the Germans from Vojvodina and was prepared to do the same with Magyars.[74] Mao ordered more than ten million Han into non-Han regions, and deported minorities from the immediate border areas. But only the Vietnamese (after dropping their very limited system of regional autonomy) unsparingly applied the policy of "indigenes out, others in." Lenin's recommendations concerning autonomy may well have prevented the parties of the Soviet Union, China, Yugoslavia, and Czechoslovakia from otherwise pursuing a policy of thorough geographic intermixing of peoples, thereby destroying once and for all the psychological vibrations emanating from contemplation of any homeland other than one coterminous with the state. Third, the fact that aversion to an alien presence in the ethnic homeland is a universal in no way leads to the conclusion that the creation of ethnically based administrative units does not serve to awaken, catalyze, focus, or strengthen such sentiments. As noted, creating such units *inter alia* adds legitimacy to ethnopolitical claims, gives precision to the area and to the human and nonhuman resources over which a proprietary right is felt, and provides institutions and symbols that can both evoke and focus loyalties. As we have seen, all Communist parties, by refusing to introduce the autonomous form, by dropping it, or by saddling it with an intensive system of risk-reducing devices, have acknowledged that the form feeds nationalism.

We have thus far confined our discussion of form and content to the intrastate scene. It is evident, however, that the Leninist dichotomy between form and content was intended to govern the relations between the Soviet fatherland (the USSR) and any states that should subsequently become Marxist-Leninist. As laid out in a 1922 letter from Stalin to a still friendly Lenin, new additions to the socialist camp were to be permitted more sovereignty than the "sovereign" union republics within the USSR. But not total sovereignty. And not for an indefinite period.

> For the nations which belonged to old Russia, one can and must consider our Soviet type of federation to be expedient as a means to international unity . . . these nationalities either had no state of their own in the past, or have lost it long since. Hence the centralized Soviet type of federation can be adapted to them without any special friction. One cannot however say the same of nationalities which did not belong to old Russia but existed as independent states, developed a state of their own and which, if they become Soviet states, will be compelled by the force of facts to establish some kind of political relations with Soviet Russia— for example a future Soviet Germany, Soviet Poland, Soviet Hungary or Soviet Finland. As soon as they have become Soviet states, these peoples who have their own state, their own army, their own finances, will hardly agree immediately to a federative union with Soviet Russia like the Bashkir or the Ukrainian Republic. . . . I do not doubt that for these nationalities the most acceptable form of association would be a confederation (a confederation of independent states).[75]

In the case of new states, form and content were to be in closer agreement than was true in the case of the republics within the USSR. However, while the gap might be smaller, in that the newly socialized nations would, during a transitional period, "have their own state, their own army, their own finances," there would still be a gap between their sovereign form and the reality of their inferior status vis-à-vis the Soviet Union. A Communist party would, of course, assume the usual vanguard role in any new Marxist state, and, in the same year as Stalin's letter, Lenin had ordained that the policy of Communist parties everywhere must be to "achieve the closest alliance, with Soviet Russia, of all the national and colonial liberation movements."[76] Also in the same year, all Communist parties, as a condition to membership in the Comintern, were required to pledge to be bound by all decisions of the Communist International and its Executive Committee, both of which were Soviet dominated.[77]

In conjunction these policies were designed to tie all Marxist-Leninist parties and, by extension, any states they might come to control, to "the Fatherland of socialism and the socialist Motherland of the international proletariat" in a subservient relationship. Although the Comintern was formally dissolved in 1943, it is evident that the Soviets intended this subservient relationship to continue. Indeed, number fourteen of the original "Conditions of Admission into the Communist International," which decreed that every party was "obliged to give unconditional support to any Soviet republic in its struggle against counter-revolutionary forces," anticipated the so-called Brezhnev Doctrine of "limited sovereignty" by nearly a half century.[78] Moreover, while the confederal form envisaged by Stalin in 1920 was never introduced per se, "the Socialist Commonwealth," with its Brezhnev corollary that no member state can secede (nor even be perceived as taking tentative, early steps towards secession) from the Commonwealth, more than fulfilled the requisites of Stalin's notion of confederation.[79]

The scheme under which new Leninist states were to be sovereign in form, dependent in content, has suffered serious setbacks. Sparsely populated and landlocked Outer Mongolia, responsive to Soviet direction since the inception of a people's republic there in the early 1920s, offered early grounds for Soviet optimism that the state form posed no innate challenge to Moscow's control. But since the advent of Leninist states in Eastern Europe and the Far East during the 1940s, challenges to this domination have proliferated. Believing he was bringing Tito to task, Stalin, in one of his greatest blunders, expelled Tito from the Cominform in 1948, only to find that he had thereby strengthened the resolve of the Yugoslav leadership to resist Moscow's domination, and that "Titoism" had become a contagious symbol of "independent Marxism-Leninism" beyond the borders of Yugoslavia.[80]

Stalin otherwise managed to maintain a tight rein over the Eastern European states, but following his death agitation for greater state independence surfaced.[81] The new hope, as well as a candid reference to past relations between the Soviet Union and the states of Eastern Europe, was sounded by the Polish CP's first secretary, Wladyslaw Gomulka, in October 1956:

> The mutual relations between the parties and states of the socialist camp do not and should not give any cause for any complications. . . . Within the framework of such relations each country should have full independence, and the right of each nation to a sovereign government in an independent country should be fully and mutually respected. This is how it should be and—I would say—this is how it is beginning to be.
>
> In the past it was unfortunately not always like this in the relations between us and our great and friendly neighbor, the Soviet Union.
>
> Stalin, as the leader of the Party and of the Soviet Union, formally recognized that all the principles enumerated above should characterize the relations between the countries of the camp of socialism. Not only did he recognize them, but he himself prolaimed them. In fact, however, these principles could not fit within the framework of what makes up the cult of personality.[82]

Ten days later, in a document paying the customary tributes to "the principles of complete equality, of respect for territorial integrity, state independence and sovereignty, and of non-interference in one anothers internal affairs," the Soviet Union announced it was sending troops into Budapest "at the request of the Hungarian people's government."[83]

Hungary's flirtation with state independence was ended by Soviet tanks in a manner calculated to inform all socialist states that their sovereignty had very definite limitations. It was therefore somewhat paradoxical that Chinese leaders, whose deference to Moscow had always been decidedly restrained, gave total verbal support to the intervention.[84] This support was later to take on heavily ironic overtones, for the growing estrangement between Peking and Moscow that developed in the late 1950s and broke into the open in 1960 was to provide smaller Leninist states with new leverage for maneuver.[85] Sharing a border with both states, North Korea was well positioned to take advantage of the competition, and Kim Il

Sung proved adroit at doing so. His regime increasingly took on the stamp of independence. And in Eastern Europe, Albania, taking advantage of the Sino-Soviet rift and the buffer location of Yugoslavia, broke completely with the Soviet Union in 1960. Rumania and Czechoslovakia also became the scenes of policies frowned upon by Moscow. Czechoslovakia's move toward greater state independence (as well as internal democratization) was squelched by Soviet forces in 1968.[86] But even the proclamation of the Brezhnev Doctrine at that time did not deter the Rumanian leadership. Nicolae Ceausescu adamantly refused to permit Soviet troops on Rumanian territory under the Warsaw Pact, maintained good relations with China, and increasingly took other foreign policy positions that clashed with the policy of the Soviet Union. Afghanistan had ostensibly become an "independent" Marxist-Leninist state through a coup d'état in 1978, but, within a year, the Soviet Union felt compelled to commit large-scale forces to what proved to be a prolonged, country-wide, antiguerrilla war in order to maintain a Leninist regime in power.

The advent of independent labor unions within Poland focused attention on that country in late 1980. The Soviets quickly made clear their profound unhappiness with this development and tensions mounted. After increasing their military strength along Poland's borders, the Soviets drew attention to the enduring significance of the Czechoslovakia-related events of 1968, with particular emphasis upon the proclamation of the Brezhnev Doctrine of limited sovereignty. In their concerted, almost desperate appeal to the Polish people to refrain from activities that might increase the likelihood of a Soviet invasion, the Polish authorities were somewhat at a disadvantage in not being able to refer directly to such a possibility. Somewhat paradoxically, the code words became a threat (from an unidentified source) to the independence and sovereignty of the homeland, although the very need to avoid giving Moscow pretense for invoking the Brezhnev Doctrine was in itself a poignant reminder that whatever independence and sovereignty Poland enjoyed was confined to the limited form permissible under that doctrine. Nevertheless, the fact that the party leadership, in time of travail, elected to fall back upon protection of the sovereignty of the homeland as the most effective means of rallying the public to heed its admonitions makes the Polish 1980 experience an excellent illustration of a broadly held desire among the general populace to bring form and content into greater harmony, by infusing the myth of independent statehood with more of the actual prerogatives of independence.

The crisis of 1980 was certainly not the first occasion on which the Polish Communist Party had felt the need to raise the specter of a threat to the independence of the homeland as a means of rallying the people. It had been the principal motif of the party's propaganda in 1956 following the Poznan riots and the ensuing thorough change in party leadership.[87] When popular dissatisfaction with progress under the new leadership had led again to violence and yet another change of leadership in 1970, the propaganda apparatus had reverted to the same theme. Indeed, it is somewhat ironic that the propaganda campaign of 1980, which also stressed defense of homeland, should be kicked off at a party conclave at which the recently deposed First Secretary had been derided for having employed the same tactic. Referring to the lack of ideological direction since 1970, one of the party's most powerful members attacked the ex-First Secretary as one who "quoted the word 'homeland' on all occasions of little significance, for example: 'homeland demands of us,' 'homeland expects of us,' 'homeland is suffering' and so on and on."[88] However, at the same meeting, it was agreed that party goals included the following:

> The ideological activity of the party should strengthen both patriotic and internationalistic principles of the functioning of the PZPR, consolidate the alliance with the USSR and other socialist countries which is of crucial importance to Poland's independence, sovereignty, security and prosperous development.[89]

A separate appeal addressed to the people by this same session of the Central Committee opened with the declaration that "the destiny of the nation and the country is at stake" and appealed to "the collective wisdom of the nation" to realize that "the development of popular rule and guarantees of our independence may be consolidated solely within the framework of a socialist state."[90] These pronouncements were made with the knowledge that the Soviet authorities had called an emergency meeting of the Warsaw Pact in Moscow for the following day in order to discuss the Polish situation. The published report of the Moscow meeting, though couched in guarded terms, left no doubt as to the determination of Moscow to intervene if the situation in Poland deteriorated:

> It was acknowledged that socialist Poland, the Polish United Workers' Party and the Polish nation can count absolutely on the fraternal solidarity and support of the countries party to the Warsaw Pact. The PZPR representatives stressed that Poland had

been and would be a socialist state, a lasting link in the community of socialist countries.[91]

With this new goad, a broad-scale propaganda compaign using nearly every agency of society was launched. Particularly important to such a campaign was the hierarchy of the Catholic church, a body which had consistently maintained that it was the true and only spokesman for, and defender of, the Polish nation, and, as such, the interpreter and defender of the nation in relations between the latter and the state and party apparatus. Although the party had never accepted such a contention, it now needed the cooperation of the church as the one agency that could conceivably reach all segments of Polish society, most particularly workers and farmers who could be expected to be very distrustful of the party. The report of a meeting held on December 8, 1980 between representatives of the church and the government announced that "the most important problem discussed was the internal stabilization of our country which is necessary for the good of our homeland." It further noted that both groups of delegates concurred on the need for unity: "Today especially all Poles should unite, no matter what their politics or philosophy. They should unite to save *the independence of our country*, and find the best way out of our crisis."[92]

With the church's support thus insured, the campaign for restraint in the name of protecting Poland's independence went into high gear. On December 12th, the Politburo of the Polish CP issued a declaration "in concern for the future of the Homeland." After calling for the full cooperation of the Polish nation, the declaration averred: "The consistent implementation of this line is in the vital interest of independent, sovereign and socialist Poland, and it reflects our patriotic, internationalist responsibility." The necessity of recognizing the vanguard role of the CP was justified in nearly identical terms: "The consolidation of the PZPR's leading role is in the most vital interest of our nation and favors the security and sovereignty of Poland."[93] On the same day as the publication of the party's declaration, there was also published a communiqué from the hierarchy of the Catholic church of Poland. The prelates noted their "great concern for the future of our homeland," and warned that "we must beware of any activities which could endanger the *independence* and *statehood* of our Homeland" (Emphasis added). Calling for sacrifices "in the name of a better future in a free homeland," the communiqué noted that "the Bishops had addressed a letter to the Nation, appealing for responsibility for the homeland, and fixed January 1, 1981 to be a day of prayer for Poland [and] that December 14, 1980 be a day of prayers for the unity of the Nation." The communiqué further noted that "the Bishops extend best wishes to all daughters and sons of our beloved homeland" and concluded with the bishops' blessings "to all inhabitants of our homeland."[94] Also on the same day, a spokesman for the Polish episcopate told Western journalists that it was necessary that Poles avoid "actions that could harm Poland's interests [and] noisy and irresponsible declarations directed against our Eastern neighbor."[95] The following day the CP's newspaper carried speeches made before the congress of the Peasant Party by the head of the party and by Communist Party First Secretary Kania. Kania's speech was full of allusions to the vital interests of the nation and the "responsibility of all Poles for the fate and state of their homeland." He recalled the glorious World War II "struggle for our homeland's independence," and called for cooperation on the part of "all the patriotic forces within our nation . . . for the sake of Poland, her security and her sovereign development."[96] In a section of his speech entitled "Strengthening the State—the Crucial Task," the head of the Peasant Party emphasized:

> The thing most precious and indispensable to a nation is its own sovereignty. Today this truth needs to be understood more widely than it has ever been in the history of People's Poland and to generate attitudes active in the defense of the state's indispensable authority and strength.

Toward the close of his speech, he sandwiched between paeans to friendship with the Soviet Union the statement that "the problem of guaranteeing our sovereignty and defensive system must always be seen as a task of the utmost importance."[97]

The verbal barrage concerned with homeland and the need to avoid imperiling it had been orchestrated with one eye nervously cast toward December 16, 1980, the day on which a monument would be dedicated to workers who had been shot during a demonstration in Gdansk ten years earlier. Authorities evidently feared that the event might touch off antiparty demonstrations on the part of the huge throng expected at the ceremony, a development that in turn would likely bring in Soviet troops. However, the theme of responsibility to the homeland, further echoed at the ceremony, had the desired defusing effect. The first speaker, Lech Wałęsa (the best-known leader of the workers' independent union movement, Solidarity), set the theme:

> From this place, in the name of patriotism and peace, I call upon all of you present here and upon all Poles of peace and good will, to assume full responsibility for the fate of our fatherland. . . . I call upon you for reason and common sense in all endeavors for the good of the fatherland. . . . I call upon you to be vigilant in defense of our security and to maintain the sovereignty of our fatherland.[98]

Party and church officials clung to the same line during the ceremony, although the bishop of Gdansk came closest to suggesting the nature of the outside pressures under which the service was being conducted. After duly noting "the duty of all Poles to ensure the good of their Homeland," the bishop observed that "there are moments in a man's life when he must remain silent," further noting that "it is difficult not to speak today." A few sentences later he added: "Our Savior gave his life for us. . . . May we give our lives for Him Our Lord Jesus Christ and for our Homeland, as it is our sacred duty to cherish her immediately after God."[99] Over the next two days, countless references to the need to protect the homeland were made at similar ceremonies throughout the country. It was therefore difficult to disagree with the statement in the December 18, 1980 issue of the party's newspaper that "it is now a truism that what Poland needs is, above all, caution, calm, political wisdom and a normal pace of life and work for our common good— the people's homeland."[100] A relieved CP First Secretary Kania, feeling that tensions had ebbed, for the first time suggested that the threat from the East had been merely a Western fabrication. He accused "leading NATO authorities and other Western political quarters" with having conducted "an alarming campaign of absurd insinuations about threats against Poland being made by our allies."[101] The First Secretary chose to overlook a *Pravda* article of the previous day in which the Soviet authorities reasserted their right to intervene in any Leninist state "upon request."[102]

The scheme to make future Leninist states sovereign in form, dependent in content did not, therefore, fare very well in practice. From the beginning, geography endowed the states of Indochina with a real bulwark against domination by Moscow (although not necessarily against domination by one of their own number). The same was true of Cuba. Albania, China, North Korea, Yugoslavia, and, to a lesser degree, Rumania, had assumed an independent posture. Afghanistan, Czechoslovakia, and Hungary had required military intervention to counter sovereign aspirations, and Poland had required an immediate and very credible threat of military force. The system of heavily guarded fences and walls erected along the entire length of East Germany's western borders and the permanent stationing of some one-half million Soviet troops on its soil denied that state even the independent form that Lenin and Stalin had envisaged. Of sixteen states, then, only Bulgaria and Mongolia can be said to have worked out as planned. In all other cases, the dichotomy between form and content could not be maintained.

THE path that our analysis of Leninist national policy has taken can be retraced in five steps:

1. Nowhere has the policy been given a fair testing, and the persistence of nationalism in all Marxist-Leninist states does not in itself establish the invalidity of the policy's underlying assumptions.

2. In the few states within which Leninist forms have ostensibly been employed, Lenin's failure to proscribe tampering with the process and to prescribe effective guidelines for differentiating permissible from impermissible tampering encouraged authorities to saddle their programs with an array of risk-reducing features that run counter to the natural process of the coming together of nations as envisaged by Lenin.

3. Lenin's sole prohibition—avoid coercion—was predicated upon a fallacious dichotomy between coercion and persuasion. It signified a narrow concern with the perceptions of the authorities, when what Lenin's policy logically required was primary concern for the perceptions of the masses. It should have been anticipated that any significant tampering with the merging process (regardless of where the mode of tampering might objectively belong on a coercion-persuasion continuum) would trigger a popular response detrimental to the notion of a natural coming together of nations.

4. Even if Lenin had proscribed all tampering with the process, his intermediate, *sine qua non* goals of economic, cultural, and political equality would have resisted fulfillment. In the most unlikely event that these goals were objectively realized, the encounter with perceptions would still be there.

5. The cornerstone of Lenin's policy—national in form, socialist in content—was, in any case, faulty. National forms (particularly language and homeland) have a national content in and by themselves. Far from exerting a deadening effect upon nationalism, encouraging national forms reinforces that phenomenon.

As was earlier noted, Lenin's plan for neutralizing nationalism flowed from his conception of nationalism as the psychological consequence of past oppression.[103] A period of equality was therefore essential in order to rid the masses of this ism that placed national consciousness above class consciousness. But a causal explanation closely tied to a sense of injustice and oppression would at best help to explain the nationalism of minorities. It has no explanatory power in the case of the nationalism of a dominant people such as the Russians, Han, Vietnamese, Serbs, Czechs, Magyars, Rumanians, etc.

It would be foolish and unfair to charge that Lenin was unaware of national proclivities on the part of dominant peoples. He must have been indelibly reminded that dominant people are in no way immune from such proclivities by his bitter disappointment in the early phases of World War I, when, contrary to his urgings and prognostications, English, French, German, and Russian members of the proletariat rallied to the national call. Moreover, Lenin occasionally referred in his writings and speeches to the nationalism of the oppressor nation.[104] Much more commonly, however, he differentiated great nation *chauvinism* from oppressed nation *nationalism*, as though they were two distinct phenomena. And indeed, logically they would have to be different phenomena, if nationalism was to be obliterated by a period of equality. As we have seen, a move toward equalization would certainly not tend to pacify nations who had been the beneficiaries of inequality. Yet nowhere does Lenin (or Stalin) offer a formula for dissolving great nation chauvinism.[105] In short, Lenin's formula for eradicating nationalism was developed against an inadequate concept of nationalism. The concept that shaped his work was at best a variety of nationalism, namely, minority nationalism.

One can only surmise as to the reasons for Lenin's failure to contemplate the whole rather than a part. One factor may have been his remarkable strategic penchant for locating and concentrating upon the most vulnerable element. It was obviously minorities, not the dominant group within the state, that sparked Lenin's imagination and led to the ascribing of great importance to national self-detemination. A second, overlapping factor may have been that the country of primary interest to Lenin was the Russian Empire, a state in which minorities comprised a most unusual numerical and strategic element. Had Lenin's preoccupation been with a China, Germany, or Japan, it is doubtful that minorities would have been so consuming an interest in his calculations, relative to the dominant group. Still a third contributing element to

Lenin's preoccupation with minority nationalism is that nearly all of his adult life was spent in plotting revolution or in consolidating power against the Whites, goals whose attainment depended heavily upon the endemic unhappiness of national minorities. Only in the last months of Lenin's life did Russian chauvinism/nationalism become an immediate, pressing concern. Even during this period, minority nationalism, agitated by Comintern orders, remained a key element in Lenin's strategy for protecting the Soviet Union from hostile states and for furthering world revolution.

Whatever the reasons for Lenin's narrow concept of nationalism, his limited focus accounts for many of the previously cited inconsistencies and shortcomings in his policy for combatting nationalism.[106] At a more fundamental level, that limited focus misled Lenin into confusing possible catalysts of nationalism with its essence. Had he been more preoccupied with Russian nationalism and less with that of the Finns and Ukrainians, he would have been far less apt to conclude that nationalism was explicable solely in terms of oppression and inequality and was therefore subject to eradication by the introduction of equality. Inequality may of course act as a catalyst and exacerbater of national tensions. But it is simply not the case, even among minorities, that the absence of inequality eradicates nationalism.[107]

This confusion of catalyst with essence accounts for Lenin's greatest presumptive error.[108] That most central piece in Lenin's policy— national in form, socialist in content—presumed that the overt symbols of national uniqueness were not tied to nationalism. Agreed, neither language nor any other single tangible national trait or institution is indispensable to the flourishing of nationalism; comparative studies show they are not. But the overt symbols of group uniqueness perpetuate and reinforce that self-identification with a particular national group, its past and its future, which is nationalism. Lenin was correct in his perception of nationalism as a matter of attitude rather than overt, group characteristics. But in mistaking a possible catalyst for the essence of nationalism, he left himself vulnerable to his most egregiously erroneous presumption: that one could have nations without having nationalism.

NOTES

1. Space does not permit a complete review of all such evidence. Examples of nationally inspired activity engaged in by the major peoples of

the Soviet Union during the 1960s and early 1970s can be found in Katz, *Handbook*, in the subsecton of each chapter, entitled "Recent Manifestations of Nationalism." More recent, large-scale demonstrations involved Georgians in 1978 (*International Herald Tribune*, April 18 and May 5, 1978, and *Keesing's Contemporary Archives* [1978], 28778); the Tadzhiks, also in 1978 (*Peking Review*, January 5, 1979); and the Letts during 1980 (*International Herald Tribune*, October 6, 1980). For a review of manifestations of ethnic strife throughout the Baltic Republics during 1979 and 1980, see *The Observer* (London), January 11, 1981. See also the article by a long-time student of Estonia who notes: "Until recently, I would have scoffed at the notion of popular uprisings in the Soviet Union, but events in my native Estonia have made me wonder. Since last fall, there has been an unprecedented outpouring of large-scale protest—massive student demonstrations, a successful strike by a thousand workers, and a letter to the Communist Party newspaper, *Pravda*, from 40 Estonian intellectuals asking for a candid discussion of Estonian-Russian relations." (Rein Taagepera in the *International Herald Tribune*, May 29, 1981.) See also "L'agitation en Estonie," 45, and "Afghanistan for the Afghans, the Baltic Region for the Balts!" in *Die Welt*, May 4, 1982. See also the account of a strike and evidence of growing anti-Russian sentiment within Estonia in the *Christian Science Monitor*, January 28, 1982. For a report of a riot in the North Ossetian Autonomous Republic, see the *London Observer*, November 29, 1981. For antagonistic attitudes among nations as perceived by émigré Germans and Lithuanians, see Kazlas, "Social Distance Among Ethnic Groups," 228–254. For an émigré's account of how Soviet "European" children learn to be prejudiced against Asian and Jewish compatriots, see Plynshch, *History's Carnival*, 8, 9, 13, 61, 68, 113, 164–168, 178. See too, d'Encausse, *Decline of an Empire*, 189, for the opinion that demonstrations have been increasing since 1967. For confirmation, see Kowalewski, "Protest Demonstrations." For a lengthy account of rising nationalism among the Great Russians, see the *New York Times*, November 12, 1978. Trials of "bourgeois nationalists" have been sporadically reported in the Soviet press, but underground (*samizdat*) literature establishes that the publicly reported cases are only a fraction of the total. (For excellent *samizdat* reporting on the trials of several Ukrainian nationalists, see *The Chornovil Papers*. For reports of the arrests of several nationalists between mid-1979 and mid-1980, see *Keesing's Contemporary Archives* [1980], 30468.) Commencing in the 1960s, the Soviet authorities permitted several surveys of national attitudes to be taken. The validity of such polls, when conducted within a "closed society," is obviously open to question. As a Soviet source has acknowledged, in such a society "a person quite often answers not what he thinks, but what he believes the researcher expects of him." (*Novyi Mir*, no 2 [1978]: 199; cited in *Radio Liberty Research*, 142/78, June 27, 1978.) It is therefore particularly noteworthy that the published results of the surveys without exception have recorded a significant level of "negative" (i.e., nationalist) attitudes. Since the authorities regularly castigate such attitudes, the number of those recorded as holding nationalist views would assuredly be substantially higher if the fear of retribution were absent. The authorities' condoning of such potentially dangerous inquiries—which in themselves contradict the official position that all hostile ethnonational sentiments have been exorcised from the "fraternal family of nations"—is an important indication of the authorities' awareness that nationalist sentiments are precariously strong and must be recognized and measured in order to be analyzed and countered. An émigré with great experience in polling within the Soviet Union has confirmed Soviet official apprehension that such polls might encourage and legitimize dissent. (*New York Times*, February 3, 1980.) Yet Soviet authorities have indicated their need to continue such studies in the 1980s. For a tabulation of several such Soviet surveys that occurred prior to 1974, see Silver "Inventory of Propositions." More recent studies have been done on the Moldavian and Georgian SSRs. Finally, the large number of Jews, Armenians, and Germans who applied for exit visas during the 1970s further attested to the strong presence of nationalism within the Soviet Union. Authorities within the Federal Republic of Germany estimated that in 1980, more than 100,000 Germans had asked to emigrate. (See *Keesing's Contemporary Archives* [1980], 30468.) In late 1982, a member of the Politburo wrote: "The problems of inter-nation relations are still among the most burning problems." (Chernenko, "60 Years," 10.)

Chinese authorities have been more prone to acknowledge a rather continuous series of separatist movements, revolts, massive transborder flights (particularly on the part of the Uighurs and Tibetans), and other manifestations of "local nationalism." (For the period 1949–1976, consult Dreyer, *China's Forty*.) In 1980 a delegation of Tibetan exiles who had been permitted a three-month tour of Tibet reported that they had confirmed that a majority of the Tibetan people desired freedom from China: "Everywhere we went the Tibetans chanted 'Long Live the Dalai Lama! We want freedom.' " (*New York Times*, August 16, 1980.) For an account of unrest in Sinkiang during 1980 and again in 1981, see *Keesing's Contemporary Archives* (1981), 30943, and (1982), 31321, and the *Washington Post*, January 18, 1982. In late 1982, the head of the CPC in the Uighur AR acknowledged that "[o]ver the last 2 years relations among nationalities had been tense" and he asserted that "those who divide the motherland and disturb unity among the nationalities must be opposed and condemned, and in serious cases, attacked without let-up." ("Stress the Key," 109, 111.) Another Chinese article written in late 1982 admitted: "Today, some separatists and others with ulterior motives continue to flaunt the misleading banner of an 'independent Tibet.' " (An Zhiguo, "Policy," 54.) The prevalence of separatist activities was reflected in the 1982 constitution's specific ban on acts that "instigate" secession. (See chapter 10.) The authorities had not found it necessary to include a specific reference to secession in any of the previous constitutions.

Nationalism was so rampant in Yugoslavia in the early 1970s that observers routinely commented on its preeminence. Referring to the level of separatist sentiment at this time, Tito remarked: "Had we not moved, in six months perhaps shooting would have broken out—civil war." (*Christian Science Monitor*, December 31, 1971.) Trials for nationalist activity continued throughout the 1970s. In 1976 members of an "Albanian National Liberation Movement" were sentenced to lengthy prison terms. (*Washington Post*, March 1, 1976.) Despite these arrests, the movement remained active and became a matter of major consternation in 1981–1982. (See, for example, *Keesing's Contemporary Archives* [1982], 31672–31673.) The manifestations of militant nationalism on the part of Albanians in Kosovo Province proved the harbinger of an outburst of nationalist activity on the part of Bosnians, Croats, Serbs, and Slovenes. By early 1983, the press was filled with articles detailing manifestations of nationalism among all four peoples. (See, for example, the several articles under Yugoslavia in *JPRS* 83173, March 31, 1983, pp. 86–104. Even the arts were said to have become infiltrated by nationalism [pp. 100-102].) An article described the situation in early 1983 as follows:

In this mosaic of ideological tendencies and collisions it should be said that it is not only Serbian nationalism that is on the offensive. Even last summer a warning was issued in a meeting of the LCY Central Committee that "nationalism is even today the most dangerous vehicle of counterrevolutionary tendencies and recently all nationalisms have become more vigorous, operating more or less covertly through legal institutions—first of all in education, culture and the press, and striving for a renewal of personnel."

Quite a few examples have also been found to support this assessment. The events in the university dormitories in Zagreb and Split are still fresh in the memory; in Croatia the church has been on a permanent offensive, and nationalism is alive even in the thesis of the "foreign exchange which has been taken away"; in Bosnia-Hercegovina there have been open and public demonstrations by nationalists, indeed even the desecration of graves; Moslem nationalists have striven to organize in their own ethnic institutions; the polemics over the Slovenian language also bore admixtures of Slovenian nationalism; in Kosovo the Irredenta is still active, but the story about threatened Serbs is still topical. . . . It nevertheless seems that at this point nationalism has penetrated most seriously certain segments of culture and creativity, but, following Marxist logic, it is obvious that it is a consequence of the general condition. A consequence of what is happening on a broader social plane, but at this point it has become so "independent" that it threatens to turn from a consequence into a cause. All of this is an occasion for more frequent comparions to be made between 1971 and the present time. (Markinovic, "Again the Same Isms," 73.)

Others also drew comparisons between the level of nationalism in 1971–72 and 1982–83. (See, for example, Galovic, "The Interest of the Working Class," 78.) The level of intergroup animosity was suggested by the description of Albanians in a resolution signed by Serbian Orthodox priests and monks:

> [W]hat is wrong with that proud and patriarchal mountain people [the Albanians] whose children, young men and adults have been setting fire to churches, vandalizing graveyards, and harassing and perfidiously murdering their neighbors for centuries? ("Appeal for Protection," 117.)

During the period of free expression in Czechoslovakia in 1968, opinion polls regularly confirmed a high incidence of national motivation on the part of the Slovaks. For polling data, consult Ulc, *Politics in Czechoslovakia*, and Skilling, *Czechoslovakia's Interrupted Revolution*. For an acknowledgment that there was still discord in the relations between Czechs and Slovaks in late 1982, see the article by the Slovak Deputy Minister of Culture (Cerevka, "Development of Nationality," 17).

Hanoi has periodically acknowledged that a national liberation guerrilla movement continues to operate among the highland peoples, and has also often accused Peking of agitation among the peoples on the Vietnamese side of the common border. (See, for example, Thanh Tin, "Central Highlands," K10, K11.) The Magyar minority within Rumania remains a heated topic between Budapest and Bucharest. (See, for example, Szaraz, "On a Curious Book," 1–15.)

2. *Program Adopted by the Twenty-second Party Congress, 1961*. Translated in *New Times* (Moscow), November 29, 1961.

3. *The Current Digest of the Soviet Press* 24, no. 5:6.

4. Ibid., 9. In 1968 Tito had also combined within a single speech a claim that the national question had been solved with an admonition that nationalism must be relentlessly fought. See Christman, *Essential Tito*, 187, 191. At the Twelfth Party Congress in 1982, the president of the party's Presidium singled out nationalism as "the most dangerous counter-revolutionary force in our multinational state and social community." (*Keesing's Contemporary Archives* (1982), 31673.)

5. A number of leading Soviet authorities on the national question hastened to embrace Brezhnev's admission of the presence of nationalism, apparently sensing that as against doctrinaires who would insist that nationalism could not be present in a socialist society, the admission offered official sanction for greater freedom to pursue their research. (See, for example, the citation of the passage by Brezhnev that we have just quoted in Bromley, *Soviet Ethnography*, 164–165. See also Zagladin, *Revolutionary Movement*, 142, 170.)

6. See Connor, "Self-Determination" and "Politics of Ethnonationalism."

7. More commonly employed coercive acts have included large-scale

purges and incarcerations, enforced deportations and migrations, and the use of the army and militia to put down or prevent demonstrations.

8. Among the afflicted states have been Austria, Belgium, Canada, Denmark, France, (post-Franco) Spain, and the United Kingdom.

9. See chapter 9.

10. See chapter 8.

11. The comment, written when Lenin's health was rapidly failing, was part of three reports that were highly critical of Stalin and were designed to deny Stalin's consolidation of power over the Soviet state.

12. In recent years, a number of Marxist-Leninist states (including China, Hungary, and especially Yugoslavia) experimented with decentralization in the economic sphere. However, in contrast with non-Marxist states, centralized planning and regulation were still rigorous. And in other pertinent areas (education policy, language policy, censorship, security, etc.), control remained in the hands of the center.

13. Soviet activists have pressed the need to intervene in the assimilation process, with barely more than a nod in the direction of inevitable, historical forces. Thus, after dwelling on the perils of nationalism, a coauthored work by nine Soviet authorities continues:

> Combatting it, we cannot afford therefore to rely on the spontaneous action of the objective law discovered by Lenin that socialism will make all economic, political and cultural thought of mankind completely international. Only purposeful and effective action by Communist Parties [can assure] socialist internationalism not only in ideology and politics, but also in the psychology of all working people, in the daily social practice of the socialist countries. (Zagladin, *Revolutionary Movement*, 169.)

The nonspontaneity of the assimilation process was also stressed by Kholmogorov in "International Traits," 38:

> The process of internationalization of the Soviet nations and nationalities is objective. It can be neither slowed nor accelerated. But this does not mean that it is spontaneous and uncontrollable, and that subjective factors exercise no influence upon it. . . . To ignore the role of subjective factors . . . leads . . . to denying the possibility of scientific control of ethnic processes. . . . Socialism is a consciously directed society.

The author does not make clear how a process that cannot be "slowed nor accelerated" can nevertheless be scientifically controlled and "consciously directed." Elsewhere, however, his comments make clear that he is indeed in favor of accelerating the process.

14. See chapter 9.

15. Ibid.

16. Rusinow (*Yugoslav Experiment*, 99, 100, 118) notes that the gap was actually widening despite fifteen years of trying to close it. See also the data in Burks, *National Problem and Future*, 55; and Lendvai, "National Tensions," 7.

17. See the tables in Katz, *Handbook*, 452–453. Soviet per capita income figures do not include income data from the unofficial, private sector, which is very important in Armenia and Georgia. However, personal savings accounts indicate greater individual wealth in these republics than in the RSFSR. Lubin ("Ethnic/Political") makes a strong case for the fact that Uzbeks earn much more than official statistics indicate.

18. See the *New York Times*, March 4, 1980.

19. Some polls have indicated that the Slovenes are the most unhappy of the state's eight major peoples. See Burks, *National Problem and Future*, 43.

20. Compare the statement (*New York Times*, November 12, 1978) that many Russians are convinced that ethnic Russians generally "live in worse conditions than many of the Soviet Union's 100 or so small ethnic groups, especially those with their own republics, such as Armenians, Ukrainians, Estonians, Georgians and Lithuanians" with the data in Katz, *Handbook*, 462. These data suggest that the Russian standard of living is well above the country's mean, and is bested only by the peoples in the Baltic Republics (and possibly Armenia and Georgia; see note 17).

21. Both Lenin and Stalin appreciated the symbolism and psychological impact of the reference to Russia in the state's official title. See chapter 8, note 52. Roy Medvedev (*On Socialist Democracy*, 87) notes that *Russia*, as an equivalent for the entire USSR, is creeping into Soviet parlance.

22. See chapter 9.

23. This line of reasoning would be even more applicable to China, where upward of 95 percent of the population spoke a Chinese dialect. By contrast, the Vietnamese CP had in French an alternative lingua franca known to Vietnamese and non-Vietnamese elites alike, but the party chose not to adopt this alternative.

24. See chapter 11.

25. See chapter 1.

26. See Szporluk, "Nationalities and Russian Problem," 31.

27. History was rewritten to make the conquest of non-Russian peoples a progressive step and any resistance to the conquest reactionary. A Soviet citizen described the rewriting of history as follows:

Alexander Nevsky, Yuri Dolgoruky, Ivan the Terrible, and Ivan Kalita were all sanctified on the grounds that "taken in historical context their lives had been progressive." At the same time various movements for national independence were vilified (Shamil and others). There were virtually no acts perpetrated by the tsarist army, administration, or diplomatic corps which the obedient hacks could not portray favorably in a clever amalgamation of Marxist language and chauvinistic ideas. Tsarist Russia disappeared; in historical studies, novels, and textbooks there was absolutely no trace of the "prison of nations," the "gendarme of Europe" crushing revolution, or the empire oppressing its colonies yet at the same time dependent on foreign capital. Historical facts were glossed over in an intolerably specious manner. It became a criminal offense to extol the local rulers in Central Asia who restricted the Russian advance, but khans who did obeisance to the tsar were graciously endowed with the epithet "progressive" (as if they had foreseen the October Revolution and the Union of the Soviet Socialist Republics!). (Raissa Lert, "Treatise on the Charms of the Knout," quoted in Medvedev, *On Socialist Democracy*, p. 361.)

For another example of historical rewriting, this one involving the Ukraine, see Barghoorn, *Soviet Russian*, 53 et seq. See also Dzubya, *Internationalism?*, 7: "To satisfy the most absurd tendency of identifying the USSR with the heritage of the former Russian Empire and of 'rehabilitating' the latter, today's historian does not interpret the 'history of the Fatherland' as the history of the Russians, Ukrainians, Georgians, Latvians, etc., respectively, but as history of the Russian Empire."

28. Cited in Karklins, *Interrelationship*, 110. See, too, the article, "Correctly Translate," 5, where the author complains that the textbooks of minorities have tended to "refuse and reject Han advanced culture." Evidently the CCP wanted Han culture to become *the* single culture of all peoples within China.

29. See, for example, the statement of Mao Tse-tung (originally made in 1940 but republished, with minor modifications, two years after the creation of the People's Republic):

Developing along the same lines as the other *great* peoples of the world, the Chinese people (*chiefly the Hans*) first went through some tens of thousands of years of life in a classless, *equalitarian*, primitive, *communistic society*. Five thousand years have gone by since the collapse of primitive *communistic society* and the transition to class society—first a slave society, then that of feudalism. In the history of Chinese civilization (chiefly that of the Hans), agriculture and handicraft have always been highly developed; many great thinkers, scientists, inventors, statesmen, men of letters, and artists have flourished, and there is a rich store of classical works. The compass was invented in China 3,000 years ago. The art of paper-making was discovered as early as 1,700 years ago. Block-printing was invented 1,200 years ago. Movable type was invented 800 years ago. Gunpowder also was used in China much earlier than in Europe. China, with a recorded history of 5,000 years, is therefore one of the oldest civilized countries in the world.

The Chinese people is not only famous throughout the world for its endurance and industriousness; it is also a freedom-loving people with a rich revolutionary tradition. The history of the Hans, for instance, shows that the Chinese people would never submit to a rule of the dark forces and that in every case they succeeded in overthrowing or changing such a rule by revolutionary means. In thousands of years of Han history, there have been hundreds of peasant insurrections against the regime of darkness imposed by the landlords and nobility. (As translated in Schram, *Political Thought of Mao*, 164–165.)

See also Chang Chih-i, *The Party* 16–17, where the vanguard role of the Han Chinese is justified by alleging that the minorities are at a lower (feudal) stage of civilization than are the Han. And see Chou En-lai's statement, in a speech attacking chauvinism, that "the Hans are greater in number and are more developed in economy and culture" than the minorities. (*Peking Review*, March 3, 1980.) Chou's speech was first made in 1957.

Similarly, Vietnamese leaders have not deigned to hide their conviction that the cultures of the "moi" (the Vietnamese term of denigration for the hill peoples) are outmoded and decadent contrasted with that of the Vietnamese and that they must be vietnamized. (See chapter 10.) The only real cultural competitors within the state, the Chinese, were pressured to emigrate.

30. Cited in Barghoorn, *Soviet Russian*, 27.

31. *Current Digest of the Soviet Press*, 23, no. 14:3. One of the stanzas of a poem that appeared in a 1964 textbook for school children, written in the Uzbek language, began: "There is a Russian people, you have a leader." Cited in Lubin, "Nationality Question as a Threat." A line in the Soviet anthem reads: "Great Russia has rallied forever/An unbreakable union of free republics."

32. Andropov, "Sixty Years of the USSR," P3.

33. "We Are the Soviet People," *JPRS* 82130, November 1, 1982, pp. 4–5.

34. Lert, "Treatise on Charms," as cited in Medvedev, *On Socialist Democracy*, 362.

35. *Sinkiang Huntsi* (1960), as cited in "Nationalities Minorities of Western China," 255. The English translation was in turn dependent upon a Russian translation that had appeared in *Kommunist*, no. 7 (1967).

36. *Summary of World Broadcasts* FE/5392 (December 17, 1976). *The Programme of the Romanian Communist Party* contains a lengthy history which, after establishing that the Rumanian people are made up of the descendents of the Dacian-Romans (i.e., after excluding the Magyar, German, and other minorities), assigns this people an almost exclusive role in the history of the state and its culture. See also the comments concerning the exclusion of Hungarian figures from the history of Transylvania in Schöpflin, *Hungarians*, 13.

37. This thesis is examined in chapter 12.

38. See chapter 9.

39. For example, in a survey conducted within Czechoslovakia shortly before the invasion in 1968, 91 percent of the Slovaks felt that fostering equality between Czechs and Slovaks was the most pressing issue; only 5 percent of the Czechs agreed. See Ulc, *Politics in Czechoslovakia*, 16.

40. Pospielovsky, "Resurgence of Nationalism," 60, 67.

41. The last complaint could be an allusion to either the nonethnic spelling of Russian in the title of the RSFSR and/or its ethnic heterogeneity. In addition to Pospielovsky ("Resurgence of Nationalism"), see Spechler, "Russia and Russians," and the *New York Times*, November 12, 1978. During Stalin's reign, Russians also complained about being ruled by a Georgian, and this despite the fact that Stalin was a Russophile who favored the Russians over all other people. See Barghoorn, *Soviet Russian*, 120.

42. There was particularly strong resentment among the Han of Kwangsi at being incorporated into an AR with the Chuang.

43. See chapter 8 and Tudjman, *Nationalism*, 131. In the early 1980s, Serbian frustration and resentment flared openly as a result of Serbs leaving Kosovo Province under Albanian pressure.

44. In the case of the Russians, see Pospielovsky, "Resurgence of Nationalism," and the *New York Times*, November 12, 1978. Aleksandr Solzhenitsyn, in a letter to the Soviet leaders on September 5, 1973, also hinted at the wisdom of falling back upon the RSFSR and possibly the Ukraine. See his *East and West*, 78 and the footnote on 108. On the growth of Serbian separatism, see Schöpflin, "National Question."

45. Solzhenitsyn, *East and West*, 180–181.

46. Ibid., 124, 140. Emphasis in original. The extract is from a letter to the Soviet leaders written in 1973, while the author was still a Soviet citizen. The reference to Russia is purposeful. He is referring to the area traditionally populated by Russians, not to the Soviet Union.

47. Whether due to a desire to placate the growing national restiveness among the Russians or to a desire to mobilize more effectively the largest and most important segment of the population for an expanded effort, paeans to the Great Russians as the vanguard people became, as earlier noted, both more commonplace and effusive with the advent of the stage of mature socialism. During the late 1970s and early 1980s, rarely did a reference to the great strides made by the Soviet people during the first sixty years of their experience fail to pay obeisance to the foremost role of the Russian people and to the "selfless assistance" that people had proffered the other nations. Passages of a book by General Secretary Brezhnev, which emphasized the debt of the non-Russians to the Great Russians, were regularly cited at length. (See, for example, the review in *JPRS* 80817 [May 14, 1982]: 9.) Another book, *The Bond of Time*, by F. Nesterov, which glorified the Russian people and the Russian past, was the recipient of a prestigious award in 1982. A guide for designing an indoctrination lecture for military recruits instructed that emphasis was to be given to the fact that "the Russian working class and the great Russian people played a prominent role in the unifying [of the Soviet peoples] according to the general admission of all Soviet peoples." (Kalinayev, "A Union of Free and Equal," 70–85.) The Russian language was extolled not only as "the language of the great Lenin [but as] the language of that magnified people which possess the richest democratic and revolutionary

traditions, as well as a great cultural heritage." (Reshidov, "Language of Our Unity and Fraternity.") And an article by a Politburo member that extolled the handling of the national question during the first sixty years of the Soviet Union noted that the "internationalist spirit," "selfless heroism," and the "uncompromising attitude toward all oppressors" of the Russian people were crucial to the creation of a "voluntary union" of free nations. (Chernenko, "Inviolable Union of Free Nations," 2–5.)

48. Minorities, whose prerevolutionary response to the carrot of independence was predicated largely upon intense dislike of the dominant group, could not now be expected to admire that same group and to accept ungrudgingly its vanguard status.

49. Marxist-Leninist regimes are, of course, also periodically reminded of this fact by the stirrings of minority nationalism at home. In the case of the Soviet Union, the pro-German activities of several non-Russian peoples in the early stages of World War II unquestionably exerted a profound impact on the perceptions of the regime.

50. The compromise of a two-house legislature (one based on population, the other on national group) is a standoff rather than a resolution of the basic dilemma. Each group would view representation in one of the houses as eminently fair and in the other as unfair. Moreover, while such a pragmatic solution might well over time acquire legitimacy when the two elements to be reconciled are, as in the case of the United States, the essentially unemotional ones of population and geography (or administrative unit), it is more doubtful that legitimacy would be accorded where the emotional factor of national group was involved. Almost by definition, matters involving the status of the nation are not to be compromised. (Since the Soviet Union's Supreme Soviet is not in any true sense of the word a policy-making body, its experience is not germane.) In any case, the bicameral approach would be inappropriate in the key decision-making organization of a Marxist-Leninist state, namely, the party. The division of power within the party would not be consonant with the Leninist principle of democratic centralism.

51. The reference to stability arises from an additional problem associated with achieving equality: its instability. Even if one were able to get all parties to agree that equality had been achieved, the fact that many of the factors used to measure equality are dynamic (not static) would make a balance inherently unstable. Thus, except on the rarest of occasions, there would be groups feeling that they were not receiving their fair share.

52. It is interesting that the great importance Lenin attached to equality in resolving the national question was predicated in part upon the mistaken assumption that the nationality question had been solved within Switzerland and that this had been due to institutionalized equality. (See "Critical Remarks on the National Question," sec. 5, "The Equality of Nations and the Rights of National Minorities," in Lenin, *Collected Works*, vol. 20, particulary pp. 40–42.) For his insight on the Swiss case, Lenin had largely

depended on a work (E. Blocher, *Die Nationalitäten in der Schweiz* [Berlin, 1910]) that had maintained that students of national relations within Switzerland agreed: "There is no national question in the East-European sense of the term. The very phrase (national question) is unknown there. . . . Switzerland left the struggle between nationalities a long way behind, in 1797–1803." Lenin favorably cited these passages, and insisted that Marxist national policy must be patterned on the Swiss model. However, while Switzerland's record of accommodating national divisions has indeed been better than that of most states, its national question has certainly never been solved. For data indicating different ethnonational attitudes and perceptions toward the state and other groups living within the country, see Schmid, *Conflict and Consensus*. See also, Connor, "Ethnonationalism within Western Europe," particularly pp. 122–125.

53. See chapter 8.

54. See chapter 9.

55. The Irish and Scots are two often-used examples. Soviet census data also show that a substantial number of people within the USSR have retained their national identity after losing their language. See also Bilinsky, *Second Soviet Republic*, 58, where the author cites statistics to demonstrate that the national background of the parents is much more decisive than language preference in determining national identity. See Kazlas, "Varieties of Nationalism and Internationalism," 17, who concludes from a survey of Soviet émigrés that language offered no hint to national attitudes. Nevertheless, some American scholars have also used linguistic assimilation as the key index to national assimilation within the Soviet Union. See, for example, the works of Brian Silver, including his article in Azrael, *Soviet Nationality*.

56. See chapter 9.

57. See, for example, King, *Minorities*, 118. Slovak treatment of all minorities (gypsies, Ruthenians, etc.) has fallen well short of Lenin's dicta concerning the need to treat minorities with special consideration in order to overcome memories of past oppression.

58. The phasing out of the autonomous region began in the early 1960s, shortly after the Sino-Soviet rift offered the Eastern European states a measure of latitude in their dealings with Moscow.

59. Chou En-lai, "Some Questions," 22. Emphasis and parenthetical material added. The reproduction of this article, more than twenty years after its origin, indicates that this extreme sensitivity to the dangers of autonomous units survived Mao's tenure. The indirect allusion to the Soviets as "imperialists" as early as 1957 is also of interest, although the CPR has been known to add and delete phrases when reproducing earlier materials.

60. Chou might also have pointed out that the word, Inner, in Inner Mongolian AR, underlined the geographic nature of that unit's title.

61. Derived from the table in Deal, "National Minority," 143–147. For

data on the ethnic heterogeneity of the autonomous districts, see chapter 9.

62. Recall, however, that the decision to drop the word Russian from the name of the state (the USSR) and the party was motivated by the desire to avoid triggering a negative response on the part of non-Russians. Moreover, as a means of weakening the claims of the Crimean Tatars (who were ordered removed from their homeland by Stalin during World War II) to a right to return to Crimea following their postwar exoneration, *The Great Soviet Encyclopedia* draws attention to the fact that the autonomous republic in which they lived had been called the Crimean ASSR. That is to say, it bore no ethnic designation, and its purely geographic title indicated that the area had been an ethnic hodgepodge over which no people could claim a special, proprietary interest. (See d'Encausse, *Decline of an Empire*, 198–199.)

63. See chapter 9.

64. *Keesing's Contemporary Archives* (1981), 30950. See also the *Washington Post*, May 3, 1982.

65. Dzyuba, *Internationalism?*, 206.

66. Those arrested for "separatism", "secession," and the like routinely demur on the ground that such a charge, even if true, could hardly be a crime. See, for example, Moroz, *Report from the Beria Reserve*, 6: "My comrades and I were convicted for 'propaganda directed toward the separation of Ukraine from the USSR.' But Article 17 of the Constitution of the USSR clearly speaks of the right of each Republic to secede from the USSR." Elsewhere (p. 9), after numbering himself among "those who dared to claim the rights proclaimed in the Constitution," Moroz adds that he refuses the interpretation, slavishly accepted by the cowardly, "according to which the phrase in the Constitution, 'Ukraine's right to secede from the USSR' is read 'keep quiet while you are still alive.' " And in a passing vignette (p. 39) Moroz relates: "When Levko Lukyanenko asked Captain Denisov, investigator of the Lviv KGB: 'For what purpose do we have Article 17, which gives each republic the right to secede freely from the USSR?' the latter replied: 'For foreign consumption.' " For an account of a constitutional lawyer within Kirgizia, who argues that the Soviet state cannot legally prosecute anyone for advocating the secession of an SSR from the USSR, see Hetmanek, "Kirgizistan and the Kirgiz," 257.

67. See the end of chapter 9. For particular complaints on Russian immigrants into Latvia, see the letter of "seventeen Latvian Communists" in Saunders, *Samizdat*, 427–440. For the Ukraine, see Dzyuba, *Internationalism?*, 110.

68. For an account of rallies under the slogan, "Russians, get out of Uzbekistan," see Carlisle, "Uzbekistan and the Uzbeks," 310. For an account of similar rallies and similar slogans some years apart within Estonia, see Taagepera, "Estonia and the Estonians," 90 ("Out, out of this republic, you who eat Estonia's bread but do not speak Estonia's language!"), and

"L'Agitation en Estonie," 45. For similar phenomena within Lithuania, see Harned, "Lithuania and the Lithuanians," 137.

69. See the *New York Times*, March 8, 1970, and June 8, 1972; the *Christian Science Monitor*, June 9, 1971, and June 30, 1972; and R. Lewis et al., *Nationality and Population*, 251, 259. On March 30, 1971, *Pravda* carried a statement by the Latvian First Secretary, which read in part:

> We cannot overlook the localistic tendencies and national narrowmind-edness that can still be encountered in the views and attitudes of some people. Such people . . . think, for example, that it would not be worth-while to build certain major industrial, power-engineering and other facilities in our republic. Why? Because, so they say, the numbers of the non-Latvian population in the Latvian Republic would increase in this connection, and the republic's nationalities composition would become mixed. The republic's party organization . . . has always resolutely opposed such sentiments and continues to do so.

70. *Current Digest of the Soviet Press* 25, no. 16 (1973):5.

71. *Basic Summarization of Experiences in Promotion of Autonomy*, 16–17.

72. See, for example, Hu, *Education of National Minorities*, 19, and Dreyer, *China's Forty*, 149–150. Frustrated with what they perceived as the emptiness of autonomy as designed by Peking, a typical evaluation by a member of a minority was that autonomy was "as useful as ears on a basket."

73. See chapter 9.

74. Ibid. Germans were also expeditiously expelled from areas in which they had traditionally predominated within Czechoslovakia and Poland.

75. Kernig, *Marxism, Communism* 3:325. The occasion for the letter was a military victory of the Red Army over Polish forces, which raised the possibility of victory over Poland.

76. See chapter 3.

77. "Conditions of Admission into the Communist International," July 1920, in Christman, *Communism*, 65–90. There were twenty-one conditions. The one cited is number sixteen.

78. See chapter 7.

79. When the Warsaw Pact and the Council of Economic Mutual Assistance (at least as Moscow originally intended them to function) are added to the relationship, it is evident that the relationship was designed to be more than a confederation.

80. The Cominform had been created in 1947. At the opening session, the chief Soviet delegate had pledged respect for the "equality" and "sovereign rights" of all members, but had then, in the words of Paul Zinner, "made it clear that the Soviet Union did not choose to abandon its task of guiding and instructing foreign Communists and that the East European Communists would do well to avail themselves of the rich experience which the Soviet Union had accumulated in its road to socialism." (Zinner, *National Communism and Popular Revolt*, 4.)

81. The surfacing was unquestionably encouraged by the rapprochement of Yugoslavia and the Soviet Union during 1955 (which *Pravda* [July 16, 1955] described as made possible by Soviet "respect for the sovereignty of all countries, large and small); by the formal dissolution of the Cominform in April 1956; and by the denunciation of Stalin and Stalinism at the Twentieth Party Congress of the Soviet CP.

82. "Address by Wladyslaw Gomulka before the Central Committee of the Polish United Workers Party," October 20, 1956, in Zinner, *National Communism and Popular Revolt*, 227–228.

83. "Declaration by the Government of the USSR on the Principles of Development and Further Strengthening of Friendship and Cooperation between the Soviet Union and other Socialist States," October 30, 1956, in ibid., 485–489.

84. The coolness traces from early Soviet resistance to Mao's leadership of the CCP, to bad advice about entering the united front with the KMT, to a surprisingly late (post-World War II) willingness of Moscow to recognize and negotiate with the KMT, to Soviet post-World War II attempts to separate Inner Mongolia from China, and to arguments over borders and special port facilities.

85. It would also prove ironic that additional support for intervention in Hungary came, *inter alia*, from Albania, Czechoslovakia, North Korea, Rumania, and Yugoslavia.

86. An article in a Ukrainian-language newspaper published within Czechoslovakia parodied the *primus inter pares* posturing of the Soviet Union. The article, written during the heady days of the 1968 spring, noted the necessity to search out all the Ukrainian bourgeois nationalists who must be lurking about: "The U.S.S.R. had Ukrainian bourgeois nationalists, and since the U.S.S.R. was a model for all to follow, the C.S.S.R. [Czechoslovakia] had to have them as well." Cited in Hodnett and Potichnj, *Ukraine and Czechoslovak Crisis*, 63.

87. For numerous illustrations of this propaganda, see Zinner, *National Communism and Popular Revolt*, particularly chapter 5.

88. "Discussion at the 7th PZPR Central Committee Plenum: Report of Mieczyslaw Moczar," *Zycie Warszawy*, December 4, 1980.

89. "Party Goals in the Fight for a Socialist Character of the Revival of Socialist Life: The Resolution by the 7th Plenum of the PZPR Central Committee," *Zycie Warszawy*, December 4, 1980.

90. "Appeal of the Central Committee of the PZPR to Create the Front of Reason and Responsibility in Defense of the Socialist Renaissance," *Zycie Warszawy*, December 4, 1980.

91. "Leaders of States Party to the Warsaw Pact Meet," *Trybuna Ludu*, December 6–7, 1980.

92. "The Meeting of the Mixed Commission of the PRL Government Representatives and the Polish Episcopate," *Trybuna Ludu*, December 9, 1980. Emphasis added.

93. *Declaration for Coordinated Activities of the Polish United Worker's Party, the United Peasant Party and the Democratic Party*, December 12, 1980, in the name of the PZPR Central Committee's Politburo, the ZSL Supreme Committee Presidium. Published in *Trybuna Ludu*, December 13–14, 1980. Although the Peasant and Democratic Parties had pre-World War II antecedents, they had become auxiliaries of the Polish CP (PZPR).

94. "The Country is in Need of Internal Peace: Plenary Conference of the Polish Episcopate," *Zycie Warszawy*, December 13–14, 1980.

95. As reported in an editorial entitled "Incorrigible and Irresponsible," in *Trybuna Ludu*, December 18, 1980.

96. "Stanislaw Kania's Speech at the VIII Congress of the ZSL," *Trybuna Ludu*, December 15, 1980.

97. "Resumé of Stanislaw Gucwa's Report Delivered at the VIII Congress of the ZSL," *Trybuna Ludu*, December 15, 1980.

98. *Slowo Powszechne*, December 17, 1980.

99. Ibid.

100. "Incorrigible and Irresponsible," *Trybuna Ludu*, December 18, 1980.

101. "The New Situation in our Country Needs a New Program. A Speech of the First Secretary of the PZPR CC on the Congress Commission" (December 20, 1980), *Trybuna Ludu*, December 22, 1980. By contrast with this after-hour denial of a threat, the authorities had earlier tried to drive home the immediacy of the threat by showing on television what was described as a current film of Soviet tanks on maneuvers within eastern Poland. But the presence of foliage and the absence of snow tipped sophisticated Poles to the fact that they were viewing old footage.

102. As reported in the *International Herald Tribune*, December 19, 1980.

103. See chapter 2.

104. See, for example, the citation from Lenin's *Collected Works* in Dzyuba, *Internationalism?*, 60–61:

> In my writings on the national question I have already said that an abstract presentation of the question of nationalism in general is of no use at all. A distinction must necessarily be made between the nationalism of an oppressor nation and that of an oppressed nation, the nationalism of a big nation and that of a small nation.
>
> In respect of the second kind of nationalism we, nationals of a big nation, have nearly always been guilty, in historic practice, of an infinite number of cases of violence; furthermore, we commit violence and insult an infinite number of times without noticing it.

105. Notice that Stalin's famous 1913 statement on how to conquer the national question refers exclusively to the nationalism of minorities. See chapter 8.

106. For example, in his preoccupation with minority nationalism, Lenin failed to consider the pressures that Communist parties would feel to offer sops to the nationalism of the "most loyal" and powerful nation in the

state, and the nationalist reaction these sops would in turn exert upon minority nationalisms. Similarly, his preoccupation caused him to ignore the impact that the state's traditional culture (essentially the culture of the dominant group) would exert upon the postrevolutionary society and his plans for ameliorating minority nationalisms.

107. See, for example, the case of the Slovenes discussed in chapter 10. Basques, Croats, and the Chinese of Malaysia are all minorities whose nationalism remains fervid despite the fact that their respective nation is better off economically than the state's dominant group.

108. Lenin's confusing of catalyst and essence brings to mind an insightful passage by Regis Debray ("Marxism and the National Question," 30):

> Marxists always complain of their inadequte theoretical understanding of the nation. But this "inadequate theory" is not accidental: the nation resists conceptualization because Marxism has no concept of nature. It has only concepts of what we produce. How could it have a concept of what we do not determine—that is, not of what we produce, but of that which produces us?

THE UNANTICIPATED SYNTHESIS

CHAPTER 12

Nationalism within the Vanguard

"KEEP the party centralized and free of all national proclivities."
This third and final prescription of Lenin for solving the national
question represented his ultimate trump card for ensuring that
nationalism would be kept in check. No matter how often Communists appeared to side with nationalism and self-determination
in a prerevolutionary situation (prescription number one) or ca-
tered to national flourishing in a postrevolutionary situation (prescription number two), there would be no likelihood that the Marxist movement would fall prey to national deviations if the party
were organized according to the principle of strict centralization
("democratic centralism"), and if party membership remained con-
ditional upon unswerving commitment to proletarian internationalism rather than to nationalism.

It would be difficult to exaggerate the significance that Lenin
attached to this prescription. Leonid Brezhnev was quite correct
when he noted in his address commemorating the fiftieth anniversary of the formation of the Soviet Union:

> As is known, Lenin repeatedly emphasized the complexity of
> the approach to nationalities problems and spoke of the need to
> show tolerance and tact toward national feelings, especially those
> of the smaller peoples, and the need gradually to foster a spirit
> of internationalism in these peoples. But Lenin always demanded
> from *Communists* of all nationalities a clear and principled position
> on the nationalities question; he allowed no backsliding or in-
> dulgences on this point. Lenin always waged a relentless struggle
> against all manifestations of nationalism and great-power chau-
> vinism in the Communists' ranks.[1]

Some of Lenin's most faithful heirs (including Brezhnev) would
come to sense that his national policy was potentially very dangerous and required a series of precautionary devices.[2] But to Lenin,
a highly centralized, monolithic party composed of people who
could be trusted to place the cause of proletarian internationalism
ahead of national considerations was the sole precaution necessary.

Even his deathbed contemplation of a Soviet Union so decentralized as to leave Moscow responsible only for military and diplomatic matters (a scenario at total odds with Lenin's often-expressed bias in favor of thoroughly integrated societies) was made palatable by his faith that a centralized, country-wide party, untainted by nationalism, would be more than equal to the task of combatting fissiparous nationalisms.[3]

Although comprising a single precautionary measure, Lenin's all-important third prescription actually contained two readily distinguishable types of command. One ("keep the Party centralized") was organizational in character and should prove easy to implement. The other ("keep the Party's membership free of the taint of nationalism"), being ideological in nature, could be more difficult to honor. And indeed, although Lenin perceived the two commands as comprising a single strategic whole,[4] there has been great variation in the degree to which the two have been observed in practice. They therefore merit separate comment.

Keeping the Party Centralized

Lenin's command to keep the party centralized was totally in accord with his earliest writings on party organization. Years before developing a profound interest in the national question, and in a tract having nothing to do with that question, Lenin had insisted that the organizational principle for the party must be iron discipline organized in the most centralized manner.[5] All that was subsequently added to this principle, with specific regard to combatting nationalism within the ranks of the vanguard, was the prohibition that the party not be organized along national lines. The catalyst for this stand was the Jewish Bund, which, prior to the revolution, was pushing for cultural autonomy outside the party (along the lines recommended by the Austrian socialists, Bauer and Renner) and for a federation along national lines within the party. With Lenin's approval, Stalin in his 1913 tract unequivocally expressed their firm opposition to both proposals. With specific regard to the organization of the party, Stalin observed:

> The Bund demands that the Social-Democratic Party should "in its organizational structure introduce demarcation according to nationalities." . . . Organizational federalism harbours the elements of disintegration and separatism. The Bund is heading for separatism. . . . We know whither the division of workers

along national lines leads. The disintegration of a united workers' party, the division of trade unions along national lines, aggravation of national friction, national strike-breaking, complete demoralization within the ranks of Social Democracy—such are the fruits of organizational federalism. . . . When the workers are organized according to nationality they segregate themselves within their national shells, fenced off from each other by organizational partitions. The stress is laid not on what is *common* to the workers but on what distinguishes them from each other. In this type of organization the worker is *primarily* a member of his nation: Jew, Pole, and so on. It is not surprising that *national* federalism in organization inculcates in the workers a spirit of national aloofness.[6]

The subsequent division of the Communist party of the Soviet Union into republican wings (that is, a Ukrainian party, a Lithuanian party, etc.) might superficially appear to contradict this prerevolutionary stand of Lenin and Stalin. In fact, however, these branches are but another illustration of the Leninist dichotomy between form and content. The republican wings of the party were designed to function as purely subordinate sections of the parent party. An accurate description of their status was offered by the party leadership as early as 1918:

> The Ukraine, Lithuania and Byelorussia exist at the present time as separate Soviet republics. Thus is solved for now the question of state structure.
> But this does not in the least mean that the Russian Communist Party [R.K.P.] should, in turn, reorganize itself as a federation of independent Communist Parties.
> The Eighth Congress of the R.K.P. resolves: there must exist a *single* centralized Communist Party with a single Central Committee leading all the party work in all sections of the RSFSR. All decisions of the R.K.P. and its directing organs are unconditionally binding on all branches of the party, regardless of their national composition. The Central Committees of the Ukrainian, Latvian, Lithuanian Communists enjoy the rights of the regional committees of the party, and are entirely subordinated to the Central Committee of the R.K.P.[7]

While subsequently honoring each newly formed union republic with what appears to be its own party, the Soviet leadership has never deviated from this early dedication to "a *single* centralized

Communist Party," headquartered in Moscow. All decisions made at the center are binding upon all republican branches. Membership policy (including decisions on purges) and appointments and dismissals of key personnel are made at the center, and, as we have seen, both the general membership and the major bodies of the republican branch parties contain a disproportionate number of nonindigenes, particularly Russians.[8] Important officeholders have been regularly rotated between the center and the branch units.[9] In short, on the matter of party organization, the Soviet leadership has been faithful to Lenin's legacy as redefined recently by a Soviet author:

> As for the fears about a possible revival of nationalistic elements in the event of the republics being recognized as independent and sovereign, Lenin argued that any centrifugal tendencies could be checked by the activity of the Communist Party, which operated on the principle of democratic centralism.[10]

The Yugoslav CP followed the Soviet model in creating branch units along territorial-national lines. Croatian and Slovene units were created as early as 1937, and by 1949 a separate branch existed for each of the six republics that constituted the Yugoslav state. In 1952 a further suggestion of decentralization was offered when the name of the parent body was changed from the Yugoslav Communist Party to the League of Communists. But behind these changes of form, control remained firmly at the center. As described by a recognized authority on Yugoslavia:

> The republic parties did not of course exercise any real powers, although each had its own Politburo and Central Committee. . . . With Party controls almost 100 percent effective throughout the country, any tendency to adopt a nationalist position, in the government or elsewhere, could be quickly brought under control.[11]

Centralization of decision-making remained the rule throughout the 1950s. Even a purely nominal concession involving the vesting of some limited power of decision-making in the republics, which was endorsed by the Sixth Party Congress in 1952, was repealed by the very next congress, meeting in 1958.[12] However, matters took a turn during the 1960s when Tito and Kardelj came to the conclusion that centralization and conformity were not the proper way to combat nationalism. On the contrary, the *Jugoslovenstvo* campaign had sharpened ethnonational identity and the centralized systems of economic decision-making had triggered a sense of competition among the nations. The answer to nationalism was now to be sought in a thoroughgoing decentralization of the society and economy. But if this switch in policy was to be given a fair chance, some decentralization of the party would probably also be necessary. Serbian leaders could be expected to be most resistant to the changes, since both *Jugoslovenstvo* and the concentration of economic decision-making in the central state apparatus favored the Serbs. However, the central apparatus of the League of Communists (just as the central apparatus of the state) was a citadel of Serbian influence, and Rankovich et al. might well use this prime center of power to cripple the intended reforms. In an apparent effort to head off or to weaken any resistance from this quarter to the new policies, which they planned to inaugurate during 1965, Tito and Kardelj drafted a resolution that for the first time gave the republican branches a measure of real authority in the decision-making process.[13] It was dutifully endorsed by the Eighth Party Congress in 1964.

Despite these precautions, effective resistance to the 1965 reforms did develop within the party. Calls for the need to observe party discipline evidently went unheeded, and the purge of Rankovich and a number of his associates followed.[14] With the most determined centrists thus eliminated, the federative principle was injected into the party at the highest level of power. At the Ninth Congress, held in 1969, an Executive Bureau was created, consisting (in addition to Tito) of two representatives from each republic and one from each autonomous republic.[15] Moreover, the republican branches were given the right to appoint their representatives to both the Presidium (the former Central Committee) and the newly created Executive Bureau.

If the leadership had hoped that greater comity would result from the party's reorganization, they were to be disillusioned. When Tito announced in late 1970 his plan for a collective presidency of the state apparatus, the ensuing violent controversy, in which sides were chosen largely in accordance with national background, thoroughly pervaded the party's ranks. By early 1971 a split in the League of Communists had become a distinct possibility.[16] Acknowledging the danger, Tito declared in April that "we shall not allow the emergence of factions pursuing different lines" and that "the line of the League of Communists is one in all the Republics."[17] In early May he specifically rejected the theory allegedly held by some members that the League of Communists should become only an alliance of six independent republican parties, adding "there is only one Yugoslav League of Communists and only one Yugoslav working class."[18]

A statement made at about this same time by a member of the party's Executive Bureau demonstrated that indeed some of those in authority were convinced that the League of Communists had already become merely a loose alliance: "We have evolved to a stage at which it is no longer thinkable that a republican Party leadership could be removed by the federal Party centre."[19] The speaker was badly mistaken. Now aware of the gravity of the situation, Tito organized resistance to those favoring decentralization of the party, and, before the year was out, a purge of party leaders was underway in Croatia, Macedonia, Serbia, and Kosovo Province.[20] During 1972 the purge also spread to Bosnia-Hercegovina, Slovenia, and Vojvodina. People more amenable to centralized power replaced those who were dismissed.

The party now moved to reassert Leninist principles of party organization. In September 1972, in a letter to all party units and members, Tito outlined the vital tasks that the party must perform. In an allusion to the need for further purges, the letter noted the necessity for certain steps to "ensure a more resolute elimination from the ranks of the League of Communists of all those elements which are alien to the ideology and policy of the League of Communists, of all those who place their egotistic and group interests above the interests of the working class and self-managing socialist community. . . . "[21] Calling also for the "consistent, practical application [of] democratic centralism," the letter insisted that there must be "determined opposition to the ideological and political disintegration of the LCY, to its conversion into a loose coalition of republican and provincial organizations and to the division of the working class according to national and republican criteria."[22]

In an interview following shortly on the heels of this letter, Tito confirmed his position.

> I see in the Press that it still happens that the Republics try to insulate themselves from the others as though the League of Communists were also some kind of federation, so that in each Republic the party can operate quite independently, without consultation, without directives which are not to some people's liking. But things cannot go on this way.

He added that all decisions must be made "on the basis of a unitary ideological guidance" and that the party must be "a cohesive force within each Republic, and also the monolithic force of our socialist country."[23]

In subsequent years, the party organization underwent an almost bewildering series of changes. Alterations approved by the Tenth Congress in 1974 for representation in the party's highest reaches underwent substantial changes at the Eleventh Congress in 1978, and Tito's death in 1980 occasioned still other adjustments.[24] The constant factors throughout all this flux were the maintenance of a system of representation according to republic and autonomous province, and the concentration of real (in contradistinction to nominal) power to select the individual members of the highest organs at the top of the hierarchy.[25] While the former aimed at assuring all of the non-Serbs that the party would not again become Serb-dominated (as it had under Rankovich), the latter was a protection against the infiltration of nationalists into inner sanctums of party power. But in any event, as Tito had demonstrated in his victorious struggle with the nationalist federalists, more important than the façade of structure is the *effective* principle of organization. At the party's Tenth Congress in 1974, Tito again took the opportunity to emphasize that it had been the principle of democratic centralism that had defeated the evil of "factionalism," and he pledged that "for our party this will in the future, too, remain the basic principle."[26] Given the faith that Tito placed in democratic centralism within the party as the ultimate instrument for preserving the Yugoslav state against the forces of nationalism, it is perhaps not surprising that four years later, in what would be his last address to a party congress, Tito should conclude his last testament by yet again stressing the need of the party to uphold "democratic centralism," which must continue to be "the basic principle of the internal relations, organizational standards and entire activity of the LCY."[27]

CZECHOSLOVAKIA offers the final case of a party with a history of branch units. A separate Slovak CP emerged from World War II but was made part of the state-wide Czechoslovak CP after the Communists came into power in 1948. While the Slovak party retained its pre-1948 name, it became in fact a subordinate branch of the state-wide party, being officially described as the "territorial organization of the KSC [Communist Party of Czechoslovakia] in Slovakia."[28] Czechs had tended to dominate the parent party.[29] Indeed, the relative unimportance of the Slovak wing, as seen from the center, was demonstrated by the KSC's overall, asymmetrical organization; the dominant Czechs apparently felt no need to create a Czech branch to balance that of the Slovaks.

During the euphoric days of outspokenness that characterized the spring of 1968, Slovak party members campaigned for truly federalizing the party, and some of the Slovak leaders requested equality of representation between Czechs and Slovaks in the highest councils of the country-wide organization.[30] As we have seen, the Soviets subsequently approved the nominal federalization of the political structure.[31] But they vetoed the desired reforms within the party.[32] Federalization of the state structure was one matter; federalization of the party was quite another.

No other party has permitted national branches. The Chinese Communist Party, for example, at a time when it was still seeking the support of minorities in its struggle to assume power, unequivocally announced in its constitution that "[t]he CCP is a unified, combat organization, built on the principle of democratic centralism [and] cannot tolerate any demand for autonomy within the Party."[33] Nor did the party subsequently budge from this stance, even though it would later acknowledge that during both the Great Leap and the Cultural Revolution, minorities had tended to describe the CCP as a Han instrument and to demand their own separate national parties.[34]

The record of Communist parties is therefore quite good with regard to respecting Lenin's injunction to keep the party centralized. With the exception of the Yugoslav scene in the 1969–1971 period, violations of the injunction have tended to be at the level of form rather than of substance. From a structural perspective, the parties have been orthodox.

Keeping the Party's Membership Free of the Taint of Nationalism

But is it enough to keep the party centralized? While in Lenin's view democratic centralism was a necessary precondition for immunizing the party from the virus of nationalism, he realized that it alone was not sufficient to guarantee immunization. In order to have the desired effect, those at the nerve center of power within the party must themselves be impervious to the virus. Otherwise, democratic centralism could become an instrument for implementing programs of national coloration. And, as Lenin was well aware, Communists were capable of being seduced by nationalist sirens. Not only the ranks of the labor parties but a number of the

luminaries of the international movement had shocked and an-
gered Lenin by surrendering to just such a seduction on the eve
of World War I.[35] And years later, after the revolution, he had
found it necessary to warn a party congress: "Scratch some Communists and you will find Great Russian chauvinists."[36] Shortly
before his death, he wrote to the highest council of the party:

> I am declaring a war not for life, but to the death, against
> Great Russian chauvinism. As soon as I rid myself of my damned
> tooth, I shall eat it with all my strong teeth. One must *absolutely*
> insist that the united Central Executive Committee be presided
> over in turn by:
> A Russian
> A Ukrainian
> A Georgian, and so on.
> *Absolutely.*[37]

The implication was clear: even the Kremlin walls surrounding the
highest organs of the party could be breached by nationalism.

That Marxist elites should be vulnerable to national instincts
should not occasion great surprise. No less than others, Communists have been born into a national group, and it would be strange
indeed were they never to feel the slightest twinge of national pride
or resentment.[38] We have had occasion to comment on the traditional tendency of the Chinese and Vietnamese to consider themselves superior to all neighboring peoples. Similarly, the missionary
or civilizing role of the Great Russian people was woven into the
rationale of the Russian Empire. Was it therefore reasonable to
expect the new elite (overwhelmingly composed of Chinese, Vietnamese, or Russians) to be unattuned totally to the ethnic vibrations
with which their traditions and youthful environment were saturated? Solzhenitsyn hoped not, as witness his letter addressed to
the Soviet leadership in 1973:

> I am writing this letter on the *supposition* that you, too, are swayed
> by this primary concern, that you are not alien to your origins,
> to your fathers, grandfathers, and great-grandfathers, to the
> expanses of your homeland; that you have not lost all feeling of
> nationality. If I am mistaken, there is no point in your reading
> the rest of this letter.[39]

A review of the writings and speeches of leaders in the Marxist-
Leninist movement supports the thesis that the topmost leadership
has not been immune to nationalist tendencies. We have seen that

the writings of the founders of scientific socialism, Marx and Engels, were peppered with national stereotypes and a most unscientific gradation of peoples according to which they were fated for greatness or extinction. Some authorities have perceived strong German nationalism at work in the writings of both men.[40] Indeed, a respected Slovak Communist scholar has dared to write that the works of Marx and Engels "were not altogether free of German arrogance."[41]

As for Lenin, the account of his prerevolutionary exile written by his wife contains several references to his nationalism. They moved to Austrian Poland because it was closer to, and more like, Mother Russia. Even there, his prejudice for all things Russian prevailed. He "starved" for Russian literature and "greedily" perused Russian periodicals. The prejudice extended to art:

> Volodya is a terrible nationalist. He wouldn't go to see the works of Polish painters for anything, but one day he got hold of a catalogue of the Tretyakov Galleries . . . and he frequently becomes absorbed in it.[42]

Stalin offers something of a paradox: a Georgian who often sounded and acted as a Great Russian nationalist.[43] It was under Stalin that Russian national character and culture were extolled, and that the Russians became loudly touted as the foremost of peoples.[44] Moreover, at the other extreme, Stalin's overzealous maltreatment of his fellow Georgians (treatment which was sufficiently excessive to cause Lenin to expend his life's last efforts attacking it as wanton and ill-advised, and which, more than three decades after Lenin's criticism, was still viewed as sufficiently wanton to earn a prime place in Khrushchev's famous post-mortem inventory of Stalin's sins) also went well beyond what could be expected of a leader, who was also a member of a minority, to convince party colleagues and the mass of Great Russians that he was personally untainted by nationalism and above favoring the minority from which he had sprung.[45] Furthermore, there is evidence that this public behavior of Stalin did in fact reflect an inner preference for the Great Russians even over his own Georgians.[46] Stalin's unnecessarily excessive eagerness to elevate the Russians to an unmistakable level of *primus inter pares*, even relative to his own nation, is indeed something of a paradox. But it is a paradox often encountered in other societies. In a manner reminiscent of the particular zeal with which converts to a religion often embrace and practice their new faith, individuals who aspire to identification as a member of a nation into which they were not born often become fanatical defenders and promoters of that nation's interests.[47] Stalin's actions appear to offer a case history of this phenomenon of the convert nationalist.

Mao's works also contain several passages reflecting a great sense of pride in Han accomplishments and virtues.[48] So too do the works of Ho Chi Minh with regard to his Vietnamese nation.[49] Communist leaders seemingly as disparate as Korea's Kim Il Sung, Hungary's Imre Nagy, Rumania's Ceausescu, and Poland's Gomulka, Gierek, and Kania made numerous unmistakably nationalist speeches and pronouncements during their tenure of office.[50] Nor did Leonid Brezhnev blanch from aping Stalin in his exaggerated praise of the virtues of the Great Russian people who stand out "above all" because of their singular "revolutionary energy, selflessness, diligence and profound internationalism."[51]

Evidence that Marxist-Leninist leaders have not been totally immune to nationally inspired emotions is therefore not hard to find. But it is dangerous to jump from this general finding to the conclusion that these leaders have allowed their national inclinations to take precedence over the interests of the world movement. If, in making decisions, the leaders have been guided by proletarian internationalism rather than by concern for the fortunes of a particular national group, then their nationalism, while of passing interest, does not constitute a violation of the Communist creed. Marx and Engels did not ordain that Communists erase all memory of their personal national heritage but only that their sole yardstick in all endeavors be the welfare of the international movement. Recall that they stipulated in the Manifesto that "Communists are distinguished . . . by this only":

1. In the national struggles of the proletarians of the different countries, they point out and bring to the front the common interests of the entire proletariat, independently of all nationality.
2. In the various stages of development which the struggle of the working class against the bourgeoisie has to pass through, they always and everywhere represent the interests of the movement as a whole.

In short, it is by their actions ye shall know them.

This standard would certainly exonerate Lenin from any charge of nationalism. Commencing with his World War I exhortation to the proletariat of his own country to work for the defeat of their state, and continuing through to his late-life excoriation of his Great

Russian brethren for chauvinism, Lenin's actions undeviatingly reflected preoccupation with the international movement.[52] But the standard is of much less help in evaluating the degree to which a number of his successors have been influenced in their actions by national considerations. A number of factors have caused these leaders to be adjudged more nationalistic than is perhaps warranted.

One factor is the difficulty in distinguishing between a person who is aware of the power of nationalism and of the wisdom of adapting it to an immediate advantage, and a devotee of nationalism. Commencing with Marx, the most effective Communist leaders appreciated the advantages to be derived from manipulating national attitudes and have striven, when it suited their ends, to cloak themselves and their activities in national garb. Foreigners, as well as conationals, have therefore often jumped to the conclusion that the leadership's goals were basically of a national nature. Thus, during the period of American involvement in Vietnam, conventional wisdom on the part of many who were opposed to the involvement held that while Ho Chi Minh was obviously a Communist, he and his colleagues were Vietnamese nationalists first and Communists second.[53] But this presupposes a communion of form and content. Whereas Stalin spoke of national in form, socialist in content, this viewpoint would hold that recent Marxist movements are Communist in name but nationalist in content. Such an inverse ordering of things is indeed possible. With regard to the Rumanian Communist leadership, for example, one author has described how what began as national manipulation may have resulted in national conviction:

> The paradox is that the architects of the new course (many of them rather emotionless one-time Stalinist *apparatchiki*) may well have viewed the use of nationalist symbolism as a tactical expedient to drum up support for a politically isolated leadership. But in acting out the role of the defender of the cultural and historical heritage the Party became absorbed by it, providing an excellent example of how behavior may ultimately influence basic attitudes. This should be taken to imply not that the Rumanian party has abandoned Marxism-Leninism in favor of ethnic particularism, but rather that it has incorporated the latter into the former. The *telos*, the ultimate goal that provides a *raison d'être* for the Party, is still the building of socialism and a collective welfare society, but the idea of the constituency that the party is

prepared to serve, even in theory, has moved from the broader concept of the international proletariat to the narrower confines of the ethnic community.[54]

A program strictly limited to the particular ethnonational community would be nationalist, whether its other sources of inspiration were Marxist-Leninist, Adam Smith, or whatever. The important point, however, is that while Communist leaders may fall victim to the national virus, the fact that they have disguised themselves as nationalists in order to manipulate national aspirations is not in itself an adequate symptom that they themselves have succumbed to the disease.[55] Their appreciation for manipulating the land-hungriness of the peasants did not mean that Lenin, Stalin, Mao, and Ho had become believers in the wisdom of indefinitely perpetuating private property. It may be equally fallacious to fail to differentiate between manipulator and believer in the case of nationalism.[56]

A second complicating factor in measuring the degree to which nationalism has motivated Marxist leaders arises from the growing number and geographic diffusion of Communist movements. The principal crucible within which and through which the various movements have operated, both before and after taking power, has been the state. In 1936 Mao ably described the necessary linkage between the state and a Marxist-Leninist movement before victory:

> The victory of the Chinese national liberation movement will be part of the victory of world Socialism, because to defeat imperialism in China means the destruction of one of its most powerful bases. If China wins its independence, the world revolution will progress very rapidly. If our country is subjugated by the enemy, we shall lose everything. For a people being deprived of its national freedom, the revolutionary task is not immediate Socialism, but the struggle for independence. We cannot even discuss Communism if we are robbed of a country in which to practice it.[57]

With victory, the state apparatus falls to the party, making the distinction between party and state all the more blurred. It is in the name of the state that the party leaders issue edicts and conduct foreign policy. Traditional Leninist strategy further contributes to the blending of state and party: in a revolutionary situation the party acts under the umbrella of a national liberation front; after the revolution, appeals to all patriotic forces become commonplace at times of crisis. As a consequence of all of this, Marxist-Leninists have often been perceived by people living both within and without the state as promoters and protectors of the national interests of those who are dominant within the particular state. Hoxha as leader of the Albanians, Mao of the Han, Ceausescu of the Rumanians, and Ho of the Vietnamese are cases in point. But can we safely conclude from (1) the fortuitous coincidence of short-range Communist party goals and long-range national goals, (2) the periodic self-description of party leaders as national patriots, and (3) popular perceptions of the leadership as nationalists on the part of the masses of the same national group (even though the people who hold these perceptions may not be Communist and may not be currently under the jurisdiction of the party), that the leaders of the party are, in fact, essentially nationalists whose actions are determined by what they perceive to be best for the nation?

The compartmentalization of Communist movements into a number of states contributes in yet another way to a presumption that the leaders are more nationalist than internationalist in orientation. Differences among the movements from one state to another are obvious to the most casual observer. Though ostensibly all are Marxist-Leninist, Chinese society bears little resemblance to the Soviets', and both differ, in turn, from Hungary's.[58] Adoption of Marxism-Leninism as official ideology has not erased the impact of national cultures and traditions. At least in part, this lack of worldwide conformity among Marxist societies is the result of purposeful policies. This is how Mao put it in 1938:

Another of our tasks is to study our historical heritage and use the Marxist method to sum it up critically. Our national history goes back several thousand years and has its own characteristics and innumerable treasures. But in these matters we are mere schoolboys. Contemporary China has grown out of the China of the past; we are Marxist in our historical approach and must not lop off our history. We should sum up our history from Confucius to Sun Yat-sen and take over this valuable legacy. This is important for guiding the great movement of today. Being Marxists, Communists are internationalists, but we can put Marxism into practice only when it is integrated with the specific characteristics of our country and acquires a definite national form. The great strength of Marxism-Leninism lies precisely in its integration with the concrete revolutionary practice of all countries. For the Chinese Communist Party, it is a matter of learning to apply the theory of Marxism-Leninism to the specific circum-

stances of China. For the Chinese Communists who are part of
the great Chinese nation, flesh of its flesh and blood of its blood,
any talk about Marxism in isolation from China's characteristics
is merely Marxism in the abstract, Marxism in a vacuum. Hence
to apply Marxism concretely in China so that its every manifestation has an indubitably Chinese character, *i.e.*, to apply Marxism
in the light of China's specific characteristics, becomes a problem
which it is urgent for the whole Party to understand and solve.
Foreign stereotypes must be abolished, there must be less singing
of empty, abstract tunes, and dogmatism must be laid to rest;
they must be replaced by the fresh, lively Chinese style and spirit
which the common people of China love. To separate internationalist content from national form is the practice of those who
do not understand the first thing about internationalism. We, on
the contrary, must link the two closely.[59]

But a Soviet dissenter has maintained that national variations were
in any case inevitable, and that they operate within a multinational
state as well as across state borders:

Truth is concrete as are the concepts of good and beauty. Truth
is also national. It is the same for all, but it has a million facets.
The mission of each nation is to recognize its own facet, which
only it can discover, and thus enrich mankind. . . . It is not enough
to introduce Marx into Byelorussia. In order for him to become
meaningful for you, he must be perceived through Byelorussian
eyes. . . . It you think he can be simply borrowed from Moscow
you are greatly mistaken. . . . Marxism (and any ism for that
matter), brought into Byelorussia, is only the comb which must
be filled with Byelorussian honey.[60]

It is far easier, of course, to say that national culture mixes with
international Marxism than it is to evaluate the impact of the former
upon the latter. But preoccupation with the national varieties of
communism is conducive to perceiving each variety as nationalist
first, Communist second. The system of Chinese communes has
visibly little in common with the 80 percent privately owned, agricultural system of Poland. One suspects that the leaders of Czechoslovakia and Hungary were as bewildered as non-Marxists by the
Great Leap Forward, the Cultural Revolution, Vietnamese "re-ed-
ucation camps," and the enforced depopulation of Cambodian cities.

Also contributing to a view of Marxist-Leninist leaders as primarily motivated by nationalist considerations are the splits and intense rivalries that have developed. Relations between People's China and the Soviet Union, and between the former and Vietnam, deteriorated to a point at which major border clashes were possible. Vietnamese forces invaded and occupied ostensibly Marxist-Leninist Cambodia. Soviet forces did likewise with regard to Hungary, Czechoslovakia, and Afghanistan. Since Tito's ouster from the Cominform in 1948, descriptions of the Second World that suggested a monolithic structure were self-evidently anachronistic. But it is a leap of impressive dimension from this truism to the conclusion that the leaders of Marxist-Leninist movements are necessarily nationalists whose thoughts and plans start and end with their nation. Surely Trotsky and the Trotskyites were no less internationalist in their objectives because of their objection to Stalin's (and therefore Moscow's) direction of the movement. Can Mao and his successors be charged with nationalism simply because they insist that the leadership of the Soviet Union has betrayed the world revolution through their "revisionism" of Marxism-Leninism? If people who disagree over the content of the national interest can nonetheless be nationalists, then certainly Marxist-Leninists can disagree over the international interest and remain internationalists.

The problem of certitude that one is in fact confronting a Communist leader who is guilty of nationalist proclivities extends even to the many individuals who have been purged over the years on the charge of nationalism, separatism, splittism, and the like. Are such charges to be taken at face value? Or are they a convenient and therefore often-resorted-to surrogate for justifying the elimination of an undesirable individual or group, although the accused are in fact innocent of national behavior? Or are the periodic purges of eminent figures a device for warning the general populace against any activities that could be perceived by the authorities as nationalist-inspired? Or some medley of the foregoing?

It is certain that the sweeping antinationalist purges carried out under Stalin (both within and without the Soviet Union) were often knowingly aimed at innocents. Beginning with Khrushchev's denunciation of Stalin at the party's Twentieth Congress, it has been acknowledged in several instances that charges had often been fabricated even to the point of falsifying documents.[61] Perhaps the best evidence we have that party officials (that is, those with the greatest access to the facts) were convinced that the charges had often been baseless was their subsequent willingness to entrust a few of those who had been purged with the most powerful positions in their respective parties.[62] A classic example occurred in China, where leaders such as Ulanfu, who were purged on charges of nationalism and separatism during the Cultural Revolution, were reelevated to their former eminence following Mao's demise.

Even less satisfactory than purges as evidence of nationalist leanings on the part of party leaders are the charges of nationalism and chauvinism hurled back and forth across state borders in the polemical disputes that have marred relations among a surprisingly large number of Marxist-Leninist states. Such accusations have been most consistently aired in the rivalry between China and the Soviet Union.[63] But they have also been prominent in the disputes between China and Vietnam, Rumania and Hungary, Hungary and Czechoslovakia, Bulgaria and Yugoslavia, and Yugoslavia and Albania.

It would, of course, be safer to impute sincerity to such allegations if they were not meant for public dissemination. As publicly aired, they sound like little more than name calling. However, it would also be dangerous to presume that the accusers believe the charges to be groundless, albeit useful, propaganda. Thus, the fact that Tito did perceive nationalism to be at work behind the actions of the Soviet leadership that led to the rupture of relations in 1948 is strongly suggested by his semiprivate comments made in 1949:

> What happened? For one thing, the Bolshevik revolutionary mind, which Lenin exemplified, was supplanted by the bureaucratic and police mind, if it can be called a mind. . . . I suppose her leaders' primacy in the International Communist Movement, their being rulers of a vast land and a great power, and winning a tremendous military victory, all this has blinded them, and they've blundered into the rankest type of nationalism: into Great Russianism, which always had imperialistic over-tones.[64]

Evaluating the degree to which the leaders of Marxist-Leninist movements have been influenced by nationalism is, therefore, a most illusive goal. At bottom, our problem is the inherent difficulty of imputing motivation. Egocentricism, ethnocentrism, conditioning in the tenets of Marxism-Leninism, and unquestionably still other forces vie for primacy in an intricate and shifting manner that probably make it impossible even for the individual leader to sort out his drives according to their influence. Sometimes these drives will be reinforcing, at other times competitive. Rationalization and self-delusion will play their roles (for example, in a Russian who comes to believe that what is good for the Soviet Union is necessarily good for the world movement). As a mass phenomenon, nationalism is normally identified through the responses of large numbers of people to national symbols and evocations. It is vastly more difficult to isolate and identify it in the case of an individual. Unquestionably, certain Marxist-Leninist leaders have been more influenced by nationalism than have others, and the same leader more influenced during one period than during another.

While the foregoing may appear somewhat pedestrian, failure to take such considerations into account has led to a number of over- and under-simplifications concerning the influence of nationalism upon Marxist leaders. Thus "Titoism" and "national communism" became almost interchangeable terms after 1948. But it is evident that "state-communism" would be a far more accurate description of what Tito strove to preserve. During his lifetime, national communism, in the form of Croatian, Slovene, and Serbian varieties, was the principal threat to Titoism, outdistancing in this regard even Moscow's version of proletarian internationalism. In his unrelenting struggle to preserve his state communism against these internal forces, Tito was unquestionably acting as an internationalist rather than a nationalist, and in his struggle against Moscow to preserve state communism, it is far easier to see the forces of egocentrism at work than those of ethnocentrism. Far from being a nationalist, Tito, throughout much of his career, did not even restrict his loyalty to Yugoslav state communism. As we have seen, the Yugoslav CP, under his direction, did not deign to resist the Axis invaders until the latter had subsequently invaded the Soviet Union, and the belated declaration of resistance to the invaders was pitched largely in terms of defense of the Soviet Union.[65] These credentials establish Tito as one of the most internationalist figures of the period.

Those who cavalierly describe Ho Chi Minh as a nationalist also ignore contrary data. We have reviewed how he voluntarily collaborated with the French colonial administration during 1937 and 1938.[66] He did so under the direction of the French CP, which in turn was following a course of action dictated by the Soviet Union. For an ostensible national liberation movement to shelve its raison d'être of political emancipation is anomalous in the extreme, and the Vietnamese Trotskyites, who scorned Ho's latest alliance as "the United Front of Treason," had a better claim to be performing as "nationalists." Moreover, Ho's image as a Vietnamese nationalist is challenged by his fluctuating position on the peoples under the aegis of his party, from the purely Vietnamese (prior to 1930), to all of the peoples of French Indochina (1930–1945), to the peoples of the state of Vietnam (1945 until his death). Quite aside from these fluctuations, documents of his lifetime substantiate that since at least 1930, Ho's plans envisaged a single Marxist-Leninist state for all of Indochina.[67] His successors' involvement in Cambodia and Laos—though hardly explicable in terms of Vietnamese nationalism—has been in thorough conformity with Ho's plans for the area.[68]

Assessing the influence of nationalism upon Marxist leaders is therefore fraught with difficulties and uncertainties. The relationship of nationalism to communism has been more subtle and complex than most of the literature indicates. Generalities to the effect that all Marxist-Leninists are primarily nationalists should be avoided. Assuming a Lenin or Tito to be motivated principally by national concerns could only produce misconceptions concerning the goals to which they were committed. Caution against too facile attributions of nationalism is therefore in order. There is good reason to conclude that nationalism has indeed permeated both the leadership and the ranks of Communist parties. But since it is prescribed strategy for Marxist-Leninists seemingly to embrace nationalism when it is useful to the movement to do so, the test of the Communist Manifesto ("By their actions ye shall know them") is not sufficient. The test must be whether their action, regardless of its national form, is evidently at odds with the ultimate goals of scientific socialism, or goes well beyond what could be justified in terms of promoting those goals. Only if one of these two conditions prevails can we speak with some certainty of nationalist motivation. Thus, we have suggested that Stalin's ardor for elevating the Great Russians to a level of eminence went well beyond what was necessary to insure the loyalty of "the most loyal nation," while unnecessarily irritating the national sensibilities of the non-Russian peoples.

Subjecting to the same test the actions of some of the individuals who have been purged for nationalism within the Soviet Union in recent decades suggests that the charges are much more apt to have substance than they did during the Stalin era. Indeed, while we have pointed out that such purges may well be a device for warning the public against the evils of nationalism, it is a risk-laden device in that it may nurture the very weed it is intended to root out. Referring to the many purges and incarcerations of Ukrainians for nationalism, one dissenter has written:

It has become evident that instead of intimidating people, you have aroused their interest. You wanted to extinguish the fire, but instead you added fuel to the flames. Nothing has contributed so much to stimulating political life in the Ukraine as your repressions. Nothing has drawn so much attention to the processes of the Ukrainian renaissance so much as your trials. To tell the truth, it was these trials that demonstrated to the public at large that political life has been revived in the Ukraine. You wanted to hide people in the Mordovian forests; instead, you placed them in a large arena for the whole world to see. It was this atmosphere of awakening produced by your repressions that created the majority of the activists in the Ukrainian renaissance. In a word, enough time has passed for you to have finally understood that you are the ones who are most hurt by the repressions. Still, you continue to hold trials. . . . What for? In order to fulfill your plan? To appease the official conscience? To find an outlet for your anger? More than likely, you do this from inertia.[69]

There is, in any case, evidence that the growing nationalism within the Soviet Union has permeated the higher echelons of the republican wings of the party. Nationalism at the top became very apparent in the Ukraine in the mid-1960s. During the first five years of the first secretaryship of Pyotr Shelest (1963–1968), the fortunes of the Ukrainians underwent a significant uplift.[70] Representation in the party and state structure increased. Contrary to official policy at the time, Shelest also strongly promoted the use of the Ukrainian language, calling for more textbooks to be published in it, and telling the Ukrainian Writers Congress that "it is necessary that we cherish and respect our beautiful Ukrainian language."[71] Before a visiting Canadian Communist delegation, he disagreed with remarks of other Soviet spokesmen to the effect that the fate of the nation does not depend upon the health of the language, insisting (in the words of the report) "that the development of Communist society must permit the fullest and freest economic and cultural development of every nation."[72] He shielded authors and others from purges for nationalist tendencies, and evidence exists that he was instrumental in the publication of the most devastatingly critical attack on Soviet national policy in the Ukraine, Ivan Dzyuba's *Internationalism or Russification?*, which he distributed among some of the party's elite. Shelest was himself purged for nationalism in 1972, but what makes his case particularly noteworthy for our purposes is that he had been a member of that most inner circle of Soviet power, the Politburo of the state-wide party, while concurrently pursuing his pro-Ukrainian activities. The same held true for Politburo member and First Secretary of the Georgian Communist Party, Vasily Mzhavanadze, who was also purged about this same time. Among the charges with evidence of validity were that the party, under Mzhavanadze, had been lenient in prosecuting nationalist behavior and in permitting the publication of nationalist tracts.[73]

Quite expectedly, symptoms of nationalism within the republican wings of the party have been most apparent in the case of those Baltic, Caucasian, and Slavic peoples who combine a highly developed sense of a national tradition with relatively good representation in the higher councils of the republican wing of the party, namely, the Armenians, Estonians, Georgians, Lithuanians, and Ukrainians.[74] Despite the pyramidal, country-wide party structure, democratic centralism, and the rotation of key personnel from outside the republics, there has been a visible tendency for these republican parties to serve as advocates of the interests of their people and to serve as a buffer between the center and their people in the case of policies viewed as detrimental to local national interests. Practicing leniency in searching out and prosecuting nationalist behavior is one facet. Earlier we reviewed how leaders of party wings have been known to resist increased investments because they feared such increases would further dilute the ethnic homogeneity of the homeland.[75] An analysis of speeches delivered at the important fiftieth celebration of the founding of the Soviet Union further attests to the breadth of the tendency for party leaders to harbor national proclivities: speeches of the First Secretaries of seven of the republican wings set forth positions that were in conflict with those enunciated by the First Secretary of the parent body, Leonid Brezhnev.[76]

Another usually overlooked indication of the influence of nationalism within the party is the impact exerted by the national question upon the careers of its top leaders. Stalin was essentially unknown prior to publication of his article on the national question in 1913. Although his rise to power within the apparatus is generally and appropriately ascribed to his becoming Secretary of the party while Lenin was still alive, his position as Commissar of Nationality Affairs in the early years of the Soviet state was also extremely important to his succession. In addition to furnishing the opportunity to increase his contacts and support among the non-Russian membership, it was to aid him more directly in the crucial period of Lenin's infirmity and death. Here is Richard Pipes's account:

In February 1923 the Plenum of the Central Committee (from which Lenin was also absent) decided to add a second chamber to the Union legislature to represent the national groups. Originally, the Communists had been hostile to the idea of a bicameral legislature, considering it a feature of a "class society" and unnecessary in the "proletarian" state. In November 1922 Stalin had stated that, although some Communists were advocating the creation of a second, upper chamber to provide representation for the nationalities as such, he felt that this view "will undoubtedly find no sympathy in the national republics, if only because the two-chamber system, with the existence of an upper chamber, is not compatible with the Soviet government, at any rate at the present stage of its development." By February, however, Stalin changed his mind in favor of a bicameral legislature, largely, in all likelihood, because it enabled him to increase his personal control over the Soviet legislature. The Council of Nationalities (*Sovet natsional'nostei*), which was approved by the party and incorporated into the Constitution, was the same Council of Nationalities that Stalin had formed as part of the Commissariat of Nationality Affairs in April 1921, with the addition of deputies from the three Union republics. The second chamber was, therefore, staffed with people who had Stalin's personal approval.[77]

The willingness to reverse position that Stalin demonstrated with regard to the Council of Nationalities was to characterize his subsequent policies on the national question. Moving from his early condonation of harsh treatment of non-Russians for which Lenin had castigated him, Stalin approved the period of "indigenization," only to revert again in the 1930s to a policy of repression. One of Stalin's most commonly self-asserted claims to greatness was that the national question had been solved during his stewardship, and two of the three principal eulogies at his funeral (those by Malenkov and Molotov) emphasized his contribution in this area. The omission from the third tribute was purposeful, for Beria, we know, had decided that a major element in his campaign to succeed Stalin would be the promise to reverse Stalin's national policy in favor of a return to "indigenization." While this policy was to prove Beria's undoing within the privacy of the Politburo, the victor in the power struggle, Khrushchev, upon coming to power also publicly embraced a more favorable stance toward national flourishing. As in the case of Stalin, this embrace was of short duration, and policy was soon deflected away from flourishing toward merging. The incumbency of his successor, Brezhnev, was also marked by an early period of sympathy toward national peculiarities, followed by a sharp retreat.

A pattern of behavior is therefore visible. Each changing of the guard (Stalin, Khrushchev, and Brezhnev) brought an abbreviated period of national flourishing followed by a swing in favor of integration. The fact that each felt compelled, prior to consolidation of his power, to express support for the national aspirations of the minorities strongly suggests the existence of constituencies of real strength within the party apparatus, wherein the constituents were motivated principally by national considerations (or who, in American political parlance, would be termed "one-issue voters").[78] This conclusion is lent great credence by Beria's flagrant appeal to non-Russians within the apparatus as a means of besting his competitors, as well as by Khrushchev's reaction to this ploy, a reaction expressing fear that the ploy might indeed work.[79] There is, to be sure, real danger in drawing analogies from democratic electoral systems by referring to the ethnic vote, etc.[80] We cannot be certain how various elements within the party make their weight felt at time of change in leadership. But the evidence seems to suggest that national orientation on the part of powerful segments of the party is recognized by the top leadership as a sufficiently influential force as to make its courting a wise maneuver during the period when the crown still rests shakily.[81]

THE most thorough case of permeation of a party apparatus by nationalism is that of Yugoslavia. Abetted, as in the case of the Soviet Union, by the organization of the party into republican wings, nationalism not only pervaded that apparatus but, on many occasions, turned the party into the principal battlefield of ethnonational struggle. Given the breadth and depth of the ethnic animosities that had surfaced during World War II and the predominant position of Serbs (particularly Serbs from Croatia) within the partisan movement and consequently within the postwar party, it is not surprising that the party, as the citadel of ultimate power, should become enmeshed in the continuing national competition. Serbs, who dominated the central party structure, would see in the party the means for insuring that Croat nationalism would not again become a menace.[82] The Croats would perceive their branch unit as a fortress for fending off Serbian domination.

Considering the country's recent agony due to extremist nationalism, it took amazingly little time for nationalism to become again a factor in the Yugoslav power struggle.[83] Although, in this new environment, the leadership must have been reluctant to draw attention to a revival of nationalism, particularly within the ostensible bastion of internationalism represented by the party, they felt compelled to do so in a warning to members as early as 1953.[84] The warning failed in its purpose, and in 1958 a letter to all party units from the Executive Committee complained that "very often, members of the leading bodies of the League of Communists fall under the influence of the petty-bourgeois intelligentsia and . . . are guilty of nationalist and chauvinist influences."[85] Additional warnings of this sort had little perceptible impact, and the republican parties increasingly demonstrated independence with regard to carrying out central directives.[86] Tito was finally forced to take action when it became manifest that the economic decentralization and other reforms that had been approved in 1965 were being frustrated by entrenched Serbian interests at the top of the central apparatus. The public became aware of the remarkable extent to which Serbian nationalism had affected policy, when Rankovich, Tito's ostensible successor, along with numerous highly placed Serbian associates, was purged for national chauvinism. With the party's scandal in the open, Tito became less reluctant to focus attention on the danger. In the summer of 1966 he criticized the growth of nationalism within the party apparatus, noting that Chetnik, Ustasha, and White Guard ideas "still smolder and, when they get the chance, flare up."[87] While such a perception would seemingly recommend a return to a recentralized structure of power, Tito and Kardelj pushed ahead with their plans for decentralization. With the central apparatus suffering from a decline in prestige because of the Rankovich scandal, the republican wings pressed their advantage.

The extent to which the wings became nationalist parties over the next few years is illustrated by the so-called "Zanko Affair." Zanko, the permanent Croatian delegate to the party conference of the state-wide party and also the vice president of the Federal Parliament, was purged of all offices and expelled from the ranks of the Croatian Communist Party in early 1970 for writing articles criticizing the reappearance of nationalism within Croatia.[88] Thus was created the rather anomalous situation of a person being purged by a Marxist-Leninist party specifically for defending internationalism against nationalism.

With the Zanko Affair, the issue of nationalism within the party focused principally upon the Croatian wing. Captured by the "national euphoria" sweeping that republic, the leadership acted increasingly as leaders of a purely nationalist movement. One nationalistic speech made by the party's chairman was punctuated with shouts from the crowd of "Long live free Croatia."[89] The First Secretary complained publicly of the disproportionately few Croats in the Yugoslav armed forces.[90] The adoption of nationalism as the guiding principle of the party appeared complete when the Croatian Central Committee in November 1971 approved a report in which it was noted that during the recent past, "a unity of nation and Party was forged and sturdily grew into a mass political movement," elsewhere called the "mass national movement."[91]

Tito had by this time become cognizant of the rapid deterioration of the party, and had, to no avail, privately warned the Croatian leadership that its house must be put in order.[92] According to his own account, however, he feared to take more positive action because of his belief that the League of Communists was not sufficiently united to take a common stand against the nationalists within the party.[93] Tito's reluctance is quite understandable, for the Croatian wing of the party was hardly the only section currently under the sway of national emotions. When Tito, with the essential backing of the military high command, finally did mount his successful campaign against entrenched nationalists, the purges that followed affected all branches of the party. The numbers associated with the purge, although not all attributable to national deviations, are impressive rough indicators of the degree to which nationalism had permeated the entire structure. In 1969 the party had 1,146,000 members. During the first stages of the nationalist purge in late 1971 and early 1972, membership dropped by 40,000. Subsequent purges were offset by new members, but in the period 1969–1974, 51,370 members were expelled for deviations from the party line, and an additional 92,400 were expelled for inactivity.[94] Included in this group were some of the most prominent Communists from all sectors of the country. Now fully aware that party membership could not be presumed to guarantee an internationalist outlook, the League of Communists went on record as demanding that "the struggle against nationalism must be unrelenting in all milieux and within every national group, and nationalism must not be underestimated for one moment, no matter what form it might take."[95] Interparty bickering along national lines continued, however, and a decade later a major purge for failing to combat nationalist forces removed the top leadership and hundreds of members of the Kosovo party apparatus.[96]

CZECHOSLOVAKIA's experience followed a similar pattern. There too, an ethnonational wing of the party became the principal agency for expressing national aspirations. In the early 1950s, the Slovak wing of the party underwent a severe purge of members charged with nationalism. Quite aside from the merits of the accusations, if their purpose was to warn Slovak Communist leaders not to serve as advocates of Slovak interests, they did not succeed for long. As First Secretary Novotny, the Czech leader of the state-wide party, remained seemingly deaf to even minor Slovak requests for a more balanced order (a deafness in itself suggestive of ethnocentrism or "great nation chauvinism"), leaders of the Slovak party became increasingly militant.[97] The dispute became public knowledge in September 1967, when the First Secretary of the Slovak party, Alexander Dubcek, attacked the policies of the Novotny regime before the Central Committee of the parent, Czechoslovak Communist Party. Among the specific charges was that investment funds that had been earmarked for Slovakia had in fact been deflected by the Czech-dominated central bureaucracy.[98] The following month, in another session of the Central Committee, Dubcek was prepared to go further. During a discussion of increased economic autonomy for Slovakia, the Slovak First Secretary asserted: "Before we can talk of economic division, we must discuss political division, starting at the top with the party leadership."[99]

The degree to which nationalism had permeated the ranks of the Slovak party is indicated by a poll of party functionaries conducted in June 1968.[100] Only 11 percent of the Slovak party members were willing to accept improvements within the basic present system. Eighty-five percent wished to go beyond anything ever permitted by a Marxist-Leninist party by introducing a truly federal system within the state-wide party. But given the jaundiced Communist view of separatist tendencies as the most insidious and extreme manifestation of nationalism, perhaps the most amazing statistic was that more than 4 percent of the party membership went on record as favoring a totally independent state for the Slovaks.

As in the cases of the Soviet Union and Yugoslavia, the national question within Czechoslovakia has also exerted a great impact upon the careers of the top leadership. Novotny's removal as First Secretary of the state-wide party was made possible only by an alliance of those Czech members of the Politburo who advocated a liberalizing of the regime (and who were in a minority among the total Czech membership) with the Slovak members, all of whom were committed to Slovak interests. This balance of forces, in turn, made it possible for Dubcek to become the first First Secretary of the Czechoslovak Communist Party to be drawn from the Slovak minority. Moscow's subsequent decision to jettison Dubcek was therefore a particularly sensitive one in Slovakia.[101] Unquestionably, this was a major consideration in the Soviet selection of Gustav Husak to succeed Dubcek. As a person who had been purged from the party in the early 1950s on charges of "Slovak nationalism" and "Titoism," Husak's appointment would neutralize any imputation of anti-Slovak motivation behind Moscow's ouster of Dubcek.

THE growth of nationalism within Communist parties has therefore been abetted by the presence of supposedly subordinate wings. But nationalism has not been confined to such parties. Indeed, the central organs of the parties with unitary structures have, on balance, been more nationalistic. As we have seen, the winged structure of the Soviet, Yugoslav, and Czechoslovak parties arose from the fact that each of the states contained at least two national groups sufficiently numerous and nationalistically motivated to make a unitary system dominated by a single group a risky approach. Since nationalism in these states constitutes a pronounced threat to the cohesion of the state, antinationalism has been a key theme in the party line. By contrast, parties in command of a state within which the dominant group's preeminence is beyond serious challenge have not perceived nationalism as a threat that must be constantly castigated. Thus, in a 1971 content analysis of the party newspaper in each of the eight Marxist-Leninist states of Eastern Europe, antinationalism was found to be the most frequent theme of articles only in Czechoslovakia and Yugoslavia. By contrast, of the eight themes used in the content survey, antinationalism placed sixth in Albania and Hungary, seventh in Bulgaria, and last (eighth) in Poland and Rumania.[102] In these more homogeneous states, any loss of influence among minorities can be more than offset by the overall gain in legitimacy that would accrue if the party could convince the masses that it was the legitimate spokesman for the dominant nation. Party leaders have therefore felt a freer rein to express their nationalism.[103] Contrast, for example, Polish First Secretary Kania's 1981 statement that "Every measure we are taking stems from the need to serve the nation, from the concern about matters of our community,"[104] with Napoleon's nationalistic justification for his highly autocratic tenure of office "We have at all times been guided by this great truth: that the sovereignty resides in the French people in the sense that everything, everything without exception, must be done for its best interests, for its well being, and for its glory."[105]

Such statements, whether made by Marxists or non-Marxists, may be a tactical maneuver rather than evidence of nationalism.[106] But they cannot be described as Leninist tactics, since Lenin had not condoned wrapping the party in national costume *after* the consolidation of power. Moreover, assertions that the party is motivated by what is best for a particular nation are self-evidently incompatible with proletarian internationalism and with the Communist Manifesto's definition of a Communist. Furthermore, the desire to have legitimacy in the eyes of the masses is a two-edged sword. If a nationalist upsurge occurs among the people, there is a strong possibility that the party leadership, responding to a mélange of motivations including the survival urge, a desire to retain power, a desire to be popular with the masses, and true national inclinations, will be swept along in the national current.

Events in Hungary during 1956 (as well as in Czechoslovakia in 1968 and Yugoslavia—particularly Croatia—in 1969-1971) illustrate this phenomenon. On October 23, a massive impromptu nationally inspired student demonstration took place in Hungary. The first reaction of the authorities was negative. The demonstrators were denounced as "fascist reactionary elements" and "counterrevolutionary gangs," and Soviet forces within Hungary were officially called upon for assistance in quelling them.[107] The First Secretary ordered the party to "oppose any attempt at creating disorder, nationalist well-poisoning, and provocation," and he reminded all members that Communists were not nationalists:

> We Communists are Hungarian patriots. . . . While we loftily proclaim that we are patriots, we also make it plain that we are not nationalists. . . . We are patriots but at the same time we are also proletarian internationalists.[108]

Despite such incantations, when threats and the usual importunities to desist in the name of the nation's best interests failed to impede the spreading national demonstrations, the leadership quickly shifted to a national stance. Within a week, the salutations customary in declarations and public addresses ("Workers, Comrades!" and "Working People of Hungary!") were replaced by "Hungarians, Friends, Comrades!", "Friends, young Hungarian Men and Girls!", "People of Hungary!", "Hungarian Brethren, Patriots! Loyal Citizens of the Fatherland!", and "Hungarian Brethren!"[109] Adopting an entirely national program, the leadership now called for the restoration of ancient national symbols and presocialist, national holidays, as well as for a revision of Soviet-Hungarian relations culminating in a declaration of neutrality and withdrawal from the Warsaw Pact. The leading party newspaper carried blatantly nationalist articles.[110] Leninist orthodoxy had been vanquished by nationalism, and Soviet troops were necessary for its reinstitution.[111]

IN contrast to the Hungarian party, in which nationalism surfaced in response to a popular nationalist movement outside the party, the Rumanian party appears to have taken the initiative in assuming the role of chief defender and advocate of the interests and aspirations of the nation. And, in doing so, the party deviated so far from Leninist internationalism as to leave little question of the authenticity of the leadership's nationalism. As noted in the previous chapter, during the 1960s and 1970s Rumania began to stress its sovereignty and independence of action in the area of foreign policy.[112] But the extent of its national deviation is best seen in its Party Program of 1974, which decidedly had more of a national than a Marxist-Leninist ring. It began with a twenty-five page account of what the General Secretary described in a preface as "the two thousand year old history of our people" prior to the party's assumption of power.[113] The fact that the beginning date of this history antecedes the creation of the party (1921) by some two millennia is significant, for the party's raison d'être was expressed in the program solely in relation to Rumanian national history. By its actions during World War II, the party was said to have established its right to take over the leadership of the Rumanian people, thus fulfilling "its historic mission of defending the national interests of the entire people."[114] This is surely an odd historical mission for a party that is ostensibly part of an antinational, international movement. Moreover, the history in the program made clear that "our people" referred to the ethnic Rumanians, a nation said to have been "born out of the fusion of the Dacians [an ancient people] with the Romans," during the period when present-day Rumania was part of the Roman Empire.[115] Rumanian legendary figures, kings, and other earlier national heroes were lauded in the program for their contribution to the unfolding Rumanian epic.[116] Class- and epoch-transcending national characteristics, "the Romanian people's way of being and thinking," were described as forged during the nation's peculiar history.[117] There was also a lengthy, ringing defense of the continuing progressive role of nations and national states.[118] It was prophesied that the national state will not even begin to disappear gradually until the stage of "mature communism." Even when this distant plateau is reached, it was stipulated that "the nation will continue to exist as a distinct entity, with its own organization, keeping its specificity."[119] All this within the program of a Communist party.[120]

In addition to symptoms of nationalism that are peculiar to one party or another, there are symptoms that are common to many or all. One of these has been the tendency of leaders to pose as protectors of the interests of members of their national group dwelling within adjacent states and, in some cases, to set forth a right to reunite the transborder segment of the nation with the larger family by annexing the territory which it populates. When such claims allude to people and territory that are presently within a non-Marxist-Leninist state, raising them can be attributed to sound Leninist strategy. But a number of such campaigns have involved only Marxist-Leninist states. Cases in point include Hungary's position concerning Magyars living within Czechoslovakia, Rumania, and Yugoslavia;[121] Bulgaria's claim that the Macedonians are Bulgars and therefore a fit subject for Sofia's concern;[122] Albania's periodic statements with regard to the Albanians within Yugoslavia;[123] the countering Chinese and Soviet propaganda barrages aimed at peoples straddling their mutual border; similar transborder appeals between China and Mongolia; and the Rumanian campaign for the return of Moldavia on the basis that most of the people living there are members of the Rumanian nation.[124] Such policies are, of course, quite incompatible with Marxism. Marx had maintained that it was life within the economic nexus that determined loyalty and identity. Notions of blood ties as a basis for drawing political borders had no place in classical Marxism.[125] Irredentism is plainly a nationalist, not a Marxist tenet.[126]

The infiltration of nationalism into various parties can also be detected in the growing tendency to make national heritage a criterion for membership and leadership. Periodic purges that appear to concentrate on Jews is one dimension of this tendency.[127] During the early 1950s, such purges occurred within the Soviet Union, Hungary, Rumania, and Czechoslovakia.[128] Since that time, Jewish membership within the Soviet party has continued to decline sharply, and the disappearance of Jews from the highest councils of power has been even more dramatic.[129] Moreover, despite a sharp decrease in the number of Jews within Eastern Europe, further attacks upon Jews within the power structure occurred within Czechoslovakia and Poland.[130] While scapegoating, in contradistinction to nationalism, is often *a* and sometimes *the* key motivation behind such campaigns, national scapegoating itself necessarily implies that national heritage is a legitimate criterion to apply within the party. This sentiment has worked to the disadvantage of several peoples. We have seen how Serbians, particularly under the protection of Rankovich, made Serbian background a prerequisite for influence in the state-wide as well as in the Serbian party, and how the Croats made their party a bastion of the Croatian nation.[131] Elsewhere, the rank and file of the Slovak party has resisted the admission of Hungarians, even though the Slovak leadership favored such admission as a means of placating and controlling the Hungarian minority.[132] Both the general membership and the upper echelons of the Rumanian party were disproportionately staffed by members of national minorities at the time of achieving political power.[133] The percentage of members represented by minorities subsequently shrunk, and although the authorities maintain that their general membership now more accurately reflects the national composition of the state's population, it is evident that effective power has been transferred to a group who perceive themselves as "born out of the fusion of the Dacians with the Romans." We have also seen how the very select few members of minorities who held positions of influence within China were purged during the Cultural Revolution.[134] And in Vietnam, the 1976 purge of old-line Communists of non-Vietnamese heritage underlined the monopoly of power enjoyed by the dominant nation.[135]

The tendency to restrict access to the fonts of power to members of particular nations harmonizes with our earlier findings concerning cadre policy.[136] There we found a proclivity to trust the dominant group ("the most loyal nation") and to distrust minorities by comparison.[137] When augmented by the personnel practices flowing from "bureaucratic ethnocentrism," the result has been to give a distinct national coloration to the power structure, including the Communist party.[138] In turn, the parties have been known to become identified with goals as unmitigatingly nationalistic as separatism and irredentism.[139]

WE began this chapter by noting that keeping the party free of all national proclivities was to Lenin an absolute imperative. Only so long as this citadel of internationalism remained impervious to the national antithesis could scientific socialism be secure. When one surveys the disarray today both within and between states led by Communist parties ostensibly committed to a single internationalist movement, the justifiability of Lenin's fears concerning the consequences of party infiltration by nationalism becomes apparent. But since Lenin was neither inexperienced nor naive regarding the appeal of nationalism, even to Communist comrades, the mystery of why and how he believed the party could be protected against infiltration by nationalism remains. Perhaps influenced by his own unquestionable dedication to internationalism, he simply presumed that there would always be a sufficient percentage of those with an international outlook among the leadership to maintain an effective vigilance against any sign of nationalism creeping into the apparatus. If so, he was mistaken, for the true internationalist, whose vision transcends the interest of his nation and state, has been a rarity indeed in the vanguard of the international proletariat.

NOTES

1. *Current Digest of the Soviet Press* 29, no. 51:9.
2. See chapter 9.
3. Ibid. See also Wolfe, *Khrushchev*, 276.
4. See chapter 2 for Lenin's concise linking of the two: "We Social Democrats are opposed to *all* nationalism and advocate centralism."
5. The tract, written in 1902, was entitled *What Is To Be Done?*
6. Stalin, *Marxism and the National Question*, 76, 104, 106. Emphasis in original.
7. Cited in Conquest, *Nation Killers*, 123. Emphasis in original. Parenthetical material added.

Lenin's adamancy concerning the maintenance of centralized power within a single state-wide party was evident in his rejection of the request of the newly formed Ukrainian party for representation in the Comintern. See Szporluk, "Nationalities and Russian Problem," 25.

8. For specifics on the ethnic composition of the republican parties, see chapter 9.
9. As noted in chapter 9, this rotation extends to the second secretary of the branch parties, who is responsible for cadre policy.
10. Gililov, "Worldwide Significance," 60. Lenin would therefore certainly applaud the following excerpt from an article that appeared in *Pravda Ukrainy* during 1969:

> In order for a socialist society to develop along the path to communism it is necessary in all cases to provide for the priority of general interests, and not to permit nationalism, localism, departmentalism, and the juxtaposing of the interests of separate regions, nations or groups to the general interests. Only a Marxist-Leninist Party can do this which as-

sumes and carries full responsibility for the development of society as a whole, a party most fully expressing the interests of the toilers of all nations, of all regions of a country, a party constructed on the basis of democratic centralism and firmly holding in its hands all the levers of leadership and social development. (Cited in Hodnett and Potichnyj, *Ukraine and Czechoslovak Crisis*, 100.)

11. Shoup, *Communism and Yugoslav National Question*, 119. At about this same time, Tito described to Stalin the power of the party as follows: "All the more or less important decisions made by the Federal Government or any inferior body, in matters of any social or State nature, are in fact decisions arrived at by the party, or else originating in the initiative of the party; and the people regards and accepts them as such." "Letter of Tito and Kardelj to Stalin and Molotov," April 13, 1948, cited in Mittelman, *Nationality Problems*. Writing in 1954, Mittelman followed the citation with the sentence: "In the field of governmental and political activity each nationality has the inalienable right to carry out the directives from above in its own language."

12. See chapter 10.

13. For details see ibid.

14. See Rusinow, *Yugoslav Experiment*, 181 et seq. By late 1965, in Rusinow's words (p. 104), "[t]here was no longer a monolithic Party in Yugoslavia."

15. Denitch (*Legitimation of a Revolution*, 128) reports that this surprising development gave rise to the quip that "Yugoslavia was indeed moving toward a multiparty system." The Executive Bureau was not destined to endure for long. It was replaced by the Executive Committee in 1974, which in turn was eradicated in 1978. However, the principle of equal representation for each republic and of one-half that representation for each of the two autonomous provinces survived Tito's passing in 1980.

16. *Keesing's Contemporary Archives* (1971), 24734.

17. Ibid.

18. Ibid., 24735.

19. Rusinow, *Yugoslav Experiment*, 196.

20. Justifying the purge in a speech to the Croatian leaders on December 1, 1971 (a speech broadcast to the entire country the following day), Tito insisted that some Croats held the view that "no one, not even the Presidency of the LCY" could overrule the republican parties. In response, Tito asserted that the party was "the one factor which does have the right to undertake ideological-political action in an all-Yugoslav framework." Cited in Rusinow, *Yugoslav Experiment*, 309.

21. *Keesing's Contemporary Archives* (1973), 25794.

22. Ibid., 25795. Earlier in the year, Tito complained that during a conference of the League (held between January 25 and 27, 1972) "no one mentioned the dictatorship of the proletariat. Many tend somehow to avoid it as they formerly avoided democratic centralism. But the dictator-

ship of the proletariat exists in our country, as indeed it must."· Cited in Rusinow, *Yugoslav Experiment*, 313.

23. *Keesing's Contemporary Archives* (1973), 25795.

24. For details on the changes made in 1974, see *Keesing's Contemporary Archives*, 26657; for 1978, see 29237; and for 1980, see 30474.

25. At the time of Tito's death, for example, the highest organ was the twenty-four member Presidium. It consisted of Tito; two representatives from each republic and one from each autonomous province; a representative of the People's Army; the presidents of the central committees of the republican parties; and the presidents of the provincial committees of the autonomous provinces. These twenty-four people were supposedly elected by the party's Central Committee, but in fact were selected by Tito and then rubber-stamped by the Central Committee.

26. *Keesing's Contemporary Archives* (1974), 26657.

27. Ibid. (1978), 29237.

28. So described in party statutes. See *Area Handbook for Czechoslovakia*, 133.

29. See chapter 9. Since 1968 the domination has not extended to the first secretaryship; Dubcek and his successor, Husak, were both of Slovak background. Both appointments, however, were unusual (the second being made by Moscow), and did not reflect the actual balance of power within the party.

30. Skilling, *Czechoslovakia's Interrupted Revolution*, 488.

31. See chapter 8.

32. Ulc, *Politics in Czechoslovakia*, 17. Ulc adds the rather odd phrase, "thus denying Czech Communists the opportunity to organize themselves separately." Given the balance of power in the party, the denial of equal status to the Slovaks (which federalism would have brought) was a far more important consequence.

33. "Constitution of the Chinese Communist Party," June 11, 1945. The entire document can be found in Brandt et al., *Documentary History*, 422 et seq. The citation is from p. 424.

34. See, for example, Moseley, *Consolidation*, 123.

35. This experience is often recalled in Soviet works as a reminder of the danger of nationalist backsliding. See, for example, Zagladin, *Revolutionary Movement*, 280: "There has been a past instance (the collapse of the Second International) when departures from class positions, a break with scientific communism, resulted in that strong and massive parties forgot the principles of proletarian internationalism, and drifted towards nationalism and chauvinism, the natural result of division." See also chapter 2.

36. "Speech Closing the Debate on the Party Programme, March 19, 1919. Eighth Congress of the RCP, March 12–23, 1919," in Lenin, *Collected Works* 3:137. Lenin added: "Many of us harbour such [Great Russian nationalist] sentiments and they must be combatted."

37. Cited by Shub, *Lenin*, 433. The principle of national rotation that

was applied to the party's top position within Yugoslavia upon the death of Tito (following his earlier instructions) was therefore not an original concept. What is remarkable is that the initiation of the rotation within Yugoslavia in 1980 was the first implementation by any Communist party of what Lenin had insisted upon *"absolutely."*

38. Frustrated nationalism (unhappiness with the plight of one's nation) has accounted for numerous youthful conversions to Marxism. This was certainly the case with Mao, who, prior to becoming a Marxist, was writing nationalist tracts deploring the subservient status of the Chinese nation and predicting that its future "will be greater than any other." (See "Great Union of the People" [1919], in Mao, *Collected Works* [Peking], vols. 1–2, particularly p. 26.)

39. Solzhenitsyn, *East and West*, 78. Emphasis in original. Near the end of his letter (p. 140), Solzhenitsyn returned to this theme: "Perhaps it will seem to you that I have deviated from my initial platform of realism? But I shall remind you of my original assumption that you are not alien to your fathers, your grandfathers, and the expanses of Russia."

Some years earlier, Vyacheslav Chornovil, a Ukrainian newsman convicted of bourgeois nationalism, addressed a letter to the First Secretary of the Ukrainian party as follows: "It is not as an ordinary journalist that I am addressing myself to you. I am addressing myself to you as one Soviet citizen to another Soviet citizen, as a Ukrainian to another Ukrainian." See the *New York Times*, February 9, 1968.

40. See, for example, Kernig, *Marxism, Communism* 8:31.

41. Cited in King, *Minorities*, 182.

42. Cited in Wolfe, *Three Who*, 567.

43. Although it is definitely played down within the Soviet Union, Lenin's national background was also far from purely Russian. His mother was Volga German and his father was partly Tatari.

44. See chapter 11.

45. This does not mean to imply that there is a pattern of behavior that is certain to placate those ruled by a nonmember of the national group. And indeed, even Stalin's extreme pro-Russian posture did not suffice to placate Russian unhappiness with his national background. (Barghoorn, *Soviet Russian*, 120.)

46. The evidence includes the many toasts and allusions to the greatness of the Great Russians. In addition, Khrushchev recounts an interesting episode. At a dinner in his quarters, Stalin suddenly berated Beria (also a Georgian) because all of his servants were Georgian rather than Russian. Stalin brushed aside Beria's statement that the servants were all faithful and devoted to him (Stalin) by indignantly asking: "Does that mean Russians aren't devoted to me?" See *Khrushchev Remembers*, 311.

47. For example, the provisional wing of the IRA (Irish Republican Army) numbers among its most radical leaders individuals of English descent, some of whom have adopted Gallic names and spelling. Stalin's early adoption of a Russian pseudonym (Stalin: Man of Steel), and his election

to retain it throughout his life in preference to his Georgian surname (Dzhughashvili) appears to fit this same behavior pattern. Lenin perceived this same phenomenon at work in Stalin and in another non-Russian, Dzerzhinsky. In a criticism naming the latter, but clearly intended to refer to Stalin as well, Lenin dictated in late 1922: "I am afraid that Comrade Dzerzhinsky also, when he went to the Caucasus to investigate the 'crimes' of those 'social nationalists,' distinguished himself there only by his one-hundred percent Russian attitude (it is common knowledge that the Russified non-Russian always likes to exaggerate when it comes to one-hundred percent Russian attitudes)." Cited in Wolfe, *Khrushchev*, 272.

48. See the section in Schram, *Political Thought of Mao* (pp. 162 et seq.) entitled "To the Glory of the Hans." There are selections extending from 1919 to 1949. See also chapter 4.

49. See footnote 8, chapter 5 and further disussion in text, chapter 5.

50. Few speeches have equaled in nationalist pathos those of Imre Nagy in the last days before Soviet troops prevailed in Hungary. In a proclamation on October 30, 1956, he appealed to "Hungarian brethren, patriots! Loyal citizens of the Fatherland! . . . My Hungarian brethren, workers, Peasants! [to] stand beside the national Government in this hour of fraternal decision." On October 31, 1956, he again addressed his "Hungarian brethren," noting that "[t]hese heroic days have brought into existence our national Government which will fight for our people's independence and freedom," and adding that "[o]ur policies will be built solidly on the will of the Hungarian people." Turning to the "smear" that he had invited Soviet troops into Hungary, he emotionally asserted: "This is a base calumny. Imre Nagy, who is a fighter for Hungarian sovereignty, Hungarian freedom, and Hungarian independence, did not call these troops. On the contrary, it was he who fought for their withdrawal." See Zinner, *National Communism and Popular Revolt*, 454, 458.

51. See chapter 11.

52. Marx and Engels are not so readily acquitted. Their harsh and historically erroneous judgments and prophecies made about peoples such as the Czechs may well have reflected the German bias detected by some authorities. Berlin's statement that "there is no trace of nationalism in Marx's conception of world progress toward communism and beyond it" appears to this writer as surprisingly out of harmony with much of Marx's writing, as traced above in chapter 1. (See Berlin, "The Bent Twig," 23.)

53. Somewhat paradoxically, an American Marxist-Leninist, writing from the vantage point of 1972, maintained as now beyond question his then contentious 1965 statement that "Ho was a nationalist above being a Communist, and a human being above being a nationalist." (See the introduction by Bruce Franklin in *Essential Stalin*, 4. Franklin meant to be complimentary, but, as a Communist, he should have been aware that to Marxist-Leninists a description of Ho as a nationalist would be an indictment, not a eulogy.)

For another illustration of the broad tendency to describe Ho as a nationalist, see the obituary-type article in the *New York Times*, September 14, 1969, entitled "Ho Chi Minh Was Noted for Success in Blending Nationalism and Communism."

54. Janos, "Ethnicity, Communism, and Political Change," 510.

55. Beginning with Napoleon, history offers several examples of leaders who disguised themselves as nationalists for purely personal gain. (See Connor, "Politics of Ethnonationalism," 7.)

56. The problem of differentiating between true and feigned nationalism within a Communist party is underscored by a 1923 directive of Stalin. He castigated one segment of party cadre ("the Rights") within the party for nationalism: "It should be borne in mind that our Communist organizations in the border districts, in the republics and regions, can develop and firmly establish themselves, can become genuine internationalist, Marxist cadres, only if they get rid of their nationalism. Nationalism is the chief ideological obstacle to the training of Marxist cadres, of a Marxist vanguard in the border regions and republics." But he then balanced this criticism by condemning others ("the Lefts") for not employing nationalism to gain the support of the masses:

> But no less, if not greater, is the sin of the "Lefts" in the border regions. While the Communist organizations in the border regions cannot grow strong and develop into genuinely Marxist cadres without ridding themselves of nationalism, these cadres themselves can become mass organizations, can rally the majority of the toiling masses around them, only if they learn to be sufficiently flexible to be able to draw into our state institutions all in-any-way reliable national elements by making concessions to them; and if they learn to combine a resolute fight against nationalism in the party with as resolute a fight in drawing into Soviet work all more or less reliable elements among the local people, the intelligentsia, and so on.
>
> The "Lefts" in the border regions are more or less free of a skeptical attitude towards the party, of a tendency to succumb to nationalism. But the sins of the "Lefts" lie in the fact that they show no flexibility in relation to the bourgeois-democratic and merely reliable elements of the population, that they are unable and unwilling to manoeuvre in order to secure the co-operation of these elements, that they distort the line of the party in the matter of gaining the support of the majority of the toiling population in the country. ("Speech Delivered at the 4th Conference of the Central Committee of the Russian Communist Party with Representatives from the National Republics and Regions," June 10, 1923, in Stalin, *Marxism: Selected Writings*, 168–169.)

In short, one must maintain a nationalist face outside the party, but never within it.

57. Snow, *Red Star*, 455.

58. Within large states, such as the USSR, the differences can also be very sharp between certain ethnic homelands—for example, Latvia and Uzbekistan.

59. Mao, *Selected Works* (Peking) 2: 209–210. The reference to Chinese Communists as "part of the great Chinese nation, flesh of its flesh, blood of its blood" could certainly also be cited as evidence of nationalism and ethnocentrism on the part of Mao.

60. Moroz, *Report from the Beria Reserve*, 53. Omission symbols in original.

61. At the Twentieth Congress, Khrushchev accused Stalin of having falsified documents in the 1951–1952 purge of "thousands of innocent" Georgians on the trumped-up charge of nationalism. We will recall that Khrushchev also maintained that Stalin's reason for exiling entire peoples to Siberia (errant nationalism leading to collaboration with the Nazis) was bogus.

62. Gomulka of Poland and Husak of Czechoslovakia offer cases in point.

63. See, for example, Roucek, "Racial Elements," particularly pp. 77–79.

64. Cited in Rusinow, *Yugoslav Experiment*, 52.

65. See chapter 6.

66. See chapter 5.

67. Although Ho's party ostensibly gave up jurisdiction over Cambodia and Laos in 1945, its 1951 platform promised to work for "an independent, free, strong, and prosperous federation of the states of Viet-Nam, Laos and Cambodia if the three people so desire." The full text of the platform can be found in Cole, *Conflict in Indo-China*, 96–106.

68. For a prediction of this extension of influence into Cambodia and Laos, made during Ho's lifetime, see Connor, "Ethnology," 80.

69. Valentyn Moroz, "New Processes Are Only Beginning," 395.

70. See Bilinsky, "Mykola Skrypnyk," particularly pp. 120–121. See also idem, "Communist Party of the Ukraine," 22. See, too, Szporluk, "Ukraine and Ukrainians," 44–45.

71. Hodnett and Potichnyj, *Ukraine and Czechoslovak Crisis*, 134. See also, in the same work, pp. 22–24.

72. Ibid., 133.

73. See, for example, the *Current Digest of the Soviet Press* 24 (May 31, 1972): 5, 30; and 25 (April 25, 1973): 6.

74. Latvia's absence from the list is undoubtedly accounted for by the particularly high incidence of people born outside of Latvia who occupy the highest offices in the Latvian party. For the specific backgrounds of these leaders, see Saunders, *Samizdat*, 436–437. As noted therein: "All the significant party and government posts have now been filled with non-Latvians and Latvians who have spent their entire lives in Russia and who arrived in Latvia only after World War II. The majority of them either do not speak any Latvian or speak very little."

75. See chapter 11.

76. *Christian Science Monitor*, February 6, 1973.

77. Pipes, *Formation*, 288.

78. At this writing it is too early to know whether Andropov fits the behavior pattern. He assumed power shortly after the party made a commitment to accelerate the fusing process during the period of mature socialism. However, his unanticipated elevation of an Azerbaijani (Geidar Aliyev) to Politburo membership was broadly interpreted as an attempt to court the elites of both the Caucasian republics and the Muslim republics of Central Asia. (See *The Times* [London], November 29, 1982, and *The Guardian* [Manchester], December 23, 1982.) Aliyev's appointment would, of course, be most popular with the Azerbaijani elite, the more so because he had publicly espoused the union of the Azerbaijani of Iran with those of the Soviet Union. Due to their shorter period of control by a Marxist-Leninist party, other states do not offer as many changes in leadership against which to test for a similar pattern of behavior. However, as will be discussed later in this chapter, the replacement of Novotny by Dubcek as First Secretary of the Czechoslovak CP was due to his standing with the Slovak constituency within the party.

In the case of Rumania, just such a pattern of behavior appears to have characterized the maneuvering for power following the demise of Gheorghiu-Dej in 1965. As noted by Gilberg ("Modernization, Human Rights, Nationalism," 197):

> During the first few years after the change in leadership, necessitated by the death of Gheorghe Gheorghiu-Dej, the new PCR head moved cautiously in his relationship with the ethnic minorities in Romania. In fact, Ceausescu attempted to improve his ties with these groups as a counterweight to his important rivals who remained at the central level as carryovers from the previous regime. As a result of this political rapprochement, the Ceausescu nationality policies during this period were markedly less stringent than had been the case during much of the Gheorghiu-Dej era.

Then, having once consolidated power, Ceausescu, following the pattern of Stalin, Khrushchev, and Brezhnev, moved toward the assimilationist end of the continuum.

The struggle for power within China, following Mao's death, does not offer so clear a picture concerning the role of minorities. The sheer numerical advantage of the Han would dictate a very limited role for the non-Han within the party. We have seen, however, that attitude toward the national question had been an issue separating the gradualists (pragmatists) from the more radical ideologues. Moreover, the great publicity given to the issue in the press, in the revised state constitutions, and in the new party constitution during 1980–1982 (see chapter 10) suggests that the attitudes of at least certain members of the minorities might have been perceived as significant to the outcome of the struggle. Teng Hsiao-p'ing (the generally acknowledged architect of the victory of the "pragmatists") was certainly attuned to the significance of getting the support of various elements in the society during the struggle by holding out the prospect of a better future. Thus those who had been encouraged by promises of greater democracy later reportedly felt that Teng had used them "temporarily for his own political ends. Now that his enemies in power have been purged and his protégés have been elevated to positions as head of the party and head of the Government, these writers argue, Mr. Deng [Teng] has succumbed to traditional tactics for stifling critics." (*New York Times*, September 30, 1981.) Whether a similar fate was eventually in store for the minorities who were being so ardently wooed during the period remained to be seen, but the general tenor of the 1982 constitution and articles appearing in early 1983 certainly suggested a swing in that direction. (See chapter 10.)

79. Given all this, it is not improbable that the national card was also played by those responsible for Khrushchev's ouster. There were several pressing reasons for Khrushchev's overthrow, including his well-publicized but woefully unrealistic schedule for surpassing U.S. production, his (subsequently jettisoned) schedule for achieving communism, and the failure of "the Virgin Lands" plan to approximate his rosy forecasts. There is no evidence that the national question was viewed within the Politburo as an additional important argument for Khrushchev's ouster. However, the fact that, upon taking power, Brezhnev adopted a markedly more lenient view of national peculiarities makes it likely that playing to national discontent within the party had been a tactic of Khrushchev's opponents. The introduction of "the voluntary principle" for attending language schools, the (1961) Party Program's emphasis upon the merging of nations, and other antinational measures had certainly left Khrushchev vulnerable on this front.

80. On the other hand, some analogies appear to possess a measure of validity. For example, the Georgian wing of the party was seen as a bastion of Beria's, and an important base of support for launching his campaign to succeed Stalin. (Following Khrushchev's victory, it was purged of his former friends.) The strategic importance of having such an initial base of support when aspiring to the country's number one office is a basic tenet of American presidential politics.

81. The fact that with consolidation of personal power Stalin, Khrushchev, and Brezhnev each adopted a hard line toward the national minorities is unquestionably also pertinent to a discussion of nationalism within the party, although here one must perforce be more speculative. There are at least three possible reasons for this common volte-face: (1) pressure from "Centrists" within the party, most of whom could be expected to be Great Russians; (2) personal ethnocentric inclinations related to the dominant national group, of which Khrushchev and Brezhnev were members by birth and Stalin by inclination; (3) awareness that playing the

national card had been a dangerous, albeit shrewd, move, and that *raison d'état* now required that fissiparous nationalist tendencies within and without the party be checked. These factors could clearly overlap and reinforce one another, as well as vary in the influence they exerted on one or another leader. But all of them are related to the presence of nationalism within the party.

82. For many revenge-minded Serbs, it would be looked upon as the means for retribution.

83. Throughout Western Europe generally, for example, nationalism did not reappear as a strong force until the mid-1960s. For details, see Connor, "Ethnonationalism in the First World"; and idem, "Political Significance of Ethnonationalism," 110–133.

84. Shoup, *Communism and Yugoslav National Question*, 189.

85. Rusinow, *Yugoslav Experiment*, 97.

86. Shoup, *Communism and Yugoslav National Question*, 208–209.

87. Cited in Vucinich, "Nationalism and Communism," 282. Chetniks, Ustashas, and White Guards were nationalist movements during World War II among Serbs, Croats, and Slovenes, respectively. YCP spokesmen regularly indentify them as "Fascists."

88. Lendvai, "National Tensions," 7–8.

89. *Keesing's Contemporary Archives* (1971), 24734.

90. Ibid. The Secretary was concomitantly a member of the Executive Bureau, the highest organ of the Yugoslav League of Communists.

91. Rusinow, *Yugoslav Experiment*, 303. The Secretary of the Croatian party had earlier maintained that nation and class had become one and the same. (Ibid., 296.)

92. His speech to the Croatian leadership, given on July 4, 1971, was not released until May 1972.

93. *Keesing's Contemporary Archives* (1972), 25214.

94. *Keesing's Contemporary Archives* (1974), 26658.

95. *Keesing's Contemporary Archives* (1973), 25794. The statement was part of a document issued by the Presidium of the League of Communists in July 1972.

96. *Keesing's Contemporary Archives* (1981), 30951, and (1982), 31673.

97. Ulc (*Politics in Czechoslovakia*, 11) states that "Novotny's outstanding lack of tact in matters of Slovak self-respect aggravated the situation to such a degree that the Slovak branch of the party emerged as a political force in opposition to Prague." At the same time, it should be noted that in this matter the Slovak party was also pressured by students, intellectuals, and other groups whose espousal of Slovak interests preceded that of the party. (See *Area Handbook for Czechoslovakia*, 120.)

98. If accurate, the charge offers an excellent illustration of the phenomenon of bureaucratic ethnocentrism that was discussed in chapter 9.

99. *Area Handbook for Czechoslovakia*, 121.

100. Skilling, *Czechoslovakia's Interrupted Revolution*, p. 523.

101. All the more so because the Soviets had been appealing to Slovak nationalism throughout 1968, as a means of driving wedges between the state's two most important peoples.

102. Volgyes, "Political Socialization in Eastern Europe," 52. Antinationalism placed fourth in East Germany, but there nationalism is equated with reunification of the two Germanys. As in the case of Czechoslovakia, it is therefore a threat to state survival.

103. In all states, leaders must be careful of the terms they use to express this nationalism. While the word *nation* is permissible, such terms as *nationalism* and *nationalist* are, of course, words of opprobrium in the Marxist-Leninist lexicon. It is therefore commonplace to substitute patriotism and patriot for them. Technically, patriotism refers to loyalty to and indentification with one's country (state), while nationalism refers to loyalty to and identification with one's own national people. But to a people who dominate a state and perceive it as essentially the state of one's own people, i.e., as its political extension or expression (for example, Albania, Bulgaria, Cambodia, China, East Germany, Hungary, Laos, Mongolia, Poland, Rumania, Vietnam, and to a lesser but important degree the Soviet Union [read: Russia]), an appeal to patriotism and an appeal to nationalism trigger the same response. Patriotism therefore has the potential for evoking a national response on the part of the dominant group while appealing to a transnational sentiment on the part of minorities.

104. Speech by Stanislaw Kania at the Democratic Party Congress, *Trybuna Ludu*, March 16, 1981.

105. "Message to the Senate" (1804), as reprinted in Herold, *Mind of Napoleon*, 72.

106. See discussion earlier in this chapter. Napoleon's assertions of dedication to the French people most assuredly fell within the category of tactics. Of Genovese descent, he fought for Corsican independence from France before concluding that the French nation was a better agent for his ambitions than was the Corsican nation.

107. See "Announcement of the Council of Ministers about the Outbreak of Disorders, October 24, 1956" and "Announcement of the Hungarian Government's Appeal for Soviet Military Assistance, October 24, 1956," in Zinner, *National Communism and Popular Revolt*, 408–409.

108. "Radio Address by Erno Gero, First Secretary of the Hungarian Worker's Party, October 23, 1956," in ibid., 403, 404, 406.

109. Ibid., 411, 416, 418, 431, 454, 450.

110. The October 28, 1956, issue of *Szabad Nep* referred to the demands of the demonstrators (who only a week earlier were "Fascists" and "counterrevolutionaries") as follows:

The demand for the equality and the independence of the country is as all-embracing as the mother tongue we speak. It is an eternal shame that there were Communists even in leading positions who did not understand the language of their own people. What has saved the Party's honor is that even under Rakosi's tyranny there were Communists, in increasing numbers until they became the majority, who as revolutionaries understood the ever faster, restless throb of the nation's heart. They placed themselves at the head of the struggle which leads the country toward socialism on a Hungarian and democratic path.

The article described the force behind the demonstrations, as "this passion which carries away a whole nation perhaps once in a century." An article in the issue of October 29, 1956, added:

> The bloody, tragic, but at the same time ennobling fight, lasting five days, was not instigated by some sort of subversive work. It was caused, alas, by our own faults and crimes. The greatest of our faults and crimes was our failure to protect the sacred flame which our ancestors had bequeathed to us—our national independence. What does the Hungarian nation want, asked the youth in March, 1848? The independence of the nation, was the answer given by Petofi and his friends in the first of his twelve points.
>
> Let us at last talk frankly. This is the first answer today too. This is the first demand of the nation.

111. An example of how opportunism and nationalism can compete is offered by Janos Kadar, who had been appointed First Secretary during the early stages of the demonstrations. At first he supported Imre Nagy and the other leaders in their national goals, but with word that the Soviets were invading in force, he quickly altered his position. Contrast, for example, his statement of support for the Hungarian government and its policies on October 30, 1956 (Zinner, *National Communism and Popular Revolt*, 455) and his radio announcement on November 1 concerning the formation of a new Communist party (ibid., 464–467) with his address of November 4 (ibid., 474–478). On November 1 he noted that "Our people have proved with their blood their intention to support unflinchingly the Government's efforts for the complete withdrawal of Soviet forces. We do not want to be dependent any longer." But by November 4 he perceived the "influence of counterrevolutionary elements" in Nagy's group. Kadar was rewarded by the Soviets for his switch. He remained in office, and at the 1969 International Meeting of Communist and Workers' Parties held in Moscow he told the audience: "It is necessary to step up the struggle against bourgeois ideas infiltrating our ranks, against revisionist and dogmatic views which distort the principles of Marxism-Leninism and lead people onto a false path. Of the bourgeois views, the nationalist views, particularly the form of nationalism expressed in anti-Sovietism, are unquestionably the most dangerous for our movement." Cited in Zagladin, *Revolutionary Movement*, 73. At the 1976 Conference of European Parties, Kadar served as the principal non-Soviet spokesman for proletarian internationalism, saying *inter alia*, "The Hungarian Socialist Workers' Party . . . rejects all bourgeois and anti-Marxist concepts of nationalism and anti-

Sovietism, knowing them to be directed against the unity of our movement and against human progress." *Keesing's Contemporary Archives* (1976), 27954.

112. See chapter 11.

113. "Programme of the Romanian Communist Party," 12.

114. Ibid., 51.

115. Ibid., 30.

116. Ibid., 33, 36.

117. Ibid., 31.

118. Ibid., 145–151.

119. Ibid., 150.

120. For a biting satire on the Rumanian leadership's nationalist pretensions and their effect upon the Magyar minority, written by a Hungarian citizen and published in Budapest, see Galabardi, "Identity," 56–63.

121. While, as noted, turning his back on Magyar nationalism in order to assume and retain power with Soviet support, Hungary's Kadar became a champion of the rights of Magyars in neighboring countries. Doing so is probably essential for any Hungarian leader desirous of enjoying a degree of legitimacy. Attitudinal surveys indicate powerful grass-roots concern with the treatment accorded Magyars within Rumania. (Blumstock, "Hungary," 371.) Although he offers no support for his statement, Ivan Volgyes ("Legitimacy and Modernization," 143) notes: "The issue of the treatment of Hungarians in Czechoslovakia, Yugoslavia and Romania is a serious one, an issue on which the legitimacy of the regime partially rests." Concerning Budapest's commentaries on the treatment of Magyars within Rumanian Transylvania, a Rumanian author (Lancranjan, *Story of Transylvania*, 163) remarked that "neither are they scientific or friendly, to say nothing of brotherly." For another article by a Hungarian, criticizing a Rumanian book for promoting an "ethnocratic state" based upon "the unity of the 'pureblooded race' in which there is no room for the *strain*, the outsider," see Szaraz, "On a Curious Book," 14. In early 1983 a Slovenian source noted that "the issue of the rights of the Hungarian national minority in Rumania . . . has been a burning issue for a long time and recently it became so acute that it was necessary to have discussions between the countries" at the highest level. The author added:

At present, it is not clear how the problem will be solved in the framework of relations between the two states, especially since it seems that the polemics are heating up especially on the part of the Hungarian side which, in various forms, has been repeatedly charging Romania with carrying on a policy of de-nationalization. In Bucharest, semi-officially, they are responding differently: they are alluding to indirect pressure from Moscow, saying that it is a process which began in 1968 when Romania condemned the Soviet intervention in Czechoslovakia. (See Sedmak, "Coolness," 2.)

122. For a Bulgarian article maintaining that Macedonia was the heartland of the Bulgarian kingdom in the tenth century, see "Stronghold of Bulgarian Spirit," 1–7.

123. A Swiss paper reported a speech delivered by Enver Hoxha in late 1982 in which the Albanian party chief berated Yugoslavia for its treatment of Albanians within Kosovo Province and declared that "Albania was not a state of three million people but a nation of six million." The reporter noted that "with these statements [Hoxha] expressed a feeling of solidarity that transcended borders." (See "Hoxha Attacks Yugoslavia Sharply, Calls Shehu an Agent," *JPRS* 82490, December 17, 1982, p. 2.)

124. Given the stark disparity in power between the two states, the Rumanian claim to Soviet Moldavia is particularly effective as an example of a Communist party pursuing an ethnonational policy despite the odds and possible consequences. Sometimes the Rumanian claims are thinly veiled. See, for example, *Romania: Documents—Events*, 15, for First Secretary Ceausescu's statement: "Historical experience teaches us that dismembering of some countries and the division of some nations has always been a break in the path of social development and hindered the peoples from mightily asserting their energies and creative capabilities in the fight for social progress, civilization and welfare." For a similar suggestion in the Party Program, see *Programme of the Romanian Communist Party*, 37:

> It is worth pointing out that Marx and Engels paid special attention to the study of Romania's history, of her economic and social development, of the evolution of the working-class movement in our country. The classics of Marxism were sympathetic to the heroic fight waged by the Romanian people against exploitation and oppression, for national and social emancipation, for union into a single national state and for shaking off the foreign yoke.

For recent articles drawing attention to the fact that Moldavians are Rumanians, see Stoicescu, "The Keen Awareness," particularly p. 61, and Ceausescu, "From Burebista's," particularly pp. 31–32. These articles hardly veil their theme of unjust Soviet control of Moldavia.

125. The appeals to blood ties or the extended family are sometimes explicit, as witness the 1958 statement of the head of the Albanian Goverment concerning Albanians in Yugoslavia:

> Had we not raised our voice in defense of our Albanian brothers in Kosovo, Montenegro, and Macedonia, we would have betrayed Marxist-Leninism. We are not chauvinists. We are not at present asking that Kosovo join with Albania. But the same mother that gave birth to us gave birth to the Albanians in Kosovo, Montenegro, and Macedonia. . . . We demand and we shall continue to demand that the Yugoslav government grant the Albanians of Kosovo, Montenegro, and Macedonia all the rights pertaining to them as a national minority. (Cited in King, *Minorities*, 144.)

Tirana's propaganda concerning the "savage policy of national oppression [which] is pursued against our Albanian brothers in Yugoslavia" increased substantially during 1981–1982. See, for example, the speech by a member of the Albanian Politburo to the Ninth Congress of Trade Unions in *JPRS* 81212, July 6, 1982, particularly p. 7. See too, the basis for the annexation of Taiwan set forth in Chou En-lai's report to the Tenth Congress of the CCP (*New York Times*, September 1, 1975): "Taiwan Province is our motherland's sacred territory, and the people of Taiwan are our kith and kin." While Taiwan is a non-Marxist-Leninist state and Chou's words might be seen as tactical, references to "kith and kin" as a basis for foreign policy are strange words to air in a party conclave. For similar terminology used by Kim Il Sung in reference to the people of South Korea, see chapter 10. See also the interview with Kim, reproduced in *Atlas* (February 1976), 19, in which Kim states that "the unification of our country rests on three major principles: peace, independence, and integration of our race."

126. In this sense, the post-World War II annexation of western Poland by the Soviet Union, which united Ukrainians, Belorussians, and Lithuanians, was a non-Marxist-like action.

127. Although Marx was himself of Jewish background, many critics have detected powerful anti-Jewish sentiments in his works, particularly in *On the Jewish Question*, which he wrote in 1843.

128. See Katz, "Jews in the Soviet Union," 359–364. For the other states of Eastern Europe, see Burks, *Dynamics of Communism*, chapter 8, and Fejto, *Juifs et l'Antisémitisme*. One of the more common aspersions cast against Jews—that they were guilty of "rootless cosmopolitanism"—is ironic in that it would indicate an internationalism rather than a nationalism.

129. Katz, "Jews in the Soviet Union," 368.

130. For a report on anti-Semitism among party officials within Czechoslovakia, see the *New York Times*, January 14, 1970. The Polish party directed a purge of Jews in 1968, and a segment of the security apparatus attempted to launch another in 1981. On the latter, see the *New York Times*, sec. 4, March 15, 1981.

131. The Macedonian party has been involved in internal struggles that go beyond the national criterion. There, clans have protested the preeminence of other clans within the party's highest organ. (See, for example, the *New York Times*, September 22, 1966.)

132. Renner, "National Minorities in Czechoslovakia," 27.

133. The precise national breakdown of the party at the end of World War II is not known, but the near exclusion of ethnic Rumanians from its key positions was apparent. See *Area Handbook for Romania*, 55; and Kovari, "Accident and Necessity," 221.

134. This is how a Soviet publication described the purging of the most important non-Han, Ulanfu:

The chauvinist witches Sabbath in Peking of the end of the sixties was accompanied by a reported assault on the traditional way of life of ethnic

Mongolians, who were subjected to crude assimilation. The Mongolians' wish to keep their mother tongue was condemned as "revisionist," and the sole Mongolian in the Central Committee of the CP of China, the only non-Chinese on that body to represent 50 million people belonging to national minorities, was depicted in Chinese propaganda as a snake trembling before giants armed with tommy-guns and Mao's little red book. (Zagladin, *Revolutionary Movement*, 125.)

Although Ulanfu and most of the other minority luminaries were rehabilitated following Mao's death, their purge highlighted the near monopoly of party power enjoyed by the Han. Their subsequent rehabilitation had little effect on this domination.

135. The fact that this purge occurred at a time when all earlier promises (autonomy, etc.) were being renounced and shortly after a number of those to be purged were assigned positions in the National Assembly of a newly united Vietnam suggests that the prominent non-Vietnamese leaders had protested concerning the treatment accorded to their people. Thus the minority leaders, the Vietnamese leaders, or (more likely) both were guilty of placing nationalism ahead of the party.

136. A variation on the tendency to exclude nonmembers of the nation from the party was an attempt by China during the 1960s and 1970s to exclude the Soviet Union from the revolutionary movement in the Third World on the basis that the Soviets were a European (that is, white) people. (Chinese posters of the period depicted pigmented Latin Americans, Africans, South Asians, and Far Eastern people marching shoulder to shoulder onward to national liberation. The accent was very much on "Colored Peoples of the World, Unite!") The Soviets showed nervous concern at this exclusion and charged the Chinese with a racial view of history in which races had been substituted for classes. (See, for example, Zagladin, *Revolutionary Movement*, 165.) For their part, the Chinese accused the Soviets of pan-Slavic racism: "Like Hitler's 'Aryan master race,' the 'pan-Slavism' of the Soviet revisionist new Tsars is exceedingly reactionary racism. They publicize these reactionary ideas only to serve expansion abroad by the handful of reactionary rulers of their 'superior race'." (*Ta King Pao*, April 23, 1970.)

137. See chapter 9.

138. There are assuredly other avenues of research that could be investigated in order to assess the impact of nationalism upon the parties. For example, one could study the degree to which a party's symbols and heroic figures reflect a national bias. Thus, by whatever test (the number of statues, published photographs and portraits, or the frequency of citation by party leaders), it is Lenin and Leninism, not Marx and Marxism, that represent the highest deity and dogma within the Soviet Union. Moreover, such tributes to Lenin are far less numerous outside of his native country (and, within that country, outside of the Russian regions). Furthermore, portraits and statues of Lenin created within other states often

do not reflect the same heroic attributes as do those in the Soviet Union. (The statue of Lenin in Nowa Huta in Poland is almost a squat caricature.) In general, the more independent a state is from Moscow's direction, the more apt it is to place an indigene first in the pantheon of Marxist deities. In China, Maoism became the principal source of inspiration, as recall the era when *Quotations from Chairman Mao* was "held aloft" by the entire citizenry. Moreover, when, following the death of "the Great Helmsman," a de-Maoization campaign began, a Chinese confederate (Chou En-lai) and his *Selected Works* were commensurately elevated. (See *The Times* [London], January 6, 1981.) Within North Korea, statues and portraits of Kim Il Sung abounded, and he, too, had his published book of quotations. Also germane is the post-Stalinist popularity of Stalin within his native Georgia, as measured by statues, portraits, etc. In what may be an apocryphal story, a Georgian party member, reminded that Stalin was "a son-of-a-bitch," is said to have retorted "Yes, but he was our son-of-a-bitch."

139. Considering the degree to which nationalism has permeated the parties, it is curious that they often go to such lengths to deny it. Thus in his speech on the fiftieth anniversary of the Soviet Union, General Secretary Brezhnev noted:

> The Party has brought about a situation in which internationalism has been transformed from the ideal of a handful of Communists into a profound conviction and norm of behavior for millions upon millions of Soviet people of all nations and nationalities. (*Applause.*) This was a genuine revolution in social consciousness, and its importance is hard to overestimate. The Party's success in accomplishing this revolution is connected in great measure with *its uncompromising attitude toward any kind of departure from the Leninist nationalities policy in its own ranks* and with the fact that the Party has resolutely fought against all kinds of deviations, firmly upholding and creatively developing the great teaching of Marxism-Leninism. (*Current Digest of the Soviet Press* 24, no. 51 [1972]: 9. Emphasis added.)

See also Zagladin, *Revolutionary Movement*, 63, 100, 109, 125, 160, 162, 191, 197, 249. The authors perceive nationalism within the ranks of the parties of Western Europe, China, Indonesia, and Yugoslavia. They acknowledge it could have become a problem within the Soviet party had the party not been vigilant. It is not made clear how such statements concerning the absence of nationalism within the party can be made compatible with the many periodic purges for nationalistic behavior.

The Unwithering National Question

LENIN's three-pronged strategy for harnessing nationalism to the cause of scientific socialism has known both success and failure. His first injunction—*prior to the assumption of power, promise all national groups the right of self-determination (expressly including the right of secession) while proffering national equality to those who wish to remain within the state*—reaped great results. The manipulation of the national aspirations of minorities was a key element in the assumption and consolidation of power by the Bolsheviks; it was an essential element in the rise to power of Mao Tse-tung; and it was likely the single most important factor in the success of the Vietnamese and Yugoslav parties.[1] Thus the four most important Marxist-Leninist movements, which can lay claim to having achieved power through their own devices, attest to the remarkable success of Lenin's first stratagem.

There was, however, a presumption underlying Lenin's first injunction that did not prove valid. Lenin had presumed that the offer of independence would not be accepted. Given the option of secession or attachment to the new revolutionary society, minorities would choose the latter. But nationalism proved far more potent than Lenin had imagined. Commenting on the havoc that self-determination had wrought, Rosa Luxemburg colorfully stated following the October Revolution:

> Nations and mini-nations are cropping up on all sides announcing their right to form states. Putrefied corpses are climbing out of age-old graves, filled with the sap of a new spring, and peoples "without a history" who never yet formed an independent state, feel a powerful urge to do so.[2]

Perceiving the array of secessions as unacceptable, the Soviet leaders set about neutralizing them through a combination of force and guile. Had the use of the first injunction ended at this point, the broken promises to the peoples of tsarist Russia—while certainly censurable and unacceptable to the peoples involved—might have been defensible in terms of *realpolitik. Raison d'état* could be offered

as a partial vindication for reneging on promises with unanticipated, disastrous results for the state. Governments have regularly
countered claims to an "inalienable, God-given right of national
self-determination" with a right and duty to maintain the political
and territorial integrity of the state with which they have been
entrusted. Had Lenin at this point simply acknowledged that he
had been wrong in his assumption that peoples would not take
advantage of the secessionist option and, as a result, that the promise to honor secession was not an apropriate instrument for revolutions elsewhere, the broken promises could be credited more to
miscalculation than to a desire to deceive. But the use of Lenin's
first injunction did not end at this point. Now made more certain
than ever of the power of the national urge and the wisdom of
harnessing it to the world revolutionary movement (as a result of
having observed the secessionist impulse at work among the peoples
of the Russian Empire), Lenin and his colleagues, through the
medium of the Comintern, ordered all Communist parties to adopt
his formula on self-determination. This was done with the awareness that the minorities, if given the possibility, would in all probability avail themselves of the right to secede. The Communist
parties of China, Vietnam, Yugoslavia, and a host of other states
subsequently pledged themselves to allow peoples to shape their
own national destiny, while fully cognizant that they did not intend
ever to permit the terms of these pledges to be carried out.

While Lenin's first injunction returned rich dividends in the case
of the Soviet Union, Yugoslavia, China, and Vietnam, it failed the
Communist parties of many other states. In general, it failed in the
case of minority people who had a viable alternative in the form
of a truly national party, and it exerted a backfire effect in the case
of the dominant group within a state, wherever that group had
become aware of the party's promise to dismember the state in the
name of national self-determination. The injunction's past record
of inutility and harmfulness in the case of parties operating within
Western Europe and North America is reflected in the fact that
none of the state-wide Communist parties of the First World currently support the Leninist notion of national self-determination
for their country's minorities. Promises pitched to ethnonational
aspirations are still very much a part of the propaganda of revolutionary movements within Third World states, and are unquestionably still an asset in many situations. However, following the
post-1954 lead of the Vietnamese CP, most of the Third World
parties have substituted the more amorphous promise of autonomy

for that of secession in their published programs. The substitution lessens the probability of alienating the state's dominant ethno-national element, while leaving the party free to promise more informally whatever level of independence appears expedient when dealing directly with a minority in its homeland. Due to its inherent shortcomings, then, Lenin's precise formula for harnessing nationalism to the revolutionary cause in a prerevolutionary situation appears out of vogue.

Lenin's second injunction—*following the assumption of power, terminate the fact (though not necessarily the fiction) of a right to secession, and begin the lengthy process of assimilation via the dialectical route of territorial autonomy for all compact groups*—has been far less successful. Nowhere has it succeeded. Indeed, nowhere has it been applied as Lenin intended. Fearing that Lenin's formula would lead unilaterally to a heightened sense of nationalism amongst nations, rather than lead them on a dialectical course toward fusion, even those few states that have paid lip service to territorial autonomy saddled their programs with risk-reducing devices that undermined in advance the hypothetical foundations upon which Leninist national policy rested. The fault is in large part Lenin's, because he failed to proscribe tampering, while offering no guidelines as to what constituted permissible/impermissible tampering. Moreover, his sole prohibition—avoid coercion—was predicated upon a nonexistent dichotomy between coercion and persuasion, and indicated a preoccupation with the perceptions of those in authority, rather than with the more vital perceptions of the masses.

Had Lenin's followers more strongly believed in his legacy on the national question and more faithfully adhered to its spirit, it is highly doubtful that his three intermediate *sine qua non* goals of economic, cultural, and political equality could have been achieved. All three goals would encounter barriers in the areas of objective reality and perceptions of that reality that were not taken into account by Lenin. Moreover, the cornerstone of Lenin's policy—a plenary distinction between form and content—was, in any case, faulty. National forms have a content of their own and serve as reminders, rallying points, and reinforcers of the national idea. Lenin's presumption that one could encourage nations without simultaneously encouraging nationalism therefore rested on shaky pillars.

The degree to which Lenin's policies have been followed varies tremendously from state to state and, within individual states, from period to period. But regardless of the approach taken, the claim of Marxist-Leninist states of having "solved" their national question is more than an overstatement. It runs contrary to the flow of events. Rather than dissipating, nationalism has been rising within Marxist-Leninist societies.

Lenin's third injunction—*keep the party free of all nationalist proclivities*—has likewise failed. Much of the inter- and intra-party disarray that has come to characterize what Lenin envisaged as a single world movement is traceable to nationalism's infiltration of the inner circles of party power.

The message that flows from the relative success of Lenin's three injunctions is that the legatees of Lenin have proven more adroit at allying themselves with nationalism than at suppressing it. When it has suited their purpose of the moment to encourage nationalism, whether at home or abroad, they have generally been remarkably successful; but when they have tried to counter it—again, whether at home or abroad—their record is certainly far from impressive. Nationalism has proven to be a much more powerful force than Marxism.[3] When communism and nationalism have been wedded in the popular mind, Communist movements have found broad acceptance. When communism and nationalism have been perceived as at odds, such movements have tended to be spurned.[4]

The Leninist scenario that called for nationalism to be restricted to the non-Marxist world and, even in the event those walls were breached, for its absolute repulsion by the party, has not materialized. As in the case of the Western, anti-Marxist policy of "containment," which was broadly criticized on the ground that effective barriers to the spread of ideologies cannot be constructed, the Leninist attempt to contain the ideology of nationalism failed. Both the outer walls of Marxist-Leninist states and the inner walls of Marxist-Leninist parties have been breached.

But where does this leave the Marxist view of history? Marx shared with Hegel a conviction that history was evolving through a dialectical pattern in a discernible direction. But in the words of the late George Sabine, "Marx removed from Hegel's theory the assumption that nations are the effective units of social history—an assumption that never had any close logical relation to his system—and replaced the struggle of nations with the struggle of social classes."[5] Perceiving nations as the principal vehicles of history may have had no logical relation to Hegel's dialectic, but we have seen how Marx and Engels presumably unconsciously assigned to nations this same august role in some of their writings and how some of Marx's successors in the Second International, particularly the

Austrian socialists, quite consciously embraced this same perception of nations as the key to historical development. More recently, ostensible Marxist-Leninists have also adopted this heresy; some have defended their position openly.[6] More commonly, however, they have manifested their conviction indirectly by taking advantage of the ambiguity and lack of precision in Lenin's national policy to defend the indefinite flourishing of nations. Behind a thin veil of Marxist-Leninist orthodoxy, a variety of neo-Hegelianism has been prospering. This should not occasion great surprise. Granted, history is too susceptible to the whims and caprices of events and individuals to be described as the inevitable unfolding of either national or socioeconomic forces. But developments since 1848 lend far greater support to a Hegelian view of history than they do to the historical analysis offered by classical Marxism.

NOTES

1. Stalin was being remarkably candid when he described the October Revolution as not just a "proletarian revolution" but as a "peasant war" and a "national war." ("October Revolution and the Middle Strata," *Pravda*, November 1, 1923. Reprinted in Stalin, *Marxism and National, Colonial Questions*, 187.) It is ironic that the two slogans of greatest appeal used by the Bolsheviks ("All land to the Peasants!" and "The Right of All Nations Freely to Secede!") were in each case appealing to sentiments that Marxists view as belonging to the bourgeois, capitalist era, namely, the desire of the peasants privately to own land and the sentiment called nationalism. The two slogans were also mainstays in the Chinese and Vietnamese campaigns to grasp power.

2. Cited in Kernig, *Marxism, Communism* 6:82.

3. Regis Debray ("Marxism and the National Question," 34) has explained this advantage in terms of nationalism's more primal history:

[H]orizontal class divisions appeared far later in social history than the segmentary cultural divisions of ethnos, nations, and peoples. And there is an anthropological law which states that the deepest layers of a national formation or of an individual personality last longest. In both psychic and social organization, ontogenetically and philogenetically, the hard core is always *archaic*. This oldest stratum is also the most active—this is a fundamental psychoanalytic and historic datum.

Elsewhere (p. 35), he added:

As a materialist, what I am maintaining is that—broadly speaking—the instinctive is determinant in relation to the conscious. What I am saying is that there is an internationalist conscience, rather than an internationalist instinct. For this fact I infer—and I think reality is with me on this—that each time national instinct conflicts with internationalist conscience, the former has a much greater mass force. That is all. Do I regret this state of affairs? Yes, I deplore it, as much as I deplore the fact that I will have to die one day; but this is ordained in my genetic code.

4. One of the more bizarre illustrations of a party's embracing the powerful force of nationalism was offered by the leadership of the Cambodian Khmer Rouge. The party had been ousted from power by Vietnamese forces in 1979, following nearly four years of Khmer Rouge rule, during which its commitment to radical policies had resulted in the dislocation of nearly the entire population and in the death of more than a conservatively estimated one to two million people. In order to gain support for a countercoup, the party warmly embraced Khmer nationalism. At a news conference called by its two principal leaders, one said: "Our main duty is not to make the socialist revolution or build socialism. Our main concern is to fight to drive all the Vietnamese forces out of Cambodia and defend our nation, our people and our race." And the other added: "If the West wants to replace us with new leaders, we have no objection, provided this person [sic] had the force to prevent Vietnam from swallowing up Cambodia. We are ready to depart for the sake of the survival of Cambodia." *New York Times*, March 1, 1980.

5. Sabine, *History of Political Thought*, 628.

6. For example, references to socioeconomic classes were strikingly absent from the view of history put forth by Rumanian CP General Secretary Ceausescu in 1975: "In the assessment of these distortions, in the whole analysis of the people's historical development we have to unabatedly set out from the fundamental principles of the outlook of dialectical and historical materialism, from the Programme of our Party which, while not neglecting the importance of personalities in the life of the nations, powerfully highlights the people's mass decisive role in the making of history, in the upward evolution of the human society." ("Speech by Nicolae Ceausescu, RCP General Secretary at Festive Meeting Marking the Anniversary of 'Stefan Gheorghi' Academy," *Romania: Documents-Events* [March 1975], 14.) See also the comments of the Rumanian party's program on the indefinite survival and progressive significance of nations (see chapter 12). During the scholarly debate on nationalism that took place in the Soviet Union in 1966–1967, there were those who pointed out that Stalin's famous definition of the nation implied that the nation was an eternal category. Several of the participants were obviously sympathetic to such a prognostication. (See Hodnett, "What's in a Nation?" particularly p. 9.) A book circulated among the highest echelon of the Ukrainian party concluded with an emotional case for the perpetuity of the Ukrainian nation:

[I]t is not a question of any organization or group of people, but of something immeasurably greater and deeper—the spontaneous, multiform, widespead, self-originating processes of a nation's "self-defence" in the face of a clear prospect of disappearing from the human family.

Engels spoke many a time about "the inevitable struggle of each people for its national existence" and also about the fact that when the life of a nation is threatened "the struggle to restore . . . national existence will absorb everything."

This constant national self-renewal, self-preservation, and self-defence is a powerful collective instinct of a people, an indestructible, unconscious, natural force like the instinct of self-preservation and the force of self-renewal of any organism.

It is these forces of national life that break through spontaneously and unexpectedly everywhere, confront purblind strategists of uniformity with inscrutable enigmas and make nonsense of all historiosophic designs of Shchedrin's town governors.

These forces are unfathomable and inexhaustible, no technique of political surveillance can keep up with them or control them.

And this is not simply an ethnographic force. Everywhere the socialist national consciousness of Ukrainians keeps awakening still more. It is inseparable from human self-knowledge. And it will keep on awakening and growing under the impact of powerful forces. . . . Stalin forgot his own admonitions and began to destroy the Ukrainian nation. And with what result? He destroyed several million Ukrainians but did not destroy the nation. And no one ever will. (Dzyuba, *Internationalism?*, 204, 205, 207.)

Milovan Djilas (*Parts of a Lifetime*, 399–400) analyzed the Yugoslavian situation in terms of the historical permanency and primacy of the nation:

Today's eruptions of nationalisms and national strife, however, do not mean that the Communists did not do anything to resolve the national question. Moreover, it would not be justified to say that the Communists made grave, essential mistakes in handling the national question. The problem cannot be presented that way because no one, not even Communists, can ever do anything beyond the scope of their ideas, interests and capacities. The revolution brought a change in the national question as well as in property relations and power.

The problem is primarily that even though social, and especially political, systems change, nations persist. That means that the national question in a multinational state can be resolved at best only for a specific period, in the framework of a specific political and social structure. Each change of the social and political order alters the relations among nations. And conversely: nations, changeable in their aspirations and potentials, influence the changing of the system.

This is what happened in Yugoslavia.

The Albanian leadership has also embraced a view of history in which the nation is the key unit. See, for example, Uci, "Folk Culture," 11–13, where the author notes that it is in the context of Albanian "ethnicity" that the masses achieve "awareness of history and of common destiny." For examples of articles extolling the Great Han nation as a historic force of destiny, see Li Hongran, "Lu Xun," 75–82, and Wang Yongan, "The Bugle," 45–47. For several other examples of a view of the nation as persevering indefinitely, see chapter 10.

Bibliography

The following is a partial listing of sources cited in the text. Extensive use was made of several newspapers of several countries, one-country and worldwide summaries of the press (such as *Current Digest of the Soviet Press, German Press Review,* and *Keesing's Contemporary Archives*), a number of foreign periodicals (such as the *Peking Review* and *Yugoslav Survey*), and translation services (such as *Foreign Broadcast Information Service [FBIS], Summary of World Broadcasts, Radio Liberty Research,* and *Joint Publications Research Service [JPRS]*).

"L'Agitation en estonie." *L'Alternative,* January–February 1981.

Allworth, Edward, ed. *Nationality Group Survival in Multi-Ethnic States.* New York: Praeger, 1977.

————. *Soviet Nationality Problems.* New York: Columbia Univ. Press, 1971.

An Zhiguo. "Policy toward Dalai Lama." *JPRS* 82455, December 14, 1982.

Andropov, Yuriy. "Sixty Years of the USSR." *FBIS,* December 21, 1982.

"Appeal for Protection of the Serbian Population and Its Shrines in Kosovo." *JPRS* 81121, June 24, 1982.

Area Handbook for Czechoslovakia. Department of the Army Pamphlet 550-158. Washington, D.C.: GPO, 1975.

Area Handbook for Hungary. Department of the Army Pamphlet 550-165. Washington, D.C.: GPO, 1973.

Area Handbook for India. 3d ed. Department of the Army Pamphlet 550-21. Washington, D.C.: GPO, 1975.

Area Handbook for Mongolia. Department of the Army Pamphlet 550-76. Washington, D.C.: GPO, 1970.

Area Handbook for the People's Republic of China. Department of the Army Pamphlet 550-66. Washington, D.C.: GPO, 1972.

Area Handbook for Romania. Department of the Army Pamphlet 550-60. Washington, D.C.: GPO, 1972.

Area Handbook for the Soviet Union. Department of the Army Pamphlet 550-95. Washington, D.C.: GPO, 1971.

Area Handbook for Yugoslavia. Department of the Army Pamphlet 550-99. Washington, D.C.: GPO, 1973.

Armstrong, John. *Ideology, Politics and Government in the Soviet Union.* 3d ed. New York: Praeger, 1974.

Ascuncion-Lande, Nobleza. "Multilingualism, Politics and 'Filipinism.' " *Asian Survey* 11 (July 1971).

Autry, Phyllis. *Yugoslavia.* London: Thames and Hudson, 1965.

Avakumovic, Ivan. *History of the Communist Party of Yugoslavia.* Vol. 1. Aberdeen: Aberdeen Univ. Press, 1964.

Avineri, Shlomo. *Karl Marx on Colonialism and Modernization.* Garden City, N.Y.: Doubleday, 1969.

Azrael, Jeremy. *Emergent Nationality Problems in the USSR.* Santa Monica: Rand Corporation, 1977.

————, ed. *Soviet Nationality Policies and Practices.* New York: Praeger, 1978.

Bagramov, E. "The Soviet Nationalities Policy and Bourgeois Falsifications." *International Affairs* (Moscow), June 1978.

Baranva, L. "The International and the National in the Socialist Way of Life." *JPRS* 81362, July 26, 1982.

Baratashvili, D. "Lenin's Doctrine of the Self-Determination of Nations and National Liberation Struggle." *International Affairs* (Moscow), December 1970.

Barghoorn, Frederick. *Politics in the USSR.* Boston: Little, Brown, 1966.

————. *Soviet Russian Nationalism.* New York: Oxford Univ. Press, 1956.

Barker, Elisabeth. *Macedonia: Its Place in Balkan Power Politics.* London: Royal Institute of International Affairs, 1950.

"Basic Summarization of Experiences in the Promotion of Autonomy in National Minority Areas." In *Current Background,* no. 264, American Consulate General, Hong Kong. October 5, 1953.

Berlin, Isaiah. "The Bent Twig." *Foreign Affairs* 51 (October 1972).

Berner, Wolfgang et al., eds. *The Soviet Union 1975–76: Domestic Policy, Economics, Foreign Policy.* London: Hurst, 1977.

Bilinsky, Yaroslav. "Assimilation and Ethnic Assertiveness among Ukrainians in the Soviet Union." In *Ethnic Minorities in the Soviet Union.* Ed. Eric Goldhagen. New York: Praeger, 1968.

————. "The Communist Party of the Ukraine after 1966." Paper prepared for discussion at the McMaster Univ. Conference on the Contemporary Ukraine. Hamilton, Ontario, October 25–27, 1974.

————. "Education of Non-Russian Peoples in the USSR, 1917–1967: An Essay." *Slavic Review* 27 (September 1968).

————. "Mykola Skrypnyk and Petro Shelest: An Essay on the Persistence and Limits of Ukrainian National Communism." In *Soviet Nationality Policies and Practices.* Ed. Jeremy Azrael. New York: Praeger, 1978.

————. *The Second Soviet Republic: The Ukraine after World War II.* New Brunswick, N.J.: Rutgers Univ. Press, 1964.

Blackstock, P., and Hoselitz, B., eds. *The Russian Menace to Europe: A Collection of Articles, Speeches, Letters and News Dispatches by Karl Marx and Friedrich Engels.* Glencoe, Ill.: Free Press, 1952.

Blaustein, A., and Flanz, G., eds. *Constitutions of the Countries of the World.* Dobbs Ferry, N.Y.: Oceana Publications.

Bloom, Solomon. *The World of Nations: A Study of the National Implications in the Work of Karl Marx.* New York: Columbia Univ. Press, 1941.

Blumstock, Robert. "Hungary." In *Survey Research and Public Attitudes in Eastern Europe and the Soviet Union*. Ed. William Welsh. Elmsford, N.Y.: Pergamon, 1981.

"Bolshevizing the Communist International." Report of the Enlarged Executive of the Communist International, March 21st to April 14th, 1925. Published by the Communist Party of Great Britain, n.d.

Booth, David. "Cuba, Color, and the Revolution." *Science and Society* 40 (Summer 1976).

Bottomore, Tom, and Goode, Patrick. *Austro-Marxism*. Oxford: Clarendon, 1978.

Bradsher, Henry. "Tibet Struggles to Survive." *Foreign Affairs* 47 (July 1969).

Brandt, Conrad; Schwartz, Benjamin; and Fairbank, John. *A Documentary History of Chinese Communism*. London: Allen and Unwin, 1952.

Braunthal, J. *History of the International. Vol. I, 1864–1914*. New York: Praeger, 1967.

Bromley, Yu. V. *Soviet Ethnography: Main Trends*. Moscow: USSR Academy of Sciences, 1976.

————. *Soviet Ethnology and Anthropology Today*. The Hague: Mouton, 1974.

Bromley, Yu. V., and Kozlov, V. "Present-day Ethnic Processes in the Intellectual Culture of the Peoples of the USSR." In *Ethnocultural Processes and National Problems in the Modern World*. Ed. I. R. Grigulevich and V. Kozlov. Moscow: Progress Publishers, 1979.

Brown, Archie, and Gray, Jack, eds. *Political Culture and Political Change in Communist States*. London: Macmillan, 1977.

Brown, Archie, and Kaser, Michael, eds. *The Soviet Union Since the Fall of Khrushchev*. 2d ed. London: Macmillan, 1978.

Bruk, S. I. "The Post-War Dynamics and Structure of the World's Population." In *Ethnocultural Processes and National Problems in the Modern World*. Eds. I. R. Grigulevich and V. Kozlov. Moscow: Progress Publishers, 1979.

Bruk, S. I., and Guboglo, M. N. "The Converging Nations in the USSR and the Main Trends in the Development of Bilingualism." In *Ethnocultural Processes and National Problems in the Modern World*. Eds. I. R. Grigulevich and V. Kozlov. Moscow: Progress Publishers, 1979.

Brzezinski, Zbigniew. *The Permanent Purge*. Cambridge: Harvard Univ. Press, 1956.

Burks, R. V. *The Dynamics of Communism in Eastern Europe*. Princeton: Princeton Univ. Press, 1961.

————. *The National Problem and the Future of Yugoslavia*. Santa Monica, Calif.: Rand Corporation, 1971.

Caldwell, John D. "Revolution and Response: The Conflict in Northeast Thailand." Ph. D. diss., University of California, Santa Barbara, 1973.

Carlisle, Donald. "Uzbekistan and the Uzbeks." In *Handbook of Major Soviet Nationalities*. Ed. Zev Katz. New York: Free Press, 1975.

Carr, Edward. *The Bolshevik Revolution*. Vol. 1. Baltimore: Penguin Books, 1966.

Ceausescu, Ilie. "From Burebista's Centralized and Independent State to the Romanian Socialist State—Unity and Continuity." *JPRS* 82763, January 31, 1983.

Central Committee of Propaganda of the Viet Nam Lao Dong Party and the Committee for the Study of the Party's History. *Thirty Years of Struggle of the Party*. Book 1. Hanoi: Foreign Languages Publishing House, n.d.

Cerevka, Vladimir. "Development of Nationality Cultures in Slovakia." *JPRS* 82763, January 31, 1983.

Chang Chih-i. "A Discussion of the National Question in the Chinese Revolution and of Actual Nationalities Policy (Draft)." In *The Party and the National Question in China*. Trans. George Moseley. Peking: China Youth Publishing House, 1956. Cambridge: MIT Press, 1966.

Chen Ren. "Respect Minority Nationality Customs, Create a New Situation in Minority Nationality Trade." *JPRS* 82540, December 27, 1982.

Chen, Theodore, ed. *The Chinese Communist Regime: Documents and Commentary*. New York: Praeger, 1967.

Ch'en, Jerome. *Mao*. Englewood Cliffs, N. J.: Prentice-Hall, 1969.

———. *Mao and the Chinese Revolution*. New York: Oxford Univ. Press, 1967.

Chernenko, Konstantin. "Inviolable Union of Free Nations." *Soviet Union*, September 1982.

———. "60 Years of the Peoples' Fraternal Friendship." *Problemy Mira I Sotsializma*, December 1982.

Chiang Kai-shek. *China's Destiny and Chinese Economic Policy*. New York: Roy Publishers, 1947.

Chinn, Jeff. *Manipulating Soviet Population Resources*. New York: Holmes and Meier, 1977.

The Chornovil Papers. New York: McGraw-Hill, 1968.

Chou En-lai. "Some Questions on Policy Toward Nationalities." *Peking Review*, March 3, 1980.

Christman, Henry, ed. *Communism in Action: A Documentary History*. New York: Bantam Books, 1969.

———. *The Essential Tito*. Newton Abbot, U.K.: David and Charles, 1970.

Chu Van Tan. "Reminiscences on the Army for National Salvation." Data Paper Number 97. South East Asia Program. Ithaca, N.Y.: Cornell University Department of Asian Studies, 1974.

Clarkson, Jesse. *A History of Russia*. New York: Random House, 1961.

Clem, Ralph. "The Ethnic Dimension of the Soviet Union." In *Contemporary Soviet Society*. Eds. Jerry Pankhurst and Michael Sacks. New York: Praeger, 1980.

———. "Population Change and Nationality in the Soviet Union, 1926–1970." Ph.D. diss., Columbia University, 1975.

Clissold, Stephen. *Whirlwind: An Account of Marshall Tito's Rise to Power.* New York: Philosophical Library, 1949.

Cohen, Jerome A. "China's Changing Constitution." *China Quarterly* 75 (December 1978).

Cole, Allen. *Conflict in Indo-China and International Repercussions: A Documentary History.* Ithaca, N.Y.: Cornell Univ. Press, 1956.

The Communist Party of the Soviet Union. Moscow: Novosti Press Agency Publishing House, 1977.

Completely Purge Liu Shao-chi for his Counter-Revolutionary Revisionist Crimes in United Front, Nationalities and Religious Work. Pamphlet compiled by the "Red Army" Corps of the K'angta Commune of the Central Institute for Nationalities, April 1967. Translation appears in *Selections from China Mainland Magazines*, no. 645 (March 3, 1969), American Consulate General, Hong Kong.

Connor, Walker. "Ethnonationalism in the First World: The Present in Historical Perspective." In *Ethnic Pluralism and Conflict in the Western World.* Ed. Milton Esman. Ithaca, N.Y.: Cornell Univ. Press, 1977.

————. "Ethnology and the Peace of South Asia." *World Politics* 22 (October 1969).

————. "A Nation is a Nation, Is a State, Is an Ethnic Group, Is a. . . ." *Ethnic and Racial Studies* 2 (July 1980).

————. "Nation-Building or Nation-Destroying?" *World Politics* 24 (April 1972).

————. "The Politics of Ethnonationalism." *Journal of International Affairs* 27, no. 1 (1973).

————. "The Political Significance of Ethnonationalism within Western Europe." In *Ethnicity in an International Context.* Eds. Abdul Said and Luiz Simmons. Edison, N.J.: Transaction Books, 1976.

————. "An Overview of the Ethnic Composition and Problems of Non-Arab Asia." *Journal of Asian Affairs* 1 (Spring 1976).

————. "Self-Determination: The New Phase." *World Politics* 20 (October 1967).

Conquest, Robert. *The Great Terror: Stalin's Purge of the Thirties.* London: Macmillan, 1968.

————. *The Nation Killers: The Soviet Deportation of Nationalities.* London: Macmillan, 1960.

————. *Soviet Nationalities Policy in Practice.* New York: Praeger, 1967.

"Correctly Translate and Publish Minority Language Textbooks." *Nationalities Research* (Peking), June 1959.

Cummins, Ian. *Marx, Engels and National Movements.* New York: St. Martin's, 1980.

Dang Thai Mai. "The Vietnamese Language, an Eloquent Expression of our National Vitality." In *Vietnamese and Teaching Vietnamese in D.R.V.N. Universities.* Hanoi: Foreign Languages Publishing House, 1968.

Deal, David. "National Minority Policy in Southwest China, 1911–1965." Ph.D. diss., University of Washington, 1971.

Debray, Regis. "Marxism and the National Question." *New Left Review* 105 (September–October 1977).

Decter, Moshe. "Jewish National Consciousness in the Soviet Union." *Soviet Jewry*, 1971.

Degras, Jane, ed. *The Communist International 1919–1943: Documents*. 3 vols. London: Oxford Univ. Press, 1956–60.

Denitch, Bogdan D. *The Legitimation of a Revolution: The Yugoslav Case*. New Haven: Yale Univ. Press, 1976.

Deshdamirov, A. "The 26th CPSU Congress on Objectives in the Study of National Relations, International and National Processes on the USSR." *Azarbayjan Kommunisti*, July 1981.

Diao, Richard K. "Minorities and the Chinese Communist Regime." In *Southeast Asian Tribes, Minorities, and Nations*. Ed. Peter Kunstadter. Princeton: Princeton Univ. Press, 1967.

Djilas, Milovan. *Parts of a Lifetime*. New York: Harcourt Brace Jovanovich, 1975.

———. *Wartime*. New York: Harcourt Brace Jovanovich, 1977.

Dobson, Richard. "Georgia and the Georgians." In *Handbook of Major Soviet Nationalities*. Ed. Zev Katz. New York: Free Press, 1975.

Doder, Dusko. *The Yugoslavs*. New York: Random House, 1978.

Dominguez, J.; Rodley, N.; Wood, B.; and Falk, R. *Enhancing Global Human Rights*. New York: McGraw-Hill, 1979.

Drew, W. J. "Sinkiang: The Land and the People." *Central Asian Review* 16, no. 3 (1968).

Dreyer, June. "Chinese Communist Policy toward Indigenous Minority Nationalities: A Study in National Integration." Ph.D. diss., Harvard University, June 1972.

———. *China's Forty Millions*. Cambridge: Harvard Univ. Press, 1976.

———. "China's Minority Nationalities in the Cultural Revolution." *China Quarterly* 8 (July–September 1968).

Dyker, David. "Yugoslavia: Unity out of Diversity?" In *Political Culture and Political Change in Communist States*. Eds. Archie Brown and Jack Gray. London: Macmillan, 1977.

Dzhafarov, Imran Bayramovich. "The Transformation of Russian into the Second Language of the Peoples of the USSR." *JPRS* 82075, October 25, 1982.

Dzyuba, Ivan. *Internationalism or Russification?* New York: Pathfinder Press, 1968.

d'Encausse, Helene Carrere. *Decline of an Empire: The Soviet Socialist Republics in Revolt*. New York: Newsweek Books, 1979.

Enloe, Cynthia. *Ethnic Soldiers: State Security in Divided Societies*. Middlesex, Eng.: Penguin Books, 1980.

Ennis, Thomas. *French Policy and Developments in Indochina*. Chicago: Univ. of Chicago Press, 1936.

Evstigneev, Iu. A. "Ethnically Mixed Marriages in Makhachkala." *Soviet Sociology* 11 (Winter–Spring 1972–73).

Fall, Bernard. "The Pathet Lao." In *The Communist Revolution in Asia*. Ed. Robert Scalapino. Englewood Cliffs, N.J.: Prentice-Hall, 1965.

———. *The Viet-Minh Regime: Government and Administration in the Democratic Republic of Vietnam*. New York: Institute of Pacific Relations, 1956.

Farmer, Donald. "The Theory and Practice of Soviet Nationality Policy." Ph.D. diss., University of Michigan, 1954.

Fedoseyev, P. "60 Years of the USSR: A New Socialist and International Community." *Pravda*, April 9, 1982.

———. "The USSR: New Social and International Community." *Slovo Lektora*, June 1982.

Fejto, François. *A History of the People's Democracy: Eastern Europe Since Stalin*. New York: Praeger, 1971.

———. *Les Juifs et l'antisémitisme dans les pays communiste*. Paris: Libraire Plan, 1960.

Fisher-Galati, Stephen. "Moldavia and the Moldavians." In *Handbook of Major Soviet Nationalities*. Ed. Zev Katz. New York: Free Press, 1975.

"For All-Round Development of Bulgaro-Yugoslav Relations." In *Declaration of the Ministry of Foreign Affairs of the People's Republic of Bulgaria*. Sofia: July 24, 1978.

Franklin, Bruce, ed. *The Essential Stalin: Major Theoretical Writings, 1905–1952*. Garden City, N.Y.: Doubleday, 1972.

Freemantle, Anne, ed. *Mao Tse-tung: An Anthology of His Writings*. New York: New American Library, Mentor Books, 1962.

Frey, Cynthia. "Yugoslav Nationalisms and the Doctrine of Limited Sovereignty." Unpublished paper, April 1973.

Galabardi, Zoltan. "Identity." *JPRS* 81186, July 1, 1982.

Galovic, Spiro. "The Interest of the Working Class and the Interest of the Nationality." *JPRS* 82961, February 28, 1983.

Giang, Nguyen K. *Le Grandes dates du parti de la classe ouvrière du Vietnam*. Hanoi: n.p., 1960.

Gilberg, Trond. "Modernization, Human Rights, Nationalism: The Case of Romania." In *The Politics of Ethnicity in Eastern Europe*. Eds. George Klein and Milan Reban. Boulder: East European Monographs, 1981 (distributed by Columbia Univ. Press).

Gililov, S. "The Worldwide Significance of the Soviet Experience in Solving the Nationalities Question." *International Affairs* (Moscow), July 1972.

Goldhagen, Eric. *Ethnic Minorities in the Soviet Union*. New York: Praeger, 1968.

Gouvernement Générale des Affaires Politiques et de la Sûreté Générale, Contributions à L'Histoire des Mouvements Politiques de l'Indochine Française. *Documents*, vol. 4 (1933).

Grigulevich, I. R. and Kozlov, V., eds. *Ethnocultural Processes and National Problems in the Modern World.* Moscow: Progress Publishers, 1979.

Groshev, I. *A Fraternal Family of Nations.* Moscow: Progress Publishers, 1967.

Hall, Paul. "Language Contact in the USSR: Some Prospects for Language Maintenance among Soviet Minority Language Groups." Ph.D. diss., Georgetown University, 1974.

Hammer, Ellen. *The Struggle for Indochina.* Stanford: Stanford Univ. Press, 1954.

Harned, Frederick. "Latvia and the Latvians." In *Handbook of Major Soviet Nationalities.* Ed. Zev Katz. New York: Free Press, 1975.

————. "Lithuania and the Lithuanians." In *Handbook of Major Soviet Nationalities.* Ed. Zev Katz. New York: Free Press, 1975.

Harrison, Selig. *In Afghanistan's Shadow: Baluch Nationalism and Soviet Temptations.* Washington, D.C.: Carnegie Endowment for World Peace, 1981.

Herold, J. Christopher. *The Mind of Napoleon: A Selection from His Writings and Spoken Words.* New York: Columbia Univ. Press, 1955.

Hetmanek, Allen. "Kirgizistan and the Kirgiz." In *Handbook of Major Soviet Nationalities.* Ed. Zev Katz. New York: Free Press, 1975.

Hirata, Lucie. "Leadership in China's Minority Nationalities Autonomous Regions." Paper presented at the Conference on Minority Relations in Asian Countries, SUNY, Buffalo, October 20—22, 1972.

Ho Chi Minh. *On Revolution: Selected Writings 1920–1966.* Ed. Bernard Fall. New York: New American Library, 1967.

Hoang Van Chi. *From Colonialism to Communism.* New York: Praeger, 1964.

Hoang Van Hoan. "Selected Works of Ho Chi Minh and Renegade Le Duan." *JPRS* 82422, December 8, 1982.

Hodnett, Grey. "What's in a Nation?" *Problems of Communism* 16 (September–October 1967).

Hodnett, Grey, and Potichnyj, Peter. *The Ukraine and the Czechoslovak Crisis.* Canberra: Australian National University, 1970.

Hoffman, George, and Neal, Fred. *Yugoslavia and the New Communism.* New York: Twentieth Century Fund, 1962.

Howard, Peter. "The Definition of a Nation: A Discussion in 'Voprosy Istorii.' " *Central Asian Review* 15, no. 1 (1967).

Hu, C. T. *The Education of National Minorities in Communist China.* Washington, D.C.: GPO, 1970.

Hung-mao Tien. "Sinicization of National Minorities in China." Paper prepared for the 1973 Annual Meeting of the American Political Science Association, New Orleans, September 1973.

Hyer, Paul, and Heaton, William. "The Cultural Revolution in Inner Mongolia." *China Quarterly* 36 (October–December 1968).

"Implement Further the Policy of Autonomy for the National Minorities Areas." *People's Daily,* September 9, 1953.

"Improve Education of Minorities." *Nationalities Research* (Min-tsu Yen-chui). Peking: n.p., June 1959.

Jackson, George. "The Green International and the Red Peasant International." Ph.D. diss., Columbia University, 1961.

Janos, Andrew. "Ethnicity, Communism, and Political Change in Eastern Europe." *World Politics* 23 (April 1971).

Jelinek, Yeshayahu. "Between Nationalism and Communism: The 'Slovak Question.' " *Canadian Review of Studies in Nationalism* 2 (Spring 1975).

Jing Wei. "Tibet: An Inside View (II): More Tibetans Assume Leadership." *Peking Review* 48 (November 29, 1982).

Johnson, A. Ross. *The Role of the Military in Communist Yugoslavia: An Historical Sketch.* Santa Monica, Calif.: Rand Corporation, 1978.

Joiner, Charles. "Administration and Political Warfare in the Highlands." *Vietnam Perspectives* 1 (November 1955).

Joncic, Koca. *The Relations between Nationalities in Yugoslavia.* Belgrade: Medunarodna Stampa—Interpress, 1967.

Jones, Ellen. "Minorities in the Soviet Armed Forces." *Comparative Strategy* 3, no. 4 (1982).

Kahin, George McT. "Minorities in the Democratic Republic of Vietnam." *Asian Survey* 12 (July 1972).

Kalinayev, A. "A Union of Free and Equal. Material for Political Classes on the Subject, 'The Friendship and Brotherhood for the Peoples of the USSR—the Source of Might of the Soviet Union and its Armed Forces. The Constitution of the USSR on the Comprehensive Development and Rapprochement of the Nations and Nationality of the USSR.' " *JPRS* 73487, March 4, 1979.

Kardelj, Edvard. *The Development of the Slovenian National Question.* 2d ed. Belgrade: Kulture, 1958.

Karklins, Rasma. "Interrelationship of Soviet Foreign and Nationality Policies: The Case of the Foreign Minorities of the USSR." Ph.D. diss., University of Chicago, 1975.

Karklins, Rasma Silde. "The Uighurs between China and the USSR." *Canadian Slavonic Papers* 16 (Summer and Fall 1975).

Katz, Zev. "Jews in the Soviet Union." In *Handbook of Major Soviet Nationalities.* Ed. Zev Katz. New York: Free Press, 1975.

————, ed. *Handbook of Major Soviet Nationalities.* New York: Free Press, 1975.

Kazlas, Juozas. "Social Distance Among Ethnic Groups." In *Nationality Group Survival in Multi-Ethnic States.* Ed. Edward Allworth. New York: Praeger, 1977.

————. "Varieties of Nationalism and Internationalism." Paper prepared for delivery at the International Political Science Association Congress, Moscow, August 12–18, 1979.

Keningshteyn, M. I. "Regulation of the Processes of Population Migration." *JPRS* 79937, January 25, 1982.

Kernig, C. D., ed. *Marxism, Communism and Western Society: A Comparative Encyclopedia*. New York: McGraw-Hill, 1973.

Khalmukhamedov, M. "Soviet Society: Complete Equality of Nations." *International Affairs* (Moscow), March 1978.

Kholmogorov, A. I. *International Traits of Soviet Nations*. Moscow: Mysl' Publishing House, 1970. Translated and published in English in three issues of *Soviet Sociology* 12 (1973).

Khrushchev, Nikita. *Khrushchev Remembers*. Boston: Little, Brown, 1970.

Kipnis, Mark. "The Georgian National Movement: Problems and Trends." *Crossroads*, Autumn 1978.

King, Robert. *Minorities under Communism*. Cambridge: Harvard Univ. Press, 1973.

Klatt, Werner, ed. *The Chinese Model*. Hong Kong: Hong Kong Univ. Press, 1965.

Klein, George, and Klein, Patricia. "Nationalism vs. Ideology: The Pivot of Yugoslav Politics." In *The Politics of Ethnicity in Eastern Europe*. Eds. George Klein and Milan Reban. Boulder: East European Monographs, 1981 (distributed by Columbia Univ. Press).

Kosing, Alfred. *Nation in History and at the Present Time*. Berlin: 1976.

Kosing, Alfred, and Schmidt, Walter. "Concerning the Development of the Socialist Nation in the German Democratic Republic." *Einheit*, no. 2 (1944).

————. "Nation and Nationality in the DDR." Neues Deutschland, February 15, 1975.

Kosolapov, Richard Ivanovich. "Class and National Relations at the Stage of Mature Socialism." *JPRS* 82853, February 11, 1983.

Kövari, Attila. "Accident and Necessity in Romanian Nationalism." *Crossroads*, Autumn 1978.

Kowalewski, D. "Protest Demonstrations in the Brezhnev Era." Paper prepared for the 1980 Annual Meeting of the American Association for the Advancement of Slavic Studies, Philadelphia.

Kozlov, V. "On the Concept of Ethnic Community." In *Soviet Ethnology and Anthropology Today*. Ed. Yu. V. Bromley. The Hague: Mouton, 1974.

Kristian, A. A. *The Right to Self-Determination and the Soviet Union*. London: Boreas, 1952.

Kristof, Ladis. "The State Idea, the National Idea and the Image of the Fatherland." *Orbis* 11 (Spring 1967).

Kunstadter, Peter, ed. *Southeast Asian Tribes, Minorities, and Nations*. Princeton: Princeton Univ. Press, 1967.

Laco, Karl. "The Czechoslovak Federation—A Form of the Leninist Solution of the Nationalities Problem." *Tvorba*, October 25, 1977.

Lal, Amrit. "Sinification of Ethnic Minorities in China." *Current Scene* 8, no. 4 (1970).

Lancranjan, Ion. *The Story of Transylvania*. Bucharest: Sport-Tourism, 1982.

Lebedinskaya, L. "The Nationality Question and the Formation of the Soviet States." *International Affairs* (Moscow), December 1972.

Lendvai, Paul. *National Tensions in Yugoslavia*. Conflict Studies No. 25 (August 1972).

Lenin, V. I. *Collected Works*. Moscow: Progress Publishers, 1966.

———. *The Right of Nations to Self-Determination: Selected Writings*. New York: International Publishers, 1951.

———. *Selected Works*. 3 vols. Moscow: Progress Publishers, 1975.

Lewis, John. *Leadership in Communist China*. Ithaca, N.Y.: Cornell Univ. Press, 1963.

———. *Major Doctrines of Communist China*. New York: Norton, 1964.

Lewis, Robert. "The Mixing of Russians and Soviet Nationalities and Its Demographic Impact." In *Soviet Nationality Problems*. Ed. Edward Allworth. New York: Columbia Univ. Press, 1971.

———. "Population Redistribution in Russia and the USSR and Its Impact on Society: 1897–1970." Paper presented at the Woodrow Wilson International Center for Scholars, Washington, D.C., August 1977.

Lewis, Robert; Rowland, Richard; and Clem, Ralph. *Nationality and Population Change in Russia and the USSR*. New York: Praeger, 1976.

Li Hongran. "Lu Xun on Patriotic Historical Figures." *JPRS* 83151, March 28, 1983.

Li Wei-han. "Report Made at the Enlarged Meeting of the Second Session of the Commission of Nationalities Affairs." In *Policies towards Nationalities of the People's Republic of China*. Peking: Foreign Languages Press, 1953.

Litvinova, Galina I., and Urlanis, B. "The Soviet Union's Demographic Policy." *Sovetskoye Gosudarstvo I Pravo*, March 1982.

Liu Ch'un. *The National Question and Class Struggle*. Peking: Foreign Languages Press, 1966.

Liu Shao-ch'i. *Internationalism and Nationalism*. Peking: Foreign Languages Press, n.d.

———. *Collected Works of Liu Shao-ch'i before 1944*. Hong Kong: Union Research Institute, 1969.

———. *Collected Works of Liu Shao-ch'i, 1945–1957*. Hong Kong: Union Research Institute, 1969.

Low, Alfred. *Lenin on the Question of Nationality*. New York: Bookman Associates, 1950.

Lubachko, Ivan. *Belorussia under Soviet Rule, 1919–1957*. Lexington: Univ. Press of Kentucky, 1972.

Lubin, Nancy. "Ethnic/Political Implications of Labor Use in Soviet Central Asia." Paper prepared for the Office of External Research (INR), U.S. Department of State, December 1981.

———. "The Nationality Question as a Threat to Political Stability in the USSR." Unpublished seminar paper, Oxford University, 1978.

Lubrano, Linda; Fisher, Wesley; Schwartz, Janet; and Tomlinson, Kate.

"The Soviet Union." In *Survey Research and Public Attitudes in Eastern Europe and the Soviet Union.* Ed. William Welsh. New York: Pergamon, 1981.

Ludz, Peter. "The SED's Concept of Nation. Deviations and Political Meanings." *Canadian Review of Studies in Nationalism* 4 (Spring 1977).

McAlister, John T. "Mountain Minorities and the Viet Minh: A Key to the Indochina War." In *Southeast Asian Tribes, Minorities, and Nations.* Ed. Peter Kunstadter. Princeton: Princeton Univ. Press, 1967.

———. "The Possibilities for Diplomacy in Southeast Asia." *World Politics* 19 (January 1967).

Maclean, Fitzroy. *Disputed Barricade: The Life and Times of Josip Broz-Tito.* London: Jonathan Cope, 1957.

Mao Tse-tung. *Collected Works of Mao Tse-tung (1917–1949).* Hong Kong: 1975. Translated by *JPRS*, 1978.

———. *Selected Works of Mao Tse-tung.* 4 vols. New York: International Publishers, 1954.

———. *Selected Works of Mao Tse-tung.* 5 vols. Peking: Foreign Languages Press, 1975.

———. *Statement Calling on the People of the World to Unite and to Oppose Racial Discrimination by U.S. Imperialism and Support the American Negroes in their Struggle Against Racial Discrimination.* Peking: Foreign Languages Press, 1964.

Markinovic, Gojko. "Again the Same Isms." *JPRS* 83103, March 21, 1983.

Marx, Karl, and Engels, Frederick. *Collected Works.* New York: International Publishers, 1975.

———. *Ireland and the Irish Question.* New York: International Publishers, 1972.

———. *Selected Works.* 3 vols. Moscow: Progress Publishers, 1969–70.

Matossian, Mary. "Armenia and the Armenians." In *Handbook of Major Soviet Nationalities.* Ed. Zev Katz. New York: Free Press, 1975.

Medvedev, Roy. *Let History Judge: The Origins and Consequences of Stalinism.* New York: Alfred Knopf, 1972.

———. *On Socialist Democracy.* New York: W. W. Norton, 1975.

Mehring, F. *Karl Marx: The Story of His Life.* Ann Arbor: Univ. of Michigan Press, 1962.

Miller, John. "Cadre Policy in Naitonality Areas: Recruitment of CPSU First and Second Secretaries in Non-Russian Republics of the USSR." *Soviet Studies* 29 (January 1977).

Mittelman, E. N. "The Nationality Problem in Yugoslavia." Ph.D. diss., New York University, 1954.

Modrzhinskaya, Ye. "The Triumph of Proletarian Internationalism and the Maneuvers of Anticommunists." *Krasnaya Zvezda* (Moscow), June 2, 1972.

Moroz, Valentyn. "The New Processes are Only Beginning." In *Samizdat:*

Voices of Soviet Opposition. Ed. George Saunders. New York: Monad Press, 1974.

————. *Report from the Beria Reserve.* Chicago: Cataract Press, 1974.

Moseley, George. *The Consolidation of the South China Frontier.* Berkeley: Univ. of California Press, 1973.

Moskin, S. E. "The 24th CPSU Congress on Intensifying the Struggle Against Nationalism and Revisionism." *JPRS* 56593, July 24, 1972.

Nagornaya, L. "National Relations in the Society of Mature Socialism." *Pravda Ukrainy*, November 15, 1981.

"The National Minorities of Western China." *Central Asian Review* 15, no. 3 (1967).

Newth, J. A. "Demographic Developments." In *The Soviet Union since the Fall of Khrushchev.* Eds. Archie Brown and Michael Kaser. 2d ed. London: Macmillan, 1978.

————. "The 1970 Soviet Census." *Soviet Studies* 24 (October 1972).

Nguyuen Khak Vien, ed. *Mountain Regions and National Minorities in the Democratic Republic of Vietnam.* Vietnamese Studies No. 15. Hanoi: Foreign Languages Publishing House, 1968.

Nguyen Van Huyen. "The Vietnamese Language, A Sharp Weapon to Build Up a National Democratic and Socialist Education." In *Vietnamese and Teaching in Vietnamese in D.R.V.N. Universities.* Hanoi: Foreign Languages Publishing House, 1968.

Nichols, James. "Minority Nationality Cadres in Communist China." Ph.D. diss., Stanford University, 1968.

Nogee, Joseph. *Man, State, and Society in the Soviet Union.* New York: Praeger, 1972.

Orleans, Leo. *Every Fifth Child: The Population of China.* London: Eyre Methuen, 1972.

Oschlies, Rolf. "Bleak Prospects for the Sorbs." *JPRS* 81546, August 4, 1982.

Osofsky, Stephen. "Soviet Criticism of China's National Minorities Policy." *Asian Survey* 14 (October 1974).

Pankhurst, Jerry, and Sacks, Michael, eds. *Contemporary Soviet Society.* New York: Praeger, 1980.

Parming, Tönu. "Roots of Nationality Differences." In *Nationality Group Survival in Multi-Ethnic States.* Ed. Edward Allworth. New York: Praeger, 1977.

Patterson, George. "Treatment of Minorities." In *The Chinese Model.* Ed. Werner Klatt. Hong Kong: Hong Kong Univ. Press, 1965.

Pavlowich, Stevan. *Yugoslavia.* London: Ernest Benn Limited, 1971.

People's Handbook. Peking: Ta-kung Pao She, 1965.

Perevedentsev, V. I. "History and Demography: On the Influence of Ethnic Factors on Geographical Population Shifts." Published in English translation. *Soviet Anthropology and Archaeology* 6 (Fall 1967).

Pipes, Richard. *The Formation of the Soviet Union*. Rev. ed. New York: Atheneum, 1968.

———. " 'Solving' the Nationality Problem." *Problems of Communism*, September–October 1967.

Plynshch, Leonid. *History's Carnival*. New York: Harcourt Brace Jovanovich, 1977.

Policies toward Nationalities of the People's Republic of China. Peking: Foreign Languages Press, 1953.

Polyakov, N. "Unmasking Mao Tse-tung's Anti-Leninist Policies." *JPRS* 48016.

Pool, Jonathan. "Soviet Language Planning: Goals, Results, Options." In *Soviet Nationality Policies and Practices*. Ed. Jeremy Azrael. New York: Praeger, 1978.

Pospielovsky, Dimitry. "The Resurgence of Nationalism in Samizdat." *Survey*, no. 1 (1973).

Possony, Stefan. "Communism and the National Question: Some Recent Developments." *Plural Societies* 6 (Autumn 1975).

Programme of the League of Yugoslav Communists. Belgrade: Edition Jugoslavija, 1958.

Programme of the Romanian Communist Party for the Building of the Multilaterally Developed Socialist Society and Romania's Advance toward Communism. Bucharest: Meridiane Publishing House, 1975.

Rakhimov, T. *Nationalizm Shovinizm—osnova politika gruppy Mao-Tze-Dun*. Moscow: Mysl' Publishing House, 1968.

Rakowska-Harmstone, Teresa. "The Dialectics of Nationalism in the USSR." *Problems of Communism*, May–June 1974.

———. *Russia and Nationalism in Central Asia: The Case of Tadzhikistan*. Baltimore: Johns Hopkins Univ. Press, 1970.

———. "The Study of Ethnic Politics in the USSR." Paper prepared for the national symposium, "The National Problem in the USSR and Eastern Europe under Brezhnev and Kosygin." University of Detroit, October 3–4, 1975.

Renner, H. "The National Minorities in Czechoslovakia after the Second World War." *Plural Societies* 7 (Spring 1976).

Reshidov, Sh. "The Language of Our Unity and Fraternity." *JPRS* 73548, May 25, 1979.

Rigby, T. H. *Communist Party Membership in the USSR*. Princeton: Princeton Univ. Press, 1968.

Rockett, R. L. *Ethnic Nationalities in the Soviet Union*. New York: Praeger, 1981.

Romania: Documents—Events. Bucharest: Agerpress, March 1975.

Rosdolsky, R. "Worker and Fatherland: A Note on a Passage in the Communist Manifesto." *Science and Society* 29, no. 3 (Summer 1965).

Roucek, Joseph. "Racial Elements in the Sino-Russian Dispute." *Contemporary Review* 210 (February 1967).

Rusinow, Dennison. *The Yugoslav Experiment, 1948–1974*. London: C. Hurst, 1977.

Rybakovskiy, Leonid. "On the Migration of the Population in the USSR." *JPRS* 79937, January 25, 1982.

Sabine, George. *History of Political Thought*. 4th ed. New York: Holt, Rinehart and Winston, 1973.

Said, Abdul, and Simmons, Luiz, eds. *Ethnicity in an International Context*. New Brunswick, N.J.: Transaction Books, 1976.

Salov, V. "Soviet Nationality Policy and the Bourgeois Falsifiers." *International Affairs* (Moscow), August 1972.

Saunders, George. "Against Russification." In *Samizdat: Voices of the Soviet Opposition*. Ed. George Saunders. New York: Monad Press, 1974.

———, ed. *Samizdat: Voices of the Soviet Opposition*. New York: Monad Press, 1974.

Scalapino, Robert. "The CCP's Provincial Secretaries." *Problems of Communism*, July–August 1976.

———. *The Communist Revolution in Asia*. 2d ed. Englewood Cliffs, N.J.: Prentice-Hall, 1969.

Schapiro, Leonard. "Keynote-Compromise." In *Man, State, and Society in the Soviet Union*. Ed. Joseph L. Nogee. New York: Praeger, 1972.

———, ed. *The U.S.S.R. and the Future*. New York: Praeger, 1963.

Schmid, Carol. *Conflict and Consensus in Switzerland*. Berkeley: Univ. of California Press, 1981.

Schöpflin, George. *The Hungarians of Rumania*. London: Minority Rights Group, 1978.

———. "The Ideology of Croatian Nationalism." *Survey* 19 (Winter 1973).

———. "The National Question in Yugoslavia." *Soviet Analyst* (London), Janury 29, 1978.

Schram, Stuart. *The Political Thought of Mao Tse-tung*. Rev. ed. New York: Praeger, 1969.

———, ed. *Chairman Mao Talks to the People: Talks and Letters: 1956–1971*. New York: Pantheon Books, 1974.

———. *Mao Tse-tung*. Baltimore: Penguin Books, 1968.

Schwartz, Henry. "Communist Language Policies for China's Ethnic Minorities: The First Decade." *China Quarterly* 12 (October–November 1962).

Sedmak, Marjan. "Coolness between Moscow and Bucharest." *JPRS* 82758, January 28, 1983.

Seitz, Paul. *Men of Dignity: The Montagnards of South Vietnam*. N.P.: Jacques Barthelemy, 1975.

Shabad, Theodore. *China's Changing Map*. Rev. ed. New York: Praeger, 1972.

Shaheen, S. *The Communist Theory of Self-Determination*. The Hague: W. Van Hoeve, Ltd., 1956.

Sheehy, Ann. "Uzbek Novel Found Ideologically Unsound." RL/337/82, Radio Liberty Research, August 20, 1982.

———. "Recent Events in Abkhazia Mirror the Complexities of National Relations in the USSR." RL/141/78, Radio Liberty Research, June 26, 1978.

Shister, G. A. "Sources for the Replenishment of Uzbekistan's Working Class during the State of Developed Socialism." *Istoriya SSSR*, November–December 1981.

Shoup, Paul. *Communism and the Yugoslav National Question*. New York: Columbia Univ. Press, 1968.

Shub, David. *Lenin: A Biography*. Baltimore: Penguin Books, 1967.

Shyrock, Richard. "Indigenous Economic Managers." In *National Group Survival in Multi-Ethnic States*. Ed. Edward Allworth. New York: Praeger, 1977.

Silver, Brian. "Inventory of Propositions Drawn from Soviet Empirical Studies on the Attitudes of Soviet Nationalities." Paper prepared for the AAASS Nationalities Project Workshop, Banff, Canada, September 1974.

———. "Language Policy and the Linguistic Russification of Soviet Nationalities." Paper prepared for the Conference on Population Change and the Soviet Nationality Question, Columbia Univ., December 5–6, 1975.

"Sinkiang Nationality Unity Gathering Reported." *JPRS* 82440, December 10, 1982.

Skilling, H. Gordon. *Czechoslovakia's Interrupted Revolution*. Princeton: Princeton Univ. Press, 1976.

Snow, Edgar. *Red Star Over China*. New York: Grove Press, 1961.

Solzhenitsyn, Aleksandr. *East and West*. New York: Harper and Row, 1980.

Spechler, Dina. "Russia and the Russians." In *Handbook of Major Soviet Nationalities*. Ed. Zev Katz. New York: Free Press, 1975.

Stalin, Joseph. *Marxism and Linguistics*. New York: International Publishers, n.d.

———. *Marxism and the National Question*. Moscow: Foreign Languages Publishing House, 1950.

———. *Marxism and the National Question: Selected Writings and Speeches*. New York: International Publishers, 1942.

———. *Marxism and the National and Colonial Questions*. New York: International Publishers, 1935.

———. *Works*. Moscow: Foreign Languages Publishing House, 1952–54.

Stanojenic, Tihomir, and Markovic, D. *Tito: His Life and Work*. Zagreb: Stuarnost, 1963.

Steiner, Eugen. *The Slovak Dilemma*. Cambridge: Cambridge Univ. Press, 1973.

Stekloff, G. *History of the First International*. New York: Russell and Russell, 1968.

Stoicescu, N. "The Keen Awareness that Dominates the Romanians' History." *JPRS* 82447, December 13, 1982.

Stone, Gerald. *The Smallest Slavonic Nation: The Sorbs of Lusatia.* London: Athlone Press, 1972.

"Stress the Key of Unity Among Nationalities; Develop the Excellent Situation in Xinjiang—Comrade Wang Enmas Answers Our Reporters' Questions." *JPRS* 83099, March 18, 1983.

"Stronghold of Bulgarian Spirit—Samuil's Fortress Memorial Complex at Foot of Belasitsa Officially Opened." *JPRS* 82464, December 14, 1982.

Sullivant, Robert. *Soviet Politics and the Ukraine 1917–1934.* New York: Columbia Univ. Press, 1962.

Sushanlo, M. Ya.; Gurevich, V. T.; Ploshkikh, V. N.; and Suprunenko, G. P. *Against Maoist Falsifications of the History of Kirghiziya.* Frunze, Kirgizistan: 1981.

Suskolov, A. A. "The 26th CPSU Congress and Tasks in the Study of Nationalities Relations in the USSR." *Sovetskaya Etnografiya*, March–April 1982.

Šuvar, Stipe. "The Relationship between the Class and the National: Some General Remarks and Reflections Concerning the Yugoslav Situation." Paper presented at the Round Table on Class and Ethnicity of the International Political Science Association, Dubrovnik, Yugoslavia, September 9–12, 1975.

Szaraz, Gyorgy. "On a Curious Book." *JPRS* 82763, January 31, 1983.

Szporluk, Roman. "Nationalities and the Russian Problem in the USSR: An Historical Outline." *Journal of International Affairs* 27, no. 1 (1973).

———. "The Nations of the USSR in 1970." *Survey* 17, no. 4 (1971).

———. "The Ukraine and the Ukrainians." In *Handbook of Major Soviet Nationalities.* Ed. Zev Katz. New York: Free Press, 1975.

Taagepera, Rein. "Estonia and the Estonians." In *Handbook of Major Soviet Nationalities.* Ed. Zev. Katz. New York: Free Press, 1975.

Terentieva, L. N. "Ethnocultural Changes among the Peoples of the Volga, Urals, and Far North of Europe." In *Ethnocultural Processes and National Problems in the Modern World.* Eds. I. R. Grigulevich and V. Kozlov. Moscow: Progress Publishers, 1979.

———. "Ethnic Self-Identification by Adolescents in Ethnically Mixed Families." *Soviet Sociology* 12 (Summer 1973).

Thanh Tin. "Central Highlands: The Security Front." *FBIS*, October 29, 1982.

Tillet, Lowell. "Nationalism and History." *Problems of Communism*, October 1967.

Tito, Josip Broz. "The National Question in the Light of the People's Liberation War." In *Govori I Clanci.* Zagreb: Naprijed, 1959.

———. "Political Report of the Central Committee of the Communist Party of Yugoslavia." Report delivered at the Fifth Congress of the CPY. Belgrade: n.p., 1948.

Tito, Josip Broz. *Selected Speeches and Articles, 1941–1961*. Zagreb: Naprijed, 1963.

————. *Selected Works on the People's War of Liberation*. Bombay: Somaiya Publications Pvt. Ltd., 1969.

————. *Tito Speaks*. London: The United Slav Committee, 1944.

Toma, Peter. "The Czechoslovak Question under Communism." *East European Quarterly* 3 (March 1969).

Tomasic, Dinko. *National Communism and Soviet Strategy*. Washington, D.C.: Public Affairs Press, 1957.

Triska, Jan, ed. *Constitutions of the Communist Party States*. Stanford: Hoover Institution Press, 1968.

Truong Chinh. *Primer for Revolt*. New York: Praeger, 1963.

Tucker, Robert C., ed. *The Marx-Engels Reader*. New York: W. W. Norton, 1972.

————. *The Soviet Political Mind*. Rev. ed. New York: W. W. Norton, 1971.

Tudjman, Franjo. *Nationalism in Contemporary Europe*. Boulder: East European Monographs, 1981 (distributed by Columbia Univ. Press).

Tung, William. *The Political Institutions of Modern China*. The Hague: Martinus Nyhoff, 1964.

Turley, William. "Vietnam Since Reunification." *Problems of Communism*, March–April 1977.

Turner, Robert. *Vietnamese Communism: Its Origins and Development*. Stanford: Hoover Institution Press, 1975.

Uci, Alfred. "Folk Culture and Its Ethnic Functions." *JPRS* 83125, March 28, 1983.

Ulc, Otto. *Politics in Czechoslovakia*. San Francisco: W. H. Freeman, 1974.

U.S. Department of the Army. *Minority Groups in North Vietnam*. DA Pamphlet 550-110, Ethnographic Study Series. Washington, D.C.: GPO, 1972.

U.S. Department of State. "Soviets Debate Manpower and Demographic Policies." Bureau of Intelligence and Research Report No. 1117, January 24, 1979.

————. "Macedonian Nationalism and the Communist Party of Yugoslavia." Unpublished mimeographed text. October 11, 1954.

————. "Political Alignments of Vietnamese Nationalists." Office of Intelligence Research Report No. 3708, October 1, 1949.

U.S. Senate Committee on Foreign Relations. *Background Information Relating to Southeast Asia and Vietnam*. 3d rev. ed. Washington, D.C.: GPO, 1967.

U.S. Senate Committee on the Judiciary. *Yugoslav Communism: A Critical Survey*. Washington, D.C.: GPO, 1961.

"Vers le renforcement du parti communiste indochinois." *Cahiers du Bolchevisme*, July 1, 1934.

Vietnamese and Teaching in Vietnamese in D.R.V.N. Universities. Hanoi: Foreign Languages Publishing House, 1968.

Volgyes, Ivan. "Political Socialization in Eastern Europe." *Problems of Communism*, January–February, 1974.

———. "Legitimacy and Modernization: Nationality and Nationalism in Hungary and Transylvania." In *The Politics of Ethnicity in Eastern Europe*. Eds. George Klein and Milan Reban. Boulder: East European Monographs, 1981 (distributed by Columbia Univ. Press).

Voropayev, A. "According to the Formulas of the Emperors, Great-Han Chauvinism in Action." *FBIS*, March 31, 1972.

Voss, A. E. "The Development of National Relations under Conditions of Mature Socialism." *JPRS* 81498, August 10, 1982.

———. "Topical Questions of Further Strengthening of Patriotic and International Education of Workers." *JPRS* 81498, August 10, 1982.

Vucinich, Wayne. "Nationalism and Communism." In *Comtemporary Yugoslavia*. Ed. Wayne Vucinich. Berkeley: Univ. of California Press, 1969.

Wales, Nym. *Red Dust: Autobiographies of Chinese Communists as Told to Nym Wales*. Stanford: Stanford Univ. Press, 1952.

Wang, Yongan. "The Bugle Call for Revolutionary Struggle." *JPRS* 82540, December 27, 1982.

Warner, Dennis. *The Last Confucian*. New York: Macmillan, 1963.

Williams, Suzanne. "The Communist Party in Yugoslavia and the Nationality Problem, 1922–1925." Master's thesis, Columbia University, 1955.

Wimbush, S. E., and Alexiev, A. *The Ethnic Factor in the Soviet Armed Forces*. Santa Monica: Rand Corporation, May 1980.

Wolfe, Bertram. *Khrushchev and Stalin's Ghost*. London: Atlantic Press, 1957.

———. *Marxism: One Hundred Years in the Life of a Doctrine*. New York: Dell Publishing, 1965.

———. *Three Who Made a Revolution*. Rev. ed. New York: Dell Publishing, 1968.

"Xinjiang Nationality Unity Gathering Reported." *JPRS* 82440, December 10, 1982.

"Yunan Racial Cadres Give Up Amidst Popular Movement." *Nationalities Solidarity* (Peking), June 1959.

Zagladin, V. V., ed. *The Revolutionary Movement of Our Time and Nationalism*. Moscow: Progress Publishers, 1975.

Zaninovich, M. G., and Brown, D. "Political Integration in Czechoslovakia: The Implications of the Prague Spring and Soviet Intervention." *Journal of International Affairs* 27, no. 1 (1973).

Zharnikov, A. Ye. "National and International and Dialectics of Their Interrelationship." *JPRS* 80851, May 19, 1982.

Zhdanko, T. A. "National State Demarcation and the Ethnic Evolution of the Peoples of Central Asia." In *Ethnocultural Processes and National Problems in the Modern World*. Eds. I. R. Grigulevich and V. Kozlov. Moscow: Progress Publishers, 1979.

Zhornitskaya, M. Ya. "The Reflections of Ethnocultural Links in Present-day Dance in the USSR." In *Ethnocultural Processes and National Problems in the Modern World*. Eds. I. R. Grigulevich and V. Kozlov. Moscow: Progress Publishers, 1979.

Zinner, Paul, ed. *National Communism and Popular Revolt in Eastern Europe: A Selection of Documents on Events in Poland and Hungary, February–November 1956*. New York: Columbia Univ. Press, 1956.

Index

Library of Congress Cataloging in Publication Data

Connor, Walker, 1926-
The national question in Marxist-Leninist
theory and strategy.

Bibliography: p.   Includes index.
1. Nationalism and socialism. 2. Marx, Karl, 1818-
1883. 3. Lenin, Vladimir Il'ich, 1870-1924. I. Title.
HX550.N3C66   1984   323.1′09171′7   83-43067
ISBN 0-691-07655-3 / ISBN 0-691-10163-9 (pbk.)